PEARSON mybusinesslab™

Improve Your Grade

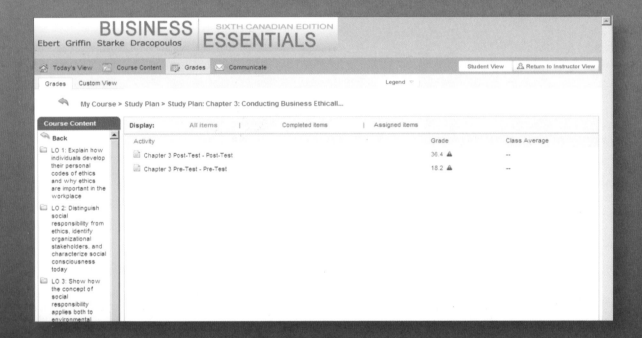

MyBusinessLab helps you focus your efforts where they are needed. Know your strengths and weaknesses before your first in-class exam.

Go to **www.pearsoned.ca/mybusinesslab** and follow the simple registration instructions on the Student Access Code Card provided with this text. Your unique access code is hidden there.

Pearson eText

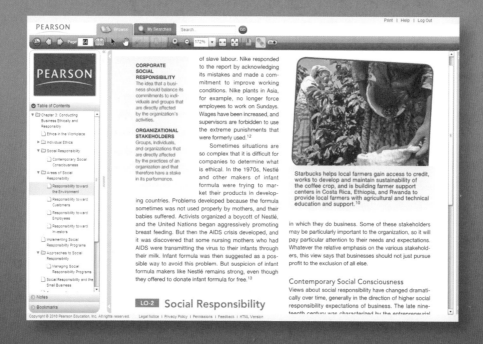

Pearson eText gives students access to the text whenever and wherever they have access to the internet. eText pages look exactly like the printed text, offering powerful new functionality for students and instructors.

Users can create notes, highlight text in different colours, create bookmarks, zoom, click hyperlinked words and phrases to view definitions, and choose single-page or two-page view.

Pearson eText allows for quick navigation using a table of contents and provides full-text search. The eText also offer links to associated media files, enabling users to access videos, animations, or other activities as they read the text.

Personalized Learning

In MyBusinessLab you are treated as an individual with specific learning needs.

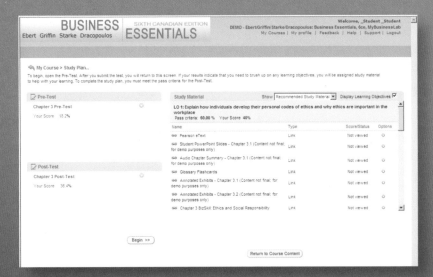

The study and assessment resources that come with your textbook allow you to review content and develop what you need to know, on your own time, and at your own pace.

MyBusinessLab provides

- Auto-graded quizzes, assignments, and mini-cases

- A personalized study plan that tells you where to study based on your quiz results

- BizSkills simulations that help you analyse and make decisions in common business situations; these assess you and include reinforcement quizzes, outlines, and glossaries

- Glossary Flashcards to help you study key terms

- Acadia/Pearson video portal featuring interviews with more than 70 executives from a variety of companies, including some featured in your textbook

- Crafting a Business Plan, including templates to guide you through the steps of creating your own business plan

Save Time. Improve Results. **www.pearsoned.ca/mybusinesslab**

BUSINESS ESSENTIALS

SIXTH CANADIAN EDITION

BUSINESS ESSENTIALS

SIXTH CANADIAN EDITION

RONALD J. EBERT
University of Missouri-Columbia

RICKY W. GRIFFIN
Texas A&M University

FREDERICK A. STARKE
University of Manitoba

GEORGE DRACOPOULOS
Vanier College

With portions of Chapter 4 written by
Monica Diochon, St. Francis Xavier University
and Entrepreneurship and New Ventures boxes written by
Sherry Finney, Cape Breton University

Pearson Canada
Toronto

Library and Archives Canada Cataloguing in Publication

Business essentials / Ronald J. Ebert ... [et al.].—6th Canadian ed.

Includes bibliographical references and indexes.
ISBN 978-0-13-706986-6

1. Industrial management—Textbooks. 2. Business enterprises—Textbooks. 3. Industrial management—Canada—Textbooks. 4. Business enterprises—Canada—Textbooks. I. Ebert, Ronald J.

HD70.C3E32 2011   658   C2010-906547-6

ISBN 978-0-13-706986-6

Vice-President, Editorial Director: Gary Bennett
Editor-in-Chief: Nicole Lukach
Acquisitions Editor: Nick Durie
Marketing Manager: Cas Shields
Developmental Editor: Pam Voves
Project Manager: Sarah Lukaweski
Production Editors: Judy Phillips, Lila Campbell
Copy Editor: Melissa Churchill
Proofreaders: Judy Phillips, Jennifer McIntyre
Compositor: MPS Limited, a Macmillan Company
Permissions and Photo Researcher: Heather Jackson
Art Director: Julia Hall
Interior Designer: Quinn Banting
Cover Designer: Anthony Leung
Cover Image: GettyImages

Dedicated to my loving companion Riley. Earning her trust showed me how simple kindness overcomes fear and begets unconditional friendship.

—R. J. E.

For Pap, who influenced my life in more ways than he ever knew.

—R.W.G.

To Ann, Eric, and Grant.

—F.A.S.

To Nitsa. Thank you for your patience and support.

—G.D.

Brief Contents

Contents

8   Managing Human Resources and Labour Relations   192

9   Motivating, Satisfying, and Leading Employees   220

Preface

Welcome to the sixth Canadian edition of *Business Essentials.* In this edition, we continue to emphasize our long-standing principle of *"Doing the Basics Best."* Cutting-edge firsts, up-to-date issues that shape today's business world, and creative pedagogy help students build a solid foundation of business knowledge. This new, sixth edition continues with the strengths that made the first five editions so successful—comprehensiveness, accuracy, currency, and readability.

What's New to the Sixth Canadian Edition

The impact of one of the most significant events of the past 70 years—**the financial crisis that began in 2008**—is examined in depth in several different chapters of the text. For example, the opening case in Chapter 16 explains the causes of the financial meltdown and its impact on banks, the stock market, sub-prime mortgages, and the economy and business in general. Chapter 16 also includes an end-of-chapter case describing the commercial paper crisis that hit Canada just prior to the more general financial crisis. The opening case of Chapter 15 describes the ups and downs of the world's stock markets during the last decade and explains how the financial crisis of 2008 led to dramatic declines in shareholder wealth. The impact of the financial crisis on business firms and on government involvement in the economy is analyzed in Chapters 1 and 2, and in other chapters as well.

The sixth Canadian edition of *Business Essentials* incorporates many of the changes suggested by professors and students who used the fifth edition. This new edition also includes changes suggested by reviewers. The following changes have been made:

■ The text contains four series of boxed inserts that are positioned at strategic points in the chapters so as to complement the main text. The first of these—entitled **"The Greening of Business"**—analyzes what businesses are doing to be more environmentally friendly. These boxed inserts identify both the opportunities and challenges that businesses are encountering as they try to be more socially responsible. The second series—entitled **"Entrepreneurship and New Ventures"**—provides all new, real-life examples of

Canadian entrepreneurs who saw an opportunity to provide a new product or service in the marketplace, and the activities they carried out in order to be successful. The third series—entitled **"Managing in Turbulent Times"**—focuses student attention on both the disappointments and unexpected opportunities that arise during economic crises such as the one that occurred during the 2008–2009 recession. The fourth series—entitled **"E-Commerce and Social Media"**—describes how rapidly changing technology has provided business firms with many new ways to connect with customers, and how the new technology has given customers a level of control over businesses that they have not previously had.

■ All of the chapter opening cases are either brand-new or updated. Opening chapter cases on **Research In Motion, Toyota, Air Canada, Tim Hortons, lululemon, Parasuco,** and others will be of great interest to students.

■ Two video cases appear at the end of each of the five major sections of the text. **Nine of these ten video cases are new**.

■ Many **new examples of business practices** have been included in each of the chapters. Some of these examples are brief and some are more detailed, but they all help students to better understand important business concepts.

■ **Three appendices are newly placed at the end of relevant chapters in the text.** The first appendix—which focuses on **Business Law**—is included at the end of Chapter 1. This appendix includes key topics such as contracts, the concept of agency, warranties, and bankruptcy. The second appendix—on **Information technology (IT)**—is included at the end of Chapter 11. It focuses on the dramatic changes in information processing that are occurring in business firms and the need to manage these changes. We discuss the impact that IT has had on the business world, the IT resources businesses have at their disposal, the threats information technology poses for businesses, and the ways in which businesses protect themselves from these threats. The third appendix—entitled **"Managing Your Personal Finances"**—is found at the end of Chapter 16. This feature has been overwhelmingly requested by students and instructors, and presents a down-to-earth, hands-on approach that will help students manage their personal finances. The practical information found in this feature includes a worksheet for determining personal net worth, insightful examples demonstrating the time value of money, a method for determining how much money to invest now in order to build a future nest egg of a certain size, suggestions on how to manage credit card debt, guidelines for purchasing a house, and a personalized worksheet for setting financial goals. This information, which complements the managing of business finances material that is presented in Chapter 16, will be immensely useful to students.

■ **Important statistics have been updated** to reflect the latest possible information on Canadian business.

■ The book has been **completely redesigned** to convey the excitement and importance of the modern business world. The book's new design and improved art will also help students to better process and understand chapter content.

■ **Large amounts of new material and new examples** that demonstrate key conceptual points are found in this new edition of the text. Illustrative (but not exhaustive) examples include the following:

Chapter 1—new material on topics such as privatization, deregulation, and nationalization; these ideas have been influenced by the recent financial crisis

Chapter 2—new material on the political-legal environment of business, the BP oil spill, and acquisitions and mergers

Chapter 3—new material on individual ethics, global warming, cap-and-trade systems, price fixing, counterfeit brands, insider trading, and misrepresentation of finances

Chapter 4—new material on small business incubators, entrepreneurship, and franchising

Chapter 5—new material on the growing importance of emerging markets in the global business context; new material on the BRIC nations (Brazil, Russia, India, and China); new material on the financial crisis in the so-called PIIGS (Portugal, Italy, Ireland, Greece, and Spain).

Chapter 6—new material on the planning activities of McDonald's (indicating how these activities demonstrate the planning model presented in the text), prediction markets, human relations skills, the impact of environmental change on companies (for example, Ontario's pharmacy rule changes), contingency planning, crisis management (for example, Toyota, McCain, and BP), and corporate culture

Chapter 9—new material on empowerment, goal setting, reinforcement theory, team management, telecommuting, and leadership styles

Chapter 10—new material on process flowcharts, new data on productivity in various countries around the world, and coverage of the problems that Toyota experienced with quality control in 2010 (opening case)

Chapter 11—new material on international accounting standards, forensic accounting, and the accounting cycle

Chapter 13—new material on branding, brand loyalty, new product development, patents and copyrights, outdoor advertising, word-of-mouth advertising, internet advertising, and online marketing

Chapter 14—new material on pricing, discounts, internet sales, and the dispute between the Competition Bureau and the Canadian Real Estate Association

Chapter 15—new material on changes in the banking industry, banks selling insurance, and venture capital firms

Major Themes

Six major themes continue to be evident in this new edition: change, international business, ethics and social responsibility, small business, information and communication technology, and the quality imperative. It is important that students understand these themes, since their careers in business will be significantly affected by them.

The Theme of Change

The dramatic changes that have been occurring during the past decade continue apace, and these changes have been complicated by the financial crisis of 2008–2009. The development of new business processes, new products, and new services all make the study of change in business exciting and necessary. In nearly every aspect of business today there are totally new ways of doing things. These new ways are replacing traditional business practices, usually with surprising speed and often with better competitive results. Given these developments, we as authors felt that our goal had to be to communicate the theme of change by describing how real-world business firms cope with the need for change. Thus, we have tried to capture the flavour and convey the excitement of the "new economy" in all of its rapidly evolving practices.

The Growth of International Business

The globalization of business is one of the dominant challenges of the twenty-first century. To keep students aware of this challenge, we've included many examples and cases that describe the experiences of Canadian companies in the global marketplace. We also describe how global companies have impacted the domestic Canadian market. In addition to these examples throughout the text, we devote an entire chapter to international business (Chapter 5, The Global Context of Business).

The Role of Ethics and Social Responsibility

The topics of business ethics and social responsibility are generating a sharply increased level of discussion and debate as a result of the highly publicized criminal trials of top managers at companies like Livent, Enron, and WorldCom, and because of the questionable financial practices that led to the economic crisis of 2008–2009. We devote an entire chapter to the discussion of ethical and social responsibility issues (Chapter 3, Conducting Business Ethically and Responsibly) because these issues are so important to modern business. Ethical issues are also raised in nearly every chapter of the text, and a team ethics exercise at the end of each chapter further focuses student attention on this important issue.

The Significance of Small Business

Since many students will not work for major corporations, we have provided coverage of both large and small companies throughout the text. In various chapters, the implications of various ideas for small business are discussed. As well, a major part of Chapter 4 (Entrepreneurship, Small Business, and New Venture Creation) contains new material focusing on small business, entrepreneurship, and new business ventures.

The Importance of Information and Communication Technology

In our information-based society, the people and organizations that learn how to obtain and use information will be the ones that succeed. The explosive growth and change in these systems is recognized as we include a rewritten appendix on the management of information at the end of Chapter 11.

The Quality Imperative

Quality and productivity became the keys to competitive success for many companies in the global marketplace during the 1990s. These topics continue to dominate the thinking of managers in the twenty-first century, and we devote a substantial part of one chapter to their coverage (Chapter 10, Operations Management, Productivity, and Quality).

Major Features of the Text

Part Opener

At the beginning of each of the five major parts of the book is a brief outline introducing the material that will be discussed in that part. These outlines give students a glimpse of the "big picture" as they start reading about a new area of the business world.

Chapter Materials

Each chapter contains several features that are designed to stimulate student interest in, and understanding of, the material being presented about business. These features are as follows:

Chapter Learning Objectives A list of numbered learning objectives is presented at the beginning of each chapter. These objectives—which help students determine what is important in each chapter—are also referenced beside headings for the relevant content in the chapter.

Chapter-Opening Case Each chapter begins with a description of a situation that is faced by a real Canadian or international company. The subject matter of the opening case is relevant to the material presented in the chapter and is designed to help students bridge the gap between theory and practice.

Boxed Inserts As noted above, four series of boxed inserts are found in the text. These boxed inserts provide interesting information on topics that are discussed in the text, and they help students understand the dynamics and complexities of the business world. Critical thinking questions are found at the end of these boxes. These questions can be used as the basis for class discussions about the implications of the material that is presented in the boxed inserts.

Examples In addition to the boxed inserts, each chapter contains numerous examples of how businesses operate so that students can gain a better understanding of the dynamics of business practice both in Canada and elsewhere. These examples—which range in length from one sentence to several paragraphs—help students understand concepts that are introduced in the text.

Key Terms In each chapter, the key terms that students should know are highlighted in the text and defined in the margin.

Figures and Tables Figures and tables are updated throughout the text.

End-of-Chapter Material

Several important pedagogical features are found at the end of each chapter. These are designed to help students better understand the contents of the chapter.

Summary of Learning Objectives The material in each chapter is concisely summarized, using the learning objectives as the organizing scheme. This helps students understand the main points that were presented in the chapter.

Questions and Exercises There are two types of questions here: "Questions for Analysis" (which require students to think beyond simple factual recall and apply the concepts they have read about), and "Application Exercises" (which require students to visit local businesses or to interview managers and gather additional information that will help them understand how business firms operate).

Team Exercises Two team exercises are included at the end of each chapter. The "Building Your Business Skills" exercise allows students to examine in detail some specific aspect of business. The exercise may ask students to work individually or in a group to gather data about an interesting business issue, and then develop a group report or a class presentation based on the information that was gathered. Each exercise begins with a list of goals, a description of the situation, a step-by-step methodology for proceeding, and follow-up questions to help students focus their responses to the challenge. The "Exercising Your Ethics" exercises ask students to take on the role of an employee, owner, customer, or investor and then examine a chapter-related business ethics dilemma through the perspective of that role. By working together as a team, students decide which outcome is ultimately best in each situation, learn how to cooperate with each other, and see an ethical dilemma from various points of view.

Business Case Each chapter concludes with a case study that focuses on a real Canadian or international company. These cases are designed to help students apply the chapter material to a real company that is currently in the news. At the end of each case, several questions guide students in their analysis.

End-of-Part Material

Crafting a Business Plan This feature, which is tailor-made to match and reinforce book content, appears at the end of each major section of the text. The business plan project is *software-independent* and provides students with an easy-to-understand template that they work from as they create their business plan. Based on reviewer feedback, the business plan project has been divided into logical sections, with each part of the project at the end of each relevant main section of the text. With five parts in all, students can gradually apply the concepts they've learned in the chapters to their business plans throughout the course. You will find the templates for the Business Plan project online in MyBusinessLab.

Video Cases At the end of each of the five major parts of the text, written summaries of two video cases are presented. The instructor can show the video in class, and then either conduct a class discussion using the questions at the end of the written case as a guide, or ask students to complete a written assignment that requires answering the questions at the end of the written case. This approach to teaching adds a positive dynamic to classes because students will be able to relate text material to actual Canadian business situations. The cases are also available through the MyBusinessLab for *Business Essentials,* Sixth Canadian Edition.

Supplemental Materials

MyBusinessLab (**www.pearsoned.ca/mybusinesslab**) is an online grading, assessment, and study tool for faculty and students. It engages students and helps them focus on what they need to study. It can help students get a better grade because they are learning in an interactive and focused environment. MyBusinessLab delivers all classroom resources for instructors and students in one place. All resources are organized by learning objective so that lectures and studying can be customized more conveniently than ever before. A complete description of the student and instructor resources available is provided on the MyBusinessLab insert included with this text.

For Instructors

Instructor's Resource Centre Instructor resources are password protected and available for download via **www.pearsoned.ca**. For your convenience, these resources are also available on the *Instructor's Resource CD-ROM* (ISBN 978-0-13-038830-8) and available online at **www.pearsoned.ca/mybusinesslab** in the instructor area.

Test Item File This substantially enhanced test bank in Microsoft Word format contains over 5100 multiple-choice, true/false, short-answer, and essay questions. The Test Item file enables instructors to view and edit the existing questions, add questions, and generate texts. This robust test bank is also available in MyTest format (see below).

MyTest The new edition test bank comes with *MyTest*, a powerful assessment-generation program that helps instructors easily create and print quizzes, test, exams, as well as homework or practice handouts. Questions and tests can all be authored online, allowing instructors ultimate flexibility and the ability to efficiently manage assessments at any time, from anywhere. MyTest can also be accessed through MyBusinessLab.

Instructor's Resource Manual The *Instructor's Resource Manual* contains chapter outlines, teaching tips, in-class exercises, and suggestions on how to use the text effectively. The manual also provides answers to the end-of-chapter questions and team exercises (including Building Your Business Skills and Exercising Your Ethics), case study questions, and the end-of-section video case questions.

PowerPoint® Presentations *PowerPoint Presentations* offer an average of 40 PowerPoint slides per chapter, outlining the key points in the text. The slides include lecture notes that provide page references to the text, summaries, and suggestions for student activities or related questions from the text.

Personal Response Questions This set of interactive Clicker PowerPoint™ Slides contains thought-provoking questions designed to engage students in the classrooms using "clickers" or classroom response systems.

CBC Video Library (DVD: ISBN 978-0-13-237727-0). The *CBC Video Library* for *Business Essentials*, Sixth Canadian Edition, includes 10 segments that focus on Canadian companies and discuss business issues from a Canadian point of view. The cases can also be viewed online at **www.pearsoned.ca/highered/videocentral** and answers to the discussion questions are provided in the Instructor's Resource Manual. Contact your Pearson Canada sales representative for details.

Acadia/Pearson Business Insider Series Videos This online selection of videos provided on MyBusinessLab contains interviews of industry leaders and top executives from Canada and abroad. The videos provide an effective link from the textbook to the real world. Included on MyBusinessLab is a table correlating pertinent videos to the chapters and topics in the textbook.

Pearson Custom Publishing (**www.prenhall.com/custombusiness**). Pearson Custom Publishing can provide you and your students with texts, cases, and articles to enhance your course. Choose material from Darden, Ivey, Harvard Business School Publishing, NACRA, and Thunderbird to create your own custom casebook. Contact your Pearson Canada sales representative for details.

Online Learning Solutions Pearson Canada supports instructors interested in using online course management systems. We provide text-related content in Blackboard/WebCT and Course Compass. To find out more about creating an online course using Pearson content in one of these platforms, contact your Pearson Canada sales representative.

Your Pearson Canada Sales Representative Your Pearson sales rep is always available to ensure you have everything you need to teach a winning course. Armed with experience, training, and product knowledge, your Pearson rep will support your assessment and adoption of any of the products, services, and technology outlined here to ensure our offerings are tailored to suit your individual needs and the needs of your students. Whether it's getting instructions on TestGen software or specific content files for your new online course, your Pearson sales rep is there to help. Ask your Pearson sales rep for details.

Technology Specialists Pearson's Technology Specialists work with faculty and course designers to ensure that Pearson technology products, assessment tools, and online course materials are tailored to meet your specific needs. This highly-qualified team is dedicated to helping schools integrate a variety of instructional materials and media formats. Your local Pearson sales rep can provide you with more details on this service program.

CourseSmart for Instructors CourseSmart goes beyond traditional expectations, providing instant, online access to the textbooks and course materials you need at a lower cost for students. And even as students save money, you can save time and hassle with a digital eTextbook that allows you to search for the most relevant content at the very moment you need it. Whether it's evaluating textbooks or creating lecture notes to help students with difficult concepts, CourseSmart can make life a little easier. See how when you visit **www.coursesmart.com/instructors.**

For Students

MyBusinessLab (**www.pearsoned.ca/mybusinesslab**) is an online grading assessment and study tool for both faculty and students. It generates a personalized study plan that focuses students on what they, individually, need to study. It engages students through an interactive and focused environment. All resources are organized by learning objective so that studying can be customized more conveniently than ever before. A complete description of the student and instructor resources available is provided on the MyBusinessLab insert included with this text.

ScanLife™ 2D Barcodes and Study on the Go Featured at the beginning and end of each chapter, the ScanLife™ barcodes provide an unprecedented seamless integration between text and online content for students.

The free, downloadable app (for instructions go here: **http://web.scanlife.com/us_en/download-application**) enables students to link to Pearson Canada's unique Study on the Go content directly from their smartphones, allowing them to study whenever and wherever they wish! Upon scanning, students can follow the online instructions to search the rich study assets, including Glossary Flashcards, Audio Summaries, and Quizzes.

Crafting a Business Plan A business plan project, tailor-made to match and reinforce book content, appears at the end of each major section of the book. The business plan project is *software-independent* and provides students with an easy-to-understand template that they work from as they create their business plans. Files to complete the project are available at **www.pearsoned.ca/mybusinesslab**.

CourseSmart for Students CourseSmart goes beyond traditional expectations, providing instant, online access to the textbooks and course materials you need at an average savings of 50%. With instant access from any computer and the ability to search your text, you'll find the content you need quickly, no matter where you are. And with online tools like highlighting and notetaking, you can save time and study efficiently. See all the benefits at **www.coursesmart.com/students.**

Acknowledgments

We owe special thanks to Melissa Churchill, copyeditor; Judy Phillips and Lila Campbell, Production Editors, Sarah Lukaweski, Project Manager; Karen Elliott and Nick Durie, Acquisitions Editors; Pamela Voves, Developmental Editor; and others at Pearson Canada who assisted with the production, marketing, and sales of this edition. In addition, we would like to acknowledge the contributions of Sherry Finney of Cape Breton University who prepared many of the Entrepreneurship and New Ventures boxed features.

We appreciate the insights and suggestions of the following individuals who provided feedback on the fifth edition or reviewed the manuscript for the new sixth edition:

Gina Grandy, Mount Allison University

Kandey Larden, Langara College

Peter Morgan, BCIT

Stephen Rose, University of Ontario Institute of Technology (UOIT)

Lucy Silvestri, Niagara College

Dan Wong, SAIT Polytechnic

Dustin Quirk, Donald School of Business – Red Deer College

Rob Anderson, Thompson Rivers University

Dr. Scott MacMillan, Saint Mary's University

Morris Nassi, Champlain College, Saint-Lambert

About the Authors

Ronald J. Ebert is Emeritus Professor at the University of Missouri-Columbia where he lectures in the Management Department and serves as adviser to students and student organizations. Dr. Ebert draws upon more than 30 years of teaching experience at such schools as Sinclair College, University of Washington, University of Missouri, Lucian Blaga University of Sibiu (Romania), and Consortium International University (Italy). His consulting alliances include such firms as Mobay Corporation, Kraft Foods, Oscar Mayer, Atlas Powder, and John Deere. He has designed and conducted management development programs for such diverse clients as the American Public Power Association, the United States Savings and Loan League, and the Central Missouri Manufacturing Training Consortium.

His experience as a practitioner has fostered an advocacy for integrating concepts with best business practices in business education. The five business books he has written have been translated into Spanish, Chinese, Malaysian, and Romanian. Dr. Ebert has served as the editor of *Journal of Operations Management*. He is a past-president and fellow of the Decision Sciences Institute. He has served as consultant and external evaluator for *Quantitative Reasoning for Business Studies*, an introduction-to-business project sponsored by the National Science Foundation.

Ricky W. Griffin is Distinguished Professor of Management and holds the Blocker Chair in Business in the Mays School of Business at Texas A&M University. Dr. Griffin currently serves as executive associate dean. He previously served as head of the Department of Management and as director of the Center for Human Resource Management at Texas A&M. His research interests include workplace aggression and violence, executive skills and decision making, and workplace culture. Dr. Griffin's research has been published in such journals as *Academy of Management Review, Academy of Management Journal, Administrative Science Quarterly,* and *Journal of Management.* He has also served as editor of *Journal of Management*. Dr. Griffin has consulted with such organizations as Texas Instruments, Tenneco, Amoco, Compaq Computer, and Continental Airlines.

Dr. Griffin has served the Academy of Management as chair of the organizational behaviour division. He also has served as president of the southwest division of the Academy of Management and on the board of directors of the Southern Management Association. He is a fellow of both the Academy of Management and the Southern Management Association. He is also the author of several successful textbooks, each of which is a market leader. In addition, they are widely used in dozens of countries and have been translated into numerous languages, including Spanish, Polish, Malaysian, and Russian.

Frederick A. Starke is Emeritus Professor of Organizational Behaviour in the Asper School of Business at the University of Manitoba. He began his career at the University of Manitoba in 1968, and has taught courses in introduction to business, organizational behaviour, organization theory, decision making, and marketing. He has served in several administrative positions, including Head of the Department of Business Administration from 1982–1987 and from 1989–1994, and as Associate Dean of the Asper School of Business from 1996–2005.

Dr. Starke earned his BA and MBA from Southern Illinois University, and his PhD in Organizational Behaviour from Ohio State University. He has published research articles in such scholarly journals as *Administrative Science Quarterly, Journal of Applied Psychology, Academy of Management Journal, Journal of Management Studies,* and *Journal of Business Venturing*. He has written articles for professional journals such as the *Journal of Systems Management, Information Executive*, and *Canadian Journal of Nursing Administration*.

Dr. Starke also writes textbooks that are used by university and community college students in business programs across Canada. These titles include *Organizational Behaviour, Business Essentials, Management*, and *Business*. Dr. Starke presents seminars on the topics of decision making and goal setting to practising managers in both the public and private sectors.

George Dracopoulos is a member of the Business Administration department at Vanier College in Montréal. He served as chairman of the department from 2004 until 2007 and is now devoting significant energy to running the International Business Exchange program. George has created links with universities throughout France and has created full-semester student exchange programs as well as two-month internship opportunities with important multinational corporations. He is a co-organizer of the national BDC/Vanier Marketing Case Competition. George also serves as a part-time lecturer at Concordia University and McGill University, teaching traditional and online courses. He earned his BA at Concordia University. He earned his MBA at McGill, as well as a graduate diploma in education and a graduate degree in applied management. Mr. Dracopoulos has taught a broad range of business courses. He is an advocate of experiential learning and dedicates a significant amount of class time to hands-on assignments. His primary interests are in the fields of marketing and management.

Outside his teaching career, Mr. Dracopoulos has worked in various marketing and sales positions. In addition to this text, he has worked on many publishing projects providing web content as well as supporting multimedia and supplemental academic material. While completing his university education, he spent a semester abroad studying management globalization issues in Europe. He has also spent a considerable amount of time coaching high-level sports and organizing events in his spare time. Recent Pearson publications include *Business in Action*, In-Class Edition, Second Canadian Edition (2009), co-authored with Courtland L. Bovée and John V. Thill.

From the Authors

Ron Ebert, Ricky Griffin, Fred Starke, and George Dracopoulos

Businesses today face constant change—change in their competitive landscape, change in their workforce, change in government regulations, change in the economy, change in technology, change in . . . well, you get the idea. As we began to plan this revision, we too recognized the need for change—changing demands from instructors, changing needs and preferences of students, and changing views on what material to cover in this course and how to cover it. These have all affected how we planned and revised the book. This time, though, we took change to a whole new level.

A new team of reviewers gave us great ideas about the content changes we needed to make, and a new editorial team was assembled to guide and shape the creation and development of the book. The business world itself provided us with dozens of new examples, new challenges, new success stories, and new perspectives on what businesses must do to remain competitive. And a new dedication to relevance guided our work from beginning to end. For example, we know that some business students will go to work for big companies. Others will work for small firms. Some will start their own business. Still others may join a family business. So we accepted the challenge of striving to make the book as relevant as possible for all students, regardless of their personal and career goals and objectives.

We met this challenge by incorporating many new features in this edition (see the Preface for a list of these new features). We also carefully reviewed the existing book line by line. New material was added and older examples were updated or replaced with newer ones. We worked extra hard to make our writing as clear and as crisp as possible. We think that these changes will help make the material even more alive and personal for you.

We believe that we have taken this book to a new, higher level of excellence. Its content is stronger, its learning framework is better, its new design is more reader-friendly, and its support materials are the best on the market. We hope that you enjoy reading and learning from this book as much as we enjoyed creating it. And who knows? Perhaps one day we can tell your story of business success to other students.

So, How Will This Text Help *You*?

The world today is populated with a breathtaking array of businesses and business opportunities. Big and small businesses, established and new businesses, broad-based and niche businesses, successful and unsuccessful businesses, global and domestic businesses—regardless of where your future plans take you, we hope that you will look back on this course as one of your positive first steps.

Keep in mind that what you get out of this course depends on at least three factors:

- One factor is this book and the information about business that you will acquire as a result of reading it.

- Another factor is your instructor. He or she is a dedicated professional who wants to help you grow and develop intellectually and academically.

- The third factor is **YOU**. Learning is an active process that requires you to be a major participant. Simply memorizing the key terms and concepts in this book may help you achieve an acceptable course grade, but true learning requires that you read, study, discuss, question, review, experience, and evaluate as you go along.

Tests and homework are necessary, but we hope that you will finish this course with new knowledge and increased enthusiasm for the world of business. Your instructor will do his or her part to facilitate your learning. The rest, then, is up to you. We wish you success.

Introducing the Contemporary Business World

In the opening cases in Chapters 1 to 5, you will read about five interesting situations: (1) opportunities and challenges in the mobile phone market, (2) inflation and deflation, (3) the unethical behaviour of business managers at Livent, (4) family business stories, and (5) Tim Hortons' international strategy. All of these situations, and many more that are described in this text, have a common thread: they all demonstrate the key elements of business, as well as the excitement and complexity of business activity. Each case tells a part of the story of our contemporary business world.

Part Summary

Part 1, Introducing the Contemporary Business World, provides a general overview of business today, including its economic roots, the environment in which it operates, the ethical problems and opportunities facing business firms, the importance of entrepreneurship and the various forms of ownership available to business firms, and the globalization of business.

■ We begin in **Chapter 1, The Canadian Business System**, by examining the role of business in the economy of Canada and other market economies. We also present a brief history of business in Canada.

■ Then, in **Chapter 2, The Environment of Business**, we examine the external environments that influence business activity. These include the economic, technological, sociocultural, legal-political, and general business environments.

■ Next, in **Chapter 3, Conducting Business Ethically and Responsibly**, we look at individual ethics and corporate social responsibility, and how these affect the firm's customers, employees, and investors.

■ In **Chapter 4, Entrepreneurship, Small Business, and New Venture Creation**, we examine the important concepts of entrepreneurship, small business, and the various forms of business ownership that have evolved to facilitate business activity.

■ Finally, in **Chapter 5, The Global Context of Business**, we look at why countries engage in international trade, how companies organize to operate internationally, the development of free trade agreements, and factors that help or hinder international trade.

chapter

1

Understanding the Canadian Business System

After reading this chapter, you should be able to:

LO-1 Define the nature of Canadian *business* and identify its main goals.

LO-2 Describe different types of global *economic systems* according to the means by which they control the *factors of production* through *input and output markets*.

LO-3 Show how *demand* and *supply* affect resource distribution in Canada.

LO-4 Identify the elements of *private enterprise* and explain the various *degrees of competition* in the Canadian economic system.

LO-5 Trace the *history of business* in Canada.

ScanLife™ Barcode: At the beginning and end of each chapter in the book, you will find a unique 2D barcode like the one above. Please go to http://web.scanlife.com/us_en/downloadapplication to see how you can download the ScanLife app to your smartphone for free. Once the app is installed, your phone will scan the code and link to a website containing Pearson Canada's Study on the Go content, including the popular study tools Glossary Flashcards, Audio Summaries, and Quizzes, which can be accessed anytime.

Opportunities and Challenges in the Mobile Phone Market

During the last decade, a Canadian company called Research In Motion (RIM) has emerged as a high-tech star in the mobile phone industry. The company was started in 1984 by two engineering students—Mike Lazaridis at the University of Waterloo and Douglas Fregin at the University of Windsor. Its first wireless handheld device—called the Inter@ctive Pager—was introduced in 1996. The now-famous BlackBerry hit the market in 1998. The BlackBerry 850, which combined email, a wireless data network, and a tiny QWERTY keyboard, was introduced in 1999. Other products have been developed since then, including the BlackBerry Pearl (2006), the BlackBerry 8300 (2008), the BlackBerry Storm 2 (2009), a 3G version of its Pearl flip phone (2010), and OS 6.0 (2010). The latter product is a touch-screen smart phone that is designed to browse the web faster than previous models. In the first quarter of 2010, RIM was one of the top five mobile phone companies in the world, and at the 2010 Wireless Enterprise Symposium trade show, Lazaridis announced RIM's plans to dominate the global smart phone market.

RIM raised $30 million from venture capital firms in the years before its initial public offering (IPO) in 1998 that raised $115 million. RIM was

How Will This Help Me?

All businesses are subject to the influences of economic forces. But these same economic forces also provide astute managers and entrepreneurs with opportunities for profits and growth. The ideas presented in this chapter will help you to better understand (1) how managers deal with the challenges and opportunities resulting from economic forces, and (2) how consumers deal with the challenges and opportunities of price fluctuations.

listed on NASDAQ in 1999 and raised another $250 million. In 2000, it raised another $950 million. As of mid-2009, RIM had 12,000 employees worldwide. In 2009, *Fortune* magazine named RIM as the fastest-growing company in the world. There are over 40 million corporate and consumer BlackBerry users, and RIM's goal is to have 100 million customers.

RIM is a remarkable Canadian success story, but industry analysts see potential challenges on the horizon for companies in the smart phone market. The market potential is huge, but competition is intense and new product introductions are occurring at a dizzying pace. For example, Nokia has introduced a smart phone—the Booklet 3G—that is designed to bridge the gap between a PC and a cellphone. The device (described as a mini-laptop) gives consumers the computing power of a PC with the mobility of a cellphone. Another new product is Motorola's Droid phone, which was launched by Verizon, the largest U.S. wireless carrier (and RIM's biggest customer). A third entry comes from Google, which has developed a touch-screen mobile phone that uses Google's own Android operating system (this product may also cause problems for Apple's iPhone). A fourth new product is Apple's iPhone, which will be a strong competitor to the BlackBerry as RIM shifts its emphasis from corporate clients to consumers.

There are also two industry trends that make it difficult to predict the future for any of the competitors in the smart phone industry. The first is the so-called "bring your own device" trend, which means that companies are shifting the responsibility for having a phone onto employees. The second trend is "sandboxing," which means separating work functions from the rest of the smart phone for security reasons, and allowing employees to use the phone at work without losing access to other applications like games or social networking. Both these trends may hurt RIM in the corporate market because employees may decide to buy something other than a BlackBerry. Some analysts are now fairly pessimistic about RIM's future; they think the company may continue to grow, but that shareholder returns will decline.

Another major area of concern is patent infringement lawsuits. During the past decade, RIM and other firms have sued and been sued for patent infringement. In 2006, RIM agreed to pay Virginia-based NTP $612.5 million for infringing on NTP's patent. RIM also sued Samsung after Samsung introduced a smart phone called the BlackJack. In 2009, Klausner Technologies filed suit against RIM for infringing one of its visual voicemail patents. These lawsuits have created great uncertainty in the smart phone industry.

Yet another problem is the negative publicity RIM received regarding stock options. In 2007, the company announced a $250 million restatement of earnings after it was learned that hundreds of stock options had been backdated (timed to a low share price to make them more lucrative for managers who received them). In 2009, Canadian regulators were seeking $80 million in penalties from co-CEOs Mike Lazaridis and Jim Balsillie, and several other executives agreed to pay penalties for backdating stock options.

All of these things have had a negative effect on RIM's stock price. In 2007, stock market analysts began saying that RIM's stock was overvalued (it was then selling for $84 per share). By August 2008, the stock had defied predictions and had increased to $123 per share, but by early 2010 it had dropped to $61 per share. RIM spent $1.2 billion to buy back some of its shares, which should have increased the share price because fewer shares were on the market, but RIM still has to demonstrate that it can compete with other companies that are bringing out new models of smart phones. In April 2010, RIM announced a series of initiatives to increase investor confidence in the company, but analysts were skeptical, and by the end of June 2010, the price of RIM's stock had declined to $54 per share.

RIM has taken several strategic actions in an attempt to improve its future prospects. Historically, RIM's international footprint has not been large (about 80 percent of RIM's revenue comes from the U.S., Canada, and the U.K.). But in 2009, RIM signed a deal with Digital China to distribute BlackBerrys in China. The potential market in China is obviously large, but consumers in China may not be willing to pay the high price of a BlackBerry. As well, the production of unauthorized copycat phones (knockoffs) is a problem in China. For example, the "BlockBerry" is one of the competing phones sold in China.

RIM is also responding to competitive threats by positioning the BlackBerry as a general purpose smart phone for the average consumer, not just business users. More stylish models are being produced and are aimed at students, "soccer moms," and consumers in general. RIM also developed a new advertising campaign, sponsored a high-profile tour of Irish rock group U2, and provided better web browsers and applications for internet shopping. RIM's security standards mean it is safe for customers to do things like shop online from their smart phone.

According to the research firm IDC, there were 450 million mobile internet users in 2009, but that number should increase to 1 billion by 2013. Over 80 percent of RIM's new subscribers are individuals, not businesses. One positive trend for RIM is increasing consumer interest in smart phones. About 40 percent of the mobile phones purchased in 2010 were smart phones, and that proportion will increase over the next few years.

LO-1 The Idea of Business and Profit

The opening case illustrates the dynamic and rapidly changing nature of modern business activity, and the opportunities and challenges that are evident. It also shows how business managers must pay attention to many different things, including the actions of competitors, rapid technological change, new product development, corporate strategy, risk management, stock prices, and a host of other variables that you will read about in this book.

Let's begin by asking what you think of when you hear the word *business*. Do you think of large corporations like Shoppers Drug Mart and Walmart, or smaller companies like your local supermarket or favourite restaurant? Do you think about successful companies like CN and Research In Motion, or less successful companies like GM Canada? Actually, each of these firms is a **business**—an organization that produces or sells goods or services in an effort to make a profit. **Profit** is what remains after a business's expenses have been subtracted from its revenues. Profits reward the owners of businesses for taking the risks involved in investing their time and money. In 2008, the most profitable Canadian companies were Encana Corp. ($6.3 billion), the Canadian Wheat Board ($5.7 billion), and Canadian Natural Resources Ltd. ($4.9 billion).[1]

The prospect of earning profits is what encourages people to start and expand businesses. Today, businesses produce most of the goods and services that we consume, and they employ many of the working people in Canada. Profits from these businesses are paid to thousands upon thousands of owners and shareholders, and business taxes help support governments at all levels. In addition, businesses help support charitable causes and provide community leadership. A 2010 study by KPMG of the G7 industrialized countries revealed that Canada ranked as the most cost-effective place to do business.[2]

In addition to for-profit business firms, there are also many not-for-profit organizations in Canada. **Not-for-profit organizations** do not try to make a profit; rather, they use the funds they generate (from government grants or the sale of goods or services) to provide services to the public. Charities, educational institutions, hospitals, labour unions, and government agencies are examples of not-for-profit organizations. Business principles are helpful to these not-for-profit organizations as they try to achieve their service goals.

LO-2 Economic Systems Around the World

A Canadian business is different in many ways from one in China, and both are different from businesses in Japan, France, or Peru. A major determinant of how organizations operate is the kind of economic system that characterizes the country in which they do business. An **economic system** allocates a nation's resources among its citizens. Economic systems differ in terms of who owns and controls these resources, known as the "factors of production" (see Figure 1.1).

Factors of Production

The key difference between economic systems is the way in which they manage the **factors of production**—the basic resources that a country's businesses use to produce goods and services. Traditionally, economists have focused on four factors of production: *labour, capital, entrepreneurs*, and *natural resources*. Newer perspectives tend to broaden the idea of "natural resources" to include all *physical resources*. In addition, *information resources* are often included now.[3]

Labour The people who work for a company represent the first factor of production—**labour**. Sometimes called *human resources*, labour is the mental and physical capabilities of people. Carrying out the business of a huge company such as Imperial Oil requires a labour force with a wide variety of skills ranging from managers to geologists to truck drivers.

Capital **Capital** refers to the funds that are needed to start a business and to keep it operating and growing.

BUSINESS An organization that seeks to earn profits by providing goods and services.

PROFIT What remains (if anything) after a business's expenses are subtracted from its sales revenues.

NOT-FOR-PROFIT ORGANIZATION An organization that provides goods and services to customers, but does not seek to make a profit while doing so.

ECONOMIC SYSTEM The way in which a nation allocates its resources among its citizens.

FACTORS OF PRODUCTION The resources used to produce goods and services: labour, capital, entrepreneurs, and natural resources.

LABOUR The mental and physical training and talents of people; sometimes called human resources.

CAPITAL The funds needed to operate an enterprise.

For example, Imperial Oil needs capital to pay for its annual drilling costs, which run into the millions of dollars each year. Major sources of capital for businesses are personal investment by owners, the sale of stock to investors, profits from the sale of products and services, and funds borrowed from banks and other lending institutions.

Entrepreneurs Entrepreneurs are people who accept the opportunities and risks involved in creating and operating businesses. Mike Lazaridis (Research In Motion), Sergie Brin and Larry Page (Google), Michael Dell (Dell Computer), and Mark Zuckerberg (Facebook) are well-known entrepreneurs.

Natural Resources Natural resources include all physical resources such as land, water, mineral deposits, and trees. Imperial Oil makes use of a wide variety of natural resources. It obviously has vast quantities of crude oil to process each year. But Imperial Oil also needs the land where the oil is located, as well as land for its refineries and pipelines.

Information Resources Information resources include the specialized knowledge and expertise of people who work in businesses, as well as information that is found in market forecasts and various other forms of economic data. Much of what businesses do results in either the creation of new information or the repackaging of existing information for new users and different audiences. The boxed insert entitled "A Shrine to Wine" gives you an opportunity to think about the importance of the factors of production in a specific business.

Types of Economic Systems
Different types of economic systems manage the factors of production in different ways. In some systems,

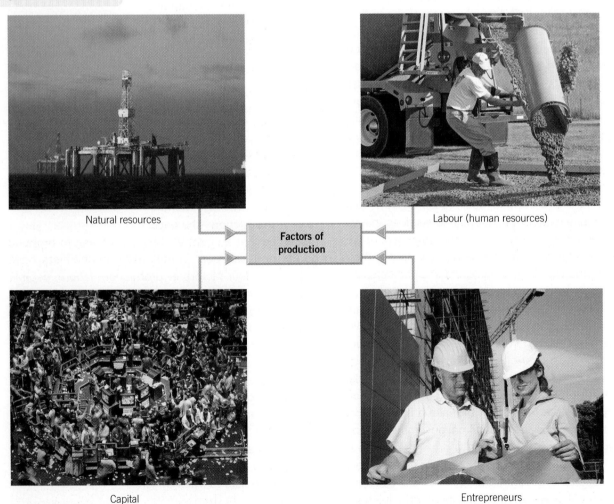

Natural resources

Labour (human resources)

Factors of production

Capital

Entrepreneurs

Figure 1.1
Factors of production are the basic resources a business uses to create goods and services. The four factors are natural resources, labour, capital, and entrepreneurs.

ownership is private; in others, the factors of production are owned by the government. Economic systems also differ in the ways decisions are made about production and allocation. A **command economy**, for example, relies on a centralized government to control all or most factors of production and to make all or most production and allocation decisions. In **market economies**, individuals—producers and consumers—control production and allocation decisions through supply and demand.

Command Economies The two most basic forms of command economies are communism and socialism. As originally proposed by nineteenth-century German economist Karl Marx, **communism** is a system in which the government owns and operates all sources of production. Marx envisioned a society in which individuals would ultimately contribute according to their abilities and receive economic benefits according to their needs. He also expected government ownership of production factors to be only temporary. Once society had matured, government would "wither away" and the workers would gain direct ownership.

COMMAND ECONOMY An economic system in which government controls all or most factors of production and makes all or most production decisions.

MARKET ECONOMY An economic system in which individuals control all or most factors of production and make all or most production decisions.

COMMUNISM A type of command economy in which the government owns and operates all industries.

ENTREPRENEURSHIP AND NEW VENTURES

A Shrine to Wine

Wine connoisseurs, also known as oenophiles, have a love of and devotion to wine, and they take just as much care in the procurement and storage of their vino as they do in the tasting. Robb Denomme and Lance Kingma own Winnipeg-based Genuwine Cellars, which sells custom-designed wine cellars, some of which have six-figure price tags. The company was started somewhat by accident in 1995 when someone asked Kingma if he thought he could build a wine cellar. He took on the challenge, and the first order led to another, and he eventually partnered with Denomme, who was just 17 at the time. As the saying goes, the rest is history. Today, the business is a multimillion-dollar operation selling to clients around the world, with the majority of sales being to the U.S.

Genuwine's international success probably wouldn't have happened, or at least not as easily, without the help of the Department of Foreign Affairs and International Trade (DFAIT). According to Robb, "Working with the TCS [Trade Commissioner Service] you get results, you get where you want to go. Trade commissioners are there to help and always get back to you with the answers you need." The TCS is a division of Foreign Affairs and its goal is to help companies succeed globally. Not only did TCS help Genuwine Cellars get connected with a business consultant, it also helped with financing. Other governmental agencies, including the Prairie Centre for Business Intelligence and the National Research Council, have also provided business support.

In addition to market development strategies, Genuwine Cellars is credited with some other good moves. "Genuwine is doing all the right things a growing company should do—lean manufacturing, continual investments in technology, importing contract manufactured goods from Asia, setting up a design office in Latin America to take advantage of a lower cost structure and access to skilled professionals, the list goes on," says Joanne MacKean, senior manager, Business Development Canada. Further, Genuwine Cellars is one of the largest wine cellar manufacturers in North America and the only company with a manufacturing facility in Canada. Very little competition, niche market, upscale consumer—so just what's "in store" for this business?

According to Denomme, the recent recession had some effect, but the company is still experiencing growth. Denomme's enthusiasm and drive are not quashed, however. He says, "You've got to keep a positive attitude." Sounds like this entrepreneur looks upon his wine glass as being half full rather than half empty.

Critical Thinking Questions

1. Discuss the factors of production as they apply to Genuwine Cellars.
2. What do you think about the company's decision to move some of its operations to Latin America because of a lower cost structure?

SOCIALISM A kind of command economy in which the government owns and operates the main industries, while individuals own and operate less crucial industries.

MARKET An exchange process between buyers and sellers of a particular good or service.

INPUT MARKET Firms buy resources that they need in the production of goods and services.

OUTPUT MARKET Firms supply goods and services in response to demand on the part of consumers.

CAPITALISM An economic system in which markets decide what, when, and for whom to produce.

But Marx's predictions were faulty. During the last 20 years, most countries have abandoned communism in favour of a more market-based economy. Even countries that still claim to be communist (for example, China, Vietnam, and Cuba) now contain elements of a market-based economy. Whether communism can be maintained alongside a market-based economy remains to be seen.

In a less extensive command economic system called **socialism**, the government owns and operates only selected major industries. Smaller businesses such as clothing stores and restaurants may be privately owned. Although workers in socialist countries are usually allowed to choose their occupations or professions, a large proportion generally work for the government. Many government-operated enterprises are inefficient, since management positions are frequently filled based on political considerations rather than ability. Extensive public welfare systems have also resulted in very high taxes. Because of these factors, socialism is generally declining in popularity.[4]

Market Economies A **market** is a mechanism for exchange between the buyers and sellers of a particular good or service. For example, the internet is a technologically sophisticated market that brings buyers and sellers together through e-commerce. People usually think of e-commerce as being business-to-consumer (B2C) transactions, such as buying books over the internet for personal use. But business-to-business (B2B) transactions are also a very important market. B2B involves businesses joining together to create e-commerce companies that make them more efficient when they purchase the goods and services they need. B2B transactions actually far exceed B2C transactions in dollar value.

In a market economy, B2C and B2B exchanges take place without much government involvement. To understand how a *market economy* works, consider what happens when a customer goes to a fruit stand to buy apples. Assume that one vendor is selling apples for $1 per kilogram, and another is charging $1.50. Both

vendors are free to charge what they want, and customers are free to buy what they choose. If both vendors' apples are of the same quality, the customer will likely buy the cheaper ones. But if the $1.50 apples are fresher, the customer may buy them instead. Both buyers and sellers enjoy freedom of choice (but they also are subject to risks, as the financial meltdown of 2008 demonstrated).

A GlobeScan poll of over 20 000 people in 20 countries asked people whether they agreed with the following statement: "The free market economy is the best system." Where do you think the highest support for the free market economy was found? Not in Canada, the United States, Germany, or Japan, but in *China*, where 74 percent of people polled agreed with the statement.[5] This is a surprising finding, given the Chinese government's strong support of the communist economic ideology. It seems hard to believe now, but before 1979, people who sold watches on street corners in China were sentenced to years of hard labour. After China's constitution was amended to legitimate private enterprise, the private sector has become incredibly productive. It is estimated that China produces 60 percent of all the toys in the world.[6] China's reputation for being a low-cost producer of goods is legendary. It is also a vast and rapidly growing market for many of the products that Canadian firms produce—chemicals, ores, cereals, and wood products.

Input and Output Markets A useful model for understanding how the factors of production work in a pure market economy is shown in Figure 1.2.[7] In the **input market**, firms buy resources from households, which then supply those resources. In the **output market**, firms supply goods and services in response to demand on the part of the households. The activities of these two markets create a circular flow. Ford Motor Co., for example, buys labour directly from households, which may also supply capital from accumulated savings in the form of stock purchases. Consumer buying patterns provide information that helps Ford decide which models to produce and which to discontinue. In turn, Ford uses these inputs in various ways and becomes a supplier to households when it designs and produces various kinds of automobiles, trucks, and sport-utility vehicles and offers them for sale to consumers.

Individuals are free to work for Ford or an alternative employer and to invest in Ford stock or alternative forms of saving or consumption. Similarly, Ford can create whatever vehicles it chooses and price them at whatever value it chooses. Consumers are free to buy their next car from Ford, Toyota, BMW, or any other manufacturer. The political basis for the free market economy is called **capitalism**, which allows private ownership of the factors of production and encourages entrepreneurship by offering profits as an incentive. This process contrasts markedly with that of a command economy, in which individuals may be told where they can and cannot work, companies may be told what they can and cannot manufacture, and consumers may have little or no choice as to what they purchase or how much they pay for items.

Mixed Market Economies Command and market economies are two extremes, or opposites. In reality, most countries rely on some form of **mixed market economy** that features characteristics of both command and market economies. One trend in mixed market economies that began in the 1990s is **privatization**—converting government enterprises into privately owned companies. In Canada, for example, the air traffic control system was privatized, and the federal government sold several other corporations, including Canadian National Railway and Air Canada. The Netherlands privatized its TNT Post Group N.V., and India privatized 18 industries, including iron, steel, machinery, and telecommunications.[8] In 2010, the Organisation for Economic Co-operation and Development (OECD) said that Canada Post's monopoly should be ended and it should be privatized.[9] However, when a worldwide recession began in 2008, the trend slowed. Government bailouts of Chrysler and GM in both

Canada and the U.S. meant that government was once again a part-owner of some business firms. A few countries are even pursuing a policy of **nationalization**—converting private firms into government-owned firms. Venezuela, for example, nationalized its telecommunications industry.

Deregulation means a reduction in the number of laws affecting business activity and in the powers of government enforcement agencies. This trend also developed during the 1990s, and deregulation occurred in many industries, including airlines, pipelines, banking, trucking, and communications. But this trend has also slowed (and even reversed in some cases) due to the 2008 recession. For example, there have been calls for a dramatic tightening up of the laws regulating business activity, particularly in the financial sector. The British Petroleum (BP) oil spill in the Gulf of Mexico in 2010 caused the U.S. government to put pressure on BP to reimburse

MIXED MARKET ECONOMY
An economic system with elements of both a command economy and a market economy; in practice, typical of most nations' economies.

PRIVATIZATION
The transfer of activities from the government to the private sector.

NATIONALIZATION
The transfer of activities from private firms to the government.

DEREGULATION
A reduction in the number of laws affecting business activity.

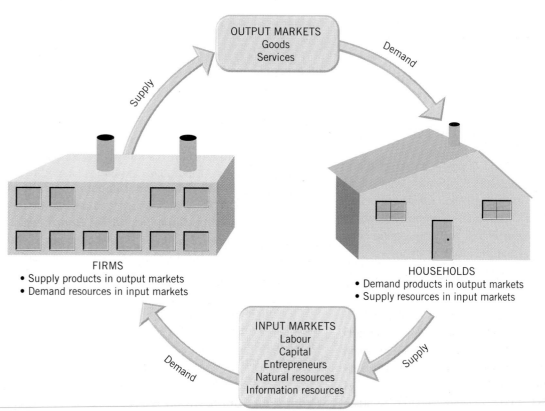

FIRMS
• Supply products in output markets
• Demand resources in input markets

HOUSEHOLDS
• Demand products in output markets
• Supply resources in input markets

Figure 1.2
Circular flow in a market economy.

individuals and businesses that were harmed by the spill. Incidents like these have created a dilemma for government policy makers; a 2009 study by the Conference Board of Canada showed that deregulation (in tandem with privatization and increased competition) caused a sharp increase in productivity in sectors like freight and airlines.[10]

As a result of the recession of 2008, mixed market econo- mies are now characterized by more government involvement than was evident just a few years ago. Governments in mixed market economies have intervened in the economic system in an attempt to sta- bilize it, but this has led to higher deficits (see Chapter 2) and more control of business activity.

Interactions between Business and Government

In Canada's mixed market economy, there are many important interactions between business and govern- ment. The ways in which government influences busi- ness and the ways business influences government are described below.

Despite becoming a territory of the communist People's Republic of China in 1997, Hong Kong remains one of the world's freest economies. In Hong Kong's Lan Kwai Fong district, for example, traditional Chinese businesses operate next door to well-known international chains.

How Government Influences Business
Government plays several key roles in the Canadian eco- nomy, and each of these roles influences business activity in some way. The roles government plays are as follows.

Government as a Customer Government buys thou- sands of different products and services from busi- ness firms, including office supplies, office buildings, computers, battleships, helicopters, highways, water treatment plants, and management and engineering con- sulting services. Many businesses depend on government purchasing, if not for their survival then at least for a cer- tain level of prosperity. Total government expenditures in 2009 were $234 billion.[11]

Government as a Competitor Government also com- petes with business through Crown corporations, which are accountable to a minister of parliament for their con- duct. Crown corporations like Hydro Quebec (revenues of $12.7 billion), Canada Post ($7.4 billion), and the Canadian Wheat Board ($8.4 billion) account for a significant amount

of economic activity in Canada.[12] Crown corporations exist at both the provincial and federal levels.

Government as Regulator Federal, and provincial governments in Canada regulate many aspects of busi- ness activity through administrative boards, tribunals, and commissions. Illustrative examples include the **Canadian Radio-television and Telecommunications Commission (CRTC)** (which issues and renews broad- cast licences) and the **Canadian Wheat Board** (which regulates the price of wheat). Provincial boards and commissions also regulate business activity, but differ- ent situations exist in different provinces. For example, the provinces of Quebec and B.C. allowed mixed martial arts events such as the UFC, but Ontario didn't (Ontario began allowing these events in 2011).[13] Reasons for regu- lating business activity include protecting competition, protecting consumers, achieving social goals, and pro- tecting the environment.

Promoting Competition Competition is crucial to a market economy, so government regulates business activity to ensure that healthy competition exists among business firms. Without these restrictions, a large company with vast resources could cut its prices and drive smaller firms out of the market. The guidelines for Canada's competition policy are contained in the Competition Act, which prohibits a variety of practices (see Table 1.1). Section 61, for example, prohibits something called *resale price maintenance*. Labatt Brewing Co. recently pled guilty to resale price maintenance and was fined $250 000 after its sales representatives gave money to store operators who agreed to not lower prices on some brands of beer. This activity meant that customers had to pay higher prices for beer.[14]

The Act prohibits agreements among companies that are designed to reduce competition. Formerly, the government had to prove that such agreements actually reduced competition, but recent changes to the legislation mean that the mere existence of a conspiracy is assumed to be proof that competition has been reduced.[15] Another big change is the dramatically increased fines for misleading marketing practices by corporations (formerly $100 000 for the first offence, but now $10 million).[16]

Businesses often complain that the Competition Bureau is too slow in approving or denying merger plans. For example, when Labatt Brewing wanted to take over Lakeport Brewing, it was told that the Competition Bureau would need up to six months to determine whether the takeover would lessen competition. Labatt therefore appealed to the Competition Tribunal to speed up the process. The Tribunal agreed with Labatt, and the merger went ahead sooner than it otherwise would have.[17] There was, however, some interesting fallout later. The federal industry minister began an investigation after a Federal Court judge accused the Competition Bureau of providing misleading information in order to get a court order for Labatt's records during its review of the proposed merger.[18]

Protecting Consumers The federal government has initiated many programs that protect consumers. Consumer and Corporate Affairs Canada administers many of these. Important legislation includes the **Hazardous Products Act** (which requires poisonous, flammable, explosive, or corrosive products to be appropriately labelled), the **Tobacco Act** (which prohibits cigarette advertising on billboards and in stores), the **Weights and Measures Act** (which sets standards of accuracy for weighing and measuring devices), the **Textile Labelling Act** (which regulates the labelling, sale, importation, and advertising of consumer textile articles),

HAZARDOUS PRODUCTS ACT Regulates banned products and products that can be sold but must be labelled hazardous.

TOBACCO ACT Prohibits cigarette advertising on billboards and in retail stores, and assigns financial penalties to violators.

WEIGHTS AND MEASURES ACT Sets standards of accuracy for weighing and measuring devices.

TEXTILE LABELLING ACT Regulates the labelling, sale, importation, and advertising of consumer textile articles.

Table 1.1	The Competition Act
Section 45	Prohibits conspiracies and combinations formed for the purpose of unduly lessening competition in the production, transportation, or storage of goods. Persons convicted may be imprisoned for up to five years or fined up to $1 million or both.
Section 50	Prohibits illegal trade practices. A company may not, for example, cut prices in one region of Canada while selling at a higher price everywhere else if this substantially lessens competition. A company may not sell at "unreasonably low prices" if this substantially lessens competition. (This section does not prohibit credit unions from returning surpluses to their members.)
Section 51	Prohibits giving allowances and rebates to buyers to cover their advertising expenses, unless these allowances are made available proportionally to other purchasers who are in competition with the buyer given the rebate.
Section 52	Prohibits marketing (promotion) activities that are false or misleading. Includes telemarketing activities.
Section 53	Prohibits the deceptive notice that a person has won a prize if the recipient is asked to pay money as a condition of winning the prize.
Section 54	Prohibits charging the higher price when two prices are shown on a product.
Section 55.1	Prohibits pyramid selling (a participant in the plan receives compensation for recruiting other individuals into the plan).
Section 61	Prohibits resale price maintenance. No person who produces or supplies a product can attempt to influence upward, or discourage reduction of, the price of the good in question. It is also illegal for the producer to refuse to supply a product to a reseller simply because the producer believes the reseller will cut the price.
Section 74	Prohibits bait-and-switch selling. No person can advertise a product at a bargain price if there is no supply of the product available to the consumer. (This tactic baits prospects into the store, where salespeople switch them to higher-priced goods.) This section also controls the use of contests to sell goods, and prohibits the sale of goods at a price higher than the advertised one.

The Hazardous Products Act requires poisonous, flammable, explosive, or corrosive products to have warning labels to protect consumers who use them.

and the **Food and Drug Act** (which prohibits the sale of food that contains any poisonous or harmful substances). Consumers are also protected by municipal bylaws such as "no smoking" bylaws.

Achieving Social Goals Social goals, which promote the well-being of Canadian society, include things like universal access to health care, safe workplaces, employment insurance, and decent pensions. All of these goals require the interaction of business firms and the Canadian government. But the decisions of foreign governments—as they pursue their own social goals—can also affect Canadian businesses. For example, when the U.S. government introduced legislation making it difficult for online gambling companies to operate in the U.S., the stock prices of Canadian firms like Cryptologic Inc. and Chartwell Technology dropped.[19]

Protecting the Environment Government legislation designed to protect the environment includes the **Canada Water Act** (which controls water quality in fresh and marine waters), the **Fisheries Act** (which controls the discharge of any harmful substance into water), and the **Environmental Contaminants Act** (which establishes regulations for

airborne substances that are a danger to human health or the environment).

Government as a Taxation Agent Taxes are imposed and collected by the federal, provincial, and local governments. **Revenue taxes** (e.g., income taxes) are levied by governments primarily to provide revenue to fund various services and programs. **Progressive revenue taxes** are levied at a higher rate on higher-income taxpayers and at a lower rate on lower-income taxpayers. **Regressive revenue taxes** (e.g., sales tax) are levied at the same rate regardless of a person's income. They cause poorer people to pay a higher percentage of their income for these taxes than rich people pay. **Restrictive taxes** (e.g., taxes on alcohol, tobacco, and gasoline) are levied partially for the revenue they provide, but also because legislative bodies believe that the products in question should be controlled.

Government as a Provider of Incentives and Financial Assistance Federal, provincial, and municipal governments offer incentive programs that attempt to stimulate economic development. The Province of Quebec, for example, has attracted video game companies like Ubisoft by giving them multimillion-dollar subsidies if they locate in the province.[20] The Provinces of Ontario and B.C. have given hundreds of millions of dollars in subsidies to film companies to motivate them to make major films in those provinces. But the government of Alberta (which spends about $20 million each year on subsidies to filmmakers) has decided not to increase the amount of its subsidies.[21]

Governments also offer incentives through the many services they provide to business firms through government organizations. Examples include the Export Development Corporation (which assists Canadian exporters by offering export insurance against non-payment by foreign buyers and long-term loans to foreign buyers of Canadian products), Natural Resources Canada (which provides geological maps of Canada's potential mineral-producing areas), and Statistics Canada (which provides data and analysis on almost every aspect of Canadian society). Industry Canada offers many different programs designed to help small businesses. The Canada Business program, for example, provides information on government programs, services, and regulations in order to improve the start-up and survival rates of small and medium-sized businesses. It also encourages businesses to focus on sound business planning and the effective use of market research. DFAIT helps Canadian companies doing business internationally by promoting Canada as a good place to invest and to carry on business activities. It also assists in negotiating and administering trade agreements.

There are many other government incentive programs, including municipal tax rebates for companies that locate in certain areas, design assistance programs, and remission of tariffs on certain advanced technology production equipment. Government incentive programs may or may not have the desired effect of stimulating the economy. They may also cause difficulties with our trading partners, as we shall see in Chapter 5. Some critics also argue that business firms are too willing to accept government assistance—either in the form of incentives or bailouts—and that managers should put more emphasis on innovation and creativity so business firms can better cope with economic difficulties when they arise, as they did during the 2008–2009 recession.

Government as a Provider of Essential Services The various levels of government facilitate business activity through the services they supply. The federal government provides highways, the postal service, the minting of money, the armed forces, and statistical data on which to base business decisions. It also tries to maintain stability through fiscal and monetary policy (discussed in Chapter 2). Provincial and municipal governments provide streets, sewage and sanitation systems, police and fire departments, utilities, hospitals, and education. All of these activities create the kind of stability that encourages business activity.

How Business Influences Government

Businesses also try to influence the government through the use of lobbyists, trade associations, and advertising. A **lobbyist** is a person hired by a company or industry to represent that company's interests with government officials. The Canadian Association of Consulting Engineers, for example, regularly lobbies the federal and provincial governments to make use of the skills possessed by private-sector consulting engineers on projects like city water systems. Some business lobbyists have training in the particular industry, public relations experience, or a legal background. A few have served as legislators or government regulators.

The federal Lobbying Act requires lobbyists to register with the Commissioner of Lobbying so it is clear which individuals are being paid for their lobbying activity. It also sets rules for accountability and transparency, and requires lobbyists to report detailed information about their communications with what are known as Designated Public Office Holders (DPOHs).[22] For many lobbying efforts, there are opposing points of view. For example, the Canadian Cancer Society and the Tobacco Institute present very different points of view on cigarette smoking and cigarette advertising.

Employees and owners of small businesses that cannot afford lobbyists often join **trade associations**, which may act as an industry lobby to influence legislation. They also conduct training programs relevant to the particular industry, and they arrange trade shows at which members display their products or services to potential customers. Most publish newsletters featuring articles on new products, new companies, changes in ownership, and changes in laws affecting the industry.

Corporations can influence legislation indirectly by influencing voters. A company can, for example, launch an advertising campaign designed to get people to write their MPs, MPPs, or MLAs demanding passage—or rejection—of a particular bill that is before parliament or the provincial legislature.

LO-3 The Canadian Market Economy

Understanding the complex nature of the Canadian economic system is essential to understanding Canadian business. In this section, we will examine the workings of our market economy, including markets, demand, supply, private enterprise, and degrees of competition.

Demand and Supply in a Market Economy

In economic terms, a **market** is not a specific place, like a supermarket, but an exchange process between buyers and sellers. Decisions about production in a market

LOBBYIST A person hired by a company or an industry to represent its interests with government officials.

TRADE ASSOCIATION An organization dedicated to promoting the interests and assisting the members of a particular industry.

MARKET An exchange process between buyers and **sellers of a particular good or service**.

DEMAND The willingness and ability of buyers to purchase a product or service.

SUPPLY The willingness and ability of producers to offer a good or service for sale.

LAW OF DEMAND The principle that buyers will purchase (demand) more of a product as price drops.

LAW OF SUPPLY The principle that producers will offer (supply) more of a product as price rises.

DEMAND AND SUPPLY SCHEDULE Assessment of the relationships between different levels of demand and supply at different price levels.

economy are the result of millions of exchanges. How much of what product a company offers for sale and who buys it depends on the laws of demand and supply.

The Laws of Supply and Demand In a market economy, decisions about what to buy and what to sell are determined primarily by the forces of demand and supply. **Demand** is the willingness and ability of buyers to purchase a product or service. **Supply** is the willingness and ability of producers to offer a good or service for sale. The **law of demand** states that buyers will purchase (demand) more of a product as its price

drops. Conversely, the **law of supply** states that producers will offer (supply) more for sale as the price rises.

Demand and Supply Schedule To appreciate these laws in action, consider the market for pizza in your town. If everyone is willing to pay $25 for a pizza (a relatively high price), the local pizzeria will produce a large supply. If, however, everyone is willing to pay only $5 (a relatively low price), the restaurant will make fewer pizzas. Through careful analysis, we can determine how many pizzas will be sold at different prices. These results, called a **demand and supply schedule**, are obtained from marketing research and other systematic studies of the market. Properly applied, they help managers understand the relationships among different levels of demand and supply at different price levels.

Demand and Supply Curves The demand and supply schedule can be used to construct demand and

E-BUSINESS AND SOCIAL MEDIA SOLUTIONS

Virtual Goods: An Emerging E-Market

Not too long ago, people doubted the commercial sales potential of bottled water because a perfectly good substitute was available for virtually no cost. At the time, many skeptics made comments like "What's next, are we going to sell air?" Today, consumers purchase approximately 200 billion litres of bottled water worldwide each year. The skeptics did not foresee an era dominated by the internet, smart phones, and social media.

At least bottled water is a physical product. But how much is an avatar worth? How much would you spend on a virtual good? If your answer is $0, you don't know what's going on in the virtual gaming world. Have you heard of Zynga? World of Warcraft? Mafia Wars? FarmVille? If you answered "no" to all these questions, you may be shocked to learn that, in 2010, virtual goods sales were expected to reach $1.6 billion in the U.S. alone, and are projected to grow to $3.6 billion by 2012.

As we've noted, a market is an exchange process between buyers and sellers of a particular good or service. This definition fits the evolving virtual goods world as well. Whether you are buying a potato to make French fries (to eat), or a virtual potato to plant in your own FarmVille virtual garden (for entertainment), you are involved in a market of buyers and sellers.

Hard-core virtual gamers are willing to spend good money to ensure that they have the best gear available in games like World of Warcraft.

Facebook links people to the virtual world and has over 500 million users. The company is now trying to capitalize on its popularity by adding a new revenue stream. It plans to charge 30 percent on virtual game props (similar to Apple's approach to apps). It is also testing the extended use of its Facebook credits. If all goes as planned, Zynga (which has 120 million game users) may be forced to adopt this model. Facebook could collect as much as $500 million over the next three years from Zynga and other gaming companies, including Electronic Arts, CrowdStar, Slide, RockYou, and Digital Chocolate. One thing is certain, there is nothing virtual about the revenue potential.

Critical Thinking Questions

1. Have you ever purchased a virtual good? If so, describe it. Were you satisfied? If not, what do you think of the prospects for this growing market?
2. What do you think of Facebook's new revenue stream model? Will it work?

supply curves for pizza. A **demand curve** shows how many products—in this case, pizzas—will be *demanded* (bought) at different prices. A **supply curve** shows how many pizzas will be *supplied* (cooked) at different prices.

Figure 1.3 shows the hypothetical demand and supply curves for pizzas in our illustration. As you can see, demand increases as price decreases, and supply increases as price increases. When the demand and supply curves are plotted on the same graph, the point at which they intersect is the **market price**, or **equilibrium**

price—the price at which the quantity of goods demanded and the quantity of goods supplied are equal. In Figure 1.3, the equilibrium price for pizzas is $10. At this point, the quantity of pizzas demanded and the quantity of pizzas supplied are the same—1000 pizzas per week.

Figure 1.3
Demand and Supply.

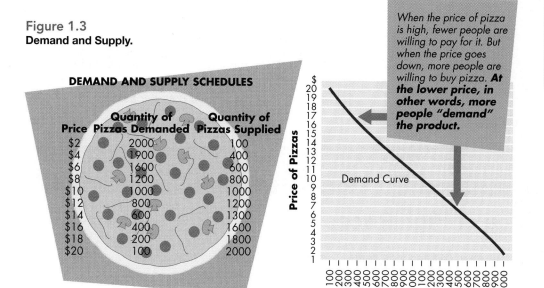

DEMAND AND SUPPLY SCHEDULES

Price	Quantity of Pizzas Demanded	Quantity of Pizzas Supplied
$2	2000	100
$4	1900	400
$6	1600	600
$8	1200	800
$10	1000	1000
$12	800	1200
$14	600	1300
$16	400	1600
$18	200	1800
$20	100	2000

*When the price of pizza is high, fewer people are willing to pay for it. But when the price goes down, more people are willing to buy pizza. **At the lower price, in other words, more people "demand" the product.***

Demand Curve

Quantity of Pizzas Demanded

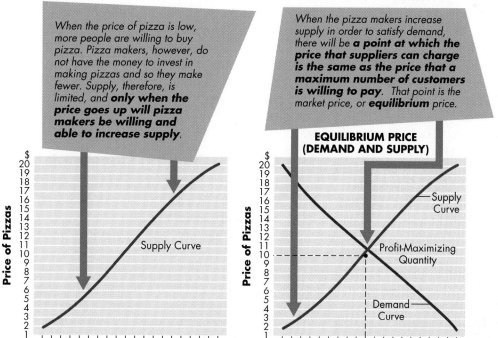

*When the price of pizza is low, more people are willing to buy pizza. Pizza makers, however, do not have the money to invest in making pizzas and so they make fewer. Supply, therefore, is limited, and **only when the price goes up will pizza makers be willing and able to increase supply**.*

Supply Curve

Quantity of Pizzas Supplied

*When the pizza makers increase supply in order to satisfy demand, there will be **a point at which the price that suppliers can charge is the same as the price that a maximum number of customers is willing to pay**. That point is the market price, or **equilibrium** price.*

EQUILIBRIUM PRICE (DEMAND AND SUPPLY)

Supply Curve

Profit-Maximizing Quantity

Demand Curve

Quantity of Pizzas

Canada is the dominant supplier of maple syrup for the world market. But variable weather conditions can create conditions of either surplus or shortage.

Surpluses and Shortages What would happen if the owner tried to increase profits by making more pizzas to sell? Or, what if the owner wanted to reduce overhead, cut back on store hours, and reduced the number of pizzas offered for sale? In either case, the result would be an inefficient use of resources. For example, if the restaurant supplies 1200 pizzas and tries to sell them for $10 each, 200 pizzas will not be purchased. The demand schedule clearly shows that only 1000 pizzas will be demanded at this price. The pizza maker will therefore have a **surplus**—a situation in which the quantity supplied exceeds the quantity demanded. The restaurant will thus lose the money that it spent making those extra 200 pizzas.

Conversely, if the pizzeria supplies only 800 pizzas, a **shortage** will result because the quantity demanded will be greater than the quantity supplied. The pizzeria will "lose" the extra money that it could have made by producing 200 more pizzas. Even though consumers may pay more for pizzas because of the shortage,

MANAGING IN TURBULENT TIMES

The High Price of High Prices

Economic theory tells us that when demand for a commodity increases, its price goes up, and people try to find substitutes that are cheaper. For example, when the price of oil is high, companies use corn to make ethanol to add to gasoline, and palm oil is used to make diesel fuel (called biodiesel). But, as more producers start using corn or palm oil, the demand for those commodities goes up and so does their price. During 2006, for example, the price of palm oil rose from less than US$400 per metric tonne to more than US$500 per metric tonne.

When prices of commodities rise rapidly, there are usually some unanticipated outcomes. One of these is increased criminal activity. As the price of stainless steel and aluminum rose during the last few years, thieves began stealing items such as beer kegs, railway baggage carts, railroad tracks, light poles, and highway guardrails. These items were then sold to scrap yards for cash.

The impact of stealing is limited to lost revenue (it's only money), but sky-high prices for food can actually threaten people's lives. Global food prices increased 83 percent between 2005 and 2008, and that put a lot of stress on the world's poorest countries. In some countries, families are spending one-half their income just on food. One culprit, ironically, is the

push to convert corn into biofuel. In countries like Haiti, Cameroon, Senegal, and Ethiopia, citizens have rioted over higher prices for important staple items such as beans and rice. In Pakistan and Thailand, army troops were deployed to prevent the theft of food from warehouses. The World Bank has identified 33 countries that are at risk for serious social upheaval because of high food prices. To cope with the problem, some countries are slashing import duties and imposing export duties. This is just the reverse of what countries normally do.

Critical Thinking Questions

1. It is obvious that negative outcomes can occur with high prices. Can high prices ever lead to positive outcomes? Explain.
2. Consider the following statement: "*The high price of commodities like copper is not a concern because we do not need copper to survive, but the high price of food is a concern because it threatens people's lives. The central governments of the world should therefore coordinate their efforts and put in place rules to ensure that food prices are kept low*." Do you agree or disagree with the statement? Explain your reasoning.

the restaurant will still earn lower profits than it would have if it had made 1000 pizzas. In addition, it may risk angering customers who cannot buy pizzas. To optimize profits, therefore, all businesses must constantly seek the right combination of price charged and quantity supplied. This "right combination" is found at the equilibrium point.

Maple syrup is a quintessential Canadian commodity (we produce 80 percent of the total world's supply), but its price fluctuates because weather influences the supply. Unfavourable weather reduced the supply in 2008, but good weather in 2009 caused yields to increase by 85 percent over 2008.[23] Price fluctuations in several other commodities are described in the boxed insert entitled "The High Price of High Prices."[24]

LO-4   Private Enterprise and Competition

Market economies rely on a **private enterprise** system— one that allows individuals to pursue their own interests with minimal government restriction. Private enterprise requires the presence of four elements: private property rights, freedom of choice, profits, and competition.

- *Private property*. Ownership of the resources used to create wealth is in the hands of individuals.[25]

- *Freedom of choice*. You can sell your labour to any employer you choose. You can also choose which products to buy, and producers can usually choose whom to hire and what to produce.

- *Profits*. The lure of profits (and freedom) leads some people to abandon the security of working for someone else and to assume the risks of entrepreneurship. Anticipated profits also influence individuals' choices of which goods or services to produce.

- *Competition*. Profits motivate individuals to start businesses, and competition motivates them to operate those businesses efficiently. **Competition** occurs when two or more businesses vie for the same resources or customers. To gain an advantage over competitors, a business must produce its goods or services efficiently and be able to sell at a reasonable profit. Competition forces all businesses to make products better or cheaper.

Degrees of Competition

Economists have identified four basic degrees of competition within a private enterprise system: perfect competition, monopolistic competition, oligopoly, and monopoly.

Perfect Competition For **perfect competition** to exist, firms must be small in size (but large in number), the products of each firm are almost identical, both buyers and sellers know the price that others are paying and receiving in the marketplace, firms find it easy to enter or leave the market, prices are set by the forces of supply and demand, and no firm is powerful enough individually to influence the price of its product in the marketplace. Agriculture is usually considered to be a good example of pure competition in the Canadian economy. There are thousands of wheat farmers, the wheat produced on one farm is essentially the same as wheat produced on another farm, producers and buyers are well aware of prevailing market prices, and it is relatively easy to get started or to quit producing wheat.

Monopolistic Competition In **monopolistic competition**, there are fewer sellers than in pure competition, but there are still many buyers. Sellers try to make their products appear to be at least slightly different from those of their competitors by tactics such as using brand names (Tide and Cheer), design or styling (Ralph Lauren and Izod clothes), and advertising (like that done by Coca-Cola and Pepsi). Monopolistically competitive businesses may be large or small, because it is relatively easy for a firm to enter or leave the market. For example, many small clothing manufacturers compete successfully with large apparel makers. Product differentiation also gives sellers some control over the price they charge. Thus, Ralph Lauren polo shirts can be priced with little regard for the price of shirts sold at the Bay, even though the Bay's shirts may have very similar styling.

Oligopoly When an industry has only a handful of very large sellers, an **oligopoly** exists. Competition is fierce

---

SURPLUS
Situation in which quantity supplied exceeds quantity demanded.

SHORTAGE
Situation in which quantity demanded exceeds quantity supplied.

PRIVATE ENTERPRISE
An economic system characterized by private property rights, freedom of choice, profits, and competition.

COMPETITION
The vying among businesses in a particular market or industry to best satisfy consumer demands and earn profits.

PERFECT COMPETITION
A market or industry characterized by a very large number of small firms producing an identical product so that none of the firms has any ability to influence price.

MONOPOLISTIC COMPETITION
A market or industry characterized by a large number of firms supplying products that are similar but distinctive enough from one another to give firms some ability to influence price.

OLIGOPOLY
A market or industry characterized by a small number of very large firms that have the power to influence the price of their product and/or resources.

because the actions of any one firm in an oligopolistic market can significantly affect the sales of all other firms.[26] Most oligopolistic firms avoid price competition because it reduces profits. For example, the four major cereal makers (Kellogg, General Mills, General Foods, and Quaker Oats) charge roughly the same price for their cereals. Rather than compete on price, they emphasize advertising, which claims that their cereals are better tasting or more nutritious than the competition's. Entry into an oligopolistic market is difficult because large capital investment is usually necessary. Thus, oligopolistic industries (such as the automobile, rubber, and steel industries) tend to stay oligopolistic. As the trend toward globalization continues, it is likely that more global oligopolies will come into being.[27]

Monopoly When an industry or market has only one producer, a **monopoly** exists. Being the only supplier gives a firm complete control over the price of its product. Its only constraint is how much consumer demand will fall as its price rises. For centuries, wine bottles were sealed using natural cork made from tree bark. But a new

technology allows wine bottles to be sealed with plastic corks that are cheaper and work just as well. The natural wine cork industry has lost its monopoly.[28] In Canada, laws such as the Competition Act forbid most monopolies. **Natural monopolies**—such as provincial electric utilities—are closely watched by provincial utilities boards, and the assumption that there is such a thing as a natural monopoly is increasingly being challenged. For example, the Royal Mail Group's 350-year monopoly of the British postal service ended in 2006, and rival companies are now allowed to compete with Royal Mail.[29] In India, private couriers like FedEx and United Parcel Service now provide more than half the delivery business in that country after they were allowed to compete with India Post, which had a monopoly on mail delivery for several hundred years.[30]

LO-5 A Brief History of Business in Canada

In this section, we will trace the broad outlines of the development of business activity in Canada. Table 1.2 highlights some important dates in Canadian business history.[31]

The Early Years
Business activity and profit from commercial fishing were the motivation for the first European involvement

Consumers often buy products under conditions of monopolistic competition. For example, there are few differences between various brands of toothpaste, cold tablets, detergents, canned goods, and soft drinks.

in Canada. In the late 1400s, ships financed by English entrepreneurs came to the coast of Newfoundland to fish. By the late 1500s, the Newfoundland coast was being visited by hundreds of fishing vessels each year.

Beginning in the 1500s, French and British adventurers began trading with the native peoples. Items such as cooking utensils and knives were exchanged for beaver and other furs. One trading syndicate made over 1000 percent profit on beaver skins sold to a Paris furrier. Trading was aggressive and, over time, the price of furs rose as more and more Europeans bid for them. Originally the fur trade was restricted to eastern Canada, but by the late 1600s, coureurs de bois were travelling far to the west in search of new sources of furs.

European settlers who arrived in Canada in the sixteenth and seventeenth centuries initially had to farm or starve. Gradually, however, they began to produce more than they needed for their own survival. The governments of the countries from which the settlers came (notably England and France) were strong supporters of the mercantilist philosophy. Under *mercantilism*, colonists were expected to export raw materials like beaver pelts and lumber at low prices to the mother country.

These raw materials were then used to produce finished goods such as fur coats, which were sold at high prices to settlers in Canada. Attempts to develop industry in Canada were thwarted by England and France, which enjoyed large profits from mercantilism. As a result, Canadian manufacturing was slow to develop.

The Factory System and the Industrial Revolution

British manufacturing took a great leap forward around 1750 with the coming of the **Industrial Revolution**. This revolution was made possible by advances in technology and by the development of the **factory system**. Instead of hundreds of workers turning out items one at a time in their cottages, the factory system brought

INDUSTRIAL REVOLUTION
A major change in goods production that began in England in the mid-eighteenth century and was characterized by a shift to the factory system, mass production, and specialization of labour.

FACTORY SYSTEM
A process in which all the machinery, materials, and workers required to produce a good in large quantities are brought together in one place.

Table 1.2	**Some Important Dates in Canadian Business History**		
1490	English fishermen active off the coast of Newfoundland	1926	U.S. replaces Great Britain as Canada's largest trading partner
1534	Account of first trading with Aboriginal peoples written by Jacques Cartier	1927	Armand Bombardier sells first "auto-neige" (forerunner of the snowmobile)
1670	Hudson's Bay Company founded	1929	Great stock market crash
1779	North West Company forms	1929–33	Great Depression
1785	Molson brewery opens	1930	Canadian Airways Limited formed
1805	First Canadian paper mill built at St. Andrew's, Quebec	1932	Canadian Radio Broadcasting Corporation formed (it became the CBC in 1936)
1809	First steamboat (the *Accommodation*) put into service on the St. Lawrence River by John Molson	1935	Bank of Canada begins operations
1817	Bank of Montreal chartered	1947–51	Early computer built at the University of Toronto
1821	Hudson's Bay Company and North West Company merge	1947	Leduc Number 1 oil well drilled in Alberta
1830–50	Era of canal building	1949	A.V. Roe (Avro) makes Canada's first commercial jetliner
1850–60	First era of railroad building	1965	Auto Pact signed with the U.S.
1855	John Redpath opens first Canadian sugar refinery in Montreal	1969	Canada becomes world's largest potash producer
1857–58	First oil well in Canada drilled near Sarnia, Ontario	1989	Free trade agreement with U.S. comes into effect
1861	Toronto Stock Exchange opens	1993	North American Free Trade Agreement comes into effect
1869	Eaton's opens for business in Toronto	2000	Tech bubble bursts; stock prices drop sharply
1880–90	First western land boom	2003	Canadian internet pharmacies begin selling prescription drugs to U.S. citizens
1885	Last spike driven to complete the Canadian Pacific Railroad	2006	Softwood lumber dispute with U.S. settled
1897–99	Klondike gold rush	2007	Canadian dollar reaches par with U.S. dollar
1917–22	Creation of Canadian National Railways	2008	Oil prices reach record high of $147 per barrel
		2008–09	Worldwide recession occurs; stock markets drop sharply

together in one place all of the materials and workers required to produce items in large quantities, along with newly created machines capable of **mass production**.

Mass production offered savings in several areas. It avoided unnecessary duplication of equipment. It allowed firms to purchase raw materials at better prices by buying large lots. And most important, it encouraged **specialization** of labour. No longer did production require highly skilled craftspeople who could do all the different tasks required to make an item. A series of semiskilled workers, each trained to perform only one task and supported by specialized machines and tools, greatly increased output.

In spite of British laws against the export of technology and manufacturing to North America, Canadian manufacturing existed almost from the beginning of European settlement. Modest manufacturing operations were evident in sawmills, breweries, grist mills for grinding grain, tanneries, woollen mills, shoemakers' shops, and tailors' shops. These operations were so successful that by 1800 exports of manufactured goods were more important than exports of fur.

With the advent of steam power in the early 1800s, manufacturing activity began to increase rapidly. By 1850, more than 30 factories—employing more than 2000 people—lined the Lachine Canal alone. Exports of timber to England in 1850 were 70 times greater than what they had been in 1800. The demand for reliable transportation was the impetus for canal building in the mid-1800s and then the railroad-building boom in the mid- and late 1800s.

The Entrepreneurial Era

One of the most significant features of the last half of the nineteenth century was the emergence of entrepreneurs willing to take risks in the hope of earning huge profits. Adam Smith in his book *The Wealth of Nations* argued that the government should not interfere in the economy but should let businesses function without regulation or restriction. This *laissez-faire* attitude was often adopted by the Canadian government. As a result,

during the **entrepreneurial era**, some individuals became immensely wealthy through their aggressive business dealings. Some railway, bank, and insurance executives made over $25 000 per year in the late 1800s, and their purchasing power was immense. Entrepreneurs such as Joseph Flavelle, Henry Pellatt, and John MacDonald lived in ostentatious mansions or castles.

The size and economic power of some firms meant that other businesses had difficulty competing against them. At the same time, some business executives decided that it was more profitable to collude than to compete. They decided among themselves to fix prices and divide up markets. Hurt by these actions, Canadian consumers called for more regulation of business. In 1889, the first anti-combines legislation was passed in Canada, and legislation regulating business has increased ever since.

The Production Era

The concepts of specialization and mass production that originated in the Industrial Revolution were more fully refined as Canada entered the twentieth century. The Scientific Management Movement focused management's attention on production. Increased efficiency via the "one best way" to accomplish tasks became the major management goal. Henry Ford's introduction of the moving assembly line in the United States in 1913 ushered in the **production era**. During the production era, less attention was paid to selling and marketing than to technical efficiency when producing goods. By using fixed workstations, increasing task specialization, and moving the work to the worker, the assembly line increased productivity and lowered prices, making all kinds of products affordable for the average person. It also increased the available labour pool because many people could be trained to carry out assembly line tasks. Formerly, the labour pool was limited because relatively few people had the high skill levels of craftspeople.

During the production era, large businesses began selling stock—making shareholders the owners—and relying on professional managers. The growth of corporations and improved production output resulting from assembly lines came at the expense of worker freedom. The dominance of big firms made it harder for individuals to go into business for themselves. Company towns run by the railroads, mining corporations, and forest products firms gave individuals little freedom of choice over whom to work for and what to buy. To restore some balance within the overall system, both government and labour had to develop and grow. Thus, this period saw the rise of labour unions and collective bargaining. We will look at this development in more detail in Chapter 8. The Great Depression of the 1930s and the Second World War caused the federal government to intervene in the economic system on a previously unimaginable scale. Today, business, government, and labour are frequently referred to by economists and politicians as the three *countervailing powers* in our society. All are big. All are strong. Yet, none totally dominates the others.

The Sales and Marketing Eras

By the 1930s, business's focus on production had resulted in spectacular increases in the amount of goods and services available for sale. As a result, buyers had more choices and producers faced greater competition in selling their wares. Thus began the so-called **sales era**. According to the ideas of that time, a business's profits and success depended on hiring the right salespeople, advertising heavily, and making sure products were readily available. Business firms were essentially production- and sales-oriented, and they produced what they thought customers wanted, or simply what the company was good at producing. This approach is still used by firms that find themselves with surplus goods that they want to sell (e.g., used-car dealerships).

Following the Second World War, pent-up demand for consumer goods kept the economy rolling. While brief recessions did occur periodically, the 1950s and 1960s were prosperous times. Production increased, technology advanced, and the standard of living rose. During the **marketing era**, business adopted a new philosophy of how to do business—use market research to determine what customers want, and then make it for them. Firms like Procter & Gamble and Molson were very effective during the marketing era, and continue to be profitable today. Each offers an array of products within a particular field (toothpaste or beer, for example), and gives customers a chance to pick what best suits their needs.

The Finance Era

In the 1980s, emphasis shifted to finance. In the **finance era** there was a sharp increase in mergers and in the buying and selling of business enterprises. Some people now call it the "decade of greed." During the finance era there was a great deal of financial manipulation of corporate assets by so-called corporate raiders. Critics charged that these raiders were simply enriching themselves and weren't creating anything of tangible value by their activity. They also charged that raiders were distracting business managers from their main goals of running the business. The raiders responded that they were making organizations more efficient by streamlining, merging, and reorganizing them.

The Global Era

During the last two decades, we have witnessed the emergence of the global economy and further dramatic technological advances in production, computer

SALES ERA
The period during the 1930s and 1940s when businesses focused on sales forces, advertising, and keeping products readily available.

MARKETING ERA
The period during the 1950s and 1960s when businesses began to identify and meet consumer wants in order to make a profit.

FINANCE ERA
The period during the 1980s when there were many mergers and much buying and selling of business enterprises.

China opened its economy to foreign investors in the 1980s and joined the World Trade Organization in 2001. Now the Chinese buy as many cars as the Germans. They also buy more cellphones than anyone anywhere, and the opening of the Chinese market has created a windfall for makers of wireless handsets, including Motorola (U.S.), Siemens (Germany), Samsung (South Korea), and Nokia (Finland).

technology, information systems, and communication capabilities. Canadians drive cars made in Japan, wear sweaters made in Italy, drink beer brewed in Mexico, and listen to stereos made in Taiwan. But we're not alone in this. In this **global era**, people around the world buy products and services from foreign companies.

While some Canadian businesses have been hurt by foreign imports, numerous others have profited by exploring new foreign markets themselves. Global and domestic competition has also forced all businesses to work harder than ever to cut costs, increase efficiency, and improve product and service quality. We will explore a variety of important trends, opportunities, and challenges of the global era throughout this book.

The Internet Era

The rapid increase in internet usage has facilitated global business activity. Both large and small businesses are not restricted to thinking only in terms of local markets. Web-based services that are offered through a web browser are helping businesses "go global."[32] The internet affects both domestic and global business activity in three major ways:

- *The internet gives a dramatic boost to trade in all sectors of the economy, especially services.* The internet makes it easier for all trade to grow, and this is particularly true for trade in services on an international scale. The growth of call centres in places like India is an example of this international trade in services.

- *The internet levels the playing field, at least to some extent, between larger and smaller enterprises, regardless of what products or services they sell.* In the past, a substantial investment was typically needed to enter some industries and to enter foreign markets. Now, however, a small business based in central Alberta, southern Italy, eastern Malaysia, or northern Brazil can set up a website and compete quite effectively with much larger businesses located around the world.

- *The internet holds considerable potential as an effective and efficient networking mechanism among businesses.* Business-to-business (B2B) networks can link firms with all of their suppliers, business customers, and strategic partners in ways that make it faster and easier for them to do business together.

PEARSON mybusinesslab

To improve your grade, visit the MyBusinessLab website at **www.pearsoned.ca/mybusinesslab**. This online homework and tutorial system allows you to test your understanding and generates a personalized study plan just for you. It provides you with study and practice tools directly related to this chapter's content. MyBusinessLab puts you in control of your own learning! Test yourself on the material for this chapter at **www.pearsoned.ca/mybusinesslab**.

Summary of Learning Objectives

1. **Define the nature of Canadian *business* and identify its main goals.** Businesses are organizations that produce or sell goods or services to make a profit. *Profits* are the difference between a business's revenues and expenses. The prospect of earning profits encourages individuals and organizations to open and expand businesses. The benefits of business activities also extend to wages paid to workers and to taxes that support government functions.

2. **Describe different types of global *economic systems* according to the means by which they control the *factors of production* through *input***

and *output markets.* An *economic system* is a nation's system for allocating its resources among its citizens. Economic systems differ in terms of who owns or controls the five basic factors of production: labour, capital, entrepreneurs, physical resources, and information resources. In *command economies*, the government controls all or most of these factors. In *market economies*, which are based on the principles of *capitalism*, individuals and businesses control the factors of production and exchange them through *input* and *output markets*. Most countries today have *mixed market economies* that are dominated by one of these systems but include elements of the other. The processes of *deregulation* and *privatization* are important means by which many of the world's planned economies are moving toward mixed market systems.

3. **Show how *demand* and *supply* affect resource distribution in Canada.** The Canadian economy is strongly influenced by markets, demand, and supply. *Demand* is the willingness and ability of buyers to purchase a good or service. *Supply* is the willingness and ability of producers to offer goods or services for sale. Demand and supply work together to set a *market* or *equilibrium price*—the price at which the quantity of goods demanded and the quantity of goods supplied are equal.

4. **Identify the elements of *private enterprise* and explain the various *degrees of competition* in the Canadian economic system.** The Canadian economy is founded on the principles of *private enterprise, private property rights, freedom of choice, profits*, and *competition*. Degrees of competition vary because not all industries are equally competitive. Under conditions of *pure competition*, numerous small firms compete in a market governed entirely by demand and supply. In *monopolistic competition*, there are a smaller number of sellers, and each one tries to make its product seem different from the products of competitors. An *oligopoly* involves only a handful of sellers who fiercely compete with each other. A *monopoly* involves only one seller.

5. **Trace the history of *business* in Canada.** Modern business structures reflect a pattern of development over centuries. Throughout much of the colonial period, sole proprietors supplied raw materials to English manufacturers. The rise of the factory system during the Industrial Revolution brought with it mass production and specialization of labour. During the entrepreneurial era in the nineteenth century, large corporations—and monopolies—emerged. During the production era of the early twentieth century, companies grew by emphasizing output and production. During the sales and marketing eras of the 1950s and 1960s, business began focusing on sales staff, advertising, and the need to produce what consumers wanted. The 1980s saw the emergence of a global economy. Many Canadian companies have profited from exporting their goods to foreign markets. The most recent development is the use of the internet to boost business activity.

Questions and Exercises

Questions for Analysis

1. On various occasions, government provides financial incentives to business firms. For example, the Canadian government provided export assistance to Bombardier Inc. with its Technology Transfer Program. Is this consistent with a basically free market system? Explain how this might distort the system.

2. In recent years, many countries have moved from planned economies to market economies. Why do you think this has occurred? Can you envision a situation that would cause a resurgence of planned economies?

3. In your opinion, what industries in Canada should be regulated by the government? Defend your arguments.

4. Familiarize yourself with a product or service that is sold under conditions of pure competition. Explain why it is an example of pure competition and identify the factors that make it so. Then do the same for a product in each of the other three competitive situations described in the chapter (monopolistic competition, oligopoly, and monopoly).

5. Analyze how the factors of production (labour, capital, entrepreneurs, natural resources, and information) work together for a product or service of your choice.

6. Government plays a variety of roles in the Canadian mixed economy (customer, regulator, taxation agent, provider of services, etc.). Consider each of the roles discussed in the text and state your view as to whether government involvement in each role is excessive, insufficient, or about right. What criteria did you use to make your assessments?

Application Exercises

7. For a product that is not discussed in Chapter 1, find an example where a surplus led to decreased prices. Then find an example where a shortage led to increased prices. What eventually happened in each case? Why? Is what happened consistent with what economic theory predicts?

8. Choose a locally owned business. Interview the owner to find out (1) how demand and supply affect the business, and (2) how each factor of production is used in the business.

9. Visit a local shopping mall or shopping area. List each store that you see and determine what degree of competition it faces in its immediate environment. For example, if there is only one store in the mall that sells shoes, that store represents a monopoly. Note those businesses with direct competitors (e.g., two jewellery stores) and show how they compete with one another.

10. Go to the library or log on to the internet and research 10 industries. Classify each according to degree of competition.

TEAM EXERCISES

Building Your Business Skills

Analyzing the Price of Doing E-Business

Goal
To encourage students to understand how the competitive environment affects a product's price.

Situation
Assume that you own a local business that provides internet access to individuals and businesses in your community. Yours is one of four such businesses in the local market. Each of the four companies charges the same price: $20 per month for unlimited DSL service. Your business also provides users with email service; two of your competitors also offer email service. One of these same two competitors, plus the third, also provides the individual user with a free, basic personal webpage. One competitor just dropped its price to $15 per month, and the other two have announced their intentions to follow suit. Your break-even price is $10 per customer. You are concerned about getting into a price war that may destroy your business.

Method
Divide into groups of four or five people. Each group is to develop a general strategy for handling competitors' price changes. In your discussion, take the following factors into account:

■ how the demand for your product is affected by price changes

■ the number of competitors selling the same or a similar product

■ the methods—other than price—you can use to attract new customers and/or retain current customers

Analysis
Develop specific pricing strategies based on each of the following situations:

■ Within a month after dropping the price to $15, one of your competitors raises its price back to $20.

■ Two of your competitors drop their prices further—to $12 per month. As a result, your business falls off by 25 percent.

■ One of your competitors that has provided customers with a free webpage has indicated that it will start charging an extra $2 per month for this optional service.

■ Two of your competitors have announced that they will charge individual users $12 per month, but will charge businesses a higher price (not yet announced).

■ All four providers (including you) are charging $12 per month. One goes out of business, and you know that another is in poor financial health.

Follow-Up Questions

1. Discuss the role that various inducements other than price might play in affecting demand and supply in the market for internet service.

2. Is it always in a company's best interest to feature the lowest prices?

3. Eventually, what form of competition is likely to characterize the market for internet service?

Exercising Your Ethics

Making the Right Decision

The Situation

Hotel S is a large hotel in a Maritime city. The hotel is a franchise operation run by an international hotel chain. The primary source of revenue for the hotel is convention business. A major tropical storm is working its way up the east coast and is about to hit the city. When that happens, heavy flooding is likely.

The Dilemma

Because Hotel S is a licensed operation, it must maintain numerous quality standards in order to keep its licence. This licence is important because the international management company handles advertising, reservations, and so on. If it were to lose its licence, it is almost certain that the hotel would have to reduce its staff.

For the past few years, members of the Hotel S team have been lobbying the investors who own the hotel to undertake a major renovation. They fear that without such a renovation, the hotel will lose its licence when it comes up for renewal in a few months. The owners, however, have balked at investing more of their funds in the hotel itself but have indicated that hotel management can use revenues earned above a specified level for upgrades.

The approaching storm has cut off most major transportation avenues and telephone service is also down. The Hotel S staff are unable to reach the general manager, who has been travelling on business. Because the city is full of conventioneers, hotel rooms are in high demand. Unfortunately, because of the disrepair at the hotel, it only has about 50 percent occupancy. Hotel S staff have been discussing what to do and have identified three options:

1. The hotel can reduce room rates in order to help both local citizens and out-of-town visitors. The hotel can also provide meals at reduced rates. A few other hotels are also doing this.
2. The hotel can maintain its present pricing policies. Most of the city's hotels are adopting this course of action.
3. The hotel can raise its rates by approximately 15 percent without attracting too much attention. It can also start charging for certain things it has been providing for free, such as local telephone calls, parking, and morning coffee. The staff members see this option as one way to generate extra profits for the renovation and to protect jobs.

Team Activity

Assemble a group of four students and assign each group member to one of the following roles:

- A member of the hotel staff
- The Hotel S manager
- A customer at the hotel
- A Hotel S investor

Action Steps

1. Before discussing the situation with your group, and from the perspective of your assigned role, which of the three options do you think is the best choice? Write down the reasons for your position.
2. Before discussing the situation with your group, and from the perspective of your assigned role, what are the underlying ethical issues, if any, in this situation? Write down the issues.
3. Gather your group together and reveal, in turn, each member's comments on the best choice of the three options. Next, reveal the ethical issues listed by each member.
4. Appoint someone to record the main points of agreement and disagreement within the group. How do you explain the results? What accounts for any disagreement?
5. From an ethical standpoint, what does your group conclude is the most appropriate action that should have been taken by the hotel in this situation?
6. Develop a group response to the following question: Can your team identify other solutions that might help satisfy both extreme views?

Are We Running Out of Oil?

Oil is a product that is much in the news these days (remember the huge oil spill in the Gulf of Mexico in 2010). Beyond the environmental issues of oil, several important questions have been raised about this important commodity: Are we running out of oil? If so, when will it happen? Is oil production going to peak and then rapidly decline? Answers to these questions are hotly debated. Much of the debate is focused on an idea called "peak oil theory," which says that oil production will soon peak and will then decline rapidly, causing a major oil crisis in the world. Opponents of the peak oil theory reject the argument and point to several predictions of peak oil theorists that have been wrong in the past. Illustrative claims of each group are summarized below.

The Arguments of Peak Oil Supporters

Those who support the idea of peak oil make the following arguments:

- Output from oil fields around the world is declining (in some fields the decline is about 18 percent a year). Declines are particularly evident in the Middle East, Europe, and the U.S. That means that 3–4 million barrels a day of new oil will have to be found for global oil production just to remain steady.

- Many big oil-producing countries are very secretive about their year-to-year production rates, so it is difficult to know just how fast their output is really declining. Their oil fields may be in worse shape than they will admit.

- Several top-level executives in the oil industry say that there is a limit to how much oil can be produced each year (about 100 million barrels per day), and that ceiling may be reached as early as 2012. The International Energy Agency (IEA) also predicts that oil production of more than 100 million barrels of oil per day will be difficult to achieve.

- Oil production will peak because of factors such as restricted access to oil fields, shortages of oil field workers, rapidly increasing costs, political crises, and complex oil field geology.

- The IEA has questioned the 174 billion barrel reserves figure commonly cited for the Alberta oil sands, saying that uncertain project economics make it unlikely that that much oil could be extracted. It says that a number closer to 15 billion barrels is more accurate.

- New oil discoveries have declined sharply. For example, new discoveries in the Middle East during

1963–1972 totalled 187 billion barrels, but new discoveries during 1993–2002 totalled only 16 billion barrels.

- In 1956, M.K. Hubbert predicted that U.S. oil production would peak in the early 1970s, and he was right. The same thing will happen with world oil production.

The Arguments of Peak Oil Opponents

Those who reject the peak oil theory make the following arguments:

- World oil production has been steadily increasing, and in 2006 was the highest in history, averaging over 85 million barrels per day (over 31 billion barrels per year). Oil output will eventually *plateau*, but it will not peak and then fall rapidly.

- A widely used measure of oil reserves is "ultimate recoverable reserves" (URR). TrendLines, a Canadian research company, notes that the world's URR is *increasing* at an increasing rate. For example, during the period 1957–2006, URR grew at an annual rate of 2.4 percent, but during 2000–2007, it grew at an annual rate of 6 percent.

- The U.S. Geological Survey (USGS) predicts that URR will grow by about 2.4 percent annually for the next few years. The URR was 1.6 trillion barrels in 1995 and was predicted to rise to 3.3 trillion barrels in 2025, but it had already reached 3.2 trillion barrels in 2006, years ahead of schedule.

- In 1979, the "life index" of oil was estimated to be about 35 years (at 1979 consumption rates). That meant that we would experience an oil crisis early in the twenty-first century. But by 2003, the life index had actually risen to 40 years, and by 2007 it had risen to 45 years. These increases have occurred even though oil consumption rates now far exceed those of 1979.

- There have been several major new discoveries in the last couple of years (for example, off the coast of Brazil and in the Gulf of Mexico). The new Gulf of Mexico oil field may contain up to 15 billion barrels of oil. If it does, that single new field would increase U.S. oil reserves by 50 percent. The new oil field off the coast of Brazil may contain 33 billion barrels of oil.

- M.K. Hubbert's prediction for *U.S.* oil production was correct, but his prediction for *world* production was far off the mark. He predicted that global oil production would peak at 12 billion barrels per year by early in the twenty-first century, but actual production in 2006 was 31 billion barrels.

Critics of peak oil also use several general arguments from economics to support their claims that the peak oil idea is not correct. First, they note that the higher the price of oil, the greater the amount that can be extracted in an economically viable way. Second, higher oil prices will also discourage consumption, and that will make the existing supply of oil last longer. Third, higher oil prices will motivate the development of alternate sources of fuel, and that will also make the existing oil supply last longer. Fourth, new technologies for extracting oil are constantly being developed and old technologies are being refined. This means that more oil can be extracted than was originally thought. For example, Canadian and Japanese researchers have succeeded in extracting natural gas from structures called gas hydrates. The energy locked in gas hydrates may exceed the total world supply of energy available from coal, oil, and natural gas combined. If this new technology becomes commercially viable, it will have a dramatic effect on the total supply of fossil fuels.

Irrespective of what the supporters and opponents of peak oil say, there is another factor that bears on this argument: the business cycle. Most of the arguments presented above were generated before the worldwide recession began in 2008. The recession substantially reduced demand for oil and caused its price to drop from $147 a barrel to less than $40 in 2008 (in 2010 the price rose again to $75). In an attempt to prop up the price, the Organization of the Petroleum Exporting Countries (OPEC) countries cut output by 4 million barrels per day. This reduced output will extend the supply of oil even further into the future. Some experts are now predicting that weak economic growth around the world will mean that the demand for oil will be low for many years to come. So, these developments support the opponents of peak oil. But peak oil supporters point out that that low demand for oil will cause less exploration for oil, and that means we will be facing an oil shortage in the future.

It is difficult to know what is going to happen, isn't it?

Questions for Discussion

1. Which group—peak oil supporters or their opponents—do you think makes more persuasive arguments about the future of oil production and the demand for oil? Explain your reasoning.

2. After considering the arguments in support of peak oil theory and the arguments against it, draw a graph that shows your predictions of world oil production from now until the year 2100. Show your prediction of annual world oil production—in billions of barrels—on the vertical axis and time on the horizontal axis. Defend your predictions.

3. Consider the following statement: "*There are so many uncertainties that must be taken into account when trying to predict world oil production that it is impossible to have any confidence in anyone's predictions.*" Do you agree or disagree with the statement? Explain your reasoning.

ScanLife

Appendix A
Business Law

The Role of Law in Canadian Society

Law is the set of rules and standards that a society agrees upon to govern the behaviour of its citizens. Both the British and the French influenced the development of law in Canada. In 1867, the British North America (BNA) Act created the nation of Canada. The BNA Act was "patriated" to Canada in 1982 and is now known as the Constitution Act. This act divides legislative powers in Canada between the federal and provincial governments.

Sources of Law

The law in Canada has evolved and changed in response to our norms and values. Our laws have arisen from three sources: (1) customs and judicial precedents (the source of common law), (2) the actions of provincial and federal legislatures (the source of statutory law), and (3) rulings by administrative bodies (the source of administrative law).

Common law is the unwritten law of England, derived from ancient precedents and judges' previous legal opinions. Common law is based on the principle of equity, the provision to every person of a just and fair remedy. Canadian legal customs and traditions derive from British common law. All provinces except Quebec, which uses the French Civil Code, have laws based on British common law, and court decisions are often based on precedents from common law. That is, decisions made in earlier cases that involved the same legal point will guide the court.

Statutory law is written law developed by city councils, provincial legislatures, and parliament. Most law in Canada today is statutory law.

Administrative law is the rules and regulations that government agencies and commissions develop based on their interpretations of statutory laws. For example, Consumer and Corporate Affairs Canada develops regulations on false advertising using federal legislation.

The Court System

In Canada, the judiciary branch of government has the responsibility of settling disputes among organizations or individuals by applying existing laws. Both provincial and federal courts exist to hear both criminal and civil cases. The Supreme Court of Canada is the highest court in Canada. It decides whether to hear appeals from lower courts.

Business Law

Business firms, like all other organizations, are affected by the laws of the country. Business law refers to laws that specifically affect how business firms are managed. Some laws affect all businesses, regardless of size, industry, or location. For example, the Income Tax Act requires businesses to pay income tax. Other laws may have a greater impact on one industry than on others. For example, pollution regulations are of much greater concern to Vale than they are to Carlson Wagonlit Travel.

Business managers must have at least a basic understanding of eight important concepts in business law:

1. contracts
2. agency
3. bailment
4. property
5. warranty
6. torts
7. negotiable instruments
8. bankruptcy

LAW The set of rules and standards that a society agrees upon to govern the behaviour of its citizens.

COMMON LAW The unwritten law of England, derived from precedent and legal judgments.

STATUTORY LAW Written law developed by city councils, provincial legislatures, and parliament.

ADMINISTRATIVE LAW The rules and regulations that government agencies and commissions develop based on their interpretations of statutory laws.

BUSINESS LAW Laws that specifically affect how business firms are managed.

Contracts

Agreements about transactions are common in a business's day-to-day activity. A **contract** is an agreement between two parties to act in a specified way or to perform certain acts. A contract might, for example, apply to a customer buying a product from a retail establishment or to two manufacturers agreeing to buy products or services from each other. A contract may be either express or implied. An **express contract** clearly specifies (either orally or in writing) the terms of an agreement. By contrast, an **implied contract** depends on the two parties' behaviours. For example, if you hire a fishing guide to help you catch fish, you have an implied contract that obligates you to pay the fishing guide for the service you receive.

A valid contract includes several elements:

■ *an agreement*—All parties must consciously agree about the contract.

■ *consideration*—The parties must exchange something of value (e.g., time, products, services, money, and so on).

■ *competence*—All parties to the contract must be legally able to enter into an agreement. Individuals who are below a certain age or who are legally insane, for example, cannot enter into legal agreements.

■ *legal purpose*—What the parties agree to do for or with each other must be legal. An agreement between two manufacturers to fix prices is not legal.

The courts will enforce a contract if it meets the criteria described above. Most parties honour their contracts, but occasionally one party does not do what it was supposed to do. **Breach of contract** occurs when one party to an agreement fails, without legal reason, to live up to the agreement's provisions. The party that has not breached the contract has three alternatives under the law in Canada: (1) discharge, (2) sue for damages, or (3) require specific performance.

An example will demonstrate these three alternatives. Suppose that Barrington Farms Inc. agrees to deliver 100 dozen long-stemmed roses to the Blue Violet Flower Shop the week before Mother's Day. One week before the agreed-upon date, Barrington informs Blue Violet that it cannot make the delivery until after Mother's Day. Under the law, the owner of Blue Violet can choose among any of the following actions.

Discharge Blue Violet can also ignore its obligations in the contract. That is, it can contract with another supplier.

Sue for Damages Blue Violet can legally demand payment for losses caused by Barrington's failure to deliver the promised goods on time. Losses might include any increased price Blue Violet would have to pay for the roses or court costs incurred in the damage suit.

Require Specific Performance If monetary damages are not sufficient to reimburse Blue Violet, the court can force Barrington to live up to its original contract.

Agency

In many business situations, one person acts as an agent for another person. Well-known examples include actors and athletes represented by agents who negotiate contracts for them. An **agency–principal relationship** is established when one party (the agent) is authorized to act on behalf of another party (the principal).

The agent is under the control of the principal and must act on behalf of the principal and in the principal's best interests. The principal remains liable for the acts of the agent as long as the agent is acting within the scope of authority granted by the principal. A salesperson for IBM, for example, is an agent for IBM, the principal.

Bailment

Many business transactions are not covered by the agency–principal relationship. For example, suppose that you take your car to a mechanic to have it repaired. Because the repair shop has temporary possession of something you own, it is responsible for your car. This is a **bailor–bailee relationship**. In a bailor–bailee relationship, the bailor (e.g., the car owner) gives possession of his or her property to the bailee (e.g., the repair shop) but retains ownership of the item. A business firm that stores inventory in a public warehouse is in a bailor–bailee relationship. The business firm is the bailor and the warehouse is the bailee. The warehouse is responsible for storing the goods safely and making them available to the manufacturer upon request.

CONTRACT An agreement between two parties to act in a specified way or to perform certain acts.

EXPRESS CONTRACT Clearly specifies the terms of an agreement.

IMPLIED CONTRACT Specifies the necessary behaviours of the parties to the contract.

BREACH OF CONTRACT When one party to an agreement fails, without legal reason, to live up to the agreement's provisions.

AGENCY–PRINCIPAL RELATIONSHIP Established when one party (the agent) is authorized to act on behalf of another party (the principal).

BAILOR–BAILEE RELATIONSHIP In a bailor–bailee relationship, the bailor (the property owner) gives possession of his or her property to the bailee (a custodian) but retains ownership of the item.

The Law of Property

Property includes anything of tangible or intangible value that the owner has the right to possess and use. **Real property** is land and any permanent buildings attached to that land. **Personal property** is tangible or intangible assets other than real property. Personal property includes cars, clothing, furniture, money in bank accounts, stock certificates, and copyrights.

Transferring Property From time to time, businesses and individuals need to transfer property to another person or business. A **deed** is a document that shows ownership of real property. It allows the transfer of title of real property.

A **lease** grants the use of an asset for a specified period of time in return for payment. The business or individual granting the lease is the lessor and the tenant is the lessee. For example, a business (the lessee) may rent space in a mall for one year from a real estate development firm (the lessor).

A **title** shows legal possession of personal property. It allows the transfer of title of personal property. When you buy a snowmobile, for example, the former owner signs the title over to you.

Warranty

When you buy a product or service, you want some assurance that it will perform satisfactorily and meet your needs. A **warranty** is a promise that the product or service will perform as the seller has promised it will.

There are two kinds of warranties—express and implied. An **express warranty** is a specific claim that the manufacturer makes about a product. For example, a warranty that a screwdriver blade is made of case-hardened steel is an express warranty. An **implied warranty** suggests that a product will perform as the manufacturer claims it will. Suppose that you buy an outboard motor for your boat and the engine burns out in one week. Because the manufacturer implies by selling the motor that it will work for a reasonable period of time, you can return it and get your money back.

Because opinions vary on what is a "reasonable" time, most manufacturers now give limited-time warranties on their products. For example, they will guarantee their products against defects in materials or manufacture for six months or one year.

Torts

A **tort** is a wrongful civil act that one party inflicts on another and that results in injury to the person, to the person's property, or to the person's good name. An **intentional tort** is a wrongful act intentionally committed. If a security guard in a department store suspects someone of shoplifting and uses excessive force to prevent him or her from leaving the store, the guard might be guilty of an intentional tort. Other examples are libel, embezzlement, and patent infringement.

Negligence is a wrongful act that inadvertently causes injury to another person. For example, if a maintenance crew in a store mops the floors without placing warning signs in the area, a customer who slips and falls might bring a negligence suit against the store.

In recent years, the most publicized area of negligence has been product liability. **Product liability** means that businesses are liable for injuries caused to product users because of negligence in design or manufacturing. **Strict product liability** means that a business is liable for injuries caused by their products even if there is no evidence of negligence in the design or manufacture of the product.

Negotiable Instruments

Negotiable instruments are types of commercial paper that can be transferred among individuals and business firms. Cheques, bank drafts, and certificates of deposit are examples of negotiable instruments.

The Bills of Exchange Act specifies that a negotiable instrument must

- be written;
- be signed by the person who puts it into circulation (the maker or drawer);

PROPERTY Anything of tangible or intangible value that the owner has the right to possess and use.

REAL PROPERTY Land and any permanent buildings attached to that land.

PERSONAL PROPERTY Tangible or intangible assets other than real property.

DEED A document that shows ownership of real property.

LEASE Grants the use of an asset for a specified period of time in return for payment.

TITLE Shows legal possession of personal property.

WARRANTY A promise that the product or service will perform as the seller has promised it will.

EXPRESS WARRANTY A specific claim that the manufacturer makes about a product.

IMPLIED WARRANTY A suggestion that a product will perform as the manufacturer claims it will.

TORT A wrongful civil act that one party inflicts on another and that results in injury to the person, to the person's property, or to the person's good name.

INTENTIONAL TORT A wrongful act intentionally committed.

NEGLIGENCE A wrongful act that inadvertently causes injury to another person.

PRODUCT LIABILITY
The liability of businesses for injuries caused to product users because of negligence in design or manufacturing.

BANKRUPTCY The court-granted permission for organizations or individuals to not pay some or all of their debts.

STRICT PRODUCT LIABILITY The liability of businesses for injuries caused by their products even if there is no evidence of negligence in the design or manufacture of the product.

NEGOTIABLE INSTRUMENTS Types of commercial paper that can be transferred among individuals and business firms.

ENDORSEMENT
Signing your name to a negotiable instrument, making it transferable to another person or organization.

INSOLVENT PERSON (OR COMPANY) One who cannot pay current obligations to creditors as they come due, or whose debts exceed their assets.

BANKRUPT PERSON (OR COMPANY) One who has either made a voluntary application to start bankruptcy proceedings (voluntary bankruptcy) or has been forced by creditors into bankruptcy (involuntary bankruptcy) by a process referred to as a receiving order.

- contain an unconditional promise to pay a certain amount of money;
- be payable on demand; and
- be payable to a specific person (or to the bearer of the instrument).

Negotiable instruments are transferred from one party to another through an endorsement. An **endorsement** means signing your name to a negotiable instrument; this makes it transferable to another person or organization. If you sign only your name on the back of a cheque, you are making a *blank* endorsement. If you state that the instrument is being transferred to a specific person, you are making a *special* endorsement. A *qualified* endorsement limits your liability if the instrument is not backed up by sufficient funds. For example, if you get a cheque from a friend and want to use it to buy a new stereo, you can write "without recourse" above your name. If your friend's cheque bounces, you have no liability. A *restrictive* endorsement limits the negotiability of the instrument. For example, if you write "for deposit only" on the back of a cheque and it is later stolen, no one else can cash it.

Bankruptcy

At one time, individuals who could not pay their debts were jailed. Today, however, both organizations and individuals can seek relief by filing for **bankruptcy**, which is the court-granted permission to not pay some or all of their debts.

Thousands of individuals and businesses file for bankruptcy each year. They do so for various reasons, including

cash flow problems, reduced demand for their products, or some other problem that makes it difficult or impossible for them to resolve their financial problems. In recent years, large businesses like Eaton's, Olympia & York, and Enron have sought the protection of bankruptcy laws. Three main factors account for the increase in bankruptcy filings:

1. The increased availability of credit
2. The "fresh-start" provisions in current bankruptcy laws
3. The growing acceptance of bankruptcy as a financial tactic

In Canada, jurisdiction over bankruptcy is provided by the Bankruptcy and Insolvency Act. An **insolvent person (or company)** is defined as one who cannot pay current obligations to creditors as they come due, or whose debts exceed their assets. A **bankrupt person (or company)** is one who has either made a voluntary application to start bankruptcy proceedings (voluntary bankruptcy) or has been forced by creditors into bankruptcy (involuntary bankruptcy) by a process referred to as a *receiving order*. A person who is insolvent may or may not be bankrupt, and a person who is bankrupt may or may not be insolvent, as there are other bases for bankruptcy under the Act. Another procedure under the Act is referred to as a *proposal*, which can delay or avoid liquidation by providing the debtor with time to reorganize affairs and/or propose a payment schedule to creditors.

On a practical basis, business bankruptcy under the act may be resolved or avoided by one of three methods:

1. Under a *liquidation plan*, the business ceases to exist. Its assets are sold and the proceeds are used to pay creditors.
2. Under a *repayment plan,* the bankrupt company works out a new payment schedule to meet its obligations. The time frame is usually extended, and payments are collected and distributed by a court-appointed trustee.
3. *Reorganization* is the most complex form of business bankruptcy. The company must explain the sources of its financial difficulties and propose a new plan for remaining in business. Reorganization may include a new slate of managers and a new financial strategy. A judge may also reduce the firm's debts to ensure its survival. Although creditors naturally dislike debt reduction, they may agree to the proposal, since getting, say, 50 percent of what you are owed is better than getting nothing at all.

The International Framework of Business Law

Laws vary from country to country, and many businesses today have international markets, suppliers, and competitors. Managers in such businesses need a basic understanding of the international framework of business law that affects the ways in which they can do business. Issues such as pollution across borders are matters of **international law**—the very general set of cooperative agreements and guidelines established by countries to govern the actions of individuals, businesses, and nations themselves.

International law has several sources. One source is custom and tradition. Among countries that have been trading with one another for centuries, many customs and traditions governing exchanges have gradually evolved into practice. Although some trading practices still follow ancient unwritten agreements, there has been a clear trend in recent years to approach international trade within a formal legal framework. Key features of that framework include a variety of formal trade agreements (see Chapter 5).

Organizations such as the WTO and EU also provide legal frameworks within which participating nations agree to abide.

INTERNATIONAL LAW The very general set of cooperative agreements and guidelines established by countries to govern the actions of individuals, businesses, and nations themselves.

chapter

2

The Environment of Business

After reading this chapter, you should be able to:

LO-1 Explain the concepts of *organizational boundaries* and *multiple organizational environments*.

LO-2 Explain the importance of the *economic environment* to business and identify the factors used to evaluate the performance of an economic system.

LO-3 Describe the *technological environment* and its role in business.

LO-4 Describe the *political–legal environment* and its role in business.

LO-5 Describe the *socio-cultural environment* and its role in business.

LO-6 Identify emerging challenges and opportunities in the *business environment*.

LO-7 Understand recent trends in the *redrawing of corporate boundaries.*

SCANLIFE

Air Canada's Challenging Environment: Competition, Economic Crisis, Fuel Prices, Volcanoes, and More

The name Air Canada does not always conjure up warm images for Canadian travellers. But it is the fifteenth largest airline in the world and it wins international awards. In 2010, it was named the "best airline in North America" by independent research firm Skytrax (which surveyed over 17 million world-wide travellers). There have been many ups and downs for Air Canada, but the company continues to control the majority of the domestic market, with WestJet as its main competitor. Back in 2004, Air Canada used bankruptcy protection to deal with major financial problems. It may be tempting to blame that dark period on general turmoil in the travel industry, following the 9/11 terrorist attacks, but placing all the blame on that significant event would be overly simplistic. The airline business is always extremely complicated; it's a difficult business environment that is shaped by relationships with many stakeholders.

Airlines must efficiently plan their capacity. They don't buy a fleet of planes overnight; airlines make projections and try to maximize the use of planes and other resources. Some of this planning is done two to five or even seven years into the future and this sort of lengthy timeline is complicated. Air Canada must contend with *competitor actions* (e.g., WestJet, Porter) at home, and on

How Will This Help Me?

By understanding the material in this chapter, you'll be better able to assess (1) the impact that events outside a business can have on its *owners* and *managers*, (2) how environmental change impacts you as a *consumer*, and (3) the challenges and opportunities that environmental change provides to you as an employee or an *investor*.

international routes (e.g., Air France, British Airways, JAL); it must deal with government regulations (e.g., tax laws, flight restrictions, and international agreements), economic conditions (e.g., recessions, fuel/food prices), and natural weather conditions (e.g., snowstorms and even volcanic ash). Let's take a closer look at these challenges.

In recent years, a major spike in fuel costs hurt air travel and caused ticket prices to skyrocket at times. The global recession, which started in 2008, decreased tourist and business travel. In fact, in 2009 the global airline business saw its most steep decline in air traffic since the Second World War. According to the International Air Transport Association (IATA), the global industry lost $10 billion that year, with additional losses expected in the $3 billion range in 2010. Air Canada worked hard to get its finances under control by creating new agreements with suppliers and major credit providers. However, in the first quarter of 2010, the airline still had an operating loss of $138 million (Air Canada pointed out that this was an improvement from the $188 million loss a year earlier indicated in the first quarter).

At home, Air Canada competes with WestJet and a host of smaller players. The rivalry has pushed it to launch its lower priced Tango fares to compete in the low-frill, budget travel segment. In addition, the company created a regional partner called Jazz mainly for short-haul flights. In order to effectively compete on the global stage Air Canada has forged alliances to cut costs. It is a founding member of the leading airline network called Star Alliance. These 26 members permit passengers on partner airlines to connect with over 1100 airports in 175 countries. The airlines code-share flights (e.g., booking Air Canada seats on a Lufthansa flight) and share airline lounges in airports around the world. In 2009, Air Canada also extended its partnerships with Continental, United, and Lufthansa to create Atlantic-Plus-Plus, which further enables it to integrate routes and compete in the transatlantic segment.

Governments are strongly linked to airline success or failure. Here are some key facts to consider. The government recently negotiated an agreement between Canada and the EU that created new opportunities by reducing restrictions for Air Canada and EU airlines. So in 2010, Air Canada launched new direct services to five popular European gateway cities: Geneva, Barcelona, Brussels, Copenhagen, and Athens. A similar deal with the United States government back in 1995 was an important step in Air Canada's extensive expansion (Air Canada is the largest airline in the U.S.–Canada transborder market, serving 60 destinations in the U.S.). Of course, the relationship with the government is not all rosy. Air Canada has stated that the government is making it impossible for the airline to be profitable with higher security charges, airport improvement fees, and federal and provincial fuel excise taxes. For example, the federal government collects over $300 million in rent from airports each year. This makes it much more expensive to land a plane in Canada than in the U.S. Air Canada pays $3400 to land an Airbus 320 in Canada's largest airports but less than half that amount ($1650) in the U.S. Total federal tax collected in Halifax alone amounted to $3.2 million in rent charges in 2009 and is expected to top $5 million by 2014. Since the airline is based in Canada, it has a tax cost disadvantage.

Weather can play a tricky role in airline operations. If you travel on a regular basis you are very familiar with airline delays. Snowstorms, severe thunder showers, icy weather, and severe winds can disrupt travel and cause delays. This creates frustrated passengers and forces airline employees and travel agents to scramble. In April 2010, a new issue hit the headlines when a volcano in Iceland halted all air travel to and from Europe for five long days, cancelling over 100 000 flights. The name of the volcano is Eyjafjallajokull (pronounced ay-yah-FYAH-lah-yer-kuhl), and customers were heard muttering similar sounds as they tried to get home. It cost the airline industry huge sums of money through no fault of its own. Air Canada lost $20 million per day; Air Transat lost approximately $750 000 per day; Air France-KLM lost an estimated $35 million per day. Airlines demanded compensation from the EU for more than $1 billion in losses. It remains to be seen what the ultimate response will be.

As you can see, airlines must create efficient strategies and plan for the unexpected. But there are so many elements far outside their control that impact success or failure. In addition to the issues mentioned above, there are the massive new security challenges, flu pandemics, and political conflict (e.g., civil war) that can erupt anywhere in the world. This is why it is so hard to find an airline that is profitable on a consistent basis. This is truly a challenging industry.

LO-1 Organizational Boundaries and Environments

As discussed in the opening case on Air Canada, all businesses, regardless of their size, location, or mission, operate within a larger external environment that plays a major role in determining their success or failure. The **external environment** consists of everything outside an organization that might affect it. Managers must understand the key features of the external environment, and then strive to operate and compete within it. No single firm can control the environment, but managers should not simply react to changes in the external environment; rather, they should be proactive and at least try to influence their environment.

To better explain the environment of business, we begin by discussing *organizational boundaries* and *multiple organizational environments*.

Organizational Boundaries

An **organizational boundary** separates the organization from its environment. Consider the simple case of a small neighbourhood grocery store that includes a retail customer area, a storage room, and the owner/manager's office. In many ways, the store's boundary coincides with its physical structure: When you walk through the door, you're crossing the boundary into the business, and when you go back onto the sidewalk, you cross the boundary back into the environment. But this is an oversimplification. During the business day, distributors of soft drinks, snack foods, ice, and bread products may enter the store, inventory their products, and refill coolers and shelves just as if they were employees. These distributors are normally considered part of the environment rather than the organization, but during the time they're inside the store, they are essentially part of the business. Customers may even assume that these distributors are store employees and ask them questions as they restock shelves.

For larger firms, the situation is even more complex. McDonald's, for example, has a contract with Coca-Cola to sell only Coke soft-drink products. McDonald's also has partnerships with Walmart and Disney that allow it to open stores inside their facilities. So when you buy a Coca-Cola soft drink from a McDonald's restaurant located inside a Walmart store or Disney theme park, you are essentially affecting, and being affected by, multiple businesses.

Multiple Organizational Environments

Organizations have multiple environments. Some, like prevailing economic conditions, affect the performance of almost every business. But other dimensions of the environment are much more specific. The neighbourhood grocery store, for example, will be influenced not only by an increase in unemployment in its area but also by the pricing and other marketing activities of its nearest competitors. As we saw in the opening case, Air Canada will be affected by competitive pressures from WestJet, from the general economic conditions (like unemployment levels and business confidence), and even from major global events like the volcanic ash that caused 100 000 flight cancellations in Europe.[1]

Figure 2.1 shows the major elements of the external environment: economic conditions, technology, political–legal considerations, social issues, the global environment, issues of ethical and social responsibility, the business environment itself, and emerging challenges and opportunities. We will cover ethical and global issues in detail in Chapters 3 and 5 respectively, so we discuss them here only as they relate directly to the other areas in this chapter.

EXTERNAL ENVIRONMENT Everything outside an organization's boundaries that might affect it.

ORGANIZATIONAL BOUNDARY That which separates the organization from its environment.

ECONOMIC ENVIRONMENT Conditions of the economic system in which an organization operates.

LO-2 The Economic Environment

The **economic environment** refers to the conditions of the economic system in which an organization operates.[2] For example, McDonald's Canadian operations are (as of this writing) functioning in an economic environment characterized by moderate growth, moderate unemployment, and low inflation. Moderate unemployment means that most people can afford to eat out, and low inflation means that McDonald's pays relatively constant prices for its supplies. But it also means that McDonald's can't easily increase the prices it charges because of competitive pressures from Burger King and Wendy's.

Economic Growth

At one time, about half the Canadian population was involved in producing the food that we eat. Today, less than 2.5 percent of the population works in agriculture because agricultural efficiency has improved so much that far fewer people are needed to produce the food we need. We can therefore say that agricultural production has *grown* because the total output of the agricultural sector has increased. We can apply the same idea to a nation's economic system, but the computations are much more complex, as we shall see.

AGGREGATE OUTPUT Total quantity of goods and services produced by an economic system during a given period.

STANDARD OF LIVING Total quantity and quality of goods and services that a country's citizens can purchase with the currency used in their economic system.

BUSINESS CYCLE Pattern of short-term ups and downs (expansions and contractions) in an economy.

GROSS DOMESTIC PRODUCT (GDP) Total value of all goods and services produced within a given period by a national economy through domestic factors of production.

Figure 2.1
Dimensions of the external environment.

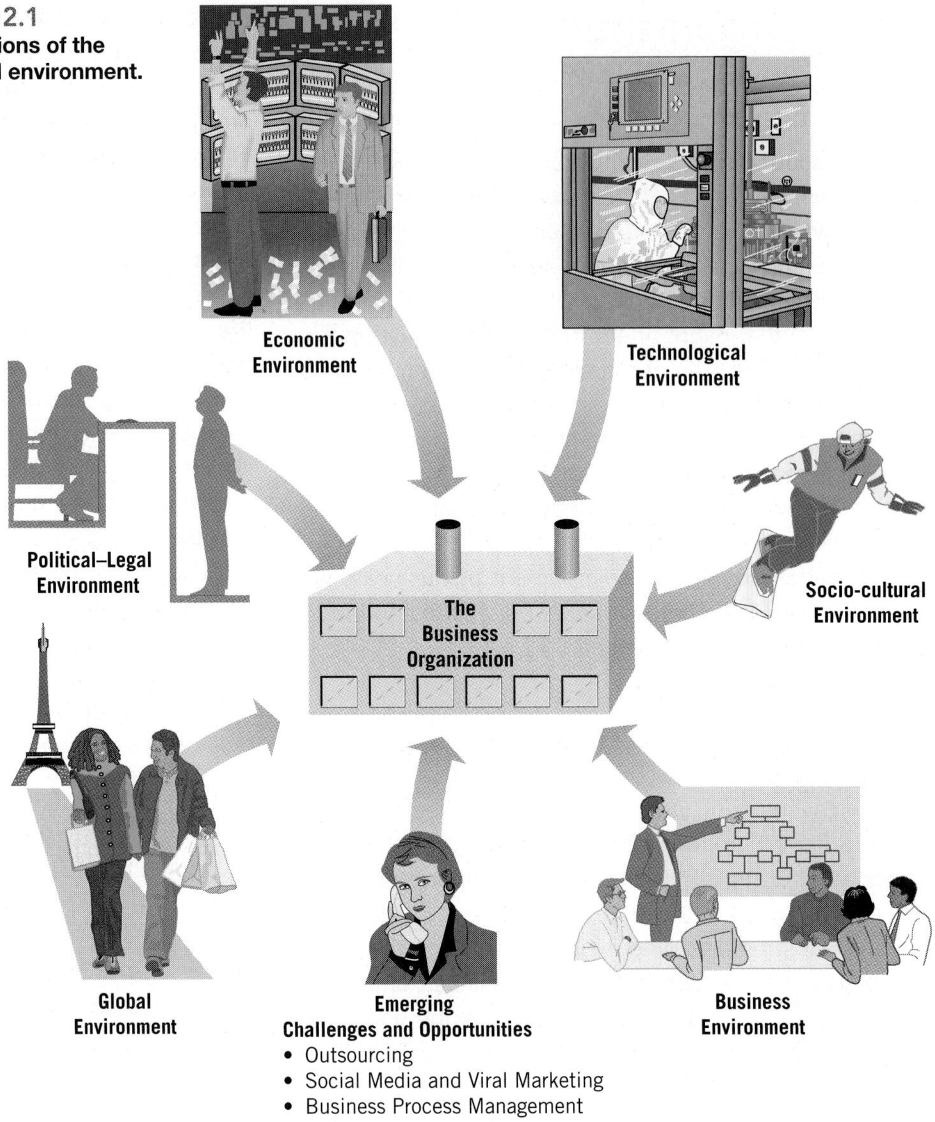

Economic Environment
Technological Environment
Political–Legal Environment
Socio-cultural Environment
The Business Organization
Global Environment
Emerging Challenges and Opportunities
• Outsourcing
• Social Media and Viral Marketing
• Business Process Management
Business Environment

Aggregate Output and the Standard of Living How do we know whether or not an economic system is growing? The main measure of *growth* is **aggregate output:** the total quantity of goods and services produced by an economic system during a given period.[3] To put it simply, an increase in aggregate output is economic growth.[4] When output grows more quickly than the population, two things usually follow: output per capita (the quantity of goods and services per person) goes up and the system provides relatively more of the goods and services that people want.[5] And when these two things occur, people living in an economic system benefit from a higher **standard of living**—the total quantity and quality of goods and services that they can purchase with the currency used in their economic system.

The Business Cycle The growth (and contraction) pattern of short-term ups and downs in an economy is called the **business cycle**. It has four recognizable phases: peak, recession, trough, and recovery (see Figure 2.2). A **recession** is usually defined as two consecutive quarters when the economy shrinks, but it is probably more helpful to say that a recession starts just after the peak of the business cycle is reached and ends when the trough is reached.[6] A **depression** occurs when the trough of the business cycle extends two or more years. Periods of expansion and contraction can vary from several months to several years. During the latter half of the 1990s, the Canadian economy was continuously expanding, leading some people to believe that the business cycle was a thing of the past. That belief was shattered twice in the last 10 years: in 2000, when the high-tech bubble burst, and in 2008, when a major financial crisis and worldwide recession occurred. Many economists predicted that the most recent recession would be long, and some compared it to the Great Depression of the 1930s.

Gross Domestic Product and Gross National Product The term **gross domestic product (GDP)** refers to the total value of all goods and services produced within a given period by a national economy through domestic factors of production. If GDP is going up, the nation is experiencing economic growth. Canada's GDP in 2009 was $1.56 trillion.[7]

GDP measures all business activity within a nation's borders and it has widely replaced **gross national product (GNP)**, which refers to the total value of all goods and services produced by a national economy within a given period regardless of where the factors of production are located. For example, the profits from a Canadian-owned manufacturing plant in Brazil are included in Canadian GNP—but not in GDP—because its output is not produced in Canada. Conversely, those profits are included in Brazil's GDP—but not GNP—because they are produced domestically (that is, in Brazil) but not by a Brazilian company.

Today, GDP is the key measure of economic growth because it tracks an economy's performance over time. However, some argue that such measures are flawed. A commission created by French president Nicolas Sarkozy and chaired by famous economist Joseph Stiglitz declared that our obsession with GDP helped contribute to the strength of the most recent recession. According to the findings, if a bit more attention had been paid to other indicators, like rising debt, governments may have reacted more cautiously. An article in *The Economist* magazine even referred to GDP as "grossly deceptive product."[8] An organization called Redefining Progress has proposed a more realistic measure to assess economic activity—the Genuine Progress Indicator (GPI). GPI treats activities that harm the environment or our quality of life as costs and gives them negative values. For example, in 2010, activities required to clean the mess from the BP Gulf of Mexico oil drilling disaster were included in measurements of economic growth.

But the oil spill was not a good thing. The GPI measure shows that while GDP has been increasing for many years, GPI has been falling for over 30 years.[9]

Real Growth Rates GDP is the preferred method of calculating national income and output. The *real growth rate of GDP—* the growth rate of GDP *adjusted for inflation and changes in the value of the country's currency—* is what counts. Remember that *growth depends on output increasing at a faster rate than population*. If the growth rate of GDP exceeds the rate of population growth, then our standard of living should be improving.

GDP per Capita **GDP per capita** means GDP per person. We get this figure by dividing total GDP by the total population of a country. As a measure of economic well-being of the average person, GDP per capita is a better measure than GDP. Norway has the highest GDP per capita of any country ($40 807), followed by the United States ($38 808), Ireland ($35 306), and Switzerland ($34 440). Canada ranked eighth at ($31 369).[10]

Real GDP **Real GDP** means that GDP has been adjusted. To understand why adjustments are necessary, assume that pizza is the only product in an economy. Assume that in 2010, a pizza cost $10 and in 2011 it cost $11.

In both years, exactly 1000 pizzas were produced. In 2010, the GDP was $10 000 ($10 × 1000); in 2011, the GDP was $11 000 ($11 × 1000). Has the economy grown? No. Since 1000 pizzas were produced in both years, aggregate output remained the same. If GDP is not adjusted for 2011, it is called **nominal GDP**, that is, GDP measured in current dollars.[11]

Purchasing Power Parity In our example, *current prices* would be 2011 prices. On the other hand, we calculate real GDP when we account for *changes in currency values and price changes*. When

Figure 2.2
The business cycle.

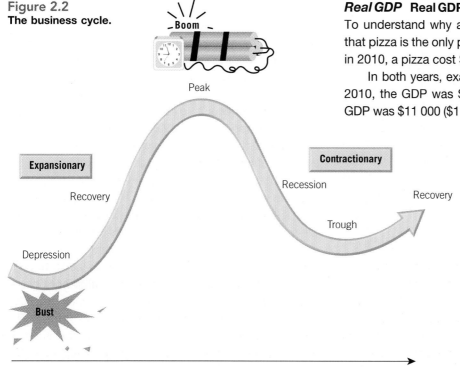

Boom

Peak

Expansionary

Recovery

Depression

Bust

Contractionary

Recession

Recovery

Trough

TIME

PURCHASING POWER PARITY
Principle that exchange rates are set so that the prices of similar products in different countries are about the same.

PRODUCTIVITY
Measure of economic growth that compares how much a system produces with the resources needed to produce it.

BALANCE OF TRADE The total of a country's exports (sales to other countries) minus its imports (purchases from other countries).

NATIONAL DEBT
The total amount of money that a country owes its creditors.

BUDGET DEFICITS
The result of the government spending more in one year than it takes in during that year.

we make this adjustment, we account for both GDP and **purchasing power parity**—the principle that exchange rates are set so that the prices of similar products in different countries are about the same. Purchasing power parity gives us a much better idea of what people can actually buy. In other words, it gives us a better sense of standards of living across the globe.

Productivity A major factor in the growth of an economic system is **productivity**, which is a measure of economic growth that compares how much a system produces with the resources needed to produce it. Let's say, for instance, that it takes one Canadian worker and one Canadian dollar to make 10 soccer balls in an eight-hour workday. Let's also say that it takes 1.2 Saudi workers and the equivalent of $1.2 (in riyals, the currency of Saudi Arabia) to make 10 soccer balls in the same eight-hour workday. We can say, then, that the Canadian soccer-ball industry is more *productive* than the Saudi soccer-ball industry.

The two factors of production in this extremely simple case are labour and capital. According to the Organisation for Economic Co-operation and Development (OECD) rankings, Canada stood in sixteenth place with a productivity ratio of 78.2 percent compared to the United States. Luxembourg was the most productive nation at 140.4 percent. Norway (136 percent) and the Netherlands (100.4 percent) were also classified above the benchmark U.S. statistics.[12]

If more products are being produced with fewer factors of production, what happens to the prices of these products? They go down. As a consumer, therefore, you would need less of your currency to purchase the same quantity of these products. Thus, your standard of living—at least with regard to these products—has improved. If your entire economic system increases its productivity, then your overall standard of living improves. In fact, the standard of living improves only through increases in productivity.[13]

The Balance of Trade and the National Debt There are several factors that can help or hinder the growth of an economic system, but here we focus on just two of them: *balance of trade* and the *national debt*.

Balance of Trade The **balance of trade** is the economic value of all the products that a country *exports* minus the economic value of its *imported* products. A negative balance of trade is commonly called a *trade deficit*, and a positive balance of trade is called a *trade surplus*. Canada traditionally has had a positive balance of trade. It is usually a *creditor nation* rather than a debtor nation. For example, Canada received $47 billion more from exports than it spent on imports in 2008, but in 2009 a long trend was reversed when Canada had a trade deficit of $4.8 billion.[14] The United States usually has a negative balance of trade; it spends more on imports than it receives for exports.[15] It is therefore a consistent *debtor nation*. A trade deficit negatively affects economic growth because the money that flows out of a country can't be used to invest in productive enterprises, either at home or overseas.

National Debt A country's **national debt** is the amount of money that the government owes its creditors. Like a business, the government takes in revenues (e.g., taxes) and has expenses (e.g., military spending, social programs). For many years, the government of Canada incurred annual **budget deficits**, that is, it spent more money *each year* than it took in. These accumulated annual deficits have created a huge national debt (estimated above $600 billion by the end of 2010). A typical recession causes an 86 percent increase in the national debt.[16]

From Confederation (1867) to 1981, the *total* accumulated debt was only $85.7 billion, but in the period 1981–1994, *annual deficits* were in the $20- to $40-billion range. But from 1997 to 2008, Canada was the only highly industrialized country in the world that had annual budget surpluses. That all changed in 2009 when the government announced a deficit of $46.9 billion. The good news, if you can call it that, was that this figure was actually 12 percent lower than initially expected.[17] The bad news was that another $49 billion deficit was projected in 2010 as well as $27.6 billion in 2011 and $17.5 billion in 2012.[18] Big increases in annual deficits are also predicted for the United States because of the multibillion-dollar bailouts that were given to companies in the financial sector. In spite of this, the United States is still able to borrow large amounts of money from countries like China because the United States is seen as a strong economy and a safe haven in troubled economic times.[19]

How does the national debt affect economic growth? When the government of Canada sells bonds to individuals and organizations (both at home and overseas), this affects economic growth because the Canadian government competes with every other potential borrower—individuals, households, businesses, and other organizations—for the available supply of loanable money. The more money the government borrows, the less money is available for the private borrowing and investment that increases productivity.

Economic Stability

A key goal of an economic system is **stability**: a condition in which the amount of money available in an economic system and the quantity of goods and services produced in it are growing at about the same rate. Several factors threaten stability—namely, *inflation, deflation,* and *unemployment.*

Inflation **Inflation** is evident when the amount of money injected into an economic system outstrips the increase in actual output. When inflation occurs, people have more money to spend, but there will still be the same quantity of products available for them to buy. As they compete with one another to buy available products, prices go up. Before long, high prices will erase the increase in the amount of money injected into the economy. Purchasing power, therefore, declines. Figure 2.3 shows how inflation has varied over the last 30 years in Canada.

Inflation varies widely across countries. One dramatic example occurred in Zimbabwe in 2008, when inflation reached an astonishing annual rate above 40 million percent (most countries have rates between 2 and 15 percent). One Zimbabwean dollar from 2005 would have been worth one trillion Zimbabwean dollars in 2008. Many workers simply stopped going to their jobs because their pay was not enough to cover their bus fare.[20] The problem was finally solved in 2009 when the government began allowing people to pay their bills using other currencies, like the U.S. dollar or the South African rand.[21]

Measuring Inflation: The CPI

The **consumer price index (CPI)** measures changes in the cost of a "basket" of goods and services that a typical family buys. What is included in the basket has changed over the years. For example, the first CPI in 1913 included items like coal, spirit vinegar, and fruit, while today the index includes bottom-freezer fridges, flat-screen TVs, energy-saving light bulbs, and laser eye surgery.[22] These changes in the CPI reflect changes that have occurred in the pattern of consumer purchases. For example, in 1961, about 53 percent of consumer spending went to necessities like food, housing, and clothing. By the turn of the century, only 40 percent of consumer spending went to necessities.[23]

STABILITY
Condition in an economic system in which the amount of money available and the quantity of goods and services produced are growing at about the same rate.

INFLATION
Occurrence of widespread price increases throughout an economic system.

CONSUMER PRICE INDEX (CPI) Measure of the prices of typical products purchased by consumers living in urban areas.

DEFLATION A period of generally falling prices.

UNEMPLOYMENT The level of joblessness among people actively seeking work in an economic system.

Deflation **Deflation** (falling prices) is evident when the amount of money injected into an economic system lags behind increases in actual output. Prices may fall because industrial productivity is increasing and cost savings are being passed on to consumers (this is good), or because consumers have high levels of debt and are therefore unwilling to buy very much (this is bad).

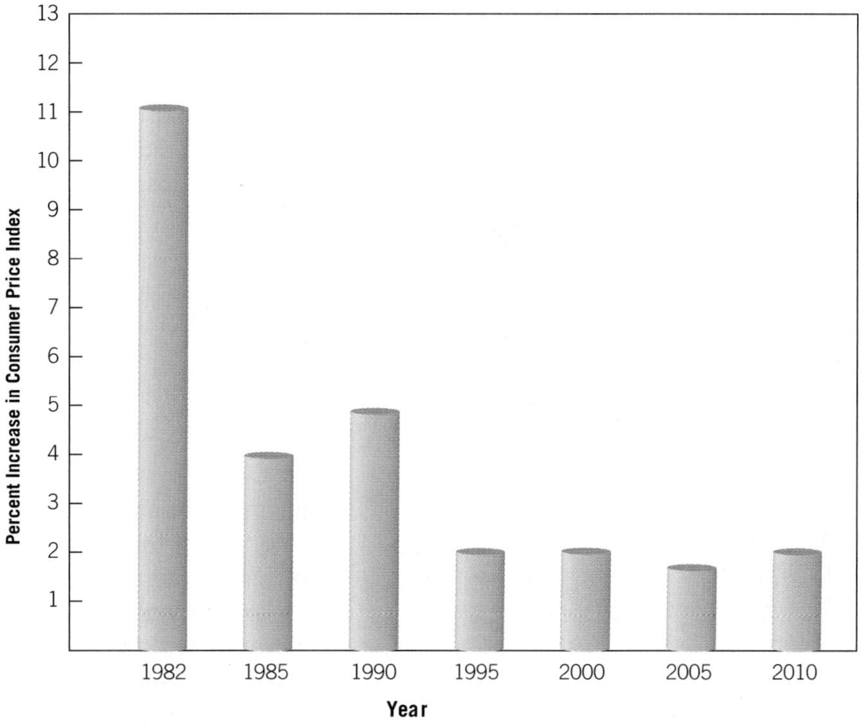

Unemployment In 2009, there were 7.7 million men and 6.9 million women (over age 25) working in Canada's labour force.[24] But there were many additional people who wanted a job but could not get one. **Unemployment** is the level of joblessness among people actively seeking work. There are various types of unemployment: *frictional unemployment* (people are out of work temporarily while looking for a new job); *seasonal unemployment* (people are out of work because of the seasonal nature of their jobs); *cyclical unemployment* (people are out of work because of a downturn in the business cycle); and *structural unemployment* (people are unemployed because they lack the skills

Figure 2.3
During the past fifteen years, the rate of price increases in Canada has been low and quite stable.

needed to perform available jobs). Unemployment rates have varied greatly over the years, as Figure 2.4 shows, with the rates for men generally being higher than the rates for women. In June 2010, the Canadian unemployment rate stood at 8.1 percent, which was higher than the 6 to 7 percent average range for the previous decade, before the recession, but was better than the rate in the Unites States, which stood at 9.7 percent and the depressing 20.1 percent rate found in Spain at the time.[25]

When unemployment is low there is a shortage of labour available for businesses. As businesses compete with one another for the available supply of labour, they raise the wages they are willing to pay. Then, because higher labour costs eat into profit margins, businesses raise the prices of their products. If prices get too high, consumers will respond by buying less. Businesses will then reduce their workforces because they don't need to produce as much. But this causes unemployment to go up and the cycle starts all over again.

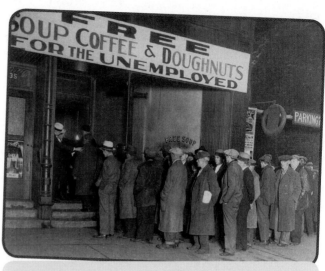

During the depression of the 1930s, unemployment was very high, with nearly one-quarter of the population unable to find work. Lines of unemployed workers outside soup kitchens were an unfortunate reality during those difficult economic times.

Managing the Canadian Economy

The federal government manages the Canadian economic system through two sets of policies: fiscal and monetary. **Fiscal policies** involve the collection and spending of government revenues. For example, when the growth rate of the economy is decreasing, tax cuts will normally stimulate renewed economic growth. **Monetary policies** focus on controlling the size of the nation's money supply. Working primarily through the Bank of Canada (see Chapter 15), the government can influence the ability and willingness of banks throughout the country to lend money. The power of the Bank of Canada to make changes in the supply of money is the centrepiece of the Canadian government's monetary policy. The principle is fairly simple:

- Higher interest rates make money more expensive to borrow and thereby reduce spending by companies that produce goods and services and consumers who buy them. When the Bank of Canada restricts the money supply, we say that it is practising a *tight monetary policy*.

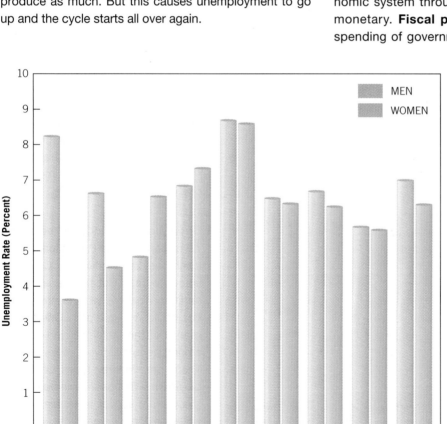

Figure 2.4
Historical unemployment rate. From 1970 to 1996, there was a steady upward trend in unemployment rates, but the rate began to decline in the late 1990s. The recession, which began in 2008, caused a clear increase in unemployment, as seen in the chart.

- Lower interest rates make money less expensive to borrow and thereby increase spending by both companies that produce goods and services and consumers who buy them. When the Bank of Canada loosens the money supply, we say that it is practising an *easy monetary policy*. When the financial crisis hit in the fall of 2008, the central banks around the world cut their interest rates in an attempt to stimulate their countries' economies.

LO-3 The Technological Environment

As applied to the environment of business, **technology** generally includes all the ways by which firms create value for their constituents. Technology includes human knowledge, work methods, physical equipment, electronics and telecommunications, and various processing systems that are used to perform business activities. Although technology is applied within organizations, the forms and availability of that technology come from the general environment. Boeing, for example, uses computer-assisted manufacturing and design techniques developed by external vendors to simulate the four miles of hydraulic tubing that run through its new 777 aircraft.

Research and Development (R&D)

Technological improvements and innovation in general are important contributors to the economic development of a country. The innovation process includes **research and development (R&D)**, which provides new ideas for products, services, and processes (see Chapter 13; the importance of R&D in the marketing of products). There are two types of R&D. **Basic (or pure) R&D** involves improving knowledge in an area without a primary focus on whether any discoveries that might occur are immediately marketable. For example, chemists in a laboratory might examine how certain chemical compounds behave. The knowledge gained from this activity might or might not result in a marketable product. **Applied R&D**, on the other hand, means focusing specifically on how a technological innovation can be put to use in the making of a product or service that can be sold in the marketplace. For example, H.J. Heinz developed a tomato that is sweeter than the variety it previously used to make its ketchup. This reduced the need for corn syrup, which had been rapidly increasing in price.[26]

R&D spending in Canada in 2009 totalled about $16.1 billion.[27] The Canadian private sector accounts for about 55 percent of R&D, the government 10 percent, and universities 34 percent.[28] In the private sector, just 100 businesses account for over half of all R&D money that is spent.[29] The largest expenditures on R&D in Canada are concentrated in industries like computer system design, information, communications equipment, and scientific research.[30]

Canada's level of R&D investment lags behind that of other countries; it typically spends less than 1 percent of GDP on R&D, while Japan, Germany, and the U.S., for example, spend from 1.5 to 2 percent of GDP. This lag exists partly because many Canadian businesses are subsidiaries of large U.S. companies that carry out their R&D in the United States. When we take into account that the GDP of these three countries is much larger than the GDP of Canada, it means that R&D spending in Canada (in absolute dollars) is a tiny fraction of what is spent by these nations.

The boxed insert entitled "The Hydrogen Fuel Cell" describes how complex and time-consuming research and development work can be.

Product and Service Technologies

Product and service technologies are employed for creating products—both physical goods and services—for customers. Although many people associate technology with manufacturing, it is also a significant factor in the service sector. Just as an automobile is built as it follows a predetermined pathway along an assembly line, a hamburger at McDonald's is cooked, assembled, and wrapped as it moves along a predefined path. The rapid advancement of the internet into all areas of business is also a reflection of the technological environment. Indeed, new technologies continue to revolutionize nearly every aspect of business, ranging from the ways that customers and companies interact to where, when, and how employees perform their work.

Companies must constantly be on the lookout for technological breakthroughs that might make their products or services obsolete and thereby threaten their survival. Many of these breakthroughs do not come from direct competitors or even from the industry the company is part of. Technology is the basis of competition for some companies, especially when their goal is to be the technology leader in their industry. A company, for example, might focus its efforts on having the most technologically advanced products on the market. Intel

TECHNOLOGY All the ways firms create value for their constituents.

RESEARCH AND DEVELOPMENT (R&D) Those activities that are necessary to provide new products, services, and proesses.

BASIC (OR PURE) R&D Improving knowledge in an area without a primary focus on whether any discoveries that might occur are immediately marketable.

APPLIED R&D Focusing specifically on how a technological innovation can be put to use in the making of a product or service that can be sold in the marketplace.

exemplifies the challenge and the risks of adopting a strategic dependence on technological leadership. Before co-founding Intel with Bob Noyce in 1968, Gordon Moore made a prediction about microprocessors (the processing components of microcomputers) that eventually became known as Moore's Law: The number of transistors in a microprocessor would double every 18 months. In effect, this rate would entail a twofold increase in processing power every 18 months—a seemingly impossible pace. Intel, however, adopted Moore's Law as a performance requirement for each new generation of processor and has kept up this pace for over 40 years.[31]

Because of the rapid pace of new developments, keeping a leadership position based on technology is increasingly difficult. **Technology transfer** refers to the process of getting a new technology out of the lab and into the marketplace where it can generate profits for the company. Efficient technology transfer means an increased likelihood of business success. A related challenge is meeting the constant demand to decrease *cycle time*—the time from beginning to end that it takes a firm to accomplish some recurring activity or function. Since businesses are more competitive if they can decrease cycle times, many companies now focus on decreasing cycle times in areas ranging

THE GREENING OF BUSINESS

The Hydrogen Fuel Cell

The hydrogen fuel cell combines hydrogen (one of earth's most common elements) with oxygen to produce electricity. The electricity generated by the fuel cell can be used to power anything that runs on electricity, including cars, and the only exhaust is warm water. When Vancouver-based Ballard Power Systems announced in the 1990s that it was developing the hydrogen fuel cell, excitement was high because automakers had tried for years to develop a new engine to replace the internal combustion engine that has powered automobiles for over a century. DaimlerChrysler and Ford Motor Co. invested hundreds of millions of dollars to pursue the development of fuel cells. Ballard sold prototypes to several public transportation companies in the U.S. and Canada, but more than 15 years have now passed, and the hydrogen fuel cell is still not ready for the mass market.

What happened? Why is the fuel cell—which looks like a fantastic product—still not widely available? Consider the daunting list of problems facing the fuel cell:

- Hydrogen must first be extracted from substances that contain it (e.g., natural gas), but stripping the hydrogen from natural gas creates carbon dioxide, which is precisely what the standard internal combustion car engines emit.

- Safety is an issue (when the word "hydrogen" is mentioned, many people immediately think of the spectacular explosion and fire that destroyed the hydrogen-powered Hindenburg airship in 1937).

- If insufficient numbers of hydrogen-dispensing gas stations are built, consumer demand will never be high enough to encourage mass production of cars that are powered by fuel cells.

- Hybrid cars like the Toyota Prius and the Honda Civic have been very successful and are providing strong competition for the hydrogen fuel cell.

The fuel cell may be commercially viable in 20 or 30 years, but there are still many developmental problems to be overcome and progress is slow. In 2008, Honda began producing the FCX Clarity, a zero-emission, fuel cell–powered car, but mass market sales are not likely until 2018. The company says that the biggest impediments to sales are the high price of the car and the lack of availability of hydrogen fuelling stations.

Maybe the hydrogen fuel cell will eventually become popular. Keep in mind what critics said when internal combustion–powered automobiles were introduced early in the twentieth century: "They'll never become popular because there would have to be gas stations all over the place." Well, now we have gas stations all over the place.

Critical Thinking Questions

1. Review the section on new product development in Chapter 13. At what stage of the new product development process is the hydrogen fuel cell?
2. Consider the following statement: *"If the fuel cell had any value, it would have been fully developed by now and there would already be many cars on the road that are powered by the fuel cell."* Do you agree or disagree with the statement? Explain your reasoning.

from developing products to making deliveries and collecting credit payments. Twenty years ago, it took automakers about five years from the decision to launch a new product until it was available in dealer showrooms. Now most companies can complete the cycle in less than two years.

LO-4 The Political–Legal Environment

The **political–legal environment** reflects the relationship between business and government, including government regulation of business. The legal system defines what an organization can and can't do. Although Canada is a free market economy, there is still significant regulation of business activity, as we saw in Chapter 1. At times government policy can be tremendously advantageous to businesses. The home renovation tax credit, which expired in 2010, brought a 30 percent sales increase for Winnipeg-based Acrylon Plastics (maker of window frames) and had hardware retailers smiling from coast to coast.[32] On the other hand, Shoppers Drug Mart was very vocal about its opposition to a new Ontario government regulation that would see generic drugs priced at as low as 25 percent of the original brand name product's cost, down from 50 percent. This regulation would have a tremendous impact on pharmacy profits.[33]

Society's general view of business (pro or anti) is also important. During periods of anti-business sentiment, companies may find their competitive activities restricted.

Political stability is also an important consideration, especially for international firms. No business wants to set up shop in another country unless trade relationships with that country are relatively well defined and stable. Thus, Canadian firms are more likely to do business in England rather than in Haiti. For example, in 2010, mining companies were concerned about rumours that members of the South African ruling government were considering nationalization (government takeover of resources, forcing private companies to sell at a price deemed fair by the government) of up to 60 percent of the country's mining sector. This was a dangerous prospect for Vancouver-based Great Basin Gold Ltd., which was developing a $230 million gold mining operation at the time.[34]

Relations between sovereign governments can also affect business activity. When Canada refused to send troops to support the U.S. invasion of Iraq, relations between the two nations were very cool for a time. Similar issues also pertain to assessments of local and provincial governments. A new mayor or provincial leader can affect many organizations, especially small firms that do

business in a single location and are susceptible to zoning restrictions, property and school taxes, and the like.

Another aspect of the political–legal environment is described in the boxed insert entitled "Nova Scotia's Golden Nectar."

LO-5 The Socio-Cultural Environment

The **socio-cultural environment** includes the customs, values, attitudes, and demographic characteristics of the society in which a company operates. The socio-cultural environment influences the customer preferences for goods and services, as well as the standards of business conduct that are seen as acceptable.

Customer Preferences and Tastes

Customer preferences and tastes vary both across and within national boundaries. In some countries, consumers are willing and able to pay premium prices for designer clothes with labels such as Armani. But the same clothes have virtually no market in other countries. Product usage also varies between nations. In China, bicycles are primarily seen as a mode of transportation, but in Canada, they are marketed primarily for recreational purposes.

Consumer preferences can also vary widely within the same country. Customs and product preferences in Quebec, for example, differ from those in other parts of Canada. In the United States, pre-packaged chilli is more popular in the southwest than in the northeast. McDonald's is just one company that is affected by socio-cultural factors. In response to concerns about nutrition and health, McDonald's has added salads to its menus and experimented with other low-fat foods. It was the first fast-food chain to provide customers with information about the ingredients in its products, and it attracted media attention when it announced that it would reduce the fat content in its popular French fries.

Consumer preferences and tastes also change over time. Preferences for colour, style, taste, and so forth change from season to season. In some years, brightly coloured clothes sell best, while in other years, people want more subdued colours. Some of these changes are driven by consumers, and some are driven by companies trying to

POLITICAL–LEGAL ENVIRONMENT Conditions reflecting the relationship between business and government, usually in the form of government regulation.

SOCIO-CULTURAL ENVIRONMENT Conditions including the customs, values, attitudes, and demographic characteristics of the society in which an organization functions.

Nova Scotia's Golden Nectar: Glen Breton Rare

Cape Breton, Nova Scotia–based Glenora Distilleries battled fiercely to keep its Glen Breton Rare Single Malt Whisky on store shelves. It's not like the product lacked demand; Glenora distils the only single-malt whisky produced in Canada. The court battle dragged on from 2000 until mid-2009. The Scotch Whisky Association, a group representing over 50 whisky distillers in Scotland, claimed the company's use of "Glen" in its brand is confusing consumers and leading them to believe that the product is distilled in Scotland.

Lauchie MacLean, Glenora's president, strongly disagreed. He argued the name referred to Glenora Distillery's home community: Glenville, Cape Breton. Fortunately, a Canadian Federal Court of Appeal's ruling, in January 2009, allowed the company to continue to use the name. This ruling was supported, in June 2009, when the Supreme Court of Canada refused to hear the case and put an end to the legal battle. This move cleared the way for Glen Breton to get a legal trademark in Canada.

The latest clash hasn't been the only form of legal restriction imposed on Glenora Distillery and other whisky producers around the globe. Distillers based in Scotland have set out to protect the use of the label "scotch." One such move was an agreement signed by Canada and the European Union in 2003 that prevented Canadian whisky distillers from using the word "scotch" in their label. This term is reserved for Scotland-based distillers only. Glenora has always complied with this ruling but wasn't ready to lie down when the association's latest assault threatened its "Glen Breton" brand. But now, the future looks bright for a company that has

had its fair share of challenges. Not only has it secured its most valuable possession, its brand name, it is also excited about the growing whisky market.

Because of increased demand in Europe and Asia, some single-malt whisky distillers have found their products in short supply. As a result, many distillers are pulling out of some markets and entering others. It's simple economics according to MacLean: "They [distillers] have an asset, and they're looking at selling that asset for the most money that they can get out of it." Glenora is a relatively small producer, but the company hopes to increase production at a later date to better match demand. Currently, Glenora is not "heavily into the Asian market," but expect that to change over the next few years.

Glenora's successes have partly been due to its entrepreneurial flexibility. The company experienced serious cash flow problems not long after its launch in 1991 because distilling doesn't happen overnight—it can take 10 to 12 years before a distillery will see revenues. However, some innovative approaches, which involved selling whisky futures and adding rum bottling and complementary tourism operations to the business, brought the company through the tough times. The business environment hasn't always been kind to Glenora, but in true entrepreneurial fashion, it has persevered. *Sláinte!*

Critical Thinking Question

1. Which of the external environments have had the most effect on Glenora Distilleries?

---

convince consumers to adopt new styles. These and many other related issues regarding businesses and their customers are explored more fully in Part IV of this book, which deals with the marketing of goods and services.

Socio-cultural factors also influence the way workers in a society feel about their jobs and organizations. In some cultures, work carries meaningful social significance, with certain employers and job titles being highly desired by workers. But in other cultures, because work is simply a means to an end, people are concerned only with pay and job security. McDonald's has occasionally struggled with its operations in the Middle East because many people there are not interested in working in food-service operations.

Ethical Compliance and Responsible Business Behaviour

An especially critical element of the socio-cultural environment is the practice of ethical conduct and social responsibility. We cover these areas in detail in Chapter 3, but they are sufficiently important that we describe a couple of points briefly here: the reporting of a company's financial position and a company's social responsibility toward citizens.

Keeping up with today's increasingly fast-paced business activities is putting a strain on the accounting profession's traditional methods for auditing, financial reporting, and time-honoured standards for professional ethics. The stakeholders of business firms—employees, stockholders, consumers, labour unions, creditors, and the government—are entitled to a fair accounting so they can make enlightened personal and business decisions, but they often get a blurred picture of a firm's competitive health. Nortel went from being the pride and joy of Canada to a historical warning. Nortel suffered at the turn of the century because the internet bubble burst. This was an external factor that had an impact on all technology companies but was not why Nortel failed; a major reason for the bankruptcy was the failure to get its financial house in order. The company made accounting restatement after restatement of its financials throughout the last decade of its existence. Restatement is a clever way of saying that the figures that the company presented to its stakeholders were inaccurate. When that happens one time it can be seen as an error. When it is repeated over time it is a clear attempt to deceive the market.

In 2010, British Petroleum (BP) was in the news for all the wrong reasons and faced the consequences of the massive Gulf of Mexico oil spill. For years, BP and other oil companies said that high-tech offshore drilling was extremely safe. But in 2010, when disaster struck, it became clear that the deep-sea environment was difficult and that BP did not have an adequate solution for the problem. For months the oil spewed into the Gulf, devastating coastlines, endangering wildlife, and battering the local fishing and tourism businesses. This failure had consequences and the various stakeholders were lining up to make BP pay. Within a few days, a Facebook page promoting a BP boycott had 360 000 supporters. Advocacy groups like Public Citizen held rallies against BP. The U.S. government was publicly pushing the company for a quick solution while demanding BP halt a $10.5 billion dividend payment to shareholders. The U.S. government was also planning a legal response to make BP pay for its mistake in the court system. The future of BP was at stake (something that was unimaginable before the crisis).[35]

The Business Environment

Business today is faster paced, more complex, and more demanding than ever before. As businesses aggressively try to differentiate themselves, there has been a trend toward higher-quality products, planned obsolescence, and product life cycles measured in weeks or months rather than years. This, in turn, has created customer expectations for instant gratification. Ultimate consumers and business customers want high-quality goods and services—often customized—with lower prices and immediate delivery. Sales offices, service providers, and production facilities are shifting geographically as new markets and resources emerge in other countries. Employees want flexible working hours and opportunities to work at home. Stockholder expectations also add pressure for productivity increases, growth in market share, and larger profits. At the same time, however, a more vocal public demands more honesty, fair competition, and respect for the environment.

A C-Suite survey found that the three most important issues facing Canadian businesses are (1) the value of the Canadian dollar, (2) a skilled labour shortage, and (3) the environment. These three issues are all important elements of the business environment.[36]

The Industry Environment

Each business firm operates in a specific industry, and each industry has different characteristics. The intensity of the competition in an industry has a big influence on how a company operates. To be effective, managers must understand the competitive situation, and then develop a competitive strategy to exploit opportunities in the industry.

One of the most popular tools to analyze competitive situations in an industry is Michael Porter's five forces model.[37] The model (see Figure 2.5) helps managers analyze five important sources of competitive pressure and then decide what their competitive strategy should be. We briefly discuss each of the elements of the model in the following paragraphs.

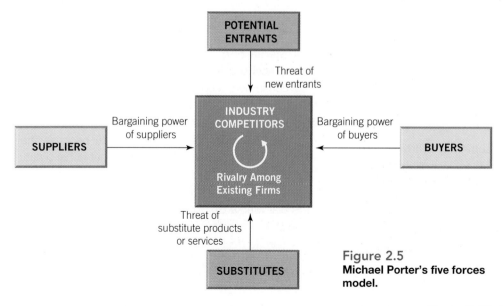

Figure 2.5
Michael Porter's five forces model.

**CORE
COMPETENCIES**
Skills and resources
with which an organiza-
tion competes best and
creates the most value
for owners.

OUTSOURCING
Strategy of paying
suppliers and distribu-
tors to perform certain
business processes
or to provide needed
materials or services.

VIRAL MARKETING
Strategy of using the
internet and word-
of-mouth marketing
to spread product
information.

Rivalry Among Existing Competitors The amount of rivalry among companies varies across industries. Rivalry can be seen in activities like intense price competition, elaborate advertising campaigns, and an increased emphasis on customer service. For many years, the rivalry among chartered accountants, certified general accountants, and certified management accountants in Canada was low-key, but it has recently become much more intense. Firms are responding by cutting costs, making pricing deals with clients, and trying to find ways to differentiate themselves from their competitors.

Threat of Potential Entrants When new competitors enter an industry, they may cause big changes. If it is easy for new competitors to enter a market, competition will likely be intense and the industry will not be that attractive. Some industries (e.g., automobile manufacturing) are very capital-intensive and are therefore difficult to enter, but others (e.g., home cleaning or lawn care services) are relatively easy to enter.

Suppliers The amount of bargaining power suppliers have in relation to buyers helps determine how competitive an industry is. When there are only a few suppliers in an industry, they tend to have great bargaining power. The power of suppliers is influenced by the number of substitute products that are available (i.e., products that perform the same or similar functions). When there are few substitute products, suppliers obviously have more power.

Buyers When there are only a few buyers and many suppliers, the buyers have a great deal of bargaining power. Retail powerhouse Walmart, for example, is often cited as a buyer that puts tremendous pressure on its suppliers to reduce their prices. Walmart can do this because it buys so much from these suppliers.

Substitutes If there are many substitute products available, the industry is more competitive. For example, various synthetic fibres can be used as substitutes for cotton. Managers use Porter's model to help them decide the level of competitive intensity in an industry. A good example is the impact of the internet on airline tickets and car rentals. By making it easier for consumers to compare prices, the internet has increased the competitive intensity of these two industries (and many others, for that matter).

In effect, the internet has increased the bargaining power of ticket buyers.

LO-6 Emerging Challenges and Opportunities in the Business Environment

The most successful firms are dealing with challenges and opportunities in today's business environment by focusing on their **core competencies**—the skills and resources with which they compete best and create the most value for owners. They outsource non-core business processes and pay suppliers and distributors to perform them, thereby increasing their reliance on suppliers. These new business models call for unprecedented coordination—not only among internal activities but also among customers, suppliers, and strategic partners—and they often involve globally dispersed processes and supply chains.

In this section, we discuss some of the most popular steps that companies have taken to respond to challenges and opportunities in the business environment. These include *outsourcing, social media and viral marketing,* and *business process management*.

Outsourcing **Outsourcing** is the strategy of paying suppliers and distributors to perform certain business processes or to provide needed materials or services. For example, the cafeteria in a museum may be important to employees and customers, but the museum's primary focus is on exhibits that will interest the general public, not on food-service operations. That's why museums usually outsource cafeteria operations to food-service management companies. The result is more attention to museum exhibits and better food service for customers. Firms today outsource numerous activities, including payroll, employee training, and research and development.

Social Media and Viral Marketing Social media sites such as Facebook are now an important part of everyday life for consumers (especially the youth market). Companies are addressing this new reality by providing content and creating links for consumers. Most organizations are being careful about their online presence because they don't want it to be seen as an imposition but rather a natural extension to their real-world relationship with clients. As we discuss throughout this book, in the E-Business and Social Media Solutions boxes, some companies are making strong inroads as this new model evolves and companies learn to deal with an empowered consumer base.

Viral marketing predates the social media craze and first gained prominence through basic email transfer; it describes word of mouth that spreads information like a virus from customer to customer, and relies on the internet to replace face-to-face communications. Messages about new cars, sports events, and numerous other goods and services travel on the internet among potential customers, who pass the information on. Using various formats—games, contests, chat rooms, and bulletin boards—marketers encourage potential customers to try out products and tell other people about them.[38] This approach has even more potential today with the likes of Twitter providing even quicker means to move messages.

Viral marketing works because people increasingly rely on the internet for information that they used to get from other media such as radio and newspapers, and because the customer becomes a participant in the process of spreading the word by forwarding information to other internet users. Take a look at the E-Business and Social Media Solutions box entitled "Corus Entertainment Looking for Listeners and Revenues in New Places."

Business Process Management A **process** is any activity that adds value to some input, transforming it into an output for a customer (whether external or internal).[39] For example, human resource departments perform interviewing and hiring processes; payroll departments perform the employee-payment process; the purchasing department performs the process of ordering materials; accounting performs the financial reporting process; and marketing performs the process of taking orders from customers.

Business process management means moving away from organizing around departments and moving toward organizing around process-oriented team structures that cut across old departmental boundaries. Often, companies begin by asking, "What must we do well to stay in business and win new orders?" Next, they identify the major processes that must be performed well to achieve these goals. Then they organize resources and skills around those essential processes. By organizing according to processes rather than functional departments, decision making is faster and more customer-oriented, materials and operations are coordinated, and products get to customers more rapidly.[40]

PROCESS Any activity that adds value to some input, transforming it into an output for a customer (whether external or internal).

BUSINESS PROCESS MANAGEMENT Approach by which firms move away from department-oriented organization and toward process-oriented team structures that cut across old departmental boundaries.

ACQUISITION The purchase of a company by another, larger firm, which absorbs the smaller company into its operations.

MERGER The union of two companies to form a single new business.

LO-7 Redrawing Corporate Boundaries

Successful companies are responding to challenges in the external environment by redrawing traditional organizational boundaries, and by joining together with other companies to develop new goods and services. Several trends have become evident in recent years: *acquisitions and mergers, divestitures and spinoffs, employee-owned corporations, strategic alliances,* and *subsidiary/parent corporations.*

Acquisitions and Mergers

In an **acquisition**, one firm simply buys another firm. For example, Kraft Foods Inc. recently bought British candy giant Cadbury for US$19 billion.[41] The transaction is similar to buying a car that becomes your property. In contrast, a **merger**

Much concern has been expressed by government officials and labour unions that the outsourcing of jobs will hurt the Canadian economy. Here, women work in one of many call centres in New Delhi, India, work that has been outsourced by Canadian and U.S. companies.

Corus Entertainment Looking for Listeners and Revenues in New Places

Do you remember when cameras were used to create photos, phones were used to make phone calls, and TVs were used to watch TV programs? Today things are different. You can watch TV on your phone, laptop, or even the LCD on your wall. Your smart phone or regular cell is a great tool for photos and your camera has an ever-increasing level of mega-pixels. As for music, it can come from your iPod, smart phone, a satellite station, or streamed from a website from your favourite station in Surrey, Saskatoon, St. John's, or even South Africa. Options are limitless. Faced with this new reality, the companies that own your favourite stations are looking for new ways to attract listeners like you.

Corus Entertainment is extending its relationship with listeners and finding ways to profit from it as well. In the early days of the internet, stations were simply excited about the chance to share music and shows with anyone who would listen online. However, this also meant that their listeners could migrate to stations from anywhere—a scary prospect. Corus Entertainment has come a long way in the last decade. Visiting one of its radio websites (e.g., Vancouver's

99.3 The Fox, Toronto's Edge 102.1, Calgary Country 105, Edmonton's 92.5 Joe FM, Winnipeg's Power 97, and Hamilton's Y108) makes it clear that even if the call letters are the same, these stations are no longer simply your father's radio station (unless Dad is especially media savvy). There are links to Facebook, Flickr, MySpace, Twitter, Viigo (for BlackBerry), YouTube, and more. There are blogs and podcasts and the tools to connect, join contests, and create virtual bonds. Corus also takes it a step further; it was the first to offer an iPhone streaming app and the first to form direct links with iTunes. You can purchase, via a special version of the Apple iTunes music store linked to your station, the song that you're currently listening to. In the process, Corus stands to add a few pennies to its bottom line.

Here is the new math that Corus and its advertising partners are studying. In 2009, Corus achieved over 7 million online listening hours per month; one out of every 20 listeners was accessing their stations through mobile devices or online, and this figure was expected to grow rapidly. However, with all of these positive signs, Corus sold its 12 Quebec-based stations to Cogeco Cable Inc. for $81 million in 2010. Corus stated that it wanted to focus on its other key markets. Was this a sign that all was not well or was Corus simply focusing on selected stations and reinvesting its new business model in key spots? This was not clear at the time. In the e-business age one thing is certain: companies must be ready to adjust and evolve in order to be successful.

An example of a Corus Entertainment radio station web site (Vancouver's 99.3 The Fox).

Critical Thinking Question

1. How do you listen to music? Have you joined or visited a social media group linked to your favourite stations? Why? Why not?

is a consolidation of two firms, and the arrangement is more collaborative. In the first quarter of 2010, there were 246 mergers and acquisitions in Canada, with a value of $19.7 billion, but this figure was much lower than the previous quarter, which had 285 deals worth $34.4 billion.[42]

When the companies are in the same industry, as when Molson Inc. merged with Adolph Coors Co., it is called a **horizontal merger**. When one of the companies in the merger is a supplier or customer to the other, it is called a **vertical merger**. When the companies are in unrelated businesses, it is called a **conglomerate merger**. A merger or acquisition can take place in one of several ways. In a **friendly takeover**, the acquired company welcomes the acquisition, perhaps because it needs cash or sees other benefits in joining the acquiring firm. But in a **hostile takeover**, the acquiring company buys enough of the other company's stock to take control even though the other company is opposed to the takeover. Montreal-based Couche-Tard has plenty of experience in the merger and takeover game (in the past 15 years it has acquired Mac's, Dairy Mart, Circle K, and Winks); it is one of the biggest convenience store operators in North America with over 5800 stores. In 2010, it made a US$1.9 billion hostile takeover bid for Iowa-based Casey's after failing to come to a friendly agreement for the 1500-store chain.[43]

A **poison pill** is a defence that management adopts to make a firm less attractive to an actual or potential hostile suitor in a takeover attempt. The objective is to make the "pill" so distasteful that a potential acquirer will not want to swallow it. BCE Inc., for example, adopted a poison pill that allowed its shareholders to buy BCE stock at a 50 percent discount if another company announced its intention to acquire 20 percent or more of BCE's shares.[44]

Divestitures and Spinoffs

A **divestiture** occurs when a company decides to sell part of its existing business operations to another corporation. For example, Unilever—the maker of Close-Up toothpaste, Dove soap, Vaseline lotion, and Q-tips—at one time owned several specialty chemical businesses that made ingredients for its consumer products. The company decided that it had to focus more on the consumer products themselves, so it sold the chemical businesses to ICI, a European chemical company.

In other cases, a company might set up one or more corporate units as new, independent businesses because a business unit might be more valuable as a separate company. This is known as a **spinoff**. For example, PepsiCo spun off Pizza Hut, KFC, and Taco Bell into a new, separate corporation now known as Yum! Brands Inc., and Canadian Pacific spun off Canadian Pacific Railway, CP Ships, Pan Canadian Petroleum, and Fording Coal.

Employee-Owned Corporations

Corporations are sometimes owned by the employees who work for them. The current pattern is for this ownership to take the form of **employee stock ownership plans**, or ESOPs. A corporation might decide to set up an ESOP to increase employee motivation or to fight a hostile takeover attempt. The company first secures a loan, which it then uses to buy shares of its stock on the open market. Some of the future profits made by the corporation are used to pay off the loan. The stock, meanwhile, is controlled by a bank or other trustee. Employees gradually gain ownership of the stock, usually on the basis of seniority. But even though they might not have physical possession of the stock for a while, they control its voting rights immediately.

A survey of 471 Canadian and U.S. companies conducted by Western Compensation & Benefits Consultants of Vancouver found that three-quarters of the companies that have adopted ESOPs have experienced improvement in both sales and profits. Charlie Spiring, the CEO of Wellington West Holdings Inc., says that one of the fundamental principles of his business is employee ownership. People really have to be entrepreneurs to work well in the company.[45]

HORIZONTAL MERGER A merger of two firms that have previously been direct competitors in the same industry.

VERTICAL MERGER A merger of two firms that have previously had a buyer–seller relationship.

CONGLOMERATE MERGER A merger of two firms in completely unrelated businesses.

FRIENDLY TAKEOVER An acquisition in which the management of the acquired company welcomes the firm's buyout by another company.

HOSTILE TAKEOVER An acquisition in which the management of the acquired company fights the firm's buyout by another company.

POISON PILL A defence that management adopts to make a firm less attractive to an actual or potential hostile suitor in a takeover attempt.

DIVESTITURE Occurs when a company sells part of its existing business operations to another company.

SPINOFF Strategy of setting up one or more corporate units as new, independent corporations.

EMPLOYEE STOCK OWNERSHIP PLANS An arrangement whereby a corporation buys its own stock with loaned funds and holds it in trust for its employees. Employees "earn" the stock based on some condition such as seniority. Employees control the stock's voting rights immediately, even though they may not take physical possession of the stock until specified conditions are met.

STRATEGIC ALLIANCE An enterprise in which two or more persons or companies temporarily join forces to undertake a particular project.

SUBSIDIARY CORPORATION One that is owned by another corporation.

PARENT CORPORATION A corporation that owns a subsidiary.

Strategic Alliances

A **strategic alliance**, or joint venture, involves two or more enterprises cooperating in the research, development, manufacture, or marketing of a product. For example, GM and Suzuki formed a strategic alliance at the Ingersoll, Ontario, plant where the Equinox and Grand Vitaras are made. Companies form strategic alliances for two main reasons: (1) to help spread the risk of a project, and (2) to get something of value (like technological expertise) from their strategic partner.

Subsidiary and Parent Corporations

A **subsidiary corporation** is one that is owned by another corporation. The corporation that owns the subsidiary is called the **parent corporation**. For example, the Hudson's Bay Company (HBC) is the parent corporation of Zellers and Home Outfitters.

PEARSON
mybusinesslab

To improve your grade, visit the MyBusinessLab website at **www.pearsoned.ca/mybusinesslab.** This online homework and tutorial system allows you to test your understanding and generates a personalized study plan just for you. It provides you with study and practice tools directly related to this chapter's content. MyBusinessLab puts you in control of your own learning! Test yourself on the material for this chapter at **www.pearsoned.ca/mybusinesslab.**

Summary of Learning Objectives

1. **Explain the concepts of *organizational boundaries* and *multiple organizational environments*.** All businesses operate within a larger *external environment* consisting of everything outside an organization's boundaries that might affect it. An *organizational boundary* is that which separates the organization from its environment. Organizations have multiple environments: economic conditions, technology, political–legal considerations, social issues, the global environment, issues of ethical and social responsibility, the business environment itself, and numerous other emerging challenges and opportunities.

2. **Explain the importance of the *economic environment* to business and identify the factors used to evaluate the performance of an economic system.** The *economic environment* is the economic system in which business firms operate. The health of this environment affects business firms. The key goals of the Canadian system are economic growth, economic stability, and full employment. *Gross domestic product (GDP)* is the total value of all goods and services produced within a given period by a national economy domestically. The government manages the economy through *fiscal* and *monetary policies*.

3. **Describe the *technological environment* and its role in business.** *Technology* refers to all the ways firms create value for their constituents, including human knowledge, work methods, physical equipment, electronics and telecommunications, and various processing systems. There are two general categories of business-related technologies: *product and service technologies* and *business process technologies*.

4. **Describe the *political–legal environment* and its role in business.** The *political–legal environment*

reflects the relationship between business and government. The legal system defines what an organization can and can't do. Various government agencies regulate important areas such as advertising practices, safety and health considerations, and acceptable standards of business conduct. Pro- or anti-business sentiment in government can further influence business activity.

5. **Describe the *socio-cultural environment* and its role in business.** The *socio-cultural environment* includes the customs, values, and demographic characteristics of society. Socio-cultural processes determine the goods and services as well as the standards of business conduct that a society values and accepts. Appropriate standards of conduct also vary across cultures. The shape of the market, the ethics of political influence, and the attitudes of its workforce are only a few of the many ways in which culture can affect an organization.

6. **Identify emerging challenges and opportunities in the *business environment*.** Successful companies are focusing on their core competencies. The innovative ways in which companies respond to emerging challenges and opportunities include *outsourcing*, *social media* and *viral marketing*, and *business process management*.

7. **Understand recent trends in the *redrawing of corporate boundaries*.** An *acquisition* occurs when one firm buys another. A *merger* occurs when two firms combine to create a new company. A *divestiture* occurs when a corporation sells a part of its existing business operations or sets it up as a new and independent corporation. When a firm sells part of itself to raise capital, the strategy is known as a *spin-off*. The *ESOP plan* allows employees to own a significant share of the corporation through trusts established on their behalf. In a *strategic alliance*, two or more organizations collaborate on a project for mutual gain.

Questions and Exercises

Questions for Analysis

1. It has been argued that inflation is both good and bad. Explain. Are government efforts to control inflation well-advised? Explain.

2. What are the benefits and risks of outsourcing? What, if anything, should be done about the problem of Canadian companies outsourcing jobs to foreign countries? Defend your answer.

3. Why is it important for managers to understand the environment in which their businesses operate?

4. Explain how current economic indicators such as inflation and unemployment affect you personally. Explain how they affect managers.

5. At first glance, it might seem as though the goals of economic growth and stability are inconsistent with one another. How can this apparent inconsistency be reconciled?

6. What is the current climate in Canada regarding the regulation of business? How might it affect you if you were a manager today?

Application Exercises

1. Select two businesses you are familiar with. Identify the major elements of their external environments that are most likely to affect them in important and meaningful ways.

2. Assume that you are the owner of an internet pharmacy that sells prescription drugs to U.S. citizens. Analyze the factors in the external environment (economic, technological, political–legal, and socio-cultural) that might facilitate your company's activities. Analyze the factors in the external environment that might threaten your company's activities.

3. Select a technology product, such as Amazon's Kindle e-reader, and research how the various environments of business (economic, technological, socio-cultural, global, political–legal, and general business) are currently impacting the sales possibilities of the product or service.

4. Interview two business owners or managers. Ask them to answer the following questions: (a) What business functions, if any, do they outsource? (b) Are they focusing more attention on business process management now than in the past? (c) How have internet applications and the growth of social media changed the way they conduct business?

Building Your Business Skills

The Letdown from Environmental Upheaval

Goal

To encourage students to understand how local events can affect other businesses.

Situation

The collapse of Enron affected literally hundreds of other businesses. While attention has been directed primarily at the demise of Arthur Andersen, many other businesses suffered as well. For example, Enron's headquarters were located in a large office building on the edge of Houston's downtown business district. Because of both Enron's rapid growth and the prosperity of its employees, numerous other service providers had set up shop nearby—a shoeshine stand, a coffee shop, a dry cleaner, and two restaurants. When Enron collapsed, the demand for services provided by these small businesses dropped sharply.

Larger businesses were also caught up in the ripple effect. Enron, for example, had bought the rights to name the new home of Houston's baseball team, the Astros, Enron Field. The Astros were forced to remove all Enron signage and seek a new sponsor. Continental Airlines dominates the air traffic market out of Houston, and Enron was one of Continental's largest corporate clients; the end of business travel by Enron managers cost the airline considerable revenue.

Method

Divide into groups of four or five students; each group should begin by doing the following:

Step 1 Identify five kinds of small businesses likely to have been affected by Enron's collapse. You can include some of those identified above, but identify at least two others.

Step 2 Identify five kinds of large businesses likely to have been affected by Enron's collapse. Again, you can use some of those identified above, but identify at least two others.

Step 3 As a group, develop answers to each of the following:

1. For each company that you identify, both small and large, describe the specific effects of the Enron collapse on its business.

2. Describe the most logical organizational response of each company to these effects.

3. What kinds of plans, if any, should each organization develop in the event of similar future events?

4. Identify businesses that might have benefited economically from the collapse of Enron.

Alternative Assignment

Select a different high-profile environmental upheaval, such as the economic crisis that nearly caused the collapse of the major North American automakers. Then proceed with Steps 1–3 above.

Follow-Up Questions

1. What does this exercise demonstrate about the pitfalls of relying too heavily on one business?

2. Could any of these businesses have been better prepared for the Enron collapse?

3. Managers must be on the alert for environmental changes that might negatively affect their business. Is it possible for a manager to spend too much time trying to anticipate future events? Why or why not?

Exercising Your Ethics

Finding the Balance

The Situation

Managers often find it necessary to find the right balance among the interests of different stakeholders. For instance, paying employees the lowest possible wages can enhance profits, but paying a living wage might better serve the interests of workers. As more businesses outsource production to other countries, these trade-offs become more complicated.

The Dilemma

The Canadian Delta Company currently uses three suppliers in Southeast Asia for most of its outsourced production. Due to increased demand for its products, it needs to double the amount of business it currently subcontracts to one of these suppliers. (For purposes of this exercise, assume that the company must award the new supplier contract to a single firm, and that it must be one of these three. You can also assume that the quality provided is about the same for all three companies.)

Subcontractor A provides a plain but clean work environment for its workers. Even though the local weather conditions are usually hot and humid, the plant is not air-conditioned. Canadian Delta safety experts have verified that the conditions are not dangerous but are definitely uncomfortable. The firm pays its workers the same prevailing wage rate that is paid by its local competitors. While it has never had a legal issue with its workforce, Subcontractor A does push its employees to meet production quotas and it has a very tough disciplinary policy regarding tardiness. An employee who is late gets probation; a second infraction within three months results in termination. This subcontractor provides production to Canadian Delta at a level such that it can attach a 25 percent mark-up.

Subcontractor B also provides a plain work environment. It pays its workers about 5 percent above local wage levels and hence is an attractive employer. Because of its higher pay, this firm is actually quite ruthless in some of its policies. For instance, any employee who reports to work more than 15 minutes late without a medical excuse is automatically terminated. This supplier's costs are such that Delta Company can achieve a 20 percent mark-up.

Subcontractor C runs a much nicer factory than either A or B, and the plant is air-conditioned. It pays its workers about 10 percent above local wage levels. The company also operates an on-site school for the children of its employees, and provides additional training for its workers so they can improve their skills. Due to its higher costs, Canadian Delta's mark-up on this firm's products is only around 15 percent.

Team Activity

Assemble a group of four students and assign each group member to one of the following roles:

- Canadian Delta executive
- Canadian Delta employee
- Canadian Delta customer
- Canadian Delta investor

Action Steps

1. Before discussing the situation with your group, and from the perspective of your assigned role, decide which firm should get the additional business. Which firm is your second choice? Write down the reasons for your position.

2. Before discussing the situation with your group, and from the perspective of your assigned role, identify the underlying ethical issues in this situation. Write down the issues.

3. Gather your group together and reveal, in turn, each member's comments on their choices. Next, reveal the ethical issues listed by each member.

4. Appoint someone to record main points of agreement and disagreement within the group. How do you explain the results? What accounts for any disagreement?

5. From an ethical standpoint, what does your group conclude is the most appropriate choice for the company in this situation? Why?

Inflation, Deflation, and the Validity of the CPI

Between 2008 and 2010, there was great fear and confusion in financial markets. The stock market saw a major decline and a major recovery and the roller coaster ride seemed far from over. It wasn't just because of the credit crisis, the housing crisis, the sovereign debt crisis, and the worldwide recession. There was also uncertainty about whether *inflation* or *deflation* was going to add to the problems that already existed. On one hand, it seemed logical to predict that inflation was going to get worse because central governments around the world cut interest rates and were injecting billions of dollars into their financial systems to get their economies moving again. On the other hand, the recession became so bad that the demand for goods and services was declining, commodity prices (including oil) were falling fast, banks were not loaning money (because they feared that borrowers wouldn't be able to repay their loans), consumers were reluctant to spend money, and everyone was hoarding cash. All of those factors suggested that deflation was going to occur.

To see how this complicated situation developed, we have to look back. In the first half of 2008, prices increased for many different products and services, including food, metals, energy, air transportation, gasoline, cable services, and mortgages. The Bank of Canada became concerned that inflation was becoming a real threat. The weakening of the Canadian dollar against the U.S. dollar also increased the threat since imported goods would be more expensive for Canadians. The International Monetary Fund (IMF) expressed concern that the strong demand for food and other resources in rapidly growing countries like India and China was going to cause increased inflation elsewhere in the world. The IMF's deputy managing director noted that there were about 50 countries in the world with inflation rates *above* 10 percent, mostly developing nations.

The interconnectedness of the global economy was also a problem. The U.S. Federal Reserve cut interest rates in an attempt to get the U.S. economy moving, but that caused the value of the U.S. dollar to decline relative to other currencies (at least for a while). That, in turn, meant that U.S. consumers would have to pay more for imported products. The rate cut also created problems for Middle Eastern and Asian countries that had pegged their dollar to the U.S. dollar in an attempt to stabilize their economies. When the United States reduced interest rates, those countries really had to follow suit; if they

didn't, people would move more money into their country (because they could earn a higher rate of return than they could in the United States). That, in turn, would create upward pressure on the currency of those Middle Eastern and Asian countries. It would also cause increased inflation because when interest rates decline, it is easier for people to borrow money.

All of these factors suggested that inflation was going to be a problem. But economic circumstances can change very quickly. Just a few months after the Bank of Canada expressed concerns about inflation, it decided to *cut* interest rates, even though doing so typically increases the chance of inflation. The Bank of Canada did this because commodity prices had suddenly declined and a worldwide recession had started. In spite of the rate cut, prices soon started dropping for meat, automobiles, computers, fresh fruit, furniture, appliances, tools, hardware, and a wide range of commodities, including oil. In China, overproduction of everything from laptop computers to building materials raised fears that many products would soon be dumped on world markets at cut-rate prices. That increased the chance of deflation (negative inflation). Support for deflation fears could be found in the fact that the rate of inflation in the U.S. economy between March 2008 and March 2009 was –0.1 percent. That was the first year of negative inflation since 1955.

Fears about deflation were not without foundation. Japan experienced deflation for 15 years after its housing bubble burst in the early 1990s. Then, just when it looked like Japan would escape from that problem, the U.S. Federal Reserve cut interest rates to almost 0 percent to get the U.S. economy moving. Japan's central bank followed suit; it didn't want the yen to rise in value because that would depress Japan's exports. But in 2010, matters were further complicated when the Bank of Canada announced it was raising rates and signalling that future rate hikes may be significant in the near term (partially because of fears of a potential housing bubble).

It is difficult to predict whether inflation or deflation is more likely partly because both situations are influenced by self-fulfilling prophecies. For example, if people think inflation is going to be a problem, they are motivated to buy things now in order to avoid paying the higher prices that they assume are soon to come. But buying things now creates more demand, and that causes prices to rise. Conversely, if people think deflation is going to occur, they are motivated to delay purchases to the time when the price will be lower. But putting off purchases lowers demand, and that causes prices to fall.

There is yet another angle to consider in this debate. According to statistician Phil Green, our measurement tool (CPI) is inaccurate and inflation is actually much higher than typically reported in the past 20 years. The way CPI is measured has changed, and some believe that governments are fudging the numbers. Green claims that the inflation rate in the U.S. was actually closer to 10 percent in 2010 if measured using traditional methods. The U.S. is not alone in this. Governments have changed the CPI equation many times in major industrialized nations.

This is no secret. But informed individuals were questioning the very integrity of this key leading indicator.

Given all this complexity, we should not be surprised if economists have trouble accurately predicting whether inflation or deflation will be the next problem we face. Inflation definitely lurks in the background. If the crisis in confidence can be overcome, people will start spending again, and with all that money that governments dished out still in the system, demand could soar and inflation could become a big problem. On the other hand, if the recession is long and deep, deflation is a distinct possibility because there will be very little demand for goods and services, and that will cause prices to fall.

Questions for Discussion

1. Based on your own observations in the marketplace, do you believe we are in an inflationary or deflationary period?

2. Go to the Bank of Canada website and find the latest inflation figures. Based on the latest statistics, is inflation or deflation a bigger problem today?

3. What do you think of Phil Green's contention that the CPI has become a deceptive tool? Do you believe that governments are purposefully massaging the numbers? If so, explain why.

SCANLIFE

chapter

3

Conducting Business Ethically and Responsibly

After reading this chapter, you should be able to:

LO-1 Explain how individuals develop their personal *codes of ethics* and why ethics are important in the workplace.

LO-2 Distinguish *social responsibility* from *ethics*, identify *organizational stakeholders*, and characterize social consciousness today.

LO-3 Show how the concept of social responsibility applies both to environmental issues and to a firm's relationships with customers, employees, and investors.

LO-4 Identify four general *approaches to social responsibility* and describe the four steps a firm must take to implement *a social responsibility program*.

LO-5 Explain how issues of social responsibility and ethics affect small businesses.

SCANLIFE

What Really Happened at Livent?

Livent Inc., a live theatre company with outlets in Toronto, Vancouver, Chicago, and New York, was founded by Garth Drabinsky and Myron Gottlieb. In 1998, questions were raised about Livent's finances by new owners who had bought into the company. Shortly thereafter, Drabinsky and Gottlieb were fired. They were eventually charged with producing false financial statements to make the company look more profitable than it actually was. The fraud allegedly cost investors and creditors $500 million. Drabinsky and Gottlieb denied any wrongdoing and claimed that the financial manipulations were carried out by subordinates without their knowledge. After a long delay, their trial finally started in 2008.

How Will This Help Me?

There is a growing dilemma in the business world today: the economic imperatives (real or imagined) facing managers versus pressures to function as good citizens. By understanding the material in this chapter, you'll be better able to assess ethical and social responsibility issues that you will face as an *employee* and as a *boss* or *business owner*. It will also help you understand the ethical and social responsibility actions of businesses you deal with as a consumer and as an *investor*.

During the trial, prosecutors called several witnesses who admitted that they had participated in the financial manipulations. But they said that they had done so at the direction of Drabinsky and Gottlieb. Some of their charges were as follows:

- A computer technician said he was asked by the accounting controller to modify accounting software so that changes could be made without auditors detecting them. He said that the vice-president, Gordon Eckstein, told him to carry out the controller's instructions.

- Gordon Eckstein said that he was told by Drabinsky and Gottlieb to carry out the fraud (Eckstein had previously pled guilty).

- John Beer, a private investigator who was hired by consulting firm KPMG's forensic unit to look into allegations of accounting manipulations, said he found a document in Drabinsky's briefcase that described $21 million of expenses that were omitted from one year's financial statements and "rolled" to the next year.

- Gary Gill, another investigator for KPMG, also testified that he saw an internal company document that contained information about financial manipulations.

- Chris Craib, Livent's accounting controller, testified that he had prepared the document and had given it to Drabinsky and Gottlieb, and that he had attended a meeting where accounting manipulations were openly discussed.

- Another accounting employee said he was amazed to learn of a plan to reclassify $10 million of expenses as fixed assets.

- Chief financial officer Maria Messina (who had formerly worked at KPMG), said she didn't tell her former colleagues about the fraud because she wanted to try to cope with it in-house (she finally exposed the fraud after new investors had taken over managing the company).

Former controller Grant Malcolm testified that he spent all of his time recording fraudulent manipulations to the company's books. He said he routinely deleted expenses for shows, or moved them to future periods, or transferred them to different shows. He said he prepared a memo for Drabinsky that summarized all the improperly transferred production costs. He also said that two advertising agencies helped with the fraud by moving their billings from an earlier year to a later year. That allowed profit to be higher in the earlier year.

Drabinsky and Gottlieb's defence attorneys repeatedly attacked the credibility of the witnesses and argued that accounting staff had circumvented the accounting controls that Drabinsky had put in place. The defence presented no witnesses and Drabinsky and Gottlieb did not testify.

In 2009, Drabinsky and Gottlieb were found guilty of fraud and forgery. Drabinsky was sentenced to seven years in jail and Gottlieb to six years. In a related case, the Institute of Chartered Accountants of Ontario found three senior Deloitte & Touche LLP auditors guilty of making errors during an audit of Livent's financial statements. The three were fined $100 000 each.

Drabinsky and Gottlieb are not the only executives who have been convicted of wrongdoing in the recent past. In 2005, Bernie Ebbers, the CEO of WorldCom, was found guilty of nine charges of securities fraud and filing false documents. He was sentenced to 25 years in prison. In 2006, Ken Lay, the CEO of Enron, was convicted of conspiracy and securities fraud, but died before he was sentenced. In 2007, Conrad Black, CEO of Hollinger International, was convicted of fraud and obstruction of justice and was sentenced to six and a half years in prison. In December 2008, Bernie Madoff, a former stockbroker and investment adviser, pled guilty to swindling investors in a $50 billion fraud. He is likely to spend the rest of his life in prison.

Ethics in the Workplace

The situation described in the opening case clearly demonstrates the controversy that often arises when dealing with the issue of ethics in business. **Ethics** are beliefs about what is right and wrong or good and bad. An individual's personal values and morals—and the social context in which they occur—determine whether a particular behaviour is perceived as ethical or unethical. In other words, **ethical behaviour** is behaviour that conforms to individual beliefs and social norms about what is right and good. **Unethical behaviour** is behaviour that individual beliefs and social norms define as wrong and bad. **Business ethics** is a term often used to refer to ethical or unethical behaviours by a manager or employee of a business.

LO-1 Individual Ethics

Because ethics are based on both individual beliefs and social concepts, they vary from person to person, from situation to situation, and from culture to culture. Differences of opinion can therefore arise as to what is ethical or unethical. For example, many people who would never think of taking a candy bar from a grocery store routinely take home pens and pads of paper from their offices. Other people who view themselves as law-abiding citizens see nothing wrong with using radar detectors to avoid speeding tickets. In each of these situations, people will choose different sides of the issue and argue that

their actions are ethical. Most Canadians would probably agree that if you see someone drop a $20 bill in a store, it would be ethical to return it to the owner. But what if you find $20 and don't know who dropped it? Should you turn it in to the lost-and-found department? Or, since the rightful owner isn't likely to claim it, would it be ethical to just keep it? In these more ambiguous situations, each person may have a different standard of ethics. The boxed insert entitled "Ethics in the YouTube Age" describes another common ethical issue.

ETHICS Individual standards or moral values regarding what is right and wrong or good and bad.

ETHICAL BEHAVIOUR Behaviour that conforms to individual beliefs and social norms about what is right and good.

UNETHICAL BEHAVIOUR Behaviour that individual beliefs and social norms define as wrong and bad.

BUSINESS ETHICS Ethical or unethical behaviours by a manager or employee of an organization.

E-BUSINESS AND SOCIAL MEDIA SOLUTIONS

Ethics in the YouTube Age

Technology has changed our lives in positive ways, but it has also made questionable practices easier to commit. YouTube, for example, is a great source of entertainment. Many of you spend considerable time watching comedians, actors, and consumer-generated videos. YouTube makes an effort to remove unauthorized copyright material, and even warns users that their account may be closed if they ignore such laws. YouTube also offers an authorized music library that enables content providers to insert music selections without fear of legal action. However, there is plenty of material on YouTube that does not meet legal requirements.

Most people consider themselves to be ethical individuals. Students are often very critical of unethical corporations that act solely to satisfy their own needs. However, ethical issues cannot simply be looked at from a convenient lens. Do you consider yourself to be an ethical person? What would you tell a friend if you saw him or her shoplifting? What would you do if you caught a co-worker stealing from your company? You may have strong, clear opinions on those issues, but how many songs and movies have you illegally downloaded?

Gary Fung, the founder of the Vancouver-based internet torrent site isoHunt, believes that illegal downloading is a legitimate right. He turned this belief into a successful business with more than 100 million users who can download TV shows, films, etc. Fung has

clearly benefited from the work of others, without paying for the content, and yet he generates millions in advertising revenue for his website. Mr. Fung is now facing a US$150 million fine for copyright infringement and damages. His success caught the attention of the Motion Picture Association of America (MPAA), which has also pursued similar sites, for instance, TorrentSpy (US$111 million fine). isoHunt may ultimately share the fate of Napster.

A popular argument that is often used to justify illegal downloading activity is that there are many wealthy artists that earn millions of dollars. However, for every successful star there are thousands of struggling musicians, actors, and artists trying to earn a living. They are not overnight successes. Perhaps your favourite song would have never been written if that artist was not able to make a basic living (from royalties) until that one big hit. Sites like isoHunt are far more likely to have an impact on an aspiring artist than they are on someone like Lady Gaga or Will Smith. So where do you stand?

Critical Thinking Questions

1. Do you believe that multimillion dollar fines on isoHunt and TorrentSpy are fair?

2. Do you believe ethics are a black-and-white issue or do you subscribe to a grey zone?

The difference between unethical and illegal behaviour can also complicate matters. When CIBC World Markets sued six former employees after they left the company and started a new rival firm, Genuity Capital Markets, CIBC was making a claim of illegal behaviour. But the defendants argued that they had done nothing illegal, or unethical for that matter, because the employees they took with them had already decided to leave CIBC.[1] But in another case, damages were awarded to RBC Dominion Securities after one of its branch managers and his subordinates abruptly left as a group to work for a competitor.[2]

Because every situation has some degree of ambiguity, societies may adopt formal laws that reflect prevailing ethical standards or social norms. For example, because most people regard theft as unethical, we have laws against such behaviour. Unfortunately, applying these laws is sometimes difficult because real-world situations can often be interpreted in different ways,

and it isn't always easy to apply statutory standards to real-life behaviour. The epidemic of financial scandals in recent years shows how willing people can be to take advantage of potentially ambiguous situations.

In some cultures, ethically ambiguous practices are hallmarks of business activity. Brazilians, for example, apply the philosophy of *jeitinho*—meaning "to find a way"—by using personal connections, bending the rules, or making a "contribution."[3] Suppose you needed to get an official document. You might start out determined to take all the proper bureaucratic steps to get it. However, when you find yourself in a complex maze of rules and regulations and think you'll never get your document, you may resort to *jeitinho* to get the job done.

Individual Values and Codes We start to form ethical standards as children in response to our perceptions of the behaviour of parents and other adults. Soon, we enter school, where we're influenced by peers, and as we grow into adulthood other experiences shape our lives and contribute to our ethical beliefs and our behaviour. We also develop values and morals that contribute to ethical standards. If you put financial gain at the top of your priority list, you may develop a code of ethics that supports the pursuit of material comfort. But if you set family and friends as a priority, you'll probably adopt different standards.

Managerial Ethics

Managerial ethics are the standards of behaviour that guide individual managers in their work.[4] Although ethics can affect managerial work in any number of ways, it's helpful to classify behaviour in terms of three broad categories.

Behaviour Toward Employees This category covers such matters as hiring and firing, wages and working conditions, privacy, and respect. Ethical and legal guidelines emphasize that hiring and firing decisions should be based solely on the ability to perform a job. A manager who discriminates against any ethnic minority in hiring exhibits both unethical and illegal behaviour. But what about the manager who hires a friend or relative when someone else might be more qualified? Such decisions may not be illegal, but in Canada they may be objectionable on ethical grounds (but not necessarily in some other countries).

Wages and working conditions, though regulated by law, are also areas for ethical controversy. Consider a manager who pays an employee less than the employee deserves because the manager knows that the employee can't afford to quit or risk his job by complaining. While some people will see this behaviour as unethical, others will see it as simply smart business. Other cases are more clear-cut. For example, Enron managers

Ethical scandals involving business leaders have made international headlines in recent years. Events ranging from the fall of Enron to the investment scam headed by Bernard Madoff (shown here) have undermined public confidence in business and its leaders. Madoff, for example, cost hundreds of major investment clients their entire life savings.

encouraged employees to invest their retirement funds in company stock and then, when financial problems began to surface, refused to permit them to sell the stock (even though top officials of the company were allowed to sell their stock).

Behaviour Toward the Organization

Ethical issues also arise from employee behaviour toward their employer, especially in such areas as conflict of interest, confidentiality, and honesty. A **conflict of interest** occurs when an activity benefits an individual at the expense of the employer. Most companies, for example, have policies that forbid company buyers from accepting gifts from suppliers. Businesses in highly competitive industries—software and fashion apparel, for example—have safeguards against designers selling company secrets to competitors. Relatively common problems in the general area of honesty include such behaviour as stealing supplies, padding expense accounts, and using a business phone to make personal long-distance calls. Most employees are honest, but most organizations are nevertheless vigilant.

Behaviour Toward Other Economic Agents

Ethics also comes into play in the relationship between the firm and its customers, competitors, stockholders, suppliers, dealers, and unions. In dealing with such agents, there is room for ethical ambiguity in just about every activity—advertising, financial disclosure, ordering and purchasing, bargaining and negotiation, and other business relationships. For example, when pharmaceutical companies are criticized

for the high prices of their drugs, they say that high prices are needed to cover the costs of research and development programs to develop new drugs. To some observers, the solution to such problems is obvious: find the right balance between reasonable pricing and *price gouging* (responding to increased demand with overly steep price increases). But like so many questions involving ethics, there are significant differences of opinion about what the proper balance is.[5]

Another area of concern is competitive espionage. In 2004, Air Canada sued WestJet for $220 million, claiming that a WestJet executive had accessed Air Canada's confidential reservation database, which contained important competitive information that would be beneficial to WestJet.[6] WestJet eventually admitted its actions were unethical and paid Air Canada $5 million to cover expenses Air Canada incurred while investigating the unauthorized accessing of its website. WestJet also agreed to contribute $10 million to children's charities.

Most people would probably see the WestJet incident as a fairly clear case of unethical behaviour. But what if a manager is given confidential information by an unhappy former employee of a competitor who wants to get revenge on his former employer? Is it okay in that case for the manager to use the information? Some people would say it's still unethical, but others might feel that since the manager didn't go looking for the information, that it's okay to use it.[7]

The intense competition between Air Canada and WestJet motivated a WestJet executive to access Air Canada's confidential reservations database in the hope of gaining a competitive edge for WestJet.

Difficulties also arise because business practices vary globally. In many countries, bribes are a normal part of doing business. German companies, for example, were formerly allowed to write off bribes as "expenses," but in 2007—after corruption laws had been changed—several executives of Siemens AG were arrested and charged with bribing foreign officials in order to obtain business.[8] In Canada and the U.S., bribes are seen as unethical and illegal. In 2006, the Gemological Institute of America (GIA) fired several employees after discovering that they had accepted bribes from diamond dealers. In return for the bribes, the GIA employees rated the dealers' diamonds higher than they should have, and this allowed the dealers to sell the diamonds for a much higher price. The GIA also banned two groups of dealers from having their diamonds rated by the GIA.[9]

Assessing Ethical Behaviour

How can we determine whether a particular action or decision is ethical or unethical? A three-step model has been suggested as a way of systematically applying ethical judgments to situations that may arise during the course of business activities.

1. Gather the relevant factual information.
2. Determine the most appropriate moral values.
3. Make an ethical judgment based on the rightness or wrongness of the proposed activity or policy.

Let's see how this process might work for a common dilemma faced by managers: expense account claims. Companies routinely cover work-related expenses of employees when they are travelling on company business and/or entertaining clients for business purposes. Common examples of such expenses include hotel bills, meals, rental cars, and so forth. Employees are expected to claim only those expenses that are work-related. For example, if a manager takes a client to dinner while travelling on business and spends $100, submitting a receipt for that dinner and expecting to be reimbursed for $100 is clearly appropriate. Suppose, however, that the manager also has a $100 dinner the next night in that same city with a good friend for purely social purposes. Submitting that receipt for full reimbursement would be seen by most managers as unethical (but some might try to rationalize that it is acceptable because they are underpaid and this is a way to increase their pay).

We can assess this situation using four ethical norms:

Utility: Does a particular act optimize what is best for those who are affected by it?

Rights: Does it respect the rights of the individuals involved?

Justice: Is it consistent with what we regard to be fair?

Caring: Is it consistent with people's responsibilities to each other?

Now, let's return to the case of the expense account. The *utility* norm would acknowledge that the manager benefits from padding an expense account, but co-workers and owners do not. Likewise, inflating an expense account does not respect the *rights* of others. It is also *unfair* and compromises the manager's responsibilities to others. This particular act, then, appears to be clearly unethical. But now suppose that the manager happens to lose the receipt for the legitimate dinner but does not lose the receipt for the social dinner. Some people will argue that it is acceptable to submit the illegitimate receipt because the manager is only doing so to be reimbursed for what he or she is entitled to. Others, however, will argue that submitting the other receipt is wrong under any circumstances. Changes in the factual information about the case may make ethical issues more or less clear-cut.

Managing Ethics in Organizations

Organizations try to promote ethical behaviour and discourage unethical behaviour, but the unethical and illegal activities of both managers and employees in recent years have motivated many firms to take additional steps to encourage ethical behaviour. Many companies, for example, establish codes of conduct and develop clear ethical positions on how the firm and its employees will conduct their business.

The single most effective step a company can take is for top management to demonstrate ethical commitment by taking decisive action when problems arise. When food products made by Maple Leaf Foods were found to be contaminated with listeria, the company took quick action to manage the crisis (see Chapter 6 for more details).[10] A now-classic illustration of decisive action occurred back in 1982, when Johnson & Johnson discovered that capsules of the company's Tylenol pain reliever had been laced with cyanide. It quickly recalled all Tylenol bottles on retailers' shelves and went public with candid information throughout the crisis.

Two of the most common approaches for formalizing ethical commitment are *adopting written codes* and *instituting ethics programs*.

Adopting Written Codes Many companies, including Johnson & Johnson, McDonald's, Starbucks, and Dell, have adopted written codes of ethics that formally acknowledge their intent to do business in an ethical manner. Figure 3.1 shows the code of ethics adopted by Mountain Equipment Co-op.

Most codes of ethics are designed to perform one or more of four functions:

1. They increase public confidence in a firm or its industry.
2. They may help stem the tide of government regulation.
3. They improve internal operations by providing consistent standards of both ethical and legal conduct.

Our Purpose

To support people in achieving the benefit of wilderness-oriented recreation.

Our **purpose** is what we resolve to do.

Our Vision

Mountain Equipment Co-op is an innovative, thriving co-operative that inspires excellence in products and services, passion for wilderness experiences, leadership for a just world, and action for a healthy planet.

Our **vision** is our picture of the future and outlines where we want to go.

Our Mission

Mountain Equipment Co-op provides quality products and services self-propelled wilderness-oriented reation, such as hiking and mountaineering, at the lowest reasonable price in an informative, respectful manner. We are a member-owned co-operative striving for social and environmental leadership.

Our **mission** tells us what business we are in, who we serv e, and how. It represents the fundamental reason for MEC's existence.

Our Values

We conduct ourselves ethically and with integrity. We show respect for others in our words and actions. We act in the spirit of community and co-operation. We respect and protect our natural environment. We strive for personal growth, continual learning, and adventure.

Our **values** influence our conduct both collectively as an organization, and individually as employees, directors and members of our community. We strive to have our actions reflect these values, demonstrate personal accountability, and be publicly defensible.

Figure 3.1
Mountain Equipment Co-op's statements of purpose, vision, mission, and values make up its code of ethics.

4. They help managers respond to problems that arise as a result of unethical or illegal behaviour.

About two-thirds of Canada's largest corporations have codes of ethics (90 percent of large U.S. firms do). More and more regulatory and professional associations in Canada are recommending that corporations adopt codes of ethics. The Canada Deposit Insurance Corp., for example, requires that all deposit-taking institutions have a code of conduct that is periodically reviewed and ratified by the board of directors. The Canadian Competition Bureau, the Canadian Institute of Chartered Accountants, and the Ontario Human Rights Commission are all pushing for the adoption of codes of ethics by corporations.[11] Many Canadian and U.S. firms are also adding a position called "ethics director" or "ethics officer."

Figure 3.2 illustrates the essential role that corporate ethics and values should play in corporate policy. It shows that business strategies and practices can change frequently and business objectives may change occasionally, but an organization's core principles and values should remain the same. For example, Google's core principle is "Don't Be Evil." Google adapts its strategies and practices to meet the challenges posed by the rapidly changing technology industry, but Google must do so in a way that does not violate its core principle.

Instituting Ethics Programs Can business ethics be "taught," either in the workplace or in schools? While business schools have become important players in the debate about ethics education, most analysts agree that companies must take the chief responsibility for educating employees. In fact, more and more firms are doing so. Imperial Oil, for example, conducts workshops for employees that emphasize ethical concerns. The purpose of these workshops is to help employees put Imperial's ethics statement into practice.

But many firms struggle with ethical dilemmas, particularly those that do business globally. Nike, for example, manufactures most of its products overseas in order to boost profitability. A few years ago, a scathing report investigating Nike's manufacturing partners in Asia called it just short

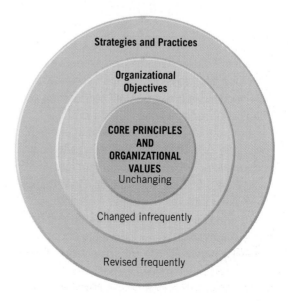

Figure 3.2
Core principles and organizational values.

of slave labour. Nike responded to the report by acknowledging its mistakes and made a commitment to improve working conditions. Nike plants in Asia, for example, no longer force employees to work on Sundays. Wages have been increased, and supervisors are forbidden to use the extreme punishments that were formerly used.[12]

Sometimes situations are so complex that it is difficult for companies to determine what is ethical. In the 1970s, Nestlé and other makers of infant formula were trying to market their products in developing countries. Problems developed because the formula sometimes was not used properly by mothers, and their babies suffered. Activists organized a boycott of Nestlé, and the United Nations began aggressively promoting breast feeding. But then the AIDS crisis developed, and it was discovered that some nursing mothers who had AIDS were transmitting the virus to their infants through their milk. Infant formula was then suggested as a possible way to avoid this problem. But suspicion of infant formula makers like Nestlé remains strong, even though they offered to donate infant formula for free.[13]

Starbucks helps local farmers gain access to credit, works to develop and maintain sustainability of the coffee crop, and is building farmer support centres in Costa Rica, Ethiopia, and Rwanda to provide local farmers with agricultural and technical education and support.

LO-2 Social Responsibility

Corporate social responsibility (CSR) refers to the way in which a business tries to balance its commitments to **organizational stakeholders**—those groups, individuals, and organizations that are directly affected by the practices of an organization and that therefore have a stake in its performance.[14] Galen Weston, the executive chairman of Loblaw Cos. Ltd., says that companies that want to be successful need to embrace CSR as part of their core strategy. It can no longer simply be an "add-on."[15]

There is a debate about which of these stakeholders should be given the most attention. One view, often called *managerial capitalism*, is held by Nobel laureate Milton Friedman, who says that a company's only social responsibility is to make as much money as possible for its shareholders, as long as it doesn't break any laws in doing so. Friedman also says that a free society is undermined when company managers accept any social responsibility other than making as much money as possible.[16]

An opposing view is that companies must be responsible to various stakeholders, including *customers, employees, investors, suppliers,* and the *local communities* in which they do business. Some of these stakeholders may be particularly important to the organization, so it will pay particular attention to their needs and expectations. Whatever the relative emphasis on the various stakeholders, this view says that businesses should not just pursue profit to the exclusion of all else.

Contemporary Social Consciousness

Views about social responsibility have changed dramatically over time, generally in the direction of higher social responsibility expectations of business. The late nineteenth century was characterized by the entrepreneurial spirit and the laissez-faire philosophy. During that era of labour strife and predatory business practices, both individual citizens and the government became concerned about uncontrolled business activity. This concern was translated into laws regulating basic business practices.

During the Great Depression of the 1930s, many people blamed the failure of businesses and banks and the widespread loss of jobs on a general climate of business greed and lack of restraint. Out of the economic turmoil emerged new laws that described an increased expectation that business should protect and enhance the general welfare of society.

During the social unrest of the 1960s and 1970s, business was often characterized as a negative social force. Eventually, increased activism prompted additional government regulation in a variety of areas. Health warnings, for example, were placed on cigarette packages, and stricter environmental protection laws were enacted.

Social consciousness and views toward social responsibility continue to evolve in the twenty-first century. The financial excesses that caused the recession of

2008–2009 resulted in new laws governing business conduct. As well, an increased awareness of the global economy and heightened campaigning on the part of environmentalists and other activists have combined to make many businesses more sensitive to various social responsibilities, not simply the pursuit of profit. For example, retailers such as Sears have policies against selling handguns and other weapons, and toy retailer Toys "R" Us refuses to sell toy guns that look too realistic. Electrolux, a Swedish appliance maker, has developed a line of water-efficient washing machines and a solar-powered lawnmower. The boxed insert entitled "This Is One Green (and Socially Responsible) Company!" describes the efforts that have been made by Mountain Equipment Co-op to protect the environment and the workers who make the products it sells.

LO-3 Areas of Social Responsibility

When defining their sense of social responsibility, most firms consider four areas: the environment, customers, employees, and investors.

Responsibility Toward the Environment

Controlling **pollution**—the release of harmful substances into the environment—is a significant challenge for contemporary business. Although noise pollution is attracting increased concern, air pollution, water pollution, and

---

THE GREENING OF BUSINESS

This Is One Green (and Socially Responsible) Company!

Mountain Equipment Co-op (MEC) was started in 1971 by four students from the University of British Columbia who were committed to protecting the environment. Unlike most corporations, MEC does not try to maximize the wealth of its members; rather, it seeks a balance between financial and social/environmental goals. MEC directs 1 percent of its sales to charity and to running energy-efficient stores. Jantzi Research Inc. rates MEC as the top company in Canada's retail sector for sustainability practices.

Some of MEC's revenue each year is allocated to sustainable community development projects, typically through donations for charitable or educational purposes. MEC's own registered charity—The MEC Endowment Fund for the Environment—was created in 1993. Each year, 0.4 percent of the previous year's sales are donated to the MEC fund. That translates into an average of $750 000 per year in contributions to environmental conservation and wilderness protection projects, research, and education.

Practising social and environmental responsibility means more than simply giving money to environmental causes and organizations. It also means being conscious of other aspects of social responsibility. For example, MEC audits its suppliers to make sure that they have programs in place to ensure that waste is disposed of in an environmentally responsible manner, do not use child labour, do not harass their workers or discriminate against them, provide workers with a healthy and safe work environment, and pay their workers fairly.

In its retail outlets, MEC practises what it preaches. The design of its buildings, and the material and construction methods used, are consistent with care for the environment. Energy efficiency, pollution control, and recycling potential are all important considerations in MEC buildings. Innovations found in MEC's green buildings include the use of geothermal energy heat pumps in Montreal, a demonstration straw-bale wall in Ottawa, and composting toilets in Winnipeg. When it was built, MEC's Winnipeg store was only the second retail building in Canada that met the national C2000 Green Building Standard (the first one was MEC's Ottawa store). (For information on other green buildings in Canada, see The Greening of Business box in Chapter 7.)

Critical Thinking Questions

1. Which of the two major views about business—"managerial capitalism" or the "variety of stakeholders" idea—would most likely be held by MEC's shareholders? Why?

2. What are the arguments for and against "managerial capitalism" and the "variety of stakeholders" idea?

3. Consider the following statement: *"Businesses should not give money to charity because (a) business executives do not have any training that would help them decide which charities to give money to, (b) businesses are biased in their decisions about which charities to give money to, and (c) business managers don't have any right to give away shareholders' money."* Do you agree or disagree with the statement? Explain your reasoning.

land pollution are the subjects of most anti-pollution efforts by business and governments.[17]

Air Pollution **Air pollution** results when a combination of factors lowers air quality. Large amounts of chemicals such as the carbon monoxide emitted by automobiles contribute to air pollution. So does smoke and other chemicals emitted by manufacturing plants. The rapid industrialization of developing countries has led to increased concerns about air pollution. In China, for example, 100 coal-fired power plants are being built each year, and each plant uses 1.4 million tons of coal and throws off 3.7 million tons of carbon dioxide. Only 5 percent of the coal-fired power plants in China are equipped with pollution-control equipment.[18] Many industrial companies were forcibly shut down by the Chinese government in advance of the 2008 Olympics in an attempt to improve air quality.

The Kyoto Summit in 1997 was an early attempt by various governments to reach an agreement on ways to reduce the threat of pollution. Australia is the world's largest greenhouse gas emitter per capita, contributing 7.3 percent of the world's total. The United States (at 6.5 percent) and Canada (at 6.4 percent) are close behind. Canada is the only one of the three leading emitters that signed the 1997 Protocol, but in 2006 the Conservative government said Canada would not be able to meet its targets for reducing pollution, and that it would continue with the Protocol only if the targets were renegotiated.[19] The meetings in Copenhagen in 2009 on this issue ended without an agreement.

The U.S.-based environmental group Nature Conservancy has recently teamed up with Indonesian logging company Sumalindo Lestari Jaya to help local villagers log a forest in a remote area of Indonesia. Why? The group believes that by working together with the company, it can better enforce sustainable practices.

The United Nations is promoting a "cap and trade" system, in which companies in industrialized countries can buy carbon credits, which essentially give them the right to pollute the atmosphere with carbon dioxide. The money collected is then used to help fund clean-air projects in developing countries that would not otherwise be affordable.[20] But critics of the plan say that the scheme is an open invitation to fraudsters. Suppose, for example, that an Indonesian forest operator sells a carbon permit to a German manufacturing firm that is releasing too much CO_2 into the atmosphere. That one transaction is fine, but what if the Indonesian firm sells the same carbon permit to manufacturers in other countries? That will make it appear like a lot more carbon dioxide has been reduced than is actually the case. Multibillion-dollar fraud has already occurred in the European Union's carbon trading market, and Europol's Criminal Finances and Technology section estimates that up to 90 percent of all carbon market volume in certain EU nations is fraudulent.[21]

Figure 3.3 shows world atmospheric carbon dioxide levels for the period between 1750 and 2000, and it offers three possible scenarios for future levels under different sets of conditions. The three projections—lowest, middle, highest—were developed by the Intergovernmental Panel on Climate Change, which calculated likely changes in the atmosphere during this century if no efforts were made to reduce *greenhouse emissions*—waste industrial gases that trap heat in the atmosphere. The criteria for estimating changes are population, economic growth, energy supplies, and technologies. The less pressure exerted by these conditions, the less the increase in CO_2 levels. Energy supplies are measured in *exajoules*—roughly the annual energy consumption of a large metropolitan area like New York or London.

Under the lowest, or best-case, scenario, by 2100 the population would only grow to 6.4 billion people, economic growth would be no more than 1.2 to 2.0 percent a year, and energy supplies would require only 8000 exajoules of conventional oil. However, under the highest, or worst-case, scenario, the population would increase to 11.3 billion people, annual economic growth would be between 3.0 and 3.5 percent, and energy supplies would require as much as 18 400 exajoules of conventional oil.

There is currently some debate about whether **global warming**—an increase in the earth's average temperature—is occurring because of increased air pollution. Most everyone agrees that global warming is a fact, but some experts argue that it is simply part of the earth's natural cycle. There *is* general agreement that global warming will benefit some people and hurt others. In normally icy Greenland, for example, the warming climate has resulted in a longer growing season for grain and vegetables, and farmers are planning to start raising cattle because of the increased forage available in the summertime. In

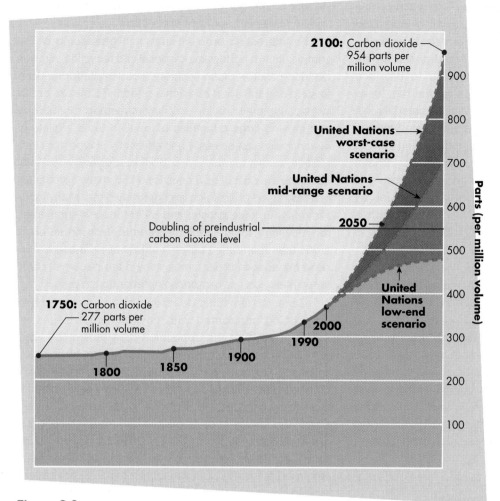

Figure 3.3
CO_2 emissions, past and future.

the Peruvian Andes, farmers did not traditionally cultivate crops above the 14 000-foot level because of the cold, but they are now planting large potato fields above 15 000 feet. But the same process that is warming Greenland and the high Andes is melting the earth's glaciers, and the water released may eventually raise sea levels to the point that many coastal cities around the world would be flooded. Even in Greenland there is a downside to global warming: the traditional lifestyle of Inuit hunters is being disrupted by the thinning ice.[22]

In difficult economic times, like those that developed in 2008–2009, the general public is less willing to make personal sacrifices in order to battle climate change. A poll of 12 000 people in 11 countries showed that less than half of the respondents were willing to make lifestyle changes to reduce carbon emissions, and only 20 percent said they would be willing to spend extra money to fight climate change.[23]

Some people think that wind power would be a good way to generate electricity while reducing air pollution. Canada is becoming a world leader in this form of power, and approximately $18 billion will be invested in wind power by 2015.[24] It is possible that 5 percent of Canada's energy needs will be supplied by wind power by 2015. However, experts note that while wind power is less polluting than coal- or gas-fired electricity generation, it is more expensive and less reliable.

Water Pollution For many years, businesses and municipalities simply dumped their waste into rivers, streams, and lakes with little regard for the effects. Thanks to new legislation and increased awareness on the part of businesses, water quality is improving in many areas. Millar Western Pulp Ltd. built Canada's first zero-discharge pulp mill at Meadow Lake, Saskatchewan. There is no discharge pipe to the river, no dioxin-forming chlorine, and next to no residue. Dow Chemical built a plant at Fort Saskatchewan that will not dump any pollutants into the nearby river.[25] But water pollution is still a problem in many areas, and occasionally a catastrophic accident occurs that pollutes large volumes of water. The BP oil spill in the Gulf of Mexico in 2010 was one such example.

Land Pollution **Toxic wastes** are dangerous chemical and/or radioactive by-products of various manufacturing processes that are harmful to humans and animals. In 2010, oil sands giant Syncrude was found guilty of causing the death of 1600 ducks that landed in a tailing pond they had mistaken for a small lake. The company faced fines of up to $800 000 under the federal Migratory Birds Act and the Alberta Environmental Protection and Enhancement Act.[26]

Changes in forestry practices, limits on certain types of mining, and new forms of solid waste disposal are all attempts to address the issue of toxic waste. A whole new industry—**recycling**—has developed as part of increased consciousness about land pollution. Plant and animal waste can be recycled to produce energy; this is referred to as **biomass**. Waste materials like sawdust, manure, and sludge are increasingly being turned into useful products. Ensyn Corp., for example, converts sawdust into liquid fuel by blasting wood waste with a sand-like substance that is heated. What's left is bio-oil.[27]

Canadian businesses are now routinely reducing various forms of pollution. However, the road to environmental purity is not easy. Under the Canadian and Ontario Environmental Protection Acts, pollution liability for a business firm can run as high as $2 million per day. To avoid such fines, companies must prove that they showed diligence in avoiding an environmental disaster such as an oil or gasoline spill.[28] The Environmental Choice program, sponsored by the federal government, licenses products that meet environmental standards set by the Canadian Standards Association. Firms whose products meet these standards can put the logo—three doves intertwined to form a maple leaf—on their products.[29]

An interesting problem that highlights some of the complexities in both waste disposal and recycling involves wooden pallets—those splintery wooden platforms used to store and transport consumer goods. Pallets are popular because they provide an efficient method for stacking and moving large quantities of smaller items. Pallets of merchandise can be easily and efficiently moved from factories to trucks to retail stores. Pallets are very recyclable, but since the cost of new ones is so low, many companies just toss used ones aside and get new ones. Many landfills refuse to take pallets, and others assess surcharges for recycling them. Ironically, some environmentalists argue that abandoned pallets actually serve a useful purpose because in urban areas, they often become refuge for animals such as raccoons and abandoned pets.[30]

Canadian firms that do business abroad are increasingly being confronted with environmental issues. In many cases, there is opposition to a project by local residents because they fear that some sort of pollution will result. For example, Calgary-based TVI Pacific Inc.'s planned open-pit mine and cyanide processing plant in the Philippines led to violent clashes between the company and the Subanon people. In Peru, indigenous groups threatened violence if Talisman Energy continued drilling for oil on their land.[31] At the annual meetings of Barrick Gold and Goldcorp Inc., protestors from several foreign countries alleged that the companies had acted in a socially irresponsible way. The mining companies responded that they had a major commitment to social responsibility, and they have recently aired videos showing how they helped Chilean earthquake victims, and how they are rehabilitating land at former mine sites.[32]

Multinational firms have also been publicly criticized. For example, Nestlé has received negative publicity on YouTube, Facebook, and Twitter claiming that the company is contributing to destruction of Indonesia's rainforest because it purchases palm oil from an Indonesian company that has cleared the rainforest to make way for a palm oil plantation.[33]

Responsibility Toward Customers

There are three key areas that are currently in the news regarding the social responsibility of business toward customers: *consumer rights, unfair pricing*, and *ethics in advertising*.

Consumer Rights **Consumerism** is a movement dedicated to protecting the rights of consumers in their dealings with businesses. Consumers have the following rights:

1. *The right to safe products.* The right to safe products is not always honoured. In 2008, 20 people died after eating meat made by Maple Leaf Foods that was

Of all roadway accidents, 25 percent are distraction-related, and the biggest distractions for motorists are handheld gadgets like cellphones and pagers. In fulfilling their responsibility to consumers, some companies are conducting tests that yield important data about roadway accidents. Ford Motor Co., for example, has a Virtual Test Track Experiment simulator that determines how often drivers get distracted. Under normal circumstances, an adult driver will miss about 3 percent of the simulated "events" (like an ice patch or a deer on the road) that Ford contrives for a virtual road trip. If they're on a cellphone, they'll miss about 14 percent. Teenagers miss a scary 54 percent of the events.

contaminated with listeria. Sales dropped by nearly 50 percent once this became public.[34] The government of China has become concerned that negative publicity about faulty toys and contaminated pet food and tooth-paste has damaged the "Made in China" label. In a surprising development, Mattel Inc. apologized to China for claiming that a recall of 18 million playsets with dangerous magnets was necessitated by poor quality control at one of its Chinese suppliers. Mattel eventually admitted that its own product design was flawed.[35]

2 *The right to be informed about all relevant aspects of a product.* Food products must list their ingredients, clothing must be labelled with information about its proper care, and banks must tell you exactly how much interest you are paying on a loan.

3 *The right to be heard.* Procter & Gamble puts a toll-free number on many of its products that consumers can call if they have questions or complaints. Many other retailers offer money-back guarantees if consumers are not happy with their purchase.

4 *The right to choose what they buy.* Central to this right is free and open competition among companies. In times past, companies divided up a market so that firms did not have to truly compete against each other. Such practices are illegal today and any attempts by business to block competition can result in fines or other penalties.

5 *The right to be educated about purchases.* All prescription drugs now come with detailed information regarding dosage, possible side effects, and potential interactions with other medications.

6 *The right to courteous service.* This right is hard to legislate, but as consumers become increasingly knowledgeable, they're more willing to complain about bad service. Consumer hotlines can also be used to voice service-related issues.

Unfair Pricing Interfering with competition can also mean illegal pricing practices. **Collusion** among companies—including getting together to "fix" prices—is against the law. Arctic Glacier Inc. of Winnipeg was one of several companies served with subpoenas by the U.S. government as it investigated collusion in the U.S. market for packaged ice. One of Arctic's employees, who claimed he was fired for refusing to take part in a conspiracy to divide up markets, went to the U.S. government and helped it in its investigation. The investigation is still under way.[36] The Canadian Competition Bureau also launched an investigation after hearing allegations from a confidential informant that Mars, Hershey, Nestlé, and Cadbury had teamed up in a candy price-fixing scheme.[37] A law firm in Toronto is organizing a class-action lawsuit against the major chocolate companies, alleging a conspiracy to fix prices.[38] Also

in 2008, Ultramar, Les Petroles Therrien Inc., and Petro-T pleaded guilty to price fixing in the retail gasoline market. Ultramar was fined $1.85 million, and the other two companies were both fined $179 000. Those who were convicted were allowed to serve their jail sentences in their communities.[39]

In 2010, new laws came into effect that are designed to make it easier for the Competition Bureau to convict price-fixers (since 1980, only three price-fixing convictions were secured in the 23 cases that came before the Competition Bureau). The maximum prison sentence for price fixing has been tripled to 14 years, and the maximum fine increased from $10 million to $25 million. But unless judges are willing to actually sentence convicted felons to serve real jail time, these changes may not have much effect.[40]

Sometimes firms come under attack for *price gouging*—responding to increased demand with steep price increases. For example, when DaimlerChrysler launched its PT Cruiser, demand for the vehicles was so strong that some dealers sold them only to customers willing to pay thousands of dollars over sticker prices. Some Ford dealers adopted a similar practice when the new Thunderbird was launched. As we saw in Chapter 1, this illustrates what can happen when there is a shortage of a product.

Ethics in Advertising There are several ethical issues in advertising, including truth-in-advertising claims, the advertising of counterfeit brands, the use of stealth advertising, and advertising that is morally objectionable.

Truth-in-Advertising Truth in advertising has long been regulated in Canada, but an increased emphasis on this issue is now becoming more noticeable on the international scene. For example, Chinese government officials investigated Procter & Gamble's claim that its Pantene shampoo made hair "10 times stronger." This came shortly after Procter & Gamble was ordered to pay a $24 000 fine after one consumer complained that SK-II skin cream was not the "miracle water" it claimed to be and that it did not make her skin "look 12 years younger in 28 days."[41] Advertising Standards Canada found that misleading advertisements in 2008 increased 31 percent over 2007.[42]

Advertising of Counterfeit Brands Another ethical issue involves the advertising and sale of counterfeit brand names. Canadians tourists who visit New York often go to booths on Canal Street, which is famous for the "bargains" that can be had on supposedly name-brand items from Cartier, Panerai, Vacheron, Mont Blanc, and Louis Vuitton. A fake Cartier Roadster watch, for example, can be bought on Canal Street for US$45, while a real one costs about US$3400. Many of the items being sold are

COLLUSION An illegal agreement among companies in an industry to "fix" prices for their products.

STEALTH
(UNDERCOVER)
ADVERTISING

Companies paying individuals to extol the virtues of their products without disclosing that they are paid to do so.

counterfeit, although it can be very hard to tell the difference between these knockoffs and the genuine article. For example, knockoffs of Suzuki motorcycles hit the market just a few weeks after the genuine product became available. These knock-offs were sold to customers as the real thing, but they had not been subjected to rigorous quality control like real Suzuki motorcycles are. Naturally, legitimate manufacturers of these high-end products are trying to stamp out this counterfeit trade in their products.[43] The boxed insert entitled "Counterfeit Products" provides more information about this issue.

Stealth (Undercover) Advertising A variation of viral marketing that we discussed in Chapter 2, **stealth advertising** involves companies paying individuals to extol the virtues of their products to other individuals who are not aware that they are listening to a paid spokesperson for the company. For example, Student Workforce hires individuals who are 18 to 30 years old to market products to other people in the same age bracket. One of the people hired is Leanne Plummer, a student at Humber College. She says that stealth advertising is more about sharing information than it is about sales.[44] One advertising agency hired models to pose as tourists. These models asked real tourists to take their picture with a new Sony Ericsson camera cellphone. The models then talked up the advantages of the new product to the unsuspecting

MANAGING IN TURBULENT TIMES

Counterfeit Products: Who's Accountable?

Counterfeit goods are a problem in many product lines, including perfume, luggage, handbags, pharmaceuticals, designer clothing, shoes, cigarettes, watches, sports memorabilia, and fine wines, to name just a few. One counterfeit group in New York imported watch components that cost it about 27 cents each and then sold them to wholesalers for $12 to $20. The wholesalers then sold them to street vendors for $20 to $30, and the street vendors sold them as Cartier watches for as much as $250. That was still well below the price of a real Cartier watch (about $1800). Wine makers are also concerned about the counterfeiting of their products because some of the top names in wine (e.g., Chateau Mouton Rothschild and Penfolds Grange) cost as much as $3000 a bottle, and this is an incentive to counterfeiters to make a lot of easy money. Wineries are fighting counterfeiting by embedding microchips in the label that can be read with an optical scanner, and by laser-etching the wine's name and vintage year into the bottle.

An FBI investigation in the U.S. revealed that up to 75 percent of sports memorabilia was fake, and the International Chamber of Commerce estimates that the counterfeit goods trade may be worth as much as $500 billion annually. The trade in counterfeit goods is harmful to *companies* (which have spent a lot of time and money developing brand-name goods), to *governments* (which are denied tax revenues because most counterfeiters do not pay taxes), and *consumers* (who pay for low-quality, and possibly unsafe, goods).

Some governments are now beginning to prosecute anyone who facilitates the sale of counterfeit products. This includes landlords who own the buildings where counterfeit goods are being sold, shipping companies, credit card companies, and others in the supply chain. There is also a move in some countries to hold the consumers who buy counterfeit goods accountable. In France and Italy, for example, it is now a crime to buy counterfeit goods.

Producers of name brands are also becoming more aggressive in trying to stop counterfeiting. Tiffany & Co., the high-end jeweller, filed a lawsuit against eBay, charging that it had ignored the sale of fake Tiffany jewellery on eBay's website. But in 2008, a U.S. federal judge ruled that Tiffany, not eBay, had the responsibility for protecting the Tiffany brand name. A court in Belgium also ruled in favour of eBay after it had been sued by L'Oréal, the cosmetics company.

Critical Thinking Questions

1. Do you think the benefits of counterfeit products exceed the costs, or vice-versa? Defend your answer.

2. Consider the following statement: *"eBay should not be responsible for monitoring the authenticity of products that are sold through its online business. The responsibility for that lies with the companies that are worried that someone is selling a counterfeit version of their product."* Do you agree or disagree with this statement? Defend your answer.

real tourists. The ethics of this are questionable when the paid individuals do not reveal that they are being paid by a company, so the recipient of the advertising is not aware that it is advertising. Commercial Alert, a U.S.-based consumer protection group, wants a government investigation of these undercover marketing tactics.[45]

Morally Objectionable Advertising A final ethical issue concerns advertising that consumers consider morally objectionable. Benetton, for example, aired a series of commercials featuring inmates on death row. The ads, dubbed "We, on Death Row," prompted such an outcry that Sears dropped the Benetton USA clothing line.[46] Other ads receiving criticism include Victoria's Secret models in skimpy underwear, and campaigns by tobacco and alcohol companies that allegedly target young people.

Responsibility Toward Employees

In Chapter 8, we will describe the human-resource management activities essential to a smoothly functioning business. These same activities—recruiting, hiring, training, promoting, and compensating—are also the basis for socially responsible behaviour toward employees.

The safety of workers is an important consideration for all organizations. The required use of hardhats is just one example of precautions that companies can take to protect workers while they are on the job.

A company that provides its employees with equal opportunities for rewards and advancement without regard to race, sex, or other irrelevant factors is meeting its social responsibilities. Firms that accept this responsibility make sure that the workplace is safe, both physically and emotionally. They would no more tolerate an abusive manager or one who sexually harasses employees than they would a gas leak.

Some progressive companies go well beyond these legal requirements, hiring and training the so-called hardcore unemployed (people with little education and training and a history of unemployment) and those who have disabilities. The Bank of Montreal, for example, sponsors a community college skills upgrading course for individuals with hearing impairments. The Royal Bank provides managers with discrimination awareness training. Rogers Communications provides individuals with mobility restrictions with telephone and customer-service job opportunities.[47]

Businesses also have a responsibility to respect the privacy of their employees. While nearly everyone agrees that companies have the right to exercise some level of control over their employees, there is great controversy about exactly how much is acceptable in areas like drug testing and computer monitoring. When the Canadian National Railway instituted drug testing for train, brake, and yard employees, 12 percent failed. Trucking companies have found that nearly one-third of truckers who had an accident were on drugs.[48]

Whistleblowers Respecting employees as people also means respecting their behaviour as ethically responsible individuals. Employees who discover that their company has been engaging in practices that are illegal, unethical, and/or socially irresponsible should be able to report the problem to higher-level management and be confident that managers will stop the questionable practices. If no one in the organization will take action, the employee might decide to inform a regulatory agency or perhaps the media.

At this point, the person becomes a **whistleblower**—an employee who discovers and tries to put an end to a company's unethical, illegal, and/or socially irresponsible actions by publicizing them. For example, John Kopchinski, a sales representative at pharmaceutical giant Pfizer, blew the whistle on the company after he learned that Pfizer was promoting certain drugs for unapproved uses. He received $5.1 million from the U.S. government for his whistleblowing efforts.[49] In Canada, Melvin Crothers discovered that a fellow WestJet employee was accessing a restricted Air Canada website in order to obtain data about Air Canada's "load factor"

CHEQUE KITING
The illegal practice of writing cheques against money that has not yet arrived at the bank on which the cheque has been written, relying on that money arriving before the cheque clears.

INSIDER TRADING
The use of confidential information to gain from the purchase or sale of stock.

(the proportion of seats filled) on certain flights. He had a conversation with a former WestJet president who was heading up an Air Canada discount airline, and that led to Air Canada filing a lawsuit against WestJet. Crothers resigned from WestJet four days later.[50]

The Investment Industry Regulatory Organization of Canada (IIROC) opened a whistleblower hotline as a result of recent securities fraud such as Ponzi schemes in both Canada and the U.S. Calls regarding market fraud are forwarded to four of the top people at the IIROC so that swift action can be taken.[51]

Responsibility Toward Investors

It may sound odd to say that a firm can be irresponsible toward investors, since investors are the owners of the company. But if the managers of a firm abuse its financial resources, the ultimate losers are the owners, since they do not receive the earnings, dividends, or capital appreciation due them. Managers can act irresponsibly in several ways.

Improper Financial Management Occasionally, organizations are guilty of financial mismanagement. For example, managers at American International Group became involved in very-high-risk insurance that caused the company to be on the hook for billions of dollars. The U.S. government ended up giving hundreds of billions of dollars to the company to keep it afloat.

Financial mismanagement can also take many other forms, including executives paying themselves outlandish salaries and bonuses, or spending huge amounts of company money for their own personal comfort. In these cases, creditors don't have much leverage and shareholders have few viable options. Trying to force a management changeover is not only difficult, it can also drive down the price of the company's stock, and this is a penalty shareholders are usually unwilling to assign themselves.

Cheque Kiting **Cheque kiting** involves writing a cheque from one account, depositing it in a second account, and then immediately spending money from the second account while the money from the first account is still in transit. A cheque from the second account can also be used to replenish the money in the first account, and the process starts all over again. This practice obviously benefits the person doing the cheque kiting, but it is irresponsible because it involves using other peoples'

money without paying for it. There has been a decline in the reporting of cheque kiting as a problem in recent years.

Insider Trading **Insider trading** occurs when someone uses confidential information to gain from the purchase or sale of stock. The most famous case is that of Martha Stewart, but there are many others as well. Barry Landen of Agnico-Eagle Mines was found guilty of insider trading when he sold shares he owned before it became publicly known that the company was going to report poor results. He was sentenced to 45 days in jail and fined $200 000.[52] In 2009, Stan Grmovsek and Gil Cornblum admitted that they carried on a 14-year insider-trading scheme. Cornblum fed confidential information on upcoming takeover bids to Grmovsek, who then purchased stock in those companies and sold it for a profit when the price went up. Cornblum committed suicide and Grmovsek received a jail sentence.[53]

Misrepresentation of Finances Certain behaviours regarding financial representation are also illegal. In maintaining and reporting its financial status, every corporation must conform to generally accepted accounting principles (see Chapter 11). Sometimes, however, unethical managers project profits far in excess of what they actually expect to earn. As we saw in the opening case, managers at Livent hid losses and/or expenses to boost paper profits. A few years earlier, the same sort of thing happened at Enron, where CFO Andrew Fastow had set up a complex network of partnerships that were often used to hide losses. This allowed Enron to report all the earnings from a partnership as its own while transferring all or most of the costs and losses to the partnership.[54]

Implementing Social Responsibility Programs

Thus far, we have discussed corporate social responsibility (CSR) as if consensus existed on how firms should behave in most situations. In fact, differences of opinion exist as to the appropriateness of CSR as a business goal. Some people oppose any business activity that cuts into profits to investors, while others argue that CSR must take precedence over profits.

Even people who share a common attitude toward CSR by business may have different reasons for their beliefs, and this influences their view about how social responsibility should be implemented. Some people fear that if businesses become too active in social concerns, they will gain too much control over how those concerns are addressed. They point to the influence many businesses have been able to exert on the government agencies that are supposed to regulate their industries. Other critics of business-sponsored social programs argue that companies lack the expertise needed. They believe that technical experts, not businesses, should decide how best to clean up a polluted river, for example.

Supporters of CSR believe that corporations are citizens just like individuals and therefore should help improve our lives. Others point to the vast resources controlled by businesses and note that since businesses often create many of the problems social programs are designed to alleviate, they should use their resources to help. Still others argue that CSR is wise because it pays off for the firm in terms of good public relations.

The late Max Clarkson, formerly a top-level business executive and director of the Centre for Corporate Social Performance and Ethics at the University of Toronto, argued that business firms that have a strong consciousness about ethics and CSR outperform firms that don't. After designing and applying a CSR rating system for companies, he found that companies that had the highest marks on questions of ethics and CSR also had the highest financial performance.[55]

LO-4 Approaches to Social Responsibility

Given these differences of opinion, it is little wonder that corporations have adopted a variety of approaches to social responsibility. As Figure 3.4 illustrates, the four stances that an organization can take concerning its obligations to society fall along a continuum ranging from the lowest to the highest degree of socially responsible practices.

Obstructionist Stance Businesses that take an **obstructionist stance** to social responsibility do as little as possible to solve social or environmental problems. When they cross the ethical or legal line that separates acceptable from unacceptable practices, their typical response is to deny or cover up their actions. Firms that adopt this position have little regard for ethical conduct and will generally go to great lengths to hide wrongdoing.

Defensive Stance An organization adopting a **defensive stance** will do everything that is required of it legally, but nothing more. Such a firm, for example, would install pollution-control equipment dictated by law, but would not install higher-quality equipment even though it might further limit pollution. Managers who take a defensive stance insist that their job is to generate profits. Tobacco companies generally take this position in their marketing efforts. In Canada and the United States, they are legally required to include warnings to smokers on their products and to limit advertising to prescribed media. Domestically, they follow these rules to the letter of the law but use more aggressive marketing methods in countries that have no such rules.

Accommodative Stance A firm that adopts an **accommodative stance** meets its legal and ethical requirements, but will also go further in certain cases. Such firms may agree to participate in social programs, but solicitors must convince them that these programs are worthy of funding. Many organizations respond to requests for donations to community hockey teams, Girl Guides, youth soccer programs, and so forth. The point, however, is that someone has to knock on the door and ask; accommodative organizations do not necessarily or proactively seek avenues for contributing.

Proactive Stance Firms that adopt the **proactive stance** take to heart the arguments in favour of CSR. They view themselves as good citizens of society and they proactively seek opportunities to contribute. The most common—and direct—way to implement this stance is by setting up a foundation to provide direct financial support for various social programs.

Keep in mind that organizations do not always fit neatly into one category or another. The Ronald McDonald House program has been widely applauded, for example, but

| Obstructionist stance | Defensive stance | Accommodative stance | Proactive stance |

LOWEST LEVEL OF SOCIAL RESPONSIBILITY

HIGHEST LEVEL OF SOCIAL RESPONSIBILITY

Figure 3.4
Spectrum of approaches to social responsibility

McDonald's has also come under fire for allegedly misleading consumers about the nutritional value of its food products. The Team Ethics exercise at the end of the chapter gives you an opportunity to think about the pros and cons of the various stances toward CSR.

Corporate Charitable Donations Donating money to different causes is one way that business firms try to show that they are socially responsible. In 2008, for example, Great-West Life, London Life, and Canada Life donated $100 000 to the Salvation Army's Christmas campaign.[56] In 2010, McDonald's raised $3 million for children's charities across Canada.[57] A survey of 93 large Canadian companies found that 97 percent made a charitable contribution of some sort, and that the median value of their contributions was $340 000.[58] Another survey of 2200 companies that was conducted by Imagine Canada found that 91 percent gave to charities or non-profit organizations. Cash donations were provided by 76 percent of the companies, products by 51 percent, and services by 43 percent. More than 80 percent of the companies said that they made contributions because it was a good thing to do, irrespective of any financial benefits they might achieve from giving.[59]

Imagine Canada's Caring Company program recommends that corporations give 1 percent of pre-tax profits to charity, but only half of the corporations met that goal in 2008. A survey conducted by the Centre for Philanthropy found that the vast majority of the money given to charities comes from individuals, not corporations. Canadians think that corporations give about 20 percent of the total, and that it should be 30 percent.[60] An Environics survey of people in 23 countries found that two-thirds of them thought that businesses are not doing enough if they simply abide by the law and provide employment.[61]

Businesses have also demonstrated a willingness to give money and products when disasters strike. When seven people died in Walkerton, Ontario, as a result of drinking contaminated water, companies such as Petro-Canada, Shoppers Drug Mart, Sobeys, and Zellers contributed products such as bleach and bottled water. And when tens of thousands of people died in the Asian tsunamis of 2004, companies from around the world rushed aid to the stricken areas. Global *Fortune 500* firms donated $580 million in drugs, cellphones, machinery, medical equipment, and water to the relief effort.[62]

Some companies go beyond simply giving money or products. For example, Unilever Canada gives employees four afternoons a year for community activities.[63] Mars Canada sets aside one day each year for employees to volunteer. Tim Horton's Children's Foundation plans to open a camp for underprivileged children in 2013 on Sylvia Lake in Manitoba. The Foundation also has a Youth Leadership Program that is currently offered at two sites in Ontario.[64] At Telus Corp.'s annual "day of service" in 2008, employees helped out at a soup kitchen.[65] Many companies take a community-based approach; they try to determine how they can achieve value for the community (and the company) with their donations of time and money.

Managing Social Responsibility Programs

There are four steps that are required in order for an organization to become truly socially responsible. First, top management must state strong support for CSR and make it a factor in strategic planning. Without the support of top management, no program can succeed.

Second, a committee of top managers needs to develop a plan detailing the level of support that will be provided. Some companies set aside a percentage of profits for social programs. Levi Strauss, for example, has a policy of giving 2.4 percent of its pre-tax earnings to worthy causes. Managers also need to set specific priorities (for example, should the firm focus on training the hard-core unemployed or supporting the arts?).

Third, a specific executive needs to be given the authority to act as director of the firm's social agenda. This individual must monitor the program and ensure that its implementation is consistent with the policy statement and the strategic plan.

Finally, the organization needs to conduct occasional **social audits**, which are systematic analyses of how a firm is using funds earmarked for its social-responsibility goals.[66] Canadian businesses also publish sustainability

Ronald McDonald House helps the families of children who are in hospital care. It is supported by McDonald's and is an example of socially responsible behaviour by a business corporation.

reports that explain how the company is performing on issues such as the environment, employee relations, workplace diversity, and business ethics. A study by Ottawa-based Stratos Inc. found that 60 percent of the 100 largest Canadian companies now report at least some sustainability performance information.[67] Social audits and sustainability reports together constitute **triple bottom line reporting**—measuring the social, environmental, and economic performance of a company.[68]

The Global 100 list of the most sustainable corporations in the world is based on factors like energy productivity (the ratio of sales to energy consumption) and water productivity (sales to water usage). In the 2010 ranking,

General Electric (U.S.) was first, Pacific Gas and Electric (U.S.) second, and TNT NV (Netherlands) third. Nine Canadian companies made the Top 100, including Enbridge (#16), EnCana (#25), and Sun Life Financial (#50).[69] Each year the Corporate Knights organization publishes its Best Corporate Citizen list. The rankings are based on an assessment of factors such as pension fund quality, board diversity, tax dollar generation, and Aboriginal relations. The top three companies in 2009 were Hydro One, Petro-Canada, and CN.[70]

ENTREPRENEURSHIP AND NEW VENTURES

How Green Is That Orange?

Ahh . . . the delicious taste of a fresh wild blueberry juice smoothie! What could be better to quench your thirst? The super juices offered by Arthur's Fresh, an Ontario-based beverage producer, offer much more than just thirst quenching. And, it's a good thing because consumers are looking for more than that these days—much more. Today's consumer insists on products that are both good for them and good for the environment. Arthur's Fresh is meeting the demands on both fronts. Its fruit smoothies are known for their nutritional benefits. Adding sugar is taboo and one 325 ml serving provides 25 to 50 percent of your required daily intake of fruits and vegetables. The product is sweet; pardon the pun! But, what's even sweeter about this product is the way it's produced.

In 2008, Travis Bell, president and founder of Arthur's Fresh, along with his brother Scott (the company CEO), decided to get serious about reducing the environmental footprint of their manufacturing business. Their strategy involved reducing bottle weight (which also reduced transportation costs and emissions), reducing packaging (e.g., plastic and cardboard), making responsible raw material sourcing decisions (like buying local), changing to bulk hauling transportation providers, and utilizing renewable energy for power generation. They expect to recover their $330 000 investment by 2011, mostly from cost savings associated with transportation and packaging.

The Packaging Association of Canada thought the changes made by the brothers were commendable, and recognized them in 2009 with an award for sustainable packaging leadership. Apparently, their

customers liked the changes too, since Arthur's Fresh has experienced a 1250 percent increase in sales since 2004. Company sales were $10 million in 2007, and in 2008 *Profit* magazine ranked Arthur's Fresh among Canada's fastest-growing companies.

The company is also involved in social responsibility initiatives that extend beyond concern for the environment. Through its Seeds of Change program, Arthur's Fresh gives at least 10 percent of its annual pre-tax profits back to the community for "kid-oriented programs." In 2008, the company was a corporate sponsor for See-Them-Run, a campaign involving two Canadians—Erin van Wiltenburg and Reuben Jentink—who ran 4200 kilometres across the African continent to raise money for youth education programs in Africa. Arthur's Fresh is also a regular donor of juice to food banks throughout the Toronto area. Along with making healthy products, and ethical procurement decisions, the company strongly believes in enriching the lives of children.

For Travis Bell, a fifth-generation fruit farmer from Goderich, Ontario, the decision to develop his part-time business to full-time operations has taken him to greener pastures in more ways than one. So, the next time you pull your chair up to the breakfast table to enjoy a glass of cold O.J., ask yourself, "Exactly how green is that orange?"

Critical Thinking Questions

1. How has Arthur's Fresh addressed the various areas of social responsibility?
2. What further actions might the company take?

LO-5 Social Responsibility and the Small Business

Small businesses face many of the same ethical and social responsibility issues as large businesses. As the owner of a small garden supply store, how would you respond to a building inspector's suggestion that a cash payment would "expedite" your application for a building permit? As the manager of a nightclub, would you call the police, refuse service, or sell liquor to a customer whose ID card looked forged? Or, as the owner of a small medical laboratory, would you actually call the board of health to make sure that it has licensed the company you want to contract with to dispose of the lab's medical waste? Is a small manufacturing firm justified in overcharging by 5 percent a customer whose purchasing agent is lax? Who will really be harmed if a small firm pads its income statement to help get a much-needed bank loan?

Can a small business afford to set CSR objectives? Should it sponsor hockey teams, make donations to the United Way, and buy light bulbs from the Lion's Club? Would you join the chamber of commerce and support the Better Business Bureau because it is the responsible thing to do, or just because it is good business? The boxed insert entitled "How Green Is That Orange?" describes the social responsibility initiatives of one small business.

PEARSON mybusinesslab

To improve your grade, visit the MyBusinessLab website at **www.pearsoned.ca/mybusinesslab**. This online homework and tutorial system allows you to test your understanding and generates a personalized study plan just for you. It provides you with study and practice tools directly related to this chapter's content. MyBusinessLab puts you in control of your own learning! Test yourself on the material for this chapter at **www.pearsoned.ca/mybusinesslab**.

Summary of Learning Objectives

1. **Explain how individuals develop their personal *codes of ethics* and why ethics are important in the workplace.** Individual codes of *ethics* are derived from social standards of right and wrong. *Ethical behaviour* is behaviour that conforms to generally accepted social norms concerning beneficial and harmful actions. Because ethics affect the behaviour of individuals on behalf of the companies that employ them, many firms are adopting formal statements of ethics. Unethical behaviour can result in loss of business, fines, and even imprisonment.

2. **Distinguish *social responsibility* from *ethics*, identify *organizational stakeholders,* and characterize social consciousness today.** *Social responsibility* refers to the way a firm attempts to balance its commitments to organizational stakeholders. One way to understand social responsibility is to view it in terms of *stakeholders*—those groups, individuals, and organizations that are directly affected by the practices of an organization and that therefore have a stake in its performance. Until the second half of the nineteenth century, businesses often paid little attention to stakeholders. Since then, however, both public pressure and government regulation, especially as a result of the Great Depression of the 1930s and the social activism of the 1960s and 1970s, have forced businesses to consider public welfare, at least to some degree. A trend toward increased social consciousness, including a heightened sense of environmental activism, has recently emerged.

3. **Show how the concept of social responsibility applies both to environmental issues and to a firm's relationships with customers, employees, and investors.** Social responsibility toward the environment requires

firms to minimize pollution of air, water, and land. Social responsibility toward customers requires firms to provide products of acceptable quality, to price products fairly, and to respect consumers' rights. Social responsibility toward employees requires firms to respect workers both as resources and as people who are more productive when their needs are met. Social responsibility toward investors requires firms to manage their resources and to represent their financial status honestly.

4. **Identify four general *approaches* to *social responsibility* and describe the four steps a firm must take to implement a *social responsibility program*.** An *obstructionist stance* on social responsibility is taken by a firm that does as little as possible to address social or environmental problems and that may deny or attempt to cover up problems that may occur. The *defensive stance* emphasizes compliance with legal minimum requirements. Companies adopting the *accommodative stance* go beyond minimum activities, if asked. The *proactive stance* commits a company to actively seek to contribute to social projects. Implementing a social responsibility program entails four steps: (1) drafting a policy statement with the support of top management, (2) developing a detailed plan, (3) appointing a director to implement the plan, and (4) conducting *social audits* to monitor results.

5. **Explain how issues of social responsibility and ethics affect small businesses.** Managers and employees of small businesses face many of the same ethical questions as their counterparts at larger firms. Small businesses face the same issues of social responsibility and the same need to decide on an approach to social responsibility. The differences are primarily differences of scale.

Questions and Exercises

Questions for Analysis

1. In what ways do you think your personal code of ethics might clash with the practices of some companies? How might you resolve these differences?

2. What kind of company wrongdoing would most likely prompt you to be a whistleblower? What kind of wrongdoing would be least likely? Explain the difference.

3. In your opinion, which area of social responsibility is most important? Why? Are there areas other than those noted in the chapter that you consider important? Describe these areas, and indicate why they are important.

4. Identify some specific social responsibility issues that might be faced by small-business managers and employees in each of the following areas: environment, customers, employees, and investors.

5. Choose a product or service and explain the social responsibility concerns that are likely to be evident in terms of the environment, customers, employees, and investors.

6. Analyze the forces that are at work from both a company's perspective and from a whistleblower's perspective. Given these forces, what characteristics would a law to protect whistleblowers have to have to be effective?

Application Exercises

7. Write a one-paragraph description of an ethical dilemma you faced recently (including the outcome). Analyze the situation using the ideas presented in the chapter. Make particular reference to the ethical norms of utility, rights, justice, and caring in terms of how they impacted the situation. What would each of these suggest about the correct decision? Is this analysis consistent with the outcome that actually occurred? Why or why not?

8. Pick a product or service that demonstrates the defensive approach to social responsibility. What has been the impact of that stance on the company that is using it? Now pick a product or service for each of the other stances (obstructionist, accommodative, and proactive) and do the same analysis. Why did

these companies adopt the particular stance they did? Have the companies that sell these products had different levels of success as a result of their social responsibility stance?

9. Develop a list of the major stakeholders of your college or university. How are these stakeholders prioritized by the school's administration? Do you agree or disagree with this prioritization? Explain your reasoning.

10. Interview the owner of a local small business. Ask the owner to (1) give his or her views on the importance of social responsibility for small businesses, (2) explain the kinds of socially responsible activities the company is currently involved in, and (3) describe the factors that facilitate and inhibit socially responsible behaviour in small businesses.

Building Your Business Skills

To Lie or Not to Lie: That Is the Question

Method

Step 1 Working with four other students, discuss ways in which you would respond to the following ethical dilemmas. When there is a difference of opinion among group members, try to determine the specific factors that influence different responses.

Goal

To encourage students to apply general concepts of business ethics to specific situations.

Background

Workplace lying, it seems, has become business as usual. According to one survey, one-quarter of working adults said that they had been asked to do something illegal or unethical on the job. Four in 10 did what they were told. Another survey of more than 2000 secretaries showed that many employees face ethical dilemmas in their day-to-day work.

- Would you lie about your supervisor's whereabouts to someone on the phone?
- Would you lie about who was responsible for a business decision that cost your company thousands of dollars to protect your own or your supervisor's job?
- Would you inflate sales and revenue data on official company accounting statements to increase stock value?
- Would you say that you witnessed a signature when you did not if you were acting in the role of a notary?
- Would you keep silent if you knew that the official minutes of a corporate meeting had been changed?
- Would you destroy or remove information that could hurt your company if it fell into the wrong hands?

Step 2 Research the commitment to business ethics at Johnson & Johnson (www.jnj.com) and Texas Instruments (www.ti.com/corp/docs/csr/corpgov/ethics/) by clicking on their respective websites. As a group, discuss ways in which these statements are likely to affect the specific behaviours mentioned in Step 1.

Step 3 Working with group members, draft a corporate code of ethics that would discourage the specific behaviours mentioned in Step 1. Limit your code to a single typewritten page, but make it sufficiently broad to cover different ethical dilemmas.

Follow-Up Questions

1. What personal, social, and cultural factors do you think contribute to lying in the workplace?

2. Do you agree or disagree with the following statement? "The term *business ethics* is an oxymoron." Support your answer with examples from your own work experience or that of a family member.

3. If you were your company's director of human resources, how would you make your code of ethics a "living document"?

4. If you were faced with any of the ethical dilemmas described in Step 1, how would you handle them? How far would you go to maintain your personal ethical standards?

Exercising Your Ethics

Assessing the Ethics of Tradeoffs

The Situation

Managers must often make choices among options that are presented by environmental circumstances. This exercise will help you better appreciate the nature and complexity of the kinds of tradeoffs that often result.

The Dilemma

You are the CEO of a medium-sized, unionized manufacturing corporation located in a town of about 15 000 people. The nearest major city is about 200 kilometres away. With about 500 workers, you are one of the five largest employers in town. A regional recession has caused two of the other largest employers to close down (one went out of business and the other relocated to another area). A new foreign competitor has set up shop in the area, but local unemployment has still risen sharply. All in all, the regional economic climate and the new competitor are hurting your business. Your sales have dropped 20 percent this year, and you forecast another drop next year before things begin to turn around.

You face two unpleasant choices:

Choice 1: You can tell your employees that you need them to take cuts in pay and benefits. You know that because of the local unemployment rate, you can easily replace anyone who refuses. Unfortunately, you may need your employees to take another cut next year if your forecasts hold true. At the same time, you do have reason to believe that when the economy rebounds (in about two years, according to your forecasts), you can begin restoring pay cuts. Here are the advantages of this choice: You can probably (1) preserve all 500 jobs, (2) maintain your own income, (3) restore pay cuts in the future, and (4) keep the business open indefinitely. And the disadvantages: pay cuts will (1) pose economic hardships for your employees and (2) create hard feelings and undercut morale.

Choice 2: You can maintain the status quo as far as your employees are concerned, but in that case, you'll be facing two problems: (1) You'll have to cut your own salary. While you can certainly afford to live on less income, doing so would be a blow to your personal finances. (2) If economic conditions get worse and/or last longer than forecast, you may have to close down altogether. The firm has a cash surplus, but because you'll have to dip into these funds to maintain stable wages, they'll soon run out. The advantages of this option: You can (1) avoid economic hardship for your workers and (2) maintain good employee relations. The downside: you will reduce your own standard of living and may eventually cost everyone his or her job.

Team Activity

Assemble a group of four students and assign each group member to one of the following roles:

- CEO of the company
- The vice-president of production
- A stockholder
- An employee who is a member of the union

Action Steps

1. Before hearing any of your group's comments on this situation, and from the perspective of your assigned role, decide which of the three options you think is the best choice. Write down the reasons for your position.

2. Before hearing any of your group's comments on this situation, and from the perspective of your assigned role, decide what the underlying ethical issues are in this situation. Write down the issues.

3. Gather the group together and reveal, in turn, each member's comments on the best choice of the two options. Next, reveal the ethical issues listed by each member.

4. Appoint someone to record the main points of agreement and disagreement within the group. How do you explain the results? What accounts for any disagreement?

5. From an ethical standpoint, what does your group conclude is the most appropriate action that should be taken by the company? (You may find the concepts of *utility*, *rights*, *justice*, and *caring* helpful in making your decision.)

Pollution on the High Seas

A study by the International Council on Clean Transportation provides some interesting statistics on the global shipping industry:

- Ships transport more than 90 percent of the world's products (by volume)

- Ships release more sulphur dioxide than all of the world's cars, trucks, and buses combined

- Only six countries in the world release more greenhouse gases than ships collectively do

- Ships produce about one-quarter of the entire world's output of nitrogen-oxide emissions (the ones that cause smog)

- Back in 1990, land-based sulphur dioxide emissions in Europe were about 10 times higher than sea-based emissions, but by 2030, sea-based emissions will exceed land-based emissions

Pollution from cargo ships is unusually high because they use bunker fuel, which is a tar-like sludge that is left over from the process of refining petroleum. Bunker fuel releases more pollutants than high-grade fuel, but ship owners use it because it is cheap. And refineries are happy to sell it to shippers because it gives them an outlet for a product that would otherwise not have a market.

While increasing concerns about the global shipping industry are evident, regulating ships on the high seas has always been something of a problem. This difficulty is obvious in the work of the International Maritime Organization, which is a United Nations agency that regulates shipping. The 167 nations that make up its membership have had extreme difficulty agreeing on what to do about the problem of pollution. For example, it took the group 17 years to agree that the sulphur content in marine fuel should not exceed 4.5 percent. But the sulphur content in bunker fuel had already been reduced to half that level by the time the regulation was passed. One frustrated member of the committee said that it spent most of one meeting discussing procedural details and the punctuation in its report.

A more effective approach is for ports to set emission rules, since cargo ships obviously have to unload their cargo *somewhere*. Some ports—particularly those in the Baltic Sea region and in the state of California—have already passed laws that prohibit ships from docking unless they use cleaner-burning fuels. California, for example, does not allow ships that use low-grade fuel to sail within 24 miles of its shores. Ports in Germany, Sweden, and Canada have also set targets to reduce air pollution from ships. But this patchwork of regulations has caused ship owners big problems, because it means that ships need to switch from low- to high-grade fuel as they sail to different locations. Because this process is complicated and dangerous, the International Association of Independent Tanker Owners and the Hong Kong Shipowners Association both think the UN should simply require ships to stop using bunker fuel.

The problem of pollution is not restricted to ships that carry *merchandise*; there is also a problem with ships that carry *people*. More than eight million passengers take an ocean voyage each year, cruising many areas of the world's oceans in search of pristine beaches and clear tropical waters. The tourists and the giant ships that carry them are usually welcomed for the revenues that they bring, but these ships also bring pollution.

A modern cruise ship generates a lot of waste—on a typical day, a ship will produce seven tons of solid garbage, 30 000 gallons of sewage, 7000 gallons of bilge water containing oil, and 225 000 gallons of "grey" water from sinks and laundries. Multiply these numbers by more than 167 ships worldwide, cruising 50 weeks per year, and the scope of the environmental damage is staggering.

Environmental groups see the top pollution-related problem as the death of marine life, including extinction. Foreign animals bring parasites and diseases, and in some cases, replace native species entirely. Bacteria that are harmless to human beings can kill corals that provide food and habitat for many species. Oil and toxic chemicals are deadly to wildlife even in minute quantities. Turtles swallow plastic bags, thinking they are jellyfish, and starve, while seals and birds drown after becoming entangled in the plastic rings that hold beverage cans.

Here again, lack of regulation is the biggest obstacle to solving the problem. Each country's laws and enforcement policies vary considerably, and even when laws are strict, enforcement may be limited. Cruise lines should be very concerned about clean seas for their own economic well-being, but this is often not the case. Intentional illegal dumping may actually be growing in scope. Over the last decade, for instance, as enforcement has tightened, 10 cruise lines have collectively paid US$48.5 million in fines related to illegal dumping. In the largest settlement to date, Royal Caribbean paid US$27 million for making illegal alterations to facilities, falsifying records, lying to the U.S. Coast Guard, and deliberately destroying evidence.

Critics are speaking out against the cruise lines' profiteering from an environment that they are destroying, but they note that the companies won't stop as long as the profits continue. Technology exists to make the waste safe, but industry experts estimate that dumping can save a firm millions of dollars annually. From that perspective, the cruise lines are making understandable decisions.

Questions for Discussion

1. What are the major legal issues in this case? What are the major ethical issues?

2. Aside from personal greed, what factors might lead a cruise line to illegally dump waste into the ocean? What factors might cause cargo ships to use low-grade fuel?

3. Are the approaches to social responsibility by the cargo and cruise lines similar or different? Explain.

4. Distinguish between ethical issues and social responsibility issues as they apply to this problem.

SCANLIFE

chapter

4

Entrepreneurship, Small Business, and New Venture Creation

After reading this chapter, you should be able to:

LO-1   Explain the meaning and interrelationship of the terms *small business, new venture creation, and entrepreneurship.*

LO-2   Describe the role of small and new businesses in the Canadian economy.

LO-3   Explain the *entrepreneurial process* and describe its three key elements.

LO-4   Describe three alternative strategies for becoming a business owner—*starting from scratch, buying an existing business, and buying a franchise.*

LO-5   Describe four forms of *legal organization* for a business and discuss the advantages and disadvantages of each.

LO-6   Identify four key reasons for success in small businesses and four key reasons for failure.

*With contributions from Dr. Monica Diochon, St. Francis Xavier University.

SCANLIFE

Parasuco Jeans: The Story of a Born Entrepreneur

Salvatore Parasuco's company recently celebrated its thirty-fifth year of operation, so his successful denim business is definitely not a new venture, but it is a great tale of entrepreneurship. Words like *drive*, *determination*, *self-starter*, and *vision* are commonly used to describe entrepreneurs. All of these terms fit the founder of Parasuco Jeans to a T. The story begins with a budding entrepreneur whose ambition is announced at a very young age when he begins selling jeans out of his high school locker in Montreal. As legend has it, he managed to convince his principal to let him sell the jeans by telling him he needed to make money to help support his family and avoid going down the wrong path. Today, Parasuco Jeans are sold in locations around the world with distribution in Canada, the United States, Europe, and Asia. The company has a particularly good presence in Italy, Hong Kong, Russia, Japan, and Korea. Celebrities such as Jessica Alba, Kate Hudson, Chris Daughtry, and many more have been photographed wearing a pair of Parasuco's trendy jeans. Yet despite the success and the longevity of the brand it does not have as much visibility across Canada as the owner thinks it deserves. He openly wonders why we Canadians (and the local media in particular) aren't as patriotic toward our homegrown brands as Americans are.

Salvatore is a Canadian whose family came here from Italy when he was just a young boy. From his humble beginnings, he learned the value of a

How Will This Help Me?

Parasuco Jeans has been successful because its entrepreneurial founder has adhered to sound business practices and made effective decisions. By understanding the material discussed in this chapter, you'll be better prepared to (1) understand the challenges and opportunities provided in new venture start-ups, (2) assess the risks and benefits of working in a new business, and (3) evaluate the investment potential inherent in a new business.

dollar and credits his father for teaching him the art of negotiation at an early age. The rise of Parasuco Jeans is not a modern-day instant success story with a major internet IPO launch. It is a story about blood, sweat, and some tears. Before getting into the denim design business, Salvatore opened a clothing store, where he learned a lot about the business that would become his life's work. Mr. Parasuco launched Santana Jeans in 1975 and changed the name to Parasuco due to legal issues in 1988. From the early days it was clear that innovation and design would be at the foundation of the company. Parasuco was the first to launch pre-washed jeans in Canada. The company was also the first brand to introduce stretch denim to the market; a product feature that is central to the company image to this day. In a recent interview, the owner talked about how customers tend to instinctively start to stretch and pull his famous jeans. Success in business requires good vision to compete. This is even more complicated in this industry because staying ahead of the fashion trends is no easy task. The guiding mission of the company is based on eight pillars of strength: (1) respect, (2) people, (3) passion, (4) promotion of innovation, (5) performance, (6) pride, (7) pursuit of excellence, and (8) professionalism. Based on a track record that spans over 35 years, it is obvious that this company has done something right in meeting customer needs. But there are significant existing domestic and emerging international competitors; there are even other major brands based in Montreal, such as Buffalo by David Bitton (which has its own niche).

Parasuco Jeans is a brand known for its provocative ads. It has shocked and pushed boundaries for years with sexy billboards, magazine spreads, and bus shelter ads. In order to gain more attention, the company placed 25 ads in giant ice blocks around the city of Toronto to coincide with Fashion Week in 2009, with a tag line to match: "Styles so hot they will melt the ice." Like most fashion companies, Parasuco uses Twitter and Facebook to build buzz and spread the word. There is also a great deal of content on YouTube, which is a testament to the brand's cult-like following.

Even the most successful businesses have their share of disappointments and failures, but true entrepreneurs know how to overcome them, reduce their losses, and to capitalize on the best available opportunity. In 2010, when Parasuco decided to close his flagship New York store, he quickly found a tenant (drugstore chain Duane Reade) that agreed to pay $1 million in rent per year, to Parasuco, who had bought the retail condominium four years earlier for about $9 million dollars. At the same time he announced intentions to build a high-end boutique hotel in Toronto. At 57 years of age, Salvatore Parasuco does not seem to be slowing down one bit; he is visibly promoting his brand and searching for new opportunities. What do you expect? Salvatore Parasuco has the DNA of a pure entrepreneur.

Small Business, New Venture Creation, and Entrepreneurship

In this chapter we examine old companies with an enduring entrepreneurial spirit (Parasuco); we look at exciting growth-oriented newcomers (Twitter); and we examine major family organizations that have stood the test of time (McCain) and a host of small organizations with dreams and aspirations. Each of these examples gives us a glimpse of an important element of the Canadian business landscape. We begin by examining the lifeblood of an economy: small business, entrepreneurship, and new ventures.

One positive result of the recent recession was a new wave of entrepreneurial efforts. In 2009, the number of self-employed Canadians increased by 115 000.[1] Every day, approximately 380 businesses are started in Canada.[2] New firms create the most jobs, are noted for their entrepreneurship, and are typically small.[3] But does this mean that most small businesses are entrepreneurial? Not necessarily.

The terms *small business, new venture*, and *entrepreneurship* are closely linked terms, but each idea is distinct. In the following paragraphs we will explain these terms to help you understand these topics and how they are interrelated.

LO-1 Small Business

Defining a "small" business can be a bit tricky. Various measures might be used, including the number of people the business employs, the company's sales revenue, the size of the investment required, or the type of ownership structure the business has. Some of the difficulties in defining a small business can be understood by considering the way the Canadian government collects and reports information on small businesses.

Industry Canada is the main federal government agency responsible for small business. In reporting Canadian small business statistics, the government relies on two distinct sources of information, both provided by Statistics Canada: the *Business Register* (which tracks businesses) and the *Labour Force Survey* (which tracks individuals). To be included in the Register, a business must have at least one paid employee, annual sales revenues of $30 000 or more, or be incorporated (we describe incorporation later in the chapter). A goods-producing business in the Register is considered small if it has fewer than 100 employees, while a service-producing business is considered small if it has fewer than 50 employees. The Labour Force Survey uses information from *individuals* to make estimates of employment and unemployment levels. Individuals are classified as self-employed if they are working owners of a business that is either incorporated or unincorporated, if they work for themselves but do not have a business (some musicians, for example, would fall into this category), or if they work without pay in a family business.[4] In its publication *Key Small Business Statistics* (www.strategis.gc.ca/sbstatistics), Industry Canada reports that there are 2.3 million "business establishments" in Canada and about 2.6 million people who are "self-employed."[5] There is no way of identifying how much overlap there is in these two categories, but we do know that an unincorporated business operated by a self-employed person (with no employees) would not be counted among the 2.3 million *businesses* in the Register. This is an important point because the majority of businesses in Canada have no employees (just the owner), nor are they incorporated.

A study by the Panel Study of Entrepreneurial Dynamics (PSED), conducted by members of the Entrepreneurship Research Consortium (ERC), tracked a sample of Canadian **nascent entrepreneurs**—people who were trying to start a business—over four years. Only 15 percent of those who reported establishing an operating business had incorporated their firm.[6]

For our purposes, we define a **small business** as an owner-managed business with less than 100 employees. We do so because it enables us to make better use of existing information, and because you are now aware of how definitions can affect our understanding of small businesses. Industry Canada estimates the percentage of small business's contribution to Canada's GDP over the past decade at 26 percent annually.[7]

Each year, the Queen's Centre for Business Venturing develops a ranking of the top 50 small- and medium-sized employers to work for. The top 10 firms in the 2010 study are shown in Table 4.1. Each of these companies exhibited superiority in employee recognition, managing performance, career opportunities, and organizational reputation.[8]

The New Venture/Firm

Various criteria can also be used to determine when a new firm comes into existence. Three of the most common are when it was formed, whether it was incorporated, and if it sold goods and/or services.[9] A business is considered to be new if it has become operational within

NASCENT ENTREPRENEURS
People who are trying to start a business from scratch.

SMALL BUSINESS
An independently owned and managed business that does not dominate its market.

Table 4.1 Top Small and Medium-Sized Employers in Canada, 2010

	Company	Location
1.	Booty Camp Fitness Inc.	Toronto, Ontario
2.	ISL Engineering and Land Services Ltd.	Edmonton, Alberta
3.	Hood Group	Sherwood Park, Alberta
4.	RL Solutions	Toronto, Ontario
5.	Radiology Consultants Associated	Calgary, Alberta
6.	Concept Electric Ltd.	Calgary, Alberta
7.	Gibraltar Solutions Inc.	Mississauga, Ontario
8.	PEOPLEsource Staffing Solutions	Toronto, Ontario
9.	EPIC Information Solutions Inc.	Winnipeg, Manitoba
10.	Vista Projects Ltd.	Calgary, Alberta

A common type of small business in Canada is the convenience store. It attracts customers from its immediate area through its long hours of operation and the product lines it carries.

the previous 12 months, if it adopts any of the main organizational forms (proprietorship, partnership, corporation, or co-operative), and if it sells goods or services. Thus, we define a **new venture** as a recently formed commercial organization that provides goods and/or services for sale.

Entrepreneurship

Entrepreneurship is the process of identifying an opportunity in the marketplace and accessing the resources needed to capitalize on that opportunity.[10] People start new businesses because they want to control their own destiny and prefer to take a chance rather than looking for a secure job. **Entrepreneurs** are people who recognize and seize these opportunities. For example, Mark Zuckerberg created Facebook, and in 2010 it had 500 million active users. He is one of the richest people in the world under the age of 30. However, it takes more than a good idea to be successful. Zuckerberg worked long hours, and he is constantly tailoring the website to suit its expanding audience.[11]

Each year, the Heritage Foundation publishes an index of economic freedom, which assesses the extent to which entrepreneurs have freedom to pursue new business opportunities. In 2010, the top three countries were Hong Kong, Singapore, and Australia, with freedom scores of 89.7, 86.1, and 82.6 respectively. Canada ranked seventh with a score of 80.4 and North Korea ranked last with a score of 1.0. Canada now ranks higher than the U.S. partly due to the U.S. government's stimulus spending, which the foundation believes will hurt the U.S. economy's long-term prospects.[12]

Small businesses often provide an environment to use personal attributes—such as creativity—that have come to be associated with entrepreneurs.[13] Because starting a business involves dealing with a great deal of uncertainty, ambiguity, and unpredictability, every new venture founder needs to exercise some of the personal attributes that entrepreneurs are noted for. But do not assume that only small business owners exhibit entrepreneurial characteristics.[14] Many successful managers in large organizations in both the public and private sectors also exhibit similar characteristics. Entrepreneurship therefore occurs in a wide range of contexts: not just in small or new commercial firms, but also in old firms, in large firms, in firms that grow slowly, in firms that grow rapidly, in non-profit organizations, and in the public sector.[15]

People who exhibit entrepreneurial characteristics and create something new within an existing firm or organization are called **intrapreneurs**. One large firm renowned for encouraging intrapreneurship is Proctor & Gamble. It has earned this reputation by having divisions that focus on creating new products for specific markets.[16] The Swiffer product line is one example. Once the basic Swiffer mop was launched successfully, a whole range of products was added, such as the Swiffer WetJet and Swiffer Dusters. A key difference between intrapreneurs and entrepreneurs is that intrapreneurs typically don't have to concern themselves with getting the resources needed to bring the new product to market, since big companies tend to have the necessary resources already available.

As we explore the entrepreneurial process later in the chapter, we will do so within a new-venture context. We begin by outlining the role of small and new businesses in the Canadian economy.

Mark Zuckerberg is the new-age entrepreneur who created Facebook, the hugely successful social networking site.

LO-2   The Role of Small and New Businesses in the Canadian Economy

As we will see in this section, small and new businesses play a key role in the Canadian economy. However, the recognition of this role has really only been acknowledged in the last two decades. Previously, large businesses were the focus of attention in terms of economic impact within industrialized nations.

Small Businesses

It may surprise you to learn that 97.8 percent of all businesses in Canada are small (they have fewer than 100 employees), and more than half of them have fewer than 5 employees. Medium-sized businesses (100–499 employees) comprise 1.9 percent of employer businesses, and large businesses (those with 500 or more employees) represent just 0.3 percent (see Figure 4.1).[17] This pattern is consistent across all provinces. While one large business has many more employees than one small business, as a group, small businesses provide more jobs than large businesses. Small businesses also lead the way when it comes to innovation and new technology.

Ontario and Quebec together account for the largest proportion of business establishments in Canada (about 57 percent), followed by the western provinces (37 percent) and the Atlantic provinces (6 percent). Northwest Territories, Yukon, and Nunavut represent just 0.3 percent of Canada's businesses.[18]

While the previous figures profile the number of businesses in Canada by size, we now look at how many people work in small- versus medium- and large-sized businesses. According to Statistics Canada, there were 10 901 100 **private sector** (companies and organizations not owned or controlled by government) employees in 2010.[19]

The distribution of employment by size of firm varies considerably across industries. Small businesses account for over two-thirds of employment in four industries: non-institutional health care (90 percent), the construction industry (77 percent), other services (73 percent), and accommodation and food (69 percent).[20] In another five industries, at least half of the workforce is employed by small businesses.

One increasingly important area is the field of green technologies and green applications for businesses of all sizes. The box entitled "Small Businesses Go Green" provides information on the growing interest around environmental concerns for small business owners.

New Ventures

New firms are not only the main source of job creation, they are also responsible for the vast majority of new products and services.[21] In 2007, small business created 100 000 jobs in Canada; this represented 40 percent of all jobs that were created that year. Between 2002 and 2006, approximately 130 000 new small businesses were started each year in Canada. During that same period, an equal number of small businesses ceased operations each year.[22]

More and more women are starting their own small businesses; women now account for half of all new businesses that are formed. According to a recent Statistics Canada report, there are about 877 000 women entrepreneurs in Canada, and 47 percent of small- and medium-sized enterprises have some degree of female ownership.[23] For example, Kyla Eaglesham, the owner of Madeleines Cherry Pie and Ice Cream Parlour, left her job as a flight attendant and opened her dessert café in Toronto's trendy Annex neighbourhood. The store attracts customers who want "a little bit of cottage country in the city."[24] However, women lead only 12 percent of the small- and medium-sized businesses that export goods and services.[25]

Female entrepreneurs are honoured each year at the Canadian Woman Entrepreneur Awards. Previous winners included Cora Tsouflidou (Montreal-based Cora Franchise Group), Teresa Coady (Vancouver-based Bunting Coady Architects), and Yvonne Tollens (Okotoks, Alberta–based ComputerAid Professional Services).[26]

Women who run businesses from their homes are sometimes called "mompreneurs."[27] The Mompreneur Networking Group

> **PRIVATE SECTOR**
> The part of the economy that is made up of companies and organizations that are not owned or controlled by the government.

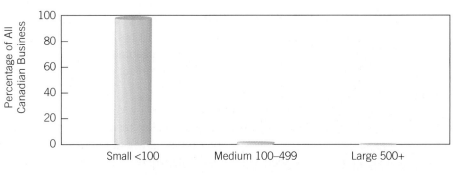

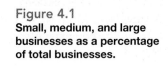

Figure 4.1
Small, medium, and large businesses as a percentage of total businesses.

Small Businesses Go Green

Small business owners have plenty of operational problems that demand their attention, so they often don't spend enough time thinking about how their company could become more eco-friendly. Even if they did find the time, they might think that they couldn't afford to go green. But there are a lot of inexpensive ways that small business owners can show concern for the environment.

Simple things like changing to energy-efficient lighting and turning off photocopiers and computers overnight is a good start. The energy departments of most provinces have websites that provide information on how companies can save money by using water and energy more efficiently. For more aggressive or longer-term projects, small business owners can access the federal government's ecoACTION program website, which contains information about programs that help organizations reduce energy costs. The ecoENERGY retrofit program, for example, provides financial incentives of up to 25 percent of project costs to help small and medium-sized companies implement energy-saving projects.

Saving energy is just one possible area for improvement. There are also many other ideas that small business owners can implement, such as using recycled paper, eco-friendly cleaning supplies, and pens made of compostable material instead of plastic. And employees can be encouraged to organize car pools, bicycle to work, or use public transit.

Green Enterprise Ontario (GEO) is a group of eco-minded businesses that pay $199 each year to belong to a network where they can trade business, advice, and referrals. All of the businesses in the group are committed to activities such as sustainable purchasing, manufacturing, and recycling of products. GEO runs regular workshops on topics of importance to small businesses—for example, finance and marketing—but it also offers information on environment and social responsibility initiatives. Chris Lowry, the coordinator of the Toronto affiliate, says that many small business owners have become interested in going green after being asked "uncomfortable" questions by their children and staff members about why they aren't doing more for the environment. Small business owners are also starting to respond to social pressure from customers.

Critical Thinking Questions

1. Find a small business in your local area that is committed to being eco-friendly. Why did the owner decide to commit to having an eco-friendly business?

2. Consider the following statement: *"It is unrealistic to expect small business owners to spend much time thinking about or implementing green practices. The failure rate of small businesses is high, so small business owners have to focus all their energies on trying to ensure the survival of their businesses. They simply don't have the time (or money) to 'go green.'"* Do you agree or disagree with the statement? Explain your reasoning.

organizes seminars and publishes *Mompreneur*, a free magazine that helps women who want to start a business. More information on mompreneurs is provided in Video Case I-1 and the Entrepreneurship and New Ventures box below.

Many young entrepreneurs are also involved in creating new ventures in Canada. Consider the following examples:

- Daisy and Adam Orser were among the winners of the BDC Young Entrepreneurs Award in 2009 for their Victoria, B.C.–based company called The Root Cellar Village Green Grocer. They are capitalizing on the movement for fresh local produce and healthier lifestyles. The company already employees 50 people and the future looks bright.[28]

- The Ben Barry Agency is an Ottawa-based modelling businesses that promotes models who are considered unorthodox—various sizes and ages, different racial backgrounds, and those who have physical disabilities. The models have appeared in government advertising campaigns and on fashion runways in shopping malls. Barry works with company management to define their clientele and then chooses models who will best reflect the store's typical shoppers.[29]

- Tell Us About Us (TUAU) is a Winnipeg-based company specializing in market research and customer satisfaction programs. Owners Tyler Gompf and Scott Griffith recently signed a seven-figure deal to provide mystery shopper service to Dunkin' Donuts,

Spotlight on Mompreneurs

An increasing number of Canadian women have decided to be stay-at-home entrepreneurs (called mompreneurs). Most of them aren't trying to be super-moms that can do everything; rather, they want to use their skills to run a business and at the same time achieve a better work-life balance. Here are some of their interesting success stories.

Laughing Belly Productions

Shirley Broback won the SavvyMom Entrepreneur of the Year Award in 2009. She earned the acknowledgement for her work in organizing the Vancouver Island Baby Fair. Shirley has put her event planning background to good use. She designs these events to provide an enjoyable family experience while providing marketing opportunities for companies that cater to the needs of pregnant women and children from birth to preschool age.

Sweetpea Baby Food

Erin Green and Tamar Wagman started their frozen baby food company from scratch and now their organic products are distributed in over 350 stores nationally with revenues that exceed $500 000. Part of their strategy focuses on an ambassador program for women from across Canada enlisted to make Sweatpea Baby Food a success. This grassroots approach makes a lot of sense. Moms love to talk about how they deal with their little ones; in return, Sweetpea provides organic products to moms as they spread the word in their yoga classes and baby groups.

Spoon Fed Soup

Carmie Nearing of Calgary had a career as a chef, but found the hours she needed to work didn't fit with raising children. She quit and got a 9-to-5 job. But that didn't satisfy her, so she decided to start her own company—called Spoon Fed Soup—to provide gourmet soups to customers. Nearing found that as her business grew, she had to hire employees and spend more and more time dealing with customers. She now realizes that she has a passion for entrepreneurship that goes beyond the simple desire to stay at home with her children.

Green Please! Inc.

Melanie Derwin of Winnipeg became interested in green living when her 20-month-old son's repeated ear and throat infections were not helped by standard antibiotics. She eventually founded Green Please! Inc., a company that provides customers with suggestions for "greening up" their lifestyle. Her company is an e-boutique offering products like bamboo crib sheets, organic cotton rattles, non-toxic toys, and organic soaps. Melanie operates on the principle that it is better to be proactive than reactive about health problems.

Some observers of the mompreneur trend have noted that things are not always as positive as they seem. Barbara Orser, a management professor at the University of Ottawa's School of Management, says that most mompreneurs work long hours, run low-growth businesses, don't make much money, and don't get benefits. She cites a Statistics Canada report showing that only 17 percent of self-employed women earn more than $30 000 per year. In spite of this, increasing numbers of women are becoming mompreneurs.

Critical Thinking Questions

1. What is the difference between small business and entrepreneurship? Are mompreneurs entrepreneurs? Explain.
2. Interview a mompreneur and ask the following questions: (a) Why did you start your business? (b) What are the advantages and disadvantages of being a mompreneur?

More and more women, like Shirley Broback, are starting and successfully operating their own small businesses. They now account for half of all new businesses that are formed.

Baskin-Robbins, and Togo's in the United States and Canada. The mystery shoppers will note any problems at a retail site and TUAU will then measure how quickly the problems are fixed.[30]

LO-3 The Entrepreneurial Process

The entrepreneurial process is like a journey (see Figure 4.2). It is influenced by the social, economic, political, and technological factors in the broader environment, but we will focus our attention on understanding the three key elements in the entrepreneurial process—the entrepreneur, the opportunity, and resources—and how they interact. As these key elements interact, they may be mismatched or well matched. For example, if an entrepreneur identifies an opportunity for a new health service but does not have the relevant background and skills to deliver the service, the business may never get off the ground. Conversely, if all three process elements are well matched, the new business will likely become operational at some point.

Since the entrepreneur is at the heart of the entrepreneurial process, considerable attention has been paid to identifying the personal characteristics of entrepreneurs. Research shows that these characteristics are wideranging. Some are behavioural (e.g., taking initiative), others are personality traits (e.g., independence), and still others are skills (e.g., problem-solving).[31] Some people think that entrepreneurs are rare; however, entrepreneurial

characteristics have been found to be widely distributed in the population.[32] We also know that personal characteristics often have less impact on a person's action than the situation a person is in.[33] What is really important is not who the person *is* but what the person *does*.[34] Entrepreneurs must (1) identify an opportunity and (2) access resources.

Identifying Opportunities

Identifying opportunities involves generating ideas for new (or improved) products, processes, or services, screening those ideas, and developing the best ones.

Idea Generation Typically, generating ideas involves abandoning traditional assumptions about how things work and how they ought to be, and seeing what others do not. If the prospective new (or improved) product, process, or service can be profitably produced and is attractive relative to other potential venture ideas, it might present an opportunity.

Where do ideas come from? Most new ventures do not emerge from a deliberate search for viable business ideas. Rather, the majority originate from events relating to work or everyday life.[35] In fact, work experience is the most common source of ideas, accounting for 45 to 85 percent of those generated. This happens because as employees of a company, prospective entrepreneurs are familiar with the product or service, the customers, the suppliers, and the competitors. They are also aware of marketplace needs, can relate those needs to personal capabilities, and can determine whether they are capable of producing products or services that can fill the void.

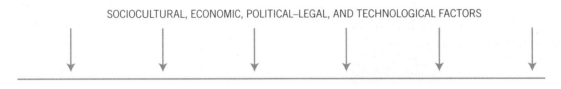

SOCIOCULTURAL, ECONOMIC, POLITICAL–LEGAL, AND TECHNOLOGICAL FACTORS

Figure 4.2
The entrepreneurial process in a new venture context.

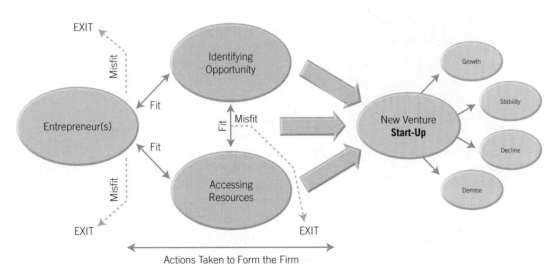

Other frequent sources of new venture ideas include a personal interest/hobby (16 percent) or a chance happening (11 percent).[36] A chance happening refers to a situation in which a venture idea comes about unexpectedly. For example, while on vacation in another country you might try a new snack food that you feel would be in demand if introduced to the Canadian market.

Screening Entrepreneurs often generate many ideas, and screening them is a key part of the entrepreneurial process. The faster you can weed out the "dead-end" venture ideas, the more time and effort you can devote to the ones that remain. The more of the following characteristics that an idea has, the greater the opportunity it presents.

The Idea Creates or Adds Value for the Customer A product or service that creates or adds value for the customer is one that solves a significant problem, or meets a significant need in new or different ways. Consider Sally Fox's idea for eliminating the dyeing process in textile operations.[37] By cross-breeding long-fibre white cotton and short-fibre coloured cotton she developed FoxFibre, an environmentally friendly new cotton fibre that is naturally grown in several colours and is long enough to be spun commercially.

The Idea Provides a Competitive Advantage That Can Be Sustained A competitive advantage exists when potential customers see the product or service as better than that of competitors. Toronto-based Sentinelle Medical is counting on a very important sustainable advantage. Cameron Piron spent 10 years developing a better cancer detection technology and another two years to get General Electric to use it in its MRI machines. He recently received the Ontario Government Innovation Award.[38] Sustaining a competitive advantage involves maintaining it in the face of competitors' actions or changes in the industry. All other things being equal, the longer markets are in a state of flux, the greater the likelihood of being able to sustain a competitive advantage. The absence of a competitive advantage or developing a competitive advantage that is not sustainable constitute two fatal flaws of many new ventures.[39]

The Idea Is Marketable and Financially Viable While it is important to determine whether there are enough customers who are willing to buy the product or service, it is also important to determine whether sales will lead to profits.[40] Estimating the market demand requires an initial understanding of who the customers are, what their needs are, and how the product or service will satisfy their needs better than competitors' products will. It also requires a thorough understanding of the key competitors who can provide similar products, services, or benefits to the target customer. For example, 10 years ago few people thought that manufacturers of cellphones would be competitors of camera manufacturers in providing real-time photos through digital imaging. Customers define the competition in terms of who can best satisfy their needs.

After learning about the competition and customers, the entrepreneur must prepare a **sales forecast**, which is an estimate of how much of a product or service will be purchased by the prospective customers for a specific period of time—typically one year. Total sales revenue is estimated by multiplying the units expected to be sold by the selling price. The sales forecast forms the foundation for determining the financial viability of the venture and the resources needed to start it.

Determining financial viability involves preparing financial forecasts, which are two- to three-year projections of a venture's future financial position and performance. They typically consist of an estimate of *start-up costs, a cash budget, an income statement*, and a balance sheet (see Chapter 11 for more details about these financial documents). These projections serve as the basis for decisions regarding whether to proceed with the venture, and, if so, the amount and type of financing to be used in financing the new business.

The Idea Has Low Exit Costs The final consideration is the venture's exit costs. Exit costs are low if a venture can be shut down without a significant loss of time, money, or reputation.[41] If a venture is not expected to make a profit for a number of years, its exit costs are high, since the project cannot be reasonably abandoned in the short term. For example, Toronto-based zero-emission car manufacturer Zenn Motors has very-long-term projections. On the other hand, if the venture is expected to make a profit quickly, its exit costs will be lower, making the idea more attractive.

Developing the Opportunity As the "dead-end" venture ideas are weeded out, a clear notion of the business concept and an entry strategy for pursuing it must be developed. The business concept often changes from what was originally envisioned. Some new ventures develop entirely new markets, products, and sources of competitive advantage once the needs of the marketplace and the economies of the business are better understood. So, while a vision of what is to be achieved is important, it is equally important to be responsive to new information and to be on the lookout for unanticipated opportunities. For example, if customers are not placing orders it is important to find out why and make adjustments.

New ventures use one or more of three main entry strategies: they introduce a totally new product or service;

> **SALES FORECAST**
> An estimate of how much of a product or service will be purchased by prospective customers over a specific period.

FRANCHISE
An arrangement that gives franchisees (buyers) the right to sell the product of the franchiser (the seller).

BUSINESS PLAN
Document in which the entrepreneur summarizes her or his business strategy for the proposed new venture and how that strategy will be implemented.

they introduce a product or service that will compete directly with existing competitive offerings but adds a new twist (customization of the standard product); or they franchise.[42] A **franchise** is an arrangement in which a buyer (franchisee) purchases the right to sell the product or service of the seller (franchiser). We discuss franchising in more detail later in the chapter.

When capital requirements are high, such as when a manufacturing operation is being proposed, there is a need for considerable research and planning. Similarly, if product development or operations are fairly complex, research and analysis will be needed to ensure that the costs associated with effectively coordinating tasks will be minimized. In these circumstances, or when the aim is to attract potential investors, a comprehensive written business plan is required. A **business plan** is a document that describes the entrepreneur's proposed business venture; explains why it is an opportunity; and outlines its marketing plan, its operational and financial details, and its managers' skills and abilities.[43] The contents of a business plan are shown in Table 4.2.

If market conditions are changing rapidly, the benefits gained from extensive research and planning diminish quickly. By the time the entrepreneur is ready to start, new competitors may have entered the market, prices may have changed, a location may no longer be available, and so on. Similarly, if the product is highly innovative, market research is of less value, since the development of entirely new products involves *creating* needs and wants rather than simply responding to existing needs. Consequently, measuring the capacity of the product or service to fill existing customer needs or wants is less critical.

Contrary to what many people think, planning does not have to be completed before action is taken. For example, if an electrical contracting business is being proposed in an area where there is a shortage of tradespeople, it would be important to seek out qualified employees prior to conducting other analyses that are needed to complete the business plan. Such early action also helps to build relationships that can be drawn on later. Obviously, some ventures do not lend themselves to early action, particularly those that are capital intensive. Since most entrepreneurs have limited resources,

---

Table 4.2 A Business Plan

A well-written business plan is formally structured, easy to read, and avoids confusion. Organizing the information into sections makes it more manageable. The amount of detail and the order of presentation may vary from one venture to another and according to the intended audience (if the plan is intended for potential investors it will require more detail than if it is intended for internal use by the entrepreneur). An outline for a standard business plan is provided below.

I.	**Cover Page:** Name of venture and owners, date prepared, contact person, his/her address, telephone and fax numbers, email address, Facebook link, and the name of the organization the plan is being presented to. The easier it is for the reader to contact the entrepreneur, the more likely the contact will occur.
II.	**Executive Summary:** A one- to three-page overview of the total business plan. Written after the other sections are completed, it highlights their significant points, and aims to create enough excitement to motivate the reader to continue.
III.	**Table of Contents:** This element lists major sections with page numbers for both the body and the appendices of the plan.
IV.	**Company Description:** Identifies the type of company: manufacturing, retail, etc. It also describes the proposed form of organization: sole proprietorship, partnership, corporation, or co-operative. A typical organization of this section is as follows: name and location; company objectives; nature and primary product or service of the business; current status (start-up, buyout, or expansion) and history, if applicable; and legal form of organization.
V.	**Product or Service Description:** Describes the product or service and indicates what is unique about it. This section explains the value that is added for customers—why people will buy the product or service; features of the product or service providing a competitive advantage; legal protection (patents, copyrights, trademarks, if relevant); and dangers of technical or style obsolescence.
VI.	**Marketing:** This section has two key parts, the market analysis and the marketing plan. The market analysis convinces the reader that the entrepreneur understands the market for the product or service and can deal effectively with the competition to achieve sales projections. The marketing plan explains the strategy for achieving sales projections.
VII.	**Operating Plan:** Explains the type of manufacturing or operating system to be used. Describes the facilities, labour, raw materials, and processing requirements.
VIII.	**Management:** Identifies the key players—the management team, active investors, and directors—and cites the experience and competence they possess. This section includes a description of the management team, outside investors and directors and their qualifications, outside resource people, and plans for recruiting and training employees.
IX.	**Financial Plan:** Specifies financial needs and expected financing sources. Presents projected financial statements, including cash budget, balance sheet, and income statement.
X.	**Supporting Details/Appendix:** Provides supplementary materials to the plan such as resumés and other supporting data.

---

it is important to concentrate on the issues that can be dealt with, *and* that will help determine whether to proceed and how to proceed.[44]

Accessing Resources

Typically, entrepreneurs acquire the various resources needed to make the venture a reality by **bootstrapping**, which means "doing more with less." Usually the term refers to financing techniques whereby entrepreneurs make do with as few resources as possible and use other peoples' resources wherever they can. However, bootstrapping can also refer to the acquisition of other types of resources, such as people, space, equipment, or materials that are loaned or provided free by customers or suppliers.

Financial Resources There are two main types of financing—*debt* and *equity* (see Chapter 15). Since a business is at its riskiest point during the start-up phase, equity is usually more appropriate and accessible than debt. However, most new venture founders prefer debt because they are reluctant to give up any control to outsiders. To obtain debt financing, the entrepreneur must have an adequate equity investment in the business—typically 20 percent of the business's value—and collateral (or security).

Collateral refers to items (assets) owned by the business (such as a building and equipment) or by the individual (such as a house or car) that the borrower uses to secure a loan or other credit. These items can be seized by the lender if the loan isn't repaid according to the specified terms. To lenders, equity investment demonstrates the commitment of the entrepreneur, as individuals tend to be more committed to a venture if they have a substantial portion of what they own invested in it.

Entrepreneurs who want to obtain financing for a start-up business must have collateral such as a house or car in order to get a loan. Would you be willing to give your house or car as collateral, knowing that if you couldn't repay the loan the bank would take your house or car?

The most common sources of *equity* financing include:

1. *Personal savings.* New venture founders draw heavily on their own finances to start their businesses. Most save as much as they can in preparation for start-up.

2. *Love money.* This type of financing includes investments from friends, relatives, and business associates. It is called "love money" because it is often given more on the basis of the relationship than on the merit of the business concept.

3. *Private investors.* One popular source of equity capital is informal capital from private investors called *angels*. Usually, these investors are financially well off individuals; many are successful entrepreneurs who wish to recycle their wealth by investing in new businesses. For example, Saxx & Co. makes high-performance men's underwear. The company was started by Trent Kitsch, who developed the idea as part of a project requirement in his MBA program. He put $18 000 of his own money into the company, but he needed a major cash injection to compete with the bigger companies in the industry. Eventually, he received $50 000 from a private investor in return for a 5 percent ownership stake in the business. Kitsch wants to get an additional $500 000, and he is willing to give an investor 15 percent of the business. He also wants a mentor who has experience in the business.[45]

4. *Venture capitalists.* Investments by venture capitalists come from professionally managed pools of investor money (venture capital). Since the risk of receiving little or no return on investment is high, only deals that present an attractive, high-growth business opportunity with a return between 35 and 50 percent are considered. Very few new ventures meet this criterion. Venture capital investment in Canada dropped to $1 billion in 2009—the lowest level in about 15 years—so angels are becoming more important in providing start-up money to entrepreneurs.[46] In a move to improve the environment and increase financing options, the Canadian government reduced red-tape hurdles for foreign venture capital firms to invest in Canada. Among other things, it eliminated a punitive 25 percent tax on capital gains aimed at foreign investors. This is good news for firms looking at the venture capital route.[47]

BOOTSTRAPPING
Doing more with less.

COLLATERAL
Assets that a borrower uses to secure a loan or other credit, and that are subject to seizure by the lender if the loan isn't repaid according to the specified repayment terms.

The most common sources of *debt* financing include:

1 *Financial institutions.* While commercial banks are the main providers of debt financing for established small businesses, it is usually difficult for a new business to borrow from a bank. Banks are risk averse, and loans to new businesses are considered very risky, largely because the business has yet to establish its ability to repay the loan. Typically, entrepreneurs have more luck obtaining financing for a new venture with a personal loan (as opposed to a business loan). The most common way to obtain a personal loan is to mortgage a house or borrow against the cash value of a life insurance policy. In addition to commercial banks, other sources of debt financing include trust companies, co-operatives, finance companies, equipment companies, credit unions, and government agencies. Since finance companies lend in high-risk situations, their interest rates tend to be high.

2 *Suppliers.* Another source of financing is suppliers who provide goods (e.g., inventory) or services to the entrepreneur with an agreement to bill them later. This is referred to as *trade credit*. Trade credit can be helpful in getting started, because inventory can be acquired without paying cash, freeing up money to pay other start-up costs. This type of financing is short term; 30 days is the usual payback period. The amount of trade credit available to a new firm depends on the type of business and the supplier's confidence in the firm. Frequently, though, a new business has trouble getting trade credit since its capacity to repay has not been demonstrated.

Besides these conventional sources of financing, the possibilities for bootstrap financing are endless. For example, an entrepreneur might require an advance payment from customers. Equipment can be leased rather than purchased (which reduces the risk of obsolete equipment). Office furniture can be rented, premises can be shared, and manufacturing can be subcontracted, thereby avoiding the expense of procuring material, equipment, and facilities. All of these activities free up cash that can then be used for other purposes.

Other Resources Businesses have other resources to help them with financing, legal, marketing, or operational advice or support. The federal and provincial governments have a wide range of financial assistance programs for small businesses. Among the various forms of assistance are low-interest loans, loan guarantees, interest-free loans, and wage subsidies. We examine three sources of information and assistance below: Business Development Bank of Canada, business incubators, and the internet.

Business Development Bank of Canada The Business Development Bank of Canada (BDC) has a mandate to help develop Canadian businesses, with a particular focus on small- and medium-sized companies. It provides financing, venture capital, and consulting strategies. The BDC provides services to over 28 000 businesses from coast to coast and serves them through over 100 branch offices. The BDC is a financial institution wholly owned by the Government of Canada. Information can be found at www.bdc.ca or by calling 1-877-BDC-Banx.[48]

Incubators Business **incubators** provide new businesses (newborns) with support to help nurture them into a successful future. The type of support varies but some key forms of assistance include consulting services, legal advice, accounting services, business contacts, clerical services, and office space. According to the Canadian Association of Business Incubation (CABI), business survival rates are greatly improved by getting involved with an incubator. Survival rates after five years stand at about 80 percent, which is far above the average rates for businesses that don't use incubators. You can learn more by visiting www.cabi.ca. Take a look at Table 4.3 for examples of incubators across the country.

The Internet There are countless resources available online that can help budding entrepreneurs gather research information, write a business plan, and access government grants. The banks all have major sites dedicated to small business and entrepreneurship resources. For example, Royal Bank of Canada (RBC) has a great site that provides checklists, business plan formats and samples, and advice on selecting business structures and more (www.rbcroyalbank.com/sme/index.html). There are also government sites such as the Canada Business

Table 4.3 Business Incubators across Canada	
Name	**Location**
NRC Institute for Fuel Cell Innovation	Victoria, British Columbia
Duncan McNeill Centre for Innovation	Edmonton, Alberta
Smart Virtual Incubation Winnipeg	Winnipeg, Manitoba
AgriTech Park	Truro, Nova Scotia
The Venture Centre	Pasadena, Newfoundland
NRC Institute for Information Technology	Fredericton, New Brunswick
Mississauga Technology Business Accelerator	Mississauga, Ontario
Saskatchewan Ideas Inc.	Saskatoon, Saskatchewan
J.-Armand-Bombardier Incubator	Montreal, Quebec
LaunchPad Incubator Facility in the Atlantic Technology Centre	Charlottetown, Prince Edward Island

Services for Entrepreneurs dedicated to providing information and advice on every aspect of starting a business, including accessing government grants (www.canadabusiness.ca/eng/).

Building the Right Team

A business may be owned by one person, but entrepreneurship is not a solo process. As we have just seen, there are various stakeholders who can provide resources to the venture. When ownership is shared, decisions must be made regarding who to share it with, how much each stakeholder will own, at what cost, and under what conditions. The form of legal organization chosen affects whether ownership can be shared and whether resources can be accessed.

Deciding whether to share ownership by forming a *venture team* involves consideration of two main issues:

- *the size and scope of the venture*—How many people does the venture require? Is it a one-person operation or does it need contributions from others? Can people be hired to fill the key roles as they are required?

- *personal competencies*—What are the talents, know-how, skills, track record, contacts, and resources that the entrepreneur brings to the venture? How do these match with what the venture needs to succeed?

The nature of the team depends upon the match between the lead entrepreneur and the opportunity and how fast and aggressively he or she plans to proceed. Most teams tend to be formed in one of two ways: (1) one person has an idea (or wants to start a business), and then several associates join the team in the first few years of operation, or (2) an entire team is formed at the outset based on such factors as a shared idea, a friendship, or an experience.

The ideal team consists of people with complementary skills covering the key success areas for the business (i.e., marketing, finance, production). Small founding teams tend to work better than big ones. It is quite common for the initial team to consist of just two people—a craftsperson and a salesperson.

If the entrepreneur does not intend to establish a high-growth venture, going solo may be a realistic option. Some new venture founders bring on additional team members only as the business can afford them. Most successful solo businesses are simple types of ventures, such as small retail stores or services.[49] The odds for survival, growth, profitability, and attracting capital are increased by a team approach.[50] Read the E-Business and Social Media Solutions case "New Age Entrepreneurs" to learn about the team and the challenges behind the popular site.

Assessing the "Fit" between Elements in the Entrepreneurial Process

Assessing the "fit" between the various elements in the entrepreneurial process is an ongoing task, since the shape of the opportunity, and consequently the resources and people needed to capitalize on it, typically changes as it is developed. It is the entrepreneur who stands to gain the most by attending to these "fits" and any changes they may require, although other stakeholders, such as investors, will be considering them as well.

The Entrepreneur–Opportunity Fit The first assessment of fit is between the entrepreneur and the opportunity. The entrepreneur needs to decide whether the opportunity is something he or she *can do* and *wants to do*. A realistic self-assessment is important. Prospective ventures that are of limited personal interest and require skills and abilities that do not fit well with those of the entrepreneur should be quickly eliminated. For example, it does little good to identify an opportunity for an ecotourism business in a wilderness area if the entrepreneur loves city life and hates spending time outdoors.

Once the entrepreneur has chosen the opportunity he or she wants to pursue, the success of the venture depends heavily upon the individual or individuals involved. No matter how good the product or service concept is, as the opportunity changes shape it may demand skills a single entrepreneur lacks. This may prompt a decision either to acquire the needed skills by forming a team or by getting further training.

New Age Entrepreneurs: The Rise of Twitter

Entrepreneurs have effective new promotion tools thanks to social media sites. But what about the entrepreneurs who created these new information highways? Biz Stone, Jack Dorsey, and Evan Williams created and launched Twitter, the micro-blogging site, in 2006. Before Twitter, Biz Stone helped launch Blogger, Odeo, Obvious, and Xanga. He is a blogging expert who has written two books on the subject. Jack Dorsey is the inventor on the software side of the business and Evan Williams is an entrepreneur who also built internet start-ups like Pyra Labs. A good team, a good idea, and a lot of entrepreneurial spirit, and the next thing you know "tweet" and "re-tweet" are part of our everyday lexicon.

So why is Twitter so popular? It is an instantaneous source of information (not all of it useful) delivered 140 characters at a time. As the website states, it allows you to stay informed on the issues that matter most to you. Today, Twitter is heavily promoting business applications complete with cases in a section called Twitter 101 for Businesses. You can read all about some of the showcase companies. For example, Best Buy has set up "real-time twelp" for instantaneous customer feedback from their "twelp force"; customers send queries to Best Buy's famous technical "geek squad" and receive quick answers to problems. There are YouTube video demonstrations to provide insight on how to maximize Twitter for small business applications. Of course, Twitter can also be used to spread negative word of mouth about organizations, so Best Buy's proactive engaging approach is quite intelligent.

Popularity does not necessarily translate into profitability. Biz Stone has faced tough questions from reporters, analysts, and even comedians. While appearing on the Stephen Colbert show, the host mocked him by joking that Biz is obviously not short for "business model." The crowd laughed and he smiled, but the issue behind the joke was very real. Popularity is great, but popularity does not pay the bills. You need a business model that can generate profits. In 2010, Twitter executives announced the creation of "promoted tweets," which enable companies to pay for their messages to be displayed in a more prominent manner on the site while providing Twitter with a new revenue stream. Starbucks and Red Bull were among the first companies to sign up. Even before this decision, companies were using Twitter's social power. Molson used Twitter to help launch Molson 67 and create pre-launch buzz. Authors and musicians use the site to generate buzz. Now Twitter appears ready to cash in on its success. Is this the beginning of sustainable revenues for Twitter? Will the tweeting masses object? It will be interesting to see how this business model evolves.

Critical Thinking Question

1. Are you in favour of promoted tweets? Debate Twitter's decision to implement this model.

The Opportunity–Resources Fit Assessing the opportunity–resources fit involves determining whether the resources needed to capitalize on the opportunity can be acquired. As the opportunity changes shape, so will the resource requirements. When challenges or risks arise, the aim is to determine whether they can be resolved and to deal with them quickly. For example, if the venture requires a greater financial investment than originally anticipated, this does not necessarily mean that the venture should be abandoned. Other options such as taking on partners or leasing rather than building a facility may be viable. Of course, some ventures may not be viable regardless of the alternatives considered.

The Entrepreneur–Resources Fit Once the resource requirements of the venture have been determined, the entrepreneur needs to assess whether he or she has the capacity to meet those requirements. For example, an entrepreneur with a stellar reputation for software development will have an easier time attracting employees for a venture specializing in software than someone with no track record. If that same entrepreneur is well connected with people in the industry, he or she will be more likely to gain commitments from customers, and in turn, investors.

Start-Up and Beyond

Entrepreneurs must make the right start-up decisions, but they must also pay attention to how the business will be run once it is started. In this section, we examine three important topics that are relevant to these issues. First, we describe the three main ways that entrepreneurs start up a small business. Next, we look at the four main organizing options that are available to entrepreneurs. We conclude the chapter with a look at the reasons for success and failure in small business.

Starting Up a Small Business

Most entrepreneurs start up a small business in one of three ways: they start from scratch, they buy an existing business, or they buy a franchise. We have already examined the "starting from scratch" alternative in detail in the preceding section, so we turn now to the latter two alternatives.

LO-4 **Buying an Existing Business** About one-third of all new businesses that were started in the past decade were bought from someone else. Many experts recommend buying an existing business because it increases the likelihood of success; it has already proven its ability to attract customers and has established relationships with lenders, suppliers, and other stakeholders. The track record also gives potential buyers a clearer picture of what to expect than any estimate of a new business's prospects.

But an entrepreneur who buys someone else's business may not be able to avoid certain problems. For example, there may be uncertainty about the exact financial shape the business is in, the business may have a poor reputation, the location may be poor, or it may be difficult to determine an appropriate purchase price.

Taking Over a Family Business A special case of buying an existing business involves family businesses. Taking over a family business poses both opportunities and challenges. On the positive side, a family business can provide otherwise unobtainable financial and management resources; it often has a valuable reputation that can result in important community and business relationships; employee loyalty is often high; and an interested, unified family management and shareholders group may emerge. Toronto-based hosiery manufacturer Phantom Industries Inc. is an example of a family-owned business that has been successful through three generations of family members.[51]

On the other hand, major problems can arise in family businesses. There may be disagreements over which family members assume control. If the parent sells his or her interest in the business, the price to be paid may be an issue. The expectation of other family members may also be problematic. Some family members may feel that they have a right to a job, promotion, and impressive title simply because they are part of the family.[52] Choosing an

appropriate successor is a key issue for continuity and it is vital to carefully groom successors over time. Finally, handling disagreements among family members about the future of the business can be a challenge. How do you fire a loved one if things are not working out?[53]

Buying a Franchise If you drive around any Canadian town or city, you will notice retail outlets with names like McDonald's, Pizza Pizza, Re/Max, Canadian Tire, Chez Cora, Comfort Inn, Second Cup, and Tim Hortons. These diverse businesses all have one thing in common: they are all franchises, operating under licences issued by parent companies to local entrepreneurs who own and manage them.

A **franchising agreement** outlines the duties and responsibilities of each party. It stipulates the amount and type of payment that franchisees must make to the franchiser. These franchise agreements have become increasingly complicated; they are often 60 or even 100 pages long. Tim Hortons avoids this trend with a streamlined contract of about 26 pages.[54] Franchisees usually make an initial payment for the right to operate an outlet. They also make royalty payment to the franchiser ranging from 2 to 30 percent of the franchisee's annual revenues or profits. The franchisee may also pay an advertising fee to the franchiser. Franchise fees vary widely, from $23 500 for a Mad Science franchise, to over $1 million for a Burger King franchise, to hundreds of millions for a professional sports franchise.

> **FRANCHISING AGREEMENT**
> Stipulates the duties and responsibilities of the franchisee and the franchiser.

Franchising is very popular in Canada. It offers individuals who want to run their own business an opportunity to establish themselves quickly in a local market.

The Advantages of Franchising

Both franchisers and franchisees benefit from the franchising way of doing business (see Table 4.4).

The Disadvantages of Franchising

There are always two sides to any story. Table 4.4 clearly outlines the obvious advantages. However, many experienced people will tell you that buying a franchise is like buying a job. The agreements are long because franchisers want to protect their image and recipes, and they want franchisees to abide by their rules. If they don't, they may be sued. If you have a great new breakfast menu idea for your store and have creative promotional ideas, then franchising may not be for you. If things go well it can be lucrative, but it is important to do your homework because there are many disappointed franchise owners out there. For example, you should carefully read the agreement and ensure that your territory is protected and that you have the right of first refusal on new potential stores within a certain distance (e.g., 10–15 kilometres or exclusivity of your particular town). Some franchisees have been shocked to see their franchiser place a new franchisee a few blocks away or even across the street. Franchisees can benefit from support and advertising, but that does not come for free. For example, a Harvey's franchisee pays a 5 percent royalty fee and a 4 percent advertising fee (based on gross sales), and these fees are payable each week in addition to regular operating costs and rent.[55] There are plenty of franchisees who belong to popular chains that are barely surviving and are wondering whatever happened to that promised success.

Is Franchising for You? Do you think you would be happy being a franchisee? The answer depends on a number of factors, including your willingness to work hard, your ability to find a good franchise to buy, and the financial resources you possess. If you are thinking seriously of going into franchising, you should consider several areas of costs that you will incur:

- the franchise sales price
- expenses that will be incurred before the business opens
- training expenses
- operational expenses for the first six months
- personal financial needs for the first six months
- emergency needs

LO-5 Forms of Business Ownership

Whether they intend to run small farms, large factories, or online e-tailers, entrepreneurs must decide which form of legal ownership best suits their goals: *sole proprietorship, partnership, corporation*, or *co-operative*.

The Sole Proprietorship The **sole proprietorship** is a business owned and operated by one person. Legally, if you set up a business as a sole proprietorship, your business is considered to be an extension of yourself

Table 4.4 The Benefits of Franchising	
For the Franchiser	**For the Franchisee**
■ The franchiser can attain rapid growth for the chain by signing up many franchisees in many different locations.	■ Franchisees own a small business that has access to big business management skills.
■ Franchisees share in the cost of advertising.	■ The franchisee does not have to build up a business from scratch.
■ The franchiser benefits from the investment money provided by franchisees.	■ Franchisee failure rates are lower than when starting one's own business.
■ Advertising money is spent more efficiently.	■ A well-advertised brand name comes with the franchise and the franchisee's outlet is instantly recognizable.
■ Franchisees are motivated to work hard for themselves, which creates profit for the franchiser.	■ The franchiser may send the franchisee to a training program run by the franchiser (e.g., the Canadian Institute of Hamburgerology run by McDonald's).
■ The franchiser is freed from all details of a local operation, which are handled by the franchisee.	■ The franchiser may visit the franchisee and provide expert advice on how to run the business.
	■ Economies in buying allow franchisees to get lower prices for the raw materials they must purchase.
	■ Financial assistance is provided by the franchiser in the form of loans; the franchiser may also help the franchisee obtain loans from local sources.
	■ Franchisees are their own bosses and get to keep most of the profit they make.

(and not a separate legal entity). Though usually small, a sole proprietorship may be as large as a steel mill or as small as a lemonade stand. While the majority of businesses in Canada are sole proprietorships, they account for only a small proportion of total business revenues.

Advantages of a Sole Proprietorship Freedom may be the most important benefit of a sole proprietorship. Sole proprietors answer to no one but themselves, since they don't share ownership. A sole proprietorship is also easy to form. If you operate the business under your own name, with no additions, you don't even need to register your business name to start operating as a sole proprietor—you can go into business simply by putting a sign on the door. The simplicity of legal setup procedures makes this form appealing to self-starters and independent spirits, as do the low start-up costs.

Another attractive feature is the tax benefits. Most businesses suffer losses in their early stages. Since the business and the proprietor are legally one and the same, these losses can be deducted from income the proprietor earns from personal sources other than the business.

Disadvantages of a Sole Proprietorship A major drawback is **unlimited liability**, which means that a sole proprietor is personally liable (responsible) for all debts incurred by the business. If the business fails to generate enough cash, bills must be paid out of the owner's pocket. Another disadvantage is lack of continuity: a sole proprietorship legally dissolves when the owner dies. Finally, a sole proprietorship depends on the resources of one person whose managerial and financial limitations may constrain the business. Sole proprietors often find it hard to borrow money to start up or expand. Many bankers fear that they won't be able to recover loans if the owner becomes disabled.

The Partnership A **partnership** is established when two or more individuals (partners) agree to combine their financial, managerial, and technical abilities for the purpose of operating a business for profit. This form of ownership is often used by professionals such as accountants, lawyers, and engineers. Partnerships are often an extension of a business that began as a sole proprietorship. The original owner may want to expand, or the business may have grown too big for a single person to handle.

There are two basic types of partners in a partnership. **General partners** are actively involved in managing the firm and have unlimited liability. **Limited partners** don't participate actively in the business, and their liability is limited to the amount they invested in the partnership. A **general partnership** is the most common type and is similar to the sole proprietorship in that all the (general) partners are jointly liable for the obligations of the business. The other type of partnership—the **limited partnership**—

consists of at least one general partner (who has unlimited liability) and one or more limited partners. The limited partners cannot participate in the day-to-day management of the business or they risk the loss of their limited liability status.

Advantages of a Partnership The most striking advantage of a general partnership is the ability to grow by adding talent and money. Partnerships also have an easier time borrowing funds than sole proprietorships. Banks and other lending institutions prefer to make loans to enterprises that are not dependent on a single individual. Partnerships can also invite new partners to join by investing money.

Like a sole proprietorship, a partnership is simple to organize, with few legal requirements. Even so, all partnerships must begin with an agreement of some kind. It may be written, oral, or even unspoken. Wise partners, however, insist on a written agreement to avoid trouble later. This agreement should answer such questions as:

- Who invested what sums of money in the partnership?

- Who will receive what share of the partnership's profits?

- Who does what and who reports to whom?

- How may the partnership be dissolved?

- How will leftover assets be distributed among the partners?

- How would surviving partners be protected from claims by surviving heirs if a partner dies?

- How will disagreements be resolved?

The partnership agreement is strictly a private document. No laws require partners to file an agreement with some government agency. Nor are partnerships regarded as legal entities. In the eyes of the law, a partnership is nothing more than two or more people working together.

UNLIMITED LIABILITY
A person who invests in a business is liable for all debts incurred by the business; personal possessions can be taken to pay debts.

PARTNERSHIP
A business with two or more owners who share in the operation of the firm and in financial responsibility for the firm's debts.

GENERAL PARTNER
A partner who is actively involved in managing the firm and has unlimited liability.

LIMITED PARTNER
A partner who generally does not participate actively in the business, and whose liability is limited to the amount invested in the partnership.

GENERAL PARTNERSHIP
A type of partnership in which all partners are jointly liable for the obligations of the business.

LIMITED PARTNERSHIP
A type of partnership with at least one general partner (who has unlimited liability) and one or more limited partners. The limited partners can not participate in the day-to-day management of the business or they risk the loss of their limited liability status.

The partnership's lack of legal standing means that the partners are taxed as individuals.

Disadvantages of a Partnership

As with sole proprietorships, unlimited liability is the greatest drawback of a general partnership. By law, each partner may be held personally liable for all debts incurred in the name of the partnership. And if any partner incurs a debt, even if the other partners know nothing about it, they are all liable if the offending partner cannot pay up. Another problem with partnerships is lack of continuity. When one partner dies or pulls out, a partnership dissolves legally, even if the other partners agree to stay to continue the business.

A related drawback is the difficulty of transferring ownership. No partner may sell out without the other partners' consent. Thus, the life of a partnership may depend on the ability of retiring partners to find someone compatible with the other partners to buy them out. Finally, a partnership provides little or no guidance in resolving conflicts between the partners. For example, suppose one partner wants to expand the business rapidly and the other wants it to grow slowly. If under the partnership agreement the two are equal, it may be difficult for them to decide what to do.

A practical illustration of the kinds of problems that can arise in partnerships is described in the Exercising Your Ethics assignment found at the end of the chapter.

The Corporation When you think of corporations you probably think of giant businesses such as Air Canada, Imperial Oil, or RIM. The very word "corporation" suggests bigness and power. Yet, the tiny corner newsstand has as much right to incorporate as does a giant oil refiner. And the newsstand and oil refiner have the same basic characteristics that all corporations share: legal status as a separate entity, property rights and obligations, and an indefinite lifespan. (See Table 4.5 for a list of the top 10 corporations in Canada.)

A corporation has been defined as "an artificial being, invisible, intangible, and existing only in contemplation of the law." As such, corporations may sue and be sued;

buy, hold, and sell property; make and sell products to consumers; and commit crimes and be tried and punished for them. Simply defined, a **corporation** is a business that is a separate legal entity, that is liable for its own debts, and whose owners' liability is limited to their investment.

Stockholders—investors who buy shares of ownership in the form of stock—are the real owners of a corporation. (The different kinds of stockholders are described in Chapter 15.) Profits may be distributed to stockholders in the form of dividends, although corporations are not required to pay dividends. Instead, they often reinvest any profits in the business. Common stockholders have the last claim to any assets if the company folds. Dividends on **common stock** are paid on a per share basis (if a dividend is declared). Thus, a shareholder with 10 shares receives 10 times the dividend paid a shareholder with one share. *Class A* common shares always have voting rights, but *Class B* common shares usually do not. Shareholder rights advocates argue that Class B common shares prevent democracy from working in companies because controlling shareholders hold most of the Class A stock and sell non-voting Class B stock to the general public. When investors cannot attend a shareholders' meeting, they can grant voting authority to someone who will attend. This procedure, called voting by *proxy*, is the way almost all individual investors vote.

The **board of directors** is the governing body of a corporation. Its main responsibility is to ensure that the corporation is run in the best interests of the stockholders. The directors choose the president and other officers of the business and delegate the power to run the day-to-day activities of the business to those officers. The directors set policy on paying dividends, on financing major spending, and on executive salaries and benefits. Large corporations tend to have large boards with as many as 20 or 30 directors. Smaller corporations, on the other

Table 4.5 Top 10 Corporations in Canada, 2009 [56]	
Company	**Sales Revenues (in billions of $)**
1. Manulife Financial Corp.	40.1
2. Royal Bank of Canada	38.1
3. Power Corp. of Canada	33.1
4. George Weston Ltd.	31.8
5. Petro-Canada	27.6
6. Sun Life Financial Inc.	27.5
7. Toronto-Dominion Bank	25.4
8. Bank of Nova Scotia	25.1
9. Suncor Energy Inc.	25.0
10. Onex Corp.	24.8

hand, tend to have no more than five directors. Usually, these are people with personal or professional ties to the corporation, such as family members, lawyers, and accountants. Each year, *The Globe and Mail* analyzes the governance practices of Canadian companies in four areas: board composition, compensation, shareholder rights, and disclosure. The top-ranked companies in 2010 were Loblaw Corp., George Weston Corp., and IamGold Corp. The lowest-ranked companies were Shaw Communications and Biovail.[57]

Inside directors are employees of the company and have primary responsibility for the corporation. That is, they are also top managers, such as the president and executive vice-president. **Outside directors** are not employees of the corporation in the normal course of its business. Attorneys, accountants, university officials, and executives from other firms are commonly used as outside directors.

Corporate officers are the top managers hired by the board to run the corporation on a day-to-day basis. The **chief executive officer (CEO)** is responsible for the firm's overall performance. Other corporate officers typically include the president, who is responsible for internal management, and various vice-presidents, who oversee functional areas such as marketing or operations.

Types of Corporations A **public corporation** is one whose shares of stock are widely held and available for sale to the general public. Anyone who has the funds to pay for them can buy shares of companies such as Petro-Canada, Bombardier, or Air Canada. The stock of a **private corporation**, on the other hand, is held by only a few people and is not generally available for sale. The controlling group may be a family, employees, or the management group. Pattison and Cirque du Soleil are two well-known Canadian private corporations.

Most new corporations start out as private corporations, because few investors will buy an unknown stock. As the corporation grows and develops a record of success, it may issue shares to the public as a way of raising additional money. This is called an **initial public offering** (IPO). IPOs are not very attractive to investors during stock market declines, but they become more popular when stock markets recover. This is one of the reasons why Porter Aviation withdrew plans for an IPO in mid-2010 because of the turbulent markets at the time.[58] However, others moved forward despite turbulent markets. Capital Power Corp. raised $500 million from its IPO and retailer Dollarama raised $300 million.[59]

A public corporation can also "go private," which is the reverse of going public. In 2008, Clearwater Seafoods announced that it would be taken private by a consortium led by Clearwater Fine Foods.[60] **Private equity firms** buy publicly traded companies and then take them private. They often make major changes to company operations in order to increase its value.

During the period from 2000 to 2005, many corporations converted to an **income trust** structure, which allowed them to avoid paying corporate income tax if they distributed all or most of their earnings to investors. For example, Bell Canada Enterprises could have avoided an $800 million tax bill in one year by becoming an income trust. The federal government estimated that it was going to lose billions of dollars of tax revenue because so many corporations were becoming income trusts. In a surprise move in 2006, the Canadian government announced that it would begin taxing income trusts more like corporations by 2011. This announcement caused a significant decline in the market value of income trusts and it also put an end to the rush to convert.[61] In 2010, income trusts were widely being ignored in the markets, however, according to Alex Sasso, of Hesperian Capital Management, there were many hidden gems in the market, such as Black Diamond Group, a provider of temporary workforce accommodation to the energy, mining, and other sectors.[62]

Formation of the Corporation The two most widely used methods to form a corporation are federal incorporation under the Canada Business Corporations Act and provincial incorporation under any of the provincial corporations acts. The former is used if the company is going to operate in more than one province; the latter is used if the founders intend to carry on business in only one province. Except for banks and certain insurance and loan companies, any company can be federally incorporated under the Canada Business Corporations Act. To do so, articles of incorporation must be drawn up. These articles include such information as the name of the corporation, the type

INSIDE DIRECTORS
Members of a corporation's board of directors who are also full-time employees of the corporation.

OUTSIDE DIRECTORS
Members of a corporation's board of directors who are not also employees of the corporation on a day-to-day basis.

CHIEF EXECUTIVE OFFICER (CEO)
The highest ranking executive in a company or organization.

PUBLIC CORPORATION
A business whose stock is widely held and available for sale to the general public.

PRIVATE CORPORATION
A business whose stock is held by a small group of individuals and is not usually available for sale to the general public.

INITIAL PUBLIC OFFERING (IPO)
Selling shares of stock in a company for the first time to a general investing public.

PRIVATE EQUITY FIRMS Companies that buy publicly traded companies and then make them private.

INCOME TRUST
A structure allowing companies to avoid paying corporate income tax if they distribute all or most of their earnings to investors.

LIMITED LIABILITY
Investor liability is limited to their personal investments in the corporation; courts cannot touch the personal assets of investors in the event that the corporation goes bankrupt.

STOCK
A share of ownership in a corporation.

DOUBLE TAXATION
A corporation must pay income taxes on its profits, and then shareholders must also pay personal income taxes on the dividends they receive from the corporation.

DIVIDENDS
The amount of money, normally a portion of the profits, that is distributed to the shareholders.

CO-OPERATIVE
An organization that is formed to benefit its owners in the form of reduced prices and/or the distribution of surpluses at year-end.

and number of shares to be issued, the number of directors the corporation will have, and the location of the company's operations. The specific procedures and information required for provincial incorporation vary from province to province.

All corporations must attach the word "Limited" (Ltd./Ltée), "Incorporated" (Inc.), or "Corporation" (Corp.) to the company name to indicate clearly to customers and suppliers that the owners have limited liability for corporate debts. The same sorts of rules apply in other countries. British firms, for example, use PLC for "public limited company" and German companies use AG for "Aktiengesellschaft" (corporation).

Advantages of Incorporation The biggest advantage of the corporate structure is **limited liability**, which means that the liability of investors is limited to their personal investment in the corporation. In the event of failure, the courts may seize a corporation's assets and sell them to pay debts, but the courts cannot touch the investors' personal possessions. If, for example, you invest $25 000 in a corporation that goes bankrupt, you may lose your $25 000, but no more. In other words, $25 000 is the extent of your liability.

Another advantage of a corporation is continuity. Because it has a legal life independent of its founders and owners, a corporation can, in theory, continue forever. Shares of stock may be sold or passed on to heirs, and most corporations also benefit from the continuity provided by professional management. Finally, corporations have advantages in raising money. By selling **stock**, they expand the number of investors and available funds. The term "stock" refers to a share of ownership in a corporation. Continuity and legal status tend to make lenders more willing to grant loans to corporations.

Disadvantages of Incorporation One of the disadvantages for a new firm in forming a corporation is the cost (approximately $2500). In addition, corporations also need legal help in meeting government regulations

because they are far more heavily regulated than are proprietorships or general partnerships. Some people say that **double taxation** is another problem with the corporate form of ownership. By this they mean that a corporation must pay income taxes on its profits, and then shareholders must also pay personal income taxes on the **dividends** they receive from the corporation. The dividend a corporation pays is the amount of money, normally a portion of the profits, that is distributed to the shareholders. Since dividends paid by the corporation are paid with after-tax dollars, this amounts to double taxation. Others point out that shareholders get a dividend tax credit, which largely offsets double taxation.

The Co-operative A **co-operative** is an incorporated form of business that is organized, owned, and democratically controlled by the people who use its products and services, and whose earnings are distributed on the basis of use of the co-operative rather than level of investment. As such, it is formed to benefit its owners in the form of reduced prices and/or the distribution of surpluses at year-end. The process works like this: Suppose some farmers believe they can get cheaper fertilizer prices if they form their own company and purchase in large volumes. They might then form a co-operative, which can be either federally or provincially chartered. Prices are generally lower to buyers and, at the end of the fiscal year, any surpluses are distributed to members on the basis of how much they purchased. If Farmer Jones bought 5 percent of all co-op sales, he would receive 5 percent of the surplus.

The co-operative's start-up capital usually comes from shares purchased by the co-operative's members. Sometimes all it takes to qualify for membership in a co-operative is the purchase of one share with a fixed (and often nominal) value. Federal co-operatives, however, can raise capital by issuing investment shares to members or non-members. Co-operatives, like investor-owned corporations, have directors and appointed officers.

Types of Co-operatives There are hundreds of different co-operatives, but they generally function in one of six main areas of business:

- *Consumer co-operatives*—These organizations sell goods to both members and the general public (e.g., Mountain Equipment Co-op).

- *Financial co-operatives*—These organizations operate much like banks, accepting deposits from members, giving loans, and providing chequing services (e.g., Vancouver City Savings Credit Union).

- *Insurance co-operatives*—These organizations provide many types of insurance coverage, such as life, fire, and liability (e.g., Co-operative Hail Insurance Company of Manitoba).

- *Marketing co-operatives*—These organizations sell the produce of their farm members and purchase inputs for the production process (e.g., seed and fertilizer). Some, like Federated Co-operatives, also purchase and market finished products.

- *Service co-operatives*—These organizations provide members with services, such as recreation.

- *Housing co-operatives*—These organizations provide housing for members, who purchase a share in the co-operative, which holds the title to the housing complex.

In terms of numbers, co-operatives are the least important form of ownership. However, they are of significance to society and to their members; they may provide services that are not readily available or that cost more than the members would otherwise be willing to pay. Table 4.6 compares the various forms of business ownership using different characteristics.

Advantages of a Co-operative Co-operatives have many of the same advantages as investor-owned corporations, such as limited liability of owners and continuity. A key benefit of a co-operative relates to its structure. Each member has only one vote in the affairs of the co-operative, regardless of how many shares he or she owns. This system prevents voting and financial control of the business by a few wealthy individuals. This is particularly attractive to the less-wealthy members of the co-operative.

Unlike corporations, which are not allowed a tax deduction on dividend payments made to shareholders, co-operatives are allowed to deduct patronage refunds to members out of before-tax income. Thus, income may be taxed only at the individual member level rather than at both the co-operative and member level.[63]

Disadvantages of a Co-operative One of the main disadvantages of co-operatives relates to attracting equity investment. Since the benefits from being a member of a co-operative arise through the level of use of the co-operative rather than the level of equity invested, members do not have an incentive to invest in equity capital of the co-operative. Another drawback is that democratic voting arrangements and dividends based purely on patronage discourage some entrepreneurs from forming or joining a co-operative.

LO-6 Success and Failure in Small Business

Of every 100 small businesses that begin operation, 96 will still be operating after one year, 85 after three years, and 67 after five years.[64] A study conducted by CIBC World Markets found that small businesses with above-average revenue growth were run by owners who had more education, used professional advisers, adopted the corporate form of ownership, did outsourcing work for other companies, had a high level of internet connectivity, and used the internet to sell outside Canada.[65]

Reasons for Success

Beyond the specific findings like the CIBC study, four general factors typically are cited to explain the success of small business owners:

1. *Hard work, drive, and dedication.* Small business owners must be committed to succeeding and be willing to put in the time and effort to make it happen. Long hours and few vacations generally characterize the first few years of new business ownership.

2. *Market demand for the product or service.* Careful analysis of market conditions can help small business people assess the probable reception of their products. If the area around a college has only one pizza parlour, a new pizzeria is more likely to succeed than if there are already 10 in operation.

3. *Managerial competence.* Successful small business people have a solid understanding of how to manage a business. They may acquire competence through training (taking courses), experience, or by using the expertise of others. Few, however, succeed alone or straight out of school. Most spend time in successful

Table 4.6 **A Comparison of Four Forms of Business Ownership**				
Characteristic	**Sole Proprietorship**	**Partnership**	**Corporation**	**Co-operative**
Protection against liability for bad debts	low	low	high	high
Ease of formation	high	high	medium	medium
Permanence	low	low	high	high
Ease of ownership transfer	low	low	high	high
Ease of raising money	low	medium	high	high
Freedom from regulation	high	high	low	medium
Tax advantages	high	high	low	high

Table 4.7 Causes of Small Business Failure

Poor management skills	Personal reasons
■ poor delegation and organizational ability ■ lack of depth in management team ■ entrepreneurial incompetence, such as a poor understanding of finances and business markets ■ lack of experience	■ loss of interest in business ■ accident, illness ■ death ■ family problems
Inadequate marketing capabilities	**Disasters**
■ difficulty in marketing product ■ market too small, non-existent, or declining ■ too much competition ■ problems with distribution systems	■ fire ■ weather ■ strikes ■ fraud by entrepreneur or others
Inadequate financial capabilities	**Other**
■ weak skills in accounting and finance ■ lack of budgetary control ■ inadequate costing systems ■ incorrect valuation of assets ■ unable to obtain financial backing	■ mishandling of large project ■ excessive standard of living ■ lack of time to devote to business ■ difficulties with associates or partners ■ government policies change
Inadequate production capabilities	
■ poorly designed production systems ■ old and inefficient production facilities and equipment ■ inadequate control over quality ■ problems with inventory control	

companies or partner with others to bring expertise to a new business.

4 *Luck.* Luck also plays a role in the success of some firms. For example, after one entrepreneur started an environmental clean-up firm, he struggled to keep his business afloat. Then the government committed a large sum of money for toxic waste clean-up. He was able to get several large contracts, and his business is now thriving.

Reasons for Failure

Small businesses fail for many *specific* reasons (see Table 4.7). Entrepreneurs may have no control over some of these factors (for example, weather, fraud, accidents),

but they can influence most items on the list. Although no set pattern has been established, four *general* factors contribute to failure:

1 *Managerial incompetence or inexperience.* Some entrepreneurs put their faith in common sense, overestimate their own managerial skills, or believe that hard work alone ensures success. If managers don't know how to make basic business decisions or don't understand basic management principles, they aren't likely to succeed in the long run.

2 *Neglect.* Some entrepreneurs try to launch ventures in their spare time, and others devote only limited time to new businesses. But starting a small business demands an overwhelming time commitment. If an entrepreneur isn't willing to put in the time and effort that a business requires, it isn't likely to survive.

3 *Weak control systems.* Effective control systems keep a business on track and alert managers to potential trouble. If the control systems don't signal impending problems, the business may be in serious trouble before obvious difficulties are spotted.

4 *Insufficient capital.* Some entrepreneurs are overly optimistic about how soon they'll start earning profits. In most cases, it takes months or even years. Amazon.com didn't earn a profit for 10 years, but obviously still required capital to pay employees and cover expenses. Experts say you need enough capital to operate six months to a year without earning a profit.[66]

On a positive note, business failures were lower than expected in the most recent recession. According to Laurie Campbell, director of the credit counselling organization Credit Canada, this was due to the fact that the recession hit the U.S. first before having an impact in Canada. Many businesses took necessary precautions to cut expenses before it hit.[67]

Summary of Learning Objectives

1. **Explain the meaning and interrelationship of the terms *small business*, *new venture creation*, and *entrepreneurship*.** A small business has less than 100 employees. A new firm is one that has become operational within the previous 12 months, has adopted any of four main organizational forms—*proprietorship, partnership, corporation,* or *co-operative*—and sells goods or services. Entrepreneurship is the *process* of identifying an opportunity in the marketplace and accessing the resources needed to capitalize on it. In relation to small and/or new businesses, entrepreneurship is the process by which a small business or a new business is created.

2. **Describe the role of small and new businesses in the Canadian economy.** While 98 percent of employer businesses in Canada are small (less than 100 employees), about half of the total private sector labour force work for small businesses. The distribution of employment by size of firm varies across industries. The small business sector's capacity for entrepreneurship and innovation accounts for much of the job creation; this sector contributes to the economy, with start-ups accounting for most of the growth. Women are playing a major role in the growth of small businesses.

3. **Explain the *entrepreneurial process* and describe its three key elements.** The entrepreneurial process occurs within a social, political, and economic context and consists of three key elements: the *entrepreneur,* the *opportunity,* and *resources*. Entrepreneurs typically access the various resources needed by bootstrapping—doing more with less. These resources are both financial and non-financial. Two types of financing—*debt* and *equity*—can be accessed from a range of sources.

4. **Describe three alternative strategies for becoming a business owner—*starting from scratch, buying an existing business,* and *buying a franchise*.** It is necessary to work through the entrepreneurial process in order to *start a business from scratch.* Whether start-up efforts will result in a new business often depends upon how well matched the entrepreneur's skills and abilities are with the opportunity and the resources required, as well as how well matched the opportunity and resources are. Some new ventures will grow; others will decline, die, or remain stable. Generally, when someone buys an *existing business,* the odds of success are better because

it has existing customers; established relationships (e.g., lenders, suppliers), and an existing track record. Potential buyers have a clearer picture of what to expect. However, the business may have a poor reputation, poor location, and it may be difficult to determine an appropriate purchase price. A special case of buying an existing business involves family businesses, which pose both opportunities and challenges. In buying a *franchise* the buyer (franchisee) purchases the right to sell the product or service of the seller (franchiser) according to the terms of the franchising agreement. In return the franchiser provides assistance with the business's start-up as well as with ongoing operations once the business opens its doors.

5. **Describe four forms of *legal organization* for a business and discuss the advantages and disadvantages of each.** *Sole proprietorships* are owned and operated by one person, are easy to set up, have low start-up costs, enjoy tax benefits, and their owners enjoy freedom. However, sole proprietorships have unlimited liability, a lack of continuity, and limited resources.

    Under a *general partnership* all partners have unlimited liability. Partnerships may lack continuity, and transferring ownership may be difficult. On the positive side, partnerships can grow by adding new talent and money, partners are taxed as individuals, and banks prefer to make loans to enterprises that are not dependent on one individual. All partnerships should have a partnership agreement.

    Corporations are separate legal entities, they have property rights and obligations, and they have indefinite life spans. They may sue and be sued; buy, hold, and sell property; make and sell products; commit crimes and be tried and punished for them. The biggest advantage of incorporation is limited liability. Other advantages include continuity, professional management, and improved ability to raise money by selling stock. Disadvantages of the corporation include high start-up costs, complexity, and *double taxation*. The vast majority of corporations are privately held. In forming a corporation, a business will incorporate federally if it is going to operate in more than one province and provincially if it is going to operate in only one province.

    A *co-operative* is an organization that is formed to benefit its owners in the form of reduced prices and/or the distribution of surpluses at year-end. On the positive side, co-operatives are democratically controlled, enjoy limited liability, continuity, and are not subject to double taxation. The main disadvantages include difficulty in raising equity. Co-operatives usually function in one of six areas of business: consumer co-operatives, financial co-operatives, insurance co-operatives, marketing co-operatives, service co-operatives, or housing co-operatives.

6. **Identify four key reasons for success in small businesses and four key reasons for failure.** Four basic factors explain most small-business success: (1) hard work, drive, and dedication; (2) market demand for the products or services being provided; (3) managerial competence; and (4) luck. Four factors contribute to small-business failure: (1) managerial incompetence or inexperience; (2) neglect; (3) weak control systems; and (4) insufficient capital.

Questions and Exercises

Questions for Analysis

1. What are some of the problems that are encountered when we try to define the term "small business"?

2. Why are new ventures the main source of job creation and new product/service ideas?

3. Do you think that you would be a successful entrepreneur? Why or why not?

4. Consider a new product or service that has recently become available for purchase by consumers. To what extent did this product or service possess the "screening" characteristics that are described in the chapter (adding value, providing competitive advantage, etc.)?

5. Using the product or service you described in Question 4, analyze the extent to which there is a good "fit" between the various elements in the entrepreneurial process.

6. Why might a private corporation choose to remain private? Why might it choose to "go public"?

Application Exercises

7. Identify three trends—whether in fashion, lifestyle, or something else—and describe at least five ideas for capitalizing on one of them.

8. Find a newspaper or magazine article that describes someone who is an entrepreneur. Use the information provided to explain what makes this person an entrepreneur.

9. Spend some time watching what people do and how they do it, and then (a) identify two ways to make what they do easier, and (b) describe two problems you observed and identify strategies for resolving those problems.

10. Interview the owners of several small businesses in your local area. Ask them what they have done to make their businesses more environmentally friendly. If they have not done anything, ask them what has prevented them from taking the initiative to be more environmentally friendly.

TEAM EXERCISES

Building Your Business Skills

Working the Internet

Goal

To encourage students to define opportunities and problems for small companies doing business on the internet.

Situation

Suppose you and two partners own a gift basket store, specializing in special-occasion baskets for individual and corporate clients. Your business is doing well in your community, but you believe there may be opportunity for growth through a virtual storefront on the internet.

Method

Step 1 Join with two other students and assume the role of business partners. Start by researching internet businesses. Look at books and articles at the library and search the following websites for help:

■ Canada Business Service Centres: www.canadabusiness.ca/eng/

- Small Business Administration (United States): www.sba.gov
- IBM Small Business Center: www.businesscenter.ibm.com
- Apple Small Business Home Page: www.apple.com/business/

These sites may lead you to other sites, so keep an open mind.

Step 2 Based on your research, determine the importance of the following small business issues:

- An analysis of changing company finances as a result of internet applications
- An analysis of your new competitive marketplace (the world) and how it affects your current marketing approach, which focuses on your local community

- Identification of sources of management advice as the expansion proceeds
- The role of technology consultants in launching and maintaining the website
- Customer service policies in your virtual environment

Follow-Up Questions

1. Do you think your business would be successful on the internet? Why or why not?

2. Based on your analysis, how will extended internet applications affect your current business practices? What specific changes are you likely to make?

3. Do you think that operating a virtual storefront will be harder or easier than doing business in your local community? Explain your answer.

Exercising Your Ethics

Public or Private? That Is the Question

The Situation

The Thomas Corporation is a very well-financed private corporation with a solid and growing product line, little debt, and a stable workforce. However, in the past few months, there has been a growing rift among the board of directors that has created considerable differences of opinion as to the future direction of the firm.

The Dilemma

Some board members believe the firm should "go public" with a stock offering. Since each board member owns a large block of corporate stock, each would make a considerable amount of money if the company went public. Other board members want to maintain the status quo as a private corporation. The biggest advantage of this approach is that the firm maintains its current ability to remain autonomous in its operations. The third faction of the board also wants to remain private but clearly has a different agenda. Those board members have identified a small public corporation that is currently one of the company's key suppliers. Their idea is to buy the supplying company, shift its assets to the parent firm, sell all of its remaining operations, terminate employees, and then outsource the production of the parts it currently buys from the firm. Their logic is that the firm would gain significant assets and lower its costs.

Team Activity

Assemble a group of four students and assign each group member to one of the following roles:

- An employee at the Thomas Corporation
- A customer of the Thomas Corporation
- An investor in the Thomas Corporation
- A board member who has not yet decided which option is best

Action Steps

1. Before discussing the situation with your group, and from the perspective of your assigned role, decide which option you think is best. Write down the reasons for your position.

2. Before discussing the situation with your group, and from the perspective of your assigned role, identify the underlying ethical issues, if any, in this situation. Write down the issues.

3. Gather your group together and reveal each member's comments on the situation. Next, reveal the ethical issues listed by each member.

4. Appoint someone to record the main points of agreement and disagreement. How do you explain the results? What accounts for any disagreement?

5. From an ethical standpoint, what is the most appropriate action that should be taken by the Thomas Corporation in this situation?

6. Develop a group response to the following question: What do you think most people would do in this situation?

Family Business

Family businesses are a prominent feature in many countries of the world. Most family businesses are small, but some are very large. In addition to the usual challenges facing business firms, family businesses often are threatened by disagreements between family members about how the business should be run. Here are some classic examples.

The Irving Family

The Irving family of New Brunswick is one of the great success stories of Canadian business. The company owns scores of businesses in oil refining, forestry, shipbuilding, food processing, publishing, transportation, and home improvement. The business was started in the nineteenth century by J.D. Irving and was expanded by his son K.C. The empire is now run by K.C.'s three sons, Arthur, J.K., and Jack, who are all in their seventies. Recently, it became clear that J.K.'s son Jim and Arthur's son Kenneth were competing for a chance to shape the company's fortunes, and they disagreed over the strategic direction the company should take. That disagreement drove a wedge between J.K. and his brothers.

This is a new situation for the Irving family, which has always presented a remarkably united front. The three brothers have a great deal of respect for each other, so when these succession tensions developed, they decided they would try to amicably divide the businesses. The energy business will go to Arthur's family, and the forestry business to J.K.'s family. Their approach contrasts sharply with what happened to the McCain family, another New Brunswick business dynasty.

The McCain Family

For many years, brothers Wallace and Harrison McCain were the key players at McCain Foods Ltd., the world's largest French fry producer. But in the mid-1990s, the two brothers had a falling out over the question of who would succeed Harrison as the CEO. Wallace wanted his son Michael to get the job, but Harrison wanted someone from outside the family to take over. After a nasty battle, Wallace was removed from the firm. He then took over Maple Leaf Foods and his son Michael eventually became CEO of that company.

The Mitchell Family

Mitchell's Gourmet Foods Inc. was a Saskatchewan-based family business. A family feud developed when

Fred Mitchell claimed that his mother and his brother Charles were trying to take control of the business from him. Both sides in the dispute then sued each other. An accommodation of sorts was reached when the disputing parties agreed to divide up the assets of the company. Fred (and his wife, LuAn) kept Mitchell's, and Charles (and his wife, Camille) kept a beef plant the company owned.

The Antinori Family

Some family businesses manage to avoid feuds. The Antinori family business in Florence, Italy, has been making wine since 1385, and for 26 generations the family has somehow managed to pass on management of the company to the next generation without getting in a big fight. How do they do it? By going against conventional wisdom—which says that you should clearly separate the family's interest from the interest of the business—and instead blurring the two interests as much as possible. For example, the current CEO and his wife live on the top two floors of their fifteenth-century mansion, and the business operates on the bottom two floors. Perhaps more importantly, the company plans far into the future for a company the grandchildren can run.

Maybe there is something about the wine business that makes family feuds less likely. For example, Catherine and Anne Monna and their father, Bernard, run Cassis Monna & Filles near Quebec City. The sisters are the fifth generation of the family to be involved in the wine business.

Questions for Discussion

1. How is running a family business different from creating a business from scratch? What are the advantages? What are the disadvantages?

2. It seems as though the Antinori family has found a way to ensure that the entrepreneurial spirit is transferred from generation to generation in a positive manner. But this contrasts heavily with the experiences of many family businesses, even some of the biggest success stories. Are entrepreneurs born to be entrepreneurs or can they be created?

3. How does financing a family business differ from financing a franchise or a new start-up? Outline the unique challenges in each of these situations.

SCANLIFE

chapter

5

The Global Context of Business

After reading this chapter, you should be able to:

LO-1 Describe the rise of international business and identify the *major world marketplaces*.

LO-2 Explain how different forms of *competitive advantage, import–export balances, exchange rates*, and *foreign competition determine how countries* and businesses respond to the international environment.

LO-3 Discuss the factors involved in conducting business internationally and in selecting the *appropriate levels of international involvement and organizational structure*.

LO-4 Describe some of the ways in which *social, cultural, economic, legal, and political differences* act as barriers to international trade.

LO-5 Explain how *free trade agreements* assist world trade.

SCANLIFE

Tim Hortons USA: Exporting a Strategic Model Is No Easy Task

When you think of Tim Hortons, what images come to mind? Students typically use the following words: hockey, Timbits, maple, Canada, doughnuts, coffee, Sidney Crosby, inexpensive. Tim Hortons is very successful in Canada, and its doughnuts have become the Canadian equivalent of American apple pie or the Big Mac. The company has worked hard to create a warm, homegrown image in the minds of the Canadian consumer. Its low-cost/high-volume approach, its tremendous channel domination, and its unapologetic links to Canadian symbols are all sources of competitive advantage for Tim Hortons in Canada. According to the website, Tim Hortons is the fourth largest quick-service restaurant chain in North America. It is the largest in Canada with over 3000 stores. To put this figure into perspective, McDonald's has approximately 1400 stores in Canada. But can Tim Hortons successfully export its business model to the U.S.?

The Challenge

The first U.S. Tim Hortons opened in Buffalo, New York, in 1984, and there are now 563 stores in 12 northern U.S. states. Recently the company announced plans to open 300 new U.S. stores, and it now seems ready for a more concentrated push into the U.S. But what approach should be used? Should the same standardized approach that has worked in Canada be used or will the model have to be adapted for the U.S. market? For obvious reasons, Tim Hortons has not focused on hockey and Canadian symbols to sell

How Will This Help Me?

Whether you see yourself living abroad, working for a big company, or starting your own business, the global economy will affect you in some way. Exchange rates for different currencies and global markets for buying and selling affect everyone, regardless of their role or perspective. The material in this chapter will help you to (1) understand how global forces impact you as a *customer*, (2) understand how globalization affects you as an *employee*, and (3) assess how global opportunities and challenges can affect you as a business owner and as an *investor*.

its doughnuts and coffee in the U.S. It might try to replace hockey with baseball, but Dunkin' Donuts already has strong grassroots links to that sport. It could wrap itself in the U.S. flag, but that would leave it open to charges of being fake, and that approach might also confuse or upset Canadians who visit the U.S. Another problem: Tim Hortons cannot rely on a large marketing channel advantage in the United States. In Canada, there is one Tim Hortons for every 11 000 consumers, but this is not the case across the border. In the U.S., there are thousands of local coffee shops in addition to major players like Dunkin' Donuts, Starbucks, and even McDonald's (especially with its recent McCafé push). In the U.S., these companies have the sort of market penetration that Tim Hortons enjoys in Canada.

So, what can be done? Until now, Tim Hortons' central message in the United States has focused on value and freshness. This was not a very original idea, but at least it was an honest approach. Unfortunately, this hasn't differentiated Tim Hortons from its competitors. Something else is needed. But what? The company is now pursuing several strategies, including the acquisition of prime locations, co-branding, and going upscale.

Acquiring Prime Locations

In 2009, Tim Hortons opened its first outlets in New York City after reaching an agreement with a former Dunkin' Donuts franchisee who owned 12 prime locations in Manhattan and Brooklyn. This gave Tim Hortons a great opportunity to develop its brand and gain exposure in this key market because prime locations are difficult to find, especially in New York City. The fact that people were already accustomed to going to these particular locations for their coffee fix should also help. As a result of this deal, Tim Hortons has some much-needed exposure, including a location in Madison Square Garden.

Co-Branding

Also in 2009, Tim Hortons and Kahala Corporation, owner of the Cold Stone Creamery—an ice cream parlour franchise—announced a co-branding agreement that would see the development of up to 100 combined stores in the U.S. At the same time, approximately 60 outlets across Canada were converted to test this new co-branded format. This should help Tim Hortons to get noticed and to improve its competitive position in the U.S. market.

Going Upscale

In 2010, Tim Hortons announced that it was planning to create upscale café/bake shops with a different menu that would include pastries baked onsite. These new stores were scheduled to open in existing markets such as New York and Michigan. The announcement raised several new questions. Could a high-end Tim Hortons work? How would the company manage the traditional stores alongside the new outlets? Would there be a sub-brand created or would it eventually transform all U.S. locations? This strategy should help relieve some of the stress of the rising food costs that have recently been squeezing low-cost food providers like Tim Hortons. But can the company manage the brand and not confuse consumers? Time will tell.

Tim Hortons is taking a concept that has worked in Canada and is trying to make it work in a foreign market. In order to succeed, Tim Hortons must develop a clear strategy that U.S. consumers can identify with. That approach is what made the company successful in Canada. Succeeding in new markets is not easy!

The Contemporary Global Economy

The total volume of world trade today is immense—around $8 trillion each year. As more firms engage in international business, the world economy is fast becoming a single interdependent system—a process called **globalization**. Even so, we often take for granted the diversity of goods and services available as a result of international trade. Your television set, your shoes, and even the roast lamb on your dinner table may all be **imports**—that is, products made or grown abroad but sold in Canada. At the same time, the success of many Canadian firms depends on **exports**—products made or grown domestically and shipped abroad.

In early 2010, China officially passed Germany as the world's top merchandise exporter; this was a clear sign of the importance of international trade.[1] However, trade between nations can be traced back at least as far as 2000 BCE, when North African tribes took dates and clothing to Assyria and Babylonia in the Middle East and traded them for olive oil and spices. International business is nothing new. But international trade has become increasingly central to the fortunes of most nations of the world, as well as businesses. Whereas in the past many nations followed strict policies to protect domestic companies, today more and more countries are aggressively encouraging international trade. They are opening their borders to foreign businesses, offering incentives for their own domestic businesses to expand internationally, and making it easier for foreign firms to partner with local firms through various alliances.

Several forces have combined to spark and sustain globalization. For one thing, governments and businesses have simply become more aware of the benefits of globalization to their countries and stockholders. For another, new technologies have made international travel, communication, and commerce easier, faster, and cheaper than ever before. Overseas phone calls and seaborne shipping costs per tonne have both declined sharply over the last several decades. Likewise, transatlantic travel once required several days aboard a ship. Today, conventional transatlantic travel takes less than a day. The internet has also torn down barriers for large and small companies. Finally, there are competitive pressures: sometimes, a firm simply must enter foreign markets just to keep up with its competitors.

Globalization is not without its critics, who charge that it allows businesses to exploit workers in less developed countries and bypass domestic environmental and tax regulations. They also charge that globalization leads to the loss of cultural heritages and often benefits the rich more than the poor. As a result, many international gatherings of global economic leaders—including the G8 and G20 meetings in Toronto in 2010—have been marked by protests and demonstrations. But despite fears and apprehensions, globalization is part of our existence and there are some interesting trends emerging. A *Globe and Mail* article listed five key trends based on a report from McKinsey: (1) the economic centre of gravity will shift away from North America/Europe/Japan to Asia and Latin America, (2) the productivity imperative (improved productivity

GLOBALIZATION Process by which the world economy is becoming a single interdependent system.

IMPORT Product made or grown abroad but sold domestically.

EXPORT Product made or grown domestically but shipped and sold abroad.

Advocates of globalization argue that increased international commerce benefits all sectors of society and should be actively encouraged. But critics, like these protestors, argue that globalization benefits only big business and is eroding distinctive national cultures.

is essential to compete in the highly competitive marketplace), (3) the global grid (increasing complex global networks of people and capital), (4) environmental sustainability will take on even more importance, and (5) there will be increased controls on businesses and markets as governments try to cope with the financial crisis.[2]

LO-1   The Major World Marketplaces

The World Bank, an agency of the United Nations, uses **per-capita income**—average income per person—to make distinctions among countries. Its current classification method consists of four categories of countries:[3]

1. *High-income countries:* have an annual per-capita income greater than U.S. $11 906. They include Canada, the United States, most countries in Europe, Australia, New Zealand, Japan, South Korea, Kuwait, the United Arab Emirates, Israel, Singapore, and Oman.

2. *Upper middle-income countries:* have an annual per-capita income between U.S. $3856 and U.S. $11 905. This group includes Columbia, Peru, Lebanon, Hungary, Poland, Turkey, Mexico, Argentina, and South Africa.

3. *Low middle-income countries:* have an annual per-capita income between U.S. $976 and U.S. $3855. This group includes Côte d'Ivoire, Guatemala, Samoa, and Thailand.

4. *Low-income countries* (often called *developing countries*): have an annual per-capita income of U.S. $975 or less. Benin, Ethiopia, Haiti, and Vietnam are among the countries in this group. Due to low literacy rates, weak infrastructures, unstable governments, and related problems, these countries are less attractive for international business. For example, the East African nation of Somalia is plagued by drought, civil war, and starvation, and plays virtually no role in the world economy.

Geographic Clusters   The world economy revolves around three major marketplaces: North America, Europe, and Asia. These clusters include relatively more of the upper-middle and high-income nations, but relatively few low- and low-middle-income countries. For instance, because Africa consists primarily of low- and low-middle-income countries, it is not generally seen as a major marketplace. The three geographic regions that do warrant this designation are home to most of the world's largest economies, biggest corporations, most influential financial markets, and highest-income consumers.

North America   The United States dominates the North American business region. It is the single largest marketplace and still enjoys the most stable economy in the world. Canada also plays a major role in the global economy. Moreover, the United States and Canada are each other's largest trading partner. Many U.S. firms, such as General Motors and Procter & Gamble, have maintained successful Canadian operations for decades, and many Canadian firms, such as Research In Motion and Scotiabank, are also major international competitors.

Mexico has become a major manufacturing centre, especially along the U.S. border, where cheap labour and low transportation costs have encouraged many firms from the United States and other countries to build factories. The auto industry has been especially active, with Daimler, General Motors, Volkswagen, Nissan, and Ford all running large assembly plants in the region. Several major suppliers have also built facilities in the area. But Mexico's role as a low-cost manufacturing centre may be usurped by China as companies begin shifting production from Mexico to China.[4]

Europe   Europe is often seen as two regions—Western and Eastern. Western Europe, dominated by Germany, the United Kingdom, France, Spain, and Italy, has long been a mature but fragmented marketplace. But the transformation of this region via the European Union (EU) (discussed later in this chapter) into an integrated economic system has further increased its importance. Major international firms, such as Unilever, Renault, Royal Dutch/Shell, Michelin, Siemens, and Nestlé, are headquartered in Western Europe.

E-commerce and technology have also become increasingly important in this region. There has been a surge in internet start-ups in southeastern England, the Netherlands, and the Scandinavian countries, and Ireland is now one of the world's largest exporters of software. Strasbourg, France, is a major centre for biotech start-ups; Barcelona, Spain, has many flourishing software and internet companies; and the Frankfurt region of Germany is dotted with both software and biotech start-ups.

Eastern Europe, once primarily Communist, has also gained importance, both as a marketplace and as a producer. Multinational corporations such as Nestlé, General Motors, and ABB Asea Brown Boveri have all set up operations in Poland. Ford, General Motors, Suzuki, and Volkswagen have all built new factories in Hungary. On the other hand, governmental instability has hampered development in Bulgaria, Albania, Romania, and other countries.

Pacific Asia Pacific Asia consists of Japan, China, Thailand, Malaysia, Singapore, Indonesia, South Korea, Taiwan, the Philippines, and Australia (which is technically not in Asia but is included because of proximity). Some experts still distinguish Hong Kong, though now part of China, as a part of the region, and others include Vietnam. Fuelled by strong entries in the automobile, electronics, and banking industries, the economies of these countries grew rapidly in the past three decades. A currency crisis in the late 1990s slowed growth in virtually every country of the region, but that crisis ran its course, and most of these countries, especially Japan and China, have since flourished.

As the trends indicate, Pacific Asia is a growing force in the world economy and a major source of competition for North American companies. The Japanese dominate the region, led by firms such as Toyota, Toshiba, and Nippon Steel. However, South Korea (with major manufacturers Samsung and Hyundai), Taiwan (with Chinese Petroleum and manufacturing for foreign firms), and Hong Kong (a major financial centre) are also successful players in the global economy. China, the world's most densely populated country, has emerged as an important market and now boasts the world's third-largest economy behind that of the United States and only slightly behind that of Japan.[5]

As in North America and Europe, technology is playing an increasingly important role in the future of this region.

In some parts of Asia, however, the emergence of technology firms has been hampered by poorly developed electronic infrastructures, slower adoption of computers and information technology, and a higher percentage of lower-income consumers.

> **BRIC** A term used to describe four important and powerful emerging markets in the business world: Brazil, Russia, India, and China.

The Rising Power of Emerging Markets: The Role of BRIC

BRIC is the term that is often used in international trade magazines and newspapers to describe the increasing importance of four specific nations in global trade: *Brazil, Russia, India,* and *China.* The BRIC concept was first used by Goldman Sachs in 2001; since that time BRIC investment funds have become an important group for money managers and international analysts. These four nations have even begun to act like a unit, and an unofficial BRIC meeting took place in 2009.

The status of these four nations has risen in international trade for different reasons. Brazil is strong in commodities and agriculture, Russia is a powerful energy supplier, and China is a major hub of manufacturing activity. India has become a leading service provider at various levels ranging from basic customer service call centres to engineering solutions providers. The growth and quick market development of the consumer market in these four nations is also providing tremendous sales opportunities for foreign companies in many industries, including car manufacturing and high-end clothing brands.[6]

The old international trading patterns and activities are changing. Once upon a time, Western companies used less developed markets to acquire natural resources supplies and to carry out simple assembly tasks. But these four nations now demonstrate relationships that are much more complex. A clear signal of this shift was evident a couple of years ago, when Indian car maker Tata acquired

The growth in international commerce has led to the emergence of several major marketplaces. Much of the international commerce in these marketplaces, in turn, is managed from major cities. Traditional centres of international commerce include New York, London, Paris, Brussels, and Tokyo. In recent years, though, cities like Shanghai, Beijing, Hong Kong, Dubai, Vancouver, Bangalore, and Kuala Lumpur have taken on increased importance. For example, international business now defines the glittering skyline of Shanghai.

ABSOLUTE ADVANTAGE
The ability to produce something more efficiently than any other country.

COMPARATIVE ADVANTAGE
The ability to produce some products more efficiently than others.

NATIONAL COMPETITIVE ADVANTAGE
International competitive advantage stemming from a combination of factor conditions; demand conditions; related and supporting industries; and firm strategies, structures, and rivalries.

Jaguar and Land Rover from Ford. Earlier that year, Tata Steel bought the Anglo Dutch steel maker Corus Group LLC for US$12.1 billion. This was not quite business as usual.[7]

Of the four countries, Russia has encountered the most profound troubles in recent years. Some analysts have even called for the exclusion of Russia from this supergroup. Among the reasons cited were corruption and excessive levels of bureaucratic red tape. For example, in 10 years in the Russian market, IKEA had been able to open only 11 stores despite major efforts to expand. Frustrated by the red tape, IKEA put further investment in Russia on hold.[8]

While China, India, and Russia have had most of the attention, it is Brazil that is now at the front of the pack in terms of optimism and opportunity. In the first quarter of 2010, Brazil's economy expanded by an impressive 9 percent, which continued a positive trend despite the world economic crisis; the growth rate averaged 10 percent for the previous three quarters as well. This was based on positive domestic demand and high levels of investment. According to Transparency International, Brazil is the least corrupt of the four BRIC nations. Brazil's rich natural resources and momentum from World Cup 2014 should help propel it for years to come.[9]

While the BRIC nations have received a lot of publicity, there are tremendous opportunities and stories of development in many nations, including South Africa, Thailand, Indonesia, and Ukraine, to name just a few. A new world order is slowly emerging, and "old" economic powers like the U.S., Japan, Germany, and even Canada are going to have to adapt.

LO-2 Forms of Competitive Advantage

No country can produce all the goods and services that its people need. Thus, countries tend to export products that they can produce better or less expensively than other countries. The proceeds are then used to import products that they cannot produce effectively. However, this general principle does not fully explain why nations export and import. Such decisions hinge partly on the kind of advantages a particular country may enjoy regarding its abilities to create and/or sell various products and resources.[10] Traditionally, economists have focused on *absolute* and *comparative advantage* to explain international trade. But because this approach focuses narrowly on such factors as natural resources and labour costs, the more contemporary view of *national competitive advantage* has emerged.

Absolute Advantage An **absolute advantage** exists when a country can produce something more cheaply and/or of higher quality than any other country. Saudi oil, Brazilian coffee beans, and Canadian timber approximate absolute advantage, but examples of true absolute advantage are rare. In reality, "absolute" advantages are always relative. For example, most experts say that the vineyards of France produce the finest wines in the world. But the growing wine businesses in California and Ontario attest to the fact that producers there can also produce very good values in wine—wines that are perhaps almost as good as French wines and that also are available in more varieties and at lower prices.

Comparative Advantage A country has a **comparative advantage** in goods that it can produce more efficiently or better than other goods. For example, if businesses in a given country can make computers more efficiently than they can make automobiles, that nation's firms have a comparative advantage in computer manufacturing. Canada has a comparative advantage in farming (because of fertile land and a temperate climate), while South Korea has a comparative advantage in electronics manufacturing (because of efficient operations and cheap labour). As a result, Canadian firms export grain to South Korea and import electronic equipment from South Korea. All countries have a comparative advantage in *some* products, but no country has a comparative advantage in *all* products. Developed countries tend to have a comparative advantage in making high-tech products, while developing countries tend to have a comparative advantage in making products that require lots of low-cost labour.

National Competitive Advantage In recent years, a theory of national competitive advantage has become a more widely accepted model of why nations engage in international trade.[11] **National competitive advantage** derives from four conditions:

1. *Factor conditions* are the factors of production that we identified in Chapter 1.

2. Demand conditions *reflect a large domestic consumer base that promotes strong demand for innovative products.*

3 Related and supporting industries *include strong local or regional suppliers and/or industrial customers.*

4 *Strategies*, *structures*, and *rivalries* refer to firms and industries that stress cost reduction, product quality, higher productivity, and innovative new products.

When all of these conditions exist in an industry, the companies in that industry are motivated to be very innovative and to excel. This, in turn, increases the likelihood that they will engage in international business. Japan, for instance, has strong domestic demand for automobiles. Its automobile producers have well-developed supplier networks, and Japanese firms have competed intensely with each other for decades. This set of circumstances explains why Japanese automobile companies such as Toyota, Honda, Nissan, and Mazda are generally successful in foreign markets.

International competitiveness refers to the ability of a country to generate more wealth than its competitors in world markets. Each year, the World Economic Forum publishes a global competitiveness ranking. The ranking is based on both hard economic data and on a poll of business leaders in many countries. In 2009, the top three countries on the list were Switzerland, the United States, and Singapore. Canada ranked ninth. Canada's high taxes, regulated industries, relatively large bureaucracy, and overly conservative capital market structure were listed as reasons for a lower rating.[12]

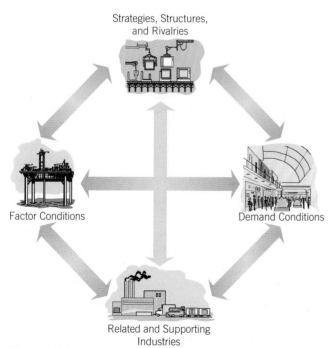

Figure 5.1
Attributes of national competitive advantage.

The Balance of Trade

A country's **balance of trade** is the difference in value between its total exports and its total imports. A country that exports more than it imports has a *favourable* balance of trade, or a **surplus**. A country that imports more than it exports has an *unfavourable* balance of trade, or a **deficit**. Canada has enjoyed a favourable balance of merchandise trade for many years, but in 2009, we had a trade deficit of $4.8 billion. The United States is by far the largest trading partner Canada has, and our overall trade balance has been generally favourable only because Canada exports so much more to the United States than it imports from it. But this is changing, partly due to the higher Canadian dollar. For years, economists had warned against Canada's dependence on the United States. Canada's nearly $47 billion surplus in 2008 turned into a deficit in large part because of a major decline in exports to the U.S. In addition, we import more from the countries of the European Union and Japan than we export to those countries, and we also import more than we export from all other countries as well (see Table 5.1).

The Balance of Payments

Even if a country has a favourable balance of trade, it can still have an unfavourable **balance of payments**. A country's balance of payments is the difference between money flowing into the country and money flowing out

INTERNATIONAL COMPETITIVENESS Competitive marketing of domestic products against foreign products.

BALANCE OF TRADE The economic value of all the products that a country exports minus the economic value of all the products it imports.

SURPLUS Situation in which a country exports more than it imports, creating a favourable balance of trade.

DEFICIT Situation in which a country's imports exceed its exports, creating a negative balance of trade.

BALANCE OF PAYMENTS Flow of all money into or out of a country.

Table 5.1 Canadian Exports to and Imports from Selected Countries, 2009

Country	Exports to (in billions of $)	Imports from (in billions of $)
United States	271.2	236.5
European Union	32.1	38.7
Japan	8.8	9.3
All others	57.4	89.6

of the country as a result of trade and other transactions. An unfavourable balance means more money is flowing out than in. For Canada to have a favourable balance of payments for a given year, the total of our exports, foreign-tourist spending in this country, foreign investments here, and earnings from overseas investments must be greater than the total of our imports, Canadian-tourist spending overseas, our foreign aid grants, our military spending abroad, the investments made by Canadian firms abroad, and the earnings of foreigners from their investments in this country. Canada has had an unfavourable balance of payments for the last two decades, but it is slowly improving. In 1999, for example, $142 billion more flowed out of Canada than flowed in, but in 2009, that amount was $103 billion.[13]

Exchange Rates

An **exchange rate** is the rate at which the currency of one nation can be exchanged for another.[14] For example, if the exchange rate between Canadian dollars and British pounds is 1 to 1.55, this means that it costs $1.55 in Canadian dollars to "buy" one British pound. Alternatively, it would cost only 0.65 of a British pound to "buy" one Canadian dollar. This exchange rate means that 0.65 of a British pound and one Canadian dollar should have exactly the same purchasing power.

The value of one country's currency relative to that of another country varies with market conditions. For example, when many English citizens want to spend pounds to buy Canadian dollars (or goods), the value of the dollar relative to the pound increases, or becomes "stronger"; *demand* for the Canadian dollar is high. It is also "strong" when there is high demand for goods manufactured in Canada. Thus, the value of the Canadian dollar rises with the demand for Canadian goods. Exchange rates typically fluctuate by very small amounts on a daily basis. More significant variations usually occur over greater spans of time.

Fluctuation in exchange rates can have an important impact on the balance of trade. Suppose, for example, that you wanted to buy some English tea for 10 British pounds per box. At an exchange rate of 1.55 Canadian dollars to the British pound, a box will cost you $15.50 (10 pounds × 1.55 = 15.50). But what if the pound gets stronger? At an exchange rate of, say, 2.1 Canadian dollars to the pound, the same box of tea would cost you $21.00 (10 pounds × 2.1 = $21.00).

Changes in the exchange rate affect more than just the price of tea. If instead the Canadian dollar gets stronger in relation to the British pound, the prices of all Canadian-made products would rise in England and the prices of all English-made products would fall in Canada. As a result, the English would buy fewer Canadian-made products, and Canadians would spend more on English-made products. The result could conceivably be a Canadian trade deficit with England. This is why the recent increase in the value of the Canadian dollar has Canadian exporters very concerned.

One of the most significant developments in foreign exchange has been the introduction of the **euro**—a common currency among 16 members of the European Union (Denmark, Sweden, and the United Kingdom do not participate). The euro was officially introduced back in 2002. The Euro has quickly become as important as the U.S. dollar and the Japanese yen in international commerce. The euro has risen in value against the U.S. and Canadian dollars since its inception. It actually stood as high as $1.73 against the Canadian dollar in 2008; however, there was a sharp drop in the Euro currency in 2010—to $1.25. This raised fears about the stability of the Eurozone (see the Managing in Turbulent Times boxed feature entitled "The Crisis in Europe").

Exchange Rates and Competition Companies that conduct international operations must watch exchange-rate fluctuations closely because these changes affect overseas demand for their products and can be a major factor in international competition. In general, when the value of a country's domestic currency rises—becomes "stronger"—companies based there find it harder to export products to foreign markets and easier for foreign companies to enter local markets. It also makes it more cost-efficient for domestic companies to move production operations to lower-cost sites in foreign countries. When the value of a country's currency declines—becomes "weaker"—just the opposite patterns occur. Thus, as the value of a country's currency falls, its balance of trade should improve because domestic companies should experience a boost in exports. There should also be a corresponding decrease in the incentives for foreign companies to ship products into the domestic market.

A good case in point is the fluctuation in the Canadian dollar relative to the American dollar. About a decade ago, as we entered the new millennium, Canadians had grown accustomed to a weak dollar—in the 65–70 cent range against the U.S. dollar. The thought of a dollar at parity with the American dollar was almost unthinkable. Yet seven years later, on November 9, 2007, the dollar reached US$1.09, a level that had not been seen for decades. That movement and strength encouraged Canadians to cross

The Crisis in Europe: Let the Name Calling Begin

P-I-I-G-S! You would expect to hear this sort of language in an elementary school playground. Lately, however, this acronym is used by reporters to identify the primary sources of the economic crisis that threatens the European Union. The villains are *Portugal, Ireland, Italy, Greece,* and *Spain.*

Why are they villains? The governments of these countries have been spending far more money than they have been taking in. In 2010, most of the headlines focused on Greece as the leading culprit. This small European nation was particularly guilty of overspending and not living up to commitments it made when it entered the Eurozone. In 2009, Greece's annual deficit was 13 percent of GDP, which is far above the Eurozone's self-imposed limit of 3 percent. When an individual has too much debt and not enough income, bankruptcy is often the only solution. Default, the national equivalent, became a very real possibility for Greece. The country's financial situation had become very bad; partially because of U.S.-based Goldman Sachs' role as an enabler (it shielded some of Greece's debt with off-balance-sheet currency swaps).

But Greece was not alone. A key measure of economic stability is the debt-to-GDP ratio. A country's debt is the accumulation of all previous deficits (total obligations) and GDP measures total goods and services produced by a nation (which relates to its ability to pay). The PIIGS had the following ratios at the beginning of 2010: Greece 125 percent, Italy 117 percent, Portugal 85 percent, Ireland 83 percent, and Spain 66 percent. While Spain was in the best shape in terms of this particular ratio, its jobless rate stood at approximately 20 percent. These scary numbers raised many questions. How should the European Union deal with the problem nations? Should it allow Greece to default on its debt? If so, would that create a domino effect, with other nations following? Should the EU bail out Greece and reward its bad behaviour? Should the EU allow one of its nations to seek help from the International Monetary Fund (IMF)?

The initial reaction to the Greek crisis by the other EU countries was to say no to any sort of bailout or support. But for countries like Germany, that have large trade surpluses within the Eurozone, it was also in their interest to support the union and not risk its potential collapse. Pressure was therefore put on the Greek government to reduce its spending and to freeze the wages of government workers. But such actions will take time to have an effect, and in the meantime, the euro was taking a major hit on currency markets. The solidarity of the Eurozone was being severely tested for the first time. After months of debate, the European Union and the IMF stepped up with a EUR$750 billion support plan (EUR$500 from the EU and EUR$250 from the IMF). But this was not the end. The situation was dangerous for the union and had major implications for the world economy.

Critical Thinking Questions

1. Should the Eurozone partners allow one of their members to face the consequences of its economic problems on their own? Debate the pros and cons.
2. Should the Eurozone partners expel members from the EU who do not meet the financial criteria set out by the EU? Explain.

---

the U.S. border and purchase everything from clothing to cars. Over the next few years the dollar retreated a bit, but a new era was upon Canadians. In mid-2010, the dollar was once again flirting with parity.[15]

These dollar fluctuations have also had a huge impact on businesses. Canadian companies are finding it harder to compete internationally, since they can no longer rely on a cheap dollar to make their products more affordable across the border and abroad. But after the initial shock, companies are learning to cope. According to chairman and CEO of Clearwater Seafoods Income Fund, "The way you deal with the stronger Canadian dollar is to increase the efficiency of your operations."[16] Other companies, like Nova Scotia–based High Liner Foods, which buys most of its raw fish on the world markets in U.S. dollars, has seen a net benefit. The rise in the Canadian dollar helped the company increase profits by 40 percent in 2009.[17]

LO-3 International Business Management

Wherever a firm is located, its success depends largely on how well it is managed. International business is challenging because the basic management responsibilities—planning, organizing, leading, and controlling—are much more difficult to carry out when a business operates in several markets scattered around the globe. (We discuss the functions of management in Chapter 6.)

Managing means making decisions. In this section, we examine the three most basic decisions that a company's management must make when faced with the prospect of globalization. The first decision is whether to "go international" at all. Often that decision is made because a company feels it has to shift its production to a low-cost foreign country in order to remain competitive. Once that decision has been made, managers must decide on the company's level of international involvement and on the organizational structure that will best meet its global needs.

"Going International"

The world economy is becoming globalized, and more and more firms are conducting international operations. As Figure 5.2 shows, several factors enter into the decision to go international. One overriding factor is the business climate in other nations. Even experienced firms have encountered cultural, legal, and economic roadblocks, as we shall see later in this chapter. In considering international expansion, a company should also consider at least two other questions: Is there a demand for its products abroad? If so, must those products be adapted for international consumption? As we saw in the opening case, these decisions can be quite complicated.

Gauging International Demand Products that are seen as vital in one country may be useless in another. Snowmobiles are popular for transportation and recreation in Canada and the northern United States, and they revolutionized reindeer herding in Lapland. But there would be no demand at all for this product in Central America. Although this is an extreme example, the point is quite basic to the decision to go international: namely, that

While Toyota markets five sport-utility vehicle models in Canada (manufacturing the RAV4 in Woodstock, Ontario, and exporting the other models to Canada), it sells only its two smallest ones at home in Japan, where crowded roads, narrow driveways, and scarce parking spaces make larger vehicles impractical.

foreign demand for a company's product may be greater than, the same as, or weaker than domestic demand. Even when there is demand, advertising may still need to be adjusted. For instance, in Canada, bicycles and small motorcycles are mainly used for recreation, but in many parts of Asia they are seen as transportation. Market research and/or the prior market entry of competitors may indicate whether there's an international demand for a firm's products. New Brunswick–based McCain Foods has worked hard to build market share in South Africa. It even developed single-sized portions of frozen vegetables to serve customers who do not have proper refrigeration. There are now 2000 McCain employees in South Africa serving eight African nations.[18]

Some products—like smart phones, Hollywood movies, and video games—are popular all over the world. Movies like *Avatar* and *Twilight* earn significant revenues in North America but generate even more revenues overseas.

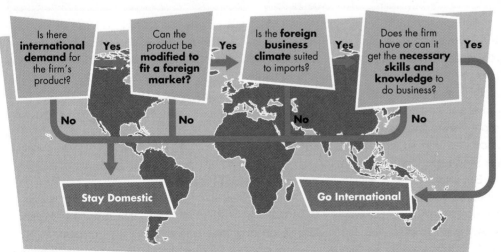

Is there **international demand** for the firm's product? → **Yes** → Can the product be **modified to fit a foreign market?** → **Yes** → Is the **foreign business climate** suited to imports? → **Yes** → Does the firm have or can it get the **necessary skills and knowledge** to do business? → **Yes** → Go International

No → No → No → No → Stay Domestic

Figure 5.2
Going international.

Adapting to Customer Needs If there is international demand for its product, a firm must consider whether and how to adapt that product to meet the special demands and expectations of foreign customers. Movies, for example, have to be dubbed into foreign languages. Likewise, McDonald's restaurants sell wine in France, beer in Germany, and meatless sandwiches in India to accommodate local tastes and preferences. Ford products must have their steering wheels mounted on the right if they are to be sold in England and Japan. When Toyota launches upscale cars at home, it retains the Toyota nameplate; those same cars are sold under the Lexus nameplate in Canada because the firm has concluded that Canadian consumers will not pay a premium price for a "Toyota." BlackBerry smart phones may originate in Waterloo, Ontario, but Research In Motion has sold over 1.2 million smart phones in Indonesia; in Jakarta, a BlackBerry is an important symbol of success. To succeed in this market, RIM adapted its approach by creating prepaid scratch cards. This enables the consumer to pay a set amount for data and email service each week or month.[19] The boxed insert entitled "Epic Entrepreneurs" describes one company's experience in going international.

ENTREPRENEURSHIP AND NEW VENTURES

Epic Entrepreneurs: Have Camera, Will Travel

Help wanted: Dynamic and innovative company seeks staff who are adventurous, love to travel, and are willing to spend most of the year in some of the world's most exotic locations, many of them very warm! Sounds like a dream job, right? Well, while there's sure to be other mandatory criteria, jobseekers interested in working for EPIC Newsgroup Inc. must meet the above demands. EPIC was started in 2004 by two young Vancouverites, Sabrina Heinekey and Tiffany Steeves. While travelling on foreign assignment, the duo realized that many countries and their respective tourism boards, corporations, ministries, and so on were not using television as a promotional medium. They decided the gap was worth pursuing, and thus their agency was launched.

EPIC is a production and media placement company that creates segments for broadcast on various channels throughout Europe, North America, Africa, the Middle East, and Asia. Generally, each year Heinekey and Steeves select up to five countries that they believe have some form of potential for international interest (e.g., developing a brand, misconception of a brand, international mystique),and they prepare a thoroughly researched media package. As an example, EPIC produced a video for Jordan's tourism board. According to Steeves, "People often lump the Middle East together as a war-torn area. Well, Jordan isn't like that at all. It's a safe, peaceful country." So sometimes their work is to help countries reposition and/or realign themselves in the international marketplace. Many of EPIC's clients were previously working under the perception that television production as a form of media exposure was difficult and out of reach; EPIC provides a solution. However, in doing so, Heinekey and Steeves haven't always found the exotic, international locations easy to navigate themselves.

The pair learned early on that young women don't often play a role in the business environment of some countries. Heinekey and Steeves state, "In some countries, for example, we've had to disprove local attitudes towards working with two women. . . . " The cultural differences regarding television as an appropriate medium have also required that they "take potential clients through a learning process." What has been their guiding philosophy in navigating these unfamiliar waters? According to Heinekey, it's their sensitivity to cultural differences and their focus on professionalism and preparation that have helped open doors for them around the globe.

"We're really doing well," says Steeves. In 2007, the Business Development Bank of Canada (BDC) applauded their success and bestowed upon them the Young Entrepreneur Award for British Columbia. In 2008, *Chatelaine* magazine named the two co-founders in an issue that profiled "80 amazing women to watch." According to BDC president and CEO Jean-René Halde, "They took an interesting concept, developed a novel product, and turned it into a thriving global enterprise."

Critical Thinking Question

1. The decision to "go international" requires a high degree of analysis and examination of factors both internal and external to the business. Assess EPIC's form of competitive advantage, level of involvement in international business, and various barriers to international trade.

Levels of Involvement in International Business

After a firm decides to go international, it must decide on the level of its international involvement. Several options are available. At the most basic level, a firm may act as an *exporter* or *importer*, organize as an *international firm*, or operate as a *multinational firm*. Most of the world's largest industrial firms are multinationals.

Exporters and Importers An **exporter** is a firm that makes products in one country and then distributes and sells them in others. An **importer** buys products in foreign markets and then imports them for resale in its home country. Exporters and importers tend to conduct most of their business in their home nations. Both enterprises entail the lowest level of involvement in international operations and are excellent ways to learn the fine points of global business.

Exporting is not limited to multinationals. Small firms also export products and services. For example, Lingo Media Inc. is the largest supplier of English-language textbooks in China's primary school system. Now this Toronto-based company has created speak2me.cn, a learning solution website that uses voice recognition. The site was created to solve a major problem in China: there is a shortage of teachers who speak English properly. The company registered 1 million users on the site in the first year alone.[20]

International Firms As firms gain experience and success as exporters and importers, they may move to the next level of involvement. An **international firm** conducts a significant portion of its business abroad. International firms also maintain manufacturing facilities overseas but their primary focus remains on their domestic market.

Multinational Firms Most **multinational firms** do not ordinarily think of themselves as having domestic and international divisions. Instead, planning and decision making are geared toward global markets.[21] The locations of headquarters are almost irrelevant. Royal Dutch/Shell, Nestlé, IBM, and Ford are well-known multinationals.

The economic importance of multinational firms should not be underestimated. Consider, for example, the economic impact of the 500 largest multinational corporations. In 2009, Royal Dutch/Shell ranked number one in the Fortune Global 500 rankings with over 102 000 employees and US$458 billion in sales. Exxon was second with 105 000 employees and US$443 billion in sales. Walmart ranked third with US$405 billion in sales and 2.1 million employees (with 700 000 international employees in its 4000 international outlets). Multinationals employ millions of people; buy supplies, parts, equipment, and materials from thousands of other firms; and pay billions of dollars in taxes. Moreover, their activities and products affect the lives of hundreds of millions of consumers, competitors, and investors (sometimes not in a very positive way).[22] Organized protests against the activities of multinational corporations have become quite common.

International Organizational Structures

Different levels of involvement in international business require different kinds of organizational structure. For example, a structure that would help coordinate an exporter's activities would be inadequate for the activities of a multinational firm. In this section, we briefly consider the spectrum of international organizational strategies, including *independent agents*, *licensing arrangements*, *branch offices*, *strategic alliances*, and *foreign direct investment*.

Independent Agents An **independent agent** is a foreign individual or organization that agrees to represent an exporter's interests in foreign markets. Independent agents often act as sales representatives: they sell the exporter's products, collect payment, and ensure that customers are satisfied. Independent agents often represent several firms at once and usually do not specialize in a particular product or market. Levi Strauss uses agents to market clothing products in many small countries in Africa, Asia, and South America.

Licensing Arrangements Canadian companies seeking more substantial involvement in international business may opt for **licensing arrangements**. Firms give individuals or companies in a foreign country the exclusive right to manufacture or market their products in that area. In return, the exporter typically receives a fee plus ongoing payments called **royalties**.[23] Royalties are usually calculated as a percentage of the licence holder's sales. For example, Can-Eng Manufacturing, Canada's largest supplier of industrial furnaces, exports its furnaces under licensing arrangements with Japan, Brazil, Germany, Korea, Taiwan, and Mexico.

Franchising is a special form of licensing that is also very popular.[24] McDonald's and Pizza Hut franchise around the world. Similarly, Accor SA, a French hotel chain, franchises its Ibis, Sofitel, and Novotel hotels.

Branch Offices Instead of developing relationships with foreign companies or independent agents, a firm may simply send some of its own managers to overseas branch offices. A company has more direct control over branch managers than over agents or licence holders. **Branch offices** also give a company a more visible public presence in foreign countries. Potential customers tend to feel more secure when a business has branch offices in their country.

When a business operates branches, plants, or subsidiaries in several countries, it may assign one plant or subsidiary the responsibility for researching, developing, manufacturing, and marketing one product or line of products. This is known as **world product mandating**.

Strategic Alliances The concept of a strategic alliance was introduced in Chapter 2. In international business, it means that a company finds a partner in a foreign country where it would like to conduct business. Each party agrees to invest resources and capital in a new business or else to cooperate in some way for mutual benefit. This new business—the alliance—is then owned by the partners, which divide its profits. For example, Canadian publisher Lingo Media Inc. is involved in a strategic alliance with the state-owned People's Education Press, which is the market leader in providing textbooks to Chinese schools.[25]

The number of strategic alliances among major companies has increased significantly over the last decade and is likely to grow even more. In many countries, including Mexico, India, and China, laws make alliances virtually the only way to do business within their borders.[26]

In addition to easing the way into new markets, alliances give firms greater control over their foreign activities than independent agents and licensing arrangements. (All partners in an alliance retain some say in its decisions.) Perhaps most important, alliances allow firms to benefit from the knowledge and expertise of their foreign partners. In India, Walmart partnered with Bharti Enterprises to build 10–15 large cash-and-carry stores. Walmart wanted to capture a share of the booming retail market without angering the local mom-and-pop merchants and middlemen that dominate the industry.[27]

Foreign Direct Investment The term **foreign direct investment (FDI)** means buying or establishing tangible assets in another country.[28] For example, Dell recently built new assembly plants in Europe and Brazil, and Volkswagen built factories in Mexico and Brazil. The establishment of branch offices in foreign countries is also a type of foreign direct investment.

As we've seen, many Canadian firms export goods and services to foreign countries, and they also set up manufacturing operations in other countries. Bombardier recently landed a $4 billion deal in China, for the sale of 80 high-speed trains. This deal was made possible because of years of direct investments and a Bombardier/China joint venture group called Bombardier Sifang (Qingdao).[29] However, a debate has been going on for many years about how FDI by foreign firms in Canada affects Canadians. The **Foreign Investment Review Agency** was established in 1973 to ensure that FDI benefited Canadians. In 1985, FIRA became **Investment Canada** and the mandate was changed to focus on attracting foreign investment. Since the late 1980s, foreign ownership of Canadian industry has again been on the rise, and now stands at approximately 30 percent.[30]

Recently, foreign buyouts of major firms like Inco, Four Seasons Hotels, and Alcan have caused some Canadian business leaders to express renewed fears about FDI in Canada. A study by Secor Consulting concluded that Canada is the easiest country in the world for foreigners to come into and take over a business. It also found that only three countries in the world were net sellers of their companies: Canada, the United States, and Great Britain.[31] The most general concern is that foreign buyouts of Canadian firms will damage the economy because the head offices will move to foreign countries and major decisions will be made there, not in Canada.

Another concern is that foreign takeovers will mean large job losses. But a Statistics Canada study showed that between 1999 and 2005, foreign companies were responsible for creating *all* of the new head offices that were created in Canada and about two-thirds of the jobs in those new head offices.[32] Another survey of 150 senior Canadian executives showed that the issue of foreign ownership ranked low on their list of perceived economic challenges.[33] Many experts argue that placing limitations on foreign investment in Canada essentially shields companies from competition and makes them less efficient.[34] Table 5.2 lists the top 10 foreign-owned companies in Canada.

BRANCH OFFICE A location that an exporting firm establishes in a foreign country to sell its products more effectively.

WORLD PRODUCT MANDATING The assignment by a multinational of a product responsibility to a particular branch.

FOREIGN DIRECT INVESTMENT (FDI) Buying or establishing tangible assets in another country.

FOREIGN INVESTMENT REVIEW AGENCY (FIRA) Established in 1973 to screen new foreign direct investment in Canada; supposed to ensure that significant benefits accrued to Canada.

Table 5.2 Top 10 Foreign-Controlled Companies in Canada, 2009

Company	Annual Revenues (in billions of $)
1. Imperial Oil	21.3
2. Walmart Canada Corp.	17.5
3. Husky Energy Inc.	15.1
4. Novelis Inc.	11.5
5. Costco Wholesale Canada	10.9
6. Direct Energy Marketing Ltd.	10.8
7. Honda Canada Inc.	9.4
8. Ford Motor Co. of Canada	9.1
9. Ultramar Ltd.	7.3
10. Canada Safeway Ltd.	6.7

LO-4 Barriers to International Trade

Whether a business is selling to just a few foreign markets or is a true multinational, a number of differences between countries will affect its international operations. How a firm responds to and manages social, economic, and political issues will go a long way toward determining its success.

Social and Cultural Differences

Any firm involved in international business needs to understand something about the society and culture in the countries it plans to operate in. Unless a firm understands these cultural differences—either itself or by acquiring a partner that does—it will probably not be successful in its international business activities.

Some differences are relatively obvious. Language barriers can cause inappropriate naming of products. In addition, the physical stature of people in different countries can make a difference. For example, the Japanese and French are slimmer and shorter on average than Canadians, an important consideration for firms that intend to sell clothes in these markets. Differences in the average age of the local population can also have ramifications for product development and marketing. Countries with growing populations tend to have a high percentage of young people. Thus, electronics and fashionable clothing would likely do well. Countries with stable or declining populations tend to have more old people. Generic pharmaceuticals might be more successful in such markets.

In addition to such obvious differences, a wide range of subtle value differences can have an important impact. For example, many Europeans shop daily. To Canadians used to weekly trips to the supermarket, the European pattern may seem like a waste of time. But for Europeans, shopping is not just "buying food." It is also meeting friends, exchanging political views, gossiping, and socializing.

What implications does this kind of shopping have for firms selling in European markets? First, those who go shopping each day do not need the large refrigerators and freezers common in North America. Second, the large supermarkets one sees in Canada are not an appropriate retail outlet in Europe. Finally, the kinds of food Europeans buy differ from those Canadians buy. While in Canada prepared and frozen foods are important, Europeans often prefer to buy fresh ingredients to do their own food preparation "from scratch." These differences are gradually disappearing, however, so firms need to be on the lookout for future opportunities as they emerge.

Even more subtle behavioural differences that can influence business activity exist. For example, crossing your legs in a business meeting in Saudi Arabia is inappropriate, because showing the sole of your foot is viewed as an insult to the other people in the room. In Portugal, it is considered rude to discuss business during dinner, and in Taiwan, tapping your fingers on the table is a sign of appreciation for a meal. In China, don't give a businessman a green hat and don't wrap a gift in white or black (a green hat on a Chinese man is said to indicate that his wife is unfaithful, and black and white are associated with death). Deals can be lost based on inadvertent cultural insults. Knowledge of local dos and don'ts is important in international business activity. Do your homework.[35]

Economic Differences

Although cultural differences are often subtle, economic differences can be fairly pronounced. In dealing with economies like those of France and Sweden, firms must be aware of when—and to what extent—the government is involved in a given industry. The French government is heavily involved in all aspects of airplane design and manufacturing.

Similarly, a foreign firm doing business in a command economy must understand the unfamiliar relationship of government to business, including a host of idiosyncratic practices. General Motors, which entered a US$100 million joint venture to build pickup trucks in China, found itself faced with an economic system that favoured state-owned companies over foreign investors. So, while its Chinese suppliers passed on inflation-based price increases for steel and energy, GM could not in turn pass increases on to Chinese consumers. With subsidized state-owned automakers charging considerably less per truck, GM had no choice but to hold its own prices—and lose money on each sale. Despite such problems, however, not all companies have had entirely negative experiences. For example, when Motorola opened a factory in

China to manufacture communication devices, it involved Chinese technicians in the production process. Chinese designers and engineers played key roles in creating an operation that integrated manufacturing, sales, research, and development.

Legal and Political Differences

Legal and political differences are often closely linked to the structure of the economic systems in different countries. These issues include *tariffs* and *quotas, local-content laws,* and *business-practice laws.*

Quotas, Tariffs, and Subsidies Even free-market economies often use some form of quota and/or tariff that affects the prices and quantities of foreign-made products in those nations. A **quota** restricts the total number of certain products that can be imported into a country. It indirectly raises the prices of those imports by reducing their supply. The ultimate form of quota is an **embargo**: a government order forbidding exportation and/or importation of a particular product—or even all the products—of a particular country. For example, many countries control bacteria and disease by banning certain plants and agricultural products.

In contrast, a **tariff** is a tax charged on imported products. Tariffs directly affect the prices of products, effectively raising the price of imports to consumers, who must pay not only for the products but also for the tariff. Tariffs may take either of two forms. A **revenue tariff** is imposed strictly to raise money for the government. Most tariffs in effect today, however, are **protectionist tariffs** meant to discourage the import of a particular product. A few years ago, the Canadian government placed a 34.6 percent tariff on barbecues made in China after complaints were received that Chinese companies were unfairly subsidizing their production.[36]

Governments impose quotas and tariffs for a wide variety of reasons. For example, the U.S. government restricts the number of Japanese automobiles that can be imported into that country. Italy imposes high tariffs on imported electronic goods, thus making them more expensive. Canada also imposes tariffs on many imported goods.

Back in 2002, the U.S. Commerce Department imposed a 29 percent tariff on softwood lumber exported from Canada to the United States (84 percent of Canadian lumber is exported to the United States). Ottawa immediately appealed the decision under the provisions of both the North American Free Trade Agreement (NAFTA) and the World Trade Organization (WTO). During 2002 and 2003, both the WTO and NAFTA ruled against the United States on various points in the appeal and said that duties on Canadian lumber must be cut drastically. In spite of these rulings, the United States continued to impose the duties. The Canadian lumber industry paid over $5.3 billion in duties to the United States.[37] A tentative resolution was reached in 2006, when the United States agreed to pay back 78 percent of the duties imposed on Canadian lumber, on the condition that Canada agree that its share of the U.S. lumber market would be capped at 34 percent.[38] Several Canadian lumber companies said that they weren't happy with that, but an agreement was eventually reached that went into effect in October 2006.[39]

A **subsidy** is a government payment given to a domestic business to help it compete with foreign firms. Bombardier has received subsidies from both federal

QUOTA A restriction by one nation on the total number of products of a certain type that can be imported from another nation.

EMBARGO A government order forbidding exportation and/or importation of a particular product.

TARIFF A tax levied on imported products.

REVENUE TARIFF A tariff imposed solely to raise money for the government that imposes it.

PROTECTIONIST TARIFF A tariff imposed at least in part to discourage imports of a particular product.

SUBSIDY A government payment to help domestic business compete with foreign firms.

The long-standing softwood lumber dispute between the United States and Canada hurt Canadian companies in the forestry industry. The dispute was settled in 2006, but much unhappiness is still evident, and critics have charged that the Conservative government caved in to American pressure.

and provincial governments. These funds and low-interest loans have helped the company compete and develop its major projects. Bombardier and its main rival, Brazil-based Embraer, have accused each other of receiving excessive unfair government support, which has led to disputes at the WTO. The end-of-chapter case addresses this dispute.

When the government of a country pays subsidies to one of its domestic companies or industries, this can have a negative effect on producers in other countries. For example, the WTO ruled that the U.S. government's subsidies to its cotton growers broke trade rules, depressed world cotton prices, and hurt Brazilian cotton producers.[40] These subsidies also hurt small cotton farmers in Africa because they caused highly productive U.S. farmers to produce a lot of cotton, which drove down the price African farmers received.[41] Canada's supply management system, which restricts imports and guarantees markets for producers of chickens, turkeys, eggs, and milk, could also come under fire since the WTO views the system as an unfair subsidy to producers.[42] More information about the WTO is available at the end of the chapter.

Protectionism—the practice of protecting domestic business at the expense of free market competition—has advocates and critics. Supporters argue that tariffs and quotas protect domestic firms and jobs. In particular, they protect new industries until they are able to compete internationally. Some claim they are necessary because other nations have such measures. Still others justify protectionism in the name of national security and argue that advanced technology should not be sold to potential enemies.

But opponents of protectionism are equally vocal. They note that protectionism reduces competition and drives up prices. They cite it as a cause of friction between nations. They maintain that while jobs in some industries would be lost if protectionism ceased, jobs in other industries would expand if all countries abolished tariffs and quotas.

Protectionism sometimes takes on almost comic proportions. Neither Europe nor the United States grows bananas, but both European and U.S. firms buy and sell bananas in foreign markets. Problems arose when the EU put a quota on bananas imported from Latin America—a market dominated by two U.S. firms, Chiquita and Dole—in order to help firms based in current and former European colonies in the Caribbean. The United States retaliated and imposed a 100 percent tariff on certain luxury products imported from Europe, including Louis Vuitton handbags, Scottish cashmere sweaters, and Parma ham.[43]

Local-Content Laws A country can affect how a foreign firm does business there by enacting **local-content laws** that require products sold in a particular country be at least partly made in that country. These laws typically mean that firms seeking to do business in a country must either invest directly or have a local joint-venture partner. In this way, some of the profits in a foreign country are shared with the people who live there. Many countries have local-content laws. In a fairly extreme case, Venezuela forbids the import of any product if a similar product is made in Venezuela. Back in 2005, Venezuela's president said he would cancel all mining licences and stop issuing new ones to foreign companies. This move was designed to protect the many small, local miners. Oil and gas licences held by foreign companies had already been cancelled.

Subsidies are designed to support domestic companies; however, in this free-trade era, governments are increasingly generous with foreign firms that can help develop local industries and provide local jobs. Warner Bros. is opening up a new studio to develop high-end video games in Montreal. Local talent, reputation, and knowledge were key factors in the decision, but government funding helped close the deal. The Quebec government provided $7.5 million to get the studio off the ground. Speed Racer is one of the games produced by Warner Bros. Interactive.

These actions make foreign companies reluctant to invest in Venezuela.[44]

Local-content laws may even exist within a country; when they do, they act just like trade barriers. In Canada, for example, a low bid on a bridge in British Columbia was rejected because the company that made the bid was from Alberta. The job was given to a B.C. company. A window manufacturer from New Brunswick lost a contract in Nova Scotia despite having made the lowest bid, and the job went to a company in Nova Scotia.

The Agreement on Internal Trade (AIT) requires all 10 Canadian provinces to remove barriers to agricultural trade. But when Quebec—which has a strong dairy lobby—prohibited margarine coloured to look like butter, it was in violation of the agreement.[45] Unilever Canada Ltd. challenged the legality of the ban on coloured margarine in 2002, but it was not until 2008 that the province of Quebec repealed the law.[46] In another case, Prince Edward Island ignored a dispute panel ruling that stated P.E.I.'s milk import restrictions also violated the AIT.[47] A third case involves the question of who is allowed to audit the financial statements of public companies. At present, only chartered accountants (CAs) are allowed to do this in Quebec. This rule is being challenged by the certified general accountants (CGAs), who have auditing rights in most other provinces.[48] If provincial governments do not honour their obligations, the AIT will become meaningless.

Business-Practice Laws Many businesses entering new markets encounter problems in complying with stringent regulations and bureaucratic obstacles. Such practices are affected by the **business-practice laws** that host countries use to govern business practices within their jurisdictions. Walmart left Germany and South Korea because it did not effectively adapt to local tastes and was unable to achieve economies of scale.[49] In Germany, for example, Walmart had to stop refunding price differences on items sold for less by other stores because the practice is illegal in Germany. In an example closer to home, mixed martial arts UFC events have been held in Montreal, Vancouver, and the U.S., but until recently they were banned in Ontario.[50]

Paying bribes to government officials to get business is another problem area. The Canadian Corruption of Foreign Public Officials Act prohibits bribery of foreign officials, but as more Canadian companies do business abroad, they find themselves competing against companies that are not reluctant to pay bribes to get business. As a result, some Canadian companies are losing business.[51] In an attempt to create fairer competition among multinational companies, ministers from the Organisation for Economic Co-operation and Development (OECD) agreed in 1997 to criminalize bribery of foreign public officials.[52] Recently, four employees of the mining giant

Rio Tinto pled guilty to bribery charges in China. Mr. Stern Hu, a top executive in charge of iron ore, was sentenced to 10 years in prison for accepting a bribe of US$146 000.[53]

Transparency International (TI), an organization devoted to stamping out global corruption, says that companies from Belgium and Canada are least likely to pay bribes to win business in foreign countries; Russian firms are most likely to pay bribes.[54] TI publishes a Corruption Perceptions Index, which ranks countries based on the amount of corruption that is perceived to exist, based on ratings by business people, academics, and risk analysts. The 2009 index showed that the least corrupt countries are New Zealand, Denmark, and Singapore, while the most corrupt countries are Myanmar, Afghanistan, and Somalia. Canada was tied for eighth least corrupt with Iceland and Australia, and the United States was nineteenth.[55]

Cartels and Dumping A **cartel** is an association of producers whose purpose is to control the supply and price of a commodity. The most famous cartel is the Organization of the Petroleum Exporting Countries (OPEC). It has given oil-producing countries considerable power in the last 25 years. At various times, other cartels have been evident in diamonds, shipping, and coffee. While nothing much can be done when governments form a cartel like OPEC, private-sector businesses can be prosecuted for doing so. In 2008 alone, the European Union imposed fines on importers of Dole and Del Monte bananas (who were fined US$95.5 million), on makers of car glass (fined $2 billion), and on makers of paraffin wax used in paper plates and cups (fined $1 billion).[56] Canada is involved in a potash cartel with Belarus and Russia (these three nations account for almost 80 percent of production); the price has quadrupled in just a few years.[57]

Many countries forbid **dumping**—selling a product abroad for less than the comparable price charged in the home country. Antidumping legislation typically defines dumping as occurring if products are being sold at prices less than fair value, or if the result unfairly harms domestic industry. Recently, the U.S. imposed duties of 10.36 to 15.78 percent on steel pipes produced in China. China denounced the U.S. protectionist approach.[58] However, the U.S. is not alone in its concerns; India has accused China of dumping products on the Indian market that it can't sell elsewhere.[59]

BUSINESS-PRACTICE LAW Law or regulation governing business practices in given countries.

CARTEL Any association of producers whose purpose is to control supply of and prices for a given product.

DUMPING Selling a product for less abroad than in the producing nation.

LO-5 Overcoming Barriers to Trade

Despite the barriers to trade described so far, international trade is flourishing. This is because both organizations and free-trade treaties exist to promote international trade. The most significant of these are the General Agreement on Tariffs and Trade (GATT), the World Trade Organization (WTO), the European Union (EU), and the North American Free Trade Agreement (NAFTA).

General Agreement on Tariffs and Trade (GATT)

Governments typically view exports as good (because they create jobs in the country) and imports as bad (because they cause job losses in the country). Because of this, governments may be tempted to erect trade barriers to discourage imports. But if every country does this, international trade is stifled. To overcome this tendency, the **General Agreement on Tariffs and Trade (GATT)**—which was often humorously referred to as the General Agreement to Talk and Talk—was signed after the Second World War. Its purpose was to reduce or eliminate trade barriers, such as tariffs and quotas. It did so by encouraging nations to protect domestic industries within agreed-upon limits and to engage in multilateral negotiations. While 92 countries signed GATT, not all complied with its rules. The United States was one of the worst offenders. A revision of GATT went into effect in 1994, but many issues remained unresolved—for example, the opening of foreign markets to most financial services.

World Trade Organization

On January 1, 1995, the **World Trade Organization (WTO)** came into existence as the successor to GATT. The 153 member countries are required to open markets to international trade, and the WTO is empowered to pursue three goals:

1. Promote trade by encouraging members to adopt fair trade practices.

2. Reduce trade barriers by promoting multilateral negotiations.

3. Establish fair procedures for resolving disputes among members.

The WTO is overseeing reductions in import duties on thousands of products that are traded between countries. Canada, the United States, and the European Union are founding members of the WTO.[60] Unlike GATT, the WTO's decisions are binding, and many people feared that it would make sweeping decisions and boss countries around. These fears were a bit overstated.[61] The WTO has served in its role as a ruling body but appeals can often drag on for years. For example, in 2010, Boeing won a ruling against Airbus because it received US$4.1 billion in loans from European governments while developing its A380 jets. Despite the ruling, there appears to be even more money being given to Airbus for development of the new A350. It has been five years since the case was first presented and it could be years before Boeing sees any rewards from the ruling.[62] The WTO also recently ruled against China and its practice of controlling access to distribution of films. China allows only 70 foreign films to be distributed in that country per year. The WTO ordered China to open distribution channels; this is seen as a big win for North American movie, music, and print distributors.[63]

The WTO has had significant trouble dealing with the issue of agricultural subsidies. Many attempts have been made during the last few years to resolve this problem (the so-called Doha Round of trade talks). The general idea was that developing countries would lower their tariffs on industrial goods, and European and American governments would lower subsidies on agricultural products. In 2008, however, these efforts collapsed, with negotiators from China and India blaming the United States, and negotiators from the United States blaming China and India.[64] In addition, WTO talks on trade liberalization have often been disrupted by protestors who resent the power of the WTO and who are concerned about what world trade is doing to both the environment and the developing countries.[65] Protestors include labour unions (which regard Third World imports as unfair), environmentalists (who are concerned about business activity harming the environment), social activists (who are concerned about poor working conditions in developing countries), and farmers (who are concerned about the effect of free trade on grain prices).

The European Union

Originally called the Common Market, the **European Union (EU)** initially included only the principal Western European nations like Italy, Germany, France, and the United Kingdom. But by 2010, 27 countries belonged to the EU (see Figure 5.3). Other countries are in the process of applying for membership, including Croatia and Turkey. The EU has eliminated most quotas and set uniform tariff levels on products imported and exported within its group. The EU is the largest free marketplace in the world and produces nearly one-quarter of total global wealth.[66]

The North American Free Trade Agreement

On January 1, 1994, the **North American Free Trade Agreement (NAFTA)** took effect. The objective of NAFTA was to create a free trade area for Canada, the United States, and Mexico. It eliminates trade barriers, promotes fair competition, and increases investment opportunities.

Surveys conducted during the early 1990s showed that the majority of Canadians were opposed to NAFTA. They feared that jobs would be lost to other countries or that Canada's sovereignty would be threatened, and that Canada would be flooded with products manufactured in Mexico, where wages are much lower. Supporters of NAFTA argued that the agreement would open up U.S. markets for Canadian products and thereby create more employment in Canada, that the agreement would not threaten Canada's sovereignty, and that NAFTA would create more employment possibilities for women.

What has actually happened since NAFTA took effect? A group of economists at the Canadian Economics Association concluded that free trade has not been as good for Canada as predicted by its supporters, nor as bad for Canada as predicted by its detractors.[67] Several specific effects are noticeable:

NORTH AMERICAN FREE TRADE AGREEMENT (NAFTA) Agreement to gradually eliminate tariffs and other trade barriers among the United States, Canada, and Mexico.

- NAFTA has created a much more active North American market.
- Direct foreign investment has increased in Canada.
- U.S. imports from (and exports to) Mexico have increased.
- Canada has become an exporting powerhouse.
- Trade between the United States and Canada has risen sharply, and Canada still enjoys a large trade surplus with the United States.

In the last few years, there is evidence that the benefits of NAFTA are slowly being eroded by ever-increasing delays at border crossings, caused mostly by heavy U.S. border security as a result of the terrorist attacks in 2001. Studies by the Conference Board of Canada and the Canadian and U.S. chambers of commerce show that companies are having difficulty taking advantage of the efficiencies of integrated supply chains because there are so many cross-border delays. Those delays are forcing companies to spend extra time and money just trying to ensure that their deliveries will get through to customers on time.[68] On the positive side, there is now an extensive Canadian presence in Mexico in everything from mining to auto parts to banking. For example, Scotiabank, the most international Canadian bank, has made great inroads in Mexico with over two million Mexican clients.[69]

Other Free Trade Agreements in the Americas

While NAFTA has been the most publicized trade agreement in the Americas, there has been a flurry of activity among other countries as well. On January 1, 1995, a free trade agreement known as Mercosur went into effect between Argentina, Brazil, Uruguay, and Paraguay. Venezuela was awaiting final approval to become the fifth member in 2010. Within the first decade of its existence, tariffs had been eliminated on 80 percent of the goods

Figure 5.3
The nations of the European Union.

traded between the original members. Brazil has proposed enlarging Mercosur into a South American Free Trade Area (SAFTA), which might eventually negotiate with NAFTA to form an Americas Free Trade Area (AFTA).

Free Trade Agreements Elsewhere

Around the world, groups of nations are banding together to form regional trade associations for their own benefit. Some examples include

- the ASEAN Free Trade Area (see Figure 5.4)
- the Asia-Pacific Economic Cooperation (many nations of the Pacific Rim, as well as the United States, Canada, and Mexico)
- the Economic Community of Central African States (many nations in equatorial Africa)
- the Gulf Cooperation Council (Bahrain, Kuwait, Oman, Qatar, Saudi Arabia, and United Arab Emirates

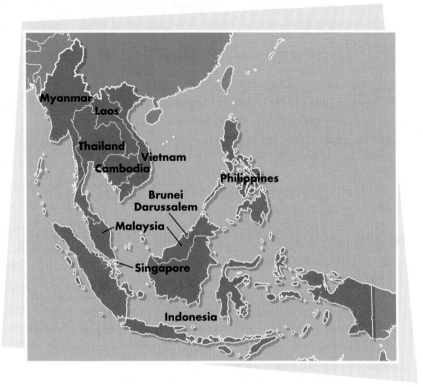

Figure 5.4
The nations of the Association of Southeast Asian Nations (ASEAN).

Summary of Learning Objectives

1. **Describe the rise of international business and identify the *major world marketplaces*.** More and more business firms are engaged in international business. The global economy is characterized by a rapid growth in the exchange of information and trade in services. The three major marketplaces for international business are *North America*, *Europe*, and *Asia–Pacific*.

2. **Explain how different forms of *competitive advantage, import–export balances, exchange rates*, and *foreign competition* determine how countries and businesses respond to the international environment.** With an *absolute advantage*, a country engages in international trade because it can produce a good or service more efficiently than any other nation. Countries usually trade because they enjoy

comparative advantages; they can produce some items more efficiently than they can produce other items. A country that exports more than it imports has a *favourable balance of trade*, while a country that imports more than it exports has an *unfavourable balance of trade*. If the exchange rate decreases, our exports become less expensive for other countries, so they will buy more of what we produce. The reverse happens if the value of the Canadian dollar increases. Changes in the exchange rate therefore have a strong impact on our international competitiveness.

3. **Discuss the factors involved in conducting business internationally and in selecting the *appropriate levels of international involvement and international organizational structure*.** In deciding whether to do business internationally, a firm must determine whether a market for its product exists abroad and whether the firm has the skills and knowledge to manage such a business. Firms must also assess the business climates in other nations and the preferred level of international involvement: (1) *exporter* or *importer*, (2) *international firm*, or (3) *multinational firm*. The choice will influence the organizational structure of its international operations, specifically, its use of *independent agents,*

licensing arrangements, branch offices, strategic alliances, and *direct investment.*

4. **Describe some of the ways in which *social, cultural, economic, legal, and political differences act as barriers to international trade*.** *Social* and *cultural differences* that can serve as barriers to trade include language, social values, and traditional buying patterns. Differences in economic systems may force businesses to establish close relationships with foreign governments before they are permitted to do business abroad. *Quotas, tariffs, subsidies,* and *local-content laws* offer protection to local industries. Differences in *business-practice laws* can make standard business practices in one nation illegal in another.

5. **Explain how *free trade agreements* assist world trade.** Several *trade agreements* have attempted to eliminate restrictions on free trade internationally. The *General Agreement on Tariffs and Trade (GATT)* was instituted to eliminate tariffs and other trade barriers among participating nations. The *European Union (EU)* has eliminated virtually all trade barriers among the 27 member nations. The *North American Free Trade Agreement (NAFTA)* eliminates many of the barriers to free trade among the United States, Canada, and Mexico.

Questions and Exercises

Questions for Analysis

1. Explain how the economic system of a country affects foreign firms interested in doing business there.

2. Assume that you are the manager of a small firm seeking to enter the international arena. What information would you need about the market that you're thinking of entering?

3. Do you think that a firm operating internationally is better advised to adopt a single standard of ethical conduct or to adapt to local conditions? Under what conditions might each approach be preferable?

4. Explain how it is possible for a country to have a positive balance of trade and a negative balance of payments.

5. Is NAFTA good or bad for Canada? Give supporting reasons for your answer.

6. The EU includes most of the Western European countries, but some (such as Switzerland) have chosen not to join. Why might that be? What are the implications for countries that do not join?

Application Exercises

7. Interview the manager of a local firm that does at least some business internationally. Identify reasons why the company decided to "go international," as well as the level of the firm's involvement and the organizational structure it uses for its international operations.

8. Select a familiar product. Using library references, learn something about the culture of India and identify the problems that might arise in trying to market this product to India's citizens.

9. What attributes of your province or region (cultural, geographical, economic, etc.) would be of interest

to a foreign firm thinking about locating there? Visit provincial government sites and find resources that are available for businesses to help them invest in your province. Identify a company that has recently invested in your province. What reasons did it give for its decision?

10. Visit the website of a major global company such as Coca-Cola and enter some of its international sites. Make sure to choose countries from different parts of the world. What are some of the differences that you see in the websites? Identify some of the similar themes and report your findings.

Building Your Business Skills

Putting Yourself in Your Place

Goal

To encourage students to apply global business strategies to a small-business situation.

Situation

Some people might say that Yolanda Lang is a bit too confident. Others might say that she needs confidence—and more—to succeed in the business she's chosen. But one thing is certain: Lang is determined to grow INDE, her handbag design company, into a global enterprise. At only 28 years of age, she has time on her side—if she makes the right business moves now.

These days, Lang spends most of her time in Milan, Italy. Backed by $50 000 of her parents' personal savings, she is trying to compete with Gucci, Fendi, and other high-end handbag makers. Her target market is women willing to spend $400 on a purse. Ironically, Lang was forced to set up shop in Italy because of the snobbishness of these customers, who buy high-end bags only if they're European-made. "Strangely enough," she muses, "I need to be in Europe to sell in North America."

To succeed, she must first find ways to keep production costs down—a tough task for a woman in a male-dominated business culture. Her fluent Italian is an advantage, but she's often forced to turn down inappropriate dinner invitations. She also has to figure out how to get her 22-bag collection into stores worldwide. Retailers are showing her bags in Italy and Japan, but she's had little luck in the United States. "I intend to be a global company," says Lang. The question is how to succeed first as a small business.

Method

Step 1 Join together with three or four other students to discuss the steps that Lang has taken so far to break into the U.S. retail market. These steps include:

- buying a mailing list of 5000 shoppers from high-end department store Neiman Marcus and selling directly to these customers; and
- linking with a manufacturer's representative to sell her line in major U.S. cities while she herself concentrates on Europe.

Step 2 Based on what you learned in this chapter, suggest other strategies that might help Lang grow her business. Working with group members, consider whether the following options would help or hurt Lang's business. Explain why a strategy is likely to work or likely to fail.

- Lang could relocate to the United States and sell abroad through an independent agent.
- Lang could relocate to the United States and set up a branch office in Italy.
- Lang could find a partner in Italy and form a strategic alliance that would allow her to build her business on both continents.

Step 3 Working alone, create a written marketing plan for INDE. What steps would you recommend that Lang take to reach her goal of becoming a global company? Compare your written response with those of other group members.

Follow-Up Questions

1. What are the most promising steps that Lang can take to grow her business? What are the least promising?

2. Lang thinks that her trouble breaking into the U.S. retail market stems from the fact that her company is unknown. How would this circumstance affect the strategies suggested in Steps 1 and 2?

3. When Lang deals with Italian manufacturers, she is a young, attractive woman in a man's world. Often, she must convince men that her purpose is business and nothing else. How should Lang handle personal invitations that get in the way of business? How can she say no while still maintaining business relationships? Why is it often difficult for women to do business in male-dominated cultures?

4. The American consulate has given Lang little business help because her products are made in Italy. Do you think the consulate's treatment of an American businessperson is fair or unfair? Explain your answer.

5. Do you think Lang's relocation to Italy will pay off? Why or why not?

6. With Lang's goals of creating a global company, can INDE continue to be a one-person operation?

Exercising Your Ethics

Weighing the Tradeoffs

The Situation

There is a small bank that is headquartered in western Canada. The firm is privately owned and all the managers own stock in the bank. The company's senior managers (and majority owners) have decided to sell the bank to a major international banking company within the next two to three years. But, the bank needs to trim its expenses in order to make it more attractive to a potential buyer.

The Dilemma

Because the bank corporation has been a locally owned and operated enterprise it has maintained a full slate of operations within the local market. For instance, its corporate offices, many banking outlets, and all of its support activities are housed locally. The latter category includes a large call centre—a staff of 30 people who handle most customer calls involving questions about their accounts.

There has been a growing trend in banking to outsource call centres to foreign countries (e.g., India). Such markets have an abundance of English-speaking employees, excellent technology, and low wages. One senior manager has argued that they should outsource the call centre immediately. This would enable the firm to lower its costs. When confronted with the prospect of cutting 30 jobs, the manager acknowledges that it will be tough but reasons that any buyer will eventually do the same.

Another vocal senior manager is opposed to this idea. This person argues that because the bank corporation was started locally and has strong ties to the local community, it should maintain its current operations until the bank is sold. He argues, if a new owner decides to cut jobs, "it will be on their conscience, not ours."

Team Activity

Assemble a group of four students and assign each group member to one of the following roles:

- Senior manager (majority owner) of the bank
- Call centre employee
- Bank customer
- Bank corporation investor

Action Steps

1. Before discussing the situation with your group, and from the perspective of your assigned role, decide whether the call centre should be outsourced immediately. Write down the reasons for your position.

2. Before discussing the situation with your group, and from the perspective of your assigned role, decide what underlying ethical issues, if any, there are in this situation. Write down the issues.

3. Gather your group together and reveal, in turn, each member's comments on whether the call centre should be outsourced immediately. Next, reveal the ethical issues listed by each member.

4. Appoint someone to record the main points of agreement and disagreement within the group. How do you explain the results? What accounts for any disagreement?

5. From an ethical standpoint, what does your group conclude is the most appropriate action for the bank to take in this situation?

6. Develop a group response to the following question: Can your team identify other solutions that might help satisfy both senior managers' views?

Bombardier's Global Strategy

Montreal-based Bombardier Inc. is a diversified Canadian company that specializes in transportation solutions, from commercial and business jets to rail transportation equipment and services. Bombardier was founded in 1942 to manufacture a now-classic Canadian product—tracked vehicles for transportation across snow-covered terrain. Many of the Bombardier snowmobiles that were manufactured decades ago can still be seen in various areas of Canada. One such half-track sits on the windswept shores of Yathkyed Lake in Nunavut, hundreds of kilometres from any town. It is a mute reminder of the important role Bombardier played in opening up Canada's remote North.

Bombardier's headquarters are in Montreal, but its employees also work in the United States, Mexico, Europe, and the Middle East. More than 90 percent of company revenues come from outside Canada. Bombardier's strategy is to achieve accelerated growth in foreign markets, so it is continually refining its strategy to find new business opportunities in global markets.

Bombardier has historically been very successful in the commercial airplane market with its regional jets, which seat 50–90 passengers. But competition is fierce. In the mid-1990s, Bombardier held two-thirds of the market; then Brazilian rival Embraer entered the market and became a strong competitor. In 2007, Embraer finally overtook Bombardier to become the market leader in regional jets. Along the way, Bombardier had complained to the World Trade Organization that the Brazilian government was unfairly subsidizing Embraer by giving it large sums of money. But the Canadian government was also giving loans to Bombardier's customers to help them purchase Bombardier's planes.

Irrespective of how the competitive wars in the regional jet market turn out, an inescapable fact is that the regional jet market is declining because airline companies want jets with longer ranges, lower operating costs, and wider cabins. Bombardier planners reasoned that if they did not develop a new jet, they would gradually be forced out of the commercial airplane business. In 2008, at the famous Farnborough International Airshow near London, England, the company announced that it would go ahead with its new transcontinental CSeries commercial jet, a plane that will seat 110–130 passengers and which is designed for transcontinental flights. The plane will be more fuel efficient than current models and much quieter due to technological improvements in the new engines. Bombardier also announced that Deutsche Lufthansa AG had signed a letter of intent (LOI) for 30 of the planes,

A photo of Bombardier's new CSeries plane. After getting an initial order from Lufthansa Bombardier began the process to produce its long awaited CSeries plane.

(Photo courtesy of Bombardier Inc. and used under license.)

as well as an option for 30 more. As of November 2010, Bombardier had recorded firm orders for 90 CSeries aircraft and options from Lufthansa, Lease Corporation International Group, and Republic Airways. Qatar Airways has also expressed strong interest in the plane.

The introduction of the CSeries aircraft means Bombardier will be going head to head with global giants Airbus and Boeing. That strategy is risky, but if it succeeds, it will mean huge sales revenues and profits for Bombardier. It will also mean that Canada is one of only three countries in the world that produce intercontinental commercial jet aircraft. Market research suggests that the market for commercial jets like the CSeries will be 5000–6000 units over the next 20 years, and Bombardier hopes to get 50 percent of that market. The price of each plane is about $59 million, so if the company achieves its market share goal, it could receive approximately $190 *billion* in revenues over the next 20 years.

That sounds impressive, but there are three areas of risk associated with Bombardier's strategy. First, there may (or may not) be competing products from other airplane manufacturers. Here, Bombardier may get lucky. There is little evidence that Airbus or Boeing is planning to develop a plane that will compete directly with the CSeries aircraft. That's because there are large order backlogs (four to five years) for both the Airbus A320 and the Boeing 737, and the companies are fully engaged trying to fill those orders. However, Embraer may be developing a jet to compete with the CSeries aircraft.

Second, there is some risk associated with Bombardier's alleged "cozy" relationship with the Canadian government. In the past, the federal government has loaned money to Bombardier's customers so they can purchase the planes and trains the company manufactures. But will the government decide to stop handing out money? When he was Opposition leader, Stephen Harper said he wanted to end this type of support to private-sector companies, but as prime minister he has now reversed his position. Industry Minister Jim Prentice says that Canada wants to maintain its position as a global supplier in the airplane business. The Liberal industry critic, Scott Brison, says the Canadian government doesn't have an industrial strategy and is just making ad hoc decisions based on which way the political winds are blowing. But given the uncertain economic times, it appears that government loans are likely to continue.

Third, there is a risk that Boeing, Airbus, and Embraer will argue at the World Trade Organization that Canada is illegally subsidizing Bombardier. There is a long and contentious history between Bombardier and Embraer about government subsidies, and each company has claimed at various times in the past that the other is being illegally subsidized by its government. The outcome of any legal action by other airplane manufacturers against Bombardier is very uncertain.

Bombardier's strategy also includes shifting some of the risk of the CSeries aircraft to suppliers and to government. The overall development cost and capital investment of the CSeries aircraft program are projected to total $3.4 billion, of which Bombardier is providing $2 billion, including $700 million in capital expenditures and $1.3 billion in non-recurring costs. The remaining $1.4 billion in CSeries aircraft program costs will be split between the government of Canada, the province of Quebec, the government of the United Kingdom (where the wings of the CSeries aircraft will be built), and suppliers. The various governments will be paid a royalty on each plane that is sold. The project will create 3500 high-paying jobs in Quebec and about 800 jobs in the United Kingdom.

Questions for Discussion

1. How does Bombardier's development of the CSeries aircraft highlight the challenges and opportunities of globalization?

2. What role will governments play in the success and failure of the CSeries aircraft? Identify the role of subsidies and debate the concept of free trade and protectionism as it relates to this case.

3. How does this case help demonstrate the important role of the WTO in the international business arena?

4. Do you think that Bombardier will be successful in its move to capture a share of this new growing market? Explain your answer. If yes, what are some of the long-term obstacles?

SCANLIFE

Part 1: The Contemporary Business World

Goal of the Exercise

In Chapter 4, we discussed how the starting point for virtually every new business is a *business plan*. Business plans describe the business strategy for any new business and demonstrate how that strategy will be implemented. One benefit of a business plan is that in preparing it, would-be entrepreneurs must develop their idea on paper and firm up their thinking about how to launch their business before investing time and money in it. In this exercise, you'll get started on creating your own business plan.

Exercise Background:
Part 1 of the Business Plan

The starting point for any business plan is coming up with a "great idea." This might be a business that you've already considered setting up. If you don't have ideas for a business already, look around. What are some businesses that you come into contact with on a regular basis? Restaurants, childcare services, and specialty stores are a few examples you might consider. You may also wish to create a business that is connected with a talent or interest you have, such as crafts, cooking, or car repair. It's important that you create a company from scratch rather than use a company that already exists. You'll learn more if you use your own ideas.

Once you have your business idea, your next step is to create an "identity" for your business. This includes determining a name for your business and an idea of what your business will do. It also includes identifying the type of ownership your business will take, topics we discussed in Chapter 4. The first part of the plan also briefly looks at who your ideal customers are, as well as how your business will stand out from the crowd. Part 1 of the plan also looks at how the business will interact with the community and demonstrate social responsibility, topics we discussed in Chapter 3. Finally, almost all business plans today include a perspective on the impact of global business, which we discussed in Chapter 5.

Your Assignment

PEARSON mybusinesslab

Step 1

To complete this assignment, you first need to download the Business Plan Student Template file from the book's MyBusinessLab. This is a Microsoft Word file you can use to complete your business plan. For this assignment, you will fill in Part 1 of the plan.

Step 2

Once you have the Business Plan Student Template file, you can begin to answer the following questions in Part 1: The Contemporary Business World.

1. What is the name of your business?

    Hint: When you think of the name of your business, make sure that it captures the spirit of the business you're creating.

2. What will your business do?

    Hint: Imagine that you are explaining your idea to a family member or a friend. Keep your description to 30 words or fewer.

3. What form of business ownership (sole proprietorship, partnership, or corporation) will your business take? Why did you choose this form?

    Hint: For more information on types of business ownership, refer to the discussion in Chapter 4.

4. Briefly describe your ideal customer. What are they like in terms of age, income level, and so on?

    Hint: You don't have to give too much detail in this part of the plan; you'll provide more details about customers and marketing in later parts of the plan.

5. Why will customers choose to buy from your business instead of your competition?

Hint: In this section, describe what will be unique about your business. For example, is the product special, or will you offer the product at a lower price?

6. All businesses have to deal with ethical issues. One way to address these issues is to create a code of ethics. List three core principles your business will follow.

   Hint: To help you consider the ethical issues that your business might face, refer to the discussion in Chapter 3.

7. A business shows social responsibility by respecting all of its stakeholders. What steps will you take to create a socially responsible business?

   Hint: Refer to the discussion of social responsibility in Chapter 3. What steps can you take to be a "good citizen" in the community? Consider also how you may need to be socially responsible toward your customers and, if applicable, investors, employees, and suppliers.

8. Will you sell your product in another country? If so, what countries and why? What challenges will you face?

   Hint: To help you consider issues of global business, refer to Chapter 5. Consider how you will expand internationally (e.g., independent agent, licensing). Do you expect global competition for your product? What advantages will foreign competitors have?

Note: Once you have answered the questions, save your Word document. You'll be answering additional questions in later chapters.

Whistleblowers at the RCMP

In 2007, four members of the RCMP went public with charges of fraud, misrepresentation, corruption, and nepotism against the leadership of the RCMP. The most senior member of the group was Fraser Macaulay, a career Mountie who had worked his way up through the ranks to become a senior human resources officer. While it is very unusual for Mounties to talk publicly about fraud, nepotism, and other criminal allegations, Macaulay said he had tried to alert his bosses to problems at the RCMP, but that he was lied to, shunned, and eventually pushed out of his job for his whistleblowing activity. Macaulay recognized that his whitle-blowing would damage the RCMP's reputation, but he came forward because he felt that doing so would eventually make the organization a better place.

Macaulay alleged that a small group of top managers used the RCMP pension fund to hire people who were related to senior members of the force, but that these people did not actually do any pension fund work. The four Mounties who testified said that when they reported this unacceptable activity to senior management, they were stonewalled and punished.

When the allegations first emerged, an internal investigation was launched by the RCMP, but then cancelled by Commissioner Zaccardelli. The Ottawa city police then conducted their own investigation, but no formal charges were laid. The auditor general eventually confirmed much of what Macaulay alleged, but by that time he had been transferred to the Department of National Defence (DND), which was known among the RCMP as the "penalty box." He is certain that he was transferred because he had been looking into pension fund irregularities. He also received a reduced performance bonus from his boss, the assistant commissioner, Barbara George. He was told that happened because he didn't support the commissioner.

During his last conversation with Commissioner Zaccardelli, Macaulay was told "it was time to go." This was an emotional conversation and Macaulay felt terrible. He told Zaccardelli that he had never lied to the commissioner before, so why did Zaccardelli think he would start now? Zaccardelli called the accusations Macaulay was making "baseless" and said that the pension fund was not at risk. Macaulay pointed out that he never said that the pension fund was at risk, but that funds were being used in an unacceptable manner and relatives of top managers were being paid for work that was not pension-fund related. Macaulay says that now it's about accountability for decisions that top managers made.

After the public investigation, Macaulay was reinstated in his former job. His boss, Barbara George, was suspended from her job for allegedly misleading the parliamentary committee that was looking into the allegations. Commissioner Zaccardelli is no longer with the RCMP.

Video Resource: "RCMP Whistleblower," *The National* (April 2, 2007).

Questions for Discussion

1. Define ethics. Explain how this idea is relevant for the situation at the RCMP.

2. Briefly describe the four criteria that can be used when trying to make an ethical decision. Which of these criteria is most relevant in the RCMP situation described above? Why?

3. What is meant by the term "whistleblowing"? Why do whistleblowers so often get into trouble when they point out questionable organizational practices?

4. Using the three-step model proposed in Chapter 3, analyze this situation. What conclusions do you reach?

Mompreneurs

The term "mompreneur" is often used to describe women who are trying to take care of kids and run a business at the same time. But just being a mom and being in business doesn't make a woman a mompreneur. Rather, a mompreneur is a woman who starts a business *because* she is inspired by being a mother. Consider two stories.

Darlene Martin

Darlene Martin has been a skating instructor for 17 years, and while the money is great, the hours are awful and Darlene has not been able to spend as much time with her daughter as she would like. So, she has started a home-based business called Bijouxbead, making and selling expensive jewellery (prices range from $100 to $1000 per piece). As a mompreneur, she wants to be able to set her own hours, and she is hoping that Bijouxbead will also make big money.

So far, Darlene has spent $75 000 on her business, and her products are carried in three high-end stores. She also sells her products at invitation-only parties. She wants her business to break even this year, and to do that she must sell $45 000 worth of product in the next five weeks. So, she's planning a big jewellery show, and she has invited over 200 people. She checks out craft shows to see how other jewellers display their products, then stops in at the boutiques that are selling her products. The boutiques take a cut of up to 50 percent of sales revenue, but at the craft show she will keep all the profit.

On sale day, family and friends help Darlene with the set-up. She has just six hours to sell $45 000 worth of beads. The first visitors are skaters and their parents. Most other visitors are family and friends (her dentist comes as well). At the end of the day, Darlene has sold just $8500 worth of products. She is far short of her goal, and she realizes that she has to do things differently in order to be successful. She wants to get more publicity for her products in magazines like *Lou Lou* and *Flair*, and she hopes to have her jewellery worn by celebrities.

Sandra Wilson

When Sandra Wilson lost her job at Canadian Airlines in the 1990s, she decided to start a home-based business that would give her flexibility and some extra income. Since she had experienced difficulty in getting non-slip soft shoes for her son Robert, she decided to make a soft shoe out of leather. She named her company Robeez. In 1994, she went to the Vancouver Gift Show trade exhibition with 20 pairs of her new footwear. They were an instant hit. Sales in the first year of her business were $20 000, and doubled every year thereafter. By 2002, sales reached $2 million. A lot of celebrity moms now use her products. She says her business was built largely on word of mouth.

Robeez is the world's leading manufacturer of soft-soled leather footwear. It employs 450 people and sells a diverse product line in 6500 stores located in North America, Europe, Australia, and parts of Asia. In 2006, Sandra sold out to Stride Rite Corporation for $30 million. She can now enjoy the fruits of her labour. She is still with Stride Rite as a consultant, and she also meets with various mompreneurs once a month to help them.

Video Resource: "Mompreneurs," *Marketplace* (February 16, 2008).

Questions for Discussion

1. What are the advantages and disadvantages of being a mompreneur?

2. Why do you think that so much publicity is currently being given to mompreneurs? Why is so little publicity given to "dadpreneurs"?

3. Consider the following statement: *"Mompreneurs say they want to spend more time with their children, but many hours of hard work are required each day in order to make a new business successful. This means that mompreneurs will not actually be able to spend any more time with their children."* Do you agree or disagree with the statement? Explain your reasoning.

The Business of Managing

Corporate culture, organizational structure, employee diversity, and motivation are four issues you will read about in the opening cases of Chapters 6 to 9. These and many other management issues must be dealt with if companies hope to grow and prosper. Managers in all business firms—indeed, in any kind of organization—must carry out the basic management functions of planning, organizing, leading, and controlling. Thcsc important functions are the focus of this section of the text.

Part Summary

Part 2, The Business of Managing, provides an overview of business management today. It includes a look at the importance of managers in business firms, how businesses are structured to achieve their goals, the management of the firm's human resources, and the importance of motivating and leading employees.

- We begin in **Chapter 6**, **Managing the Business Enterprise**, by describing how managers set goals and choose corporate strategies. The basic functions of management—planning, organizing, leading, and controlling—are examined, as are the different types and levels of managers that are found in business firms, and the corporate culture that is created in each firm.

- In **Chapter 7**, **Organizing the Business Enterprise**, we look at the basic organizational structures that companies have adopted, and the different kinds of authority that managers can have. The impact of the informal organization is also examined.

- In **Chapter 8**, **Managing Human Resources and Labour Relations**, we explore the activities that are necessary to effectively manage employees, including assessing employee needs, training, promoting, and compensating employees. We also look at the union movement in Canada, why and how workers organize, how government legislation has affected workers' rights to organize into unions, and how management and labour interact.

- In **Chapter 9**, **Motivating, Satisfying, and Leading Employees**, we examine the important issues of motivation and leadership. We look at the reasons why firms should establish good relationships with their employees, how managers' attempts to maintain productivity can affect their relations with employees, and the approaches to leadership that have developed over time.

chapter

6

Managing the Business Enterprise

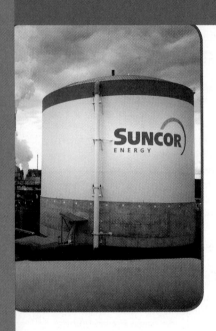

After reading this chapter, you should be able to:

LO-1 Describe the four activities that constitute the *management process*.

LO-2 Identify *types of managers* by level and area.

LO-3 Describe the five basic *management skills*.

LO-4 Explain the importance of *goal setting and strategic management* in organizational success.

LO-5 Discuss *contingency planning and crisis management* in today's business world.

LO-6 Explain the idea of *corporate culture* and why it is important.

SCANLIFE

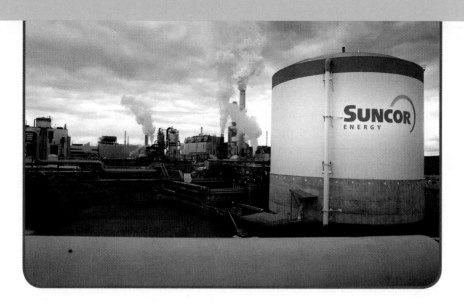

Corporate Culture

The term "corporate culture" refers to the shared experiences, values, norms, and ethical stance that characterize an organization. It is important for managers to understand the concept of corporate culture because culture influences the behaviour of employees, and that, in turn, influences corporate performance. Consider these examples of corporate culture:

- At WestJet, employees have a big stake in the company's success because of profit-sharing, and they contribute ideas about how to best run the airline. For example, a group has formed that calls itself the WestJesters. They do things like develop the cornball jokes that WestJet flight attendants tell during flights.

- The culture of the Toronto Blue Jays Baseball Club is making employees feel like they are part of a family. To facilitate the culture, former CEO Paul Godfrey invited small groups of employees to have "snacks with the president" so they could talk about how the operation of the organization. Godfrey encouraged questions from employees on virtually any topic.

- The culture of Suncor is open and non-bureaucratic, and the company has a clear strategy that employees can relate to. The company hires many new people, so it must take steps to ensure that the new employees understand the "soul" of Suncor.

- At Wellington West Holdings Inc., the culture is simple, personal, and fun.

Companies that focus largely on one type of product (for example, Starbucks) may have a fairly homogeneous culture throughout the organization. But large companies with many different divisions and many different types of customers (for example, the Royal Bank of Canada) are likely to have several different subcultures because the various divisions pursue different goals, and because different types of people are found in the different divisions.

How Will This Help Me?

After reading this chapter, you will have a clearer understanding of how to effectively carry out various management responsibilities. From the perspective of a *consumer* or *investor*, you'll be better able to assess and appreciate the quality of management in various companies.

Culture Surveys

Waterstone Human Capital is a Toronto-based executive search firm that publishes a 10 Most Admired Corporate Cultures list each year. Companies on the list in 2009 included Ceridian Canada, Acklands-Grainger Inc., Corus Entertainment, Starbucks Canada, and Walmart Canada. The 10 companies on the list had compound annual growth rates for the period 2005–2008 that were triple those of the TSX/S&P index.

Many companies do not systematically monitor their corporate culture, but Starbucks does. Once every 18 months, employees fill out a Partner View survey, which contains questions that are designed to help the company determine whether it is making progress toward one of its key values—providing a work environment where people treat one another with respect and dignity. The survey is voluntary, but about 90 percent of employees fill it out (on company time). One reason the participation rate is so high is that the company actually pays attention to what employees say in the survey. For example, when one survey showed that employees were not clear about career progression possibilities in the company, Starbucks held career fairs in several Canadian cities where company managers spoke with employees about management opportunities at Starbucks.

Some culture surveys assess the business culture of countries rather than individual businesses. In summarizing the perceptions of 4875 people from 22 countries, the 2010 Edelman Trust Barometer ranked Canada and Sweden as the most trusted business cultures, and Russia and China as the least trusted cultures. Survey respondents said that trust—being able to count on business to do the right thing—was even more important than the quality of goods that companies produce.

Cultural Change

Companies sometimes decide that they need to change their culture. A realization of the need for change usually comes after top management sees that changes in the company's external environment are going to require some sort of response from the company. But just because someone recognizes the need for change does not mean that the change will actually be implemented; changing an organization's culture can be very difficult.

In 2007, several RCMP officers alleged that senior management was covering up mismanagement of the RCMP's pension and insurance plans. As a result of these charges, lawyer David Brown was appointed by the government to look into the matter. His report concluded that Commissioner Giuliano Zaccardelli had exercised absolute power, that no one questioned his management style, and that there was a "tone" at the top of the organization that resulted in little respect for employees and put pressure on them to not challenge authority. The report also said that whistleblowers within the RCMP were punished when they pointed out that there were problems. The report concluded that the culture and management structure at the RCMP was "horribly broken." These developments are discouraging, since a few years earlier the RCMP had completed a "visioning" process that resulted in a new mission statement, a new set of core values, and a commitment to the communities where it worked. At that time, it was reported that the culture of the RCMP was quite different from what it was in the days when military tradition dominated the organization, but subsequent events suggested that the culture had not actually changed.

Who Are Managers?

All businesses depend on effective management. Regardless of the type of business they work in, managers perform many of the same basic functions, are responsible for many of the same tasks, and have many of the same responsibilities. All managers must make plans, organize their work, direct the work of subordinates, and control operations.

Although our focus is on managers in *business* settings, the principles of management apply to all kinds of organizations. Managers work in charities, churches, community organizations, educational institutions, and government agencies. The prime minister of Canada, the president of the University of Toronto, the executive director of the United Way, the dean of your business school, and the chief administrator of your local hospital are all managers. Remember, too, that managers bring to small

As top managers (a) Marjorie Scardino (CEO of Pearson PLC), (b) Calin Rovinescu (president and CEO of Air Canada), and (c) James Sinegal (co-founder and CEO of Costco) are important resources for their companies. They set the strategic direction for their companies and provide leadership to other managers. They are also accountable to shareholders, employees, customers, and other key constituents for the performance and effectiveness of their businesses.

organizations many of the skills that they bring to large ones. Regardless of the nature and size of an organization, managers are among its most important resources.

LO-1 The Management Process

Management is the process of planning, organizing, leading, and controlling an enterprise's financial, physical, human, and information resources to achieve the organization's goals. There are two important overall points to keep in mind when thinking about the management process. First, the planning, organizing, leading, and controlling aspects of a manager's job are interrelated. This means that a manager is likely to be engaged in all these activities during the course of any given business day.

Second, there is a difference between management effectiveness and management efficiency. **Efficiency** means achieving the greatest level of output with a given amount of input. **Effectiveness**, on the other hand, means achieving organizational goals that have been set. Thus, efficiency means doing things right, while effectiveness means doing the right things. A manager who focuses on being effective will likely also be efficient, but a manager who focuses on being efficient may or may not be effective. The box entitled "What Do Managers Actually Do?" explains the nature of managerial jobs.

Planning

Planning is the process of determining the firm's goals and developing a strategy for achieving those goals. The planning process involves five steps:

- In *step 1*, goals are established for the organization. A commercial airline, for example, may set a goal to fill 90 percent of the seats on each flight.

- In *step 2*, managers identify whether a gap exists between the company's desired and actual position. For example, the airline may analyze load data and find that only 73 percent of the seats on the average flight are filled.

- In *step 3*, managers develop plans to achieve the desired objectives. For example, the airline may reduce fares on heavily travelled routes in order to increase the percentage of the seats that are filled.

- In *step 4*, the plans that have been decided upon are implemented. For example, the fare from Toronto to Montreal may be reduced by 10 percent.

- In *step 5*, the effectiveness of the plan is assessed. The airline would measure the percentage of seats that were filled after the change was implemented to determine whether the goal was reached.

McDonald's experience in Canada over the past decade demonstrates the importance of planning. Until 2002, McDonald's was the largest fast-food chain in Canada. But then it was overtaken by Tim Hortons. In response to this development, McDonald's set a goal to reinvent itself and begin to grow again (*step 1*). The gap between where McDonald's was and where it wanted to be (*step 2*) was obvious, so McDonald's top managers developed a strategic plan (called "Plan to Win") in order to achieve the new objective (*step 3*). This involved developing many new menu items (like the Angus Burger, new salads, and snack wraps), renovating restaurants to look more like contemporary cafés or bistros (with polished stone tabletops and fireplaces), letting franchisees target local tastes with their menus (like the McLobster sandwich in the Maritimes), and

MANAGEMENT
The process of planning, organizing, leading, and controlling a business's financial, physical, human, and information resources in order to achieve its goals.

EFFICIENCY
Achieving the greatest level of output with a given amount of input.

EFFECTIVENESS
Achieving set organizational goals.

PLANNING That portion of a manager's job concerned with determining what the business needs to do and the best way to achieve it.

STRATEGIC PLANS
Plans that reflect decisions about resource allocations, company priorities, and steps needed to meet strategic goals.

staying open longer (60 percent of McDonald's restaurants are now open 24 hours a day). These plans were implemented beginning in 2003 and 2004 (*step 4*). The effectiveness of the plan has now been assessed (*step 5*). Sales were $2.9 billion in 2008 (a record) and $3 billion in 2009 (another record). These sales levels were achieved in spite of the recession of 2008–2009. McDonald's was one of only two companies in the Dow Jones Industrial Average whose stock price rose during 2008 (the other was Walmart).[1]

Because it may be difficult to predict which plans will be successful, some managers use *prediction markets* to help assess future possibilities. This approach involves creating a market where people can buy "shares" in various answers to important questions that need to be answered. At Cisco Systems, for example, 20 employees

in a chip-design unit bought shares based on how many defects they thought they would find in a new product (each share represented a range of possible number of defects). The winner of the game received an iPod. The actual number of defects found in the new chip was in the range that was predicted by the group. Other companies that use prediction markets include Microsoft, Best Buy, and Hewlett-Packard.[2]

A Hierarchy of Plans Plans can be made on three general levels, with each level reflecting plans for which managers at that level are responsible. These levels constitute a hierarchy because implementing plans is practical only when there is a logical flow from one level to the next. **Strategic plans** reflect decisions about resource allocations, company priorities, and the steps needed to meet strategic goals, and are usually set by top management. Procter & Gamble's strategy to have its products rank first or second in their category is an example of a

MANAGING IN TURBULENT TIMES

What Do Managers Actually Do?

Henry Mintzberg of McGill University conducted a detailed study of the work of five chief executive officers and found that managers work at an unrelenting pace; their activities are characterized by brevity, variety, and fragmentation; they have a preference for "live" action; they emphasize work activities that are current, specific, and well-defined; and they are attracted to verbal media.

Mintzberg says that a manager's formal authority and status give rise to three *interpersonal roles*: (1) *figurehead* (duties of a ceremonial nature, such as attending a subordinate's wedding); (2) *leader* (being responsible for the work of the unit); and (3) *liaison* (making contact outside the vertical chain of command). These interpersonal roles give rise to three *informational roles*: (1) *monitor* (scanning the environment for relevant information); (2) *disseminator* (passing information to subordinates); and (3) *spokesperson* (sending information to people outside the unit). The interpersonal and informational roles allow the manager to carry out four *decision-making roles*: (1) *entrepreneur* (improving the performance of the unit); (2) *disturbance handler* (responding to high-pressure disturbances, such as a strike at a supplier); (3) *resource allocator* (deciding who will get what in the unit); and (4) *negotiator* (working out

agreements on a wide variety of issues, such as the amount of authority an individual will be given).

Managers in a study conducted by Pace Productivity felt that they should have spent about half their time on activities such as managing staff, providing direction, and coaching, but that they actually were able to spend less than 20 percent of their time on "people management." Managers also thought that they should have spent about 6 percent of their time on administrative tasks, but they actually spent 25 percent of their time on those activities. The amount of time managers thought they should spend on planning was about the same as what they actually spent. Consistent with Mintzberg's original findings, the Pace data also showed that managers' lives are very hectic, and their focus shifts rapidly from activity to activity. For example, Pace identified 43 different activities that lasted an average of just 16 minutes each.

Critical Thinking Questions

1. Why is the work of managers important?
2. Why do you think managers spend less time on "people management" than they think they should, and more time on administrative tasks than they think they should?

strategic plan. We look at strategic planning later in this chapter. **Tactical plans** are shorter-range plans concerned with implementing specific aspects of the company's strategic plans. They typically involve upper and middle management. Coca-Cola's decision to increase sales in Europe by building European bottling facilities is an example of tactical planning. **Operational plans**, which are developed by middle and lower-level managers, set short-term targets for daily, weekly, or monthly performance. McDonald's, for example, establishes operational plans when it explains precisely how Big Macs are to be cooked, warmed, and served.

Organizing

Organizing is the process of deciding which jobs must be performed, and how these jobs should be coordinated so that the company's goals are reached. Most businesses prepare organization charts that diagram the various jobs within the company and how those jobs relate to one another. These charts help everyone understand their job and to whom they report. In many larger businesses, roles and reporting relationships may be too complex to draw as a simple box-and-line diagram.

To help you appreciate the importance of the organizing function, consider the example of Hewlett-Packard (HP). The company was once one of the leading-edge, high-tech firms in the world, but it lost its lustre a few years ago. HP had long prided itself on being a corporate confederation of individual businesses, and sometimes these businesses ended up competing with each other. This approach had been beneficial for much of the firm's history. It was easier for each business to make its own decisions quickly and efficiently, and the competition kept each unit on its toes. By the late 1990s, however, problems had become apparent, and no one could quite figure out what was going on. Ann Livermore, then head of the firm's software and services business, realized that the structure that had worked so well in the past was now holding the company back. To regain its competitive edge, HP needed an integrated, organization-wide strategy. Livermore led the charge to create one organization united behind one strategic plan. Eventually, a new team of top managers was handed control of the company, and every major component of the firm's structure was reorganized. The firm is now back on solid footing and has regained its place as one of the world's top technology businesses.[3] We explore the organizing function in more detail in Chapter 7.

Leading

When **leading**, managers guide and motivate workers to meet the company's objectives. Legendary leaders like

Sam Walton (Walmart) and Clive Beddoe (WestJet) were able to unite their employees in a clear and targeted manner, and motivate them to work in the best interests of their employer. While managers do have the power to give orders and demand results, leading goes beyond merely giving orders. Leaders must also have the ability to motivate their employees to set challenging goals and to work hard to achieve them. This is likely to lead to organizational success, which in turn means that employees will respect their leaders, trust them, and believe that by working together, both the firm and its employees will benefit. We discuss the important topic of leadership more fully in Chapter 9.

Controlling

Controlling is the process of monitoring a firm's performance to make sure that it is meeting its goals. Managers at WestJet and Air Canada, for example, focus relentlessly on numerous indicators of performance that they can measure and adjust. Everything from on-time arrivals to baggage-handling

TACTICAL PLANS Generally, short-range plans concerned with implementing specific aspects of a company's strategic plans.

OPERATIONAL PLANS Plans setting short-term targets for daily, weekly, or monthly performance.

ORGANIZING That portion of a manager's job concerned with mobilizing the necessary resources to complete a particular task.

LEADING That portion of a manager's job concerned with guiding and motivating employees to meet the firm's objectives.

CONTROLLING That portion of a manager's job concerned with monitoring the firm's performance and, if necessary, acting to bring it in line with the firm's goals.

Japanese organizations don't usually like radical restructuring, but when Senichi Hoshino took over the hapless Hanshin Tigers, he axed 24 of the team's 70 players and replaced them with free agents. He required everyone on the roster to compete for a position, tracked performance daily, and made individual coaches directly responsible for seeing that players executed certain skills. Soon after that, the Tigers won the pennant.

errors to the number of empty seats on an airplane to surveys of employee and customer satisfaction are regularly and routinely monitored. If on-time arrivals start to slip, managers focus on the problem and get it fixed. No single element of the firm's performance can slip too far before it's noticed and fixed.

Figure 6.1 illustrates the control process, which begins when management establishes standards (often for financial performance). If, for example, a company sets a goal of increasing its sales by 20 percent over the next five years, an appropriate standard to assess progress toward the 20 percent goal might be an increase of about 4 percent a year. Managers then measure actual performance each year against standards. If the two amounts agree, the organization continues along its present course. If they vary significantly, however, one or the other needs adjustment. If sales have increased 3.9 percent by the end of the first year, things are probably fine. But if sales have dropped 1 percent, some revision in plans is needed.

Controlling applies to many activities, including the college or university courses that you are now taking. The instructor first indicates the knowledge areas where you must show competence, and the level of competence you must show. Next, the instructor measures your performance, usually through assignments and exams. The instructor then determines whether your performance meets the standard. If your performance is satisfactory (or unsatisfactory), you receive feedback in the form of a passing (or failing) grade in the course.

Control can also show where performance is better (or worse) than expected, and can serve as a basis for providing rewards or reducing costs. For example, when the distributor of the surprise hit movie *The March of the Penguins* saw how popular the movie was becoming, the firm was able to increase advertising and distribution, making the niche movie into a major commercial success. In contrast, when the sales of the Chevrolet Super Sport Roadster (a classic, late-1940s pickup-style vehicle with a two-seat roadster design) were much lower than expected, production of the vehicle was suspended.

LO-2 Types of Managers

Although all managers plan, organize, lead, and control, not all managers have the same degree of responsibility for each activity. Moreover, managers differ in the specific application of these activities. Thus we can differentiate between managers based on their *level* of responsibility and their *area* of responsibility.

Levels of Management

The three basic levels of management are top, middle, and first-line management. As Figure 6.2 shows, in most firms there are more middle managers than top managers and more first-line managers than middle managers. Moreover, as the categories imply, the authority of managers and the complexity of their duties increase as we move up the pyramid.

Figure 6.2
Most organizations have three basic levels of management.

Figure 6.1
The control process.

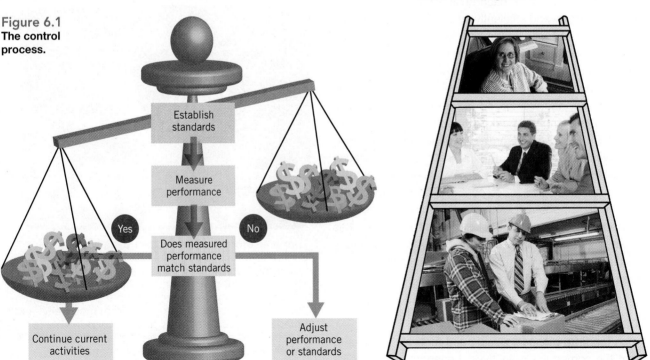

Top Managers The managers who guide the fortunes of companies are **top managers**. Top managers set policies, formulate strategies, oversee significant decisions, and represent the company in its dealings with other businesses and government.[4] Top managers are responsible to the board of directors and stockholders for the firm's overall performance and effectiveness. Common titles for top managers include president, vice-president, chief executive officer (CEO), chief operating officer (COO), and chief financial officer (CFO). CEOs are the link between the organization and its markets and customers.[5]

Each year, *Canadian Business* develops an All-Star Execs list by examining financial data of Canadian companies, and by consulting with a panel of business leaders to determine which executives performed unusually well. In 2009, the top managers were Mayo Schmidt (CEO of Viterra), Colleen Johnston (CFO of TD Bank Financial Group), and Larry Conlee (COO of Research In Motion).[6]

Middle Managers Although below the ranks of the top executives, **middle managers** still occupy positions of considerable autonomy and importance. Titles such as plant manager, operations manager, and division manager are typical of middle-management positions. The producer of a Lion's Gate film like *Precious* is a middle manager. In general, middle managers are responsible for implementing the strategies, policies, and decisions made by top managers. For example, if top management decides to bring out a new product in 12 months or to cut costs by 5 percent, middle management will have to decide to increase the pace of new product development or to reduce the plant's workforce.

First-Line Managers Individuals with titles such as *supervisor*, *office manager*, and *group leader* are **first-line managers.** Although they spend most of their time working with and supervising the employees who report to them, first-line managers' activities are not limited to those

activities. At a building site, for example, the project manager not only ensures that workers are carrying out construction as specified by the architect but also interacts extensively with materials suppliers, community officials, and middle and top managers at the home office. The manager of a Canadian Tire store and the flight-services manager for a specific Air Canada flight are first-line managers. Table 6.1 summarizes the duties of the three basic levels of management.

Areas of Management

Within any large company, the top, middle, and first-line managers work in a variety of areas, including human resources, operations, information, marketing, and finance.

Human Resource Managers **Human resource managers** can be found in most companies; they hire employees, train them, evaluate their performance, decide how they should be compensated, and deal with labour unions (if the workforce is unionized). Large firms may have several human resource departments, each dealing with specialized activities. Imperial Oil, for example, has separate departments to deal with recruiting and hiring, wage and salary levels, and labour relations. Smaller firms may have a single department, while very small organizations may have a single person responsible for all human resource activities. Chapters 8 and 9 address human resource management issues.

TOP MANAGERS Those managers responsible for a firm's overall performance and effectiveness and for developing long-range plans for the company.

MIDDLE MANAGERS Those managers responsible for implementing the decisions made by top managers.

FIRST-LINE MANAGERS Those managers responsible for supervising the work of employees.

HUMAN RESOURCE MANAGERS Those managers responsible for hiring, training, evaluating, and compensating employees.

Table 6.1 **The Three Levels of Management**

Level	Examples	Responsibilities
Top managers	President, vice president, treasurer, chief executive officer (CEO), chief financial officer (CFO)	■ Responsible for the overall performance and effectiveness of the firm ■ Set general policies, formulate strategies, and approve all significant decisions ■ Represent the company in dealings with other firms and with government bodies
Middle managers	Plant manager, operations manager, division manager, regional sales manager	■ Responsible for implementing the strategies and working toward the goals set by top managers
First-line managers	Supervisor, office manager, project manager, group leader, sales manager	■ Responsible for supervising the work of employees who report to them ■ Ensure employees understand and are properly trained in company policies and procedures

OPERATIONS MANAGERS Those managers responsible for controlling production, inventory, and quality of a firm's products.

INFORMATION MANAGERS Those managers responsible for the design and implementation of systems to gather, process, and disseminate information.

MARKETING MANAGERS Those managers responsible for developing, pricing, promoting, and distributing goods and services to buyers.

FINANCIAL MANAGERS Those managers responsible for planning and overseeing the financial resources of a firm.

TECHNICAL SKILLS Skills associated with performing specialized tasks within a firm.

Operations Managers **Operations managers** are responsible for a company's system for creating goods and services. This includes production control, inventory control, and quality control, among other duties. Manufacturing companies like Steelcase, Bristol Aerospace, and Sony need operations managers at many levels. Such firms typically have a vice-president for operations (top), plant managers (middle), and supervisors (first-line). In recent years, sound operations management practices have also become increasingly important to service-producing organizations like hospitals, the government, and colleges and universities. Operations management is the subject of Chapter 10.

Information Managers Dramatic increases in both the amount of information available to managers and the ability to manage it have led to the emergence of **information managers**. These managers are responsible for designing and implementing various systems to gather, process, and disseminate information. Federal Express, for example, has a chief information officer. Middle managers engaged in information management help design information systems for divisions or plants. Computer systems managers within smaller businesses or operations are first-line managers. Information management is discussed in Appendix B.

Marketing Managers Marketing includes the development, pricing, promotion, and distribution of products and services. **Marketing managers** are responsible for getting these products and services to buyers. Marketing is especially important for firms producing consumer products, such as Procter & Gamble, Coca-Cola, and Sun Ice. These firms may have large numbers of marketing managers at various levels. For example, a large firm will probably have a vice-president for marketing (top manager), regional marketing managers (middle managers), and several district sales managers (first-line managers). We examine marketing in Chapters 12–14.

Financial Managers Management of a firm's finances is extremely important to its survival. Nearly every company

has **financial managers** to plan and oversee its financial resources. Levels of financial management may include a vice-president for finance (top), division controller (middle), and accounting supervisor (first-line). For large financial institutions, effective financial management is the company's reason for being. Chapters 15 and 16 describe financial management in detail.

Other Managers Some firms have more specialized managers. Chemical companies like CIL have research and development managers, for example, whereas companies like Petro-Canada and Apple have public relations managers. The range of possibilities is almost endless, and the areas of management are limited only by the needs and imagination of the company.

LO-3 Basic Management Skills

The degree of success that people achieve in management positions is determined by the skills and abilities they possess. Effective managers must have several skills: *technical*, *human relations*, *conceptual*, *time management*, and *decision-making skills*.

Technical Skills

Technical skills help people to perform specialized tasks. A secretary's ability to type, an animator's ability to draw a cartoon, and an accountant's ability to audit a company's records are all technical skills. People develop their technical skills through education and experience. The secretary, for example, probably took an office systems technology course and has had many hours of practice both on and off the job. The animator may have had training in an art school and probably learned a great deal from experienced animators on the job. The accountant earned a university degree and a professional certification.

As Figure 6.3 shows, technical skills are especially important for first-line managers. Most first-line managers spend considerable time helping employees solve work-related problems, monitoring their performance, and training them in more efficient work procedures. Such managers need a basic understanding of the jobs they supervise. As a manager moves up the corporate ladder, however, technical skills become less and less important. Top managers, for example, often need only a general familiarity with the mechanics of basic tasks performed within the company. A top manager at Disney, for example, probably can't draw Mickey Mouse or build a ride for Disney World.

TOP MANAGEMENT

Technical

Human Relations

Conceptual

MIDDLE MANAGEMENT

Technical

Human Relations

Conceptual

FIRST-LINE MANAGEMENT

Technical

Human Relations

Conceptual

Figure 6.3
Different levels in an organization require different combinations of managerial skills.

Human Relations Skills

Human relations skills help managers to lead, motivate, communicate with, and get along with their subordinates. Managers with poor human relations skills will likely have conflicts with subordinates, cause valuable employees to quit or transfer, and contribute to poor morale. Figure 6.3 shows that human relations skills are important at all levels of management. This is true because all managers in the hierarchy act as "bridges" between their bosses, their subordinates, and other managers at the same level in the hierarchy. A study by DDI Canada found that the top reason for managerial failure was poor people skills.[7]

To improve their insights into employee needs and company operations, some managers have decided to work alongside entry-level employees on a temporary basis. When the CEO of 7-Eleven (Joseph De Pinto) worked undercover at a 7-Eleven outlet, he discovered how hard the people worked, and why the location was selling so much coffee. Larry O'Donnell, the CEO of Waste Management, did jobs like sorting trash, picking up paper at a landfill, and cleaning portable toilets. The experience taught him the pressure for production that employees had to cope with, and he introduced changes based on what he had learned on the job.[8]

Conceptual Skills

Conceptual skills refer to a person's ability to think in the abstract, to diagnose and analyze various situations, and to see beyond the present situation. Conceptual skills help managers recognize new market opportunities and threats. For example, in e-commerce businesses, conceptual skills help mangers foresee how a particular business application will be affected by, or can be translated to, the internet. Figure 6.3 shows that top managers depend most on conceptual skills, and first-line managers least, but at least some conceptual skills are needed in almost any management job.

Time Management Skills

Time management skills refer to the productive use that managers make of their time. In 2009, for example, the CEO of Thomson Reuters Corp., Thomas Glocer, was paid $36.6 million.[9] Assuming that he worked 50 hours a week and took two weeks' vacation, Glocer earned about $14 640 per hour, or about $244 per minute. Any time that he wastes represents a large cost to Thomson Reuters and its stockholders.

To manage time effectively, managers must address four leading causes of wasted time:

- *Paperwork.* Some managers spend too much time deciding what to do with letters and reports. Most documents of this sort are routine and can be handled quickly. Managers must learn to recognize those documents that require more attention.

- *The telephone.* Experts estimate that managers are interrupted by the telephone every five minutes. To manage time more effectively, they suggest having a secretary screen all calls and setting aside a certain block of time each day to return the important ones.

- *Meetings.* Many managers spend as much as four hours per day in meetings. To help keep this time productive, the person handling the meeting should specify a clear agenda, start on time, keep everyone focused on the agenda, and end on time.

- *Email.* With the introduction of devices like the BlackBerry, managers are relying more heavily on email and other forms of electronic communication. But many email messages are not important, and some are

HUMAN RELATIONS SKILLS Skills in understanding and getting along with people.

CONCEPTUAL SKILLS Abilities to think in the abstract, diagnose and analyze various situations, and see beyond the present situation.

TIME MANAGEMENT SKILLS Skills associated with the productive use of time.

downright trivial. As the number of electronic messages grows, the potential time wasted also increases.

Decision-Making Skills

Decision-making skills help managers define problems and select the best course of action. It is a critical management skill because decision making affects all the functions of management. The Alternative Board (TAB) is devoted to improving management decision making and has 1000 peer groups around North America. These peer groups—which are attended by managers who are looking for solutions to problems that they are experiencing—provide a forum for discussions among managers who have had similar problems.[10]

The Pittsburgh Steelers are one of the most successful franchises in the history of professional football. They have won more Super Bowls (six) than any other team. The Rooney family has owned and managed the team since 1933. They have demonstrated technical and decision-making skills in selecting and retaining the best players for the team. In 2009, the Steelers won another Super Bowl.

The Rational Decision-Making Process Figure 6.4 shows the steps in the rational decision-making process. The key elements of each step are described below.

Recognizing and Defining the Decision Situation The first step in rational decision making is recognizing that a decision is necessary. There must be some stimulus or spark to initiate this process. For example, when equipment malfunctions, managers must decide whether to repair it or to replace it. The stimulus for a decision may

Figure 6.4
Steps in the rational decision-making process.

Step	Detail	Example
1. Recognizing and defining the decision situation	Some stimulus indicates that a decision must be made. The stimulus may be positive or negative.	The plant manager sees that employee turnover has increased by 5 percent.
2. Identifying alternatives	Both obvious and creative alternatives are desired. In general, the more important the decision, the more alternatives should be generated.	The plant manager can increase wages, increase benefits, or change hiring standards.
3. Evaluating alternatives	Each alternative is evaluated to determine its feasibility, its satisfactoriness, and its consequences.	Increasing benefits may not be feasible. Increasing wages and changing hiring standards may satisfy all conditions.
4. Selecting the best alternative	Consider all situational factors and choose the alternative that best fits the manager's situation.	Changing hiring standards will take an extended period of time to cut turnover, so increase wages.
5. Implementing the chosen alternative	The chosen alternative is implemented into the organizational system.	The plant manager may need permission from corporate headquarters. The human resource department establishes a new wage structure.
6. Following up and evaluating the results	At some time in the future, the manager should ascertain the extent to which the alternative chosen in step 4 and implemented in step 5 has worked.	The plant manager notes that six months later, turnover dropped to its previous level.

be either a problem or an opportunity. A manager facing cost overruns on a project is faced with a problem decision, while a manager who is trying to decide how to invest surplus funds is faced with an opportunity decision.

Understanding precisely what the problem or opportunity is comes from careful analysis and thoughtful consideration of the situation. Consider the international air travel industry. Because of the growth of international travel related to business, education, and tourism, global carriers like Singapore Airlines, KLM, JAL, British Airways, and American Airlines need to increase their capacity for international travel. Because most major international airports are already operating at or near capacity, adding a significant number of new flights to existing schedules is not feasible. As a result, the most logical alternative is to increase capacity on existing flights. Thus, Boeing and Airbus, the world's only manufacturers of large commercial aircraft, recognized an important opportunity and defined their decision situation as how best to respond to the need for increased global travel capacity.[11]

Identifying Alternatives Once the need for a decision has been recognized and defined, the second step is to identify possible alternative courses of effective action. In general, the more important the decision, the more attention is directed to developing alternatives. If the decision involves a multimillion-dollar relocation, a great deal of time and expertise should be devoted to identifying alternatives, but if the decision involves choosing a name for the company softball team, much less resources should be devoted to the task (although there may be a lot of arguing about what the name should be!).

Managers must accept that factors such as legal restrictions, moral and ethical norms, and available technology can limit their alternatives. For example, after assessing the question of how to increase international airline capacity, Boeing and Airbus identified three alternatives: They could independently develop new large planes, they could collaborate in a joint venture to create a single new large plane, or they could modify their largest existing planes to increase their capacity.

Evaluating Alternatives Once alternatives have been identified, they must be thoroughly evaluated to increase the chance that the alternative finally chosen will be successful. During its analysis

of alternatives, Airbus concluded that it would be at a disadvantage if it tried to simply enlarge its existing planes, because the competitive Boeing 747 is already the largest aircraft being made and could readily be expanded. Boeing, meanwhile, was seriously concerned about the risk inherent in building a new and even larger plane, even if it shared the risk with Airbus as a joint venture.

Selecting the Best Alternative Choosing the best available alternative is a key activity in decision making. Even though many situations do not lend themselves to objective mathematical analysis, managers and leaders can often develop subjective estimates for choosing an alternative. Decision makers should also remember that finding multiple acceptable alternatives may be possible, so selecting just one alternative and rejecting all the others might not be necessary. For example, Airbus proposed a joint venture with Boeing, but Boeing decided that its best course of action was to modify its existing 747 to increase its capacity. Airbus then decided to proceed on its own to develop and manufacture a new jumbo jet called the A380. Meanwhile, Boeing decided that in addition to modifying its 747, it would also develop a new plane (the 787).

Implementing the Chosen Alternative After an alternative has been selected, managers must implement it. In the case of an acquisition, for example, managers must decide how to integrate the activities of the new business into the firm's existing organizational framework. One of the key considerations during implementation is employee resistance to change. The reasons for such resistance include insecurity, inconvenience, and fear of the unknown. Managers must also recognize that even

After a long decision-making process, Airbus decided to design its own new jumbo jet. Boeing, meanwhile, went through a similar decision-making process but concluded that the risks were too great to gamble on such an enormous project. Instead, the company decided to modify its existing 747 design and develop a new fuel-efficient aircraft called the 787.

when all alternatives have been evaluated as precisely as possible and the consequences of each alternative have been weighed, unanticipated consequences are still likely. For example, both Boeing and Airbus have experienced unexpected delays in bringing their new planes to market.

Following up and Evaluating the Results

The final step in the decision-making process requires managers to evaluate the effectiveness of their decision—that is, they should make sure that the chosen alternative has served its original purpose. If an implemented alternative appears not to be working, they can respond in several ways. One possibility is to adopt an alternative that had previously been discarded. Or they might recognize that the situation was not correctly defined to begin with and start the process all over again. In the Boeing/Airbus case, both companies are getting some feedback about whether or not they made a good decision. For example, increasing fuel prices may mean that the 787 was the best decision because it is so fuel efficient.

Behavioural Aspects of Decision Making Most managers try to be logical when they make decisions. But even when they try, they may not succeed. When Starbucks opened its first coffee shops in New York, it relied on scientific marketing research, taste tests, and rational deliberation in making a decision to emphasize drip over espresso coffee. However, that decision proved wrong when it became clear that New Yorkers strongly preferred the same espresso-style coffees that were Starbucks' mainstays in the west. Hence, the firm had to reconfigure its stores hastily to meet customer preferences.

To complicate matters, non-logical and emotional factors often influence managerial decision making. These factors include *organizational politics*, *intuition*, *escalation of commitment*, and *risk propensity*.

Organizational Politics The term **organizational politics** refers to the actions that people take as they try to get what they want. These actions may or may not be beneficial to the organization, but they do influence decision making, particularly if the person taking the action is a powerful manager.

Intuition Managers sometimes decide to do something because it "feels right" or they have a "hunch." **Intuition** is usually based on years of experience and practice in making decisions in similar situations. Such an inner sense may actually help managers make an occasional decision without going through a rational sequence of steps. For example, the New York Yankees once contacted three major sneaker manufacturers—Nike, Reebok, and Adidas—and informed them that they were interested in signing a sponsorship deal. While Nike and Reebok were carefully and rationally assessing the possibilities, managers at Adidas quickly responded to the idea and ended up hammering out a contract while the competitors were still analyzing details.[12] These occasional successes can be very dramatic, but they should not cause managers to rely too heavily on intuition.

Escalation of Commitment When a manager makes a decision and then remains committed to its implementation in spite of clear evidence that it was a bad decision, **escalation of commitment** has occurred.[13] A good example of this is Expo '86, the world's fair that was held in British Columbia. When the project was first conceived, the deficit was projected at about $56 million. Over the next few years, the projected deficit kept rising until it was over $300 million. In spite of that, the project went forward. Managers can avoid overcommitment by setting specific goals ahead of time that deal with how much time and money they are willing to spend on a given project. These goals make it harder for managers to interpret unfavourable news in a positive light.

Risk Propensity **Risk propensity** refers to how much a manager is willing to gamble when making decisions. Managers who are very cautious when making decisions are more likely to avoid mistakes, and they are unlikely to make decisions that lead to big losses (or big gains). Other managers are extremely aggressive in making decisions and are willing to take risks.[14] They rely heavily on intuition, reach decisions quickly, and often risk big money on their decisions. These managers are more likely than their conservative counterparts to achieve big successes, but they are also more likely to incur greater losses.[15] The organization's culture is a prime ingredient in fostering different levels of risk propensity.

LO-4 Strategic Management: Setting Goals and Formulating Strategy

Strategic management is the process of effectively aligning the organization with its external environment. The starting point in strategic management is setting goals that a business wants to achieve. Every business needs goals. Remember, however, that deciding what it intends to do is only the first step for an organization. Managers must also make decisions about what actions will and will not achieve company goals. Decisions cannot be made on a problem-by-problem basis or merely to meet needs as they arise. In most companies, a broad program underlies those decisions. That program is called a **strategy**—the broad set of organizational plans for implementing the decisions made for achieving organizational goals.

Setting Business Goals

Goals are performance targets, the means by which organizations and their managers measure success or failure at every level. Managers must understand the purposes of goal setting and the kinds of goals that need to be set.

The Purposes of Goal Setting There are four main purposes in organizational goal setting:

1. *Goal setting provides direction, guidance, and motivation for all managers.* For example, each manager at Kanke Seafood Restaurants Ltd. is required to work through a goal-setting exercise each year. Setting and achieving goals is the most effective form of self-motivation.

2. *Goal setting helps firms allocate resources.* Areas that are expected to grow, for example, will get first priority. Thus, 3M allocates more resources to new projects with large sales potential than to projects with low growth potential.

3. *Goal setting helps to define corporate culture.* General Electric's goal, for instance, is to push each of its divisions to number one or number two in its industry. The result is a competitive (and often stressful) environment, and a culture that rewards success and has little tolerance for failure.

4. *Goal setting helps managers assess performance.* If a unit sets a goal of increasing sales by 10 percent in a given year, managers in that unit who attain or exceed the goal can be rewarded. Units failing to reach the goal will also be compensated accordingly.

Kinds of Goals Goals differ from company to company, depending on the firm's vision and mission. Every organization has a **vision (or purpose)** that indicates *why* it exists and what kind of organization it wants to be. For example, businesses seek profit, universities discover and transmit new knowledge, and government agencies provide services to the public. Most organizations also have a **mission statement**—a statement of *how* they will achieve their purpose. DaimlerChrysler's mission statement emphasizes

"delighted customers," while Atco Ltd.'s mission is to provide products and services to the energy and resource industries, and to invest in energy-related assets in North America. Mission statements often include some statement about the company's core values and its commitment to ethical behaviour.

Two business firms can have the same vision—for example, to sell watches at a profit—yet have very different missions. Timex sells low-cost, reliable watches in outlets ranging from department stores to corner drugstores. Rolex, on the other hand, sells high-quality, high-priced fashion watches through selected jewellery stores. Regardless of a company's purpose and mission, it must set long-term, intermediate, and short-term goals.

- **Long-term goals** relate to extended periods of time — typically five years or more into the future. American Express, for example, might set a long-term goal of doubling the number of participating merchants during the next 10 years.

- **Intermediate goals** are set for a period of one to five years into the future. Companies usually have intermediate goals in several areas. For example, the marketing department's goal might be to increase sales by 3 percent in two years. The production department might want to decrease expenses by 6 percent in four years. Human resources might seek to cut turnover by 10 percent in two years. Finance might aim for a 3 percent increase in return on investment in three years.

- Like intermediate goals, **short-term goals**—which are set for perhaps one year—are developed for several different areas. Increasing sales by 2 percent this year, cutting costs by 1 percent next quarter, and reducing turnover by 4 percent over the next six months are all short-term goals.

Whatever the time frame of the goals that are set, research shows that managers who set **SMART goals** (goals that are Specific, Measurable, Achievable, Realistic,

STRATEGY The broad set of organizational plans for implementing the decisions made for achieving organizational goals.

VISION (OR PURPOSE) A statement indicating why an organization exists and what kind of organization it wants to be.

MISSION STATEMENT An organization's statement of how it will achieve its purpose in the environment in which it conducts its business.

LONG-TERM GOALS Goals set for extended periods of time, typically five years or more into the future.

INTERMEDIATE GOALS Goals set for a period of one to five years.

SHORT-TERM GOALS Goals set for the very near future, typically less than one year.

SMART GOALS Goals that are Specific, Measurable, Achievable, Realistic, and Time-framed.

and *Time*-framed) have higher performance than managers who don't. The boxed insert entitled "Setting Green Goals" describes the importance of setting goals that take the environment into account.

Formulating Strategy

After a firm has set its goals, it must develop a strategy for achieving them. In contrast to planning, strategy is wider in scope, and is a broad program that describes how a business intends to meet its goals, how it will respond to new challenges, and how it will meet new needs. Developing a strategy may not be easy (see the boxed insert entitled "Print Media").

Strategy formulation involves three basic steps: (1) setting strategic goals, (2) analyzing the organization and its environment, and (3) matching the organization and its environment (see Figure 6.5).

Setting Strategic Goals **Strategic goals** are long-term goals derived directly from the firm's mission statement. General Electric, for example, is pursuing four strategic goals to ensure continued success for the company: an emphasis on quality control, an emphasis on selling services and not just products, concentrating on niche acquisitions, and global expansion.

THE GREENING OF BUSINESS

Setting Green Goals

The logic of goal setting is being applied to make businesses greener. Consider the following:

- Walmart set a goal to reduce the amount of packaging used by 5 percent throughout its huge supply chain; it wants to achieve that goal by 2013.
- The province of Ontario has set a goal to reduce plastic bag usage by 50 percent by 2012.
- Scotiabank has set a goal to be in the top 10 percent of the companies listed on the Dow Jones Sustainability World Index.
- Employees on different floors of the Air Miles building in Toronto compete to see who can reduce energy usage the most in a specific month.

For some organizations, the setting of green goals is closely tied to their success. For example, the CEO of Honda, Takeo Fukui, recognized that Toyota's popular Prius hybrid automobile outsold Honda's hybrid car by a wide margin during the last decade, so he set a goal to make Honda the greenest company in the automobile industry. Honda has set a goal to sell 500 000 hybrid automobiles each year (Toyota's goal is one million). In 2008, Honda introduced its Clarity FCX, which is the most advanced green vehicle ever made. It is powered by a hydrogen fuel cell that generates no pollution at all. Honda also launched a new gas–electric hybrid in 2009, and plans to launch several other hybrids by 2015.

Rona Inc., the home renovation chain, has set a goal of doing business only with suppliers who address environmental sustainability, and who do not contribute to deforestation. The goal for 2009 was to have all the plywood panels Rona sells made only from lumber that comes from forests that have been certified as sustainable. In 2010, the same goal was applied to spruce, pine, and fir. By 2012, Rona's goal is to have 25 percent of its total wood sales come from forests that are certified by the Forest Stewardship Council.

Green goals may be imposed on companies by external groups. In 2007, for example, the federal government notified Canada's biggest industrial polluters that they had six months to provide emissions data that the government would use in setting new emission reduction targets. Discussions also continue at the international level about what the goal for emissions should be, but to date there has been no agreement. A spokesman for 77 developing nations says that unless there is a goal, there can be no progress.

Critical Thinking Questions

1. What are the advantages associated with setting green goals? Are there disadvantages? Explain.
2. What difficulties might Rona encounter as it tries to reach the goal of having 25 percent of its total wood sales come from forests that are certified by the Forest Stewardship Council?
3. What are the advantages of the government setting emission reduction targets? What are the disadvantages?

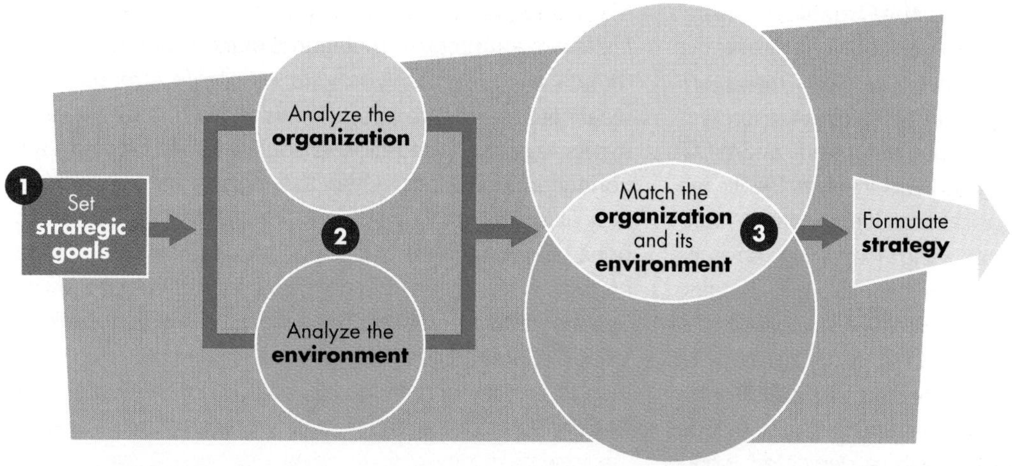

Figure 6.5
Strategy formulation.

E-BUSINESS AND SOCIAL MEDIA SOLUTIONS

Print Media: Are E-Readers the Solution or a New Problem?

The publishing business is dealing with significant changes that will require serious strategic thinking. Consider these facts:

- According to the Audit Bureau of Circulations, which measures statistics for 57 Canadian and 472 American magazines, the industry is suffering. Newsstand sales were down and ad page revenues were down 21 percent in Canada in 2009.

- According to the Newspaper Association of America, readership has fallen by more than 700 000 per year since 2000. Classified ad revenue is down 40 percent in the last decade because of online competitors like craigslist, Monster, and AutoTrader. Rupert Murdoch recently declared that news aggregator sites like Google and Digg.com are kleptomaniacs that steal content. As the owner of NewsCorp, a major media giant, his intention is to erect pay walls around his media sites.

- Book publishers and bookstore owners are also under pressure. According to Heather Reisman of Indigo Books, the e-reader threat may cause a 15 percent decline in book sales over the next five years. Others predict digital sales will comprise 25 percent of the market in three years and as high as 80 percent in 10 years.

There are several new electronic devices that are having a big impact on the publishing industry, including Kindle (with a grey and black screen can be read in direct sunlight), the iPad (which provides a colour touch screen and serves as a web surfer, video console, and iPod), Kobo (a Kindle-like competitor that undercut the competition in 2010 with a price of $150), the Sony Reader, Nook (Barnes and Noble), Eee Pad (AsusTek), and the Skiff. The EnTourage eDGe is an interesting dual screen reader that looks like a book. Imagine reading the newspaper on the bus without elbowing the person next to you each time you flip a page. Imagine packing one e-reader rather than three or four books on your next trip. Actually, you don't have to imagine it.

The online world has been having a negative impact on print media for some time, but the introduction of e-readers was a new tipping point. How will the print media providers and the technology device creators develop a strategic, sustainable model? The model must satisfy the needs of consumers, columnists, authors, and technology companies alike. Developing such a strategy is not easy. Major publishers like Macmillan used the iPad launch to negotiate higher prices on e-books than had previously been dictated by Amazon (because of its virtual monopoly). Five top publishers—including Penguin and HarperCollins—were on board for the launch of the iPad. Newspapers and magazine companies were even keener to form partnerships, since the iPad was seen as a way to display content in a new, exciting, and accessible fashion.

Critical Thinking Questions

1. How do you think e-readers will impact the print industry? In the short term? In the long term?
2. Which print media source (newspapers, magazines, or books) is more likely to benefit from the widespread adoption of e-readers? Why?

SWOT ANALYSIS Identification and analysis of organizational strengths and weaknesses and environmental opportunities and threats as part of strategy formulation.

ORGANIZATIONAL ANALYSIS The process of analyzing a firm's strengths and weaknesses.

ENVIRONMENTAL ANALYSIS The process of scanning the environment for threats and opportunities.

CORPORATE-LEVEL STRATEGY Identifies the various businesses that a company will be in, and how these businesses will relate to each other.

BUSINESS-LEVEL (COMPETITIVE) STRATEGY Identifies the ways a business will compete in its chosen line of products or services.

FUNCTIONAL STRATEGIES Identify the basic courses of action that each department in the firm will pursue so that it contributes to the attainment of the business's overall goals.

CONCENTRATION STRATEGY Involves focusing the company on one product or product line.

Analyzing the Organization and Its Environment After strategic goals have been set, managers assess both their organization and its environment using a **SWOT analysis**. This involves identifying organizational *Strengths* and *Weaknesses*, and identifying environmental *Opportunities* and *Threats*. Strengths and weaknesses are factors *internal* to the firm, and are assessed using **organizational analysis**. Strengths might include surplus cash, a dedicated workforce, an ample supply of managerial talent, technical expertise, or weak competitors. For example, Pepsi's strength in beverage distribution through its network of soft-drink distributors was successfully extended to distribution of its Aquafina brand of bottled water. Weaknesses might include a cash shortage, aging factories, and a poor public image. Garden.com's reliance on the internet-based e-tailing model became its downfall when the dot-com bubble burst.

Opportunities and threats are factors *external* to the firm, and are assessed using **environmental analysis**. *Opportunities* include things like market demand for new products, favourable government legislation, or shortages of raw materials that the company is good at producing. For example, when Pepsi managers recognized a market opportunity for bottled water, they moved quickly to launch their Aquafina brand and to position it for rapid growth. *Threats* include new products developed by competitors, unfavourable government regulations, and changes in consumer tastes. For example, in 2010, the Province of Ontario proposed new legislation that sharply reduced the revenue that pharmacies would receive for dispensing prescription drugs. Some external threats are unpredictable, like the volcanic eruption in Iceland in 2010 that halted air travel in Europe for a week. Commercial airlines lost hundreds of millions of dollars of revenue, while alternative service providers like trains saw demand for their services soar.

Matching the Organization and Its Environment The final step in strategy formulation is matching environmental threats and opportunities with corporate strengths and weaknesses. Matching companies with their environments lays the foundation for successfully planning and conducting business. Over the long term, this process may also determine whether a firm typically takes risks or behaves more conservatively. Just because two companies are in the same industry does not mean that they will use the same strategies. The Toronto-Dominion Bank, for example, aggressively expanded into the U.S. retail banking industry by acquiring U.S. banks, but the Royal Bank of Canada has been much less aggressive in this area.[16]

Levels of Strategy

There are three levels of strategy in a business firm (see Figure 6.6). A **corporate-level strategy** identifies the various businesses that a company will be in, and how these businesses will relate to each other. A **business-level (competitive) strategy** identifies the ways a business will compete in its chosen line of products or services. **Functional strategies** identify the basic courses of action that each department in the firm will pursue so that it contributes to the attainment of the business's overall goals.

Corporate-Level Strategies There are several different corporate-level strategies that a company might pursue, including *concentration*, *growth*, *integration*, *diversification*, and *investment reduction*.

Concentration A **concentration strategy** involves focusing the company on one product or product line that it knows very well. Organizations that have successfully pursued a concentration strategy include McDonald's and Canadian National Railway.

Figure 6.6
Hierarchy of strategy.

Functional Strategy

Business or Competitive Strategy

Corporate Strategy

Growth Companies have several growth strategies available to them, including **market penetration** (boosting sales of present products by more aggressive selling in the firm's current markets), **geographic expansion** (expanding operations in new geographic areas), and **product development** (developing improved products for current markets). These three strategies focus on internal activities that will result in growth.

Integration There are two basic integration strategies. **Horizontal integration** means acquiring control of competitors in the same or similar markets with the same or similar products. For example, Hudson's Bay Company owns Zellers and Home Outfitters (Déco Découverte in Quebec). **Vertical integration** means owning or controlling the inputs to the firm's processes and/or the channels through which the products or services are distributed. Oil companies like Shell not only drill and produce their own oil but also sell it through company-controlled outlets across Canada. These two strategies focus on external activities that will result in growth.

Diversification Diversification helps the firm avoid the problem of having all of its eggs in one basket by spreading risk among several products or markets. *Related diversification* means adding new, but related, products or services to an existing business. For example, Maple Leaf Gardens Ltd., which already owned the Toronto Maple Leafs, acquired the Toronto Raptors basketball team. *Conglomerate diversification* means diversifying into products or markets that are not related to the firm's present businesses.

Investment Reduction Investment reduction means reducing the company's investment in one or more of its lines of business. One investment-reduction strategy is *retrenchment*, which means the reduction of activity or operations. For example, Federal Industries formerly was a conglomerate with interests in trucking, railways, metals, and other product lines, but it has now retrenched and focuses on a more limited set of products and customers. *Divestment* involves selling or liquidating one or more of a firm's businesses. For example, BCE sold its Yellow Pages and White Pages for $4 billion.

Business-Level (Competitive) Strategies Whatever corporate-level strategy a firm decides on, it must also have a competitive strategy. A *competitive strategy* is a plan to establish a profitable and sustainable competitive position.[17] Michael Porter identifies three competitive strategies. **Cost leadership** means becoming *the* low-cost leader in an industry. Walmart is the best-known industry cost leader. Montreal-based Gildan Activewear is dedicated to achieving the lowest possible costs in producing its T-shirts. The company has captured 29 percent of the U.S. imprinted T-shirt market with this strategy.[18]

A firm using a **differentiation strategy** tries to be unique in its industry along some dimension that is valued by buyers. For example, Caterpillar emphasizes durability, Volvo stresses safety, Apple stresses user-friendly products, and Mercedes-Benz emphasizes quality. A **focus strategy** means selecting a market segment and serving the customers in that market niche better than competitors. Before it was acquired by Nexfor, Fraser Inc. focused on producing high-quality, durable, lightweight paper that is used in bibles.

Functional Strategies Each business's choice of a competitive strategy (cost leadership, differentiation, or focus) is translated into supporting functional strategies for each of its departments to pursue. A *functional strategy* is the basic course of action that each department follows so that the business accomplishes its overall goals. To implement its cost-leadership strategy, for example, Walmart's distribution department pursued a functional strategy of satellite-based warehousing that ultimately drove distribution costs down below those of its competitors.

The strategy of one small business is described in the boxed insert entitled "From a Missouri Garage to Hollywood."

MARKET PENETRATION Boosting sales of present products by more aggressive selling in the firm's current markets.

GEOGRAPHIC EXPANSION Expanding operations in new geographic areas or countries.

PRODUCT DEVELOPMENT Developing improved products for current markets.

HORIZONTAL INTEGRATION Acquiring control of competitors in the same or similar markets with the same or similar products.

VERTICAL INTEGRATION Owning or controlling the inputs to the firm's processes and/or the channels through which the products or services are distributed.

DIVERSIFICATION Expanding into related or unrelated products or market segments.

INVESTMENT REDUCTION Reducing the company's investment in one or more of its lines of business.

COST LEADERSHIP Becoming the low-cost leader in an industry.

DIFFERENTIATION STRATEGY A firm seeks to be unique in its industry along some dimension that is valued by buyers.

LO-5 Contingency Planning and Crisis Management

Most managers recognize that even the best-laid plans sometimes simply do not work out. When Walt Disney announced plans to launch a cruise line using Disney characters and themes, managers began aggressively developing and marketing packages linking three- and four-day cruises with visits to Disney World in Florida. The inaugural sailing was sold out more than a year in advance. But three months before the first sailing, the shipyard constructing Disney's first ship (the *Disney Magic*) notified the company that it was behind schedule and that delivery would be several weeks late. Because Disney had no other ship, it had no choice but to refund the money it had collected as pre-booking deposits for its first 15 cruises. The 20 000 displaced customers were offered big discounts if they rebooked on a later cruise, but many of them blamed Disney's poor planning for the problem. Fortunately for Disney, the *Disney Magic* was eventually launched and has now become very popular and very profitable.[19]

Two common methods of dealing with the unknown and unforeseen are *contingency planning* and *crisis management*.

Contingency Planning

Contingency planning tries to identify in advance the important aspects of a business or its markets that might change, and how the company will respond if such changes actually occur. Suppose, for example, that a

Commercial airlines have contingency plans to deal with problems like major snowstorms. These contingency plans involve making sure that planes are not stranded at airports that are experiencing snow delays.

ENTREPRENEURSHIP AND NEW VENTURES

From a Missouri Garage to Hollywood

The feature films *The Red Canvas* and *Way of the Guardian* were not developed by your typical Hollywood production team. For starters, one of the films' co-creators lives and works in Missouri. Adam Boster and his partner, Ken Chamitoff, started Photo-Kicks—a marketing company specializing in action photography—in their garages in 2002. From their beginnings as photographing students at local martial arts schools, Boster and Chamitoff built Photo-Kicks into a multimillion-dollar business employing photographers, graphic designers, and marketers throughout the United States and Canada. In 2007, Photo-Kicks came in at number 592 on *Inc.* magazine's list of the 5000 fastest-growing private companies in America.

Just a quick glance at the many photographs on display at the Photo-Kicks website (www.photo-kicks.com) provides an eye-opening introduction to action photography. Athletes young and old punch, kick, and leap their way across the frames. But it's the countless other services that Photo-Kicks provides its customers that have allowed it to grow so rapidly.

Photo-Kicks bills itself as "a fully equipped graphic design and marketing organization," creating such products as customized logos, brochures, websites, posters, and trading cards.

Then, of course, there are the movies. *Way of the Guardian* began as a card game and animated series also developed by Boster and Chamitoff. *The Red Canvas* is more personal. It tells the story of a struggling immigrant who finds success and redemption in the sport of mixed martial arts. Chamitoff acknowledges that the film could not have happened without the years he and Boster spent travelling the country photographing martial arts students. "I learned the stories of every person I encountered," said Chamitoff. "Those stories shaped not only *The Red Canvas* but Photo-Kicks as well."

Critical Thinking Question

1. What are the key differences between the various types of corporate and business-level strategies? Which strategies is Photo-Kicks pursuing?

company develops a plan to create a new division, and it expects sales of this new division to reach a level of $1 million in sales revenue by the end of the first year. But suppose that sales revenues are only $500 000 by the end of the first year. Does the company abandon the business, invest more in advertising, or wait to see what happens in the second year? Any of these alternatives is possible. However, things will go more smoothly if managers have decided *in advance* what to do in the event of lower-than-expected sales. Contingency planning can help them do exactly that.

In the summer of 2008, a strike at the Potash Corp. of Saskatchewan created a shortage of potassium acetate, which is the key ingredient in runway de-icer that airports use to prevent airplanes from sliding off runways in sub-freezing weather. The strike ended in November 2008, but by then airports were having trouble obtaining potassium acetate. The U.S. Federal Aviation Administration informed all airports that they should develop contingency plans to get their potassium acetate from alternate sources. Cryotech Technologies, the biggest supplier of potassium acetate to airports, responded by getting supplies of a corn-based de-icer instead.[20]

Crisis Management

Crisis management involves an organization's plan for dealing with emergencies that require an immediate response. The listeria contamination problem at Maple Leaf Foods in 2008 is an example of a crisis that needed to be effectively managed. CEO Michael McCain acted quickly to handle the crisis and did not hide behind lawyers or let financial implications get in the way of his decisions. The company recalled 686 000 kilograms of tainted meat (which cost the company $19 million). McCain publicly apologized at news conferences and in televi-

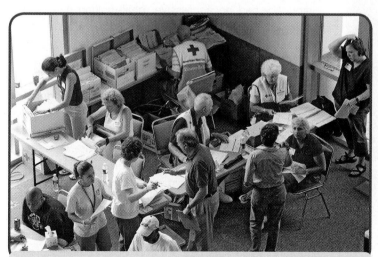

Crisis management involves an organization's methods for dealing with emergencies. Here, Red Cross volunteers organize and file paperwork submitted by Hurricane Katrina victims in Texas.

sion commercials, and assured consumers that the company would solve the problem.[21] By January 1, 2009, a survey revealed that 78 percent of respondents had recently purchased a Maple Leaf product. That was up from only 20 percent in September 2008.[22]

In 2010, Toyota faced a crisis when consumers began reporting that some models of its cars were accelerating out of control (see the opening case in Chapter 10 for details). Also in 2010, BP faced a crisis when an explosion and fire at a drilling rig in the Gulf of Mexico resulted in the death of 11 workers and a huge oil spill. The intense news coverage of the oil spill, as well as some poorly chosen remarks by BP's CEO, created significant public relations problems for BP. The company is likely facing many lawsuits with huge financial implications.

To prepare for emergencies better, many organizations maintain crisis plans. These plans—which are designed to help employees cope when disaster strikes—typically outline who will be in charge in different kinds of circumstances, how the organization will respond, and the plans that exist for assembling and deploying crisis-management teams.

LO-6 Management and the Corporate Culture

Just as every individual has a unique personality, every company has a unique identity. This is its **corporate culture**—the shared experiences, stories, beliefs, and norms that characterize it. The opening case provides several examples of corporate cultures. Here are some more:

- Magna International, a large Canadian producer of auto parts, is a firm with a strong culture. Its founder, Frank Stronach, is well known for his views about employees, working conditions, daycare centres, unions, the free enterprise system, and profit distribution.[23]

- Four Seasons Hotels and Resorts has a different, but equally strong, culture. Managers are judged by deeds, not words, and act as role models; employees take their cues from the managers.[24]

- At Toyota's Cambridge, Ontario, plant the corporate culture stresses values, principles, and trust. The culture is one of continuous improvement.[25]

- At WestJet Airlines the corporate culture emphasizes profit maximization. Most of the employees own shares in the company, and all of them get to keep some of the profits. This is a powerful incentive for them to work productively.[26]

In 2008, executives at 340 Canadian companies participated in the Waterstone Human Capital corporate culture survey and expressed the following views:[27]

- Eighty-two percent said that culture has a strong or very strong impact on corporate performance (but only 36 percent of executives felt that the culture of their company was strong).

- Three-year average revenue growth for the top 10 firms on the list was 63 percent higher than that of the 60 largest public companies in Canada that are listed on the S&P/TSX.

- Fifty-three percent felt that a strong culture reduced turnover, and 57 percent felt that a strong culture gave employees a sense of belonging. This finding is important, since an online survey conducted by Ipsos-Reid found that many workers feel that they don't fit in well at work.[28]

A strong corporate culture guides everyone to work toward the same goals and helps newcomers learn accepted behaviours. Cameron Herold—a Vancouver entrepreneur who has had a string of successes in franchising, including College Pro Painters, Boyd Autobody, and 1-800-GOT-JUNK—says that a cult-like culture is crucial for attracting great employees. He says what's

A business's founder or CEO plays a major role in shaping the company's culture. For example, Apple co-founder and CEO Steve Jobs helped establish an informal and laidback culture at the company. Casual business attire and an open-door policy help him maintain that same culture today. And that culture, in turn, helps Apple continue to attract and retain talented people.

needed is a culture that is "more than a business and slightly less than a religion."[29]

In a strong culture where financial success is the key issue, newcomers quickly learn that they are expected to work long, hard hours and that the "winner" is the one who brings in the most revenue. But if quality of life is more fundamental to the culture, newcomers learn that it's acceptable to balance work and non-work activities.

Communicating the Culture and Managing Change

Managers must carefully consider the kind of culture they want for their organization, then work to nourish that culture by communicating with everyone who works there. Walmart, for example, assigns veteran managers to lead employees in new territories. As we saw in the opening case, Starbucks Coffee surveys employees every 18 months regarding several aspects of its culture. Royal Bank of Canada and Four Seasons Hotels and Resorts also survey their employees to determine how well they are progressing toward their corporate culture goals.[30]

Communicating the Culture To use its culture to full advantage, managers must accomplish several tasks, all of which hinge on effective communication. First, managers themselves must have a clear understanding of the culture. Second, they must transmit the culture to others in the organization. Communication is thus one aim in training and orienting newcomers. A clear and meaningful statement of the organization's mission is also a valuable communication tool. Finally, managers can maintain the culture by rewarding and promoting those who understand it and work toward maintaining it.

Managing Change An organization may experience difficulty when trying to change its culture. For example, CIBC historically had an aggressive, deal-making culture that caused it to compete head to head with large Wall Street companies in the U.S. But after several major failures in the U.S., CIBC tried to become much more conservative.[31] But as the commercial paper crisis unfolded in 2007 (see Chapter 16), it became clear that CIBC was going to incur billions of dollars of losses because of its exposure to subprime mortgages in the U.S. This happened in spite of CIBC's supposed shift to a low-risk culture.[32]

In 2006, the Brazilian mining company Vale bought Inco, one of Canada's most famous companies. But frictions soon arose because the cultures of the two companies were quite different. Inco had a culture that encouraged the exchange of ideas and a decentralized decision-making structure, while Vale had a much more centralized decision-making structure. Vale executives imposed their culture on Inco executives, who were now expected to obey orders. One former Inco manager noted that many Inco managers left the company after Vale took charge.[33]

Summary of Learning Objectives

1. **Describe the four activities that constitute the management process.** *Management* is the process of planning, organizing, leading, and controlling an organization's financial, physical, human, and information resources to achieve the organization's goals. *Planning* means determining what the company needs to do and how best to get it done. *Organizing* means determining how best to arrange a business's resources and the necessary jobs into an overall structure. *Leading* means guiding and motivating employees to meet the firm's objectives. *Controlling* means monitoring the firm's performance to ensure that it is meeting its goals.

2. **Identify *types of managers* by level and area.** Managers can be differentiated in two ways: by level and by area. By level, *top managers* set policies, formulate strategies, and approve decisions. *Middle managers* implement policies, strategies, and decisions. *First-line managers* usually work with and supervise employees. By area, managers focus on marketing, finance, operations, human resource, and information. Managers at all levels may be found in every area of a company.

3. **Describe the five basic *management skills.*** Most managers agree that five basic management skills are necessary for success. *Technical skills* are needed to perform specialized tasks ranging from typing to auditing. *Human relations skills* are needed to understand and get along with other people. *Conceptual skills* allow managers to think in the abstract, to diagnose and analyze various situations, and to see beyond present circumstances. *Decision-making skills* allow managers to define problems and to select the best course of action. *Time management* skills refer to managers' ability to make productive use of the time available to them.

4. **Explain the importance of *goal setting and strategic management* in organizational success.** *Goals*—the performance targets of an organization—can be *long term, intermediate,* and *short term.* They provide direction for managers, they help managers decide how to allocate limited resources, they define the corporate culture, and they help managers assess performance. *Strategic management* involves three major activities: setting strategic goals, analyzing the organization and its environment, and matching the organization and its environment. The strategies that are decided upon are then translated into *strategic, tactical,* and *operational plans.*

5. **Discuss *contingency planning* and *crisis management* in today's business world.** To deal with crises or major environmental changes, companies develop *contingency plans* and plans for *crisis management. Contingency planning* tries to identify in advance the important aspects of a business or its markets that might change, and how the company will respond if such changes actually occur. *Crisis management* means developing methods and actions for dealing with an emergency that requires an immediate response. To prepare for such emergencies, organizations develop crisis plans.

6. **Explain the idea of corporate *culture* and why it is important.** *Corporate culture* is the shared experiences, stories, beliefs, and norms that characterize an organization. A strong, well-defined culture can help a business reach its goals and can influence management styles. Culture is determined by several factors, including top management, the organization's history, stories and legends, and behavioural norms. If carefully communicated and flexible enough to accommodate change, corporate culture can be managed for the betterment of the organization.

Questions and Exercises

Questions for Analysis

1. How are the five basic management *skills* related to the four *functions* of management? Give several specific examples.

2. What is the relationship between Mintzberg's *roles* of management and the more traditional *functions* of management? Use examples to clarify your answer.

3. Identify the managers by level and area at your college or university.

4. Can you identify any organizations where the technical skills of top managers are more important than human relations or conceptual skills? Can you identify organizations where conceptual skills are not important?

5. What differences might you expect to find in the corporate cultures of a 100-year-old manufacturing firm based in Winnipeg and a five-year-old e-commerce firm based in Ottawa?

6. Consider the various corporate-level strategies discussed in the text (concentration, growth, integration, diversification, investment reduction). What is the relationship between these various strategies? Are they mutually exclusive? Are they complementary? Defend your answer.

Application Exercises

7. Interview an administrator at your college or university. Ask the administrator to give his or her views on the college or university's strengths and weaknesses, and on the threats and opportunities the school is facing. Then use this information to write up a SWOT analysis for the school.

8. Review the example of the decisions made by Airbus and Boeing regarding new large aircraft. Then research the most current information on the status of the two planes. Which company seems to have made the better decision?

9. Choose two companies in the same industry—for example, fast food, electronics, retailing—and compare and contrast the corporate cultures of the two companies.

10. Select any group of which you are a member (your company, your family, your church, or a club). Explain the relevance of the management functions of planning, organizing, directing, and controlling for that group.

TEAM EXERCISES

Building Your Business Skills

Speaking with Power

Goal

To encourage students to appreciate effective speaking as a critical human relations skill.

Background

A manager's ability to understand and get along with supervisors, peers, and subordinates is a critical human relations skill. At the heart of this skill, says Harvard University professor of education Sarah McGinty, is the ability to speak with power and control. McGinty defines "powerful speech" in terms of the following characteristics:

- The ability to speak at length and in complete sentences
- The ability to set a conversational agenda
- The ability to deter interruption
- The ability to argue openly and to express strong opinions about ideas, not people
- The ability to make statements that offer solutions rather than pose questions
- The ability to express humour

Taken together, says McGinty, "all this creates a sense of confidence in listeners."

Method

Step 1 Working alone, compare your own personal speaking style with McGinty's description of powerful speech by taping yourself as you speak during a meeting with classmates or during a phone conversation. (Tape both sides of the conversation only if the person to whom you are speaking gives permission.) Listen for the following problems:

- Unfinished sentences
- An absence of solutions
- Too many disclaimers ("I'm not sure I have enough information to say this, but . . .")
- The habit of seeking support from others instead of making definitive statements of personal conviction (saying, "As Emily stated in her report, I recommend consolidating the medical and fitness functions," instead of, "I recommend consolidating the medical and fitness functions.")
- Language fillers (saying, "you know," "like," and "um" when you are unsure of your facts or uneasy about expressing your opinion)

Step 2 Join with three or four other classmates to evaluate each other's speaking styles.

- Have a 10-minute group discussion on the importance of human relations skills in business.
- Listen to other group members, and take notes on the "power" content of what you hear.
- Offer constructive criticism by focusing on what speakers say rather than on personal characteristics

(say, "Bob, you sympathized with Paul's position, but I still don't know what you think," instead of, "Bob, you sounded like a weakling.").

Follow-Up Questions

1. How do you think the power content of speech affects a manager's ability to communicate? Evaluate some of the ways in which effects may differ among supervisors, peers, and subordinates.

2. How do you evaluate yourself and group members in terms of powerful and powerless speech? List the strengths and weaknesses of the group.

3. Do you agree or disagree with McGinty that business success depends on gaining insight into your own language habits? Explain your answer.

4. In our age of computers and email, why do you think personal presentation continues to be important in management?

5. McGinty believes that power language differs from company to company and that it is linked to the corporate culture. Do you agree, or do you believe that people express themselves in similar ways no matter where they are?

Exercising Your Ethics

Clean Up Now, or Clean Up Later?

The Situation

The top management team of a medium-sized manufacturing company is on a strategic planning "retreat" where it is formulating ideas and plans for spurring new growth in the company. As one part of this activity, the team, working with the assistance of a consultant, has conducted a SWOT analysis. During this activity, an interesting and complex situation has been identified. Next year, the federal government will be issuing new—and much more stringent—pollution standards for the company's industry. The management team sees this as a potential threat in that the company will have to buy new equipment and change some of its manufacturing methods in order to comply with the new standards.

The Dilemma

One member of the team, James Smith, has posed an interesting option—not complying. His logic can be summarized as follows:

1. The firm has already developed its capital budgets for the next two years. Any additional capital expenditures will cause major problems with the company's cash flow and budget allocations.

2. The company has a large uncommitted capital budget entry available in three years; those funds could be used to upgrade pollution control systems at that time.

3. Because the company has a spotless environmental record so far, James Smith argues that if the company does not buy the equipment for three years, the most likely outcomes will be (a) a warning in year 1; (b) a small fine in year 2; and (c) a substantial fine in year 3. However, the total amounts of the years 2 and 3 fines will be much lower than the cost of redoing the company budgets and complying with the new law next year.

Team Activity

Assemble a group of four students and assign each group member to one of the following roles:

- Management team member
- Lower-level employee at the company
- Company customer
- Company investor

Action Steps

1. Before hearing any of your group's comments on this situation, and from the perspective of your assigned role, decide whether James Smith's suggestion regarding ignoring pollution standards is a good one. Write down the reasons for your position.

2. Before hearing any of your group's comments on this situation, and from the perspective of your assigned role, decide what are the underlying ethical issues in this situation. Write down the issues.

3. Gather your group together and reveal, in turn, each member's comments on James Smith's suggestion. Next, reveal the ethical issues listed by each member.

4. Appoint someone to record main points of agreement and disagreement within the group. How do you explain the results? What accounts for any disagreement?

5. From an ethical standpoint, what does your group conclude is the most appropriate action that should be taken by the company in this situation?

6. Develop a group response to the following question: What are the respective roles of profits, obligations to customers, and obligations to the community for the firm in this situation?

The Business of Bagging Customers

Coach Inc. started out in 1941 making virtually indestructible, high-quality handbags. In the 1970s it was bought by Sara Lee Corp., a big company that was pursuing a strategy of diversification. Because Coach was just one of literally dozens of businesses owned by Sara Lee, it suffered from the lack of focused management attention. Coach's CEO, Lew Frankfort, knew that his company's success depended on finding the right industry niche. In 2000, he convinced Sara Lee to spin off Coach as an independent company.

By 2007, Coach had sales of $2.6 billion, and the company's net income growth had averaged 51 percent per year for the previous five years. In spite of the recession that started in 2008, the company planned to open many new stores in North America and in China. And it had big plans to compete with the best-known brand names in the industry. For example, just a few years ago in China, Louis Vuitton had the largest market share (33 percent), followed by Gucci and Prada (more than 10 percent each). Coach had only 2 percent. But by 2007, Coach's market share had increased to 12 percent, Louis Vuitton's share had dropped to 27 percent, and Gucci and Prada had less than 10 percent each.

These successes have come in the high-fashion business, where fickle customers and rapid changes make planning difficult. Most fashion designers—Ralph Lauren, Donna Karan, Prada, Gucci, Fendi—have adopted a design-driven business model, in which the designer dictates style to the customers. Coach, however, has taken a different approach. The company asks the customers what they want and then provides it. Coach's customer focus has created a competitive advantage for the firm, which annually sells $865 of merchandise for every square

foot of store space, compared to an industry average of $200–$300.

Frankfort introduced many new analytical tools for tracking market trends, evaluating effectiveness, and managing risk. The firm's leaders look at sales data for each store and each product type on a daily basis (several times a day during busy seasons). But extensive and intensive customer research remains the cornerstone of his planning. Indeed, the company spends $2 million per year on surveys. The surveys are supplemented with one-on-one interviews with customers from locations around the world, to quiz them on everything from appearance and quality to the correct length for a shoulder strap.

"The tremendous amount of testing they do differentiates them from a lot of other fashion companies," says industry analyst Robert Ohmes. Analyst Bob Drbul says, "Their execution and business planning is in the league of a Walmart or a Target" (two much larger firms known for their effective business planning). To test new products, Coach shows them to selected buyers in 12 worldwide markets to gauge initial customer reaction. An initial demand forecast is then made, and six months before introduction, they are tested in another 12 markets. At launch time, sales are monitored closely and adjustments made quickly.

For example, when an unexpected spike in sales was investigated, managers found that buying by Hispanic customers was on the increase. Within a week, the firm had moved up the opening date of a South Miami store and began advertising in Spanish for the first time. Frankfort understands that, to be effective, plans must be translated into appropriate actions. "Not only do you need to know your business and your customers . . . you also need to be nimble to adapt," he says.

A host of other changes have also aided Coach in its rapid rise. Lew Frankfort hired a former Tommy Hilfiger designer, Reed Krakoff, to update the firm's classic but clunky styles. "Something was missing," says Krakoff. "I had to take these ideas and make them fun—young in spirit." Instead of introducing new products twice a year (which is a common practice in the fashion industry), Coach releases new styles monthly. Customers now have a reason to visit the stores more often. Outsourcing the production function allowed the company to increase gross profit margins by 24 percent over five years. The firm has diversified into many other related lines of business, including shoes, jewellery, furniture, and more. There is even a Coach car, a co-branded Lexus, with a Coach leather interior.

Women's Wear Daily, the bible of the fashion industry, recently named Coach as the "most splurge-worthy luxury brand." Customers agree. Investors too like Coach. The firm's share price rose an astonishing 900 percent during its first four years as an independent firm. Krakoff gives the credit for the firm's achievements to Frankfort's planning skills, saying, "The key to Lew's success . . . is his ability to orchestrate a decision-making process that is both inclusive and incisive."

Questions for Discussion

1. Describe examples of each of the management functions illustrated in this case.

2. Which management skills seem to be most exemplified in Lew Frankfort?

3. Explain the role of goals and strategy in the success of Coach.

4. What corporate culture issues might exist when a former division of a big company is spun off?

SCANLIFE

chapter

7

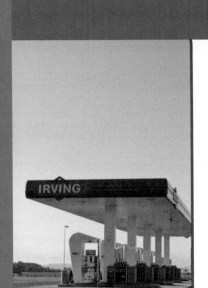

Organizing the Business Enterprise

After studying this chapter, you should be able to:

LO-1 Discuss the elements that influence a firm's *organizational structure*.

LO-2 Explain how *specialization* and *departmentalization* are the building blocks of organizational structure.

LO-3 Distinguish between *responsibility* and *authority* and explain the differences in decision making in *centralized* and *decentralized organizations*.

LO-4 Explain the differences between *functional, divisional, project*, and *international organization structures*, and describe the most popular forms of organizational design.

LO-5 Understand how the *informal organization* is different from the formal organization.

SCANLIFE

Reorganizing the Irving Empire

The Irving family of New Brunswick is a legendary success story in Canadian business. The company owns nearly 300 businesses in areas as diverse as oil refining, forestry, shipbuilding, food processing, publishing, transportation, and home improvement, and it has dominated corporate life in New Brunswick for decades. The company represents Canada's third largest fortune, and is valued at about $6 billion. The company was founded by J.D. Irving in 1882 when he opened a sawmill in Bouctouche, New Brunswick. The business expanded dramatically under his son K.C. Irving, who then passed it on to his sons J.K. (Jim), Arthur, and J.E. (Jack). These three brothers have five sons working in the business. The two most active are Jim (J.K.'s son), who oversees the forestry operations, and Kenneth (Arthur's son), who heads the oil and gas operation, and who was seen as a strong modernizing force in the company.

In July 2010, two unexpected events took place: Jack Irving died, and Kenneth announced that he was taking a leave of absence from the company. In recent years, tensions had developed between Ken and Jim regarding the strategic direction of the company because they each wanted more control over the business. These tensions also made relations between J.K. and his brothers more difficult, and threatened the company's tradition of passing on control of the company to the next generation.

Originally, K.C. Irving set up a structure that saw J.K. (and later his son Jim) running the forestry empire, trucking, food processing, and newspapers. Arthur (and later his son Kenneth) was in charge of oil refineries and service stations. Jack's responsibilities were in construction, steel, and real estate. The grand plan began to fall apart when Jim began to feel restricted by the structure because it tied his strategy to Ken's. As well, the third brother—Jack—began to feel like an also-ran in the company. As a result, a coalition—composed of Arthur and Jack and their families—developed and began to oppose Jim and his family.

These tensions were surprising because the Irving family had always presented a united front. But once the conflict became public, the key players in the business decided to avoid the problems that many other family businesses have faced when family members disagree. To their credit, the brothers wanted to avoid a bitter family feud like the one that engulfed the McCain brothers in the 1990s. So, they started talking about how to achieve an amicable parting of the ways. They basically decided to

How Will This Help Me?

Companies frequently introduce changes to improve their organizational structures. By understanding the material in this chapter, as an *employee*, you'll understand your "place" in the organization that employs you. As a *boss* or *owner*, you'll be better equipped to decide on the optimal structure for your own organization.

restructure the company and let the two main parts go their separate ways. Jim and his family took control of the forestry end of the business, and Ken and his family took over the oil and gas business.

The restructuring is a bit complicated because the various businesses in the family empire are controlled by trusts that were set up by K.C. Irving many years ago. In order to divide the company, the dozens of family members who have an interest will have to agree on what the restructuring will look like. Irving descendants will likely be offered cash or business interests in return for the original trusts being phased out.

The complexity involved in dividing up the trusts is only one problem. The other is the shifting fortunes of the two main businesses (energy and forestry). In 2007, the energy business was in good shape (because of high oil prices), while forestry was suffering (the high Canadian dollar had a negative effect on exports of lumber). This was just the reverse of the situation that existed in the 1990s, when forestry was booming and the energy business was suffering (partly because of cost overruns on a new refinery that was being built in St. John). At that time, the energy business needed a bailout, and the forestry side of the business provided it. By 2009, however, oil prices had dropped dramatically and so had the Canadian dollar, so the fortunes of the two main parts of the Irving empire were converging once again.

ORGANIZATIONAL STRUCTURE The specification of the jobs to be done within a business and how those jobs relate to one another.

ORGANIZATION CHART A physical depiction of the company's structure showing employee titles and their relationship to one another.

What Is Organizational Structure?

Organizational structure is the specification of the jobs to be done within a business and how those jobs relate to one another. This definition will be clear if we consider the following analogy. In many ways, a business is like an automobile. All automobiles have an engine, four wheels, fenders, and other structural components, an interior compartment for passengers, and various operating systems including those for fuel, braking, and climate control. Each component has a distinct purpose, but it must also work in harmony with the others. Similarly, all businesses have common structural and operating components, each of which has a specific purpose. Each component must fulfill its own purpose while simultaneously fitting in with the others. And, just like automobiles made by different companies, how these components look and fit together varies from company to company.

Every institution—be it a for-profit business like Irving Oil, a not-for-profit organization like the University of Saskatchewan, or a government agency like the Canadian Wheat Board—must develop an appropriate structure for its own unique situation. What works for Air Canada is not likely to work for the Canada Revenue Agency. Likewise, the structure of the Red Cross will not likely work for the University of Toronto.

LO-1 Determinants of Organizational Structure

How is an organization's structure determined? Does it happen by chance or is there some logic that managers use to create structure? Or does it develop by some combination of circumstance and strategy? Ideally, managers should carefully assess a variety of important factors as they plan for and then create a structure that will allow their organization to function efficiently. But with the busyness that is evident in most organizations, structure may develop without sufficient planning.

What factors influence structure? The organization's *purpose*, *mission*, and *strategy* are obviously important. A dynamic and rapidly growing enterprise, for example, needs a structure that contributes to flexibility and growth, while a stable organization with only modest growth will function best with a different structure. Size, technology, and changes in environmental circumstances also affect structure. A large manufacturing firm operating in a strongly competitive environment requires a different structure than a local barbershop or video store.

Whatever structure an organization adopts, it is rarely fixed for long. Indeed, most organizations change their structures almost continually. Ford Motor Co. has, for example, initiated several major structural changes in just the last 15 years. In 1994, the firm announced a major restructuring plan called Ford 2000, which was intended to integrate all of Ford's vast international operations into a single, unified structure by 2000. By 1998, however, midway through implementation of the plan, top Ford executives announced further modifications, and in 2001 still more changes were announced that were intended to boost the firm's flagging bottom line and stem a decline in product quality.[1, 2] The problems that developed in the automobile industry in 2008 resulted in further significant structural changes.

The Chain of Command

Most businesses prepare **organization charts** that illustrate the company's structure and show employees where they fit into the firm's operations. Figure 7.1 shows the organization chart for a hypothetical company. Each box represents a job within the company. The solid lines that connect the boxes define the **chain of command**, or the reporting relationships within the company. Thus, each plant manager reports directly to the vice-president of production who, in turn, reports to the president. When the chain of command is not clear, many different kinds of problems can result. An actual organization chart would, of course, be far more complex and include individuals at many more levels. Large firms cannot easily draw an organization chart with everyone on it.

The Building Blocks of Organizational Structure

Whether a business is large or small, the starting point in developing its organizational structure is determining who will do what and how people performing certain tasks can most appropriately be grouped together. Job specialization and departmentalization represent the basic building blocks of all businesses.

LO-2 Specialization

Job specialization is the process of identifying the specific jobs that need to be done and designating the people who will perform them. In a sense, all organizations have only one major "job"—say, making a profit by manufacturing and selling men's and boys' shirts. But this big job must be broken into smaller components, and each component is then assigned to an individual. Consider the manufacturing of men's shirts. Because several steps are required to produce a shirt, each job is broken down into its component parts—that is, into a set of tasks to be completed by a series of individuals or machines. One person, for example, cuts material for the shirt body, another cuts material for the sleeves, and a third cuts material for the collar. Components are then shipped to a sewing room, where a fourth person assembles the shirt. In the final stage, a fifth person sews on the buttons.[3]

Specialization and Growth In a very small organization, the owner may perform every job. As the firm grows, however, so does the need to specialize jobs so that others can perform them. Consider the case of Mrs Fields Gifts, producer of gourmet cookies. When Debbi Fields opened her first store, she did everything herself: bought the equipment, negotiated the lease, baked the cookies, operated the store, and kept the records. As the business grew, however, she found that her job was becoming too much for one person. She first hired a bookkeeper to handle her financial records, then an in-store manager and a cookie baker. Her second store required another set of employees—another manager, another baker, and some salespeople. While Fields focused her attention on other expansion opportunities, she turned promotions over to a

Figure 7.1

An organization chart shows key positions in the organization and interrelationships among them. An actual organization chart would, of course, be far more complex and include individuals at many more levels. Indeed, because of their size, larger firms cannot easily draw a diagram with everyone on it.

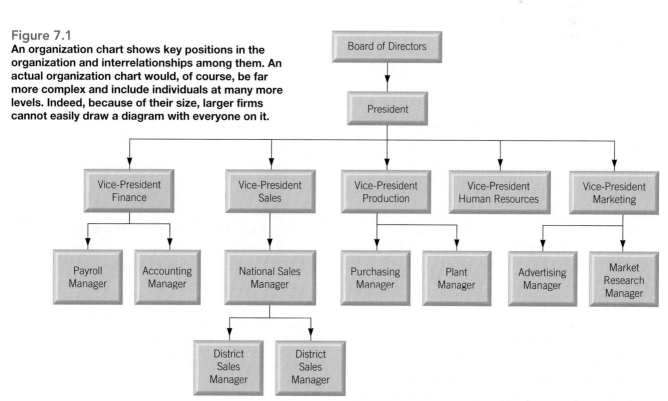

When Walt Disney and his brother Roy made Mickey Mouse's debut in *Steamboat Willie* in 1933, they handled every step of the creative process. Today, it takes hundreds of people to create an animated film like 2009's *Up*.

professional advertising director. Thus the job that she once did all by herself was increasingly broken down into components and assigned to different individuals.

Job specialization is a natural part of organizational growth. It is neither a new idea nor limited to factory work. It carries with it certain advantages—individual jobs can be performed more efficiently, the jobs are easier to learn, and it is easier to replace people who leave the organization. But if job specialization is carried too far and jobs become too narrowly defined, people get bored, become less satisfied with their jobs, and lose sight of how their contributions fit into the overall organization.

Departmentalization

After jobs are specialized, they must be grouped into logical units. This process is called **departmentalization**. Companies benefit from departmentalization because top managers can see more easily how various units are performing. Departmentalization allows the firm to treat a department as a **profit centre**—a separate unit responsible for its own costs and profits. Thus, by assessing profits from sales in a particular area—say, men's clothing—Sears can decide whether to expand or curtail promotions in that area.

Managers group jobs logically, according to some common thread or purpose. In general, departmentalization occurs along *functional*, *customer*, *product*, *process*, or *geographic* lines (or any combination of these).

Functional Departmentalization Many service and manufacturing companies develop departments based on a group's functions or activities—**functional departmentalization**. Such firms typically have a production department, a marketing and sales department, a personnel department, and an accounting and finance department.

These departments may be further subdivided, just as a university's business school may be subdivided into departments of accounting, finance, marketing, and management.

Customer Departmentalization Some retail stores actually derive their generic name—department stores—from the manner in which they are structured. Stores like HMV are divided into departments—a classical music department, an R&B department, a pop department, and so on. Each department targets a specific customer category (people who want different genres of music).

Customer departmentalization makes shopping easier by providing identifiable store segments. Thus, a customer shopping for Shania Twain's latest CD can bypass World Music and head straight for Country. Stores can also group products in locations designated for deliveries, special sales, and other service-oriented purposes.

Nissan has developed an assembly process that is so efficient that it can turn out a vehicle in 10 fewer hours than Ford can. The key is the organization of the workstations. At this station, workers install just about everything that the driver touches inside the truck cab. Other stations take care of the whole vehicle frame, the entire electrical system, or completed doors.

Many department stores are departmentalized by product. Concentrating different products in different areas of the store makes shopping easier for customers.

the production process used. Vlasic, a pickle maker, has separate departments that transform cucumbers into fresh-packed pickles, relishes, or pickles cured in brine.

Geographic Departmentalization Some firms may be divided according to the area of the country—or even the world—they serve. This is known as **geographic departmentalization**. In 2009, Nike introduced a new structure that was organized around six geographic regions: North America, Western Europe, Eastern/Central Europe, Greater China, Japan, and emerging markets.[5] Levi Strauss has one division for the United States, one for Europe, and one for the Asia-Pacific region. PepsiCo has three geographic divisions: Americas Food, Americas Beverages, and International. The Managing in Turbulent Times boxed insert below describes some dilemmas that companies face when they try to choose between product and geographic departmentalization.

Because different forms of departmentalization offer different advantages, larger companies tend to adopt different types of departmentalization at various levels of the corporation. For example, the company illustrated in Figure 7.2 uses functional departmentalization at the top level, geographic departmentalization in its production department, and product departmentalization in its marketing unit.

PRODUCT DEPART-MENTALIZATION Departmentalization according to the products being created or sold.

PROCESS DEPART-MENTALIZATION Departmentalization according to the production process used to create a good or service.

GEOGRAPHIC DEPARTMENTAL-IZATION Departmentalization according to the area of the country or world supplied.

In general, the store is more efficient and customers get better service—in part because salespeople tend to specialize and gain expertise in their departments.[4]

Product Departmentalization **Product departmentalization means** dividing an organization according to the specific product or service being created. A bank, for example, may handle consumer loans in one department and commercial loans in another. 3M, which makes both consumer and industrial products, operates different divisions for Post-it brand sticky notes, Scotch-Brite scrub sponges, and the Sarns Sternal Saw II.

Process Departmentalization **Process departmentalization** means dividing the company according to

Figure 7.2
Most organizations use multiple bases of departmentalization. This organization, for example, is using functional, geographic, and product departmentalization.

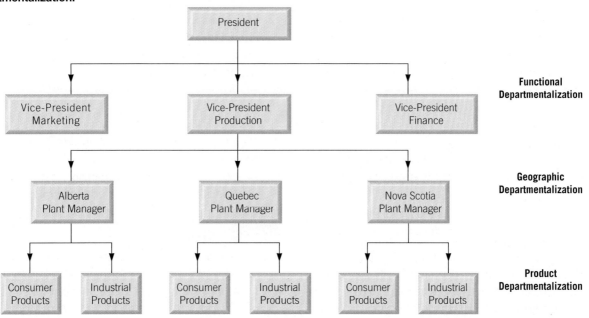

Product vs. Geographical Departmentalization: What's the Right Choice?

Geographical departmentalization became popular many years ago as companies expanded their operations across national borders. Since relatively limited communications made it difficult to take the pulse of consumer needs or monitor operations abroad, it made sense to let local managers in foreign countries run their regional or country businesses as more or less autonomous companies. However, two trends are making this structure less popular today. First, information technology is reducing the impediments to cross-border communication. Second, global competition is so intense that firms can't afford to miss an opportunity to quickly transfer product improvements from one region to another.

For example, the Canadian Imperial Bank of Commerce (CIBC) reorganized in order to break down the walls between the conservative and traditional retail/commercial banking side, and the more volatile investment banking side. The company is now organized around product lines. Exide Technologies, the world's largest producer of automotive and industrial batteries, has also shifted from geographical to product departmentalization. Previously, Exide's structure consisted of about 10 "country organizations." The head of each country organization had considerable latitude to make decisions that were best for that person's country. It also meant that each country manager focused on products that were marketable in that country. Under the new product system, global business units have been formed to oversee the company's various product lines such as car and industrial batteries. But the change has not been without problems. For example, a top executive got upset when his unit was made subordinate to a newly acquired unit. It wasn't long before Exide was tinkering with its organization chart again.

Either approach—products or geography—can cause problems if taken to an extreme. If a company organizes by products, it can standardize manufacturing, introduce new products around the world faster, and eliminate overlapping activities. But if too much emphasis is placed on product and not enough on geography, a company is likely to find that local decision making is slowed, pricing flexibility is reduced, and products are not tailored to meet the needs of a specific country's customers.

Ford Motor Company experienced exactly these problems when it decided to move toward the product model. The reorganization saved the company $5 billion in its first few years of operation, but Ford's market share declined during the same period. This is what we would expect to happen when too much emphasis is placed on product departmentalization. Ford responded to this drop in market share by giving executives in various regions more authority to decide what types of vehicles were best for their local market. In other words, it moved back a bit toward the geographical model.

Critical Thinking Question

1. In your own words, explain the dilemma that managers face when they are trying to decide between product departmentalization and geographical departmentalization.

Establishing the Decision-Making Hierarchy

A major question that must be asked about any organization is this: *Who makes which decisions?* This leads to a consideration of the decision-making hierarchy, which generally results from a three-step process:

1. *Assigning tasks:* determining who can make decisions and specifying how they should be made.

2. *Performing tasks:* implementing decisions that have been made.

3. *Distributing authority:* determining whether the organization is to be centralized or decentralized.

LO-3 Assigning Tasks

The question of who is supposed to do what and who is entitled to do what in an organization is complex. In any company with more than one person, individuals must work out agreements about responsibilities and authority. **Responsibility** is the duty to perform an assigned task, while **authority** is the power to make the decisions necessary to complete the task. The amount of authority and responsibility a person has must be consistent. Imagine a mid-level buyer for the Bay who encounters an unexpected opportunity to make a large purchase at an extremely good price but does not have the authority to make such a purchase without confirmation from above. The company's policies on delegation and authority are inconsistent, since the buyer is *responsible* for purchasing clothes that will be sold in the upcoming season but lacks the *authority* to make the needed purchases.

Performing Tasks

When appropriate levels of responsibility and authority are not clearly spelled out, difficulties arise between managers and subordinates around the issues of delegation and accountability. **Delegation** begins when a manager assigns a task to a subordinate. **Accountability** then falls to the subordinate, who must complete the task. If the subordinate does not perform the assigned task properly and promptly, he or she may be reprimanded, punished, or possibly even dismissed.

Some managers have trouble delegating tasks because (a) they assume that subordinates can never do anything as well as the manager can; (b) they fear that their subordinates will "show them up" in front of others by doing a superb job; or (c) they want to control everything. Managers who fail to delegate don't have time to do long-range planning, and they may be uninformed about important industry trends and competitive products because they are too involved in day-to-day operations.

There are remedies for these problems. First, managers should recognize that they cannot do everything themselves. Second, if subordinates cannot do a job, they should be trained so that they can assume more responsibility. Third, managers should recognize that if a subordinate performs well, that reflects favourably on the manager. Effective managers surround themselves with a team of strong subordinates, and then delegate sufficient authority to those subordinates so they can get the job done. There are four things to keep in mind when delegating:

- decide on the nature of the work to be done
- match the job with the skills of subordinates
- make sure the person chosen understands the objectives he or she is supposed to achieve
- make sure subordinates have the time and training necessary to do the task

Distributing Authority

In a **centralized organization**, top management retains the right to make most decisions that need to be made. Most lower-level decisions must be approved by upper management before they can be implemented.[6] McDonald's, for example, uses centralization as a way to standardize its operations. All restaurants must follow precise steps in buying products and making and packaging burgers and other menu items. Most advertising is handled at the corporate level, and any local advertising must be approved by a regional manager. Restaurants even have to follow prescribed schedules for facilities' maintenance and upgrades like floor polishing and parking lot cleaning.[7]

In a **decentralized organization**, more decision-making authority is delegated to managers at lower levels in the hierarchy. The purpose of decentralization is to make a company more responsive to its environment. At FedEx, the commitment to decentralization promotes innovation. Managers are encouraged and rewarded for questioning, challenging, and developing new ideas, which are always given serious consideration. Developments have included teaming up with Motorola and Microsoft to create a proprietary pocket-size PC, sending package information to cell phones, and creating software products for small business logistics.[8]

There are both advantages and disadvantages of decentralization, and they can clearly be seen in the long history of General Motors. In the 1920s, GM's legendary president, Alfred Sloan, introduced a decentralized structure that gave each car division considerable autonomy to produce cars that would attract whatever market segment

McDonald's emphasis on centralization ensures standardization in its product offerings. Customers will have a consistent dining experience whenever and wherever they eat at a McDonald's restaurant.

SPAN OF CONTROL
The number of people managed by one manager.

DOWNSIZING
The planned reduction in the scope of an organization's activity.

LINE AUTHORITY
An organizational structure in which authority flows in a direct chain of command from the top of the company to the bottom.

LINE DEPARTMENT
A department directly linked to the production and sale of a specific product.

the division was pursuing. It worked so well that GM became the largest automobile manufacturer in the world by the middle of the twentieth century.

But all this autonomy resulted in widely differing car designs that were very expensive to produce. As decades passed, costs soared and competition from cost-conscious Japanese automakers became ferocious. GM's sales and overall profitability plummeted. In response, GM took away much of the autonomy that managers in various international divisions had and instituted a requirement that its worldwide units work much more closely together to design cars that could be sold (with modest variations) worldwide. A "Global Council" in Detroit now makes key decisions about how much will be spent on new car development. When GM engineers at its Daewoo joint venture with South Korea wanted to develop a sport utility vehicle especially suited for the South Korean market, the request was denied.[9] But even these actions were not sufficient to stem GM's decline, and in 2008 the company was bailed out by the U.S. and Canadian governments and entered bankruptcy protection as it tried to recover. By 2010, the company's performance had improved somewhat, but there were still great concerns about its survival.

Span of Control The **span of control** refers to how many people work for any individual manager. The span of control may be *wide* (many subordinates reporting to a boss) or *narrow* (few subordinates reporting to a boss). Factors influencing the span of control include employees' abilities, the supervisor's managerial skills, the nature of the tasks being performed, and the extent to which tasks are interrelated. For example, when many employees perform the same simple task or a group of interrelated assembly-line tasks, a wide span of control is possible. Because all the jobs are routine, one supervisor may well control an entire assembly line having 40 or more workers. Since tasks are interrelated—if one workstation stops, they all stop—having one supervisor ensures that all stations receive equal attention. In contrast, when jobs are not routine, or when they are unrelated, a narrower span of control is preferable.

Downsizing—the planned reduction in the scope of an organization's activity—affects the span of control. When downsizing involves cutting large numbers of managers, entire layers of management are eliminated. When this happens, the remaining managers often end up with larger spans of control. Because spans of control are wider, corporate structures are flatter after downsizing.

Three Forms of Authority

As individuals are delegated responsibility and authority, a complex web of interactions develops. These interactions may take one of three forms of authority: *line*, *staff*, or *committee and team*. All three forms of authority may be found in a single company, especially if it is a large one.

Line Authority **Line authority** is authority that flows up and down the chain of command (refer to Figure 7.1). Most companies rely on **line departments**, those that are directly linked to the production and sale of specific products. For example, Clark, an equipment manufacturer, has a division that produces forklifts and small earth movers (see Figure 7.3). In this division, line departments include purchasing, materials handling, fabrication, painting, and assembly (all of which are directly linked to production), along with sales and distribution (both of which are directly linked to sales).

Each line department is essential in achieving the goals the company has set. Line employees are the

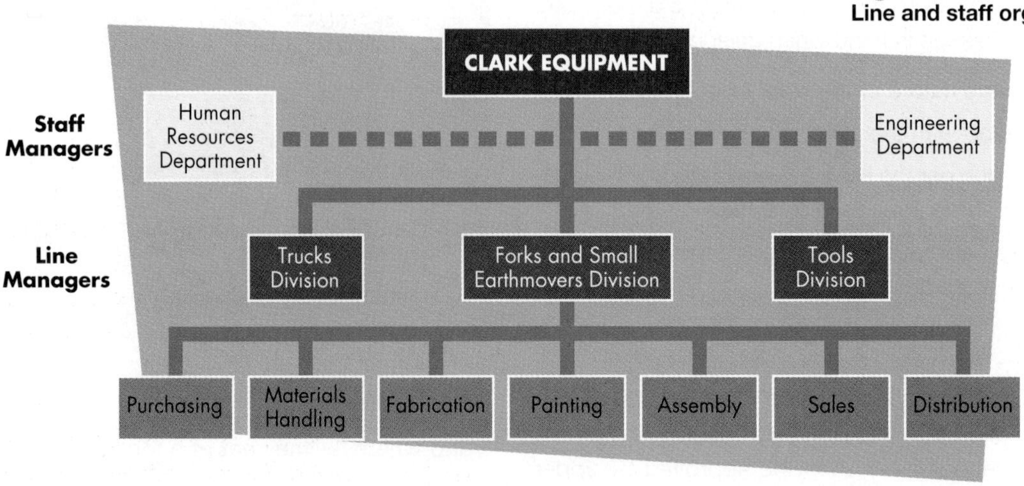

Figure 7.3
Line and staff organization.

"doers" and producers in a company. If any line department fails to complete its task, the company cannot sell and deliver finished goods. Thus, significant authority is usually delegated to line departments.

Staff Authority Companies often employ individuals with technical expertise in areas like law, accounting, marketing research, and human resources. These experts may be given **staff authority**; that is, they help line departments in making decisions, but they do not have the authority to make the final decision. For example, if the fabrication department at Clark has an employee with a drinking problem, the line manager of the department might consult a human resource staff expert for advice on how to handle the situation. The staff expert might suggest that the worker stay on the job but enter a counselling program. But if the line manager decides that the job is too dangerous to be handled by a person whose judgment is impaired by alcohol, the line manager's decision will most likely prevail.

Typically, line authority is represented on organization charts by solid lines, while staff authority is shown by dotted lines. Line managers are directly involved in producing the firm's products or services, while staff members generally provide services to management. But remember this: the goals of the organization influence the distinction between line and staff authority. At Aluminum Company of Canada, for example, the director of personnel has staff authority because the personnel department supports the primary function of the company (the production and marketing of aluminum). But at Office Overload the director of personnel is a line manager because the primary goal of

that firm is to provide personnel to other firms.

Committee and Team Authority More and more organizations have started to use **committee and team authority**—authority granted to committees or work teams that play central roles in the firm's daily operations. A committee, for example, may consist of top managers from several major areas of the company. If the work of the committee is especially important, and if the committee will be working together for an extended time, the organization may even grant it special authority as a decision-making body that goes beyond the individual authority possessed by each of its members.

Teams are also used at the operating level. Groups of operating employees are often empowered to plan and organize their own work and to perform that work with a minimum of supervision. As with permanent top management committees, the organization will usually find it beneficial to grant special authority to operating work teams so that they may function more effectively.[10] More detailed information about teams is presented in Chapter 9.

Business firms are increasingly using work teams and allowing groups of employees to plan and organize their own work with a minimum of supervision. This contributes to employee empowerment.

LO-4 Basic Organizational Structures

A glance at the organization charts of many organizations reveals what appears to be an almost infinite variety of structures. However, closer examination shows that most of them fit into one of four basic categories: *functional*, *divisional*, *project*, or *international*.

The Functional Structure
In the **functional structure**, the various units in the organization are formed based on the key functions that must be carried out to reach organizational goals. The functional structure makes use of departmentalization by function. An example of a functional structure was shown in Figure 7.1. The advantages and disadvantages of the functional structure are summarized in Table 7.1.

The Divisional Structure
The **divisional structure** divides the organization into several divisions, each of which operates as a semi-autonomous

Table 7.1 Advantages and Disadvantages of a Functional Structure

Advantages	Disadvantages
1. It focuses attention on the key activities that must be performed.	1. Conflicts may arise among the functional areas.
2. Expertise develops within each function.	2. No single function is responsible for overall organizational performance.
3. Employees have clearly defined career paths.	3. Employees in each functional area have a narrow view of the organization.
4. The structure is simple and easy to understand.	4. Decision making is slowed because functional areas must get approval from top management for a variety of decisions.
5. It eliminates duplication of activities.	5. Coordinating highly specialized functions may be difficult.

PROJECT ORGANIZATION
An organization that uses teams of specialists to complete specific projects.

unit and profit centre. Divisions in organizations can be based on products, customers, or geography. In 2008, Teck Resources Ltd. (formerly Teck Cominco Ltd.) reorganized its business into separate product divisions for gold, copper, zinc, metallurgical coal, and energy. The company felt that the new structure would increase its competitiveness and allow it to act on opportunities in the five different commodity segments.[11] A few years earlier, Bell Canada created three divisions based on which *customers* were being served: consumers, small- and medium-sized businesses, and large corporations. This structure replaced the former divisional structure that was geographically based.[12] Whatever basis is used, divisional performance can be assessed easily each year because the division operates as a separate company.

Divisionalized companies can buy, sell, create, and disband divisions without disrupting the rest of their operations. Different divisions can sponsor separate advertising campaigns and foster different corporate identities. They can also share certain corporate-level resources (such as market research data). But unhealthy competition may develop between divisions, and the efforts of one division may be duplicated by those of another. At PepsiCo, for example, each of the company's three major beverage brands—Pepsi, Gatorade, and Tropicana—formerly operated as independent divisions. But this independence became a problem because the three brands were competing for the same resources and there was very little coordination and sharing of

information between the divisions. Now, all three brands are in one division so that a unified approach to brand management is achieved.

The advantages and disadvantages of the divisional structure are summarized in Table 7.2.

Project Organization

A typical organization is characterized by unchanging vertical authority relationships because the organization produces a product or service in a repetitive and predictable way. Procter & Gamble, for example, produces millions of tubes of Crest toothpaste each year using standardized production methods. The company has done this for years and intends to do so indefinitely. But some organizations find themselves faced with new product opportunities, or with projects that have a definite starting and ending point. These organizations often use a project structure to deal with the uncertainty encountered in new situations. **Project organization** involves forming a team of specialists from different functional areas of the organization to work on a specific project.[13] A project structure may be temporary or permanent; if it is temporary, the project team disbands once the project is completed and team members return to their regular functional area or are assigned to a new project.

Project organization is used extensively by Canadian firms in the construction of hydroelectric generating stations like those developed by Hydro-Québec on the La Grande River, and by Manitoba Hydro on the Nelson River. Once the generating station is complete, it becomes part of the traditional structure of the utility. Project organization is also used at Genstar Shipyards Ltd. in Vancouver.

Table 7.2 Advantages and Disadvantages of a Divisional Structure

Advantages	Disadvantages
1. It accommodates change and expansion.	1. Activities may be duplicated across divisions.
2. It increases accountability.	2. A lack of communication among divisions may occur.
3. It develops expertise in the various divisions.	3. Adding diverse divisions may blur the focus of the organization.
4. It encourages training for top management.	4. Company politics may affect the allocation of resources.

The project organization structure is very useful for construction projects like this hydroelectric generating station on the La Grande River in Quebec. The construction of installations like this has a specific beginning and ending point. Once completed, the generating station becomes part of the traditional organization structure of the provincial utility.

Each ship that is built is treated as a project and supervised by a project manager, who is responsible for ensuring that the ship is completed on time and within budget.[14] Project organization has also proven useful for coordinating the many elements needed to extract oil from the tar sands.

A **matrix organization** is a variation of the project structure in which the project manager and the regular line managers share authority. When a project is concluded, the matrix is disbanded. Ford, for example, uses a matrix organization to design new car models. A design team composed of people from engineering, marketing, operations, and finance is created to design the new car. After the team's work is completed, team members move back to their permanent functional jobs.

Martha Stewart Living Omnimedia, Inc. has created a permanent matrix organization for its lifestyle business. The company is organized broadly into media and merchandising groups, each of which has specific products and product groups. Layered on top of this structure are teams of lifestyle experts organized into groups such as cooking, crafts, weddings, and so forth (see Figure 7.4). Although each group targets specific customer needs, they all work across all product groups. A wedding expert, for example, might contribute to an article on wedding planning for a Martha Stewart magazine, develop a story idea for a Martha Stewart cable television program, and supply content for a Martha Stewart website. This same individual might also help select fabrics suitable for wedding gowns that are to be retailed.[15]

The matrix structure is not always effective. In 2009, Carol Bartz—the new CEO at Yahoo!—announced a restructuring that was designed to make managers more accountable and to speed up decision making. The new structure essentially did away with the matrix structure and workers no longer report to multiple bosses.[16]

International Organization

There are several types of **international organizational structures** that have emerged as competition on

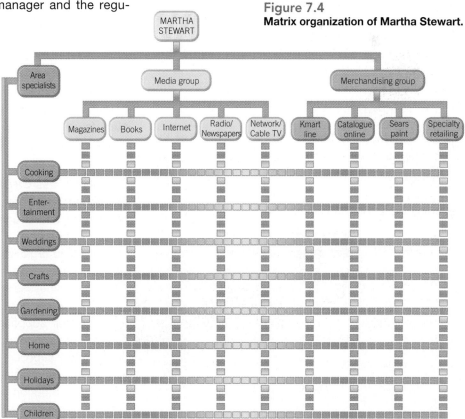

Figure 7.4
Matrix organization of Martha Stewart.

All the signs at this 8000 square metre store in Numazu identify it as a Seiyu outlet run by Japan's fifth-largest supermarket chain. However, Wal-Mart owns 38 percent of Seiyu, and this giant store is part of Wal-Mart's effort to enter the world's second-largest retail market.

Danone Group, for instance, has two major product groups: dairy products (Danone yogourt), and bottled water (Evian). Danone's structure does not differentiate internationally, but rather integrates global operations within each product group.[17]

Some companies adopt a truly global structure in which they acquire resources (including capital), produce goods and services, engage in research and development, and sell products in whatever local market is appropriate, without any consideration of national boundaries. Until a few years ago, for example, General Electric (GE) kept its international business operations as separate divisions. Now, however, the company functions as one integrated global organization. GE businesses around the world connect and interact with each other constantly, and managers freely move back and forth among them.[18]

Another kind of "structure" is described in the boxed insert entitled "Green Structures."

a global scale becomes more intense and companies experiment with the ways in which they might respond. For example, when Walmart opened its first store outside the United States in the early 1990s, it set up a special projects team to handle the logistics. As more stores were opened during the next decade, the firm created a small international department to handle overseas expansion. By then, however, international sales and expansion had become such a major part of Walmart's operations that the firm created a separate international division headed up by a senior vice-president. International operations are now so important to Walmart that the international division has been further divided into geographic areas where the firm does business, such as Mexico and Europe. Walmart's structure is of the general type shown in Figure 7.5.

Other companies have adopted variations of the basic international structure. The French food giant

Organizational Design for the Twenty-First Century

As the world grows increasingly complex and fast paced, companies continue to seek new forms of organization that permit them to compete effectively. Among the most popular of these new forms are the *boundaryless organization*, the *team organization*, the *virtual organization*, and the *learning organization*.

Boundaryless Organization

The *boundaryless organization* is one in which traditional boundaries and structures are minimized or eliminated altogether. For example, General Electric's fluid organizational structure, in which people, ideas, and information flow freely between businesses and business groups, approximates this concept. Similarly, as firms partner with their suppliers in more efficient ways, external boundaries disappear. Some of Walmart's key suppliers are tied directly into the retailer's information system. As a result, when Walmart distribution centres start running low on, say, Wrangler blue jeans, the manufacturer receives

Figure 7.5
International division structure.

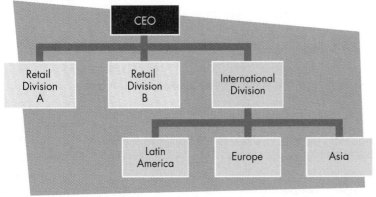

Green Structures

The term "organizational structure" is commonly used to explain *theoretical* concepts like departmentalization, authority, responsibility, and the hierarchical patterns within organizations. But organizations also need *physical* structures like offices and factories to do their work, and managers in both the public and private sector are beginning to realize that their physical structures present significant opportunities to be eco-friendly. In Charlottetown, P.E.I., for example, a federal government office building has been constructed with photovoltaic panels that produce 8–10 percent of the building's power needs. Delta Whistler Village Suites installed a hybrid heating system that has reduced greenhouse gases by 45 percent and saved the hotel $70 000 in energy costs. At the University of Toronto, over 90 percent of the heating requirements for the engineering and computer science building are being recovered from a nearby boiler plant.

Manitoba Hydro's new building in Winnipeg contains a geothermal heating and air conditioning system that provides 100 percent of the energy needed to air-condition the building in the summer and 60 percent of the energy needed to heat the building in winter. The building is so energy efficient that it uses just 91 kilowatt hours of energy per square metre of floor space (the Model National Energy Code standards say that a building should not use more than 295 kilowatt hours). In 2009, the building won the Council on Tall Buildings and Urban Habitat's Best Tall Building award for the Americas. The Council gives only four such awards each year—one for the Americas, one for Asia and Australia, one for Europe, and one for the Middle East and Africa.

Sunova Credit Union's branch in Oak Bank, Manitoba, received the Platinum (highest) rating from the Leadership in Energy and Environmental Design (LEED) organization. Some automobile dealers are also seeking certification from LEED for buildings at their dealerships, and LEED standards were important in the planning of the facilities and venues for the 2010 Winter Olympics in B.C.

Some architects think that over the next decade it may be possible to have buildings that require no energy at all from public utilities. Gerrit de Boer, president of Toronto-based Idomo Furniture Company, says that his firm will be "off the grid" within 10 years as a result of the geothermal heating system and the photovoltaic solar array that are being installed in the company's 200 000-square-foot building.

Critical Thinking Questions

1. What are the advantages of "green" buildings? Are there any disadvantages? Explain.
2. Consider the following statement: "*It is very expensive to build eco-friendly buildings, so expenditures like these should generally not be made. Rather, companies should focus on upgrading their production facilities so they can make higher quality, lower-priced products for consumers and more profits for their shareholders.*" Do you agree or disagree with the statement? Explain your reasoning.

---

the information as soon as the retailer does. Wrangler proceeds to manufacture new inventory and restock the distribution centre without Walmart having to place a new order.

Team Organization

Team organization relies almost exclusively on project-type teams, with little or no underlying functional hierarchy. People "float" from project to project as dictated by their skills and the demands of those projects. At Cypress Semiconductor, units or groups that become large are simply split into smaller units. Not surprisingly, the organization is composed entirely of small units. This strategy allows each unit to change direction, explore new ideas, and try new methods without having to deal with a rigid bureaucratic superstructure. Although few large organizations have actually reached this level of adaptability, Apple and Xerox are among those moving toward it.

Virtual Organization

Closely related to the team organization is the virtual organization. A *virtual organization* has little or no formal structure. Typically, it has only a handful of permanent employees, a very small staff, and a modest administrative facility. As the needs of the organization change, its managers bring in temporary workers, lease facilities, and outsource basic support services to meet the demands of each unique situation. As the situation changes, the temporary workforce changes in parallel, with some people leaving the organization and others entering it. Facilities and subcontracted services also change. In other words, the virtual organization exists only in response to its own needs.

Global Research Consortium (GRC) is a virtual organization. GRC offers research and consulting services to firms doing business in Asia. As clients request various services, GRC's staff of three permanent employees subcontracts the work to an appropriate set of several dozen independent consultants and/or researchers with whom it has relationships. At any given time, therefore, GRC may have several projects underway and 20 or 30 people working in various capacities. As the projects change, so does the composition of the organization. Figure 7.6 illustrates the basic structure of a virtual organization.

Learning Organization

A *learning organization* facilitates the lifelong learning and personal development of all of its employees while continually transforming itself to respond to changing demands and needs. The most frequent goals are improved quality, continuous improvement, and performance measurement. The idea is that the most consistent and logical strategy for achieving continuous improvement is to constantly upgrade employee talent, skill, and knowledge. For example, if each employee in an organization learns one new thing each day and can translate that knowledge into work-related practice, continuous improvement will logically follow.

In recent years, many different organizations have implemented this approach on various levels. Shell, for example, purchased an executive conference centre called the Shell Learning Center. The facility boasts state-of-the-art classrooms and instructional technology, lodging facilities, a restaurant, and recreational amenities such as a golf course, swimming pool, and tennis courts. Line managers at the firm rotate through the centre and serve as teaching faculty. All Shell employees routinely attend training programs, seminars, and related activities, gathering the latest information they need to contribute more effectively to the firm.

LO-5 The Informal Organization

The formal organization of a business is the part that can be seen and represented on the organization chart. The structure of a company, however, is not limited to the organization chart and the formal assignment of authority. Frequently, the **informal organization**—the everyday social interactions among employees that transcend formal jobs and job interrelationships—effectively alters a company's formal structure. Indeed, the informal organization is sometimes more powerful than the formal structure. The team ethics exercise at the end of this chapter presents an interesting situation that illustrates the informal organization.

Is the informal organization good or bad? On the positive side, the informal organization can help employees feel that they "belong," and it gives them an outlet for "letting off steam" in a safe environment. It also provides information that employees are interested in hearing. On the negative side, the informal organization can reinforce office politics that put the interests of individuals ahead of those of the company. Likewise, a great deal of harm can be caused by distorted or inaccurate information communicated without management input or review. For example, if the informal organization is generating false information about impending layoffs, valuable employees may act quickly (and unnecessarily) to seek other employment. Two important elements of the informal organization are *informal groups* and the *organizational grapevine*.

Informal Groups *Informal groups* are simply groups of people who decide to interact among themselves even though they may not be required to do so by the formal organization. They may be made up of people who work together in a formal sense or who simply get together for lunch, during breaks, or after work. They may talk about business, the boss,

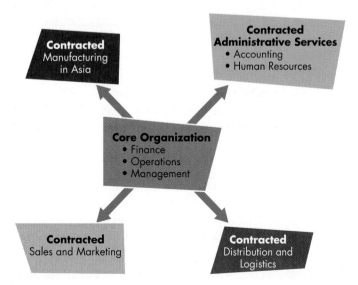

Figure 7.6
The virtual organization.

The grapevine is a powerful communications network in most organizations. These workers may be talking about any number of things—an upcoming deadline on an important project, tonight's hockey game, the stock market, rumours about an impending takeover, gossip about who's getting promoted, or the weather.

or non-work related topics such as families, movies, or sports. For example, at the New York Metropolitan Opera, musicians and singers play poker during the intermissions. Most pots are in the $30 to $40 range. Luciano Pavarotti, the famed tenor, once played (he lost big).[19]

The Organizational Grapevine The **grapevine** is the informal communication network that runs through the entire organization.[20] The grapevine is found in *all* organizations, and it does not always follow the same patterns as formal channels of authority and communication. Formerly, when people gathered around the water cooler or on the golf course to exchange gossip and pass on information, they had names and faces. But with the internet (a worldwide grapevine), you may not know who you are talking to, or how reliable the person providing the information is.[21]

Because the grapevine typically passes information orally, messages may become distorted in the process. In addition to miscommunication and attempts by some people to manipulate it for their own ends, the grapevine may carry rumours with absolutely no basis in fact. Such rumours are most common when there is a complete lack of information. Human nature abhors a vacuum and the grapevine may fill the vacuum with *something*, even if that something is just rumours. Baseless rumours can be very hard to kill, however.

Attempts to eliminate the grapevine are fruitless, but managers do have at least some control over it. By maintaining open channels of communication and responding vigorously to inaccurate information, they can minimize the damage the grapevine can do. In fact, the grapevine can actually be an asset. By getting to know the key people who are part of the grapevine, the manager can partially control the information received and use the grapevine to determine employee reactions to new ideas (e.g., a change in human resource policies or benefit packages). Wise managers will tune in to the grapevine's message because it is often a corporate early-warning system. Ignoring this valuable source of information can cause managers to be the last to know that they are about to get a new boss, or that they have a potentially fatal image problem.

Summary of Learning Objectives

1. **Discuss the elements that influence a firm's *organizational structure*.** Every business needs structure to operate. *Organizational structure* varies according to a firm's mission, purpose, and strategy. Size, technology, and changes in environmental circumstances also influence structure. In general, while all organizations have the same basic elements, each develops the structure that contributes to the most efficient operations.

2. **Explain how *specialization* and *departmentalization* are the building blocks of organizational structure.** As a firm grows, it usually has a greater need for people to perform specialized tasks (specialization). It also has a greater need to group types of work into logical units (departmentalization). Common forms of departmentalization are *customer, product, process, geographic,* and *functional*. Large businesses often use more than one form of departmentalization.

3. **Distinguish between *responsibility* and *authority* and explain the differences in decision making in *centralized* and *decentralized organizations*.** *Responsibility* is the duty to perform a task, while *authority* is the power to make the decisions necessary to complete tasks. *Delegation* begins when a manager assigns a task to a subordinate; *accountability* means that the subordinate must complete the task. *Span of control* refers to the number of people who work for a manager. The more people supervised by a manager, the wider his or her span of control. Wide spans are usually desirable when employees perform simple or unrelated tasks. When jobs are diversified or prone to change, a narrower span is generally preferable.

   In a *centralized organization*, only a few individuals in top management have real decision-making authority. In a *decentralized organization*, much authority is delegated to lower-level management. Where both *line* and *line-and-staff* authority exist in an organization, *line departments* generally have authority to make decisions while *staff departments* have a responsibility to advise. *Committee and team authority* empowers committees or work teams to make decisions about various aspects of operations.

4. **Explain the differences between *functional, divisional, project,* and *international organization structures,* and describe the most popular forms of organizational design.** In a *functional organization*, authority is usually distributed among such basic functions as marketing and finance. In a *divisional organization*, the various divisions operate in a relatively autonomous fashion. In *project organization*, a company creates project teams to address specific problems or to complete specific projects. A company that has divisions in many countries may require an additional level of *international organization* to coordinate those operations. Four of the most popular forms of organizational design are (1) boundaryless organizations (traditional boundaries and structures are minimized or eliminated), (2) team organizations (relying on project-type teams, with little or no functional hierarchy), (3) virtual organizations (which have little formal structure and only a handful of permanent employees, a small staff, and a modest administrative facility), and (4) learning organizations (which facilitate employees' lifelong learning and personal development while transforming the organization to meet changing demands and needs).

5. **Understand how the *informal organization* is different from the formal organization.** The *informal organization* consists of the everyday social interactions among employees that transcend formal jobs and job interrelationships. The informal organization exists within the formal structure of every organization and cannot be suppressed. Effective managers work with the informal organization and try to harness it for the good of the formal organization.

Questions and Exercises

Questions for Analysis

1. Explain the significance of size as it relates to organizational structure. Describe the changes that are likely to occur as an organization grows.

2. Why do some managers have difficulties in delegating authority? Why does this problem tend to plague smaller businesses?

3. Describe a hypothetical organization structure for a small printing firm. Describe changes that might be necessary as the business grows.

4. Compare and contrast the matrix and divisional approaches to organizational structure. How would you feel personally about working in a matrix organization in which you were assigned simultaneously to multiple units or groups?

5. If a company has a formal organization structure, why is the informal organization so important?

6. The argument has been made that, compared to the functional organization structure, the divisional structure does a better job of training managers for top-level positions. Do you agree or disagree with this argument? Explain your reasoning.

Application Exercises

7. Draw up an organization chart for your college or university.

8. Consider the organization where you currently work (or one where you previously worked). Which of the four basic structural types was it most consistent with (functional, divisional, project, international)? What was the basis of departmentalization in the organization? Why was that particular basis used?

9. Interview the manager of a local service business (for example, a fast-food restaurant). What types of tasks does this manager typically delegate? Is the appropriate authority also delegated in each case? What problems occur when authority is not delegated appropriately?

10. Review the discussion of intrapraneurs in Chapter 4. Then identify a person who has succeeded as an intrapreneur. In what ways did the structure of the intrapreneur's company help this individual succeed? In what ways did the structure pose problems?

TEAM EXERCISES

Building Your Business Skills

Getting with the Program

Goal

To encourage students to understand the relationship between organization structure and a company's ability to attract and keep valued employees.

Situation

You are the founder of a small but growing high-tech company that develops new computer software. With your current workload and new contracts in the pipeline, your business is thriving, except for one problem: you cannot find computer programmers for product development. Worse yet, current staff members are being lured away by other high-tech firms. After suffering a particularly discouraging personnel raid in which competitors captured three of your most valued employees, you schedule a meeting with your director of human resources to plan organizational changes designed to encourage worker loyalty. You already pay top dollar, but the continuing exodus tells you that programmers are looking for something more.

Method

Working with three or four classmates, identify some ways in which specific organizational changes might improve the working environment and encourage employee loyalty. As you analyze the following factors, ask yourself the obvious question: If I were a programmer, what organizational changes would encourage me to stay?

- *Level of job specialization*. With many programmers describing their jobs as tedious because of the focus on detail in a narrow work area, what changes, if any, would you make in job specialization? Right now, for instance, few of your programmers have any say in product design.

- *Decision-making hierarchy*. What decision-making authority would encourage people to stay? Is expanding employee authority likely to work better in a centralized or decentralized organization?

- *Team authority*. Can team empowerment make a difference? Taking the point of view of the worker, describe the ideal team.

- *Intrapreneuring*. What can your company do to encourage and reward innovation?

1. With the average computer programmer earning nearly $70 000, and with all competitive firms paying top dollar, why might organizational issues be critical in determining employee loyalty?

2. If you were a programmer, what organizational factors would make a difference to you? Why?

3. As the company founder, how willing would you be to make major organizational changes in light of the shortage of qualified programmers?

Exercising Your Ethics

To Poach, or Not to Poach

The Situation

The Hails Corporation, a manufacturing plant, has recently moved toward an all-team-based organization structure. That is, all workers are divided into teams. Each team has the autonomy to divide up the work assigned to it among its individual members. In addition, each team handles its own scheduling for members to take vacations and other time off. The teams also handle the interviews and hiring of new team members when the need arises. Team A has just lost one of its members, who moved to another city to be closer to his ailing parents.

The Dilemma

Since moving to the team structure, every time a team has needed new members, it has advertised in the local newspaper and hired someone from outside the company. However, Team A is considering a different approach to fill its opening. Specifically, a key member of another team (Team B) has made it known that she would like to join Team A. She likes the team members, sees the team's work as being enjoyable, and is somewhat bored with her team's current assignment.

The concern is that if Team A chooses this individual to join the team, several problems may occur. For one thing, her current team will clearly be angry with the members of Team A. Further, "poaching" new team members from other teams inside the plant is likely to become a common occurrence. On the other hand, though, it seems reasonable that she should have the same opportunity to join Team A as an outsider would. Team A needs to decide how to proceed.

Team Activity

Assemble a group of four students and assign each group member to one of the following roles:

- Member of Team A
- Member of Team B
- Manager of both teams
- Hails investor

Action Steps

1. Before hearing any of your group's comments on this situation, and from the perspective of your assigned role, decide whether you think that the member of Team B should be allowed to join Team A. Write down the reasons for your position.

2. Before hearing any of your group's comments on this situation, and from the perspective of your assigned role, determine the underlying ethical issues, if any, in this situation. Write down the issues.

3. Gather your group together and reveal, in turn, each member's comments on the situation. Next, reveal the ethical issues listed by each member.

4. Appoint someone to record main points of agreement and disagreement within the group. How do you explain the results? What accounts for any disagreement?

5. From an ethical standpoint, what does your group conclude is the most appropriate action that should be taken by Hails in this situation? Should Team B's member be allowed to join Team A?

6. Develop a group response to the following questions: Assuming Team A asks the Team B member to join its team, how might it go about minimizing repercussions? Assuming Team A does not ask the Team B member to join its team, how might it go about minimizing repercussions?

Structure Evolves at Frantic Films

Frantic Films is a Winnipeg-based film and TV production company. Shortly after its founding in 1997, the company was named one of Canada's Hottest 50 Start-Ups by *Profit* magazine. By 2004, it ranked twenty-third on the list of Canada's fastest-growing companies, and in 2005 it ranked fifth on the list of Manitoba's fastest-growing companies. Frantic has also received numerous awards; a partial list includes the following:

- National Research Council recognition as a Canadian innovation leader
- Lions Gate Innovative Producers Award
- New Media Visionary Award nomination
- Blizzard Award (for the documentary series *Quest for the Bay*)
- Finalist for the Ernst & Young Entrepreneur of the Year Award (multiple years)

Frantic Films started as a private corporation that was owned and managed by three principal shareholders—

Jamie Brown (chief executive officer), Chris Bond (president), and Ken Zorniak (chief operating officer). It originally had three divisions—visual effects, live action, and TV commercials—(see Figure 7.7), but the visual effects division was sold in 2007.

The TV commercial division (Frantic Films Commercial Projects Inc.) produces television commercials for local Winnipeg companies, as well as for national and international clients. It also provides visual effects for commercials produced by other companies. The writers, producers, designers, compositors, animators, and editors create award-winning spots for local, national, and international companies as diverse as the Royal Winnipeg Ballet, the Disney Channel, and Procter & Gamble Canada.

The live action division (Frantic Films Live Action Productions Inc.) produces and owns programs that are broadcast in over 40 countries. The division first develops the ideas for a program, then promotes the idea to broadcasters and financiers. If there is a strong

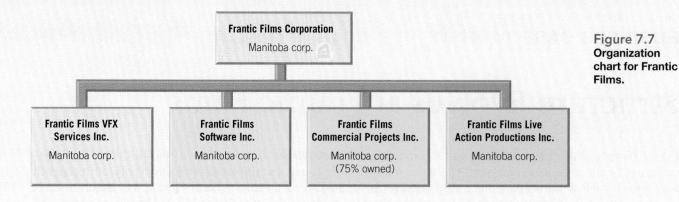

Figure 7.7
Organization
chart for Frantic
Films.

interest, a budget is provided and the division produces the program. Frantic has produced documentary programs such as *Pioneer Quest* (one of the highest rated documentary series ever broadcast on a Canadian specialty channel), lifestyle series (*'Til Debt Do Us Part*), television movies (*Zeyda and the Hitman*), and feature films (*Lucid*). Once a program is completed, rights are transferred to the releasing company and the individual, single-purpose production companies created for each show are wound up.

Until 2007, the *visual effects* division (Frantic Films VFX Services Inc.) produced visual effects for TV and movies. Using visual effects software packages such as Maya, Houdini, Fusion, and 3ds Max, the division established a reputation as one of the top visual effects providers in North America. The majority of the employees at Frantic were in this division. Its output included visual effects for films like *Superman Returns*, *Stay*, *X-Men 3*, *The Italian Job*, *Catwoman*, *The Core*, *Swordfish*, *Mr. Magorium's Wonder Emporium*, and *Across the Universe*. The division used a matrix structure to complete film projects. This meant that a project team, made up of specialists in areas like 3D animation, 2D animation, compositing, and hardware/software support, was put together. When the project was completed, the team disbanded and its members were assigned to other projects. These teams were typically given specific goals to achieve, and then the team members used their technical expertise to decide how they could best achieve the goal.

Recently, a software division has been created (Frantic Films Software Inc.). It employs seven individuals with specialized expertise, some of whom are computer science grads. When software division employees discovered that off-the-shelf software did not meet their needs, they began creating their own new stand-alone software to enhance certain visual effects like virtual water and smoke. This software was used to create the fluid-based character Tar Monster in the movie *Scooby-Doo II*.

Each of the divisions at Frantic Films operates fairly independently, but the company is still small enough that individuals from one division sometimes get involved in decisions in other divisions. For example, since the company does not have a marketing vice-president,

marketing decisions are often made jointly by Brown, Bond, and Zorniak for each of the divisions.

In 2007, the visual effects division was sold to Prime Focus Ltd., a leader in India's post-production and visual effects services. Office space and a receptionist are now shared with Prime Focus. Jamie Brown says the change will allow the company to get a larger slice of the visual effects pie by pooling its resources with those of Prime Focus. At about the same time as the visual effects division was sold, it was announced that COO Ken Zorniak and president Chris Bond would remain with the company as employees, not owners.

When the company was first formed, the authority structure was quite centralized because the principal shareholders had both the expertise to make decisions and the motivation to do so. But Brown thinks it is important to increase the involvement of lower-level workers in decisions, so he is trying to delegate more authority to them. Some progress has been made in this area. For example, managers in some of the divisions were given the authority to spend up to $5000 without having to get the approval of top management. This change was made because the top managers found that they were spending too much time discussing whether to approve requests for relatively small amounts of money. So, they essentially delegated more authority to division managers by giving them the discretion to make spending decisions. Brown also encourages employees to make recommendations on various issues to top management. He recognizes that giving employees more discretion can sometimes lead to less-than-optimal decisions, but he also wants to give people more experience in making decisions that affect the company.

Like all rapidly growing companies, Frantic Films has experienced certain growing pains with regard to its organizational structure. For example, offices were set up in California and British Columbia to get more visual effects business in those local areas, but until recently, there have not been dedicated salespeople responsible for generating work there. While employees in those offices have been fully employed, they are more costly. The original idea was to have them obtain work that could be sent to the lower-cost Winnipeg office, but more work is being done by a growing workforce in the satellite offices.

Top management is now in the process of determining the changes that are needed to make the organization's structure more effective.

Another structural issue is the division of duties between Brown, Bond, and Zorniak. When the company first formed, all three principals were involved in decision making for all the divisions. But as the company grew, each individual gradually became more focused. For example, Brown had primary responsibility for the live action division, while Zorniak and Bond had primary responsibility for the visual effects division.

Questions for Discussion

1. What are the four basic types of organizational structures? Which of these basic structural types seems most like the structure that Frantic Films has adopted?

2. What are the advantages and disadvantages of the organizational structure at Frantic Films?

3. What is the difference between a centralized company and a decentralized company? Where is Frantic Films positioned on the centralization-decentralization continuum? Explain.

SCANLIFE

chapter

8

Managing Human Resources and Labour Relations

After reading this chapter, you will be able to:

LO-1 Define *human resource management*, discuss its strategic significance, and explain how managers plan for human resources.

LO-2 Identify the issues involved in *staffing* a company, including internal and external recruiting and *selection*.

LO-3 Discuss different ways in which organizations go about developing the capabilities of employees and managers.

LO-4 Discuss the importance of *wages and salaries, incentives*, and *benefit programs* in attracting and keeping skilled workers.

LO-5 Describe some of the key legal issues involved in hiring, compensating, and managing workers in today's workplace.

LO-6 Discuss *workforce diversity*, the management of *knowledge workers*, and the use of *contingent* and *temporary workers* as important changes in the contemporary workplace.

LO-7 Trace the evolution of, and discuss trends in, *unionism* in Canada.

LO-8 Describe the *major laws governing unionism*.

LO-9 Identify the steps in the *collective bargaining process*.

SCANLIFE

Are More Cracks Appearing in the Glass Ceiling?

Back in the 1990s, much was written about how a "glass ceiling"—the invisible barrier that prevents women from moving into the very top jobs in business firms—was starting to break down. Dramatic changes occurred in the automobile business, for example, Maureen Kempston Darkes was appointed CEO of General Motors of Canada and Bobbie Gaunt became CEO of Ford Motor Company of Canada. These were major changes in an industry that had been very male-dominated. Other high-profile appointments have continued to be evident. For example, in 2008 Monique Leroux was appointed CEO of Desjardins Group, Quebec's largest financial institution. She is the first woman to lead a top 10 financial institution in Canada. A year earlier, Cynthia Carroll shattered another ceiling when she became the first female CEO to lead a global mining company, Anglo American PLC. This was quite significant when you consider that Ontario legislation did not even permit women to work underground until 1979. It has not been quite that difficult in other areas. In 2010, Kathleen Taylor took over as CEO of the Four Seasons hotel chain, in an industry that has long been favourable to women.

So progress is evident. But it is also slow. A Statistics Canada report showed that women aged 25–29 who worked full time earned only 85 percent of what men earned. That gap is the same size it was five years earlier. During the last few years, other studies have revealed some other interesting statistics:

- Women with advanced degrees earn 96 percent of what men earn; women with bachelor's

How Will This Help Me?

Effectively managing human resources is critical to the success of organizations. A firm that handles this activity well has a better chance for success than a firm that simply goes through the motions. After reading the material in this chapter, you'll be better able to understand—from the perspective of a *manager*—the importance of properly managing human resources in a department or business you own or supervise. You'll also understand—from the perspective of an *employee*—why your employer has adopted certain approaches to dealing with issues like hiring, training, compensation, and benefits.

degrees earn 89 percent; and at the trades certificate level, women earn just 65 percent of what men earn.

- The average single woman earns 99 percent of what the average man earns.

- In law firms, women comprise 50 percent of associates but only 16 percent of partners. Women also drop out of practice at two or three times the rate of men. In contrast, more than half of all senior management positions at Vancouver City Savings Credit Union and Coast Capital Savings Credit Union are occupied by women.

- No member state in the Organisation for Economic Co-operation and Development (OECD) has been able to erase the wage gap; in the OECD as a whole, the difference is about 15 percent.

- For men aged 55–64, the proportion of potential years of work spent actually working is 92.3 percent, but for women aged 55–64, the ratio is only 64.2 percent.

- Compared to men, the average woman has less labour market experience, is less likely to work full time, and is more likely to leave the labour force for long periods of time.

A study that analyzed the pay earned by males and females at equivalent levels of responsibility found that base pay rates were not much different, but men received bonuses that often doubled their total pay while women received bonuses that only slightly increased their total pay.

Various reasons have been proposed for pay inequity and the under-representation of women in the top ranks of management. They include simple male bias against promoting women; the "old boys network"; women dropping out of the workforce to have children; lack of organizational support and role models for women; stereotyping; partners who don't help at home; and a work culture that's not compatible with family life. Some researchers say that both men and women are ambitious, competent, and competitive, but men carry everything to an extreme. For men, winning is everything and they feel the need to decisively defeat their opponents (think sports). This line of thinking says that male hormones (notably testosterone) cause men to have an extremely strong drive for dominance, status, power, and control, and that kind of behaviour is rewarded in organizations.

In this same vein, another study found that women don't aspire to top management positions like men do. About one-third of men surveyed said they aspired to positions like chief executive officer or chief operations officer, but only about one-fifth of women wanted such a job title. Age was also a factor: 89 percent of women aged 25–34 aspired to top positions, but only 58 percent of women aged 45–55 had such aspirations. This suggests that the issue is generational, and that more and more women are going to be appointed to top jobs as time passes because they have different attitudes about the desirability of top management jobs. There is also the matter of overcoming traditions and expectations. Cynthia Carroll may have broken the glass ceiling in the mining field, but the rest of the statistics in the industry are still quite unfavourable. Only 14 percent of the labourers and 1 percent of geological engineers are women.

For change to occur, structural action is needed. There have been some positive steps. For example, the Iron Ore Company of Canada teamed up with a community college in Labrador City to create an apprenticeship program that actively recruits and attracts young women. There are some systematic obstacles still in place but actions like these are slowly eliminating barriers even in traditionally male-dominated industries.

HUMAN RESOURCE MANAGEMENT (HRM) Set of organizational activities directed at attracting, developing, and maintaining an effective workforce.

LO-1 The Foundations of Human Resource Management

Human resource management (HRM) is the set of organizational activities directed at attracting, developing, and maintaining an effective workforce. Human resource management takes place within a complex and ever-changing environmental context and is increasingly being recognized for its strategic importance.[1]

The Strategic Importance of HRM

Human resources are critical for effective organizational functioning. HRM (or *personnel*) was once relegated to second-class status in many organizations, but its importance has grown dramatically in the last two decades, stemming from increased legal complexities, the recognition that human resources are a valuable means for improving productivity, and an awareness of the costs associated with poor human resource management.

Managers now realize that the effectiveness of their HR function has a substantial impact on a firm's bottom-line performance. Poor human resource planning can result in spurts of hiring followed by layoffs—a process that is costly in terms of unemployment compensation payments, training expenses, and morale. Haphazard compensation systems do not attract, keep, and motivate good employees, and outmoded recruitment practices can expose the firm to expensive and embarrassing legal action. Consequently, the chief human resource executive of most large businesses is a vice-president directly accountable to the CEO, and many firms are developing strategic HR plans that are integrated with other strategic planning activities.

Human Resource Planning

Planning is the starting point in attracting qualified human resources. Human resource (HR) planning involves *job analysis*, *forecasting* the demand for and supply of labour, and *matching* supply and demand.

Job Analysis **Job analysis** is a systematic analysis of jobs within an organization. A job analysis is made up of two parts:

1. The **job description** lists the duties of a job, its working conditions, and the tools, materials, and equipment used to perform it.

2. The **job specification** lists the skills, abilities, and other credentials needed to do the job.

Job analysis information is used in many HR activities. For instance, knowing about job content and job requirements is necessary to develop appropriate selection methods and job-relevant performance appraisal systems and to set equitable compensation rates.

Forecasting HR Demand and Supply After managers fully understand the jobs to be performed within an organization, they can start planning for the organization's future HR needs. The manager starts by assessing trends in past HR usage, future organizational plans, and general economic trends. A good sales forecast is often the foundation, especially for smaller organizations. Historical ratios can then be used to predict demand for types of employees, such as operating employees and sales representatives. Large organizations use much more complicated models to predict HR needs.

Forecasting the supply of labour involves two tasks:

- Forecasting *internal supply*—the number and type of employees who will be in the firm at some future date

- Forecasting *external supply*—the number and type of people who will be available for hiring from the labour market at large

The simplest approach merely adjusts present staffing levels for anticipated turnover and promotions. Large organizations often use extremely sophisticated models to keep track of the present and future distributions of professionals and managers. This allows the company to spot areas where there will eventually be too many qualified professionals competing for too few promotions or, conversely, too few good people available to fill important positions. Research In Motion and about 550 high-tech companies are located in Canada's "technology triangle" (Kitchener, Waterloo, and Cambridge, Ontario). At the beginning of 2010, unemployment was high but there were about 1500–2000 high-tech, high-paying jobs open in the region. Why? These jobs are highly specialized and require experienced workers, so there was a bit of a mismatch in supply and demand at the time.[2]

Replacement Charts At higher levels of the organization, managers plan for specific people and positions. The technique most commonly used is the **replacement chart,** which lists each important managerial position, who occupies it, how long he or she will probably stay in it before moving on, and who is now qualified or soon will be qualified to move into it. This technique allows ample time to plan developmental experiences for people identified as potential successors to critical managerial jobs. WestJet had a smooth transition of power when Sean Durfy took over as CEO from Clive Beddoe. In 2010, when Mr. Durfy had to leave abruptly for personal reasons, after just 18 months on the job, Gregg Saretsky took over. He was regarded as the logical successor, having been hired nine months earlier as vice-president of WestJet Vacations, but nobody expected him to get the CEO opportunity so quickly.[3]

Skills Inventories To facilitate planning and to identify people for transfer or promotion, some organizations also have **employee information systems**, or **skills inventories**. These systems are usually computerized and contain information on each employee's education, skills, work experience, and career aspirations. Such a system can quickly locate every employee in the company who is qualified to fill a position requiring, say, a degree in chemical engineering, three years of experience in an oil refinery, and fluency in French.

Forecasting the external supply of labour is more difficult. For example, how does a manager predict how many electrical engineers will be seeking work in Ontario or British Columbia three years from now? To get an idea of the future availability of labour, planners must rely on information from outside sources, including population and demographic statistics and figures supplied by colleges and universities on the number of students in major fields. These statistics show that Canada is soon likely to face a severe labour shortage with baby boomers reaching retirement age.[4] The recession of 2008–2009 meant a surplus of labour, but as the economy improves we are starting to see strong hiring needs in the mining, construction, wholesale, and retail trade sectors.[5]

Matching HR Supply and Demand After comparing future demand and internal supply, managers can make plans to navigate predicted shortfalls or over-staffing. If a shortfall is predicted, new employees can be hired, present employees can be retrained and transferred into understaffed areas, individuals approaching retirement can be persuaded to stay on, or labour-saving or productivity-enhancing systems can be installed.

If the organization needs to hire, the external labour-supply forecast helps managers plan how to recruit according to whether the type of person needed is readily available or scarce in the labour market. The use of temporary workers also helps managers by giving them extra flexibility in staffing. If overstaffing is expected to be a problem, the main options are transferring the extra employees, not replacing individuals who quit, encouraging early retirement, and laying people off.

Before we take a closer look at the recruiting process, read the boxed insert entitled "Green Recruiting." It illustrates the increasing importance of environmental considerations in recruiting.

Staffing the Organization

Once managers have decided what positions they need to fill, they must find and hire individuals who meet the job requirements. A study by the Canadian Federation of Independent Business found that the top three characteristics employers are looking for are a good work ethic, reliability, and willingness to stay on the job.[6] Staffing of the business is one of the most complex and important aspects of good human resource management. In this section, we will describe both the process of acquiring staff from outside the company (*external staffing*) and the process of promoting staff from within (*internal staffing*); both start with effective recruiting.

LO-2 Recruiting Human Resources

Recruiting is the process of attracting qualified people to apply for available jobs. Some recruits are found internally; others come from outside the organization.

Internal recruiting means considering present employees as candidates for openings. Promotion from within can help build morale and keep high-quality employees from leaving. In unionized firms, the procedures for notifying employees of internal job-change opportunities are usually spelled out in the union contract. For higher-level positions, a skills inventory system may be used to identify internal candidates, or managers may be asked to recommend individuals who should be considered.

External recruiting means attracting people outside the organization to apply for jobs. External recruiting methods include advertising, campus interviews, employment agencies or executive search firms, union hiring halls, referrals by present employees, and hiring "walk-ins" (people who show up without being solicited). Private employment agencies can be a good source of clerical and technical employees, and executive search firms specialize in locating top-management talent. Newspaper and job-search website ads are often used because they reach a wide audience and thus allow minorities "equal opportunity" to learn about and apply for job openings.

At a job fair, candidates browse through the positions available and talk face to face with recruiters. Job fairs are cheaper than posting jobs with an employment agency or headhunter. **Internships**—short-term paid positions where students focus on a specific project—are increasingly popular. If the individual works out well, the company often hires the student full time after graduation.

Green Recruiting

When Chad Hunt went looking for a job after graduating from university, one key criterion he used was the prospective employer's environmental impact. He eventually took a job with Husky Injection Molding Systems because of the company's emphasis on protecting the environment. Dirk Schlimm, vice-president of corporate affairs for Husky, says that when prospective hires are asked during job interviews why they want to work for Husky, they often mention the company's environmental responsibility program.

Sara Wong said it was the zero-waste program at Hudson's Bay Company (HBC) that caught her attention when she was job hunting. Bob Kolida, the senior vice-president for human resources at HBC, says workers today are more vocal about their desire to work for a green employer. When they visit the company's website, they often click on the corporate social responsibility report.

In a survey conducted by Monster.ca, 78 percent of respondents said they would quit their current job if they could get one at a company that had an environmentally friendly focus. In a second survey, 81 percent of the respondents said that their current employer was not environmentally friendly, and only 18 percent said their employer was "extremely green."

Gabriel Bouchard, Monster.ca's vice-president and general manager, says that employers need to recognize that an environmentally friendly workplace is important to both current employees and job candidates. Bob Willard, who has written books about how businesses can benefit by going green, says that Canadians in general have become more concerned about the environment, and they want to work for companies that share their concerns. So, there is a connection between being green and being a desired employer.

Over half a million Canadians are now employed in environment-related jobs, many of which didn't even exist a generation ago (e.g., consultants for home energy efficiency). According to the Environmental Careers Organization of Canada, the top five green careers are environmental engineer, environmental technologist, conservation biologist, geographic information system analyst, and environmental communications officer.

Ontario has set up a new $650 million fund to secure the next generation of high-paying jobs. Ontario's premier said the money will be used to develop clean and green technologies and businesses. The world is looking for innovative ways to conserve energy and to fight global warming, and *some* place is going to secure thousands of new jobs by developing new solutions. Ontario wants to be that place.

Critical Thinking Questions

1. What are the advantages of working for an environmentally friendly company? Are there any disadvantages?

2. Consider the following statement: "*All the publicity about graduates looking for jobs at environmentally friendly companies is exaggerated. Since being green is the thing to do, many graduates are merely claiming they want to work for an environmentally friendly company, even though most of them really don't care that much about the environment.*" Do you agree or disagree with the statement? Explain your reasoning.

At Bayer Inc. in Toronto, interns are paid at about the same level as full-time employees.[7]

The biggest change in recent years has been the influential impact of internet recruiting. Companies like Monster.ca and Workopolis.ca have become key sources. Internet recruiting gives employers and those seeking employment a fast, easy, and inexpensive way of interacting. But there are drawbacks. For example, employers often receive applications from unqualified people, and those seeking a job often find that they receive no response to their application. Adding to the complexity of the recruitment process is the growing use of social media by job searchers and recruiters. Read the following E-Business and Social Media Solutions boxed insert titled "Job Recruitment in the Social Media Era."

Selecting Human Resources

Once the recruiting process has attracted a pool of applicants, the next step is to select someone to hire. The intent of the selection process is to gather information from applicants that will predict their job success and then to hire the candidates likely to be most successful.

The process of determining the predictive value of information is called **validation.**

To reduce the element of uncertainty, managers use a variety of selection techniques, the most common of which are shown in Figure 8.1. Each organization develops its own mix of selection techniques and may use them in almost any order.

Application Forms The first step in selection is asking the candidate to fill out an application form. An

E-BUSINESS AND SOCIAL MEDIA SOLUTIONS

Job Recruitment in the Social Media Era

The internet has transformed the job recruitment process. Online recruitment sites like Monster.ca and Workopolis made the first revolutionary impression and changed the traditional job-hunting process a few years ago. However, the best way to find a job is through a personal contact. Since social media plays a big role in the private lives of job hunters and HR officers, it is only natural that this relationship would transfer into the job-search process. Some sites like LinkedIn were designed with business networking in mind; others like Facebook and Twitter are evolving. Here are some examples.

- Razor Suleman runs I Love Rewards Inc., a Toronto-based company that consults companies on employee incentives and recognition programs. When the company needed to hire 17 people he did not place ads in a national paper (approximate cost $5000) or use an internet job site (approximate cost $700). Instead, he asked employees to put job postings on Facebook, share them with their LinkedIn networks, and tweet them to friends. He expects this approach to yield 1000 applicants at a minimal cost. It costs on average $2000 to fill a clerical job and $35 000 to fill an executive position using traditional means.

- Mark Buell got a job as a social media communications officer in Ottawa after reading a tweet from one of his contacts. He wasn't looking for a job but used this inside track to apply for the job before it was posted. After his initial interview he sent them a link to his Twitter account to help demonstrate who he is. It worked; his tweets helped him secure the job.

- Future Shop turned to social media to help attract 5000 people for the holiday season. The company has over 17 000 followers on its Facebook page.

- Shannon Yelland found a job at Vancouver-based ActiveState Software Inc. by using her Twitter account proactively. She updated her profile and let people know that she was looking for an online marketing position in Vancouver. She conducted a search on Twitter and Twitter directory sites twellow and tweepsearch. She quickly received tips from her 4000 Twitter followers, including some recruiters.

- U.S. Cellular in Chicago moved to online recruiting years ago but still spent about $4 million annually to post and screen resumés on Monster.ca, CareerBuilder, and Yahoo!HotJobs. When the company had to cut the budget below $1 million, it turned to social media. Many of their new hires come from LinkedIn, where the company signed a $60 000 deal to have access to all 42 million members.

Canadians are among the world's busiest users of social media. LinkedIn has over 2 million members in Canada. The company, which helps professionals connect online, recently announced that it would open an office here. But, the story does not end with the popular social media sites. The online options are endless and are increasingly tailored to people's needs. For example, TheLadders.com and BlueSteps.com are sites dedicated to helping people find executive-level jobs ($100 000+).

Yes, social media sites are increasingly being used by job seekers, but recruiters are also using sites to discover who candidates really are. You might keep that in mind before posting material online that may hurt your future prospects.

Critical Thinking Questions

1. Have you ever used a social media or online recruiting site to find a job? In your opinion how effective are these tools?
2. Should recruiters be legally permitted to conduct background checks on candidates based on publicly available information on social media sites? Does this prospect worry you?

While internet solutions are taking a major role in recruitment, the old application process is still alive and well.

application form is an efficient method of gathering information about the applicant's previous work history, educational background, and other job-related demographic data. It should not contain questions about areas unrelated to the job, such as gender, religion, or national origin. Application-form data are generally used informally to decide whether a candidate merits further evaluation, and interviewers use application forms to familiarize themselves with candidates before interviewing them.

Tests Employers sometimes ask candidates to take tests during the selection process. Tests of ability, skill, aptitude, or knowledge relevant to a particular job are usually the best predictors of job success, although tests of general intelligence or personality are occasionally useful as well. At Astral Media, job candidates are required to take a series of tests that measure verbal and numerical skills, as well as psychological traits.[8] Some companies administer tests to determine how well applicants score on the "big five" personality dimensions discussed in Chapter 9. These scores are used to help make hiring decisions. In addition to being validated, tests should be administered and scored consistently. All candidates should be given the same directions, allowed the same amount of time, and offered the same testing environment, including temperature, lighting, and distractions.

Figure 8.1
General steps in the selection process.

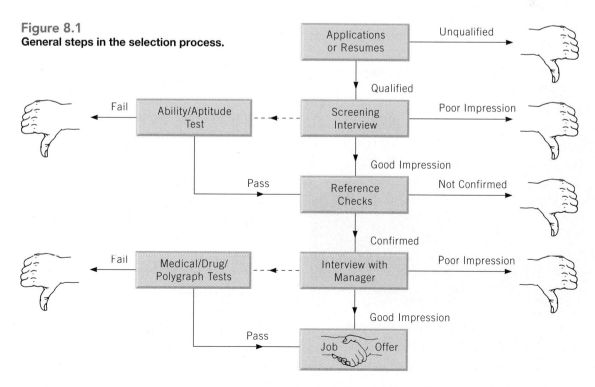

ASSESSMENT CENTRE A series of exercises in which management candidates perform realistic management tasks while being observed by appraisers.

VIDEO ASSESSMENT Involves showing potential hires videos of realistic work situations and asking them to choose a course of action to deal with the situation.

BEHAVIOUR-BASED INTERVIEWING An approach to improving interview validity by asking questions that focuses the interview much more on *behaviour* than on what a person says.

An **assessment centre** is a series of exercises in which candidates perform realistic management tasks under the watchful eye of expert appraisers. During this time, potential managers take selection tests, engage in management simulations, make individual presentations, and conduct group discussions. Assessors check to see how each participant reacts to stress or to criticism by colleagues. A relatively new type of test is **video assessment**, which involves showing potential hires videos of realistic work situations and asking them to choose a course of action to deal with the situation.

Interviews The interview is a popular selection device, but it is sometimes a poor predictor of job success because biases inherent in the way people perceive and judge others on first meeting affect subsequent evaluations. Many companies are placing more emphasis on testing and less emphasis on interviewing because job candidates are becoming clever at giving all the "right" answers during interviews.[9] Interview validity can be improved by training interviewers to be aware of potential biases, and by writing out questions in advance and asking all interviewees the same set of questions.

Interviewers can also increase interview validity by asking "curveball" questions—that is, questions that job applicants would never expect to be asked—to see how well they think on their feet. Questions such as "How would you move Mount Fuji?" or "How would you sell me a glass of water?" are curveball questions.[10]

Another approach to improving interview validity is **behaviour-based interviewing**. Instead of asking a traditional interview question like "Do you often take the initiative?" behaviour-based interviewing asks, "Tell me about a situation where you became aware of a problem. What did you do?" This approach puts a spotlight on behaviour rather than on what a person says. It can be used to test for technical skills (e.g., accounting, welding, or computer programming), management skills (e.g., organizing, motivating others, or communicating), and individual skills (e.g., dependability, discipline, or the ability to work on a team).

Other Techniques Organizations also use other selection techniques that vary with the circumstances. A manufacturer afraid of injuries to workers on the job might require new employees to have a physical examination. This gives the company some information about whether the applicants are physically fit to do the work and what (if any) pre-existing injuries they might have.

Drug tests are coming under fire. According to the Canadian Human Rights Commission policy, pre-employment drug testing and random drug testing are not permitted. However, recent legal decisions make this anything but a black-and-white issue. Rulings related to the Greater Toronto Airport Authority (GTAA) and Goodyear Canada are open to other interpretations. The decisions upheld the rights of these organizations to use drug and alcohol testing for safety-sensitive positions and as a post-treatment check for employees with a history of drug abuse. However, it was also deemed unreasonable to deny selection because of a pre-employment positive drug test. This is an area of law that will continue to evolve and be debated.[11]

Reference checks with previous employers are also used but may be of limited value because individuals are likely to provide the names of only those references who will give them positive recommendations. It is also getting harder to get good reference information because many HR people are worried about legal rulings south of the border as high as $1.4 million. Many legal experts say that the fear is unwarranted; the law protects them in giving honest, even if negative, information.[12]

LO-3 Developing Human Resources

After a company has hired new employees, it must acquaint them with the firm and their new jobs. This process begins with a formal orientation to welcome the

An in-depth interview with a prospective employee is often part of the recruiting process, particularly for managerial jobs.

employee and transfer information about the company history, structure, culture, benefits programs, and much more. Managers also take steps to train employees and develop necessary job skills. In addition, every firm has some system for performance appraisal and feedback.

Training and Development

On-the-job training occurs while employees are in the actual work situation. Much on-the-job training is informal, as when one employee shows another how to operate the photocopy machine. Training may also be formal, as when a trainer shows employees how to operate a new software program. In **job rotation**, employees learn a wide array of tasks and acquire more abilities as they are moved from one job to another.

Off-the-job training is performed at a location away from the work site. For example, **vestibule training** involves employees performing work under conditions closely *simulating* the actual work environment. Montreal-based CAE is famous for building flight simulators that enable airline pilots to learn how to fly a new jet without ever leaving the ground. CAE also develops mock-up operating rooms where medical students can learn in a simulated environment.[13]

Management development programs try to enhance conceptual, analytical, and problem-solving skills.

Most large companies run formal in-house management development programs or send managers to programs on university campuses. Some management development takes place informally, often through processes such as networking and mentoring. **Networking** refers to informal interactions among managers for the purpose of discussing mutual problems, solutions, and opportunities. Networking takes place in a variety of settings, both inside and outside the office. **Mentoring** means having a more experienced manager sponsor and teach a less experienced manager. The fast pace of technology has even created an interesting twist to mentoring, with many companies employing a reverse mentoring approach in which younger, more tech-savvy employees mentor senior staff members on everything from viral marketing to blogging to the use of Facebook and YouTube.[14]

Team Building and Group-Based Training

Since more and more organizations are using teams as a basis for doing work, it should not be surprising that many of the same companies are de veloping training programs specifically designed to facilitate cooperation among team members.

One popular method involves various outdoor training exercises. Some programs involve a group going through a physical obstacle course that requires climbing, crawling, and other physical activities. Outward Bound and several other independent companies specialize in offering these kinds of programs to client firms like Xerox and Burger King. Participants, of course, must see the relevance of such programs if they are to be successful. Firms don't want employees returning from team-building programs to report merely that the experience "was childlike and fun and fairly inoffensive."[15]

Evaluating Employee Performance

Performance appraisals are designed to show how well workers are doing their jobs. Typically, the appraisal process involves a written assessment issued on a regular basis. As a rule, however, the written evaluation is only one part of a multi-step process. The appraisal process begins when a manager defines performance standards for an employee. The manager then observes the employee's performance. If the standards are clear, the manager should have little difficulty comparing expectations with performance. The process is completed when the manager and employee meet to discuss the appraisal.

It is best to rely on several information sources when conducting appraisals. A system called **360-degree feedback** gathers information from supervisors, subordinates, and co-workers. The most accurate information comes from individuals who have known the person being appraised for one to three years. Eight or 10 individuals should take part in the evaluation.[16]

Performance appraisal in many organizations tends to focus on negatives. As a result, managers may have a tendency to avoid giving feedback because they know that an employee who receives negative feedback may be angry, hurt,

ON-THE-JOB TRAINING Those development programs in which employees gain new skills while performing them at work.

JOB ROTATION A technique in which an employee is rotated or transferred from one job to another.

OFF-THE-JOB TRAINING Those development programs in which employees learn new skills at a location away from the normal work site.

VESTIBULE TRAINING A work simulation in which the job is performed under conditions closely simulating the actual work environment.

MANAGEMENT DEVELOPMENT PROGRAMS Development programs in which managers' conceptual, analytical, and problem-solving skills are enhanced.

NETWORKING Informal interactions among managers, both inside and outside the office, for the purpose of discussing mutual problems, solutions, and opportunities.

MENTORING Having a more experienced manager sponsor and teach a less experienced manager.

PERFORMANCE APPRAISALS A formal program for evaluating how well an employee is performing the job; helps managers to determine how effective they are in recruiting and selecting employees.

360-DEGREE FEEDBACK Gathering information from a manager's subordinates, peers, and superiors when assessing the manager's performance.

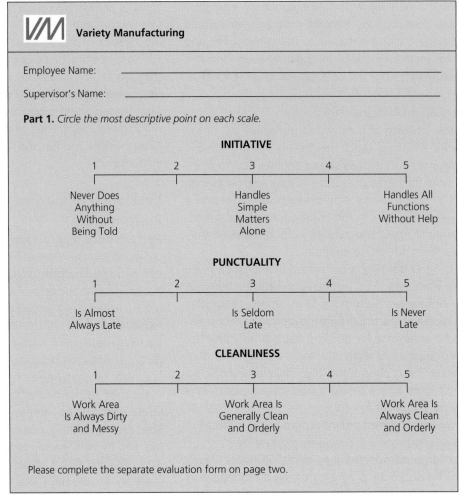

Figure 8.2
Performance rating scale.

discouraged, or argumentative. But clearly, if employees are not told about their shortcomings, they will have no concrete reason to try to improve and receive no guidance as to *how* to improve. In a recently released book, Professor Samuel Culbert from UCLA argues that the traditional performance review approach is both flawed and damaging; 80 to 90 percent of employees and managers dislike and are stressed by the ritual. According to Culbert, companies should focus more on "performance previews" and use a continuous feedback approach.[17]

Methods for Appraising Performance The **simple ranking method** requires a manager to rank-order from top to bottom or from best to worst each member of a particular workgroup or department. The individual ranked first is the top performer; the individual ranked second is the second-best performer, and so forth. Another ranking method, the forced distribution method, involves grouping employees into predefined frequencies of performance ratings. Those frequencies are determined in advance and are imposed on the rater. A decision might be made, for instance, that 10 percent of the employees in a workgroup will be categorized as outstanding, 20 percent as very good, 40 percent

as average, 20 percent as below average, and the remaining 10 percent as poor. The forced distribution method is familiar to students because it is the principle used by professors who grade on a so-called "bell curve" or "normal curve."

One of the most popular and widely used methods is the **graphic rating scale**, which consists simply of a statement or question about some aspect of an individual's job performance. Figure 8.2 shows a sample graphic rating scale.

The **critical incident method** focuses attention on an example of especially good or poor performance on the part of the employee. Raters then describe what the employee did (or did not do) that led to success or failure. This technique not only provides information for feedback but defines performance in fairly clear behavioural terms.

LO-4 Compensation and Benefits

Compensation refers to the rewards that organizations provide to individuals in return for their willingness to perform various jobs and tasks within the organization.

Compensation includes a number of different elements, including base salary, incentives, bonuses, benefits, and other rewards. The compensation received by CEOs can be extremely large, especially when bonuses are included. The most highly paid executives in the 2009 *Globe and Mail* Survey of Compensation were Aaron Regent of Barrick Gold (who earned $24.2 million), Hunter Harrison of Canadian National Railway ($17.3 million), and Gerald Swartz of Onex Corp. ($16.7 million).[18] Critics have frequently questioned the wisdom of giving executives such large amounts of money, but most attempts to rein in executive salaries have failed. In 2009, there was a huge outcry in the United States about bonuses paid to executives of AIG, a company that was in deep financial trouble and had been bailed out by taxpayers. Shareholders at CIBC and the Royal Bank of Canada passed motions demanding that the companies give them a voice in executive compensation through non-binding shareholder votes.[19] In Sweden, Norway, and the Netherlands, shareholders have a binding vote on executive pay packages. Whether binding or non-binding, investor feedback may help boards of directors rein in executive compensation that is perceived as too high.[20]

Determining Basic Compensation

Wages generally refer to hourly compensation paid to operating employees. Most of the jobs that are paid on an hourly wage basis are lower-level and/or operating-level jobs. In 2008, the average hourly wage in manufacturing was $21.66, while in retailing it was only $14.87. The manufacturing sector is shrinking, and retailers are now the biggest employers in Canada.[21]

Rather than expressing compensation on an hourly basis, the organization may instead describe compensation on an annual or monthly basis. Many college and university graduates, for example, compare job offers on the basis of annual **salary**, such as $40 000 versus $38 000 a year.

Companies often use **pay surveys** to determine pay levels. These surveys show the compensation that is being paid to employees by other employers in a particular geographic area, an industry, or an occupational group. For example, the Canadian Federation of Business School Deans publishes an annual summary of salaries for professors teaching in business schools in Canadian universities. The internet allows job seekers and current employees to more easily get a sense of what their true market value is. If they can document the claim that their value is higher than what their current employer now pays or is offering, they are in a position to demand a higher salary.

Another means of determining basic compensation is **job evaluation**, a method for determining the relative value or worth of a job to the organization so that individuals who perform it can be compensated appropriately. In other words, it is concerned with establishing internal pay equity. There should be a logical rank-ordering of compensation levels from the most valuable to the least valuable jobs throughout the organization.

Incentive Programs

Employees feel better about themselves and their company when they believe that they are being fairly compensated. However, studies have shown that beyond a certain point, more money will not produce better performance. As well, money motivates employees only if it is tied directly to performance. The most common method of establishing this link is the use of **incentive programs**—special pay programs designed to motivate high performance. Some programs are available to individuals, whereas others are distributed on a companywide basis.

Individual Incentives Under a **piece-rate incentive plan**, employees receive a certain amount of money for every unit they produce. An assembly-line worker might be paid $1 for every 12 units of a product successfully

WAGES Dollars paid based on the number of hours worked.

SALARY Dollars paid at regular intervals in return for doing a job, regardless of the amount of time or output involved.

PAY SURVEYS A survey of compensation paid to employees by other employers in a particular geographic area, an industry, or an occupational group.

JOB EVALUATION A method for determining the relative value or worth of a job to the organization so that individuals who perform it can be appropriately compensated.

INCENTIVE PROGRAMS Special compensation programs designed to motivate high performance.

PIECE-RATE INCENTIVE PLAN A compensation system in which an organization pays an employee a certain amount of money for every unit produced.

Individual incentive plans have been a big part of professional sports for many years. Some players receive multimillion-dollar annual compensation for outstanding individual performance.

completed. Sales employees are often paid a **bonus**—a special payment above their salaries—when they sell a certain number or certain dollar amount of goods for the year. Bonuses are also given in non-sales jobs. For example, many baseball players have contract clauses that pay them bonuses for hitting over 300, making the all-star team, or being named Most Valuable Player. Despite public outcries, large bonuses at the "Big Six" Canadian banks continue to rise. For example, in 2010, the Royal Bank of Canada was expected to pay $1.87 billion in bonuses, up from $1.7 billion a year earlier.[22]

With **pay for performance** (or **variable pay**) schemes, managers are rewarded for especially productive output—for producing earnings that significantly exceed the cost of bonuses. Such incentives go to middle managers on the basis of company-wide performance, business-unit performance, personal record, or all three factors. Eligible managers must often forgo merit or entitlement raises (increases for staying on and reporting to work every day), but many firms say that variable pay is a better motivator because the range between generous and mediocre merit raises is usually quite small.

Team and Group Incentives Some incentive programs apply to all the employees in a firm. Under **profit-sharing plans**, profits earned above a certain level are distributed to employees. At the Great Little Box Company in Richmond, B.C., 15 percent of company profits are split evenly among staff. The company also has an "open book" policy of providing financial information to employees

so they can relate financial performance of the company to their share of the profits.[23]

Gainsharing plans distribute bonuses to employees when a company's costs are reduced through greater work efficiency. **Pay-for-knowledge plans** encourage workers to learn new skills and to become proficient at different jobs. These workers receive additional pay for each new skill or job they master.

Benefits

Benefits are rewards, incentives, and other things of value that an organization gives to employees in addition to wages, salaries, and other forms of direct financial compensation. Because these benefits have tangible value, they represent a meaningful form of compensation even though they are not generally expressed in financial terms. According to a PricewaterhouseCoopers survey, some of the top benefits sought, other than money, were gift cards, extra vacation days, and being fast-tracked for promotion.[24]

Mandated Protection Plans **Protection plans** assist employees when their income is threatened or reduced by illness, disability, unemployment, or retirement. **Employment insurance** provides a basic subsistence payment to employees who are unemployed but are actively seeking employment. Both employers and employees pay premiums to an employment insurance fund. As of 2010, employee premiums were $1.73 per hundred dollars of earnings, and employer premiums were $2.42.[25]

The **Canada Pension Plan** provides income for retired individuals to help them supplement their personal savings, private pensions, part-time work, etc. It is funded through employee and employer taxes that are withheld from payroll. In 2009, the Canada Pension Plan had a surplus of almost $127 billion.[26]

Workers' compensation is mandated insurance that covers individuals who suffer a job-related illness or accident. Employers bear the cost of workers' compensation insurance. The premium is related to each employer's past experience with job-related accidents and illnesses. For example, a steel company might pay $20 per $100 of wages, while an accounting firm might pay only $0.10 per $100 of wages.

Optional Protection Plans Health insurance is the most important type of coverage, and has expanded in recent years to include vision care, mental health services, dental care, and prescription drugs. Employee prescription drug plan costs are doubling about every five years, and companies are increasingly concerned about their ability to offer this kind of coverage.[27] Pension liabilities are also a problem.

Paid Time Off *Paid vacations* are usually for periods of one, two, or more weeks. Most organizations vary the amount of paid vacation with an individual's seniority, but some companies are reducing the time required to qualify for paid vacations. At Carlson Wagonlit Travel Canada, employees get four weeks of paid vacation after working at the company for just five years. Formerly, 10 years of service was required.[28]

Another common paid time off plan is *sick leave*, which is provided when an individual is sick or otherwise physically unable to perform his or her job. Sometimes an organization will allow an employee to take off a small number of days simply for "personal business." The Catholic Children's Aid Society provides its child protection workers with time off when they need it because they routinely face high-stress situations.[29]

Some companies go even further and offer their employees paid or unpaid sabbaticals to help them rejuvenate themselves and increase their enthusiasm for their jobs. Employees at Procter & Gamble are eligible for a 12-week unpaid sabbatical after they have worked for the company for one year.[30]

Other Types of Benefits In addition to protection plans and paid time off, many organizations offer a number of other benefit programs. **Wellness programs**, for example, concentrate on preventing illness in employees rather than simply paying their expenses when they become sick.

Cafeteria-style benefit plans allow employees to choose the benefits they really want. The organization typically establishes a budget, indicating how much it is willing to spend, per employee, on benefits. Employees are then presented with a list of possible benefits and the cost of each. They are free to put the benefits together in any combination they wish. The range and significance of possible benefits is evident in the boxed insert entitled "The Importance of Perks."

LO-5 The Legal Context of HRM

HRM is heavily influenced by federal and provincial law, so managers must be aware of the most important and far-reaching areas of HR regulation. These include *equal employment opportunity, comparable worth, sexual harassment, employee health and safety,* and *retirement.*

Equal Employment Opportunity

The basic goal of all **equal employment opportunity regulations** is to protect people from unfair or inappropriate discrimination in the workplace. Note that differentiating between employees—for example, giving one person a raise and denying the raise to another person—is not illegal. As long as the basis for this distinction is purely

job related (i.e., based on performance or qualifications) and is applied objectively and consistently, the action is legal and appropriate. Problems arise when distinctions among people are not job related. In such cases, the resulting discrimination is illegal.

Anti-Discrimination Laws The key federal anti-discrimination legislation is the **Canadian Human Rights Act** of 1977 (each province has also enacted human rights legislation). The goal of the Act is to ensure that any individual who wishes to obtain a job has an equal opportunity. The Act applies to all federal agencies, federal Crown corporations, any employee of the federal government, and business firms that do business inter-provincially. The Act prohibits a wide variety of practices in recruiting, selecting, promoting, and dismissing personnel. It specifically prohibits discrimination on the basis of age, race and colour, national and ethnic origin, physical handicap, religion, gender, marital status, or prison record (if pardoned). Some exceptions to these blanket prohibitions are permitted. Discrimination cannot be charged if a blind person is refused a position as a bus driver or crane operator. Likewise, a firm cannot be charged with discrimination if it does not hire a deaf person as an audio engineer.

Difficulties in determining whether discrimination has occurred are sometimes dealt with by using the concept of **bona fide occupational requirement**. That is, an employer may choose one person over another based on overriding characteristics of the job in question. If a fitness centre wants to hire only women to supervise its women's locker room and sauna, it can do so without being discriminatory because it established a bona fide occupational requirement.

Enforcement of the federal Act is carried out by the Canadian Human Rights Commission. The commission can either respond to complaints from individuals who believe they have been discriminated against, or launch an investigation on its own if it has reason to believe that

WELLNESS PROGRAMS A program that concentrates on preventing illness in employees rather than simply paying their expenses when they become sick.

CAFETERIA-STYLE BENEFIT PLANS A flexible approach to providing benefits in which employees are allocated a certain sum to cover benefits and can "spend" this allocation on the specific benefits they prefer.

EQUAL EMPLOYMENT OPPORTUNITY REGULATIONS Regulations to protect people from unfair or inappropriate discrimination in the workplace.

CANADIAN HUMAN RIGHTS ACT Ensures that any individual who wishes to obtain a job has an equal opportunity to apply for it.

BONA FIDE OCCUPATIONAL REQUIREMENT When an employer may choose one applicant over another based on overriding characteristics of the job.

EMPLOYMENT EQUITY ACT OF 1986 Federal legislation that designates four groups as employment dis- advantaged—women, visible minorities, Aboriginal people, and people with disabilities.

discrimination has occurred. If a claim of discrimination is substantiated, the offending organization or individual may be ordered to compensate the victim.

The **Employment Equity Act of 1986** addresses the issue of discrimination in employment by designating four groups as employment-disadvantaged— women, visible minorities, Aboriginal people, and people

with disabilities. These four groups contain six of every 10 individuals in the Canadian workforce, and it is estimated that their underemployment costs the Canadian economy around \$50 billion each year.[31] Companies covered by the Employment Equity Act are required to publish statistics on their employment of people in the four designated groups. In 2010, the Royal Bank of Canada received an award from Catalyst recognizing the bank's success in promot- ing diversity. For example, women at RBC now occupy nearly 40 percent of executive roles in the company, and this figure is growing.[32]

MANAGING IN TURBULENT TIMES

The Importance of Perks

The list of perks that Canadian companies might offer employees is very long. It includes things like unlim- ited sick days, on-site childcare, eldercare benefits, counselling, flexible work schedules, free beverages, concierge services, laundry pickup and delivery, train- ing and development opportunities, exercise facilities, on-site pet care, and wellness programs, to name just a few. The extent of these perks varies widely across companies.

Giving discounts to employees is a long-stand- ing practice at some firms. Consider the following examples:

- lululemon gives employees a 60 percent discount on high-end clothing (plus two free weekly yoga lessons)

- Starbucks employees receive free beverages dur- ing their work shifts (plus one pound of coffee or one box of tea each week)

- Employees at Toronto-Dominion Bank can get fixed-rate mortgages for 1.5 percentage points below the posted rate (they can also get a Visa card with an interest rate as low as 5 percent)

- Fairmont Hotels & Resorts gives its employees discounts on rooms, food, and drink

Wellness programs—which concentrate on pre- venting illness in employees rather than simply paying their expenses when they become sick—have become increasingly popular. Labatt Brewing Company employs a full-time fitness coordinator who schedules nutritionists and massage therapists for employees.

Childcare and eldercare perks are also being more frequently offered to employees. The childcare

centre run by Husky Injection Molding Systems in Bolton, Ontario, provides on-site haircuts, music les- sons, and a pajama party on Valentine's Day. Any orga- nization that wants to be considered "family friendly" must have some type of childcare benefits, and being a family-friendly company is increasingly becoming a competitive advantage.

A study done for *Report on Business* magazine found that many of the traditional things that manag- ers have assumed are important to employees—for example, fair pay, financial incentives like share owner- ship plans, and the opportunity for further training and education—are, in fact, important. However, employ- ees also want to balance work and personal activities. A Canada@Work study done by Aon Consulting found that when employers recognize employee needs out- side the workplace, employees are more likely to stay with the company, and are more likely to recommend the company as a good place to work. Overall, compa- nies need to have a "people-first" attitude about their employees, and perks play a significant role in this.

But what about companies that are struggling financially? Can they afford to give perks? The good news is that there are cost-effective perks that can be used. The most powerful—and least expensive—perk can be time off. Experts suggest, for example, that up to 20 percent of workers would be willing to work fewer hours for lower pay.

Critical Thinking Questions

1. What are the advantages of perks? What are the disadvantages?
2. What other incentives might a company be able to offer its best workers to retain them?

Comparable Worth

Comparable worth is a legal concept that aims at paying equal wages for jobs that are of comparable value to the employer. This might mean comparing dissimilar jobs, such as those of secretaries and mechanics or nurses and electricians. Proponents of comparable worth say that all the jobs in a company must be evaluated and then rated in terms of basic dimensions such as the level of skill they require. All jobs could then be compared based on a common index. People in different jobs that rate the same on this index would be paid the same. Experts hope that this will help to reduce the gap between men's and women's pay. In a long-standing comparable worth dispute, the Supreme Court of Canada ruled that flight attendants at Air Canada—who have been trying for years to achieve pay equity with male-dominated groups of employees—could compare their pay with the pay of ground crews and pilots because all these employees work for the same company.[33]

Critics of comparable worth object on the grounds that it ignores the supply and demand aspects of labour. They say that legislation forcing a company to pay people more than the open market price for their labour (which may happen in jobs where there is a surplus of workers) is another example of unreasonable government interference in business activities. They also say that implementing comparable worth will cost business firms too much money. A study prepared for the Ontario Ministry of Labour estimated that it would cost approximately $10 billion for the public and private sectors in Ontario to establish equitable payment for jobs of equal value.

Sexual Harassment

Within the job context, **sexual harassment** refers to requests for sexual favours, unwelcome sexual advances, or verbal or physical conduct of a sexual nature that creates an intimidating or hostile environment for a given employee. The Canadian Human Rights Act takes precedence over any policies that a company might have developed on its own to deal with sexual harassment problems.

Quid pro quo harassment is the most blatant form of sexual harassment. It occurs when the harasser offers to exchange something of value for sexual favours. A male supervisor, for example, might suggest to a female subordinate that he will recommend her for promotion or give her a raise in exchange for sexual favours. The creation of a **hostile work environment** is a subtler form of sexual harassment. A group of employees who continually make off-colour jokes and decorate the work environment with questionable photographs may create a hostile work environment for a colleague. Regardless of the pattern, the same bottom-line rules apply: sexual harassment is illegal, and the organization is responsible for controlling it. If a manager is found guilty of sexual harassment, the company is liable because the manager is an agent of the company.

Debrahlee Lorenzana made news when she sued Citibank and claimed that she was fired because her voluptuous body had become a workplace distraction. Debrahlee clearly stated that she followed the company dress code but admittedly dressed provocatively like a Playboy model. Her enemies were calling her an attention-seeking gold digger who was fired for poor performance. The ruling on this case will be closely followed and discussed.[34]

Employee Health and Safety

Employee health and safety programs help to reduce absenteeism and turnover, raise productivity, and boost morale by making jobs safer and

COMPARABLE WORTH A legal idea that aims to pay equal wages for work of equal value.

SEXUAL HARASSMENT Requests for sexual favours, unwelcome sexual advances, or verbal or physical conduct of a sexual nature that creates an intimidating or hostile environment for a given employee.

QUID PRO QUO HARASSMENT Form of sexual harassment in which sexual favours are requested in return for job-related benefits.

HOSTILE WORK ENVIRONMENT Form of sexual harassment deriving from off-colour jokes, lewd comments, and so forth.

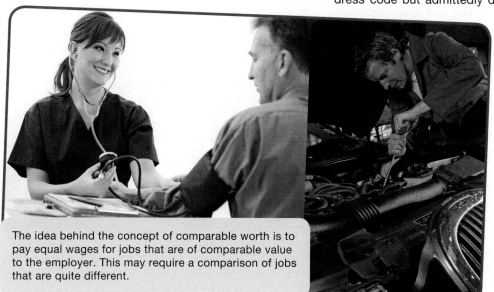

The idea behind the concept of comparable worth is to pay equal wages for jobs that are of comparable value to the employer. This may require a comparison of jobs that are quite different.

more healthful. In Canada, each province has developed its own workplace health and safety regulations. The Ontario Occupational Health and Safety Act illustrates current legislation in Canada. It requires all employers to ensure that equipment and safety devices are used properly. Employers must also show workers the proper way to operate machinery. At the job site, supervisors are charged with the responsibility of ensuring that workers use equipment properly. The Act also requires workers to behave appropriately on the job. Employees have the right to refuse to work on a job if they believe it is unsafe; a legal procedure exists for resolving any disputes in this area. In most provinces, the Ministry of Labour appoints inspectors to enforce health and safety regulations. If the inspector finds a sufficient hazard, he or she has the authority to clear the workplace. Inspectors can usually arrive at a firm unannounced to conduct an inspection.

Some industrial work—logging, construction, fishing, and mining—can put workers at risk of injury in obvious ways. But other types of work—such as typing or lifting—can also cause painful injuries. **Repetitive strain injuries (RSIs)** occur when workers perform the same functions over and over again. These injuries disable more than 200 000 Canadians each year and account for nearly half of all work-related lost-time claims.

Retirement

Until the 1990s, Canadian courts generally upheld 65 as the mandatory retirement age, but most Canadian provinces have now abolished mandatory retirement. In 2009, Nova Scotia became the latest province to remove this provision. In spite of this, workers are actually retiring earlier than they used to. In the late 1970s, the average retirement age in Canada was 65, but by 2009 it had dropped to 62.[35] A Statistics Canada study showed that "boomer" couples are unlikely to retire at the same time, with the woman often staying in the workforce longer than her husband.[36]

Some managers fear that the abolition of mandatory retirement will allow less productive employees to remain at work after age 65, but research shows that the employees who stay on the job past 65 are usually the most productive ones. But there are two other interesting facts that should not be ignored: workers over age 65 are nearly four times as likely to die from work-related causes as are younger workers, and older workers have double the health care costs that workers in their forties do.[37]

LO-6 New Challenges in the Changing Workplace

As we have seen throughout this chapter, HR managers face various challenges in their efforts to keep their organizations staffed with effective workers. To complicate matters, new challenges arise as the economic and social environments of business change. Several of the most important HRM issues facing business today are *managing workforce diversity, managing knowledge workers,* and *managing contingent and temporary workers.*

Managing Workforce Diversity

One extremely important set of human resource challenges centres on **workforce diversity**—the range of workers' attitudes, values, beliefs, and behaviours that differ by gender, race, age, ethnicity, physical ability, and other characteristics. The situation for visible minorities is currently one of the most publicized aspects of diversity. Consider these facts:

■ By 2015, 20 percent of Saskatchewan's population will be Aboriginal.

■ In 2001, approximately 4 million Canadians were visible minorities; by 2017, that number could increase to as much as 8.5 million.

■ Visible minorities currently make up more than 40 percent of the population of Vancouver.

Many Canadian organizations have evolved from dealing with diversity to proactively embracing the business benefits of a diverse workforce.

- By 2017, visible minorities will form more than 50 percent of the populations of Toronto and Vancouver.
- By 2017, 22 percent of the total Canadian population will be visible minorities.[38]

In the past, organizations tended to work toward homogenizing their workforces, getting everyone to think and behave in similar ways. Organizations are now increasingly recognizing that diversity can be a competitive advantage. By hiring the best people available from every group rather than hiring from just one or a few groups, a firm can develop a higher-quality workforce. Similarly, a diverse workforce can bring a wider array of information to bear on problems and can provide insights on marketing products to a wider range of consumers.

Managing Knowledge Workers

Traditionally, employees added value to organizations because of what they did or because of their experience. In the "information age," however, many employees add value because of what they *know*.[39]

The Nature of Knowledge Work These employees are usually called **knowledge workers**, and the skill with which they are managed is a major factor in determining which firms will be successful in the future. Knowledge workers, including computer scientists, engineers, and physical scientists, provide special challenges for the HR manager. They tend to work for high-tech firms and are usually experts in some abstract knowledge base. They often prefer to work independently and tend to identify more strongly with their profession than with the organization that pays them—even to the extent of defining performance in terms recognized by other members of their profession.

As the importance of information-driven jobs grows, the need for knowledge workers increases. But these employees require extensive and highly specialized training, and not every organization is willing to make the human capital investments necessary to take advantage of these employees. Even after knowledge workers are on the job, training updates are critical to prevent their skills from becoming obsolete. The failure to update such skills not only results in the loss of competitive advantage, it also increases the likelihood that knowledge workers will move to another firm that is more committed to updating their knowledge.

Knowledge Worker Management and Labour Markets Organizations that need knowledge workers must introduce regular market adjustments (upward) to pay them enough to keep them. This is especially critical in areas in which demand is growing, as even entry-level salaries for these employees are skyrocketing. Once an employee accepts a job with a firm, the employer faces yet another dilemma. Once hired, workers are subject to the company's internal labour market, which is not likely to be growing as quickly as the external market for knowledge workers as a whole. Consequently, the longer knowledge workers remain with a firm, the further behind the market their pay falls—unless it is regularly adjusted upward.

> **KNOWLEDGE WORKERS** Workers who are experts in specific fields like computer technology and engineering, and who add value because of what they know, rather than how long they have worked or the job they do.

Managing Contingent Workers

A contingent worker is one who works for an organization on something other than a permanent or full-time basis. Categories of contingent workers include part-time workers, independent contractors (freelancers), on-call workers, temporary employees (usually hired through outside "temp" agencies), contract workers, and guest workers (foreigners working in Canada for a limited time).

Trends in Contingent Employment Contingent employment is on the rise in Canada. Part-time employment in all categories was nearly 7 percent higher in 2009 than in 2005.[40] In Canada, there is increasing demand for temporary workers in top management because the economic downturn has created a lot of turnover in this area. These "temps at the top" usually stay for a year or less until a permanent person is found.[41]

The number of guest workers in Canada—one category of contingent workers—is increasing. They work in all kinds of industries, including agriculture, manufacturing, and services. Each year there are over 150 000 guest workers in Canada. The number is predicted to rise in the future.[42]

Management of Contingent Workers The effective management of contingent workers requires consideration of three issues. First, careful planning must be done so the organization brings in contingent workers only when they are actually needed and in the quantity needed to complete necessary tasks. Second, the costs and benefits of using contingent workers must be understood. Many firms bring in contingent workers in order to reduce labour costs, but if contingent workers are less productive than permanent workers, there may be no gain for the organization. Third, contingent workers should be integrated into the mainstream activities of the organization as much as possible. This involves deciding how they will be treated relative to permanent workers. For example, should contingent workers be invited to the company holiday party?

Should they have the same access to employee benefits? Managers must develop a strategy for integrating contingent workers according to some sound logic and then follow that strategy consistently over time.[43]

LO-7 Dealing with Organized Labour

A **labour union** is a group of individuals working together to achieve shared job-related goals, such as higher pay, shorter working hours, greater benefits, or better working conditions.[44] Labour unions grew in popularity in Canada in the nineteenth and early twentieth centuries. At that time, work hours were long, pay was minimal, and working conditions were often unsafe. Workers had no job security and received few benefits. Many companies employed large numbers of children and paid them poverty-level wages. If people complained, they were fired.

Unions forced management to listen to the complaints of all workers rather than to just those few who were brave enough to speak out. Thus the power of unions comes from collective action. **Collective bargaining** is the process by which union leaders and company management negotiate terms and conditions of employment for those workers represented by unions. We discuss the role of **collective bargaining** in detail below.

Unionism Today

Although 4.6 million workers belonged to unions in 2009, union membership as a proportion of the non-agricultural workforce (called *union density*) has stagnated, and less than one-third of Canadian workers belong to unions. From 1970 to 2009, union density has ranged from 27.2 percent to 30.5 percent. In the United States, union density is even lower (12.1 percent).[45]

The highest rates of unionization are found in Newfoundland (37.7 percent) and Quebec (37.5 percent). The lowest rates are found in Alberta (23.0 percent) and New Brunswick (26.4 percent). The public sector is quite heavily unionized (72.7 percent), but the private sector is not (18.1 percent).[46] In some occupations like teaching and nursing over 80 percent of workers are unionized. In other occupations like management and food and beverage services, less than 10 percent of workers belong to unions.[47]

Many years ago, unions routinely won certification votes. But in recent years, they have had less success. One reason is that today's workforce is increasingly diverse. Women and ethnic minorities have weaker traditions of union affiliation than white males (who dominated the blue-collar jobs in the past). The workforce is also increasingly employed in the service sector, which traditionally has been less heavily unionized.

Another reason for declining unionization is that companies have become far more aggressive in opposing unions. Federal and provincial labour legislation restricts what management of a company can do to keep out a union, but companies are free to pursue certain strategies to minimize unionization, such as creating a more employee-friendly work environment. For example, Japanese manufacturers who have set up shop in North America have avoided unionization efforts by the United Auto Workers (UAW) by providing job security, higher wages, and a work environment in which employees are allowed to participate and be actively involved in plant management. The case at the end of the chapter explores union management issues in detail.

Trends in Union–Management Relations The problems that have been experienced by unions have caused some significant changes in union–management relations. Not so long ago, most union–management bargaining was very adversarial, with unions making demands for dramatic improvements in wages, benefits, and job security. But with organizational downsizing and a decade of low inflation in Canada, many unions today find themselves able to achieve only modest improvements in wages and benefits. A common goal of union strategy is therefore to preserve what has already been won. For example, unions are well aware that companies have an incentive to relocate jobs to lower-wage foreign countries, so unions have to work hard to keep jobs in Canada and thus maintain job security for members.

Today, unions must cooperate with employers if both companies and unions are to survive and prosper. The goal is to create win-win partnerships in which managers and workers share the same goals: profitability, growth, and effectiveness, with equitable rewards for everyone. Even in those sectors of the economy where unions remain quite strong—most notably in the automobile and steel industries—unions have changed their tactics. In the automobile industry, Buzz Hargrove, former president of the Canadian Auto Workers, has urged members of the union bargaining team to come up with new ideas for improving quality and productivity so that Canadian factories will be more attractive for new investment.[48]

The Future of Unions

Despite declining membership and loss of power, labour unions remain a significant factor in Canadian business. The labour organizations in the Canadian Labour Congress and independent major unions such as the International Brotherhood of Teamsters and the Canadian Union of Public Employees can disrupt the economy by refusing to work. The votes of their members are still sought by politicians at all levels. In addition, the concessions they have won—better pay, shorter working hours, and safer working conditions—now cover many non-unionized workers as well.

The big question is this: Will unions be able to cope with the many challenges that are currently facing them, or will their power continue to dwindle? The challenges facing unions are many, including the decline of the so-called "smokestack industries" (where union power has traditionally been very strong), employment growth in service industries (where union power has traditionally not been strong), the globalization of business (which has raised the very real possibility of more jobs being moved to areas of the world with lower labour costs), and technological change (which often reduces the number of workers that are needed).

LO-8 The Legal Environment for Unions in Canada

Political and legal barriers to collective bargaining existed until well into the twentieth century (see Table 8.1). Courts held that some unions were conspirators in restraint of trade. Employers viewed their employees' efforts to unionize as attempts to deprive the employers of their private property. The employment contract, employers contended, was between the individual worker and the employer—not between the employer and employees as a group. The balance of bargaining power was very much in favour of the employer.

The employer–employee relationship became much less direct as firms grew in size. Managers were themselves employees, and hired managers dealt with other employees. Communication among owners, managers, and workers became more formalized. Big business had more power than workers did. Because of mounting public concern, laws were passed to place workers on a more even footing with employers.

The **Constitution Act** (originally the BNA Act), passed in 1867, has also affected labour legislation. This Act allocated certain activities to the federal government (e.g., labour legislation for companies operating inter-provincially) and others to individual provinces (labour relations regulations in general). Thus, labour legislation comes from both the federal and provincial governments but is basically a provincial matter. That is why certain groups of similar employees might be allowed to go on strike in one province but not in another.

Federal Legislation—The Canada Labour Code

The **Canada Labour Code** is a comprehensive piece of legislation that applies to the labour practices of firms operating under the legislative authority of parliament. In 2005, a sweeping review of the Canada Labour Code was announced by the federal Minister of Labour. One of the issues that the review will focus on is whether managers and supervisors should also be protected by labour code restrictions on the number of hours they work each week, and whether they should receive overtime pay. The issue came to the forefront after the Manitoba Labour Board

CONSTITUTION ACT Divided authority over labour regulations between the federal and provincial governments.

CANADA LABOUR CODE Legislation that applies to the labour practices of firms operating under the legislative authority of parliament.

Table 8.1 Historical Steps for Canadian Labour Legislation

Date	Legislation	Accomplishments/Goals
1900	Conciliation Act	■ designed to help settle labour disputes through voluntary conciliation ■ first step in creating more favourable labour conditions
1907	Industrial Disputes Investigation Act	■ compulsory investigation of labour disputes by a government-appointed board before any strike action (found to violate a provision of the British North America [BNA] Act).
1943	Privy Council Order 1003	■ recognized the right of employees to bargain collectively ■ prohibited unfair management labour practices ■ established a labour board to certify bargaining authority ■ prohibited strikes and lockouts (except in collective bargaining agreements [CBAs])

ruled that Sharon Michalowski, a manager at Nygard International, was entitled to overtime pay, even though she was a manager and had signed a contract stipulating that she would work whatever hours were required to earn her annual salary of $42 000.[49] As of 2009, managers were still not covered by the provisions of the Canada Labour Code.

The Canada Labour Code has four main sections: fair employment practices; standard hours, wages, vacations, and holidays; safety of employees; and Canada industrial relations regulations.

Fair Employment Practices This section prohibits an employer from either refusing employment on the basis of a person's race or religion or using an employment agency that discriminates against people on the basis of their race or religion. These prohibitions apply to trade unions as well, but not to non-profit, charitable, and philanthropic organizations. Any individual who believes a violation has occurred may make a complaint in writing to Labour Canada. The allegation will then be investigated and, if necessary, an Industrial Inquiry Commission will be appointed to make a recommendation in the case. Since 1982, fair employment practices have been covered by the Canadian Human Rights Act; they are also covered by the Canadian Charter of Rights and Freedoms.

Standard Hours, Wages, Vacations, and Holidays This section deals with a wide variety of mechanical issues such as standard hours of work (8-hour day and 40-hour week), maximum hours of work per week (48), overtime pay (at least one and a half times the regular pay), minimum wages, equal wages for men and women doing the same jobs, vacations, general holidays, and parental leave. The specific provisions are changed frequently to take into account changes in the economic and social structure of Canada, but their basic goal is to ensure consistent treatment of employees in these areas.

Safety of Employees This section requires that every person running a federal work project do so in a way that will not endanger the health or safety of any employee. It also requires that safety procedures and techniques be implemented to reduce the risk of employment injury. This section requires employees to exercise care to ensure their own safety; however, even if it can be shown that the employee did not exercise proper care, compensation must still be paid. This section also makes provisions for a safety officer whose duty is to assure that the provisions of the

code are fulfilled. The safety officer has the right to enter any federal project "at any reasonable time."

Canada Industrial Relations Regulations The final major section of the Canada Labour Code deals with all matters related to collective bargaining.

Provincial Labour Legislation

Each province has enacted legislation to deal with the personnel practices covered in the Canada Labour Code. These laws vary across provinces and are frequently revised; however, their basic approach and substance is the same as in the Canada Labour Code. Certain provinces may exceed the minimum code requirements on some issues (e.g., minimum wage).

LO-9 Collective Bargaining

People often associate collective bargaining with the specific act of signing of a contract between a union and a company or industry. In fact, collective bargaining is an ongoing process involving both the drafting and administration of the terms of a labour contract.

Reaching Agreement on the Contract's Terms

The collective bargaining process begins when the union is recognized as the exclusive negotiator for its members. The bargaining cycle begins when union leaders meet with management representatives to begin working on a new contract. By law, both parties must negotiate "in good faith." When each side has presented its demands, sessions focus on identifying the *bargaining zone*. This process is shown in Figure 8.3. For example, although an

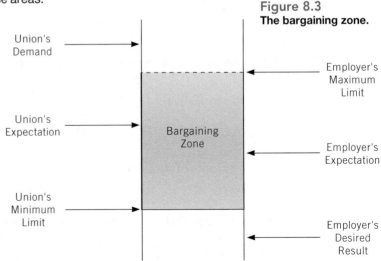

Figure 8.3
The bargaining zone.

employer may initially offer no pay raise, it may expect that it may eventually have to grant a raise of up to 6 percent. Likewise, the union may initially demand a 10 percent pay raise while expecting to accept a raise as low as 4 percent. The bargaining zone, then, is a raise between 4 and 6 percent. Obviously, compromise is needed on both sides if agreement is to be reached. The new tentative agreement is then submitted for a ratification vote by union membership.

Contract Issues

Most of the issues in the labour contract arise from demands that unions make on behalf of their members. Issues that are typically most important to union negotiators include *compensation, benefits,* and *job security. Certain management rights* issues are also negotiated in most bargaining agreements.

Compensation The most common issue is compensation. Unions want their employees to earn higher wages immediately, so they try to convince management to raise wages for all or some employees. Of equal concern to unions is future compensation that is to be paid during subsequent years of the contract. One common tool for securing wage increases is a **cost-of-living adjustment (COLA)**. Most COLA clauses tie future raises to the *Consumer Price Index (CPI),* a government statistic that reflects changes in consumer purchasing power.

A **wage reopener clause** is now included in some labour contracts as well. Such a clause allows wage rates to be renegotiated at preset times during the life of the contract. For example, a union might be uncomfortable with a long-term contract based solely on COLA wage increases.

Benefits Benefits that are commonly addressed during negotiations include insurance, retirement benefits, paid holidays, working conditions, and the cost of supplementary health care (prescription drugs, eye care, dental care, etc.). The health care issue is becoming increasingly contentious during negotiations because the cost of health care is rapidly increasing. For example, General Motors spends more on health care benefits for its 1.1 million workers than it does on steel. And insurance premiums for drug plans are doubling every five years.[50]

Job Security In some cases, a contract may dictate that if the workforce is reduced, seniority will be used to determine which employees keep their jobs. Unions are also increasingly setting their sights on preserving jobs for workers in Canada in the face of business efforts to outsource production in some sectors to countries where labour costs are cheaper. For example, Gildan Activewear outsources much of its production to low-wage countries in the Caribbean.

Other Union Issues Other possible issues might include such specific details as working hours, overtime policies, rest periods, differential pay plans for shift employees, the use of temporary workers, grievance procedures, and allowable unionactivities (dues collection, union bulletin boards, etc.). In addition, some contracts are beginning to include formal mechanisms for greater worker input into management decisions.

Management Rights Management wants as much control as possible over hiring policies, work assignments, and so forth. Unions, meanwhile, often try to limit management rights by specifying hiring, assignment, and other policies. At one Chrysler plant the contract stipulates that three workers are needed to change fuses in robots: a machinist to open the robot, an electrician to change the fuse, and a supervisor to oversee the process. Such contracts often bar workers in one job category from performing work that falls within the domain of another. Unions try to secure jobs by defining as many different categories as possible (the Chrysler plant has over 100). Of course, management resists this practice, which limits flexibility and makes it difficult to reassign workers.

When Bargaining Fails

An impasse occurs if management and labour fail to agree on a new contract. Although it is generally agreed that both parties suffer when an impasse is reached and action is taken, each side can employ several tactics to support its cause until the impasse is resolved.

Union Tactics A **strike** occurs when employees temporarily walk off the job and refuse to work. In 2008, 500 workers at Potash Corporation of Saskatchewan (Potash-Corp) were on strike for 99 days. They eventually agreed to a new contract that was not much different from the one management had offered during negotiations.[51] Strike

COST-OF-LIVING ADJUSTMENT (COLA) A contract clause specifying that wages will increase automatically with the rate of inflation.

WAGE REOPENER CLAUSE A contract clause that allows wage rates to be renegotiated at preset times during the life of the contract.

STRIKE A tactic of labour unions in which members temporarily walk off the job and refuse to work, in order to win concessions from management.

PICKETING A tactic of labour unions in which members march at the entrance to the company with signs explaining their reasons for striking.

BOYCOTT Union members agree not to buy the product of the firm that employs them.

WORK SLOWDOWN Workers perform their jobs at a much slower pace than normal.

LOCKOUT A tactic of management in which the firm physically denies employees access to the workplace to pressure workers to agree to the company's latest contract offer.

STRIKEBREAKER An individual hired by a firm to replace a worker on strike; a tactic of management in disputes with labour unions.

EMPLOYERS' ASSOCIATIONS A group of companies that get together to plan strategies and exchange information about how to manage their relations with unions.

DECERTIFICATION The process by which employees terminate their union's right to represent them.

MEDIATION A method of settling a contract dispute in which a neutral third party is asked to hear arguments from both the union and management and offer a suggested resolution.

VOLUNTARY ARBITRATION A method of settling a contract dispute in which the union and management ask a neutral third party to hear their arguments and issue a binding resolution.

actions are growing in China as well, in industries ranging from car manufacturing to electronics to hospitality management.[52] During a strike, unions may picket or launch a boycott. **Picketing** involves having workers march at the entrance to the company with signs explaining their reasons for striking. The most strike-prone sectors in Canada are mining and transport/communication.[53]

During a strike, workers are not paid and the business is usually unable to produce its normal range of products and services. After a strike is over, employees may exhibit low morale, anger, increased absenteeism, and decreased productivity. In these situations, care must be taken to improve communications between management and workers. Sometimes a union is not permitted to strike. The Province of Nova Scotia passed a law that forbids strikes by health care workers in that province.[54] Hospital workers cannot strike in Alberta, P.E.I., or Ontario either. Strikes may also be illegal if the union does not go through certain necessary steps before striking.

A **boycott** occurs when union members agree not to buy the product of the firm that employs them. Workers may also urge other consumers to shun their firm's product.

In a **work slowdown**, workers perform their jobs at a much slower pace than normal. A variation is the "sickout," during which large numbers of workers call in sick.

Management Tactics Management can also respond forcefully to an impasse. A **lockout** occurs when employers physically deny employees access to the workplace. Management might lock workers out if they fear that workers will damage expensive equipment. Petro-Canada workers were locked out of a refinery for more than a year. The company kept the refinery running by using replacement workers.[55] As an alternative to a lockout, firms can hire temporary or permanent replacements (**strikebreakers**) for the absent employees. However, the use of replacement workers is illegal in Quebec and British Columbia.

Companies can also lessen the impact of unions by contracting out—to non-union contractors—a lot of assembly work they used to do themselves. This results in fewer union workers within the company. Companies can also join **employers' associations**—groups of companies that get together to plan strategies and exchange information about how to manage their relations with unions.

The threat of **decertification**—the process by which employees legally terminate their union's right to represent them—is also a deterrent to unions. For example, the Manitoba Labour Board decertified Local 832 of the United Food and Commercial Workers for workers at the Hampton Inn & Suites in Winnipeg. The workers said they weren't getting value for the dues they were paying to the union.[56]

In extreme cases, management may simply close down a plant if an agreement cannot be reached with the union. For example, Magna International decided to shut down a plant in Syracuse, New York, when a deal could not be reached with the United Auto Workers union.[57] Maple Leaf Foods closed its Edmonton hog processing plant when the workers went on strike there. That cost 850 workers their jobs. In 2009—when GM and Chrysler were thinking of declaring bankruptcy—there was speculation that they would be able to dissolve high-cost union collective agreements ("union busting") as part of the bankruptcy plan. But Canadian laws are different from U.S. laws, and collective agreements are not necessarily negated when a bankruptcy occurs.

Mediation and Arbitration

Rather than using their weapons on one another, labour and management can agree to call in a third party to help resolve a dispute. In **mediation**, the neutral third party (a mediator) advises the parties about how to reach a settlement. The mediator cannot impose a settlement. When the United Steelworkers union and PotashCorp were initially unable to reach a collective agreement, both parties asked for a mediator to help them with their contract talks.[58] In **voluntary arbitration**, the neutral third party (an arbitrator) dictates a settlement between two sides that have agreed to submit to outside judgment. Air Canada and the Canadian Union of Public Employees requested that an arbitrator decide on an exit package for terminated Air Canada employees when the company cut 2000 jobs.[59] In some cases, arbitration is legally required to settle bargaining disputes. This **compulsory arbitration** is used to settle disputes between government and public employees such as firefighters and police officers.

COMPULSORY ARBITRATION A method of settling a contract dispute in which the union and management are forced to explain their positions to a neutral third party, which issues a binding resolution.

PEARSON
mybusinesslab

To improve your grade, visit the MyBusinessLab website at **www.pearsoned.ca/mybusinesslab**. This online homework and tutorial system allows you to test your understanding and generates a personalized study plan just for you. It provides you with study and practice tools directly related to this chapter's content. MyBusinessLab puts you in control of your own learning! Test yourself on the material for this chapter at **www.pearsoned.ca/mybusinesslab**.

Summary of Learning Objectives

1. **Define *human resource management*, discuss its strategic significance, and explain how managers plan for human resources.** Human resource management, or HRM, is the set of organizational activities directed at attracting, developing, and maintaining an effective workforce. HRM plays a key strategic role in organizational performance. Planning for human resource needs entails several steps: (1) conducting a *job analysis*, (2) forecasting demand and supply, and (3) matching HR supply and demand.

2. **Identify the issues involved in *staffing* a company, including internal and external recruiting and *selection*.** Recruiting is the process of attracting qualified persons to apply for open jobs. *Internal recruiting* involves considering present employees for new jobs. It builds morale and rewards the best employees. *External recruiting* means attracting people from outside the organization. Key selection techniques include *application forms, tests,* and *interviews*. The techniques must be valid predictors of expected performance.

3. **Discuss different ways in which organizations go about developing the capabilities of employees and managers.** Nearly all employees undergo some initial *orientation* process. Many employees are also given the opportunity to acquire new skills through various *work-based* and/or *instructional-based* programs.

4. **Discuss the importance of *wages and salaries, incentives*, and *benefit programs* in attracting and keeping skilled workers.** *Wages and salaries, incentives,* and *benefit packages* may all be parts of a company's *compensation program.* By providing competitive compensation levels, a business can attract and keep qualified personnel. Incentive programs can also motivate people to work more productively. *Indirect compensation* also plays a major role in effective and well-designed compensation systems.

5. **Describe some of the key legal issues involved in hiring, compensating, and managing workers in today's workplace.** Managers must obey a variety of federal and provincial laws in the areas of *equal opportunity* and *equal pay, sexual harassment,* and *comparable worth.* Firms are also required to provide employees with safe working environments, as per the guidelines of provincial occupational health and safety acts.

6. **Discuss *workforce diversity*, the management of *knowledge workers*, and the use of *contingent* and *temporary workers* as important changes in the contemporary workplace.** *Workforce diversity* refers

to the range of workers' attitudes, values, beliefs, and behaviours that differ by gender, race, ethnicity, age, and physical ability. Many firms now see diversity as a source of competitive advantage and work actively to achieve diversity in their ranks. Additional challenges exist in managing *knowledge workers* (rapidly increasing salaries and high turnover). *Contingent workers* are hired to supplement an organization's permanent workforce. The use of contingent workers gives managers flexibility; also these workers are usually not covered by employers' benefit programs—two reasons why their numbers are growing.

7. **Trace the evolution of, and discuss trends in, *unionism* in Canada.** The first unions were formed in the early nineteenth century in the Maritime provinces. Labour organizations sprang up and faded away during the nineteenth century and unions began to develop in the twentieth century. Since the mid-1970s, labour unions in Canada have had difficulty attracting new members. Membership as a percentage of total workforce has declined. Increasingly, unions recognize that they have lost significant power and that it is in everyone's best interests to work with management instead of against it.

8. **Describe the *major laws governing unionism.*** *Privy Council Order 1003* gave unions the right to bargain collectively in Canada. *The Constitution Act of 1867* allows the federal government to pass labour legislation (e.g., the *Canada Labour Code*) for companies that operate inter-provincially, and allowed the provincial governments to pass legislation (e.g., the *Ontario Labour Relations Act*) for companies that operate in only one province.

9. **Identify the steps in the *collective bargaining process.*** Once certified, the union engages in collective bargaining with the organization. The initial step is reaching agreement on a *labour contract.* Contract demands usually involve wages, job security, or management rights.

Both labour and management have several tactics that can be used against the other if negotiations break down. Unions may attempt a *strike,* a *boycott,* or a *slowdown.* Companies may hire *strikebreakers* or *lockout* workers.

In extreme cases, mediation or arbitration may be used to settle disputes. Once a contract has been agreed on, union and management representatives continue to interact to settle worker grievances and interpret the contract.

Questions and Exercises

Questions for Analysis

1. Why is a good employee–job match important? Who benefits more, the organization or the employee? Why?

2. What benefits do you consider most and least important in attracting workers? In keeping workers? In motivating workers to perform their jobs well? How much will benefit considerations affect your choice of an employer after graduation?

3. Select a job currently held by you or a close friend. Draw up a job description and job specification for this position.

4. Why is the formal training of workers so important to most employers? Why don't employers simply let people learn about their jobs as they perform them?

5. Suppose you are a manager in a non-unionized company. You have just heard a rumour that some of your workers are discussing forming a union. What would you do? Be specific.

6. What training do you think you are most likely to need when you finish school and start your career?

Application Exercises

7. Interview a human resource manager at a local company. Select a position for which the firm is currently recruiting applicants and identify the steps in the selection process.

8. Interview the managers of two local companies, one unionized and one non-unionized. Compare the wage and salary levels, benefits, and working conditions of workers at the two firms.

9. Obtain a copy of an employment application. Examine it carefully and determine how useful it might be in making a hiring decision.

10. Consider the following statement: *"Many years ago, workers were treated very badly by management compared to the way they are treated now. Since unions exist largely to protect workers from unreasonable behaviour by management, the need for unions has disappeared."* Do you agree or disagree with this statement? Explain your position.

Building Your Business Skills

A Little Collective Bargaining

The Purpose of the Assignment

To encourage students to understand why some companies unionize and others don't.

The Situation

You've been working for the same non-union company for five years. Although there are problems, you like your job and have confidence in your ability to get ahead. Recently, you've heard rumblings that a large group of workers want to call for a union election. You're not sure how you feel about this because none of your friends or family is a union member.

Assignment

Step 1 Come together with three other "co-workers" who have the same questions as you. Each person should target four companies to learn their union status. Avoid small businesses; choose large corporations such as Canadian National Railway, Bombardier, and Walmart. As you investigate, answer the following questions:

- Is the company unionized?
- Is every worker in the company unionized or only selected groups of workers? Describe the groups.
- If a company is unionized, what is the union's history in that company?
- If a company is unionized, what are the main labour–management issues?
- If a company is unionized, how would you describe the current status of labour–management relations? For example, is it cordial or strained?
- If a company is not unionized, what factors are responsible for its non-union status?

To learn the answers to these questions, contact the company, read corporate annual reports, search the company's website, contact union representatives, or do research on a computerized database.

Step 2 Go to the website of CUPE (www.cupe.ca) to learn more about the current status of the union movement. Then, with your co-workers, write a short report about the advantages of union membership.

Step 3 Research the disadvantages of unionization. A key issue to address is whether unions make it harder for companies to compete in the global marketplace.

Follow-Up Questions

1. Based on everything you have learned, are you sympathetic to the union movement? Would you want to be a union member?
2. Are the union members you spoke with satisfied or dissatisfied with their union's efforts to achieve better working conditions, higher wages, and improved benefits?
3. What is the union's role when layoffs occur?
4. Based on what you have learned, do you think the union movement in Canada will stagnate or thrive in the years ahead?

Exercising Your Ethics

Handling the Layoffs

The Situation

The CEO of a moderate-sized company is developing a plan for laying-off employees. He wants each manager to rank his or her employees according to the order in which they should be laid off, from first to last.

The Dilemma

One manager has just asked for help. He is new to his position and has little experience to draw from. The members of the manager's team are as follows:

- Tony Jones: white male, 10 years with the company, average performer, reportedly drinks a lot after work

- Amanda Wiggens: white female, very ambitious, three years with the company, above-average performer, puts in extra time at work; is known to be abrasive when dealing with others
- George Sinclair: Aboriginal, 20 years with the company, average performer, was previously laid off but called back when business picked up
- Dorothy Henderson: white female, 25 years with the company, below-average performer, has filed five sexual harassment complaints in the last 10 years
- Wanda Jackson: black female, eight years with the company, outstanding performer, is rumoured to be looking for another job
- Jerry Loudder: white male, single parent, five years with the company, average performer
- Martha Strawser: white female, six years with company, excellent performer but spotty attendance, is putting husband through university

Team Activity

Assemble a group of four students. Your group has agreed to provide the manager with a suggested rank ordering of the manager's employees.

Action Steps

1. Working together, prepare this list, ranking the manager's employees according to the order in which they should be laid off, from first to last. Identify any disagreements that occurred along the way, and indicate how they were resolved.

2. As a group, discuss the underlying ethical issues in this situation and write them down.

3. As a group, brainstorm any legal issues involved in this situation and write them down.

4. Do the ethical and legal implications of your choices always align?

5. Do the ethical and performance implications of your choices always align?

BUSINESS CASE 8

Reports from the Walmart–Union Battlefield

In 2009, an arbitrator ruled that workers in the United Food and Commercial Workers (UFCW) in Saint-Hyacinthe, Quebec, would not receive the wage and benefits increase they had hoped to get from Walmart. In rejecting the union's demands, the arbitrator portrayed Walmart as a good employer and concluded that Walmart's performance-based compensation system had to be retained because it was part of the culture of the company. The arbitrator also noted that Walmart sometimes paid its employees more than competitors like Zellers did. The arbitrator's ruling is the latest round in the intense battle that is taking place between the UFCW and Walmart. The UFCW is committed to organizing Walmart's employees, while Walmart's management aggressively fights every UFCW attempt. The fight has been bitter at times, and the eventual outcome is not yet clear. Each side has had both victories and defeats. In 2010, this battle was intensifying even as Walmart was announcing further Canadian expansion with another 6500 employees needed to staff 35–40 planned superstores.

The Quebec Labour Relations Board certified the UFCW as the sole bargaining agent for about 150 workers at a Walmart store in Gatineau in December 2008. That required Walmart to negotiate with the union regarding a collective agreement. If the past is any indication, the negotiations are going to be very difficult. Here's why.

In August 2005, the UFCW was certified as the sole bargaining agent for nine tire and lubrication workers at another Walmart in Gatineau. The UFCW and Walmart then tried to negotiate a collective agreement, but failed. In August 2008, an arbitrator imposed an agreement that, among other things, raised workers' wages from $9.25 an hour to $11.54 an hour over three years. Two months later Walmart closed the store.

Until the mid-1990s, Walmart had never had a union in any of its stores in the United States, Canada, Puerto Rico, Argentina, Brazil, or Mexico. It had been able to resist unions partly by promoting its family-like culture. The company argued that forcing employees to work under a collective agreement would reduce their motivation and damage the company's successful formula for keeping customers happy. In 1996, management first began hearing rumours that the Canadian Auto Workers (CAW) union was approaching employees at the Windsor, Ontario, store about unionizing. During the organizing drive, there was much squabbling among employees, and when the certification vote was held, the workers voted 151–43 against joining the union. In spite of this, the Ontario Labour Relations Board certified the union as the employees' bargaining agent on the grounds that the company had intimidated employees during the membership drive. A first collective agreement was approved, but in April 2000 the union was officially decertified.

In 2003, the Labour Relations Board of British Columbia found Walmart guilty of an unfair labour practice, namely, that it undermined a union-organizing drive at the Walmart store in Quesnel, British Columbia. As part of its decision, the board required Walmart management to schedule an employee meeting and read aloud the board's decision to employees.

During 2003 and 2004, the UFCW made efforts to organize Walmart stores in Saskatchewan, British Columbia, and Manitoba. Walmart won a victory in Saskatchewan when it successfully challenged the constitutionality of that province's labour law, which restricts employer–employee communication during an organizing drive. Walmart argued that workers should hear the whole story before voting.

The UFCW's strategy has been to organize stores in Canada because labour laws are stronger here than they are in the United States. In Quebec, for example, the card-based certification system allows workers to unionize by signing cards rather than having an actual vote. UFCW president Wayne Hanley calls this a "luxury" that does not now exist for unions in the United States (but the U.S. Congress is considering passage of such a bill). The UFCW is particularly interested in unionizing Walmart's Supercentres in Alberta, British Columbia, and Ontario. That battle will be intense because Walmart is deeply committed to its strategy of providing customers with very low prices.

There is also a lot at stake for the UFCW. Food workers make up about 60 percent of UFCW membership, and 40 percent of those work for Loblaw. But Loblaw management has become more aggressive in dealing with unions because its market share is under attack from Walmart. When 800 workers went on strike in Quebec, Loblaw closed 13 Maxi outlets there until the strike was resolved. The UFCW also has to cope with declining unionization rates in the retail food industry. In the 1980s, 60–70 percent of food workers were unionized, but now only 40–50 percent are.

Walmart is not the only company where unions are trying to gain a foothold. Ken Lewenza, the new president of the Canadian Auto Workers (CAW), said that employees at WestJet are "ripe" for organizing. The CAW already represents call centre workers and customer service agents at Air Canada, and the CAW wants to organize the same types of workers at WestJet. The idea is being played down by WestJet, which says that it has a very positive corporate culture, a profit-sharing plan, and a share purchase program in which 80 percent of its employees take part. The Pro-Active Communication Team (PACT)—a non-union group that represents about 6300 WestJet workers—also represents workers' concerns, and the president of PACT sits on WestJet's board of directors.

Questions for Discussion

1. From a practical perspective explain why Walmart is so intent on fighting unionization attempts in Canada.

2. Why is the UFCW's battle with Walmart so important to the union? Take a look at its strategic approach of focusing on union-friendly Canadian provinces.

3. Debate the following controversial statement: *"Unions are divisive and they artificially inflate wages and make companies less competitive."*

SCANLIFE

Motivating, Satisfying, and Leading Employees

After reading this chapter, you should be able to:

LO-1 Identify and discuss the basic *forms of behaviour* that employees exhibit in organizations.

LO-2 Describe the nature and importance of *individual differences* among employees.

LO-3 Explain the meaning and importance of *psychological contracts* and the person–job fit in the workplace.

LO-4 Identify and summarize the most important models of *employee motivation*.

LO-5 Describe the *strategies* used by organizations to improve job satisfaction and employee motivation.

LO-6 Define *leadership* and distinguish it from *management*.

LO-7 Summarize the *approaches to leadership* that developed during the twentieth century.

LO-8 Describe the most recent ideas about effective leadership.

SCANLIFE

What Do Employees Want?

Every manager wants to have employees who are satisfied and highly motivated because such employees exhibit positive behaviours, such as persisting even in the face of difficulties, being involved in continuous learning and improvement, and constantly finding ways to improve quality and productivity. These behaviours, in turn, lead to several positive outcomes for the organization: higher customer satisfaction, greater profits, higher quality, and lower employee turnover. But how do managers achieve the goal of having highly motivated and satisfied workers? The most general answer: give employees what they want (within reason, of course).

But what do employees want? Managers often assume that they know what employees want, but consider the results of two surveys. The Canadian Payroll Association analyzed the frequency with which 39 specific benefits were provided by *companies* to their employees. The top five most common items were term life insurance, car allowances, tuition fees, disability-related employment benefits, and professional membership dues. But another survey of *worker* opinions found that they rated flexible working hours, casual dress, unlimited internet access, opportunities to telecommute, and nap time as the most desirable. There are obviously major differences in these two lists, so managers are having some difficulty assessing what employees want.

How Will This Help Me?

The connections that employees have with their jobs can go a long way toward determining how happy they are with their work. Some people love their jobs, while others hate theirs. Most people, however, fall somewhere in between. After studying the information in this chapter, you'll be better able to understand (1) your own feelings toward your work from the perspective of an *employee,* (2) the feelings of others toward their work from the perspective of a *manager or an owner,* (3) how you can more effectively function as a *leader,* and (4) how your manager or boss strives to motivate you through his or her own leadership.

Several other studies are consistent with this conclusion. For example, a Sirota Survey Intelligence study that assessed employee satisfaction levels at 237 companies found that only 14 percent of these companies had workforces that could be classified as "enthusiastic." When the stock prices of 28 companies with enthusiastic workforces were compared to the average for publicly traded companies, it was found that they outperformed the average prices by more than two and a half times, while companies with *unenthusiastic* workforces lagged far behind the average stock prices. Companies with enthusiastic workforces also had fewer customer complaints, lower employee turnover, and higher quality in their products.

Another study of more than 3000 Canadian employees that was conducted by Watson Wyatt Canada revealed the following:

- 46 percent would consider changing jobs if a comparable job became available
- Only 40 percent of employees believe they have real opportunities for advancement with their current employer
- Only 27 percent of employees see any connection between their job performance and their pay

In yet another study, the Gallup Organization focused on the attitudes of 7200 workers in Canada, the U.S., and Great Britain. The survey revealed that on most measures of job satisfaction, Canadian workplaces ranked behind those of the U.S. For example, only 47 percent of Canadian workers were completely satisfied with their boss, while 60 percent of American workers were. Only 29 percent of Canadian workers were completely satisfied with their opportunities for promotion, while 40 percent of Americans were. And 37 percent of Canadian workers were completely satisfied with the recognition they received, while 48 percent of Americans were. Canadian workers were also less satisfied than U.S. workers on several other issues, including the flexibility of their work hours, workplace safety, relationships with co-workers, and the amount of vacation time they received (even though they usually received more than Americans).

Most employees start work with considerable enthusiasm, but they often lose it. Much of the blame is laid at the feet of managers whose attitudes and behaviours depress employee enthusiasm. These include failing to express appreciation to employees for a job well done, assuming that employees are lazy and irresponsible, treating employees as disposable objects, failing to build trust with workers, and quickly laying people off when the business gets into trouble. Managerial assumptions about employee satisfaction with pay can be particularly problematic. For example, many managers assume that workers will never be satisfied with their pay. But only a minority of workers rate their pay as poor or very poor, and many rate it as good or very good. A Kelly Workforce Index study showed that 58 percent of Canadian workers would be willing to accept a lower wage if they felt their work contributed something important to their organization. A poll by the staffing firm Randstad USA found that 57 percent of workers would be willing to work overtime without pay to impress their boss so that they would be less likely to laid off as a result of the economic downturn.

One of the simplest ways for managers to motivate workers is to praise them. Yet this occurs far less often than it should. A *Globe and Mail* web poll showed that 27 percent of the 2331 respondents had *never* received a compliment from their boss. Another 10 percent had not received a compliment in the last year, and 18 percent had not received a compliment in the last month. This result is disturbing, since another survey showed that 89 percent of employees rate recognition of their work as "very important" or "extremely important."

When there is a disconnect between what companies provide for workers and what they really want, we should not be surprised if motivation and satisfaction levels of workers are not high. The real question is this: In the most general sense, what can be done to make worker and company needs more consistent? Part of the answer is provided in yet another survey, this one based on responses by 8000 Canadians. That survey found that the three most important things (for employees of all ages) were to be treated with respect, to be dealt with fairly, and to feel a sense of "connection" with the organization they worked for. All of these are things on which managers can have a very positive influence. And that is what this chapter is all about.

LO-1 Forms of Employee Behaviour

Employee behaviour is the pattern of actions by the members of an organization that directly or indirectly influences the organization's effectiveness. **Performance behaviours** are those that are directly involved in performing a job. An assembly-line worker who sits by a moving conveyor and attaches parts to a product as it passes by has relatively simple performance behaviours, but a research-and-development scientist who works in a lab trying to find new scientific breakthroughs that have commercial potential has much more complex performance behaviours.

Other behaviours—called **organizational citizenship**—provide positive benefits to the organization in more indirect ways. An employee who does satisfactory work in terms of quantity and quality, but refuses to work overtime, won't help newcomers learn the ropes, and is generally unwilling to make any contribution beyond the strict performance requirements of the job is not a good organizational citizen. In contrast, an employee with a satisfactory level of performance who works late when the boss asks and takes time to help newcomers learn their way around is a good organizational citizen.

Counterproductive behaviours are those that detract from organizational performance. **Absenteeism** occurs when an employee does not show up for work. When an employee is absent, legitimately or not, that person's work does not get done and a substitute must be hired to do it, or others in the organization must pick up the slack. **Turnover** occurs when people quit their jobs. It results from a number of factors, including aspects of the job, the organization, the individual, a poor person–job fit, the labour market, and family influences. One survey of 660 workers showed that 84 percent who worked for a "kind" manager planned to stay with their company a long time, while only 47 percent of those who worked for a "bully" said they planned to stay.[1]

Other forms of counterproductive behaviour are also costly. *Theft and sabotage,* for example, result in direct financial costs for an organization. *Sexual and racial harassment* also cost an organization, both directly (through financial liability if the organization responds inappropriately) and indirectly (by lowering morale, producing fear, and driving off valuable employees). *Workplace aggression and violence* are also counterproductive.

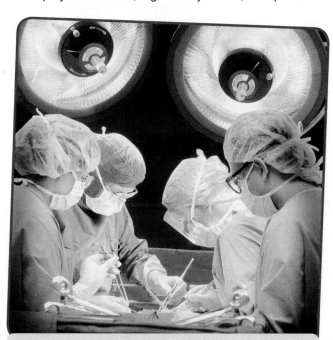

For some jobs, performance behaviours can be narrowly defined and easily measured. For many other jobs, such as those held by scientists or doctors, however, performance behaviours are less objective, more diverse, and more difficult to assess.

LO-2 Individual Differences among Employees

Individual differences are physical, psychological, and emotional attributes that vary from one person to another. The individual differences that characterize a specific person make that person unique. *Personality* and *attitudes* are two main categories of individual differences.

Personality

Personality is the relatively stable set of psychological attributes that distinguish one person from another. In recent years, researchers have identified five fundamental traits that are especially relevant to organizations. These

---

EMPLOYEE BEHAVIOUR The pattern of actions by the members of an organization that directly or indirectly influences the organization's effectiveness.

PERFORMANCE BEHAVIOURS The total set of work-related behaviours that the organization expects employees to display.

ORGANIZATIONAL CITIZENSHIP Positive behaviours that do not directly contribute to the bottom line.

COUNTERPRODUCTIVE BEHAVIOURS Behaviours that detract from organizational performance.

ABSENTEEISM When an employee does not show up for work.

TURNOVER Annual percentage of an organization's workforce that leaves and must be replaced.

INDIVIDUAL DIFFERENCES Personal attributes that vary from one person to another.

PERSONALITY The relatively stable set of psychological attributes that distinguish one person from another.

"big five" personality traits (shown in Figure 9.1) can be summarized as follows:

- *Agreeableness* is a person's ability to get along with others. A person with a high level of agreeableness is gentle, cooperative, forgiving, understanding, and good-natured in their dealings with others. A person with a low level of agreeableness is often irritable, short-tempered, unco-operative, and generally antagonistic toward other people. Highly agreeable people are better at developing good working relationships with co-workers, whereas less agreeable people are not likely to have particularly good working relationships.

- *Conscientiousness* refers to the number of things a person tries to accomplish. *Highly conscientious* people tend to focus on relatively few tasks at one time; as a result, they are likely to be organized, systematic, careful, thorough, responsible, and self-disciplined. *Less conscientious* people tend to pursue a wider array of tasks; as a result, they are often more disorganized and irresponsible, as well as less thorough and self-disciplined. Highly conscientious people tend to be relatively higher performers in a variety of different jobs.

- *Emotionality* refers to the degree to which people tend to be positive or negative in their outlook and behaviours toward others. People with *positive* emotionality are relatively poised, calm, resilient, and secure; people with negative emotionality are more excitable, insecure, reactive, and subject to mood swings. People with positive emotionality are better able to handle job stress, pressure, and tension. Their stability might also cause them to be seen as more reliable than their less stable counterparts.

- *Extraversion* refers to a person's comfort level with relationships. *Extroverts* are sociable, talkative, assertive, and open to establishing new relationships, while *introverts* are much less sociable, talkative, and assertive, and more reluctant to begin new relationships. Extroverts tend to be higher overall job performers than introverts and are more likely to be attracted to jobs based on personal relationships, such as sales and marketing positions.

- *Openness* reflects how open or rigid a person is in terms of his or her beliefs. People with *high* levels of openness are curious and willing to listen to new ideas and to change their own ideas, beliefs, and attitudes in response to new information. People with *low* levels of openness tend to be less receptive to new ideas and less willing to change their minds. People with more openness are often better performers due to their flexibility and the likelihood that they will be better accepted by others in the organization.

Emotional Intelligence *Emotional intelligence,* while not part of the "big five," also plays a large role in employee personality. **Emotional intelligence**, or **emotional quotient (EQ)**, refers to the extent to which people possess *self-awareness* (the ability to understand their mood), *self-regulation* (the ability to control disruptive impulses), *motivation* (a passion for work), *empathy* (the ability to understand the emotional makeup of others), and *social*

Figure 9.1
The "big five" personality traits.

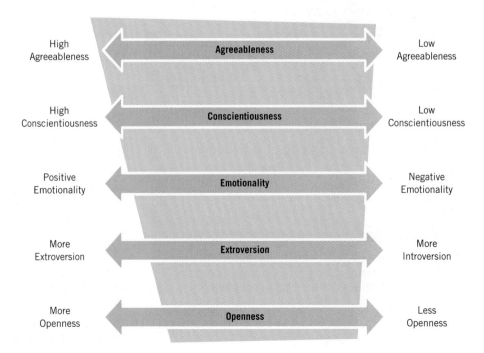

skill (proficiency in managing relationships).[2] Research suggests that people with high EQs may perform better than others, especially in jobs that require a high degree of interpersonal interaction and that involve influencing or directing the work of others. EQ appears to be something that isn't biologically based but which can be developed.[3]

Attitudes

People's attitudes also affect their behaviour in organizations. **Attitudes** reflect our beliefs and feelings about specific ideas, situations, or other people. People in organizations have attitudes about many different things: their salary, their promotion possibilities, their boss, their employee benefits, and so on. Especially important attitudes are *job satisfaction* and *organizational commitment*.

- **Job satisfaction** reflects the extent to which people have positive attitudes toward their jobs. (A related concept—*morale*—refers to the overall attitude people have toward their workplace.) A Workopolis survey of 577 Canadians showed that 53 percent loved their jobs, 16 percent kept their job simply because it helped pay the bills, and 14 percent felt that their current job had the potential to lead to something better.[4] A 2010 survey of workers in 23 countries found that workers in Norway, Denmark, and Canada were the most satisfied with their current employer.[5] Satisfied employees tend to be absent less often, to be good organizational citizens, and to stay with the organization. Dissatisfied employees may be absent more often, may experience stress that disrupts co-workers, and may be continually looking for another job. Contrary to what a lot of managers believe, however, high levels of job satisfaction do not automatically lead to high levels of productivity.

- **Organizational commitment** (also called *job commitment*) reflects an individual's identification with the organization and its mission. Highly committed employees see themselves as true members of the firm, overlook minor sources of dissatisfaction, and see themselves remaining members of the organization. Less committed employees are more likely to see themselves as outsiders, to express more dissatisfaction about the work situation, and to not see themselves as long-term members of the organization. One way to increase employee commitment is to give employees a voice. BBVA, Spain's second largest bank, accomplishes this by including employees in the performance evaluation process. Not only is the employee's own self-evaluation considered, but co-workers also answer questions about each employee's performance. Infosys Technologies in Bangalore, India, started a Voice of Youth program, which gives top-performing young employees a seat on its management council.[6]

LO-3 Matching People and Jobs

Given the array of individual differences that exist across people and the many different forms of employee behaviour that can occur in organizations, it is important to have a good match between people and the jobs they are performing. Two key methods for facilitating this match are *psychological contracts* and the *person–job fit*.

Psychological Contracts

A **psychological contract** is the set of expectations held by an employee concerning what he or she will contribute to an organization (referred to as *contributions*) and what the organization will provide to the employee (referred to as *inducements*). If either party perceives an inequity in the contract, that party may seek a change. The employee, for example, might ask for a pay raise, a promotion, or a bigger office, or might put forth less effort or look for a better job elsewhere. The organization can also initiate change by training workers to improve their skills, transferring them to new jobs, or terminating them. Unlike a business contract, a psychological contract is not written on paper, nor are all of its terms explicitly negotiated. Figure 9.2 illustrates the essential features of a psychological contract.

The downsizing and cutbacks that have occurred in Canadian businesses in recent years have complicated the process of managing psychological contracts. Many organizations, for example, used to offer at least some assurance of job security as a fundamental inducement to employees. Now, however, because job security is lower, alternative inducements (like improved benefits, more flexible working hours, bonuses, etc.) may be needed.

The Person–Job Fit

The **person–job fit** refers to the extent to which a person's contributions and the organization's inducements match one another. Each employee has a specific set of needs that he or she wants fulfilled, and a set of job-related

ATTITUDES
A person's beliefs and feelings about specific ideas, situations, or people.

JOB SATISFACTION
Extent to which people have positive attitudes toward their jobs.

ORGANIZATIONAL COMMITMENT
An individual's identification with the organization and its mission.

PSYCHOLOGICAL CONTRACT
The set of expectations held by an employee concerning what he or she will contribute to an organization (contributions) and what the organization will provide the employee (inducements) in return.

PERSON–JOB FIT
The extent to which a person's contributions and the organization's inducements match one another.

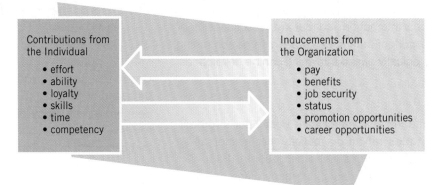

Figure 9.2
The psychological contract.

Contributions from the Individual
- effort
- ability
- loyalty
- skills
- time
- competency

Inducements from the Organization
- pay
- benefits
- job security
- status
- promotion opportunities
- career opportunities

behaviours and abilities to contribute. If the organization can take perfect advantage of those behaviours and abilities and exactly fulfill those needs, it will have achieved a perfect person–job fit. A good person–job fit can result in higher performance and more positive attitudes, whereas a poor person–job fit can have just the opposite effect.

Motivation in the Workplace

Motivation is the set of forces that causes people to behave in certain ways. While one worker may be motivated to work hard to produce as much as possible, another may be motivated to do just enough to get by. As we saw in the opening case, effective managers recognize that different employees have different needs and are motivated by different things. One company that stopped handing out T-shirts with the company logo on them found that professional workers didn't much care, but immigrant workers in entry-level jobs were unhappy because the T-shirts had symbolic value for them (they apparently made them feel like they belonged in Canada).[7] This example, and thousands more, show that managers must think very carefully about how to motivate employees.

Over the last century, many theories have been proposed to explain the complex issue of motivation. In this section, we will focus on three major approaches that reflect a chronology of thinking in the area of motivation: *classical theory/scientific management, early behavioural theory,* and *contemporary motivational theories.*

Classical Theory

In the **classical theory of motivation**, it is assumed that workers are motivated solely by money. In his book *The Principles of Scientific Management* (1911), industrial

engineer Frederick Taylor proposed a way for both companies and workers to benefit from this view of life in the workplace.[8] If workers are motivated by money, Taylor reasoned, then paying them more would prompt them to produce more. Meanwhile, the firm that analyzed jobs and found better ways to perform them would be able to produce goods more cheaply, make higher profits, and thus pay—and motivate—workers better than its competitors.

Taylor's approach is known as **scientific management**, and his ideas captured the imagination of many managers in the early twentieth century. Soon, plants across Canada and the United States were hiring experts to perform **time-and-motion studies**, which were the first "scientific" attempts to break jobs down into easily repeated components and to devise more efficient tools and machines for performing them. [9]

The Hawthorne studies were an important step in developing an appreciation for the human factor at work. These women worked under different lighting conditions as researchers monitored their productivity. The researchers were amazed to find that productivity increased regardless of whether lighting levels increased or decreased.

Courtesy of AT&T Archives and History Center

Early Behavioural Theory

In 1925, a group of Harvard researchers began a study at the Hawthorne Works of the Western Electric Company. Their intent was to examine the relationship between changes in the physical environment and worker output, with an eye to increasing productivity. The results of the experiment at first confused, then amazed, the scientists. Increasing lighting levels improved productivity, but so did lowering lighting levels. And against all expectations, raising the pay of workers failed to increase their productivity. Gradually they pieced together the puzzle: the explanation for the contradictory findings lay in workers' response to the attention being paid to them. In essence, the researchers determined that almost any action on the part of management that made workers believe they were receiving special attention caused worker productivity to rise. This result, known as the **Hawthorne effect**, convinced many managers that paying attention to employees is indeed good for business.

Following the Hawthorne studies, managers and researchers alike focused more attention on the importance of good human relations in motivating employee performance. Stressing the factors that cause, focus, and sustain workers' behaviour, most motivation theorists became concerned with the ways in which management thinks about and treats employees. The major motivation theories that were proposed during the 1940s and 1950s include the *human resources model,* the *hierarchy of needs model,* and the *two-factor theory.*

LO-4   The Human-Resources Model: Theories X and Y   Behavioural scientist Douglas McGregor concluded that managers had different beliefs about how best to use the human resources at a firm's disposal. He classified these beliefs into sets of assumptions that he labelled "Theory X" and "Theory Y."[10] Managers who subscribe to **Theory X** tend to believe that people are naturally lazy and uncooperative and must therefore be either punished or rewarded to be made productive. Managers who subscribe to **Theory Y** tend to believe that people are naturally energetic, growth-oriented, self-motivated, and interested in being productive.

McGregor generally favoured Theory Y beliefs, and argued that Theory Y managers are more likely to have satisfied, motivated employees. Of course, Theory X and Y distinctions are somewhat simplistic and offer little concrete basis for action. Their value lies primarily in their ability to highlight and analyze the behaviour of managers in light of their attitudes toward employees.

Maslow's Hierarchy of Human Needs Model Psychologist Abraham Maslow's **hierarchy of human needs model** proposed that people have a number of different needs that they attempt to satis-fy in their work.[11] He classified these needs into five basic types and suggested that they are arranged in a hierarchy of importance, where lower-level needs must be met before a person will try to satisfy those on a higher level (see Figure 9.3).

■ *Physiological needs* are those concerned with survival; they include food,

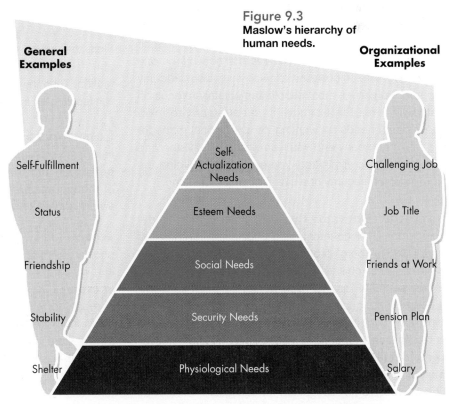

Figure 9.3
Maslow's hierarchy of human needs.

General Examples — Self-Fulfillment, Status, Friendship, Stability, Shelter

Self-Actualization Needs, Esteem Needs, Social Needs, Security Needs, Physiological Needs

Organizational Examples — Challenging Job, Job Title, Friends at Work, Pension Plan, Salary

water, shelter, and sleep. Businesses address these needs by providing both comfortable working environments and salaries sufficient to buy food and shelter.

■ *Security needs* include the needs for stability and protection from the unknown. Many employers thus offer pension plans and job security.

■ *Social needs* include the needs for friendship and companionship. Making friends at work can help to satisfy social needs, as can the feeling that you "belong" in a company.

■ *Esteem needs* include the needs for status, recognition, and self-respect. Job titles and large offices are among the things that businesses can provide to address these needs.

■ *Self-actualization needs* are needs for self-fulfillment. They include the needs to grow and develop one's capabilities and to achieve new and meaningful goals. Challenging job assignments can help satisfy these needs.

According to Maslow, once needs at one level have been satisfied, they cease to motivate behaviour. For example, if you feel secure in your job, a new pension plan will probably be less important to you than the chance to make new friends and join an informal network among your co-workers. If, however, a lower-level need suddenly becomes unfulfilled, most people immediately refocus on that lower level. For example, if you are trying to meet your esteem needs by working as a divisional manager at a major company and you learn that your division and your job may be eliminated, you might very well find the promise of job security at a new firm very motivating.

Two-Factor (Motivator–Hygiene) Theory After studying a group of accountants and engineers, psychologist Frederick Herzberg proposed the **two-factor theory**, which says that job satisfaction and dissatisfaction depend on two separate factors: *hygiene factors* (such as working conditions, quality of supervision, interpersonal relations, pay, and job security) and *motivating factors* (such as recognition, responsibility, advancement, and achievement).[12] Motivation factors cause movement along a continuum from *no satisfaction* to *satisfaction*. For example, if workers receive no recognition for successful work, they

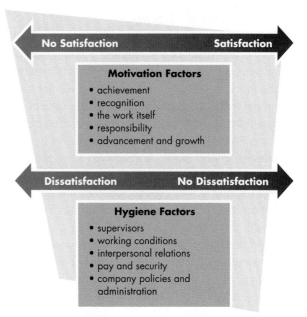

Figure 9.4
Two-factor theory of motivation.

may not be satisfied, but neither will they be dissatisfied. If recognition is provided, they will likely become more satisfied. Hygiene factors cause movement along a different continuum, one from *no dissatisfaction* to *dissatisfaction*. For example, workers will be dissatisfied if they feel that working conditions are poor, but if working conditions are improved, workers will not become *satisfied*; rather, they will no longer be *dissatisfied*. Overall, motivation factors are directly related to the *work* that employees actually perform, while hygiene factors refer to the *environment* in which they perform it (see Figure 9.4).

This theory thus suggests that managers should follow a two-step approach to enhancing motivation. First, they must ensure that hygiene factors are acceptable. This practice will result in an absence of dissatisfaction. Then they must introduce motivating factors. This will result in an increase in satisfaction.

Contemporary Motivation Theory

In recent years, other, more complex models of employee behaviour and motivation have been developed. Two of the more interesting and useful ones are *expectancy theory* and *equity theory*.

Expectancy Theory **Expectancy theory** suggests that people are motivated to work toward rewards they want and which they believe they have a reasonable chance—or expectancy—of obtaining.[13] A reward that seems out of reach, for example, is not likely to be motivating even if it is intrinsically positive (see Figure 9.5). Suppose that an assistant department manager learns that a division manager has retired and that the firm is looking for a replacement. Even though she wants the job, the assistant manager does not apply for it because she doubts

Individual Effort		Individual Performance		Organizational Rewards		Personal Goals

Effort–Performance Issue

Performance–Reward Issue

Rewards–Personal Goals Issue

Figure 9.5
Expectancy theory mode.

that she would be selected. Then she learns that the firm is looking for a production manager on a later shift. She thinks that she could get this job but does not apply for that one because she does not want to change shifts. But when she learns of an opening one level higher—full department manager—in her own division she applies for this job because she both wants it and thinks that she has a good chance of getting it.

Expectancy theory helps to explain why some people do not work as hard as they can when their salaries are based purely on seniority. Because they are paid the same whether they work very hard or just hard enough to get by, there is no financial incentive for them to work harder. Similarly, if hard work will result in one or more *undesirable* outcomes—say, a transfer to another location or a promotion to a job that requires more travel—employees may not be motivated to work hard.

Equity Theory **Equity theory** focuses on social comparisons—people evaluating their treatment by the organization relative to the treatment of others. This approach says that people begin by analyzing what they contribute to their jobs (time, effort, education, experience, and so forth) relative to what they get in return (salary, benefits, recognition, security). The result is a ratio of contribution to return. Employees compare their own ratios to those of other employees. Depending on their assessments, they experience feelings of equity or inequity.[14]

For example, suppose a new college graduate gets a starting job at a large manufacturing firm. His starting salary is $38 000 per year, he gets a compact company car, and he shares an office with another new employee. If he later learns that another new employee has received the same salary, car, and office arrangement, he will feel equitably treated. But if he finds out that another newcomer received $40 000, a full-size company car, and a private office, he may feel inequity.

When people feel that they are being inequitably treated, they may do various things to restore fairness. For example, they may ask for a raise, reduce their work effort, work shorter hours, or complain to their boss. They may also rationalize their situation, find a different comparison person, or simply quit.

LO-5 Strategies for Enhancing Motivation

Understanding what motivates workers and provides job satisfaction is only part of the manager's job. The other part is to apply that knowledge. Experts have suggested—and many companies have instituted—a wide range of programs designed to make jobs more interesting and rewarding and the work environment more pleasant. Six of the most common strategies are *reinforcement/behaviour modification, goal setting, participative management and empowerment, team management, job enrichment and redesign,* and *modified work schedules.*

Reinforcement/Behaviour Modification

Many managers try to control or modify workers' behaviour through rewards and punishments. To do this, managers must first define the specific behaviours that they want employees to exhibit (working hard, being courteous to customers, stressing quality, etc.) and the specific behaviours they want to eliminate (wasting time, being rude to customers, ignoring quality, etc.). Then they can "shape" employee behaviour by using reinforcement.

Reinforcement means applying (or withholding) positive (or negative) consequences in order to motivate employees to exhibit behaviour the manager wants. A manager has four basic reinforcement options: (1) *positive reinforcement* (apply positive consequences when employees exhibit desired behaviours), (2) *punishment* (apply negative consequences when employees exhibit undesirable behaviours), (3) *omission* (withhold positive consequences when employees exhibit undesirable behaviours), and (4) *negative reinforcement* (withhold negative consequences when employees exhibit desired behaviours).

Managers generally prefer positive reinforcement because it contributes to good employer–employee relationships. It generally works best when people are learning new behaviours, new skills, or new jobs.

Managers generally dislike punishing employees, partly because workers may respond with anger, resentment, hostility, or even retaliation.

Positive reinforcement is evident at Maple Leaf Sports & Entertainment, where workers receive "good job" cards when they do outstanding work. These cards can be redeemed for prizes.[15] WestJet rewarded its employees with a $500 travel credit when they helped deal with major flight disruptions caused by bad weather during a winter storm.[16] Positive reinforcement need not be monetary to be effective. Calgary-based Pacesetter Directional and Performance Drilling rewards top employees with time off from work, and Markham, Ontario–based Nobis, a manufacturer of hats and apparel, rewards employees by allowing them to name hats after family and friends.[17] The boxed insert entitled "Employee Engagement" provides further information about rewards.

Goal-Setting Theory

Goal-setting theory focuses on setting goals that will motivate employees. Research has shown that SMART goals (*S*pecific, *M*easurable, *A*chievable, *R*ealistic, and *T*ime-framed) are most likely to result in increased

---

ENTREPRENEURSHIP AND NEW VENTURES

Employee Engagement: The Ultimate Win–Win

A Toronto-based company called I Love Rewards sells solutions for businesses wishing to improve their corporate culture and employee motivation levels. They do this primarily through the development of web-based employee rewards- or incentive-based systems that are customized to suit their clients' needs. Client employees are awarded points for performance, and these points can be redeemed for rewards, including brand-name merchandise and travel, which have been carefully selected with the employee demographic in mind.

If companies can motivate their customers with rewards-based systems, why can't it work for employees? Companies like Microsoft, Rogers Communications, and Marriott have bought into the concept, and have contracted I Love Rewards to develop incentive-based packages for their employees. News of the successes of this high-growth company is travelling quickly. In the first quarter of 2009, I Love Rewards reported a 187 percent increase in gross billings year over year. But the future didn't always look so bright for Razor Suleman's agency.

In 2005, Suleman found himself wrestling with his own employee morale and motivation issues. In a span of six months, his company experienced almost 50 percent employee turnover. The answer: Suleman decided to incorporate his marketing expertise into his own HR practices. One technique was to introduce group interviews. Suleman decided to directly involve as many as 10 to 12 current employees of his company in interviewing prospective employees. Employees "sell" the company to the applicant, and by doing so, the company brand is reinforced internally. Further, having so many staff members directly involved in hiring helps to ensure that new hires will fit in with the company culture. Other newly introduced incentives include flextime and at least four weeks of vacation for new hires. Employee involvement extends as well to participation in setting objectives (this is reinforced by an employee share ownership program). Employees are also privy to the company's financial statements and can query management on any budget line expense.

Suleman's new strategy has paid off. In addition to reduced turnover and increased morale, his company has been named on Canada's Top 100 Employers list produced by *Maclean's* magazine. *Profit* magazine has also included I Love Rewards on its list of Fastest Growing Companies, and WorldBlu, a U.S.-based social enterprise has included the company on its Most Democratic Workplaces list. According to WorldBlu, the current economic crisis has dictated the need for a new business model that promotes transparency and accountability, and I Love Rewards' new business model is built on these principles. These characteristics, combined with I Love Rewards' authentic democratic practices, emphasis on culture, and focus on people and recognition has created a winning combination.

Suleman is now excited about the future of his business. His new strategies for employee engagement may have been just the competitive advantage and vehicle for growth his company was looking for.

Critical Thinking Question

1. Which of the strategies for enhancing job satisfaction and morale has Razor Suleman employed?

Research has shown that goals that are specific, measurable, and moderately difficult to achieve result in high performance for employees.

the proposed objectives for his or her division to the appropriate regional manager. This process continues all the way up to the vice-president of sales, who gives final approval to the overall sales objectives of the company for the coming year.[19]

Participative Management and Empowerment

Participative management and empowerment involves tapping into workers' knowledge about the job, encouraging them to be self-motivated and to make suggestions for improvements, and giving them more authority and responsibility so that they feel they are a real part of the company's success. In 2009, Texas-based WorldBlu published a list of the 100 most democratic workplaces in the world. Seven Canadian companies made the list, including 1-800-GOT-JUNK?, I Love Rewards, and TakingITGlobal.[20]

There are many other examples of empowerment in Canadian and international businesses:

- At WestJet, front-line staff have the right to issue travel credits to customers they feel have not been treated properly. WestJet thinks that the goodwill generated by the practice will increase repeat business.[21]

- At Toronto's Delta Chelsea Hotel, employees noticed that in the summer months there were fewer business guests and more vacationers' children in the hotel. As a result of employee suggestions, the hotel installed a waterslide, appointed a "kids' concierge," and set up a game room for teens to better serve this market segment.[22]

employee performance. It is also true that on occasion, goal setting may lead to bad behaviour on the part of managers. For example, if managers are told they will receive a bonus if they achieve a certain level of sales revenue, they may focus all their attention on generating *sales revenue,* and not pay any attention to *profits.* At Enron, managers received large bonuses for achieving revenue goals even though the company was failing.[18]

One of the most popular methods for setting performance goals is called **management by objectives (MBO)**, which involves managers and subordinates in setting goals and evaluating progress. The motivational impact is perhaps the biggest advantage of MBO. When employees work together with managers to set goals, they learn more about company-wide objectives, feel that they are an important part of a team, and see how they can improve company-wide performance by achieving their own goals.

Investors Group Financial Services has used MBO for many years to motivate its sales force in selling financial services. The MBO process begins when the vice-president of sales develops general goals for the entire sales force. Sales reps review their financial accomplishments and think through their personal and financial goals for the coming year. They then meet with their division managers and reach a consensus about the specific goals the sales reps will pursue during the next year. Each division manager then forwards

Participative management gets employees involved in analyzing problems, and suggesting solutions. This increases employee satisfaction with, and commitment to, decision that are made.

■ At ING Direct Canada, a webpage has been set up that allows employees to submit ideas for peers to vote on. An innovation team then evaluates the ideas.[23]

■ AES Corporation is a large energy company where multifunctional teams manage themselves without the assistance of any legal, human resources, or other functional department, or any written policies or procedures. No one person is in charge of the teams. As a result of this structure (some call it "empowerment gone mad"), employees exhibit flexibility and continuous learning.[24]

To enhance employee productivity, some companies are now using **wikis**—websites that allow employees to add content on issues that are of interest to the business. This is part of a move to "mass collaboration" that is going on in businesses.[25] Another technique to encourage participative management is the **quality circle**, a group of employees who meet regularly to consider solutions for problems in their work area. At Great-West Life Assurance Company, for example, quality circles are made up of

---

MANAGING IN TURBULENT TIMES

Encouraging Employees to Share Ideas

Empowerment can be a tricky process, particularly in an era when layoffs are common and employees may not trust management, so managers who assume that all workers want to be empowered may be in for a rude shock. Consider these examples:

■ One employee who cut metal shafts for industrial pumps at Blackmer in Grand Rapids, Michigan, had a reputation for being both fast and accurate in his work. He refused to share his knowledge with management (or his fellow workers) because he feared that management would use the knowledge to speed up the workflow and that he would then have to work faster.

■ A long-time employee at a small Canadian manufacturing plant taught a younger replacement worker how to run a complicated machine. Shortly thereafter, the older worker became ill and was off work for several weeks. When he returned, he found that the younger worker had essentially taken over his job. The older worker had this to say: "To pass on your experience or your knowledge to others, or to pass on to your fellow workers your secrets, how you assemble it faster, better, or more efficiently for the company, be careful; tomorrow you might have lost your job."

Workers fear that if they share their knowledge, management will use that knowledge to increase output, which will mean that management can get by with fewer workers, so some people will lose their jobs. Workers may also refuse to share their knowledge because they are convinced that management doesn't think they have anything to contribute. At the Blackmer plant, for example, workers were surprised when a new plant manager asked for their input, because they had never been asked before.

Another problem is identified by Robin Miller, the executive director of the Winnipeg-based Centre for Education and Work, who says that there is a lot of "informal learning" that goes on in companies, but it is not generally recognized or rewarded in Canadian workplaces. If informal learning is not rewarded, we should not be surprised if employees do not share with management the efficient shortcuts they have discovered that allow them to work faster.

The culture of a country may also moderate the positive effects of empowerment initiatives. One study of a company with operations in the U.S., Mexico, Poland, and India found that empowerment was negatively related to job satisfaction in India, but positively related to job satisfaction in the U.S., Mexico, and Poland.

Critical Thinking Questions

1. Why do some workers refuse to share their job knowledge with either their co-workers or with management? What can management do to encourage workers to share their job knowledge?

2. Consider the following statement: *"Companies provide jobs for people, so they have every right to expect that employees will do things like share their job knowledge with their co-workers because this will make the company more successful and allow it to continue to provide jobs."* Do you agree or disagree with the statement? Explain your reasoning.

volunteers who meet once a week (on company time) to consider ways to do higher quality, more effective work.

As positive as these developments are, managers must remember that not all employees want to be "empowered." Some will be frustrated by responsibilities they are not equipped to handle, and others will be dissatisfied if they see the invitation to participate as more symbolic than real. A good approach is to invite participation if employees want to have input, and if participation will have real value for an organization. The boxed insert entitled "Encouraging Employees to Share Ideas" describes some of the problems that can arise with empowerment.

Team Management

Companies have traditionally given individual employees the responsibility to complete certain tasks, but in recent years, an emphasis on teams has become increasingly common. These teams take a variety of forms. **Problem-solving teams** focus on developing solutions to specific problems. They are based on the idea that the best solutions to problems are likely to come from the employees who actually do the work. For example, at the Bowmanville, Ontario, plant of St. Mary's Cement Inc., members of various departments joined a problem-solving team whose goal was to find ways to reduce the company's energy bills. After analyzing the situation, the committee developed a list of energy-saving initiatives and created plans to implement them. Over a recent three-year period, the initiatives saved the company $800 000.[26]

The problem-solving idea is developed even further in **self-managed teams**, which set their own goals, select their own team members, evaluate their own performance, and generally manage themselves. At Johnsonville Foods,

This team of workers at Germany's Apollo car production plant work together to design and manufacture the Apollo sports car. Such teams often help firms make decisions more effectively, enhance communication, and lead to increased employee motivation and satisfaction.

self-managing teams recruit, hire, evaluate, and terminate low performers on their own.[27]

Project teams (also called **venture teams**) work on specific projects like developing new processes, new products, or new businesses. The classic example of a project team is the one that developed IBM's first personal computer many years ago. **Transnational teams**, which are composed of members from many different countries, have also become common. For example, Fuji-Xerox sent 15 engineers from Tokyo to New York to work with U.S. engineers as they developed a "world copier," a product which became a big success.[28] **Virtual teams** are groups of geographically dispersed co-workers that are assembled to accomplish a specific task, using a combination of telecommunications and information technologies. These teams are becoming increasingly popular because of globalization.

Teams provide monetary benefits for companies that use them, but they can also provide non-monetary benefits such as increasing motivation and job satisfaction levels for employees, enhancing companywide communication, and making members feel like they are an integral part of the organization.[29] But, as with participative management, managers must remember that teams are not for everyone, nor are they effective in every situation.[30] At Levi Strauss, for example, individual workers who performed repetitive tasks like sewing zippers into jeans were paid according to the number of jobs they completed each day. In an attempt to boost productivity, company management reorganized everyone into teams of 10 to 35 workers and assigned tasks to the entire team. Each team member's pay was determined by the team's level of productivity. But faster workers became resentful of slower workers because they reduced the group's total output. Slower workers, meanwhile, resented the pressure put on them by faster-working coworkers. As a result, motivation, satisfaction, and morale all dropped, and Levi Strauss eventually abandoned the teamwork plan altogether.[31]

Teams work best when successful task completion requires input from several people, when there is

JOB ENRICHMENT
A method of increasing employees' job satisfaction by extending or adding motivating factors such as responsibility or growth.

JOB REDESIGN
A method of increasing employees' job satisfaction by improving the person–job fit through combining tasks, creating natural work groups, and/or establishing client relationships.

FLEXTIME
A method of increasing employees' job satisfaction by allowing them some choice in the hours they work.

interdependence between tasks (as in team sports), and when working together can accomplish tasks that an individual could not do alone (as in a hospital surgical team).[32]

Job Enrichment and Redesign

While MBO programs and participative management can work in a variety of settings, job enrichment and job redesign programs can increase satisfaction only if a job lacks motivating factors to begin with.[33] **Job enrichment** means adding one or more motivating factors to a job. In a now-classic study, a group of eight typists worked in isolated cubicles taking calls from field sales representatives and then typing up service orders. They had no client contact, so if they had a question about the order, they had to call the sales representative. They also received little performance feedback. Interviews with these workers suggested that they were bored with their jobs and did not feel valued. As part of a job enrichment program, each typist was paired with a small group of designated sales representatives and became a part of their team. Typists were also given permission to call clients directly if they had questions about the order. Finally, a new feedback system was installed to give the typists more information about their performance. As a result, their performance improved and absenteeism decreased markedly.[34]

In general terms, job enrichment is accomplished by **job redesign**, which involves combining tasks to increase job variety, forming natural work groups, and establishing client relationships. By redesigning work to achieve a more satisfactory person–job fit, job redesign motivates individuals who have a high need for growth or achievement.[35]

Combining Tasks This involves enlarging jobs and increasing their variety to make employees feel that their work is more meaningful. In turn, workers are more motivated. For example, the job done by a computer programmer who maintains computer systems might be redesigned to include some system design and development work. The programmer is then able to use additional skills and is involved in the overall system package.

Forming Natural Workgroups People who do different jobs on the same project are good candidates for natural workgroups. These groups help employees get an overview of their jobs and see their importance in the total structure. They also help managers, and the firm in general, because

the people working on a project are usually the most knowledgeable about it and are thus able to solve problems related to it. Consider a group where each employee does a small part of the job of assembling iPhones. One worker may see his job as working on the internal components, while another worker may see her job as working on the external components. The jobs could be redesigned to allow the group to decide who does what and in what order. The workers can exchange jobs and plan their work schedules. Now they all see themselves as part of a team that assembles iPhones.

Establishing Client Relationships A third way of redesigning a job is to establish client relationships, that is, to let employees interact with customers. This approach increases the variety of a job. It also gives workers greater feelings of control over their jobs and more feedback about their performance. Instead of responding to instructions from marketing managers on how to develop new products, software writers at Lotus are encouraged to work directly with customers. Similarly, software writers at Microsoft watch test users work with programs and discuss problems with them directly rather than receive feedback from third-party researchers.

Modified Work Schedules

Many companies are experimenting with different work schedules. Several types of modified work schedules have been tried, including *flextime, compressed workweeks, telecommuting,* and *workshare programs.*

Flextime **Flextime** allows people to pick their working hours. Figure 9.6 illustrates how a flextime system might

Best Buy is taking modified schedules and alternative workplaces to new extremes with its corporate "results-only-work environment" or ROWE. Under ROWE, Best Buy employees can work anytime, anywhere, as long as they achieve results. The program has been so successful that Best Buy has begun introducing the program into its retail stores.

be arranged and how different people might use it. The office is open from 6 a.m. until 7 p.m. Core time is 9 a.m. until 11 a.m. and 1 p.m. until 3 p.m. Joe, being an early riser, comes in at 6 a.m., takes an hour lunch between 11 a.m. and noon, and finishes his day by 3 p.m. Sue, on the other hand, prefers a later day. She comes in at 9 a.m., takes a long lunch from 11 a.m. to 1 p.m., and then works until 7 p.m. Pat works a more traditional day from 8 a.m. until 5 p.m.

About 70 percent of North American firms offer some variation of flextime.[36] Flextime programs give employees more freedom in their professional and personal lives and allow workers to plan around the work schedules of spouses and the school schedules of young children. The increased feeling of freedom and control over their work life also reduces individuals' levels of stress. Flextime also offers advantages to the company. For example, a Toronto company doing business in Vancouver will benefit if some employees come in at 10 a.m. and work until 7 p.m. to account for the time difference between the two cities. Companies can also benefit from the higher levels of commitment and job satisfaction among flextime workers. In large urban areas, flextime programs reduce traffic congestion that contributes to lost work time.

Compressed Workweeks In the **compressed workweek**, employees work fewer days per week, but more hours on the days they do work. The most popular compressed workweek is four days, 10 hours per day, which is used in many companies and municipalities. In 2008, Chrysler began talking with the Canadian Auto Workers Union about instituting the practice because it would cut energy costs and give employees an additional day off each week. Workers at Babcock & Wilcox Canada also negotiated a four-day, 10-hour-per-day contract.[37]

Telecommuting A third variation in work design is **telecommuting**, which allows people to do some or all of their work away from their office. The availability of networked computers, fax machines, cellular telephones, and overnight delivery services makes it possible for many independent professionals to work at home or while travelling. A survey conducted by WorldatWork found that 40 percent of Canadian businesses offer some form of telecommuting for their employees.[38] In certain business functions—for example, customer service and telemarketing—most employees are telecommuters.[39]

When telecommuting is introduced, some managers are concerned that employees will not work as hard at home as they will in the office, but that fear has gradually diminished. When Ikon Office Solutions Inc. implemented a telecommuting program for 250 of its sales staff, the president of the company said there were some initial concerns that telecommuters might not work as hard from home, but they are actually very productive.[40]

Employees like telecommuting because it saves them time and money, and companies like it because it boosts productivity and saves them money as well. A survey by the Computing Technology Industry Association found that two-thirds of employers felt that telecommuting boosted employee productivity and saved the company money.[41] Bell Canada, for example, has reduced its real estate expenses by having 2000 of its workers work at home.[42] Some workers do report feeling isolated and "out of the loop" when they do not see co-workers

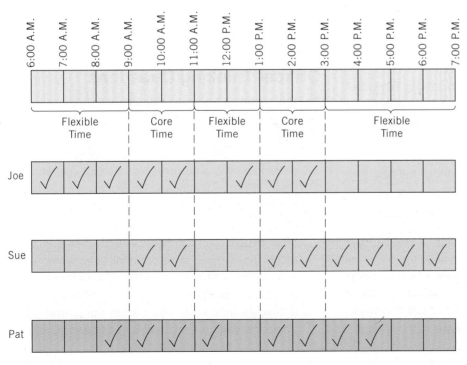

Figure 9.6
Flextime schedules include core time, when everyone must be at work, and flexible time, during which employees can set their own working hours.

very often. To avoid this problem, B.C. Tel and Bentall Development Inc. jointly developed a satellite telecommuting office in Langley, British Columbia. It allows workers who used to commute to Burnaby or Vancouver to reduce their travel time considerably and still be able to interact with other workers.[43]

But telecommuting may not be for everyone. Would-be telecommuters must ask themselves several important questions: Can I meet deadlines even when I'm not being closely supervised? What will it be like to

be away from the social context of the office five days a week? Can I renegotiate family rules so my spouse doesn't come home expecting to see dinner on the table just because I've been home all day?

Additional information about telecommuting is provided in Business Case 9 at the end of this chapter. The boxed insert entitled "The Four-Day Workweek and Telecommuting" raises interesting ecology issues.

Workshare Programs A fourth type of modified work schedule—**worksharing** (also called **job sharing**)—allows two people to share one full-time job. For example, two people might share a position advising the human

---

THE GREENING OF BUSINESS

The Four-Day Workweek and Telecommuting: Are They Really Green?

Recently, the four-day workweek has been promoted as good not only for employee morale and satisfaction but also for the environment. One argument is that since workers will be driving to work only four days each week instead of five, they will be using less gas and therefore putting fewer greenhouse gases into the atmosphere. But whether the four-day workweek really saves gas obviously depends on what workers do on the fifth day. If they drive their SUV 400 kilometres to go visit relatives, they will burn more gas than they would have by simply driving to and from work. On the other hand, maybe they would have taken such a trip on the weekend if they had to work a traditional five-day workweek.

A second argument is that a four-day workweek will mean less electricity use by businesses because machines, computers, and heating systems will be turned down or off on the fifth day. But there may be no actual savings because factory machines have already run for 40 hours as a result of the four previous days at 10 hours. Other electricity savings may also be elusive unless the company is committed to turning down the heat and turning off the lights on the fifth day. But that may be impossible, because there always seem to be office staff who need to be at work on the fifth day. Also, even if workers do stay at home on the fifth day, they may do other tasks that require an equivalent amount of electricity or gas that they would have consumed at work (e.g., renovating their home).

It is difficult to determine if the four-day workweek is better for the environment than the traditional five-day workweek. But *telecommuting* may actually be an effective strategy because workers who telecommute don't come into the office very often. If they are at home working, they will not be driving their car, so that should also save gas. As well, companies that encourage telecommuting can save considerable money on real estate and other operating costs. But even here, we need to analyze what individual workers do as alternate activities before we can conclude that telecommuting is good for the environment.

Critical Thinking Questions

1. Using material contained in this insert as well as other material that you find, develop a list of arguments that the four-day workweek is better for the environment than the five-day workweek. Then develop a list of arguments that the four-day workweek is no better for the environment than the five-day workweek. Which list is most persuasive?

2. Using material contained in this insert, as well as other material you can find, develop a list of arguments that suggest telecommuting is better for the environment than making people come to the traditional workplace. Then develop a list of arguments that suggest telecommuting is not better than the traditional system. Which list is most persuasive?

resource department. One person works Monday through Wednesday noon, and the other works Wednesday noon through Friday. A Statistics Canadasurvey showed that 8 percent of all part-time workers in Canada share a job with someone.[44] People who share jobs are more likely to be women, to be university educated, and to have professional occupations such as teaching and nursing. In addition, job sharers earned more than regular part-time workers.

LO-6 Leadership and Motivation

Leadership refers to the processes and behaviours used by managers to motivate, inspire, and influence subordinates to work toward certain goals. People often assume that "leadership" and "management" mean the same thing, but they are really different concepts. A person can be a manager, a leader, or both.[45] Consider a hospital setting. The chief of staff (chief physician) of a large hospital is clearly a manager by virtue of the position the person occupies. But this individual may or may not be respected or trusted by others, and may have to rely solely on the authority vested in the position to get people to do things. Thus, being a manager does not ensure that a person is also a leader. In contrast, an emergency-room nurse with no formal authority may be quite effective at taking charge of a chaotic situation and directing others in how to deal with specific patient problems. Others in the emergency room may respond because they trust the nurse's judgment and have confidence in the nurse's decision-making skills. In this case, the emergency-room nurse is a leader but not a manager. Finally, the head of pediatrics, supervising a staff of 20 other doctors, nurses, and attendants, may also enjoy the staff's complete respect, confidence, and trust. They readily take the head's advice, follow directives without question, and often go far beyond what is necessary to help carry out the unit's mission. In this case, the head of pediatrics is both a manager and a leader. The key distinctions between leadership and management are summarized in Table 9.1.

LEADERSHIP The process of motivating others to work to meet specific objectives.

Organizations need both management *and* leadership if they are to be effective. Leadership is necessary to create and direct change and to help the organization get through tough times, and management is necessary to achieve coordination and systematic results and to handle administrative activities during times of stability and predictability.[46] Management—in conjunction with leadership—can help achieve planned orderly change. Leadership—in conjunction with management—can keep the organization properly aligned with its environment. Bothmanagers and leaders play a major role in establishing the moral climate of the organization and in determining the role of ethics in its culture.[47]

LO-7 Approaches to Leadership

Political, religious, and business leaders have influenced the course of human events throughout history,

Table 9.1 Kotter's Distinctions between Management and Leadership

Activity	Management	Leadership
Creating an Agenda	Planning and budgeting. Establishing detailed steps and timetables for achieving needed results; allocating the resources necessary to make those needed results happen.	Establishing direction. Developing a vision of the future, often the distant future, and strategies for producing the changes needed to achieve that vision.
Developing a Human Network for Achieving the Agenda	Organizing and staffing. Establishing some structure for accomplishing plan requirements, staffing that structure with individuals, delegating responsibility and authority for carrying out the plan, providing policies and procedures to help guide people, and creating methods or systems to monitor implementation.	Aligning people. Communicating the direction by words and deeds to all those whose cooperation may be needed to influence the creation of teams and coalitions that understand the vision and strategies and accept their validity.
Executing Plans	Controlling and problem solving. Monitoring results vs. plan in some detail, identifying deviations, and then planning and organizing to solve these problems.	Motivating and inspiring. Energizing people to overcome major political, bureaucratic, and resource barriers to change, by satisfying very basic, but often unfulfilled, human needs.
Outcomes	Produces a degree of predictability and order and has the potential to consistently produce major results expected by various shareholders (e.g., for customers, always being on time; for stockholders, being on budget).	Produces change, often to a dramatic degree, and has the potential to produce extremely useful change (e.g., new products that customers want, new approaches to labour relations that help make a firm more competitive).

TRAIT APPROACH
A leadership approach focused on identifying the essential traits that distinguished leaders

BEHAVIOURAL APPROACH
A leadership approach focused on determining what behaviours are employed by leaders.

TASK-ORIENTED LEADER BEHAVIOUR
Leader behaviour focusing on how tasks should be performed in order to meet certain goals and to achieve certain performance standards.

EMPLOYEE-ORIENTED LEADER BEHAVIOUR
Leader behaviour focusing on satisfaction, motivation, and well-being of employees.

AUTOCRATIC STYLE
A form of leader behaviour in which the manager issues orders and expects them to be obeyed without question.

DEMOCRATIC STYLE A form of leader behaviour in which the manager requests input from subordinates before making decisions, but the manager retains the decision-making power.

FREE-REIN STYLE
A form of leader behaviour in which the manager serves as an adviser to subordinates who are given a lot of discretion when making decisions.

SITUATIONAL (CONTINGENCY) APPROACH TO LEADERSHIP
Leadership approach that assumes that appropriate leader behaviour varies from one situation to another.

but careful scientific study of leadership began only about a century ago. In the following paragraphs, we briefly summarize the development of this research.

The Trait Approach In the first two decades of the twentieth century, researchers believed that leaders had unique traits that distinguished them from non-leaders (the **trait approach**). Many traits were proposed as important, but as time passed the list became so long that it lost any practical value. The trait approach was all but abandoned by the middle of the twentieth century, but in recent years it has resurfaced. Some researchers now argue that certain traits (for example, intelligence, drive, motivation, honesty, integrity, and self-confidence) provide the *potential* for effective leadership, but only if the person is really motivated to be a leader. The implication is that people without these traits are not likely to be successful leaders even if they try.[48] Recall that the *emotional intelligence* idea that was discussed earlier in this chapter identified five somewhat different traits of successful leaders.[49]

The Behavioural Approach Because the trait approach was a poor predictor of leadership success, attention shifted from managers' *traits* to their *behaviours*. The goal of the **behavioural approach** was to determine how the behaviours of effective leaders differed from the behaviours of less effective leaders. This research led to the identification of two basic forms of leader behaviour: **task-oriented** (the manager focuses on how tasks should be performed in order to achieve important goals) and **employee-oriented** (the manager focuses on the

satisfaction, motivation, and well-being of employees). Task-oriented managers tend to have higher performing subordinates, while employee-oriented managers tend to have more satisfied subordinates.

Researchers have also identified three main leadership styles: the **autocratic style** (the manager issues orders and expects them to be obeyed without question), the **democratic style** (the manager requests input from subordinates before making decisions but retains final decision-making power), and the **free-rein style** (the manager serves as an adviser to subordinates who are given a lot of discretion when making decisions). Most leaders tend to regularly use one style, and may in fact find it difficult to change from one style to another. But some leaders do manage to change their style. For example, Andrall (Andy) Pearson was an abrasive, numbers-oriented, hard-to-please manager when he was president and COO of PepsiCo. But now, as director of Yum Brands, he has softened and transformed and seems to truly care about employees.[50]

The Situational Approach to Leadership As time passed, researchers began to realize that different combinations of leader behaviour might be effective in different situations. For instance, if workers are satisfied but are not very motivated to work hard, a leader should most likely focus on task-focused behaviours in order to improve productivity. If worker productivity is high, but workers are stressed out about their jobs and have low levels of job satisfaction, the leader should most likely concentrate on employee-focused behaviours so as to improve their job satisfaction. This line of thinking led to the development of the **situational** (or **contingency**) **approach to leadership**.

The contingency approach was first proposed as a continuum of leadership behaviour (see Figure 9.7). At one extreme, the leader makes decisions alone; at the other extreme the leader has employees make decisions with only minimal guidance from the leader. Each point on the continuum is influenced by *characteristics of the leader* (including the manager's value system, confidence in subordinates, personal inclinations, and feelings of security), *characteristics of the subordinates* (including the subordinates' need for independence, readiness to assume responsibility, tolerance for ambiguity, interest in the problem, understanding of goals, knowledge, experience, and expectations), and the *characteristics of the situation* (including the type of organization, group effectiveness, the problem itself, and time pressures). Thus, many variables beyond the leader's behaviour were considered. Later models proposed additional factors (in the leader, in the subordinates, and in the environment) that influenced subordinate satisfaction and productivity.

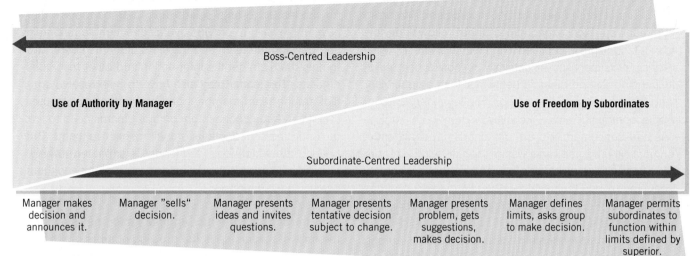

Figure 9.7
The leadership continuum.

LO-8 Recent Trends in Leadership

During the late twentieth and early twenty-first centuries, many new ideas about leadership have been developed. We conclude this chapter with a brief discussion of several of these ideas.

Transformational Leadership **Transformational leadership** is the set of abilities that allows a leader to recognize the need for change, to create a vision to guide that change, and to execute the change effectively. In contrast, **transactional leadership** involves routine, regimented activities that are necessary during periods of stability.

Many leaders may find it difficult to exercise both types of leadership. For example, when Michael Eisner took over the Walt Disney organization in the early 1990s, the company was stagnant and was heading into decline. Relying on transformational skills, Eisner turned things around in dramatic fashion. Among many other things, he quickly expanded the company's theme parks, built new hotels, improved Disney's movie business, created a successful Disney cruise line, launched several other major initiatives, and changed the company into a global media powerhouse. But when the firm began to plateau and needed some time to let the changes all settle in, Eisner was unsuccessful at changing his own approach from transformational leadership to transactional leadership and was pressured into retiring.

Charismatic Leadership **Charismatic leadership** is a type of influence based on the leader's personal charisma. Figure 9.8 portrays the three key elements of charismatic leadership that most experts acknowledge today.[51]

TRANSFORMATIONAL LEADERSHIP The set of abilities that allows a leader to recognize the need for change, to create a vision to guide that change, and to execute the change effectively.

TRANSACTIONAL LEADERSHIP Comparable to management, it involves routine, regimented activities.

CHARISMATIC LEADERSHIP Type of influence based on the leader's personal charisma.

Figure 9.8
Charismatic leadership.

The Charismatic Leader

Envisioning	Energizing	Enabling
• articulating a compelling vision	• demonstrating personal excitement	• expressing personal support
• setting high expectations	• expressing personal confidence	• empathizing
• modelling consistent behaviours	• seeking, finding, and using success	• expressing confidence in people

Charismatic leaders have a high level of self-confidence and a strong need to influence others. They also communicate high expectations about follower performance and express confidence in their followers. A highly charismatic supervisor will generally be more successful in influencing a subordinate's behaviour than a supervisor who lacks charisma. Steve Jobs, the legendary CEO of Apple, commands a cult-like following from both employees and consumers. He exhibits charisma, confidence, originality, brilliance, and vision. He is clearly a leader who can deliver success in businesses that are rapidly changing, highly technical, and demanding. Yet he has also been portrayed as intimidating, power-hungry, and an aggressive egotist.[52]

Charismatic leadership ideas are popular among managers today and are the subject of numerous books and articles.[53] One concern is that some charismatic leaders will inspire such blind faith in their followers that the followers may engage in inappropriate, unethical, or even illegal behaviours simply because the leader instructs them to do so. This tendency likely played a role in the collapse of both Enron and Arthur Andersen, as people followed orders from their charismatic bosses to hide information, shred documents, and mislead investigators. The film *Enron: The Smartest Guys in the Room* documents this problem.

Leaders as Coaches Many organizations are now attempting to become less hierarchical—that is, to eliminate the old-fashioned command-and-control mentality often inherent in bureaucratic organizations—and to motivate and empower individuals to work independently. This changes the role of leaders. Whereas leaders were once expected to control situations, direct work, supervise people, closely monitor performance, make decisions, and structure activities, many leaders today are being asked to become *coaches* instead of *overseers*.[54]

Consider the parallel with an athletic team. The coach selects the players for the team and decides on the general direction to take (such as emphasizing offence versus defence). The coach also helps develop player talent and teaches team members how to execute specific plays. But at game time, it's up to the players to execute plays and get the job done. While the coach may get some of the credit for the victory, he or she didn't actually score any of the points.

For business leaders, a coaching perspective calls for the leader to help select team members and other new employees, to provide overall direction, to help train and develop the team and the skills of its members, and to help the team get the information and other resources it needs. The leader may also have to help resolve conflict among team members and mediate other disputes that arise. And coaches from different teams need to link the activities and functions of their respective teams. But beyond these activities, the leader is expected to keep a low profile and let the group get its work done without overly close supervision.

Gender and Leadership Another factor that is altering the face of leadership is the growing number of women advancing to the highest levels in organizations. Given that most leadership theories and research studies have focused on male leaders, developing a better understanding of how women lead is clearly an important next step. For example, do women and men lead differently? Some early observers, for instance, predicted that (consistent with prevailing stereotypes) female leaders would be relatively warm, supportive, and nurturing as compared to their male counterparts. But in reality, research suggests that female leaders are not necessarily more nurturing or supportive than male leaders. Likewise, male leaders are not systematically more harsh, controlling, or task focused than female leaders. Women do seem to have a tendency to be more democratic when making decisions, whereas men have a tendency to be somewhat more autocratic.[55]

Andrea Jung (left), CEO of Avon Products, and Angela Merkel (right) chancellor of Germany, are exceptional leaders. Jung has transformed Avon and made it a powerhouse in its industry, and Merkel was recently names to TIME magazine's list of "people who shape our world."

Cross-Cultural Leadership *Culture* is a broad concept that encompasses both international differences and diversity-based differences within one culture. For instance, when a Japanese firm sends an executive to head up the firm's operation in Canada, that person will need to be sensitive to the cultural differences that exist between the two countries and consider changing his or her leadership style accordingly. Japan is generally characterized by *collectivism* (group before individual), whereas Canada is based more on *individualism* (individual before group). The Japanese executive, then, will find it necessary to recognize the importance of individual contributions and rewards and the differences in individual and group roles that exist in Japanese and Canadian businesses.

Cross-cultural factors also play a growing role in organizations as their workforces become more diverse. Most leadership research, for instance, has analyzed white male leaders because those individuals dominated leadership positions in North America. But as Asians, Blacks, Aboriginals, and Hispanics achieve leadership positions, it will be necessary to reassess how applicable current models of leadership are when applied to an increasingly diverse pool of leaders.

Canadian versus American Management Styles The management styles of Canadian managers might look a lot like that of Americans, but there are several notable differences. In general, Canadian managers are more subtle and subdued than American managers, more committed to their companies, less willing to mindlessly follow the latest management fad, and more open to different cultures because of the multicultural nature of Canada.[56] The Global Leadership and Organizational Behavior Effectiveness study also found that Canadian managers are very oriented toward fairness, are less likely to protect their own interests above those of their teams, and put more emphasis on long-term goals rather than short-term gratification.[57] All of these characteristics are advantageous for Canadian companies that will increasingly be competing in global markets.

During the last few years, many Canadian-born managers have achieved significant success in companies that operate internationally. These include Bob Kelly (CEO of the Bank of New York Mellon Corp.), Henry McKinnell (former CEO of Pfizer), Steven McArthur (president of Expedia), Patricia Arnold (vice-president of Credit Suisse First Boston), Clara Furse (former CEO of the London Stock Exchange), Simon Cooper (CEO of Ritz-Carlton Hotel), and Dominic Barton (chairman of McKinsey & Company's Asia Region).[58]

Strategic Leadership **Strategic leadership**—which focuses on leadership in top management—is a leader's ability to understand the complexities of both the organization and its environment in order to lead change toward enhanced competitiveness. Steve Jobs, CEO of Apple, is an effective strategic leader. A few years ago, Jobs recognized the potential growth of MP3 players and the fact that those devices used technology that is similar to that found in computers. He therefore directed the development of the Apple iPod, the iPhone, and iTunes, which have become enormously successful and profitable products. When Jobs became ill in 2009, observers worried that Apple would lose its competitive advantage.

Ethical Leadership In the wake of recent corporate scandals at firms like Enron, Boeing, and WorldCom, faith in business leaders has been shaken. High standards of ethical conduct are therefore being held up as a prerequisite for effective leadership. More specifically, business leaders are being called on to maintain high ethical standards for their own conduct, to unfailingly exhibit ethical behaviour, and to hold others in their organizations to the same standards—in short, to practice **ethical leadership**.

The behaviours of top leaders are being scrutinized more than ever, and those responsible for hiring new leaders are looking more closely at the backgrounds of those being considered. The emerging pressure for stronger corporate governance models is likely to further increase the commitment to select for leadership positions only those individuals with high ethical standards and to hold them more accountable for both their actions and the consequences of those actions.

Virtual Leadership Finally, **virtual leadership** is also emerging as an important issue for organizations. In earlier times, leaders and their followers worked together in the same physical location and engaged in personal (i.e., face-to-face) interactions on a regular basis. But in today's world, leaders and their followers may work in locations that are far from one another. Such arrangements might include people telecommuting from a home office one or two days a week to people actually living and working far from company headquarters and seeing one another in person only very infrequently.

How do managers carry out leadership activities when they do not have regular personal contact with their followers? And how do they help mentor and

STRATEGIC LEADERSHIP Leader's ability to understand the complexities of both the organization and its envrionment, and to lead change in the organization so as to enhance its competitiveness.

ETHICAL LEADERSHIP Leader behaviours that reflect high ethical standards.

VIRTUAL LEADERSHIP Leadership in settings where leaders and followers interact electronically rather than in face-to-face settings.

develop others? Communication between leaders and their subordinates is more important than ever, and it will still occur, but it may be largely by telephone and email. In the future, leaders may simply have to work harder at creating and maintaining relationships with their employees that go beyond words on a computer screen. While nonverbal communication, such as smiles and handshakes, may not be possible online, managers can make a point of adding a few personal words in an email to convey appreciation, reinforcement, or constructive feedback. Building on this, managers should also take advantage of every opportunity whenever they are in face-to-face situations to go further than they might formerly have done.

Beyond these simple prescriptions, there is not much theory or research to guide managers functioning in a virtual world. Hence, as electronic communication continues to pervade the workplace, researchers and managers alike need to work together to first help frame the appropriate issues and questions regarding virtual leadership, and then to help address those issues and answer those questions.

Summary of Learning Objectives

1. **Identify and discuss the basic *forms of behaviour* that employees exhibit in organizations.** *Employee behaviour* is the pattern of actions by the members of an organization that directly or indirectly influences the organization's effectiveness. *Performance behaviours* are the total set of work-related behaviours that the organization expects employees to display. *Organizational citizenship* refers to the behaviour of individuals who make a positive overall contribution to the organization. *Counterproductive behaviours* are those that detract from, rather than contribute to, organizational performance.

2. **Describe the nature and importance of *individual differences* among employees.** *Individual differences* are personal attributes that vary from one person to another. *Personality* is the relatively stable set of psychological attributes that distinguish one person from another. The *"big five" personality traits* are *agreeableness, conscientiousness, emotionality,* *extraversion,* and *openness. Emotional intelligence,* or *emotional quotient (EQ),* refers to the extent to which people are self-aware, can manage their emotions, can motivate themselves, express empathy for others, and possess social skills. *Attitudes* reflect our beliefs and feelings about specific ideas, situations, or other people. Especially important attitudes are *job satisfaction* and *organizational commitment.*

3. **Explain the meaning and importance of *psychological contracts* and the *person–job fit* in the workplace.** A *psychological contract* is the overall set of expectations held by employees and the organization regarding what employees will contribute to the organization and what the organization will provide in return. A good *person–job fit* is achieved when the employee's contributions match the inducements the organization offers. Having a good match between people and their jobs can help enhance performance, job satisfaction, and motivation.

4. **Identify and summarize the most important *models of employee motivation.*** *Motivation* is the set of forces that cause people to behave in certain ways. Early approaches to motivation were first based on the assumption that people work only for money, and then on the assumption that social needs are the primary way to motivate people. The *hierarchy of human needs* model holds that people at work try to satisfy one or more of five different needs. The *two-factor theory* argues that job satisfaction is influenced by *motivation factors* such as recognition for a job well done, while job dissatisfaction depends on *hygiene factors* such as working conditions. *Expectancy theory* suggests that people are motivated to work toward rewards that they desire and have a reasonable expectancy of obtaining. *Equity theory* focuses on social comparisons—people evaluating their treatment by the organization relative to the treatment of others.

5. **Describe the *strategies* used by organizations to improve job satisfaction and employee motivation.** *Reinforcement* involves applying (or withholding) positive (or negative) consequences in an attempt to motivate employees to exhibit behaviour the manager wants. *Goal setting* involves setting SMART goals that will motivate workers to high performance. *Participative management and empowerment* involves tapping into workers' knowledge about the job, encouraging them to be self-motivated, and giving them more authority and responsibility so that they feel they are a real part of the company's success. *Team management* means forming teams of employees and empowering the team to make decisions on issues like production scheduling, work procedures, work schedules, and the hiring of new employees. *Job enrichment* means adding motivating factors to job activities. *Modified work schedules*—such as *work sharing (job sharing)*, *flextime*, and *telecommuting* increase employee satisfaction by providing increased flexibility to workers.

6. **Define *leadership* and distinguish it from *management.*** *Leadership* refers to the processes and behaviours used by a person in order to motivate, inspire, and influence the behaviours of others. Leadership and management are not the same thing. *Leadership* involves such things as developing a vision, communicating that vision, and directing change. *Management*, meanwhile, focuses more on outlining procedures, monitoring results, and working toward outcomes.

7. **Summarize the *approaches to leadership* that developed during the twentieth century.** The *trait approach to leadership* focused on identifying the traits of successful leaders. Recent research has focused on traits such as emotional intelligence, drive, honesty and integrity, self-confidence, and charisma. The *behavioural approach* identified two common leader behaviours: *task-focused* and *employee-focused* behaviours. Three leadership styles—autocratic, democratic, and free-rein—were also identified. The *situational approach to leadership* assumes that factors in the leader, factors in the followers, and factors in the situation determine which leadership behaviour is most effective.

8. **Describe the most recent ideas about effective leadership.** *Transformational leadership* (as distinguished from *transactional leadership*) focuses on the set of abilities that allows a leader to recognize the need for change, to create a vision to guide that change, and to execute the change effectively. *Charismatic leadership* is influence based on the leader's personal charisma. Leaders are often expected to play the role of *coach,* which involves selecting team members; providing direction, training, and developing; and allowing the group to function autonomously. Research on *gender and leadership* is re-examining assumptions about how men and women lead. *Cross-cultural leadership* is becoming increasingly important as companies become more diverse in a globalized economic system. *Strategic leadership* is the leader's ability to lead change in the organization so as to enhance its competitiveness. *Ethical leadership* requires that leaders maintain high ethical standards for their own conduct, and to hold others in their organizations to the same standards. *Virtual leadership* is becoming important as more leaders and their followers work in physically separate places.

Questions and Exercises

Questions for Analysis

1. Describe the psychological contract you currently have or have had in the past with an employer. If you have never worked, describe the psychological contract that you have with the instructor in this class.

2. Explain how each of the "big five" personality traits influence leadership effectiveness.

3. How is the job enrichment/job redesign approach to motivation different from the modified work schedules

(flextime, compressed workweek) approach to motivation? Are there similarities between the two approaches? Explain.

4. How can participative management programs enhance employee satisfaction and motivation? Why do some employees not want to get involved in participative management?

5. What is the relationship between performance behaviours and organizational citizenship behaviours? Which are more important to an organization?

6. Describe the type of circumstance in which it would be appropriate to apply each of the theories of motivation discussed in this chapter. Which theory would be easiest to use? Which one would be hardest? Why?

Application Exercises

7. Identify two Canadian and two U.S. *managers* who you think would also qualify as great *leaders*. Explain your choices.

8. Ask a manager what traits he or she thinks are necessary for success. How does the manager's list compare with the "big five" list in this chapter? How many differences are there? Why would these differences exist?

9. Interview the human resource manager of a local company and ask what strategies the company uses to enhance employee job satisfaction.

10. Interview a manager and ask whether he or she believes that leadership can be taught. What are the implications of the manager's answer?

TEAM EXERCISES

Building Your Business Skills

Too Much of a Good Thing

Goal
To encourage students to apply different motivational theories to a workplace problem involving poor productivity.

Situation
Consider a small company that makes its employees feel as if they are members of a large family. Unfortunately, this company is going broke because too few members are working hard enough to make money for it. They are happy, comfortable, complacent—and lazy. With sales dropping, the company brings in management consultants to analyze the situation and make recommendations. The outsiders quickly identify a motivational problem affecting the sales force: sales reps are paid a handsome salary and receive automatic year-end bonuses regardless of performance. They are also treated to bagels every Friday and regular group birthday lunches that cost as much as $200 each. Employees

feel satisfied, but have little incentive to work very hard. Eager to return to profitability, the company's owners wait to hear your recommendations.

Method
Step 1 In groups of four, step into the role of management consultants. Start by analyzing your client's workforce motivation problems from the following perspectives (the questions focus on key motivational issues):

- *Job satisfaction and morale.* As part of a long-standing family-owned business, employees are happy and loyal, in part because they are treated so well. Can high morale have a downside? How can it breed stagnation, and what can managers do to prevent stagnation from taking hold?

- *Theory X versus Theory Y.* Although the behaviour of these workers seems to make a case for Theory X, why is it difficult to draw this conclusion about a company that focuses more on satisfaction than on sales and profits?

- *Two-factor theory.* Analyze the various ways in which improving such motivational factors as recognition, added responsibility, advancement, and growth might reduce the importance of hygiene factors, including pay and security.

- *Expectancy theory.* Analyze the effect on productivity of redesigning the company's sales force compensation structure; namely, by paying lower base salaries while offering greater earnings potential through a sales-based incentive system. How would linking performance with increased pay that is achievable through hard work motivate employees? How would the threat of job loss motivate greater effort?

Step 2 Write a short report based on your analysis, and make recommendations to the company's owners. The goal of your report is to change the working environment in ways that will motivate greater effort and generate greater productivity.

Follow-Up Questions

1. What is your group's most important recommendation? Why do you think it is likely to succeed?

2. Changing the corporate culture to make it less paternalistic may reduce employees' sense of belonging to a family. If you were an employee, would you consider a greater focus on profits to be an improvement or a problem? How would it affect your motivation and productivity?

3. What steps would you take to improve the attitude and productivity of long-time employees who resist change?

Exercising Your Ethics

Taking One for the Team

The Situation

You are a skilled technician who has worked for a major electronics firm for the past 10 years. You love your job—it is interesting, stimulating, and enjoyable, and you are well paid for what you do. The plant where you work is one of five manufacturing centres your firm operates in a major metropolitan area. The firm is currently developing a new prototype for one of its next-generation products. To ensure that all perspectives are reflected, the company has identified a set of technicians from each plant who will work together as a team for the next two months.

The Dilemma

You have just met with your new teammates and are quite confused about what you might do next. As it turns out, the technicians from two of the manufacturing centres have heard rumours that your company is planning to

close at least three of the centres and move production to a lower-cost factory in another country. These individuals are very upset. Moreover, they have made it clear that they (1) do not intend to put forth much extra effort on this project and (2) they are all looking for new jobs. You and the other technicians, though, have heard none of these rumours. Moreover, these individuals seem as excited as you about their jobs.

Team Activity

First, working alone, write a brief summary of how you would handle this situation. For instance, would you seek more information or just go about your work? Would you start looking for another job, would you try to form a subgroup just with those technicians who share your views, or would you try to work with everyone?

Second, form a small group with some of your classmates. Share with each other the various ideas you each identified. Then, formulate a group description of what you think most people in your situation would do. Finally, share your description with the rest of the class.

What about Telecommuting?

On any given day, many business offices are vacant because employees are either at off-site meetings, travelling, on vacation, out sick, or attending training sessions. Many companies now recognize that there are advantages for both employees and for the company if they allow employees to work from home and telecommute. About 1.5 million Canadians work at home at least one or two days a week, and some work from home almost all the time. Consider three fairly typical stories.

Edward Moffat works for Sun Microsystems of Canada. He signed up for the company's "open work" program, which allowed him to work largely from home (or anywhere for that matter). He wasn't in the office much anyway because he travelled a lot. Now he works out of his Brampton, Ontario, home 9 days out of 10. He doesn't have to pay $300 per month in highway tolls, his gas costs and car maintenance costs have gone way down, and he spends less on lunch. He thinks all those things combined save him about $50 per day. He also gets to see his wife and children more frequently. The company estimates that telecommuting saved it $71 million in real estate costs alone (because fewer employee offices are needed), and the turnover rate is half what it is for non-telecommuters.

Sylvie Bolduc decided to take advantage of Bell Canada's telework option, partly because she was sick of the 90-minute drive to work every day. She says she is a disciplined person and doesn't feel the need to constantly interact with co-workers. She has online meetings with staff on a regular basis, and makes trips to the office every two weeks to catch up on other developments. She says she wants to work like this the rest of her life. Bell's program means that 11 000 tons of greenhouse gases are not being put into the atmosphere because fewer employees are driving to and from work.

Deborah Corber started telecommuting at her job when her family relocated to her hometown of Montreal. Later, she worked out of her home after she started her own consulting firm. She says the biggest challenge was isolation because she likes bouncing ideas off colleagues. She also had trouble separating her personal and professional life, and felt that she was spending way too much time in her home office. In 2007, she decided to stop working at home, and she now shares space with several colleagues in an office close to her home.

These three stories show how varied employee experiences are with the idea of telecommuting. They also show that there are both advantages and disadvantages associated with telecommuting.

Advantages for employees:

- health benefits (lower stress levels)
- lower costs (reduced car expenses)
- better use of time (no commuting long distances)
- better use of time (no interruptions)

Disadvantages for employees:

- feeling "out of the loop" (not being knowledgeable about important business issues or interesting personal gossip)
- having difficulty separating personal and professional life (work intrudes at home)
- feeling ill-suited for telework (lack of discipline and feeling lonesome)
- finding it difficult to work closely with colleagues when necessary
- fear of career derailment

Advantages for the employer:

- increases productivity (two-thirds of employers surveyed said that employee productivity went up)
- cost savings (fewer offices and office supplies are needed; lower vehicle expenses)
- lower electric bills (fewer lights and computers are turned on in offices)
- access to qualified staff (who otherwise wouldn't be available because they don't live in the area or don't want to drive so far to work)

- lower travel expenses (teleconferencing, email, networking systems take the place of travel)
- lower employee turnover

Disadvantages for the employer:

- requires a change in management thinking (forces managers to adopt an attitude of trust regarding employees)
- many managers still think if they can't see employees, they aren't working (may threaten the control of bosses who are used to having employees in sight)
- bosses have to spend more time with subordinates on the phone or other media (they may prefer face-to-face communication)
- bosses don't know when employees are actually working
- telecommuting may not work well for companies where customers are frequently in the office
- telecommuting may not work well if colleagues frequently need intense face-to-face collaboration to complete rush jobs on time

These advantages and disadvantages mean that telecommuting must be carefully thought through so that it is beneficial to both employees and to the company. It does *not* mean simply telling workers that they can now work at home. Rather, there must be a clear understanding between the bosses and workers about things like the nature of the arrangement, the type of tasks that can be completed away from the office, maintaining safety and confidentiality in the employee's home office, what telecommuting might mean for the employee's career path, and so on.

Questions for Discussion

1. How is telecommuting different from other forms of modified work schedules? How is it similar?

2. Do you think that telecommuting will become more prominent in the future? Explain the reasons for your position.

3. Interview a friend or relative who telecommutes in their job. What advantages and disadvantages do they see in such an arrangement? Compare their responses with the advantages and disadvantages listed above. If there are major differences, try to explain them.

SCANLIFE

Part 2(A): The Business of Managing

Goal of the Exercise

In Part 1 of the business plan project, you formulated a basic identity for your business. Part 2(a) asks you to think about the goals of your business, some internal and external factors affecting the business, and the organizational structure of the business.

Exercise Background: Part 2(a) of the Business Plan

As you learned in Chapter 6, every business sets goals. In this part of the plan, you'll define some of the goals for your business. Part 2(a) also asks you to perform a basic SWOT analysis for your business. As you'll recall from Chapter 6, a SWOT analysis looks at the business's *strengths, weaknesses, opportunities,* and *threats*. The strengths and weaknesses are internal factors—things that the business can control. The opportunities and threats are generally external factors that affect the business:

Socio-cultural forces—Will changes in population or culture help your business or hurt it?

Economic forces—Will changes in the economy help your business or hurt it?

Technological forces—Will changes in technology help your business or hurt it?

Competitive forces—Does your business face much competition or very little?

Political–legal forces—Will changes in laws help your business or hurt it?

Each of these forces will affect different businesses in different ways, and some of these may not apply to your business at all.

Part 2(a) of the business plan also asks you to determine how the business is to be run. One thing you'll need to do is create an organizational chart to get you thinking about the different tasks needed for a successful business. You'll also examine various factors relating to operating your business.

Your Assignment

mybusinesslab

Step 1

Open the saved Business Plan file you began working on in Part 1. You will continue to work from this file.

Step 2

For the purposes of this assignment, you will answer the questions in Part 2(a): The Business of Managing:

1. Provide a brief mission statement for your business.

    Hint: Refer to the discussion of mission statements in Chapter 5. Be sure to include the name of your business, how you will stand out from your competition, and why a customer will buy from you.

2. Consider the goals for your business. What are three of your business goals for the first year? What are two intermediate- to long-term goals?

    Hint: Refer to the discussion of goal setting in Chapter 5. Be as specific and realistic as possible with the goals you set. For example, if you plan on selling a service, how many customers do you want by the end of the first year, and how much do you want each customer to spend?

3. Perform a basic SWOT analysis for your business, listing its main strengths, weaknesses, opportunities, and threats.

    Hint: We explained previously which factors you should consider in your basic SWOT analysis. Look around at your world, talk to classmates, or talk to your instructor for other ideas in performing your SWOT analysis.

4. Who will manage the business?

    Hint: Refer to the discussion of managers in Chapter 6. Think about how many levels of management as well as what kinds of managers your business needs.

5. Show how the "team" fits together by creating a simple organizational chart for your business. Your chart should indicate who will work for each manager, as well as each person's job title.

   Hint: As you create your organizational chart, consider the different tasks involved in the business.

To whom will each person report? Refer to the discussion of organizational structure in Chapter 7 for information to get you started.

Note: Once you have answered the questions, save your Word document. You'll be answering additional questions in later chapters.

Part 2(B): The Business of Managing

Goal of the Exercise

At this point, your business has an identity and you've described the factors that will affect your business and how you will operate it. Part 2(b) of the business plan project asks you to think about your employees, the jobs they will be performing, and the ways in which you can lead and motivate them.

Exercise Background: Part 2(b) of the Business Plan

To complete this part of the plan, you need to refer to the organizational chart that you created in Part 2(a). In this part of the business plan exercise, you'll take the different job titles you created in the organizational chart and give thought to the *skills* that employees will need to bring to the job *before* they begin. You'll also consider *training* you'll need to provide *after* they are hired, as well as how you'll compensate your employees. Part 2(b) of the business plan also asks you to consider how you'll lead your employees and keep them happy and motivated.

Your Assignment

mybusinesslab

Step 1

Open the Business Plan file you have been working on.

Step 2

For the purposes of this assignment, you will answer the questions in Part 2(b): The Business of Managing:

1. What do you see as the "corporate culture" of your business? What types of employee behaviours, such as organizational citizenship, will you expect?

   Hint: Will your business demand a casual environment or a more professional environment? Refer to the discussion on employee behaviour in Chapter 9 for information on organizational citizenship and other employee behaviours.

2. What is your philosophy on leadership? How will you manage your employees on a day-to-day basis?

   Hint: Refer to the discussion on leadership in Chapter 9 to help you formulate your thoughts.

3. Looking back at your organizational chart in Part 2(a), briefly create a job description for each team member.

   Hint: As you learned in Chapter 8, a job description lists the duties and responsibilities of a job; its working conditions; and the tools, materials, equipment, and information used to perform it. Imagine your business on a typical day. Who is working, and what are each person's responsibilities?

4. Next, create a job specification for each job, listing the skills and other credentials and qualifications needed to perform the job effectively.

   Hint: As you write your job specifications, consider what you would write if you were making an ad for the position. What would the new employee need to bring to the job in order to qualify for the position?

5. What sort of training, if any, will your employees need once they are hired? How will you provide this training?

   Hint: Refer to the discussion of training in Chapter 8. Will you offer your employees on-the-job training? Off-the-job training? Vestibule training?

6. A major factor in retaining skilled workers is a company's compensation system—the total package of rewards that it offers employees in return for their labour. Part of this compensation system includes wages/salaries. What wages or salaries will you offer for each job? Why did you decide on that pay rate?

   Hint: Refer to Chapter 8 for more information on forms of compensation.

7. As you learned in Chapter 8, incentive programs are special programs designed to motivate high performance. What incentives will you use to motivate your workforce?

   Hint: Be creative and look beyond a simple answer, such as giving pay increases. Ask yourself, who are my employees and what is important to them? Refer to Chapter 8 for more information on the types of incentives you may want to consider.

Note: Once you have answered the questions, save your Word document. You'll be answering additional questions in later chapters.

Flair Bartending

More than 20 years ago, Tom Cruise played a flashy bartender in the movie *Cocktail*. That style of bartending actually has a name—it's called "flair bartending." Gavin MacMillan is the top-ranked Canadian flair bartender, and second-ranked in the world. He's also an author and the owner of a bartender-for-hire business called Movers and Shakers. Now he's developing a brand-new idea for a bartender school called Bartender 1. Eventually, he wants to franchise the idea across Canada and the U.S., and around the world.

Potential franchisees will like his idea to use an actual bar to teach students flair bartending. Gavin doesn't rent space; rather, he borrows a bar for an evening to hold his classes. On one Monday evening, he is at a Toronto bar that is closed, but he has talked the owner into letting him run his class there for free. In return, the bar gets first pick of the graduates of Gavin's bartending school. In his first class of 12 students, Gavin has incurred $11 000 of expenses, but he receives only $6 000 in revenues. He hopes to reduce the cost of running future classes by reusing demonstration equipment. He needs to prove this concept will really work before trying to franchise it.

There is no problem finding students who want to be bartenders, but there is a problem finding people who can be instructors. There are only about 10 flair bartenders in Toronto and 40 in all of Canada. Finding teachers is not Gavin's only problem. He is a perfectionist who is always fussing over the little things. Sometimes he focuses so much on the details that he doesn't see the big picture. A third problem is his lack of time to do all the things he wants to do.

He has designed, built, and financed a portable bar that he hopes to sell to golf courses and hotels. He brings his idea to a business group that he joined, and which runs entrepreneurial self-help sessions. He says that he wants to make 10 of the portable bars in

order to be more cost-effective, and he wants the other participants in the group to help him with ideas to market the bar. But one of the group members questions whether Gavin should even pursue the idea because he already has too many balls in the air. He needs to prioritize.

Two months later, Gavin is conducting a two-day bartending course at the University of Guelph. His school is now making money, and everything is going well because he listened to the advice to focus on just a few projects. He has stopped putting energy into his portable bar for the moment, and he has begun delegating duties to others.

Gavin says he wants to make his business a great success. He is thinking big. He wants to earn enough money to buy a yacht with a helicopter pad on it.

Video Resource: "Flair Bartending," *Dreamers and Schemers* (November 8, 2006).

Questions for Discussion

1. What are the "Big 5" personality traits? How do you think Gavin MacMillan would score on each of these five traits? What might this imply for his success as an entrepreneur?

2. Do a little research and find out what the difference is between extrinsic motivation and intrinsic motivation. Do you think Gavin MacMillan is extrinsically or intrinsically motivated?

3. Gavin MacMillan says that he wants to eventually have a yacht with a helicopter pad on it. How does setting a goal like this motivate a person?

4. What recommendations would you have for Gavin MacMillan in the area of being more focused in his goal setting?

Clash of the Co-workers

Venture conducted a survey to determine workers' perceptions of the main causes of conflict in the workplace. Respondents were presented with a list of 10 common worker complaints and asked to list their top three. The top three vote-getters were: (1) people who talk too loud on the phone, (2) office gossip, and (3) co-workers who waste your time. *Venture* further examined the impact of office gossip, and also looked at the issues of co-workers who don't pull their weight, and clashes between older and younger workers.

Office Gossip

Office gossip can poison a workplace. A tanning salon owner who had worked hard to build her company encountered big problems when employees starting spreading rumours about each other. After one salon manager disciplined a worker, other workers began spreading rumours that the salon manager was incompetent. When the owner became aware of the large amount of gossip that was evident at the company, she called all employees into the head office and asked them to sign a contract that prohibited gossip. One behaviour that is prohibited is talking about a co-worker when that co-worker isn't present. A year after introducing the contract idea, the salon owner is getting calls from other companies asking about the policy.

Bob Summerhurst, an HR specialist, says that gossip occurs when bosses play favourites or when they don't communicate properly. Any information void will be filled with gossip, and that gossip is often negative. His solution is not a ban on gossip, but rather regular meetings of managers and employees.

Co-Workers Who Don't Pull Their Weight

Jerry Steinberg, a Vancouver teacher, says that workers with children are often treated as "special" and he thinks it's not fair. He says an extra burden is being borne by people like himself when they are asked to work a few extra hours a week to cover for parents who are tending to their children. The problem is worst during the holiday season because people with no children are asked to work holidays so that workers with children can spend time with their kids.

Steinberg is speaking up about his concerns. He has started a website called No Kidding where child-free members can vent their frustrations about the unfair treatment they are receiving at their place of work. But Steinberg says it's hard to stand up for yourself because you don't want to rock the boat or be a whiner. He recognizes that it sounds heartless to be unsympathetic to parents' wishes to spend time with their children. But he also observes that these people made a choice to have children, and they shouldn't expect to have an advantage because they made that choice. He is also unhappy about the extra benefits that parents get. He has a simple solution for that problem: Give each employee a certain dollar amount that they can spend on whatever benefits they want.

The Generation Gap

People in their 20s have generally grown up in an environment where their baby boomer parents gave them lots of things. Now those young people are entering the workforce, and they want more things: benefits, money, authority, and free time. And they want them right now.

Consider John and Ryan, who are recent college grads. They are part of a generation that is a problem for business. They feel that they work very hard, but they don't necessarily want to do what their predecessors did (like wearing a suit and tie to work, or working from 9 to 5). Mike Farrell, who researches attitudes of young people, notes that most young people are plugged in and well informed, and these are qualities that employers crave. Theresa Williams, who hires workers for the Halifax *Chronicle-Herald*, recognizes that young people today are different from their predecessors. For example, they don't seem grateful to be offered a job like people in her generation were. She tries to overcome the difficulties in recruiting young people by emphasizing the good working conditions at the *Chronicle-Herald*.

The way students look for jobs is also changing. The job fair approach is still used, but some companies find it doesn't attract the kind of employees they want. One company therefore came up with a gimmick: it posted a job competition on the internet, with the prize being a job for a year, a free apartment, and a trip home for the holidays. The two winners—John and Ryan—moved to Halifax. A year later, they moved out of their free apartment, but stayed on with the company. Now they are helping to design this year's job competition, and they're on board with "the old guys."

Video Resource: "Clash of the Co-workers," *Venture* (March 26, 2006).

Questions for Discussion

1. What are the various forms of employee behaviour that can be observed in organizations, and what is their impact on organizations? Identify the forms of employee behaviour evident in each of the three situations described above, and how they affected the organization in which they occurred.

2. What is the difference between management and leadership? What is the relevance of management and leadership in each of the situations described above?

3. What is the difference between the formal organization and the informal organization? How is the distinction relevant for each of the three situations described above?

4. Consider the following statement with respect to the first incident described above (office gossip): *"The grapevine carries a lot of inaccurate information that prevents employees from doing their jobs well. To overcome this problem, managers should provide accurate information through formal communication channels, and that will negate the need for the grapevine."* Do you agree or disagree with the statement? Explain your reasoning.

Managing Operations and Information

To be successful, Canadian business firms must produce high-quality goods and services, and they must achieve high levels of productivity when doing so. Businesses must also manage information and report their activity to various stakeholders. The opening cases in the chapters in this section describe the challenges and opportunities that exist when business firms manage operations and information.

Part Summary

Part 3, Managing Operations and Information, provides an overview of two key issues that are important to a firm's survival: the efficient production of high-quality goods and services, and understanding the basic principles of accounting.

- In **Chapter 10, Operations Management, Productivity, and Quality**, we examine how business firms manage the production of both physical goods and intangible services, and how they plan, organize, and control the production process. Included in this chapter is a discussion of the importance of both productivity and quality, and the various approaches that companies have taken to improve the productivity and quality of their output.

- In **Chapter 11, Understanding Accounting**, we examine the role of accountants in gathering, assembling, and presenting financial information about a company. We also look at the tools accountants use, the statements they prepare to report a firm's financial standing, and their use of ratio analysis to assess a firm's financial strength.

chapter 10

Operations Management, Productivity, and Quality

After reading this chapter, you will be able to:

LO-1 Explain the meaning of the term *production* (or *operations*) and describe the four kinds of *utility* it provides.

LO-2 Identify the characteristics that distinguish *service operations* from *goods production* and explain the main differences in the *service focus*.

LO-3 Describe two types of *operations processes*.

LO-4 Describe the factors involved in *operations planning* and *operations control*.

LO-5 Explain the connection between *productivity* and *quality*.

LO-6 Understand the concept of *total quality management* and describe nine tools that companies can use to achieve it.

LO-7 Explain how a *supply chain strategy* differs from traditional strategies for coordinating operations among businesses.

SCANLIFE

Too Many Recalls

During the last decade, Toyota has been extremely successful in the marketplace, and in 2009 it overtook General Motors as the largest car manufacturer in the world. Toyota has received lots of positive publicity about "The Toyota Way," which emphasizes efficient production methods, continuous improvement, and high-quality products. Toyota's production system was so impressive that executives from other automobile companies regularly toured Toyota's manufacturing plants in an attempt to discover Toyota's secret.

But trouble started for Toyota in mid-2009 when it reported the first operating loss in its history. Things got worse in November 2009, when Toyota announced that it was recalling more than 5 million of its cars because accelerator pedals were getting jammed in the driver's side car mat and causing the car to surge forward uncontrollably. That was bad enough, but in January 2010 Toyota announced another recall—this one involving 2.3 million vehicles (270 000 in Canada)—that also had to do with jamming accelerators. Production and sales were halted on eight of Toyota's most popular vehicles: the Corolla, RAV4, Camry, Avalon, Matrix, Highlander, Tundra, and Sequoia. These models account for 60 percent of Toyota sales in Canada. In February 2010, the highly publicized Prius was also recalled, and later Sienna vans.

These recalls created an uproar among Toyota owners, who were suddenly scared to drive their cars. Toyota worked frantically with its supplier, CTS Corp., to figure out a way to fix the problem. The solution was to insert a steel reinforcement bar in the accelerator pedal assembly, which reduced the tension that was

How Will This Help Me?

You will benefit in three ways by reading and understanding methods that managers use for managing production operations and improving quality: (1) as an *employee*, you'll get a clearer picture of why everyone in a business should be concerned about productivity and quality, and how your job depends on the goods and services your company provides; (2) as a *manager*, you'll understand that if companies want to remain competitive they must continually analyze their production methods so they can efficiently produce high-quality products and services; and (3) as a *consumer*, you'll gain an appreciation of the significant efforts that companies expend in order to efficiently produce high-quality goods and services for consumers.

causing the pedal to stick. CTS began producing the redesigned pedal in just a few days. Toyota admitted that the accelerator had a design flaw and that CTS was not at fault (CTS also produces accelerator pedals for Honda and Nissan and no problems have been found in those cars). In an effort to reassure the public, senior executives from the company went on TV to tell customers that they were going to fix the problem quickly and get redesigned accelerator pedals onto the recalled cars.

The recall was a public relations nightmare for Toyota because the company had always emphasized its reputation for producing high-quality automobiles. In 2009, Toyota had 10 cars rated as the best in 18 vehicle categories by J.D. Power and Associates, and many consumers in Canada and the U.S. did, in fact, have the perception that Toyota produced higher-quality cars than those produced by Ford, Chrysler, and GM. But this incident has changed those perceptions. In May 2010, a *Consumer Reports* survey found that Toyota lost the top spot in terms of customer loyalty (it was passed by both Ford and Honda). And in the 2010 Initial Quality Survey conducted by J.D. Power and Associates, Chrysler, Ford, and GM had fewer design-related problems and defects than their foreign competitors. That was the first time in nearly 50 years that domestic carmakers had beaten foreign rivals in quality.

A Canadian class-action lawsuit against Toyota and CTS Corp. claimed that Toyota knew (or should have known) that there were design defects in the electronic throttle control system. Toyota also faced a lawsuit in the U.S. because of 19 deaths caused by jammed accelerators. The law firm bringing the suit claimed that Toyota knew about the defect, but didn't do anything about it.

Toyota is not alone in having quality problems that require the recall of products. Consider what happened to Mattel, the company that makes the famous Barbie doll and many other popular toys. In the 1990s, Mattel began contracting out its manufacturing activities to companies in China in an effort to reduce costs and to remain competitive. Before long, however, the company had to recall some toys because of safety concerns. During the past few years, these recalls have increased substantially, and millions of toys that were made in China have since been recalled. Products like Barbie doll accessories and small cars—totalling 11.5 million pieces—were recalled in 2007 because they contained lead paint and small magnets that could be easily removed and possibly swallowed by children.

When analyzing why quality problems arise, it is important to understand the distinction between toy design and toy manufacturing. Toy *design* occurs at toy companies like Mattel. Design problems can be things like sharp edges on a toy that could lead to a cut, small detachable parts (balls and beads), long strings that could cause strangulation, and buttons (a choking hazard). In contrast, toy *manufacturing* is carried out by manufacturers (who are often overseas). Manufacturing problems include the use of substandard material (which causes parts to break), faulty electric circuits, and lead paint that is not approved. Manufacturing defects occur because of errors or negligence, and manufacturers can prevent defects with proper attention to quality control.

Mattel initially blamed the Chinese manufacturers for the quality problems, but when independent researchers looked at the situation and concluded that most of the problems were design problems, not manufacturing problems, Mattel had to backpedal. The Chinese manufacturer did use lead paint in the toys, but that did not relieve Mattel of the responsibility for its presence in the toys. Mattel needed to develop proper systems to engage more directly and closely with its overseas manufacturers.

Mattel does deserve credit for later publicly admitting that it was its design flaw that caused the problem, and for taking steps to ensure that all of the affected products were recalled. The company announced the recall by placing ads on high-traffic internet sites, created a website that clearly outlined the recall, and also provided consumers with downloadable application forms and paid shipping mailers. In addition, Mattel's CEO took responsibility for the recall, and in a prepared public apology stated that the company "takes full responsibility for these recalls and apologizes personally to you, the Chinese people, and all of our customers who received the toys." This type of public admission of guilt was unprecedented in recent history. For its efforts in ensuring that all the affected toys were safely removed from stores and homes, Mattel was named one of the "World's Most Ethical Companies" in 2009 by Ethisphere.

LO-1 What Does "Production" Mean Today?

Everywhere you go today, you encounter businesses that provide goods and services to their customers. You wake up in the morning, for example, to the sound of your favourite radio station. You stop at the corner store for a newspaper on your way to the bus stop, where you catch the bus to work or school. Your instructors, the bus driver, the clerk at the 7-Eleven store, and the morning radio announcer are all examples of people who work in **service operations**. They provide you with tangible and intangible service products, such as entertainment, transportation, education, and food preparation. Firms that make tangible products—radios, newspapers, buses, textbooks—are engaged in **goods production.**

Although the term *production* has historically referred to the production of physical goods, the concept as we now use it also includes services. Many of the things that we need or want, from health care to fast food, are produced by service operations. As a rule, service-sector managers focus less on equipment and technology than on the human element in operations. Why? Because success or failure may depend on provider–customer contact. Employees who deal directly with customers affect customer feelings about the service. As we will see, a key difference between production and service operations is the customer's level of involvement in the production process. But provider–customer contact is also important in the production of physical goods (see the boxed insert entitled "Open Source Automobile Manufacturing").

Although companies are typically classified as either goods producers or service providers, the distinction is often blurred. All businesses are service operations to some extent. When you think of General Electric, for example, you most likely think of appliances and jet engines. However, GE is not just a producer of physical goods. GE's "growth engines"—its most vibrant business activities—are service operations, including media and entertainment (NBC Universal), consumer and commercial finance, investment, transportation services, health care information, and real estate, which account for the majority of the company's revenues.[1]

The boxed insert entitled "The Unicycle Motorbike" describes one entrepreneur's efforts to produce a physical product that is environmentally friendly.

Creating Value through Production

To understand production processes, you need to understand the importance of products—both goods and services. Products provide businesses with economic results (profits, wages, goods purchased from other companies), and products provide customers with **utility** (want satisfaction).

By making a product available at a time when consumers want it, production creates **time utility**, as when a company turns out ornaments in time for Christmas. By making a product available in a place convenient for consumers, production creates **place utility**, as when a local department store creates a "Trim-a-Tree" section. By making a product that consumers can take pleasure in owning, production creates **ownership (possession) utility**, as when you take a box of ornaments home and decorate your tree. By turning raw materials into finished goods, production creates **form utility**, as when an

General Electric (GE) can be classified as both a goods producer (for example of the GE Wind Turbine) and a service provider (for example, of media and entertainment shows such as Saturday Night Live).

ornament maker combines glass, plastic, and other materials to create tree decorations.

Operations (or **production**) **management** is the systematic direction and control of the processes that transform resources into finished goods and services.

As Figure 10.1 shows, **production managers** must bring raw materials, equipment, and labour together under a production plan that effectively uses all the resources available in the production facility. As the demand for a product increases, managers must schedule and control work to produce the amount required. Meanwhile, they must control costs, quality levels, inventory, and plant and equipment.

LO-2 Differences between Service and Manufacturing Operations

Both service and manufacturing operations transform raw materials into finished products. In service operations, however, the raw materials, or inputs, are not things like glass or steel. Rather, they are people who have either unsatisfied needs or possessions needing care or alteration. In service operations, finished products or outputs are people with needs met and possessions serviced.

Thus, there is at least one obvious difference between service and manufacturing operations. Whereas goods are *produced*, services are *performed*. Service operations are

---

E-BUSINESS AND SOCIAL MEDIA SOLUTIONS

Open Source Automobile Manufacturing

In the early 1900s, Henry Ford revolutionized the automobile industry by applying the assembly-line approach to manufacturing, bringing prices down, and making cars more affordable for the masses. What would he think of the latest innovation in the industry: open-source design? Jay Rogers, of Local Motors, is building a community of engineers to design cars. Local Motors is a mass participation designer and niche product provider that has developed a unique solution for a very old industry.

Open-source is usually associated with new technology; it became popular in the 1990s with the creation of software programs like Linux (computer operating system) and Mozilla (Firefox), the popular web browser. The approach is gaining popularity in various areas as companies tap into the power of the internet and social media. *Crowdsourcing* involves posting challenges or questions in the form of an open call. This can be accomplished in an unsophisticated manner through general sites like wikiHow and Yahoo! Answers. But companies like Toronto-based Innovations Exchange have gone a step further and created a website to link companies with a community of marketers, engineers, and designers to build customer solutions. Organizations pay to post challenges and then individuals or teams tackle the problems. For example, two New York college buddies earned a prize (US$40 000) for creating a better yogourt container. Now, yogourt containers are one thing, but can this really work for car manufacturers?

Automobile manufacturing has traditionally been characterized by secrecy. Designs are tightly guarded until they are unveiled at major car shows. Local Motors is flipping this traditional approach around. It posts a challenge (competition rules and an ignition kit) that addresses a certain car component and invites engineering volunteers to upload sketches and ideas. Participants can submit their designs for assessment and feedback. The final designs are then posted in the "design garage" to be evaluated and voted on by the community and the company. Prizes are awarded to the winners. Once there is enough support for a model, the car is manufactured in limited batches.

According to Jay Rogers, this unique development approach reduces his breakeven point to as little as 200 cars per model. Inclusiveness is part of the DNA of this company, and activity does not end with the design. Car owners can be involved in the actual manufacturing process (up to 60 hours) under the supervision of staff. This approach appeals to the typical car enthusiast, who is likely to offer opinions on the site. Local Motors aims to revolutionize the industry by using radical design, production, and engineering concepts. It's off to a good start.

Critical Thinking Questions

1. What do you think of this approach to car manufacturing and design?
2. Do you believe that this approach can work for major manufacturers like GM or Honda?

Figure 10.1
The transformation system.

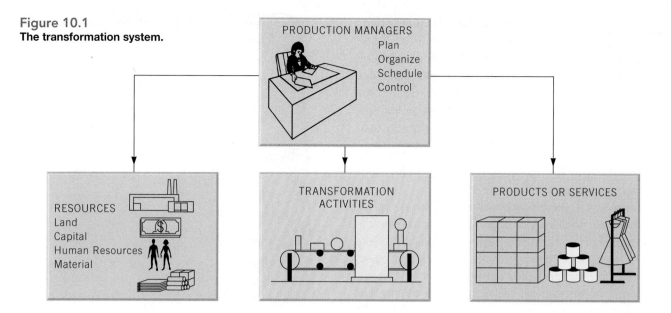

ENTREPRENEURSHIP AND NEW VENTURES

The Unicycle Motorbike

The Uno, touted as the world's first unicycle motorbike, was invented by Ben Gulak, a 19-year-old student from Milton, Ontario. Eye-catching because of its space-age design and reminiscent of something you might have seen on the once-popular TV cartoon show *The Jetsons,* the Uno is an electric-powered motorcycle that uses gyroscope technology. It's kind of like the Segway (an electric scooter) in that it's controlled completely through body movements.

Gulak made a conscious decision to ensure his invention provided more than just transportation. It had to possess the cool factor because "if something doesn't look cool, people just won't be interested." Gulak got the idea for the bike while on a family vacation in China in 2006. Struck by the unbelievable pollution he saw there, he decided to develop an environmentally friendly alternative vehicle for densely populated urban centres. A test run of a prototype resulted in a chipped kneecap, but he didn't let that slow him down. The gyro control system needed some fine-tuning so that the machine would move more smoothly. He also had a custom motorcycle manufacturer build the body parts out of foam and fibreglass, based on Gulak's drawings. The Uno can travel up to 15 m.p.h., but Gulak is aiming to reach 40 m.p.h. It can run for about 2.5 hours on a single charge.

So far, Gulak's parents have bankrolled his research efforts to the tune of $50 000. But that money is now gone, and the bike is not quite ready for production. So, how does a 19-year-old get the money to advance his prototype development? He applies to CBC's *Dragon's Den,* of course! In November 2008, Gulak wowed the dragons with his Uno prototype, and on-air he landed a $1.25 million investment to be used for research purposes. In exchange, the dragons were given a 20 percent stake in his business. Since the show, however, four of the dragons have reneged on their offers and now dragon Brett Wilson is the only investor remaining. According to Wilson, "Now it's just me and I'm in for $250 000." However, Gulak has not let this setback dampen his enthusiasm. "I really believe in this product and would really like to see it to production," he says.

Popular Science magazine listed the Uno among the top ten inventions for 2008. And, a profile on the Discovery Channel and a request to do an appearance on the *Tonight Show* in the U.S. haven't been bad for publicity either. Who knows? With the right combination of engineering and business skills, Gulak just might be able to make this machine fly someday.

Critical Thinking Question

1. Discuss the concepts of production value, transformation, and operations planning as they apply now, or may in the future, to the production of Gulak's Uno. Could any of these factors be reasons why the dragons backed out of the deal?

OPERATIONS PROCESS A set of methods and technologies used in the production of a good or a service.

more complicated than goods production in four aspects: (1) interacting with consumers, (2) the intangible and unstorable nature of some services, (3) the customer's presence in the process, and (4) service quality considerations.

Interacting with Consumers Manufacturing operations emphasize outcomes in terms of physical goods—for example, a new jacket. But the products of most *service* operations are really combinations of goods and services—both making a pizza *and* delivering (serving) it. Service workers need different skills. For example, gas company employees may need interpersonal skills to calm frightened customers who have reported gas leaks. Thus, the job includes more than just repairing pipes. In contrast, factory workers who install gas pipes in manufactured homes without any customer contact don't need such skills.

Services Can Be Intangible and Unstorable Often, services can't be touched, tasted, smelled, or seen, but they're still there. An important satisfier for customers, therefore, is the *intangible* value they receive in the form of pleasure, gratification, or a feeling of safety. For example, when you hire an attorney, you purchase not only the intangible quality of legal expertise but also the equally intangible reassurance that help is at hand.

Many services—such as trash collection, transportation, child care, and house cleaning—can't be produced ahead of time and then stored for high-demand periods. If a service isn't used when available, it's usually wasted. Services, then, are typically unstorable.

The Customer's Presence in the Operations Process Because service operations transform customers or their possessions, the customer is often present in the operations process. To get a haircut, for example, most of us have to go to the barbershop or hair salon. As physical participants in the operations process, consumers can affect it. As a customer, you expect the salon to be conveniently located (place utility), to be open for business at convenient times (time utility), to provide safe and comfortable facilities, and to offer quality grooming (form utility) at reasonable prices (value for money spent). Accordingly, the manager sets hours of operation, available services, and an appropriate number of employees to meet customer requirements. But what happens if a customer, scheduled to receive a haircut, also asks for additional services, such as highlights or a shave, when he or she arrives? In this case, the service provider must balance customer satisfaction with a tight schedule. High customer contact has the potential to significantly affect the process.

The growth of e-commerce has introduced a "virtual presence" of the customer, as opposed to a physical

The hair styling service being provided to this customer illustrates the three key features of service operations: *intangibility* (customer pleasure or satisfaction with the service), *customization* (the service each person gets is customized for them), and *unstorability* (the service cannot be produced ahead of time).

presence. Consumers interact electronically, in real time, with sellers, collecting information about product features, delivery availability, and after-sales service. Many companies have invited "the virtual customer" into their service systems by building customer-communications relationships. For example, the online travel agency Expedia.ca responds to your personalized profile with a welcome email letter, presents you with a tailor-made webpage the next time you sign in, offers chat rooms in which you can compare notes with other customers, and notifies you of upcoming special travel opportunities.

Service Quality Considerations Consumers use different measures to judge services and goods because services include intangibles, not just physical objects. Most service managers know that quality of work and quality of service are not necessarily the same thing. Your car, for example, may have been flawlessly repaired (quality of work), but you'll probably be unhappy with the service if you're forced to pick it up a day later than promised (quality of service).

LO-3 Operations Processes

An **operations process** is a set of methods and technologies used in the production of a good or a service. At the most fundamental level, operations processes for the production of physical products are either *make-to-order* (producing custom-designed products for special order) or *make-to-stock* (producing standard items in large quantities for consumers in general). We can classify services according to the *extent of customer contact* required.

Goods-Producing Processes Operations processes in manufacturing firms can be classified based on the kind of *transformation technology* that is used, or based on whether the operations process combines resources or breaks them into component parts.

Types of Transformation Technologies Manufacturers use the following types of transformation technologies to turn raw materials into finished goods:

- In *chemical processes,* raw materials are chemically altered. Such techniques are common in the aluminum, steel, fertilizer, petroleum, and paint industries.
- *Fabrication processes* mechanically alter the basic shape or form of a product. Fabrication occurs in the metal forming, woodworking, and textile industries.
- *Assembly processes* put together various components. These techniques are common in the electronics, appliance, and automotive industries.
- In *transport processes,* goods acquire place utility by being moved from one location to another. For example, bicycles are routinely moved by trucks from manufacturing plants to consumers through warehouses and discount stores.
- *Clerical processes* transform information. Combining data on employee absences and machine breakdowns into a productivity report is a clerical process. So is compiling inventory reports at a retail outlet.

Analytic versus Synthetic Processes An **analytic process** breaks down basic resources into their component parts. For example, Rio Tinto Alcan manufactures aluminum by extracting it from an ore called bauxite. The reverse approach, a **synthetic process**, combines a number of raw materials to produce a finished product such as fertilizer or paint.

Service-Producing Processes

One useful way of classifying services is to determine whether a given service can be provided without the customer being part of the production system.

High-Contact Processes Think for a moment about the service provided by your local public transit system. When you purchase transportation, you must board a bus or train, so public transit is a **high-contact system**. For

ANALYTIC PROCESS Any production process in which resources are broken down into their component parts.

SYNTHETIC PROCESS Any production process in which resources are combined.

HIGH-CONTACT SYSTEM A system in which the service cannot be provided without the customer being physically in the system (e.g., transit systems).

As these photos show, various industries use different transformation techniques: chemical (top left), fabrication (top centre), assembly (top right), transport (bottom left), and clerical (bottom right).

this reason, transit managers must worry about the cleanliness of the trains and buses and the appearance of the stations. This is usually not the case in low-contact systems. Large industrial concerns that ship coal in freight trains, for example, are generally not concerned with the atmosphere inside those trains. Dental and medical services, hair salons, and guided tours are also high-contact systems.

Low-Contact Processes Consider the cheque-processing operations at your bank. Workers sort the cheques that have been cashed that day and dispatch them to the banks on which they were drawn. This operation is a **low-contact system** because customers are not in contact with the bank while the service is performed. They receive the service—their funds are transferred to cover their cheques—without ever setting foot in the cheque-processing centre. Gas and electric utilities, auto repair shops, and lawn care services are also low-contact systems.

Business Strategy as the Driver of Operations

There is no one standard way for doing production. Rather, it is a flexible activity that can be moulded into many shapes to give quite different capabilities for different purposes. How, then, do companies go about selecting the kind of production that is best for them? Its design is best driven from above by the firm's business strategy.

In this section we present examples of four firms—two in goods production and two in services—that have contrasting business strategies and, as we shall see, have chosen different operations capabilities. All four firms are successful, but they've taken quite different operations paths to get there. As shown in Table 10.1, each company has identified a business strategy that it can use for attracting customers in its industry. For Toyota, *quality*

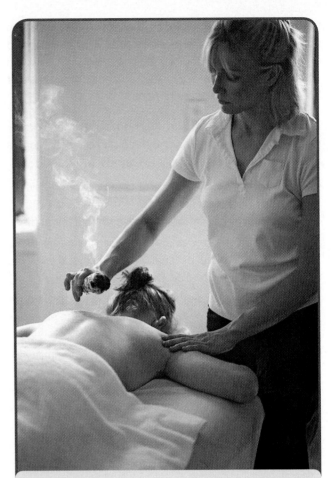

In a high-contact service, the customer must be present in the operations process.

was chosen as the strategy for competing in selling cars. The U.S.-based Save-A-Lot grocery stores, in contrast to others in the grocery industry, offer customers *lower prices*. The *flexibility* strategy at 3M emphasizes new product development in an ever-changing line of products for home and office. FedEx captures the overnight delivery market by emphasizing delivery *dependability*.

Business Strategy Determines Operations Capabilities Successful firms design their operations to support the company's business strategy.[2] In other words,

Table 10.1 **Business Strategies That Win Customers for Four Companies**		
Company	**Strategy for Attracting Customers**	**What the Company Does to Implement Its Strategy**
Toyota	Quality	Cars perform reliably, have an appealing fit-and-finish, and consistently meet or exceed customer expectations at a competitive price
Save-A-Lot	Low Price	Foods and everyday items offered at savings up to 40 percent less than conventional food chains
3M	Flexibility	Innovation, with more than 55 000 products in a constantly changing line of convenience items for home and office
FedEx	Dependability	Every delivery is fast and on time, as promised

production operations are adjusted to support the firms' target markets. Since the four firms have different business strategies, we should expect to see differences in their operations. The top-priority **operations capability (production capability)**—the activity or process that production must do especially well, with high proficiency—is listed for each firm in Table 10.2, along with key operations characteristics for implementing that capability. Each company's operations capability matches up with its business strategy so that the firm's activities—from top to bottom—are focused in a particular direction.

As you can see in Table 10.2, Toyota's top priority is quality, so its operations—inputs, transformation activities, and outputs—are devoted first and foremost to quality. All production processes, equipment, and training are designed to build better cars. The entire culture supports a quality emphasis among employees, suppliers, and dealerships. As noted in the opening case, Toyota had a significant setback with respect to quality in 2010, but its problems will likely motivate its managers to redouble their efforts to produce high-quality cars. If Toyota had chosen to compete as the low-price car in the industry, as some successful car companies do, then a cost-minimization focus would have been appropriate, and Toyota's operations would have a different form.

Expanding into Additional Capabilities Over time, excellent firms learn how to achieve more than just one competence. For example, in addition to dependability, FedEx is noted for world-class service quality and cost containment, too. But in its earlier years, its primary and distinguishing capability was dependability, the foundation upon which future success was built.

LO-4 Operations Planning

Managers from many departments contribute to the firm's decisions about operations management. As Figure 10.2 shows, however, no matter how many decision makers are involved, the process can be described as a series of logical steps. The success of any firm depends on the final result of this logical sequence of decisions.

The business plan and forecasts developed by top managers guide operations planning. The business plan outlines goals and objectives, including the specific goods and services that the firm will offer. Managers also develop

Table 10.2 Operations Capabilities and Characteristics for Four Companies

Operations Capability	Key Operations Characteristics
Quality (Toyota)	▪ High-quality standards for materials suppliers
	▪ Just-in-time materials flow for lean manufacturing
	▪ Specialized, automated equipment for consistent product build-up
	▪ Operations personnel are experts on continuous improvement of product, work methods, and materials
Low Cost (Save-A-Lot)	▪ Avoids excessive overhead and costly inventory (no floral departments, sushi bars, or banks that drive up costs)
	▪ Limited assortment of products, staples, in one size only for low-cost restocking, lower inventories, and less paperwork
	▪ Many locations; small stores—less than half the size of conventional grocery stores—for low construction and maintenance costs
	▪ Reduces labour and shelving costs by receiving and selling merchandise out of custom shipping cartons
Flexibility (3M)	▪ Maintains some excess (expensive) production capacity available for fast start on new products
	▪ Adaptable equipment/facilities for production changeovers from old to new products
	▪ Hires operations personnel who thrive on change
	▪ Many medium- to small-sized facilities in diverse locations, which enhances creativity
Dependability (FedEx)	▪ Customer automation: uses electronic and online tools with customers to shorten shipping time
	▪ Wireless information system for package scanning by courier, updating of package movement, and package tracking by customer
	▪ Maintains a company air force, global weather forecasting centre, and ground transportation for pickup and delivery, with backup vehicles for emergencies
	▪ Each of 30 automated regional distribution hubs processes up to 45 000 packages per hour for next-day deliveries

long-range production plans through **forecasts** of future demand for both new and existing products. Covering a period of two to five years, the production plan specifies the number of plants or service facilities and the amount of labour, equipment, transportation, and storage that will be needed to meet demand. It also specifies how resources will be obtained. There are five main categories of operations planning: *capacity, location, layout, quality,* and *methods planning.*

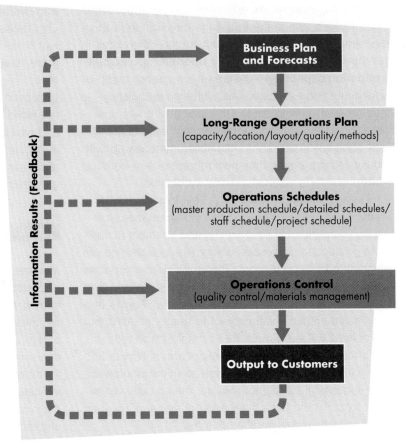

Figure 10.2
Operations planning and control.

Capacity Planning

The amount of a product that a company can produce under normal working conditions is its **capacity**. A firm's capacity depends on how many people it employs and the number and size of its facilities.

Capacity Planning for Producing Goods Capacity planning means ensuring that a firm's capacity just *slightly* exceeds the normal demand for its product. If capacity is too small to meet demand, the company must turn away customers, and it will forgo profit opportunities. If capacity is too large, the firm wastes money by having a plant that is too large and has too many employees.

Capacity Planning for Producing Services In low-contact systems, capacity should be set at the level of *average demand.* Orders that arrive faster than expected can be set aside in a "to be done" file and processed later during a slower period. In high-contact systems, managers must plan capacity to meet *peak demand.* A supermarket, for instance, has far more cash registers than it needs on an average day. But on a Saturday morning or during the three days before Christmas, all registers will be running at full speed. By introducing self-service check-in machines and manned "bag drop" stations, Alaska Airlines doubled its capacity, halved its staffing needs, and cut costs, all the while speeding travellers through the check-in process.[3]

Location Planning

Because the location of a factory, office, or store affects its production costs and flexibility, sound location planning is crucial. Depending on the site of its facility, a company should be capable of producing a low-cost product or may find itself at an extreme cost disadvantage relative to its competitors.

Location Planning for Producing Goods In goods-producing operations, location decisions are influenced by proximity to raw materials and markets, availability of labour, energy and transportation costs, local regulations and taxes, and community living conditions. Slovakia, for example, is fast becoming the "Detroit" of Europe. With an existing Volkswagen plant producing 850 000 cars a year, two more giant automakers—Peugeot Citroën (French) and Hyundai Motor Company (Korean)—opened new plants in 2006. Slovakia has a good supply of skilled workers, a good work ethic, wages below those of the surrounding countries, a good railroad system, and nearby access to the Danube River.[4]

Location Planning for Producing Services Low-contact services can be located near resource supplies, labour, or transportation outlets. For example, the typical Walmart distribution centre is located near the hundreds of Walmart stores it supplies, not near the companies that supply the distribution centre. Distribution managers regard Walmart stores as their customers. To better serve them, distribution centres are located so that truckloads of merchandise flow quickly to the stores.

On the other hand, high-contact services must locate near the customers who are a part of the system. Accordingly, fast-food restaurants such as Taco Bell, McDonald's, and Burger King have begun moving into non-traditional locations with high traffic—dormitories, hospital cafeterias, museums, and shopping malls.

Layout Planning

Once a site has been selected, managers must decide on plant layout. Layout of machinery, equipment, and supplies determines whether a company can respond quickly and efficiently to customer requests for more and different products, or whether it will find itself unable to match competitors' production speed or convenience of service.

Layout Planning for Producing Goods In facilities that produce goods, layout must be planned for three types of space:

1. *Productive facilities:* workstations and equipment for transforming raw materials
2. *Non-productive facilities:* storage and maintenance areas
3. *Support facilities:* offices, restrooms, parking lots, cafeterias, and so forth

When producing goods, alternatives for layout planning include *process, cellular,* and *product layouts.*

Process Layouts In a **process layout**, which is well suited to *job shops* specializing in custom work, equipment and people are grouped according to function. In a woodworking shop, for example, machines cut the wood in an area devoted to sawing, sanding occurs in a dedicated area, and jobs that need painting are taken to a dust-free area where all the painting equipment is located. The various tasks are each performed in specialized locations.

The job shop produces many one-of-a-kind products, and each product requires different kinds of work (see Figure 10.3a). Whereas Product X needs only three production steps prior to packaging, Product Y needs four. Machine shops, custom bakeries, and dry cleaning shops often feature process layouts.

Cellular Layouts The **cellular layout** is used when a group of similar products follows a fixed flow path. A

clothing manufacturer, for example, may establish a cell, or designated area, dedicated to making a family of pockets—for example, pockets for shirts, coats, blouses, trousers, and slacks. Within the cell, various types of equipment (e.g., for cutting, trimming, and sewing) are arranged close together in the appropriate sequence. Figure 10.3b shows two production cells, one each for Products X and Y, while all other smaller-volume products are produced elsewhere in the plant.

Product Layouts In a **product layout**, equipment and people are set up to produce one type of product in a fixed sequence of steps that are arranged according to its production requirements (see Figure 10.3c). Product layouts are efficient for producing large volumes of product quickly and often use **assembly lines**. Automobile, food processing, and television assembly plants use product layouts. In an attempt to improve productivity even more, many companies have introduced **lean manufacturing**, which emphasizes the elimination of all forms of waste, including overproduction, excess inventory, and wasted motions. In spite of its recent quality problems, Toyota is the recognized leader in lean manufacturing. Bombardier Aerospace (Montreal) and St. Joseph's Healthcare (Hamilton) are two Canadian organizations that have adopted Toyota's ideas about lean manufacturing.[5] Louis Vuitton, the maker of luxury handbags, has adopted lean manufacturing in order to quickly respond to changes in customer preferences.[6]

Other Developments in Layout Flexibility With a **flexible manufacturing system (FMS)**, a single factory can produce a wide variety of products. Automobile manufacturers, for example, now build several models of cars using the same basic "platform" (the underbody of the car). Nissan, Toyota, and Honda make the majority of their cars using FMS, and North American carmakers are now rapidly adopting the strategy.[7] The Oakville,

PROCESS LAYOUT
A way of organizing production activities such that equipment and people are grouped together according to their function.

CELLULAR LAYOUT
Used to produce goods when families of products can follow similar flow paths.

PRODUCT LAYOUT
A way of organizing production activities such that equipment and people are set up to produce only one type of good.

ASSEMBLY LINE
A type of product layout in which a partially finished product moves through a plant on a conveyor belt or other equipment.

LEAN MANUFACTURING A system designed for smooth production flows that avoid inefficiencies, eliminate unnecessary inventories, and continuously improve production processes.

FLEXIBLE MANUFACTURING SYSTEM (FMS)
A production system that allows a single factory to produce small batches of different goods on the same production line.

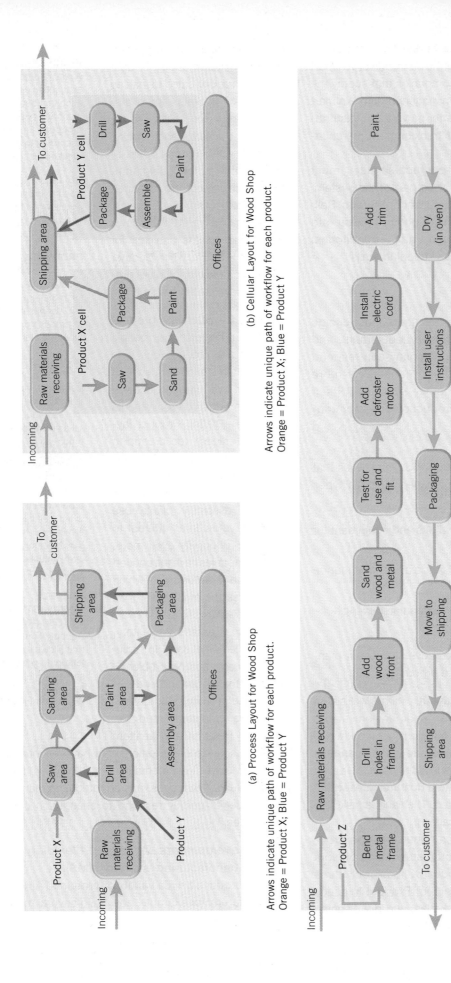

Figure 10.3
Layouts for producing goods.

(a) Process Layout for Wood Shop

Arrows indicate unique path of workflow for each product.
Orange = Product X; Blue = Product Y

(b) Cellular Layout for Wood Shop

Arrows indicate unique path of workflow for each product.
Orange = Product X; Blue = Product Y

(c) Product Layout—Assembly Line

Arrows indicate the fixed path of workflow for all units of Product Z

Ontario, Ford plant is the first flexible assembly plant in Canada.[8]

Some companies have experimented with so-called **soft manufacturing**—reducing huge FMS operations to smaller, more manageable groups of machines. Automation is less likely to fail when relegated to jobs it does best, while human workers perform the assembly-line jobs that require dexterity and decision making. Both are supported by networks of computers programmed to assist in all sorts of tasks.

The very latest development is the **movable factory**. Because FMS is so expensive, some developing countries with lots of labour but little capital are buying up equipment from industrialized countries that is still relatively modern and then using it to produce new and untested products in their own country. For example, a used press from the Buffalo-Niagara region, which is capable of shaping steel with its 14 000 tonnes of pressure per square inch, will be used to manufacture the internal workings of new Chinese nuclear power plants.[9]

Layout Planning for Services In a low-contact system like the mail-processing facility at UPS or FedEx, the system looks very much like a product layout in a factory. Machines and people are arranged in the order in which they are used in the mass processing of mail. In contrast, FedEx Kinko's Office and Print Centers use process layouts for diverse custom jobs. Specific functions such as photocopying, computing, binding, photography, and laminating are each performed in specialized areas of the store.

High-contact service systems are arranged to meet customer needs and expectations. For example, a cafeteria focuses both layout and services on the groups that constitute its primary market—families and elderly people. As shown in Figure 10.4, families enter to find an array of highchairs and rolling baby beds that make it convenient to wheel children through the line. Meanwhile, servers are willing to carry trays for elderly people and for those pushing strollers.

Quality Planning

In planning production systems and facilities, managers must keep in mind the firm's quality goals.[10] Thus any complete production plan includes systems for ensuring that goods are produced to meet the firm's quality standards. The issues of productivity and quality are discussed in more detail later in this chapter.

Methods Planning

In designing production systems, managers must clearly identify all production steps and the specific methods for performing them. They can then work to reduce waste, inefficiency, and poor performance by examining procedures on a step-by-step basis, an approach sometimes called *methods improvement.*

Methods Improvements in Goods Improvement of production for goods begins when a manager documents the current method using a diagram called the *process flow chart*. The chart identifies the sequence of production activities, movements of materials, and work performed at each stage as the product flows through production. The flow can then be analyzed to identify wasteful activities, sources of delay in production flows, and other inefficiencies.

Methods Improvements in Services Similar procedures are useful in designing and evaluating low-contact service systems. At a bank, for example, the cash-management

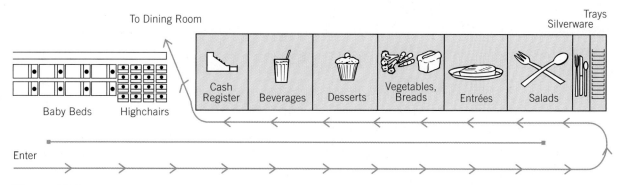

Figure 10.4
Layout of a typical Piccadilly cafeteria.

**MASTER PRODUC-
TION SCHEDULE**
Schedule showing
which products will be
produced, when pro-
duction will take place,
and what resources
will be used.

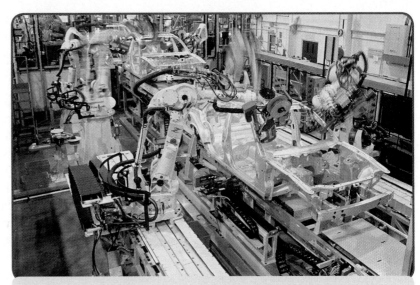

For its new XJ sedan, Jaguar wanted to use an aluminum unibody construction because it is lighter and more efficient than steel. But spot welding weakens aluminum, so at its factory in Castle Bromich in the United Kingdom, engineers built an assembly line of 88 robots equipped with tools to drive more than 3,000 rivets into each car.

unit collects accounts receivable for corporate clients; the sooner cheques are collected and deposited, the sooner the client begins collecting interest.In high-contact services, the demands of systems analysis are somewhat different. Here, the steps in the process must be analyzed to see where improvements can be made. Consider the traditional checkout method at hotels. The process flowchart in Figure 10.5 shows five stages of customer activities. A more efficient checkout method eliminates steps 1, 2, 3A, and 5. Customers now scan their bills on the TV in their rooms before departure. If the bill is correct, no further checkout is required, and the hotel submits the charges against the credit card the customer showed at check-in.

Operations Scheduling

Once plans identify the necessary resources and how to use those resources to reach a firm's quantity and quality goals, managers must develop timetables for acquiring the resources. This aspect of operations is called *scheduling*.

Scheduling Goods Operations

A **master production schedule** shows which products will be produced, when production will occur, and what resources will be used during the scheduled time period. Consider the case of Logan Aluminum Inc., which produces coils of aluminum that its main customers, Atlantic Richfield and Alcan Aluminum, use to produce aluminum cans. Logan's master schedule extends out to 60 weeks and shows which types of coils, and how many of each, will be made during each week.

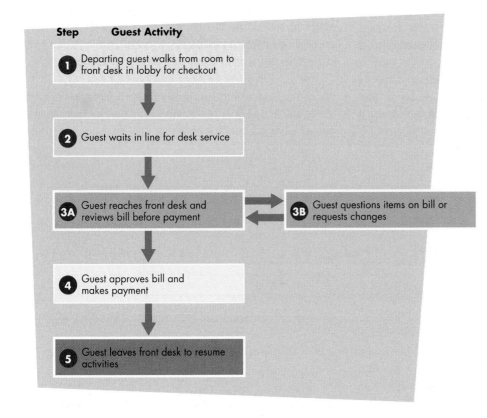

Step	Guest Activity
1	Departing guest walks from room to front desk in lobby for checkout
2	Guest waits in line for desk service
3A	Guest reaches front desk and reviews bill before payment
3B	Guest questions items on bill or requests changes
4	Guest approves bill and makes payment
5	Guest leaves front desk to resume activities

Figure 10.5
Flowchart of traditional guest checkout.

This information is not complete, however. For example, manufacturing personnel must also know on which days each type of coil will be run. Machine start-up and stop times must be assigned, and employees must be given scheduled work assignments. Short-term *detailed schedules* answer questions like these on a daily or weekly basis. These schedules use incoming orders and weekly sales forecasts to determine what size and variety of coils to make within a specified time period.

Scheduling Service Operations

In low-contact services, *work scheduling* may be based either on the desired completion date or on the time of order arrival. For example, several cars may be scheduled for repairs at a local garage. Thus, if your car is not scheduled for work until 3:30 p.m., it may sit idle for several hours even if it was the first to be dropped off. In such businesses, reservation and appointment systems can help to smooth demand.

In high-contact services, the customer is part of the system and must be accommodated. Thus, precise scheduling of services may not be possible in high-contact systems. For example, if a hospital emergency room is overloaded, patients cannot be asked to make an appointment and come back later.

LO-5 Operations Control

Operations control requires production managers to monitor production performance by comparing results with detailed plans and schedules. If schedules or quality standards are not met, these managers must take corrective action. **Follow-up**—checking to ensure that production decisions are being implemented—is an essential and ongoing facet of operations control. Operations control involves *materials management* and *production process control.* Both activities ensure that schedules are met and that production goals are fulfilled, both in quantity and in quality.

Materials Management

Materials management involves planning, organizing, and controlling the flow of materials. Even before production starts, materials management focuses on product design by emphasizing materials **standardization**—the use, where possible, of standard and uniform components rather than new or different components. Standardization simplifies paperwork, reduces storage requirements, eliminates unnecessary material flows, and saves money by reducing the number of different parts that are needed. The five major areas of materials management are *transportation, warehousing, inventory*

control, supplier selection, and *purchasing.*

- **Transportation** includes the means of transporting resources to the company and finished goods to buyers.
- **Warehousing** is the storage of both incoming materials for production and finished goods for physical distribution to customers.
- **Inventory control** includes the receiving, storing, handling, and counting of all raw materials, partly finished goods, and finished goods. It ensures that enough material inventories are available to meet production schedules.
- **Supplier selection** means finding and choosing suppliers of services and materials to buy from. It includes evaluating potential suppliers, negotiating terms of service, and maintaining positive buyer–seller relationships.
- **Purchasing** is the acquisition of all the raw materials and services that a company needs to produce its products; most large firms have purchasing departments to buy proper materials in the amounts needed. The boxed insert entitled "For the Greener Good" describes the purchasing strategies of Walmart as it tries to reduce its environmental footprint.

Production Process Control

Tools for process control include *worker training, just-in-time production systems, material requirements planning,* and *quality control.*

Worker Training When providing services, employees are both the producers of the product and the salespeople.

Thus, human relations skills are vital for anyone who has contact with the public. Managers realize how easily service employees with poor attitudes can reduce sales. Conversely, the right attitude is a powerful sales tool. Disney World has a team of sweepers constantly at work picking up bits of trash as soon as they fall to the ground. When visitors have questions about directions or time, they often ask one of the sweepers. Because their responses affect visitors' overall impressions of Disney World, sweepers are trained to respond in appropriate ways. Their work is evaluated and rewarded based on strict performance appraisal standards.[11]

Just-in-Time Production Systems To minimize manufacturing inventory costs, many companies use **just-in-time (JIT) production systems**. JIT brings together all the needed materials and parts at the precise moment they are required for each production stage, not before. JIT reduces inventory of goods in process to practically nothing, and saves money by replacing stop-and-go production with smooth movement. Once smooth movements become the norm, disruptions become more visible and thus are resolved more quickly. At Mount Sinai Hospital in Toronto, individual suppliers no longer go to the hospital to deliver the items. Rather, all suppliers deliver their products to Livingston Healthcare Services Inc., which stores these items and fills Mount Sinai's order once each day. Mount Sinai no longer keeps any inventory.[12] Sobeys, the grocery chain, has invested in more efficient inventory management that has allowed it to reduce the size of storage rooms

THE GREENING OF BUSINESS

For the Greener Good

When retail giant Walmart decided to make changes to the way it conducts business in an effort to be more environmentally friendly, critics and supporters alike could not have fathomed the effect it would have on their suppliers, employees, and consumers. In 2005, Walmart unveiled an environmental plan that was designed to boost energy efficiency, cut down on waste, and reduce greenhouse gases. The decision to be environmentally friendly throws the burden back onto their suppliers, because Walmart closely monitors its overseas suppliers to make sure they meet social and environmental standards. More specifically, Walmart announced it would evaluate the suppliers not only on price but also on the environmental sustainability of their packaging.

The result? Walmart saw unprecedented amounts of innovation in packaging in the first six months of 2007, more than in the previous five years combined. The changes have also impacted Walmart's bottom line by lowering shipping costs and reducing waste, which in turn reduces expenses. Walmart says its goal is to reduce packaging by 5 percent by 2013. If everyone complies, this is a very attainable target.

It might seem that so much change so fast would be disruptive to operations. But it was business as usual. Walmart used the same *tactics* it uses to show its commitment to low prices, but the environmental *message* was different. Skeptics have been pleasantly surprised by the shift in focus, but some are concerned about the success and sustainability of Walmart's suppliers. Historically, Walmart's aggressive approach has been criticized for pushing some companies toward drastic changes in the name of cost savings, and in some cases, for driving companies out of business. Even with all this negative publicity, critics now concede that Walmart has the potential to use its power for good by persuading suppliers to make the necessary changes that will reduce greenhouse gas emissions.

Making changes to packaging could, in some cases, lead to production changes in the product itself. Walmart believes that there are financial incentives for every company that makes environmentally friendly changes to its production processes.

Critical Thinking Questions

1. Walmart has mandated very strict policies regarding packaging. Explain the consequences of these policies for Walmart's suppliers.
2. As a consumer, would you make a conscious choice to shop only at stores that sell environmentally friendly products? Why or why not?

Just-in-time (JIT) production, a type of lean manufacturing, brings together all needed materials at the precise moment they are required for each stage in the production process.

by 10 percent because products now move more quickly to the shelves.[13]

Material Requirements Planning **Material requirements planning (MRP)** uses a **bill of materials** that is basically a "recipe" for the finished product. It specifies the necessary raw materials and components (ingredients), the order in which they should be combined (directions), and the quantity of each ingredient needed to make one "batch" of the product (say, 2000 finished telephones). The recipe is fed into a computer that controls inventory and schedules each stage of production. The result is fewer early arrivals, less frequent stock shortages, and lower storage costs.

Manufacturing resource planning (also called **MRP II**), is an advanced version of MRP that ties together all parts of the organization into the company's production activities. For example, MRP inventory and production schedules are translated into cost requirements for the financial management department and personnel requirements for the human resources department. Information on capacity availability for new-customer orders goes to the marketing department.

Quality Control **Quality control** refers to the management of the production process so as to manufacture goods or supply services that meet specific quality standards. McDonald's, for example, is a pioneer in quality control in the restaurant industry. The company oversees everything from the farming of potatoes for French fries to the packing of meat for Big Macs. Quality-assurance staffers even check standards for ketchup sweetness and French fry length. We discuss quality control in more detail in the following section, where we focus on the connection between productivity and quality.

The Productivity–Quality Connection

Productivity measures how much is produced relative to the resources used to produce it. By using resources more efficiently, the quantity of output will be greater for a given amount of input. But unless the resulting goods and services are of satisfactory quality, consumers will not want them. **Quality**, then, means fitness for use—offering features that consumers want.

Meeting the Productivity Challenge

A nation's productivity determines how large a piece of the global economic resource pie it gets. A country with more resources has more wealth to divide among its citizens. A country whose productivity fails to increase as rapidly as that of other countries will see its people's standard of living fall relative to the rest of the world.

Measuring Productivity How do we know how productive a country is? Most countries use **labour productivity** to measure their level of productivity:

$$\text{labour productivity of a country} = \frac{\text{gross domestic product}}{\text{total number of workers}}$$

MATERIAL REQUIREMENTS PLANNING (MRP) A method of inventory control in which a computerized bill of materials is used to estimate production needs so that resources are acquired and put into production only as needed.

BILL OF MATERIALS Production control tool that specifies the necessary ingredients of a product, the order in which they should be combined, and how many of each are needed to make one batch.

MANUFACTURING RESOURCE PLANNING (MRP II) An advanced version of MRP that ties together all parts of the organization into the company's production activities.

QUALITY CONTROL The management of the production process so as to manufacture goods or supply services that meet specific quality standards.

QUALITY A product's fitness for use in terms of offering the features that consumers want.

LABOUR PRODUCTIVITY Partial productivity ratio calculated by dividing gross domestic product by total number of workers.

The focus on labour, rather than on other resources (such as capital or energy), is popular because most countries keep records on employment and hours worked.

Productivity among Global Competitors Productivity levels vary widely from country to country. A 2008 study of the productivity of 35 countries, which was carried out by the Organisation for Economic Co-operation and Development (OECD), showed that productivity was highest in Luxembourg and lowest in Chile (see Figure 10.6). Canada ranked fifteenth.[14]

Back in 1960, Canada ranked third among the 20 countries that were then part of the OECD, but Canada now ranks only seventeenth among the 30 countries that are currently part of the OECD. Since the late 1980s, all but two OECD countries have had better productivity records than Canada. During 2000–2010, Canadian productivity grew at an annual rate of 1 percent, while the U.S. achieved a 2.5 percent growth rate.[15]

These trends are a big concern because without strong productivity growth rates, the standard of living of Canadians will fall. Michael Porter, a Harvard University expert on international competitiveness, says that Canada has historically lived off its rich diet of natural resources, but in the future it will have to put more emphasis on innovation if it hopes to be successful in international markets.[16]

Domestic Productivity Nations must pay attention to their domestic productivity regardless of their global standing. A country that improves its ability to make something out of its existing resources can increase the wealth of all its inhabitants. Conversely, a decline in productivity shrinks a nation's total wealth. Additional wealth from higher productivity can be shared among workers (as higher wages), investors (as higher profits), and customers (as stable prices). When productivity drops, however, wages can be increased only by reducing profits (penalizing investors) or by increasing prices (penalizing customers).

Manufacturing versus Service Productivity Manufacturing productivity is higher than service productivity. For many years, it was widely believed that the service sector suffered from "Baumol's Disease," named after economist William Baumol. He argued that since the service sector focused more on hands-on activity that machines couldn't replace, it would be more difficult to increase productivity in services. Baumol noted, for example, that it would always require four musicians to play a Mozart quartet. But the Opera Company of Brooklyn is challenging that notion. It now puts on the opera *The Marriage of Figaro* with only 12 musicians and a technician who oversees a computer program that plays all the other parts. The orchestra's productivity has increased sharply because it does not have to pay for the usual complement of musicians.[17]

Industry Productivity Industries differ in terms of their productivity. Agriculture is more productive in Canada than in many other nations because we use more sophisticated technology. In an effort to increase productivity, Canfor Corporation developed a system called Genus, which it is using to manage its forestry operations. Genus, a computerized database containing geographic information and other essential data about Canfor's vast lumber and pulp operations in British Columbia and Alberta, will be used as a strategic planning tool to determine how the company should adjust its logging plans to reflect market demand.[18]

Company Productivity High productivity gives a company a competitive edge because its costs are lower. As a result, it can offer its product at a lower price (and gain more customers), or it can make a greater profit on each item sold. The productivity of individual companies is therefore important to investors, workers, and managers.

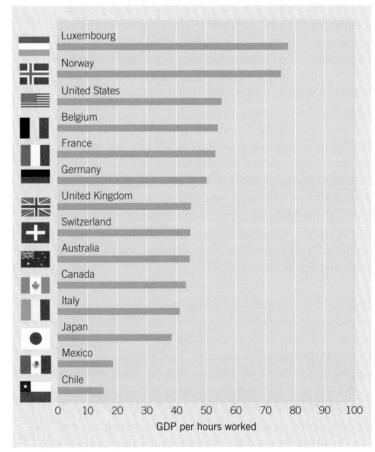

Figure 10.6

International productivity comparisons, 2008 (selected countries).

Meeting the Quality Challenge

Business has not always recognized the importance of quality. In the decades after the Second World War, American business consultant W. Edwards Deming tried to persuade U.S. firms that they needed to improve quality at least as much as quantity. Like many a prophet, he was not honoured in his homeland. But his arguments won the Japanese over. Through years of meticulous hard work, Japan's manufacturers have changed "Made in Japan" from a synonym for cheap, shoddy merchandise into a hallmark of reliability. Eventually, North American businesses came to understand that Deming was right.

Quality advocates such as Joseph Juran and Kaoru Ishikawa introduced methods and tools for implementing quality. Ishikawa, for example, developed "fishbone diagrams," also known as "cause-and-effect diagrams" or "Ishikawa diagrams," that help employees figure out the causes of quality problems in their work areas. The diagram in Figure 10.7, for instance, was designed to help an airport manager find out why the facility had so many delayed departures. Focusing on five major categories of possible causes, the manager then noted several potential causes of the problem in each. (It turns out that there weren't enough tow trucks to handle baggage transfers.)[19]

LO-6 Managing for Quality

Total quality management (TQM) includes all of the activities necessary for getting high-quality goods and services into the marketplace. TQM emphasizes that no defects are tolerable, and that employees are responsible for maintaining quality standards. For example, at Toyota's Cambridge, Ontario, plant workers can push a button or pull a rope to stop the production line when something is not up to standard.[20]

A customer focus is the starting point for TQM. It includes using methods for determining what customers want, and then making sure that all the company's activities and people are focused on fulfilling those needs. Total participation is critical; if all employees are not working toward improved quality, the firm is wasting potential contributions from its human resources, and is missing a chance to become a stronger competitor in the marketplace. TQM in today's competitive markets demands unending and continuous improvement of products, after-sales services, and all of the company's internal processes, such as accounting, delivery, billing, and information flow.

Consider the example of Standard Aero in Winnipeg, which is in the business of aircraft overhaul. When the company instituted TQM, the process began with the formation of a "change council" consisting of the CEO and five senior managers. Next, a nine-person task force was formed that consisted of employees who had done the full range of jobs on one of Standard's major overhaul contracts. The task force's first job was to find out what the customer wanted. It did this by designing a

TOTAL QUALITY MANAGEMENT (TQM) A concept that emphasizes that no defects are tolerable and that all employees are responsible for maintaining quality standards.

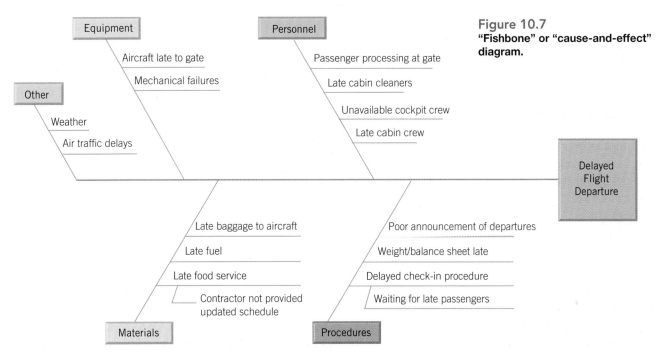

Figure 10.7
"Fishbone" or "cause-and-effect" diagram.

questionnaire and visiting customer plants around the world to gather information. It also worked within Standard Aero to determine exactly how the company did its aircraft overhaul work. After weeks of analysis, the task force was able to reduce the time required for overhaul work significantly. For example, the number of times a certain gearbox was handled as it moved through the repair process was reduced by 84 percent.[21]

Planning for Quality Planning for quality should begin before products are designed or redesigned. Managers need to set goals for both quality levels and quality reliability in the beginning. **Performance quality** refers to the features of a product and how well it performs. For example, Maytag gets a price premium because its washers and dryers offer a high level of performance quality. Customers perceive Maytag products as having more advanced features and being more durable than other brands.

Performance quality may or may not be related to quality reliability in a product. **Quality reliability** refers to the consistency or repeatability of performance. At Courtyard by Marriott hotels, for example, consistency is achieved by maintaining the same features at all of Marriott's nearly 700 locations (high-speed internet access, meeting space, access to an exercise room and swimming pool, and 24-hour access to food).

Organizing for Quality Having a separate "quality control" department is no longer enough. Everyone from the chair of the board to the part-time clerk—purchasers, engineers, janitors, marketers, machinists, and other personnel—must work to assure quality. At Germany's Messerschmitt-Boelkow-Blohm aerospace company, for example, all employees are responsible for inspecting their own work. The overall goal is to minimize eventual problems by making the product correctly from the beginning.

Leading for Quality Too often, firms fail to take the initiative to make quality happen. Leading for quality means that managers must inspire and motivate employees throughout the company to achieve quality goals. They need to help employees see how they affect quality

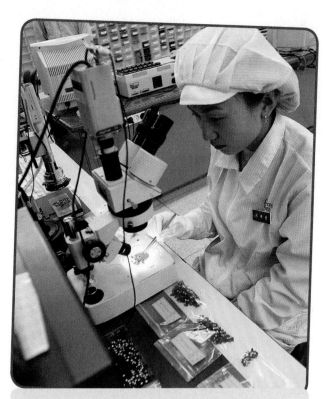

Quality control means taking action to ensure that operations produce products that meet specific quality standards.

and how quality affects their jobs and their company. If managers succeed, employees will ultimately accept **quality ownership**—the idea that quality belongs to each person who creates or destroys it while performing a job.

Controlling for Quality By monitoring its products and services, a company can detect mistakes and make corrections. To do so, however, managers must first establish specific quality standards and measurements. In a bank, for example, supervisors periodically evaluate transactions against a checklist. Specific aspects of each teller's work—appearance, courtesy, efficiency, and so on—are recorded. The results, reviewed with employees, either confirm proper performance or indicate changes that are needed to bring performance up to standards.

When safety and quality procedures are not regularly monitored, human and environmental disasters may result. In 2010, for example, an oil-drilling rig in the Gulf of Mexico that was leased by BP exploded and killed 11 workers. Millions of litres of oil escaped into the ocean, creating an environmental catastrophe. A *Wall Street Journal* investigation found that several quality and safety checks had not been carried out at the rig, partly because the drilling was behind schedule.[22]

Tools for Quality Assurance

In managing for quality, companies rely on assistance from proven tools. Often, ideas for improving both the product and the production process come from **competitive product analysis**. For example, Toshiba will take apart a Xerox photocopier and test each component to see how it compares with Toshiba's competing product. It can then decide which Toshiba product features are satisfactory, which product features need to be upgraded, and whether Toshiba's production processes need improvement.

There are many specific tools that can be used to achieve the desired level of quality: *value-added analysis, statistical process control, quality/cost studies, quality improvement teams, benchmarking, getting closer to the customer, ISO 9000:2000 and ISO 14000, re-engineering,* and *adding value through supply chains*.

Value-Added Analysis **Value-added analysis** means evaluating all work activities, material flows, and paperwork to determine the value that they add for customers. Value-added analysis often reveals wasteful or unnecessary activities that can be eliminated without harming customer service. For example, when Hewlett-Packard reduced its customer contracts from 20 pages to as few as 2, computer sales rose by more than 18 percent.

Statistical Process Control Companies can improve uniformity in their outputs by understanding the sources of variation. **Statistical process control (SPC)** methods—especially process variation studies and control charts—

allow managers to analyze variations in production data.

Process Variation While some amount of **process variation** is acceptable, too much can result in poor quality and excessive operating costs. Consider the box-filling operation for Honey Nuggets cereal. Each automated machine fills two 400-gram boxes per second. Even under proper conditions, slight variations in cereal weight from box to box are normal. Equipment and tools wear out, the cereal may be overly moist, and machinists make occasional adjustments. But how much variation is occurring? How much is acceptable?

Information about variation in a process can be obtained from a *process capability study.* Boxes are taken from the filling machines and weighed. The results are plotted, as in Figure 10.8, and compared with the upper and lower *specification limits* (quality limits) for weight. These limits define good and bad quality

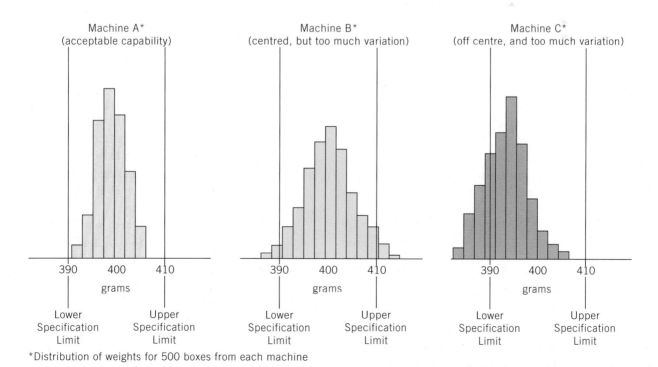

Machine A*
(acceptable capability)

Machine B*
(centred, but too much variation)

Machine C*
(off centre, and too much variation)

390   400   410
grams

390   400   410
grams

390   400   410
grams

Lower Specification Limit   Upper Specification Limit

Lower Specification Limit   Upper Specification Limit

Lower Specification Limit   Upper Specification Limit

*Distribution of weights for 500 boxes from each machine

Figure 10.8
Process variation in box filling for Honey Nuggets cereal.

CONTROL CHART
A statistical process control method in which results of test sampling of a product are plotted on a diagram that reveals when the process is beginning to depart from normal operating conditions.

QUALITY/COST STUDIES A method of improving product quality by assessing a firm's current quality-related costs and identifying areas with the greatest cost-saving potential.

INTERNAL FAILURES Expenses incurred during production and before bad product leaves the plant.

EXTERNAL FAILURES Allowing defective products to leave the factory and get into consumers' hands.

BENCHMARKING Comparing the quality of the firm's output with the quality of the output of the industry's leaders.

for box filling. Boxes with more than 410 grams are a wasteful "giveaway." Underfilling has a cost because it is unlawful.

In Figure 10.8, we see that none of Machine A's output violates the quality limits, and it is fully capable of meeting the company's quality standards. But Machines B and C have problems and cannot reliably meet Honey Nuggets' quality standards. The company must take special—and costly—actions to sort the good from the bad boxes before releasing the cereal for shipment.

Control charts Knowing that a process is capable of meeting quality standards is not enough. Managers must still monitor the process to prevent its going astray during production. To detect the beginning of bad conditions, managers can check production periodically and plot the results on a **control chart**. For example, several times a day, a machine operator at Honey Nuggets might weigh several boxes of cereal together to ascertain the average weight.

Quality/Cost Studies for Quality Improvement Statistical process controls help keep operations up to existing capabilities. But in today's competitive environment, firms must consistently *raise* quality capabilities. Managers thus face the challenge of identifying the improvements that offer the greatest promise. **Quality/cost studies** are helpful to managers because they not only identify a firm's current costs but also reveal areas with the largest cost-saving potential.[23]

For example, Honey Nuggets must determine its costs for **internal failures**. These are expenses—including the costs of overfilling boxes and the costs of sorting out bad boxes—incurred during production and before bad product leaves the plant. Despite quality control procedures, however, some bad boxes may get out of the factory, reach the customer, and generate complaints from grocers and customers. These are **external failures** that occur outside the factory. The costs of correcting them—refunds to customers, transportation costs to return bad

boxes to the factory, possible lawsuits, factory recalls—should also be tabulated in the quality/cost study.

Quality Improvement Teams Quality improvement (QI) teams are groups of employees from various work areas who meet regularly to define, analyze, and solve common production problems. Their goal is to improve both their own work methods and the products they make.[24] Many QI teams organize their own work, select leaders, and address problems in the workplace. Motorola, for example, sponsors company-wide team competitions to emphasize the value of the team approach, to recognize outstanding team performance, and to reaffirm the team's role in the company's continuous-improvement culture. Teams get higher marks for dealing with projects closely tied to Motorola's key initiatives.[25]

Benchmarking With **benchmarking**, a company compares its current performance against its own past performance (internal benchmarking), or against the performance of its competitors (external benchmarking). As an example of the former, the percentage of customer phone calls last month requiring more than two minutes of response time may be compared to the required response time the month before that. As an example of the latter, Toronto Hospital gathered performance data on 26 indicators from various Canadian hospitals so it could determine how well it was performing compared to other organizations in the health-care industry.[26]

Getting Closer to the Customer Says one advocate of quality improvement, "Customers are an economic asset. They're not on the balance sheet, but they should be." Struggling companies have often lost sight of customers as the driving force behind all business activity. Such companies may design products that customers do not want, ignore customer reactions to existing products, or fail to keep up with changing tastes. Meanwhile, successful businesses take steps to know what their customers want in the products they consume.

Caterpillar Financial Services won a Malcolm Baldrige National Quality Award—the prestigious award for excellence in quality—for high ratings by its customers (dealers and buyers of Caterpillar equipment). Buying and financing equipment from Caterpillar Financial became easier as it moved its services increasingly online. Customers now have 24/7 access to information on how much they owe on equipment, and they can make payments around the clock. In the past, the 60 000 customers had to phone a representative, who was often unavailable, for these services, resulting in delays and wasted time. The improved online system is testimony to Caterpillar Financial's dedication in knowing what customers want and then providing it.[27]

At Greyhound Lines of Canada, the marketing and operations vice-president wanted to drive home the point to managers that clean restrooms are important to customers. He warned regional managers that he would visit bus depots on one hour's notice to see if the restrooms were clean enough to eat dinner in. Within weeks, photos of regional managers having dinner in spotless restrooms began pouring in to the vice-president's office.[28]

ISO 9000:2000 and ISO 14000 DuPont had a problem: A moulding press used to make plastic connectors for computers had a 30-percent defect rate. Efforts to solve the problem went nowhere until, as part of a plant-wide quality program, press operators were asked to submit detailed written reports describing how they did their jobs. After comparing notes, operators realized that they were incorrectly measuring the temperature of the moulding press; as a result, temperature adjustments were often wrong. With the mystery solved, the defect rate dropped to 8 percent.

The quality program that led to this solution is called *ISO 9000*—a certification program attesting to the fact that a factory, a laboratory, or an office has met the rigorous quality management requirements set by the International Organization for Standardization. ISO 9000 (pronounced *ICE-o nine thousand*) originated in Europe as an attempt to standardize materials received from suppliers in such high-tech industries as electronics, chemicals, and aviation. Today, more than 160 countries have adopted ISO 9000 as a national standard, and more than 400 000 certificates have been issued.[29]

The latest version, *ISO 9000:2000,* indicates that it was revised in 2000. Revised standards allow firms to show that they follow documented procedures for testing products, training workers, keeping records, and fixing defects. To become certified, companies must document the procedures followed by workers during every stage of production. The purpose is to ensure that a manufacturer's product is exactly the same today as it was yesterday and as it will be tomorrow. Ideally, standardized processes would ensure that goods are produced at the same level of quality even if all employees were replaced by a new set of workers.

The **ISO 14000** program certifies improvements in *environmental* performance. Extending the ISO approach into the arena of environmental protection and hazardous

waste management, ISO 14000 requires a firm to develop an *environmental management system (EMS),* which is a plan documenting how the company has acted to improve its performance in using resources (such as raw materials) and in managing pollution. A company must not only identify hazardous wastes that it expects to create, but it must also stipulate plans for treatment and disposal. ISO 14000 covers practices in environmental labelling—the use of such terms as *energy efficient* and *recyclable*—and assesses the total environmental impact of the firm's products, not just from manufacturing but also from use and disposal.

ISO 14000
Certification program attesting to the fact that a factory, laboratory, or office has improved environmental performance.

BUSINESS PROCESS RE-ENGINEERING
Redesigning of business processes to improve performance, quality, and productivity.

SUPPLY CHAIN (VALUE CHAIN) Flow of information, materials, and services that starts with raw materials suppliers and continues through other stages in the operations process until the product reaches the end customer.

Business Process Re-engineering **Business process re-engineering** focuses on improving business processes by rethinking each of its steps, starting from scratch. *Re-engineering* is the fundamental rethinking and radical redesign of business processes to achieve dramatic improvements as measured by cost, quality, service, and speed.[30] The example given above of Caterpillar's change-over to an online system for customers is illustrative. Caterpillar reengineered the whole payments and financing process by improving equipment, retraining employees, and connecting customers to its databases. As the example illustrates, redesign is guided by a desire to improve operations and thereby provide higher-value services for the customer.

Adding Value through Supply Chains Managers sometimes forget that a company belongs to a network of firms that must coordinate their activities. As each firm performs its transformation processes, it relies on others in the network. A **supply chain** (or **value chain**) for any product is the flow of information, materials, and services that starts with raw-materials suppliers and continues adding value through other stages in the network of firms until the product reaches the end customer.[31]

Figure 10.9 shows the supply chain activities involved in supplying baked goods to consumers. Each stage adds value for the final customer. The chain begins with raw materials (grain harvested from the farm). It also includes additional storage and transportation activities, factory operations for baking and wrapping, and

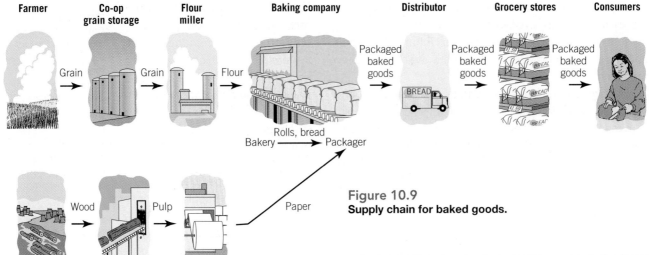

| Farmer | Co-op grain storage | Flour miller | Baking company | Distributor | Grocery stores | Consumers |

Grain → Grain → Flour →

Rolls, bread
Bakery ──────→ Packager

Packaged baked goods → Packaged baked goods → Packaged baked goods →

Wood → Pulp →

Paper

Forester · Pulp maker · Paper factory

Figure 10.9
Supply chain for baked goods.

distribution to retailers. Each stage depends on the others for success in getting fresh-baked goods to consumers.

LO-7 **Supply chain management (SCM)** tries to improve the overall flow through a system composed of companies working together. Because customers ultimately get better value, SCM gains competitive advantage for each supply-chain member.[32] A traditionally managed bakery, for example, would focus simply on getting production inputs from flour millers and paper suppliers and supplying baked goods to distributors. Unfortunately, this approach limits the chain's performance and doesn't allow for possible improvements when activities are more carefully coordinated. Supply chain management can improve performance and, as a result, provide higher quality at lower prices.

An innovative supply chain strategy was at the heart of Michael Dell's vision when he established Dell. The process starts when customer orders are automatically translated into updated production schedules in the factory. These schedules are used not only by operations managers at Dell but also by such parts suppliers as Sony, which adjust its own production and shipping activities to better meet Dell's production needs. In turn, parts suppliers' updated schedules are transmitted to their materials suppliers, and so on up the chain. As Dell's requirements change, suppliers up and down the chain synchronize their schedules to produce only the right materials and parts. As a result, Dell's prices are low and turnaround time for shipping PCs to customers is reduced to a matter of hours instead of days.

Fashion house Louis Vuitton, which produces upscale products like its Reade totebag, used to focus mainly on product image and product design. When an item became a hot seller, retailers often ran out of product because the company's production system and supply chain was not responsive to increased consumer demand. Vuitton has therefore revamped its systems in order to ensure that retailers always have a supply of in-demand Vuitton products on their shelves. Other luxury-goods manufacturers like Armani, Gucci, and Versace are also doing the same thing.[33]

Summary of Learning Objectives

1. **Explain the meaning of the term *production* (or *operations*) and describe the four kinds of *utility* it provides.** *Production* (or *operations*) refers to the processes and activities for transforming resources into finished services and goods for customers. Production creates *time utility* (products are available when customers want them), *place utility* (products are available where they are convenient for customers), *ownership utility* (customers benefit from possessing and using the product), and *form utility* (products are in a form that is useful to the customer).

2. **Identify the characteristics that distinguish *service operations* from *goods production* and explain the main differences in the *service focus*.** In service production, raw materials are not things but rather people, so services are performed, while goods are produced. Also, services are largely *intangible*, more likely than physical goods to be *customized* to meet the purchaser's needs, and more *unstorable* than most products. Because services are intangible, for instance, providers work to ensure that customers receive value in the form of pleasure, satisfaction, or a feeling of safety. Service providers also focus on the *customer-service link*, often acknowledging the customer as part of the operations process.

3. **Describe two types of *operations processes*.** In manufacturing, *analytic* processes break down resources into component parts and *synthetic* processes combine raw materials to produce a finished product. Services use either *high-contact* processes (the customer is in the system while the service is being performed) or *low-contact* processes (the customer is not in the system while the service is being performed).

4. **Describe the factors involved in *operations planning* and *operations control*.** *Operations planning* involves *forecasting* (determining future demand for products), *capacity planning* (calculating how much of a product can be produced), *location planning* (analyzing proposed facility sites), *layout planning* (designing a facility to enhance production efficiency), *quality planning* (ensuring that products meet a firm's quality standards), and *methods planning* (identifying specific production steps and methods for performing them). *Operations control* requires production managers to monitor production performance (by comparing results with detailed plans and schedules) and then to take corrective action as needed. *Materials management* involves the planning, organizing, and controlling of the flow of materials. There are several tools for helping managers control operations processes, including *worker training* programs, *just-in-time (JIT) production systems, material requirements planning (MRP),* and *quality control.*

5. **Explain the connection between *productivity* and *quality*.** *Productivity* is a measure of economic performance; it compares how much is produced with the resources used to produce it. *Quality* is a product's fitness for use. However, an emphasis solely on productivity or solely on quality is not enough. Profitable competition in today's business world demands high levels of both productivity and quality.

6. **Understand the concept of *total quality management* and describe nine tools that companies can use to achieve it.** *Total quality management (TQM)* includes all the activities that are necessary for getting high-quality goods and services into the marketplace. Tools that are available to managers include *value-added analysis, statistical process control methods, quality/cost studies, quality improvement teams benchmarking, getting closer to the customer, ISO 9000:2000, re-engineering, and supply chain management.*

7. **Explain how a *supply chain strategy* differs from traditional strategies for coordinating operations among businesses.** The *supply chain strategy* is based on the idea that members of the supply chain can gain competitive advantage by working together as a coordinated system of units. Sharing information allows companies to reduce inventories, improve quality, and speed the delivery of products to consumers.

Questions and Exercises

Questions for Analysis

1. What are the resources needed and the finished "products" that are produced in the following services: real estate firm, child care facility, bank, city water and electric department, and hotel?

2. Find examples of a synthetic production process and an analytic process. Then classify each according to whether it is chemical, fabrication, assembly, transport, or clerical. Explain your reasoning.

3. Pick three products (not services) that you regularly use. Then do some research to determine which of the basic production processes are used to produce these products (chemical, fabrication, assembly, transport, or clerical processes). To what extent are multiple processes used in the production of the product?

4. Pick three services (not goods) that you regularly use. Explain what customization, unstorability, and intangibility mean for each of the services. How do these factors influence the way the service is delivered to customers?

5. Develop a service flow analysis for some service that you use frequently, such as buying lunch at a cafeteria, having your hair cut, or riding a bus. Identify areas of potential quality or productivity failures in the process.

6. Historically, high productivity in the service sector has been difficult to achieve. Why was this so? What might be changing in this area that will cause service productivity to increase during the next decade?

Application Exercises

7. Develop a list of internal customers and internal suppliers for the organization where you work. Identify areas of potential quality improvement in these internal customer–supplier relationships.

8. Choose a consumer item and trace its supply chain. Identify at least four upstream stages in the chain. Can you make recommendations that would improve the supply chain?

9. Interview the owner of a local service business, such as a laundry or dry-cleaning shop. Identify the major

decisions that were necessary in planning its service operations.

10. Think of an everyday activity—either personal or professional—that you would like to do more efficiently. Describe how you would use methods planning to achieve increased efficiency in that activity. Draw a process flowchart that shows the stages in the activity you chose, and then explain how you would use it.

TEAM EXERCISES

Building Your Business Skills

Making Your Benchmark in the World

Goal

To encourage students to understand ways in which benchmarking can improve quality and productivity.

Situation

As the director of maintenance for a regional airline, you are disturbed to learn that the cost of maintaining your 20-plane fleet is skyrocketing. A major factor is repair time; when maintenance or repairs are required, work often proceeds slowly. As a result, additional aircraft are required to meet the schedule. To address the problem,

you decide to use a powerful total quality management tool called benchmarking. You will approach your problem by studying ways in which other companies have successfully managed similar problems. Your goal is to apply the best practices to your own maintenance and repair operation.

Method

Step 1 Working with three or four other students, choose your benchmarking target from among the following choices:

- The maintenance and repair operations of a competing airline
- The pit crew operations of a race car team
- The maintenance and repair operations of a national trucking company

Write a memo explaining the reasons for your choice.

Step 2 Write a list of benchmarking questions that will help you learn the best practices of your targeted company. Your goal is to ask questions that will help you improve your own operation. These questions will be asked during on-site visits.

Step 3 As part of a benchmarking project, you will be dealing with your counterparts in other companies. You have a responsibility to prepare for these encounters, and you must remember that what you learn during the exchange process is privileged information. Given these requirements, describe the steps you would take before your first on-site visit and outline your benchmarking code of ethics.

Follow-Up Questions

1. Why is benchmarking an important method for improving quality?

2. Why did you make your benchmarking choice? Explain why the company you selected holds more promise than other companies in helping you to solve your internal maintenance problems.

3. What kind of information would help you to improve the efficiency of your operations? Are you interested in management information, technical information, or both?

4. In an age of heightened competition, why do you think companies are willing to benchmark with each other?

Exercising Your Ethics

Calculating the Cost of Conscience

The Situation

Product quality and cost affect every firm's reputation and profitability, as well as the satisfaction of customers. This exercise will expose you to some ethical considerations that pertain to certain cost and service decisions that must be made by operations managers.

The Dilemma

As director of quality for a major appliance manufacturer, Ruth was reporting to the executive committee on the results of a program for correcting problems with a newly redesigned compressor that the company had recently begun putting in its refrigerators. Following several customer complaints, the quality lab had determined that some of the new compressor units ran more loudly than expected. One corrective option was simply waiting until customers complained and responding to each complaint if and when it occurred. Ruth, however, decided that this approach was inconsistent with the company's policy of being the high-quality leader in the industry. Insisting on a proactive, "pro-quality" approach, Ruth initiated a program for contacting all customers who had purchased refrigerators containing the new compressor.

Unfortunately, her "quality-and-customers-first" policy was expensive. Service representatives across Canada had to phone every customer, make appointments for home visits, and replace original compressors with a newer model. Because replacement time was only 30 minutes, customers were hardly inconvenienced, and food stayed refrigerated without interruption. Customer response to the replacement program was overwhelmingly favourable.

Near the end of Ruth's report, an executive vice-president was overheard to comment, "Ruth's program has cost this company $400 million in service expenses." Two weeks later, Ruth was fired.

Team Activity

Assemble a group of four students and assign each group member to one of the following roles:

- Ruth
- Ruth's boss
- A customer
- A company investor

Action Steps

1. Before hearing any of your group's comments on this situation, and from the perspective of your assigned role, take a moment to consider whether Ruth's firing is consistent with the company's desire for industry leadership in quality. Write down the reasons for your position.

2. Before hearing any of your group's comments on this situation, and from the perspective of your assigned role, consider what underlying ethical issues, if any, exist in this situation. Write down the issues.

3. Gather your group together and reveal, in turn, each member's comments on Ruth's firing. Next, reveal the ethical issues listed by each member.

4. Appoint someone to record the main points of agreement and disagreement within the group. How

do you explain the results? What accounts for any disagreement?

5. From an ethical standpoint, what does your group conclude is the most appropriate action that should have been taken by the company in this situation?

6. Develop a group response to the following question: What are the respective roles of profits, obligations to customers, and employee considerations for the firm in this situation?

Quality Problems in Service Businesses

In September 2006, the U.S. Federal Aviation Administration (FAA) gave airlines until March 2008 to inspect a certain bundle of wires located near the main landing gear in all MD-80 airliners, and, if improperly secured, to repair the bundle. Eighteen months later, some 250 000 travellers found themselves stranded as American Airlines grounded its fleet of MD-80s and cancelled nearly 3300 flights in a hurried effort to comply with the FAA directive.

How could the United States' largest carrier make such a costly and seemingly avoidable mistake? Shortly before the deadline to repair the wiring, the FAA was embarrassed by revelations that another carrier, Southwest Airlines, had violated federal regulations by flying planes that had missed their scheduled inspections. Suddenly, the FAA found itself under fire from the U.S. Congress for failing to keep closer tabs on airlines. It is not surprising, then, that the FAA became extra vigilant in inspecting the MD-80s—more vigilant, it seems, than carriers such as American had come to expect.

None of this may be much consolation to frustrated travellers. According to Bren Bowen, co-author of the 2008 Airline Quality Rating (AQR), 2007 "was the worst year ever for the U.S. airlines." The AQR measures such performance indicators as the percentage of flights arriving on time, the amount of mishandled baggage, and the number of complaints ranging from high fares to misleading advertising to discriminatory practices. Such a varied list of concerns is a reminder that the fundamental service an airline provides—getting people from point A to point B—is only the beginning of operational performance and quality. As the American Airlines incident illustrates, however, even this fundamental service is impossible to provide without a strong emphasis on quality practices.

In Canada, a different part of the travel industry is under scrutiny: travel companies and booking agents. When Conquest Vacations suddenly ceased operations in April 2009, many travellers were stranded in hotels in Mexico, the Dominican Republic, and Cuba. Many of

these Canadians were told by hotel officials that they had to pay for their room after Conquest folded because their bill had not been paid by the travel company.

The Ontario government established the Travel Industry Council of Ontario (TICO) to ensure that (a) fair business practices and ethical behaviour are adhered to, and (b) Canadian travellers are not scammed or taken advantage of. But Conquest's sudden shutdown meant that TICO was not given proper notice and therefore could not provide sufficient information to travellers. The outcome has left many critics questioning the usefulness of the travel council. There is now concern about the travel industry in general, and many people are asking if there are going to be additional travel businesses that suddenly cease operations.

These problems have arisen at a time when the travel business is hurting because of the recession. Intense competition has driven down vacation prices and consumers are looking for the lowest all-inclusive deals. In an effort to remain competitive, tour companies are laying off staff and reducing their prices to below cost. Transat A.T. Inc. cut 53 administrative jobs at their Montreal, Toronto, and Vancouver office locations, while U.S. airline subsidiary Air Transat cut about 30 administrative positions. Analyst David Newman of National Bank Financial indicated that the restructuring efforts will eliminate duplicate functions, merge divisions, and centralize administrative and support operations in a bid to "flatten the management structure."

Travel companies have assured consumers that the changes they are making will strengthen their service offering, but many customers are feeling uncertain about the level of service quality they can expect.

Customer complaints about poor service quality are obviously not limited to the travel business. To observe consumer unhappiness in action, go to Complaints.com, a forum for people who have had bad consumer experiences. Enter "missed appointment" or "late repairman" in the search engine and you will get pages of hits. Typical is this complaint about a failed window installation: "I then made an appointment for [an] employee to come to my house the next day between 2 p.m. and 4 p.m. . . . I took a day off from work and stayed home to wait for the [company] truck. Four p.m. came and went. No one from [the company] showed up or called."

ConsumerAffairs.com, an advocacy group for customers who have received poor service or purchased shoddy merchandise, also details numerous incidents in which people were left waiting helplessly for repair people who were late for scheduled appointments. Part of the problem is that the company that manufactures a product may not be the same company that provides service for that product. This is often the case with mass-produced products purchased in department stores or wholesale outlets. General Electric may make a refrigerator, but a GE repair person is not located in every town where that refrigerator is sold. Outside contractors must then be hired to perform repairs, and they may lack the specific expertise required to do the job in a timely manner.

It's not only products in need of installation or repair that can cause customers' frustrations over missed appointments. How many hours have you spent waiting in crowded doctors' offices, overbooked salons, and slow-service restaurants? In each case, even if the quality of the product or service turns out to be excellent, you may still feel dissatisfied with the overall quality of the experience. For service providers in particular, that is a failure that can be as costly as producing a defective product.

Questions for Discussion

1. What is the definition of "quality"? How do the incidents described above illustrate a lack of quality? What would constitute high quality? Explain.

2. Why do quality problems arise?

3. Consider the following statement: *"It is very difficult and expensive for companies to produce high-quality goods and services. But consumers want high-quality products at low prices, and they expect far too much from companies in terms of product quality, given the price they are willing to pay. Consumers should be more realistic in their expectations."* Do you agree or disagree with the statement? Explain your reasoning.

SCANLIFE

chapter

11

Understanding Accounting

After reading this chapter, you should be able to:

LO-1 Explain the role of *accountants* and distinguish among the three types of *professional accountants* in Canada.

LO-2 Explain how the *accounting equation* is used.

LO-3 Describe three basic *financial statements* and show how they reflect the activity and financial condition of a business.

LO-4 Explain the key standards and principles for reporting financial statements.

LO-5 Explain how computing *financial ratios* can help in analyzing the financial strengths of a business.

SCANLIFE

What's the Latest on Pension Accounting?

The dramatic decline of the stock market in 2008 created large pension shortfalls because the market value of the assets that pension plans held declined sharply. The Ontario Teachers' Pension Plan, for example, posted an 18 percent loss in 2008 (the fund's value declined by $21 billion), and the Ontario Municipal Employees Retirement System (OMERS) lost 15.3 percent. As of 2008, GM Canada's pension plan was under-funded by more than $6 billion, which meant that workers would receive only 50 percent of what they thought they were going to get. The Canada Pension Plan (CPP) has also been hard hit. During the second quarter of fiscal 2009, the CPP fund declined in value by 6.7 percent ($7.9 billion).

In 2007, the typical pension plan was 96 percent funded (i.e., the market value of a pension plan's assets nearly equalled its liabilities), but in 2008 the typical pension plan was only 59 percent funded. By 2009, the typical pension plan had improved to 74 percent funded because the stock market had gained back some of what it lost in 2008. But more than half of all pension plans still are less than 80 percent funded, and they will need to achieve returns of 7.5 percent annually for the next 15 years just to return to fully funded status.

The problems in pension plans have been caused by a variety of factors, but two stand out. First, recent returns on investments held by pension plans have been much lower than anticipated. In the 1990s, returns on pension plan investments averaged 11 percent (higher than the 7.5 percent that had been predicted). But during the economic downturn of 2001–2003, the average rate of return for pension plan investments was just 3.1 percent, well below the 7 percent that had been assumed. And during 2008–2009, pension funds *lost* 15 to 30 percent of their value. Second, because pension plan investments had achieved such high returns in the 1990s, many companies took contribution

How Will This Help Me?

By understanding the material presented in this chapter, you'll benefit in three ways: (1) if you're an *entrepreneur* thinking about starting your own business, you'll discover your obligations for reporting your firm's financial status, (2) as an *employee* or *manager*, you'll better understand how your company's operations influence its financial performance, and (3) as an *investor*, you'll learn how to interpret financial statements so that you can evaluate a company's financial condition and its prospects for the future.

"holidays" and did not contribute anything to the plans they were sponsoring. With the lower investment returns of the twenty-first century, pension surpluses quickly became pension deficits.

The simplest solution to the pension problem is to drop defined *benefit* pension plans (which guarantee employees a certain level of income during retirement) and replace them with defined *contribution* pension plans (which simply require a company to contribute a certain amount of money each year). With defined contribution plans, the company's liability is known, but the value of the pension when an employee retires is unknown (its value is determined solely by the rate of return that the investments in the plan have achieved). Defined contribution plans obviously reduce uncertainty for the company, but increase uncertainty for retirees.

Companies are, in fact, shifting to defined contribution pension plans. In the United States, for example, there were 112 000 defined benefit plans in 1985, but now there are fewer than 30 000. The move away from defined benefit plans is also occurring in Canada, although at a slower rate. But the change is likely to accelerate, since Canadian legislation requires companies to bear the full financial burden of pension deficits. The current crisis in defined benefit plans means that over the next five years, billions of extra dollars will have to be put into those plans to make up for past investment losses. Companies, therefore, have an incentive to move away from defined benefit plans and toward defined contribution plans because with the latter they at least know what their contribution requirements are.

Canadian accounting rules may also need to be re-examined. Under current rules, companies can delay recognizing changes in the value of their pension plans. Using a practice called "smoothing," companies can spread the reporting of changes over several years. When stock markets were booming, no one scrutinized pension plans much because their value was going up. But when stock markets started dropping, large liabilities began building up (but companies kept that information off their balance sheets). National Bank Financial studied 79 Canadian companies—representing 80 percent of the capitalization of the S&P/TSX—and found that their off-balance-sheet pension deficits totalled $21 billion.

Canadian and international accounting regulators are working on changes to accounting rules that will bring more realism to pension reporting. The most obvious change involves ending the practice of smoothing and reporting pension fund returns as they actually take place. This means that income from the pension fund would be reported as investment income and the costs of running the pension fund would be reported as expenses. Regulators recognize that a change like this will increase the volatility in the earnings that corporations report, but they point out that investors will be able to more clearly see what is happening (good or bad) in a company's pension fund. Unfortunately, the economic problems that developed in 2008 made it very difficult to end the practice of smoothing. In fact, companies were given even more time (10 years) to make up for pension shortfalls.

What Is Accounting?

Accounting is a comprehensive information system for collecting, analyzing, and communicating financial information. It measures business performance and translates the findings into information for management decisions. Accountants prepare performance reports for owners, the public, and regulatory agencies. To perform these functions, accountants keep records of such transactions as taxes paid, income received, and expenses incurred, and they analyze the effects of these transactions on particular business activities. By sorting, analyzing, and recording thousands of transactions, accountants can determine how well a business is being managed and how financially strong it is. **Bookkeeping** is just one phase of accounting—the recording of accounting transactions.

Because businesses engage in many thousands of transactions, ensuring that financial information is consistent and dependable is mandatory. This is the job of the **accounting information system (AIS)**: an organized procedure for identifying, measuring, recording, and retaining financial information so that it can be used in accounting statements and management reports. The system includes all of the people, reports, computers, procedures, and resources for compiling financial transactions.[1] The boxed insert entitled "The Green

Revolution Hits Accounting" describes several ways that accountants are becoming more environmentally responsible.

Users of accounting information are numerous:

- *Business managers* use accounting information to set goals, develop plans, set budgets, and evaluate future prospects.

- *Employees and unions* use accounting information to get paid and to plan for and receive such benefits as health care, insurance, vacation time, and retirement pay.

- *Investors and creditors* use accounting information to estimate returns to stockholders, determine a company's growth prospects, and determine whether it is a good credit risk before investing or lending.

- *Tax authorities* use accounting information to plan for tax inflows, determine the tax liabilities of individuals and businesses, and ensure that correct amounts are paid on time.

- *Government regulatory agencies* rely on accounting information to fulfill their duties. Provincial securities regulators, for example, require firms to file financial disclosures so that potential investors have valid information about a company's financial status.

The Green Revolution Hits Accounting

In accounting, there is one important activity that impacts the environment, and that is the use of paper for all those financial statements. But the electronic revolution has provided accountants with the opportunity to reduce paper waste; to quickly respond to clients; to reduce the costs associated with storing, tracking, and accessing documents; and to work virtually anywhere in the world via the internet. Traditional accounting firms spend a lot of valuable time handling paperwork such as invoices. A paperless system eliminates the need to store paper invoices by storing their digital images and retrieving the images as needed. Firms now have easier access to more data, facilitating analyses that can save thousands of dollars.

There are real incentives for companies to embrace environmentally friendly business practices like saving paper. But careful thought has to be given to how this will be done because of the well-known tendency of human beings to resist change. To resolve any resistance that is based on *technical* concerns, management must ensure that the IT infrastructure is working properly and that there is an adequate storage and security system. To deal with resistance that is based on *emotional* concerns, management needs to provide incentives to motivate people to change to the new system. Digital files, for example, reduce the need to travel in order to share documents with clients and other associates. This also enables companies to reduce their dependency on a traditional work environment because more employees can choose to work flexible hours and have a more balanced work and family life. Another incentive is the increased efficiency that will be evident with the use of electronic technology. Increased efficiency means that a given amount of work can be done with fewer people than were previously needed, and this will increase competitiveness.

It is anticipated that accounting firms will increasingly train their clients to perform more of the initial data entry to allow for the electronic exchange of information. Firms will no longer be limited by geographic boundaries. They can also bill for higher-level accounting tasks and be much more selective about their clients. These new methods will help eliminate the bottom 10 to 20 percent of unproductive clients and allow more time to cultivate the profitable files.

Critical Thinking Questions

1. There are clearly benefits for firms that embrace green accounting practices, but are there also benefits to clients? If so, describe them.
2. Why might there be reluctance on the part of accounting firms or their clients to embrace green initiatives like paperless systems?

LO-1 Who Are Accountants and What Do They Do?

At the head of the accounting system is the **controller**, who manages all of the firm's accounting activities. As chief accounting officer, the controller ensures that the accounting system provides the reports and statements needed for planning, controlling, and decision-making activities. This broad range of activities requires different types of expertise among accounting specialists. We begin our discussion by distinguishing between the two main fields of accounting: *financial* and *managerial*. Then we discuss the different functions and activities of the three professional accounting groups in Canada.

Financial and Managerial Accounting

As we have just seen, it is important to distinguish between users of accounting information who are outside a company and users who are inside the company.

A financial report is an integral component of the financial accounting system.

goals, salespeople need data on past sales by geographic region. Purchasing agents use information on material costs to negotiate terms with suppliers.

Professional Accountants

Three professional accounting organizations have developed in Canada to certify accounting expertise.

Chartered Accountants The Canadian Institute of Chartered Accountants (CICA) grants the **chartered accountant (CA)** designation. To achieve this designation, a person must earn a university degree, then complete an educational program and pass a national exam. About half of all CAs work in CA firms that offer accounting services to the public; the other half work in government or industry. CA firms typically provide audit, tax, and management services. CAs focus on external financial reporting, that is, certifying for various interested parties (stockholders, lenders, the Canada Revenue Agency, etc.) that the financial records of a company accurately reflect the true financial condition of the firm. In 2008, there were about 74 000 CAs in Canada.[2]

Certified General Accountants The Certified General Accountants Association of Canada grants the **certified general accountant (CGA)** designation. To become a CGA, a person must comlete an education program and pass a national exam; to be eligible, a person must have an accounting job with a company. CGAs can audit corporate financial statements in most provinces. Most CGAs work in private companies, but there are a few CGA firms. Some CGAs also work in CA firms. CGAs also focus

Financial Accounting A firm's **financial accounting system** is concerned with *external* users of information such as consumer groups, unions, stockholders, and government agencies. Companies prepare and publish income statements and balance sheets at regular intervals, as well as other financial reports that are useful for stockholders and the general public. All of these documents focus on the activities of the company *as a whole*, rather than on individual departments or divisions.

Managerial Accounting In contrast, **managerial** (or **management**) **accounting** serves *internal* users. Managers at all levels need information to make decisions for their departments, to monitor current projects, and to plan for future activities. Other employees also need accounting information. Engineers, for instance, want to know the costs for materials and production so that they can make product operation improvements. To set performance

on external financial reporting, and emphasize the use of the computer as a management accounting tool. In 2008, there were about 71 000 CGAs in Canada, the Caribbean, and China.[3]

Certified Management Accountants The Society of Management Accountants of Canada grants the **certified management accountant (CMA)** designation. To achieve the designation, a person must have a university degree, pass a two-part national entrance examination, and complete a strategic leadership program while gaining practical experience in a management accounting environment. CMAs work in organizations of all sizes, and focus on applying best management practices in all of the operations of a business. CMAs bring a strong market focus to strategic management and resource deployment, synthesizing and analyzing financial and non-financial information to help organizations maintain a competitive advantage. CMAs emphasize the role of accountants in the planning and overall strategy of the firm in which they work. In 2008, there were about 40 000 CMAs in Canada, with an additional 10 000 students in the program.[4]

Accounting Services

CAs and CGAs usually perform several accounting services for their clients. The most common of these are auditing, tax services, and management services.

Auditing In an **audit**, accountants examine a company's AIS to ensure that it adheres to **generally accepted accounting principles (GAAP)**—a body of theory and procedure developed and monitored by the CICA. An audit involves examination of receipts such as shipping documents, cancelled cheques, payroll records, and cash receipts records. In some cases, an auditor may physically check inventories, equipment, or other assets, even if it means descending 200 metres into an underground mine. At the end of an audit, the auditor will certify whether the client's financial reports comply with GAAP.

International accounting standards In a globalized economy, users of financial information want assurances that accounting procedures are comparable from country to country. So, the International Accounting Standards Board (IASB) has developed International Financial Reporting Standards (IFRS), a sort of "global GAAP," which is now being used by more than 100 countries.[5] Canadian companies adopted the IFRS on January 1, 2011, but it required a lot of work to determine how to present accounting information in a way that satisfies the new standards.[6] IASB financial statements require an income statement, balance sheet, and statement of cash flows, which are similar to those that have historically been developed by Canadian accountants, but a uniform format is not required and there is a lot of variety. Some accounting experts argue that IFRS gives managers too much leeway to report the figures they want, and that means less protection for investors.[7] The U.S. resisted the adoption of IFRS, and in 2010 the IASB announced that it would no longer pursue convergence of standards with the U.S. as a key objective.[8]

The new IASB standards may have a noticeable impact on the way Canadian companies report some financial results. For example, suppose a company has a customer loyalty plan that gives customers points for purchases they make, and then these points can be redeemed for free products. If a customer makes $1000 in purchases and earns points that can be redeemed for $25 worth of merchandise, the company may have historically counted the $1000 as sales revenue and then also counted the $25 as sales revenue when the points were redeemed. But under the new IFRS, companies cannot add the $25 to the original $1000. The new rules will reduce the apparent same-stores sales growth numbers for these companies.[9]

Detecting fraud In recent years, there has been much publicity about the alleged failure of auditors to detect fraud. Therefore, when audits are being conducted, **forensic accountants** may be used to track down hidden funds in business firms. Because white-collar crime is on the increase, the number of forensic accountants has increased in recent years. The boxed insert entitled "Opportunities in Forensic Accounting" gives more information on this interesting career path.

Tax Services Tax services include helping clients not only with preparing their tax returns but also in their tax planning. Tax laws are complex, and an accountant's advice can help a business structure (or restructure) its operations and investments and save millions of dollars in taxes. To serve their clients best, of course, accountants must stay abreast of changes in tax laws—no simple matter.

CERTIFIED MANAGEMENT ACCOUNTANT (CMA)
An individual who has completed a university degree, passed a national examination, and completed a strategic leadership program; works in industry and focuses on internal management accounting.

AUDIT
An accountant's examination of a company's financial records to determine if it used proper procedures to prepare its financial reports.

GENERALLY ACCEPTED ACCOUNTING PRINCIPLES (GAAP)
Standard rules and methods used by accountants in preparing financial reports.

Management Consulting Services **Management consulting services** range from personal financial planning to planning corporate mergers. Other services include plant layout and design, marketing studies, production scheduling, computer feasibility studies, and design and implementation of accounting systems. Some CA firms even assist in executive recruitment. Small wonder that the staffs of CA firms include engineers, architects, mathematicians, and even psychologists.

Private Accountants

Private accountants are salaried employees who deal with a company's day-to-day accounting needs. Large businesses employ specialized accountants in such areas as budgets, financial planning, internal auditing, payroll, and taxation. In a small firm, a single individual may handle all accounting tasks. The work of private accountants varies, depending on the nature of the specific business and the activities needed to make that business a success. An internal auditor at Petro-Canada,

MANAGING IN TURBULENT TIMES

Opportunities in Forensic Accounting

Anyone who watches television knows about the forensic investigations that police officers conduct as they try to catch the bad guys (think *CSI: Miami*). It's pretty interesting stuff. But did you know that forensics is also very relevant to the field of accounting? The numerous corporate financial scandals of the last few years have caused an increase in demand for forensic accountants—individuals who investigate the financial transactions of companies in order to determine if something fishy is going on. According to the latest Kroll Global Fraud Report, companies lost an average of $8.2 million to fraud in the past three years, largely because of the credit crunch and tough economic climate.

Fraud examiners interview high-level executives, pursue tips from employees or outsiders, and comb through emails, searching for suspicious words and phrases. The CA designation in investigative and forensic accounting (CA IFA) provides in-depth knowledge and experience in investigative and forensic accounting. This is accomplished through a profession-endorsed certification process that has ongoing experience and education requirements. Individuals who pursue a career in IFA are well positioned to practise in areas such as fraud and economic loss quantification. Some of their responsibilities include testifying as expert witnesses, investigating and analyzing financial evidence, and getting involved in criminal investigations (especially in the rapidly evolving area of computer and internet fraud).

Most of the publicity about financial scandals focuses on large companies, but forensic investigation is needed in businesses of all shapes and sizes.

The Atlantic Lottery Corporation, for example, hired a forensic accounting firm to review the operations of its small, individually owned lottery retail outlets when reported winnings were higher than statistically possible. That led to widespread concerns that some retailers were cheating by pocketing prizes won by other players who weren't properly notified of their winnings.

At the other end of the size scale, a major multinational consumer-goods producer became concerned when one of its best-known products began to lose market share in Europe because a competitor was selling its brand at a substantially lower price. Kroll was asked to determine whether the competitor's actions were legitimately supported by lower production costs or whether they reflected unfair market practices. After considerable research, Kroll discovered that the competitor had indeed found a novel means of production that sharply reduced its costs without reducing the quality of its product. Kroll recommended that the company license the technology so that it could also achieve lower costs.

Critical Thinking Questions

1. Visit the Canadian Institute of Chartered Accountants (www.cica.ca) website. How much emphasis is placed on forensic accounting? How does a person become a forensic accountant?
2. Interview a forensic accountant and ask the following questions: (a) What general approach do forensic accountants take when investigating the financial statements of companies? and (b) What specific techniques are used to determine whether accounting fraud has occurred?

for example, might fly to the Hibernia site to confirm the accuracy of oil-flow meters on the offshore drilling platform. But a supervisor responsible for $200 million in monthly accounts payable to vendors and employees may travel no further than the executive suite.

The Accounting Cycle Private accountants use a six-step process to develop and analyze a company's financial reports (see Figure 11.1). The first step is to analyze data that are generated as a result of the company's regular business operations (sales revenue, income tax payments, interest income, inventory purchases, etc.). These transactions are entered in a *journal* (which lists them in chronological order) and then in a *ledger* (which shows the increases and decreases in the various asset, liability, and equity accounts). Then the ledger amounts for each account are listed in a *trial balance* (which assesses the accuracy of the figures). Financial statements (balance sheet, income statement, and statement of cash flows) are then prepared, using GAAP. The last step in the process involves analyzing the financial statements (for example, by using ratio analysis). Many years ago, these steps were done laboriously by hand, but now computers are used to help private accountants efficiently work through the six steps.

LO-2 The Accounting Equation

All accountants, whether public or private, rely on record keeping. Underlying all record-keeping procedures is the most basic tool of accounting: the **accounting equation**. At various points in the year, accountants use the following equation to balance the data pertaining to financial transactions:

$$\text{Assets} = \text{Liabilities} + \text{Owners' equity}$$

After each transaction (e.g., payments to suppliers, sales to customers, wages to employees), the accounting equation must be in balance. To understand the importance of this equation, we must understand the terms *assets*, *liabilities*, and *owners' equity*.[10]

Assets and Liabilities

An **asset** is any economic resource that is expected to benefit a firm or an individual who owns it. Assets include land, buildings, equipment, inventory, and payments due to the company (accounts receivable). A **liability** is a debt that the firm owes to an outside party.

Owners' Equity

You may have heard of the equity that a homeowner has in a house—that is, the amount of money that could be made by selling the house and paying off the mortgage. Similarly, **owners' equity** is the amount of money that owners would receive if they sold all of a company's assets and paid all of its liabilities. We can rewrite the accounting equation to highlight this definition:

$$\text{Assets} - \text{Liabilities} = \text{Owners' equity}$$

If a company's assets exceed its liabilities, owners' equity is *positive*; if the company goes out of business, the owners will receive some cash (a gain) after selling assets and paying

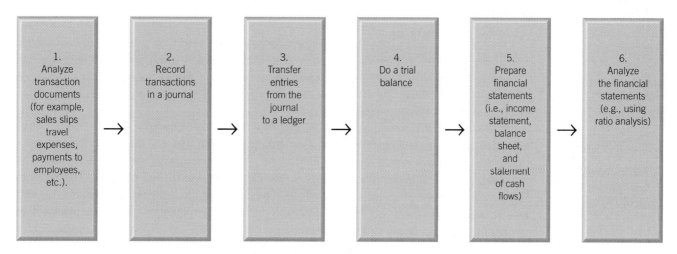

Figure 11.1
The accounting cycle.

The inventory at this auto dealership is among the company's assets. The cars constitute an economic resource because the firm will benefit financially as it sells them.

DOUBLE-ENTRY ACCOUNTING SYSTEM A bookkeeping system, developed in the fifteenth century and still in use, that requires every transaction to be entered in two ways—how it affects assets and how it affects liabilities and owners' equity—so that the accounting equation is always in balance.

FINANCIAL STATEMENTS Any of several types of broad reports regarding a company's financial status; most often used in reference to balance sheets, income statements, and/or statements of cash flows.

BALANCE SHEET A type of financial statement that summarizes a firm's financial position on a particular date in terms of its assets, liabilities, and owners' equity.

CURRENT ASSETS Cash and other assets that can be converted into cash within a year.

LIQUIDITY The ease and speed with which an asset can be converted to cash; cash is said to be perfectly liquid.

ACCOUNTS RECEIVABLE Amounts due to the firm from customers who have purchased goods or services on credit; a form of current asset.

MERCHANDISE INVENTORY The cost of merchandise that has been acquired for sale to customers but is still on hand.

PREPAID EXPENSES Includes supplies on hand and rent paid for the period to come.

off liabilities. If liabilities outweigh assets, owners' equity is *negative*; assets are insufficient to pay off all debts. If the company goes out of business, the owners will get no cash and some creditors won't be paid. Owners' equity is meaningful for both investors and lenders. Before lending money to owners, for example, lenders want to know the amount of owners' equity in a business. Owners' equity consists of two sources of capital:

1. The amount that the owners originally invested.

2. Profits earned by and reinvested in the company.

When a company operates profitably, its assets increase faster than its liabilities. Owners' equity, therefore, will increase if profits are retained in the business instead of paid out as dividends to stockholders. Owners' equity also increases if owners invest more of their own money to increase assets. However, owners' equity can shrink if the company operates at a loss or if owners withdraw assets.

LO-3 Financial Statements

If a business purchases inventory with cash, cash decreases and inventory increases. Similarly, if the business purchases supplies on credit, supplies increase and so do accounts payable. Since every transaction affects two accounts, **double-entry accounting systems** are used to record the dual effects of financial transactions. These transactions are reflected in three important **financial statements**: *balance sheets*, *income statements*, and *statements of cash flows*.[11]

Balance Sheets

Balance sheets supply detailed information about the accounting equation factors: assets, liabilities, and owners' equity. Figure 11.2 shows the balance sheet for Perfect Posters.

Assets As we have seen, an asset is any economic resource that a company owns and from which it can expect to derive some future benefit. Most companies have three types of assets: *current*, *fixed*, and *intangible*.

Current Assets **Current assets** include cash, money in the bank, and assets that can be converted into cash within a year. They are normally listed in order of **liquidity**, that is, the ease with which they can be converted into cash. Business debts, for example, can usually be satisfied only through payments of cash. A company that needs cash but does not have it—in other words, a company that is not liquid—may be forced to sell assets at sacrifice prices or even go out of business.

By definition, cash is completely liquid. *Marketable securities* (e.g., stocks or bonds of other companies, government securities, and money market certificates) are slightly less liquid but can be sold quickly if necessary. Three other non-liquid assets are **accounts receivable** (amounts due from customers who have purchased goods on credit), **merchandise inventory** (merchandise that has been acquired for sale to customers and is still on hand), and **prepaid expenses** (supplies on hand and rent paid for the period to come). Figure 11.2 shows that Perfect Posters' current assets as of December 31, 2009, totalled $57 210.

Fixed Assets Fixed assets (e.g., land, buildings, and equipment) have long-term use or value. As buildings and equipment wear out or become obsolete, their value depreciates. Various methods can be used to calculate depreciation, but in its simplest sense, **depreciation** means determining an asset's useful life in years, dividing its worth by that many years, and then subtracting the resulting amount each year. The asset's remaining value therefore decreases each year. In Figure 11.2,

Perfect Posters shows fixed assets of $107 880 after depreciation.

Intangible Assets Although their worth is hard to set, intangible assets have monetary value. **Intangible assets** usually include the cost of obtaining rights or privileges such as patents, trademarks, copyrights, and franchise fees. **Goodwill** is the amount paid for an existing business beyond the value of its other assets. Perfect Posters has no goodwill assets, but it does own trademarks and patents for specialized storage equipment. These intangible assets are worth $8000. Larger companies have intangible assets that are worth much more.

FIXED ASSETS
Assets that have long-term use or value to the firm, such as land, buildings, and machinery.

DEPRECIATION
Distributing the cost of a major asset over the years in which it produces revenues; calculated by each year subtracting the asset's original value divided by the number of years in its productive life.

INTANGIBLE ASSETS
Non-physical assets, such as patents, trademarks, copyrights, and franchise fees, that have economic value but whose precise value is difficult to calculate.

GOODWILL The amount paid for an existing business beyond the value of its other assets.

Figure 11.2
Perfect Posters' balance sheet shows clearly that the firm's total assets equal its total liabilities and owners' equity.

□□□□□□□□ **Perfect Posters, Inc.**			
555 Riverview, Toronto, Ontario			

Perfect Posters, Inc.
Balance Sheet
As of December 31, 2009

Assets

Current Assets:			
Cash		$7,050	
Marketable securities. . . .		2,300	
Accounts receivable.	$26,210		
Less: Allowance of			
doubtful accounts.	(650)	25,560	
Merchandise inventory.		21,250	
Prepaid expenses		1,050	
Total current assets			$57,210
Fixed Assets:			
Land		18,000	
Building	65,000		
Less: Accumulated			
depreciation	(22,500)	42,500	
Equipment	72,195		
Less: Accumulated			
depreciation	(24,815)	47,380	
Total fixed assets. . .			107,880
Intangible Assets:			
Patents	7,100		
Trademarks	900		
Total intangible			
assets			8,000
Total assets			$173,090

Liabilities and Owners' Equity

Current liabilities:			
Accounts payable.	$16,315		
Wages payable.	3,700		
Taxes payable.	1,920		
Total current liabilities			$21,935
Long-term liabilities:			
Notes payable, 8%			
due 2010	10,000		
Bonds payable, 9%			
due 2012	30,000		
Total long-term			
liabilities			40,000
Total liabilities			$61,935
Owners' Equity			
Common stock, $5 par	40,000		
Additional paid-in capital	15,000		
Retained earnings	56,155		
Total owners' equity			111,155
Total liabilities and owners' equity . . .			$173,090

CURRENT LIABILITIES Any debts owed by the firm that must be paid within one year.

ACCOUNTS PAYABLE Amounts due from the firm to its suppliers for goods and/or services purchased on credit; a form of current liability.

LONG-TERM LIABILITIES Any debts owed by the firm that are not due for at least one year.

PAID-IN CAPITAL Any additional money invested in the firm by the owners.

RETAINED EARNINGS A company's net profits less any dividend payments to shareholders.

INCOME STATEMENT (PROFIT-AND-LOSS STATEMENT) A type of financial statement that describes a firm's revenues and expenses and indicates whether the firm has earned a profit or suffered a loss during a given period.

REVENUES Any monies received by a firm as a result of selling a good or service or from other sources such as interest, rent, and licensing fees.

REVENUE RECOGNITION The formal recording and reporting of revenues in the financial statements.

Liabilities **Current liabilities** are debts that must be paid within one year. These include **accounts payable** (unpaid bills to suppliers for materials, as well as wages and taxes that must be paid in the coming year). Perfect Posters has current liabilities of $21 935.

Long-term liabilities are debts that are not due for at least one year. These normally represent borrowed funds on which the company must pay interest. Perfect Posters' long-term liabilities are $40 000.

Owners' Equity The final section of the balance sheet in Figure 11.2 shows owners' equity broken down into *common stock*, *paid-in capital*, and *retained earnings*. When Perfect Posters was formed, the declared legal value of its common stock was $5 per share. By law, this $40 000 ($5 multiplied by 8000 shares) cannot be distributed as dividends. **Paid-in capital** is additional money invested in the firm by its owners. Perfect Posters has $15 000 in paid-in capital.

Retained earnings are net profits minus dividend payments to stockholders. Retained earnings accumulate when profits, which could have been distributed to stockholders, are kept instead for use by the company. At the close of 2009, Perfect Posters had retained earnings of $56 155.

LO-4 Income Statements

The **income statement** is sometimes called a **profit-and-loss statement**, because its description of revenues and expenses results in a figure showing the firm's annual profit or loss. In other words,

Revenues − Expenses = Profit (or loss)

Popularly known as "the bottom line," profit or loss is probably the most important figure in any business enterprise. Figure 11.3 shows the 2009 income

statement for Perfect Posters, whose bottom line that year was $12 585. The income statement is divided into three major categories: *revenues*, *cost of goods sold*, and *operating expenses*.

Revenues When a law firm receives $250 for preparing a will or when a supermarket collects $65 from a customer buying groceries, both are receiving **revenues**—the funds that flow into a business from the sale of goods or services. In 2009, Perfect Posters reported revenues of $256 425 from the sale of art prints and other posters.

Revenue Recognition and Matching **Revenue recognition** is the formal recording and reporting of revenues in the financial statements. Although any firm earns revenues continuously as it makes sales, earnings are not reported until the earnings cycle is completed. Revenues are recorded for the accounting period in which sales are completed and collectible (or collected).

🞏🞏🞏🞏🞏🞏🞏🞏🞏🞏🞏🞏 **Perfect Posters, Inc.**
555 Riverview, Toronto, Ontario

Perfect Posters, Inc.
Income Statement
Year ended December 31, 2009

Revenues (gross sales).			$256,425
Costs of goods sold:			
Merchandise inventory,			
January 1, 2009	$22,380		
Merchandise purchases			
during year.	103,635		
Goods available for sale.		$126,015	
Less: Merchandise inventory,			
December 31, 2009		21,250	
Cost of goods sold			104,765
Gross profit			**151,660**
Operating expenses:			
Selling and repackaging expenses:			
Salaries and wages.	49,750		
Advertising.	6,380		
Depreciation—warehouse and			
repackaging equipment.	3,350		
Total selling and repackaging			
expenses.		59,480	
Administrative expenses:			
Salaries and wages.	55,100		
Supplies.	4,150		
Utilities	3,800		
Depreciation—office equipment .	3,420		
Interest expense	2,900		
Miscellaneous expenses.	1,835		
Total administration expenses.		71,205	
Total operating expenses.			130,685
Operating income (income before taxes). . .			20,975
Income taxes.			8,390
Net income.			**$12,585**

Figure 11.3

Perfect Posters' income statement. The final entry on the income statement, the bottom line, reports the firm's profit or loss.

The **matching** principle states that expenses will be matched with revenues to determine net income for an accounting period.[12] This principle is important because it permits the user of the statement to see how much net gain resulted from the assets that had to be given up to generate revenues during the period covered in the statement.

Cost of Goods Sold In Perfect Posters' income statement, the **cost of goods sold** category shows the costs of obtaining materials to make the products sold during the year. Perfect Posters began 2009 with posters valued at $22 380. Over the year, it spent $103 635 to purchase posters. During 2009, then, the company had $126 015 worth of merchandise available to sell. By the end of the year, it had sold all but $21 250 of those posters, which remained as merchandise inventory. The cost of obtaining the goods sold by the firm was thus $104 765.

Gross Profit (or Gross Margin) To calculate **gross profit** (or **gross margin**), subtract the cost of goods sold from revenues. Perfect Posters' gross profit in 2009 was $151 660 ($256 425 minus $104 765). Expressed as a percentage of sales, gross profit is 59.1 percent ($151 660 divided by $256 425).

Gross profit percentages vary widely across industries. In retailing, Home Depot reports 30 percent; in manufacturing, Harley-Davidson reports 34 percent; and in pharmaceuticals, American Home Products reports 75 percent. For companies with low gross margins, product costs are a big expense. If a company has a high gross margin, it probably has low cost-of-goods-sold but high selling and administrative expenses.

Operating Expenses In addition to costs directly related to acquiring goods, every company has general expenses ranging from erasers to the president's salary. Like cost of goods sold, **operating expenses** are resources that must flow out of a company for it to earn revenues. As you can see in Figure 11.3, Perfect Posters had operating expenses of $130 685 in 2009. This figure consists of $59 480 in selling and repackaging expenses and $71 205 in administrative expenses.

Selling expenses result from activities related to selling the firm's goods or services. These may include salaries for the sales force, delivery costs, and advertising expenses. General and administrative expenses, such as management salaries, insurance expenses, and maintenance costs, are expenses related to the general management of the company.

Operating Income and Net Income Sometimes managers calculate **operating income**, which compares the gross profit from business operations against operating expenses. This calculation for Perfect Posters ($151 660 minus $130 685) reveals an operating income, or *income before taxes*, of $20 975. Subtracting income taxes from operating income ($20 975 minus $8390) reveals **net income** (also called **net profit** or **net earnings**). In 2009, Perfect Posters' net income was $12 585.

Statements of Cash Flows

In order to survive, a business must earn a *profit* (that is, its sales revenues must exceed its expenses), but it must also make sure it has *cash* available when it needs it (for example, to pay employees). Cash flow management requires the development of a **statement of cash flows**, which describes a company's yearly cash receipts and

MATCHING Expenses should be matched with revenues to determine net income for an accounting period.

COST OF GOODS SOLD Any expenses directly involved in producing or selling a good or service during a given time period.

GROSS PROFIT (GROSS MARGIN) A firm's revenues (gross sales) less its cost of goods sold.

OPERATING EXPENSES Costs incurred by a firm other than those included in cost of goods sold.

OPERATING INCOME Compares the gross profit from business operations against operating expenses.

NET INCOME (NET PROFIT OR NET EARNINGS) A firm's gross profit less its operating expenses and income taxes.

STATEMENT OF CASH FLOWS A financial statement that describes a firm's generation and use of cash during a given period.

At the end of its accounting period, this pharmaceuticals company will subtract the cost of making the goods that it sells from the revenues it receives from sales. The difference will be its gross profit (or gross margin).

cash payments. It shows the effects on cash of three important business activities:

- *Cash flows from operations.* This part of the statement is concerned with the firm's main operating activities: the cash transactions involved in buying and selling goods and services. It reveals how much of the year's profits result from the firm's main line of business (for example, Jaguar's sales of automobiles) rather than from secondary activities (for example, licensing fees that a clothing firm paid to Jaguar for using the Jaguar logo on shirts).

- *Cash flows from investing.* This section reports net cash used in or provided by investing. It includes cash receipts and payments from buying and selling stocks, bonds, property, equipment, and other productive assets.

- *Cash flows from financing.* The final section reports net cash from all financing activities. It includes cash inflows from borrowing or issuing stock, as well as outflows for payment of dividends and repayment of borrowed money.

The overall change in cash from these three sources provides information to lenders and investors. When creditors and stockholders know how firms obtained and used their funds during the course of a year, it is easier for them to interpret the year-to-year changes in the firm's balance sheet and income statement.

The Budget: An Internal Financial Statement

In addition to financial statements, managers need other types of accounting information to aid in internal planning, controlling, and decision making. Probably the most crucial internal financial statement is the budget. A **budget** is a detailed statement of estimated receipts and expenditures for a period of time in the future. Although that period is usually one year, some companies also prepare budgets for three- or five-year periods, especially when considering major capital expenditures.

Budgets are also useful for keeping track of weekly or monthly performance. Procter & Gamble, for example, evaluates all of its business units monthly by comparing actual financial results with monthly budgeted amounts. Discrepancies in "actual versus budget" totals signal

potential problems and initiate action to get financial performance back on track.

LO-5 Analyzing Financial Statements

Financial statements present a great deal of information, but what does it all mean? How, for example, can statements help investors decide what stock to buy or help managers decide whether to extend credit? Statements provide data, which in turn can be used to compute solvency, profitability, and activity ratios that are useful in analyzing the financial health of a company compared to other companies, and to check a firm's progress by comparing its current and past statements.

Solvency Ratios

What are the chances that a borrower will be able to repay a loan and the interest due? This question is first and foremost in the minds of bank lending officers, managers of pension funds and other investors, suppliers, and the borrowing company's own financial managers. **Solvency ratios** measure the firm's ability to meet its debt obligations.

Short-Term Solvency Ratios **Short-term solvency ratios** measure a company's liquidity and its ability to pay immediate debts. The most commonly used ratio is the **current ratio**, which reflects a firm's ability to generate cash to meet obligations through the normal, orderly process of selling inventories and collecting revenues from customers. It is calculated by dividing current assets by current liabilities. The higher a firm's current ratio, the lower the risk to investors. For many years, the guideline was a current ratio was one of 2:1 or higher—which meant that current assets were at least double current liabilities. More recently, many firms that are financially strong operate with current ratios of less than 2:1.

How does Perfect Posters measure up? Look again at the balance sheet in Figure 11.2. Judging from its current assets and current liabilities at the end of 2009, we see that the company looks like a good credit risk:

$$\frac{\text{Current assets}}{\text{Current liabilities}} = \frac{\$57\,210}{\$21\,935} = 2.61$$

Long-Term Solvency A firm that can't meet its long-term debt obligations is in danger of collapse or takeover—a risk that makes creditors and investors quite cautious. To evaluate a company's risk of running into this problem, creditors turn to the balance sheet to see the extent to which a firm is financed through borrowed money. Long-term solvency is calculated by dividing **debt**—total liabilities—by owners' equity. The lower a firm's debt, the lower the risk to investors and creditors. Companies with **debt-to-equity ratios** above 1.0 may be relying too much on debt. In the case of Perfect Posters, we can see from the balance sheet in Figure 11.2 that the debt-to-equity ratio calculates as follows:

$$\frac{\text{Debt}}{\text{Owners' equity}} = \frac{\$61\ 935}{\$111\ 155} = \$0.56$$

Sometimes, high debt can be not only acceptable but also desirable. Borrowing funds gives a firm **leverage**—the ability to make otherwise unaffordable investments. In *leveraged buyouts*, firms have sometimes taken on huge debt in order to get the money to buy out other companies. If owning the purchased company generates profits above the cost of borrowing the purchase price, leveraging makes sense. Unfortunately, many buyouts have caused problems because profits fell short of expected levels or because rising interest rates increased payments on the buyer's debt.

Profitability Ratios

Although it is important to know that a company is solvent, safety or risk alone is not an adequate basis for investment decisions. Investors also want some measure of the returns they can expect. Return on equity, return on sales, and earnings per share are three commonly used **profitability ratios** (sometimes these are called *shareholder return ratios* or *performance ratios*).

Return on Equity Owners are interested in the net income earned by a business for each dollar invested. **Return on equity** measures this performance by dividing net income (recorded on the income statement, Figure 11.3) by total owners' equity (recorded on the balance sheet, Figure 11.2). For Perfect Posters, the return-on-equity ratio in 2009 is:

$$\frac{\text{Net income}}{\text{Total owners' equity}} = \frac{\$12\ 585}{\$111\ 155} = 11.3\%$$

Is this ratio good or bad? There is no set answer. If Perfect Posters' ratio for 2009 is higher than in previous years, owners and investors should be encouraged. But if 11.3 percent is lower than the ratios of other companies in the same industry, they should be concerned.

Return on Sales Companies want to generate as much profit as they can from each dollar of sales revenue they receive. The **return on sales** ratio is calculated by dividing net income by sales revenue (see Figure 11.3). For Perfect Posters, the return on sales ratio for 2009 is:

$$\frac{\text{Net income}}{\text{Sales revenue}} = \frac{\$12\ 585}{\$256\ 425} = 4.9\%$$

Is this figure good or bad? Once again, there is no set answer. If Perfect Posters' ratio for 2009 is higher than in previous years, owners and investors should be encouraged, but if 4.9 percent is lower than the ratios of other companies in the same industry, they will likely be concerned.

Earnings per Share **Earnings per share**—which is calculated by dividing net income by the number of shares of common stock outstanding—influences the size of the dividend a company can pay to its shareholders. Investors use this ratio to decide whether to buy or sell a company's stock. As the ratio gets higher, the stock value increases because investors know that the firm can better afford to pay dividends. The market value of a stock will typically decline if the latest financial statements report a decline in earnings per share. For Perfect Posters, we can use the net income total from the income statement in Figure 11.3 to calculate earnings per share as follows:

$$\frac{\text{Net income}}{\text{Number of common shares outstanding}}$$

$$= \frac{\$12\ 585}{\$8000} = \$1.57 \text{ per share}$$

Activity Ratios

Activity ratios measure how efficient a company is in using the resources that it has. Potential investors want to know which company gets more "mileage" from its resources. For example, suppose that two firms use the same amount of resources or assets. If Firm A generates greater profits or sales, it is more efficient and thus has a better activity ratio.

One of the most important activity ratios is the **inventory turnover ratio**, which calculates the average number of times that inventory is sold and restocked during the year.[13] Once a company knows its *average inventory* (which is calculated by adding end-of-year inventory to beginning-of-year inventory and dividing by 2), it can calculate the inventory turnover ratio, which is expressed as the cost of goods sold divided by average inventory:

$$\frac{\text{Cost of goods sold}}{\text{Average inventory}} =$$

$$\frac{\text{Cost of goods sold}}{(\text{Beginning inventory} + \text{Ending inventory}) \div 2}$$

To calculate Perfect Posters' inventory turnover ratio for 2009, we take the merchandise inventory figures for the income statement in Figure 11.3. The ratio can be expressed as follows:

$$\frac{\$104\ 765}{(\$22\ 380 + \$21\ 250) \div 2} = 4.8$$

In other words, new merchandise replaces old merchandise every 76 days (365 days divided by 4.8). The 4.8 ratio is below the industry average of 7.0 for comparable wholesaling operations, indicating that the business is somewhat inefficient.

The inventory turnover ratio measures the average number of times that a store sells and restocks its inventory in one year. The higher the ratio, the more products that get sold and the more revenue that comes in. In almost all retail stores, products with the highest ratios get the shelf space that generates the most customer traffic and sales.

PEARSON mybusinesslab

To improve your grade, visit the MyBusinessLab website at **www.pearsoned.ca/mybusinesslab.** This online homework and tutorial system allows you to test your understanding and generates a personalized study plan just for you. It provides you with study and practice tools directly related to this chapter's content. MyBusinessLab puts you in control of your own learning! Test yourself on the material for this chapter at **www.pearsoned.ca/mybusinesslab.**

Summary of Learning Objectives

1. **Explain the role of *accountants* and distinguish among the three types of *professional accountants* in Canada.** By collecting, analyzing, and communicating financial information, accountants provide business managers and investors with an accurate picture of a firm's financial health. *Chartered Accountants* (CAs) and *Certified General Accountants* (CGAs) provide accounting expertise for client organizations that must report their financial condition to external stakeholders. *Certified Management*

Accountants (CMAs) provide accounting expertise for the firms that employ them.

2. **Explain how the *accounting equation* is used.** Accountants use the following equation to balance the data pertaining to financial transactions:

Assets − Liabilities = Owners' Equity

After each financial transaction (e.g., payments to suppliers, sales to customers, wages to employees), the accounting equation must be in balance. If it isn't, then an accounting error has occurred. The equation also provides an indication of the firm's financial health. If assets exceed liabilities, owners' equity is positive; if the firm goes out of business, owners will receive some cash (a gain) after selling assets and paying off liabilities. If liabilities outweigh assets, owners' equity is negative; assets aren't enough to pay off debts. If the company goes under, owners will get no cash and some creditors won't be paid, thus losing their remaining investments in the company.

3. **Describe three basic *financial statements* and show how they reflect the activity and financial condition of a business.** The *balance sheet* summarizes a company's assets, liabilities, and owners' equity at a given point in time. The *income statement* details revenues and expenses for a given period of time and identifies any profit or loss. The *statement of cash flows* reports cash receipts and payment from operating, investing, and financial activities.

4. **Explain the key standards and principles for reporting financial statements.** Accountants follow standard reporting practices and principles when they prepare financial statements. Otherwise, users wouldn't be able to compare information from different companies, and they might misunderstand—or

be led to misconstrue—a company's true financial status. *Revenue recognition* is the formal recording and reporting of revenues in financial statements. The earnings cycle is complete when the sale has been made, the product is delivered, and the sale price has been collected or is collectible. This practice assures interested parties that the statement gives a fair comparison of what was gained for the resources that were given up. The *matching* principle states that expenses will be matched with revenues to determine net income for an accounting period. This permits the user of the statement to see how much net gain resulted from the assets that had to be given up to generate revenues during the period covered in the statement.

5. **Explain how computing *financial ratios* can help in analyzing the financial strengths of a business.** Drawing upon data from financial statements, ratios can help creditors, investors, and managers assess a firm's finances. The *current*, *liquidity*, and *debt-to-owners' equity ratios* all measure solvency, a firm's ability to pay its debt in both the short and long runs. *Return on sales*, *return on equity*, and *earnings per share* are all ratios that measure profitability. The *inventory turnover ratio* shows how efficiently a firm is using its funds.

Questions and Exercises

Questions for Analysis

1. Balance sheets and income statements are supposed to be objective assessments of the financial condition of a company. But the accounting scandals of the last few years show that certain pressures may be put on accountants as they audit a company's financial statements. Describe these pressures. To what extent do these pressures make the audit more subjective?

2. If you were planning to invest in a company, which of the three types of financial statements would you want most to see? Why?

3. A business hires a professional accountant like a CA or CGA to assess the financial condition of the

company. Why would the business also employ a private accountant?

4. Why does the double-entry system reduce the chances of mistakes or fraud in accounting?

5. How do financial ratios help managers to monitor their own efficiency and effectiveness?

6. Explain the difference between financial and managerial accounting. In your answer, describe the different audiences for the two types of accounting and the various individuals involved in the process.

Application Exercises

7. Dasar Co. reports the following data in its September 30, 2010, financial statements:

- Gross sales $225 000
- Current assets 40 000
- Long-term assets 100 000
- Current liabilities 16 000
- Long-term liabilities 44 000
- Owners' equity 80 000

- Net income 7 200
- Number of common shares 5 000

Compute the following ratios: current ratio, debt-to-equity, return on owners' equity, and earnings per share.

8. Interview an accountant at a local manufacturing firm. Determine what kinds of budgets the firm uses, and the process by which budgets are developed. Also

determine how budgeting helps managers plan their business activities. Give specific examples.

9. Interview the manager of a local retail or wholesale business. Ask the manager about the company's primary purpose for taking inventory, and how often this is done.

10. Interview the manager of a local business and ask about the role of ethics in the company's accounting practices. How important is ethics in accounting? What measures does the firm take to ensure that its internal reporting is ethical? What steps does the company take to maintain ethical relationships in its dealing with external CA or CGA firms?

Building Your Business Skills

Putting the Buzz in Billing

Goal
To encourage students to think about the advantages and disadvantages of using an electronic system for handling accounts receivable and accounts payable.

Method
Step 1 As the CFO of a utility company, you are analyzing the feasibility of switching from a paper to an electronic system. You decide to discuss the ramifications of the choice with three associates (choose three classmates to take on these roles). Your discussion requires that you research electronic payment systems now being developed. Specifically, using online and library research, you must find out as much as you can about the electronic bill-paying systems being developed by companies like VISA International, Intuit, IBM, and the Checkfree Corporation.

Step 2 After you have researched this information, brainstorm the advantages and disadvantages of switching to an electronic system.

Follow-Up Questions
1. What cost savings are inherent in the electronic system for both your company and its customers? In your answer, consider such costs as handling, postage, and paper.

2. What consequences would your decision to adopt an electronic system have on others with whom you do business, including manufacturers of cheque-sorting equipment, Canada Post, and banks?

3. Switching to an electronic system would mean a large capital expense for new computers and software. How could analyzing the company's income statement help you justify this expense?

4. How are consumers likely to respond to paying bills electronically? Are you likely to get a different response from individuals than you get from business customers?

Exercising Your Ethics

Confidentially Yours

The Situation
Accountants are often entrusted with private, sensitive information that should be used confidentially. In this exercise, you're encouraged to think about ethical considerations that might arise when an accountant's career choices come up against a professional obligation to maintain confidentiality.

The Dilemma
Assume that you're the head accountant in Turbatron, a large electronics firm that makes components for other manufacturing firms. Your responsibilities include preparing Turbatron's financial statements that are then audited for financial reporting to shareholders. In addition, you regularly prepare confidential budgets for internal use by managers responsible for planning departmental activities, including future investments in new assets. You've also worked with auditors and CA consultants that assess financial problems and suggest solutions.

Now let's suppose that you're approached by another company, Electrolast, one of the electronics industry's most successful firms, and offered a higher-level position. If you accept, your new job will include developing Electrolast's financial plans and serving on the strategic planning committee. Thus, you'd be involved not only in developing strategy but also in evaluating the competition, perhaps even using your knowledge of Turbatron's competitive strengths and weaknesses.

Your contractual commitments with Turbatron do not bar you from employment with other electronics firms.

Team Activity

Assemble a group of four to five students and assign each group member to one of the following roles:

- Head accountant (leaving Turbatron)
- General manager of Turbatron
- Shareholder of Turbatron
- Customer of Turbatron
- General manager of Electrolast (if your group has five members)

Action Steps

1. Before hearing any of your group's comments on this situation, and from the perspective of your assigned role, decide if there are any ethical issues confronting the head accountant in this situation. If so, write them down.

2. Return to your group and reveal ethical issues identified by each member. Were the issues the same among all roles or did differences in roles result in different issues?

3. Among the ethical issues that were identified, decide as a group which one is most important for the head accountant. Which is most important for Turbatron?

4. What does your group finally recommend be done to resolve the most important ethical issue(s)?

5. What steps do you think Turbatron might take in advance of such a situation to avoid any difficulties it now faces?

BUSINESS CASE 11

Who Will Take the Blame?

The negative publicity that has been given to firms like Livent, Enron, Parmalat, and WorldCom during the last decade has made for very interesting reading, but it has also made auditors nervous. More and more investors are asking questions like, "How much confidence can I really have when I read in an auditor's statement that a company's practices adhere to generally accepted accounting principles?" or "How can a company go bankrupt shortly after having its books audited by an independent auditor?" Two recent high-profile cases have been evident at Lehman Brothers in the U.S. and Livent in Canada.

In 2008, an executive at Lehman Brothers wrote a letter to senior management expressing his concern that the company was concealing the true risks on its balance sheet and therefore misleading investors about its financial condition. The board of directors instructed the company's auditors (Ernst & Young) to interview the executive and investigate his concerns. The auditors did so, but when they met with the board of directors, the auditors did not mention the executive's allegations. Not too long afterward, Lehman Brothers went bankrupt.

In 2010, a report by a bankruptcy-court examiner concluded that Lehman's auditors knew of accounting irregularities but did nothing about them. In its defence, Ernst & Young pointed out that Lehman's management had concluded that the allegations originally made by the executive were unfounded. It also noted that its review of the executive's allegations was not completed because Lehman Brothers went bankrupt. As of mid-2010, authorities were in the process of deciding whether to prosecute some of Lehman's top executives for manipulating the company's financial statements. If they decide to go ahead with the prosecution, it is likely that the executives will use the defence that they relied on the firm's auditors to determine if financial reporting had been properly done (Ernst & Young said that some questionable transactions complied with generally acceptable accounting principles). When executives blame the auditors and the auditors blame the executives, it is very frustrating. *Someone* is to blame for the problems.

The case of Livent Inc.—a live theatre company that formerly had theatres in Vancouver, Toronto, and

was fined $100 000, and was required to pay costs of $417 000. Deloitte appealed the ICAO's decision, arguing that the faulty audit didn't necessarily mean there was professional misconduct.

The CEO of Deloitte says that there is an "expectation gap" between what the investing public expects and what external auditors can possibly deliver. While auditors simply certify the accuracy of a company's financial statements (based on information provided by the company), investors want auditors to certify that a company is actually financially healthy. He also says that it is not reasonable to hold auditing firms accountable for the illegal and secretive behaviour of corporate executives. He does agree that auditing firms will have to improve the rigour of their audits, and he said that Deloitte has been working hard to overcome any existing deficiencies. The company has appointed an ethics officer in each of its national companies, has added more resources to audit teams, and re-checks initial audit results.

The CEO's explanation sounds pretty reasonable, but people still want to know how cases like Livent, Parmalat, and Enron happen even after the companies' financial statements have been audited by an independent accounting firm. One answer is that auditors are sometimes tempted to "look the other way" when they encounter questionable practices. But *why* would accounting firms not point out questionable accounting practices when they find them? One reason is that many accounting firms have historically also done management consulting for the firms they are auditing. The fees generated from this management consulting can be very lucrative, and often exceed the auditing fees the accounting firm receives. Accountants are human beings, so we should not be surprised if they worry that their clients will be upset if auditors question certain accounting practices. And if clients get upset enough, they may not give the accounting firm any more management consulting contracts. The obvious solution to this problem is to prohibit accounting firms from doing both auditing and management consulting for a given client. The Canadian Imperial Bank of Commerce no longer allows its auditors to do any management consulting for CIBC.

One very specific Canadian response is the establishment of the Canadian Public Accountability Board (CPAB), which oversees supervision, inspection, and discipline of Canada's largest accounting firms. Accounting firms must get CPAB clearance before their clients' financial statements are accepted. In short, the auditors are going to be audited. Since the CPAB was formed, several individuals have had their chartered accountant certifications revoked as a result of professional misconduct or violation of securities laws.

New York—further illustrates the tendency to shift the blame for problems to someone else. Livent went bankrupt in the late 1990s amid charges of questionable accounting practices. After nearly a decade of court delays, two of its executives—Garth Drabinsky and Myron Gottlieb—were found guilty in 2009 of defrauding investors and creditors out of $500 million. Investors lost 95 percent of their investment after Livent first disclosed accounting irregularities in 1998. (For more details about the Livent case, see the opening case in Chapter 3.)

Several years before the 2009 court ruling, the Institute of Chartered Accountants of Ontario (ICAO) had already taken disciplinary action against Livent's senior vice-president of finance, who was a chartered accountant. He was fined $25 000 and expelled from the ICAO after admitting that he had filed false financial statements and fraudulently manipulated Livent's books. The ICAO then laid charges of professional misconduct against three partners at Deloitte & Touche, the accounting firm that was auditing Livent. (Deloitte also faced several other lawsuits, including one resulting from the collapse of the Italian dairy firm Parmalat. In that case, investors sued Parmalat executives and two partners in Deloitte's Italian branch for allegedly conspiring to hide nearly $17 billion of debt.)

At a disciplinary hearing, the lawyer for Deloitte & Touche argued that the ICAO charges were "rubbish," and that the allegations were simply differences of opinion regarding the application of generally accepted accounting principles. He also pointed out that Livent managers had admitted lying to Deloitte auditors to prevent them from finding out about Livent's real financial condition. In 2007, the ICAO decided that the three partners at Deloitte were guilty of professional misconduct during their audit of Livent's books (a report stating the ICAO's reasons for their decision was published some months later). Each partner received a written reprimand,

We should not conclude from all of this that doom and gloom reigns in the auditing business. In fact, things are looking up, partly because of the Sarbanes-Oxley Act, which was passed by the U.S. Congress in 2002 and is designed to restore public trust in corporate accounting practices. Section 404 of the Act requires U.S.-listed companies to analyze their reporting controls and to make any improvements that are necessary. At each year-end, auditors must certify these controls. Many people in the accounting field believe that Canadian legislators will soon introduce similar legislation. That will affect over 4000 Canadian corporations, which in turn will create a substantial increase in demand for the services of auditors. Canadian public accounting firms have already begun recruiting more staff. The increased demand for accountants who are knowledgeable about Sarbanes-Oxley is particularly evident in places like Calgary, the home of many Canadian companies that are listed on U.S. stock exchanges.

Questions for Discussion

1. What role does the Institute of Chartered Accountants of Ontario (ICAO) play in ensuring full disclosure on the part of accountants and auditors? How does the ICAO monitor auditor activity and maintain integrity within the accounting profession? What is its relationship to the CPAB?

2. What are some ways to ensure that an auditing firm does not find itself in the position that Deloitte & Touche did in the Livent case?

3. Do you think business practices like disclosure and auditing proceedings will change as a result of the Sarbanes-Oxley Act? Do you think the number of fraud allegations will decline? Explain your answers.

4. There has been much publicity in the last few years about white-collar fraud. Give some examples of fraud that you are familiar with. What role, if any, did accounting fraud play in these cases?

SCANLIFE

Appendix B
Using Technology to Manage Information in the Internet and Social Media Era

Throughout the text we examine how the internet and the emergence of social media have improved communications, revolutionized distribution, augmented human resources practices, revolutionized industries (and threatened others), developed new marketing communication channels, and changed the most basic business systems. In this appendix we will begin by providing additional information about the internet and social media. We will also examine the evolving role of technology in managing information.

Internet Usage

Before we look into the specifics, let's examine some of the key Canadian internet statistics. In 2009, approximately 80 percent of Canadians (21.7 million) over the age of 16 used the internet. That figure was up from 73 percent two years earlier. The statistics are even more impressive for higher income families; 94 percent of Canadians that live in households with incomes above $85 000 are connected (only 56 percent for households with incomes below $30 000 per year).[1] These figures will continue to increase in the next few years. The federal government has set its sights on increasing and improving the connectivity in rural settings; it invested in 52 projects worth over $225 million in 2010. At the time, it cost approximately $89 per month for 5Mbps (megabits per second) in most rural areas, but consumers could get 10Mbps for about $47 a month in most cities, or get 50mbps (10 times quicker speed) for about the same fee. The improved infrastructure will help increase rural access and build further opportunities for companies wishing to sell to rural Canadian clients and also provide more incentive and opportunity for small businesses to operate in rural settings.[2]

The Impact of Information Technology (IT)

No matter where we go, we can't escape the impact of **information technology (IT)**—the various devices for creating, storing, exchanging, and using information in diverse modes, including visual images, voice, multimedia, and business data. We see ads all the time for the latest smart phones, iPods, laptops, iPads, netbooks, and software products, and most of us connect daily to the internet (many of you never disconnect). Email and BlackBerry (BBM) messaging have become staples in business, and even such traditionally "low-tech" businesses as hair salons and garbage collection companies are becoming dependent on the internet, computers, and networks. As consumers, we interact with databases every time we withdraw money from an ATM, order food at McDonald's, use an Apple application to order food or movie tickets, or check on the status of a package at UPS or FedEx.

IT has had an immense effect on businesses—in fact, the growth of IT has changed the very structure of business organizations. Its adoption has altered the workforces in many companies, contributed to greater flexibility in dealing with customers, and changed the way that employees interact with each other. E-commerce has created new market relationships around the globe. We begin by looking at how businesses are using IT to bolster productivity, improve operations and processes, create new opportunities, and communicate and work in ways not possible before.

The Impact of the Internet on Marketing

E-commerce refers to buying and selling processes that make use of electronic technology, while **internet marketing** refers to the promotional efforts of companies to sell their products and services to consumers over the internet.[3]

While internet marketing has some obvious advantages for both buyers (access to information, convenience, etc.) and sellers (reach, direct distribution, etc.) it also has weaknesses, including profitability problems (many internet marketers are still unprofitable and the failure rates are high); information overload (consumers may not know what to do with all the information available to them), and somewhat limited markets (consumers who use the web are typically more highly educated).

In addition to these weaknesses, internet marketers must also cope with consumer concerns about two security-related issues. An Angus Reid/Globe and Mail poll of 1500 Canadians found that their main concern about internet marketing was security. People who had made at least one purchase on the internet were more likely to list security as their top concern than were those who had never purchased anything on the internet. In particular, people were concerned that their credit card number might end up in the wrong hands, and that their privacy would be invaded if they purchased on the internet.[4]

Consumers also object to spyware software, which monitors websites they visit and observes their shopping habits. This software is often implanted on their personal computers as they wander through the web. It then generates pop-up advertisements that are targeted to that particular consumer. Because people are often unaware that such spyware is on their computer, the technique has generated anger among consumers. Consumers can, however, get free anti-spyware software that removes spyware from their computer. Spyware is also a concern for companies that sell from their own websites because the pop-ups are designed to divert web surfers from the products offered by the website.[5]

Creating Portable Offices: Providing Remote Access to Instant Information

The packing list for Barry Martin's upcoming fishing trip reflects his new outlook on how he gets his work done. It reads, in part, as follows: (1) fly rod, (2) dry-pack food, (3) tent, and (4) BlackBerry. Five years ago, a much longer list would have included a cellphone, road and area maps, phone directory, appointments calendar, office files, and client project folders, all of which are now replaced by just one item—his BlackBerry—a wireless hand-held messaging device that allows him to take the office with him wherever he goes. Even in the Canadian wilderness, Martin can place phone calls and read new email messages. Along with internet browsing, there's access to desktop tools—such as an organizer and an address book—for managing work and staying in touch with customers, suppliers, and employees from any location. The mobile messaging capabilities of devices like the BlackBerry offer businesses powerful tools that save time and travel expenses.[6] As we describe in Chapter 12's E-Business and Social Media Solutions box, "Apps, Apps, and More Apps," the range of current applications is immense and enlarging to meet the needs of business and consumers.

E-COMMERCE
Buying and selling processes that make use of electronic technology.

INTERNET MARKETING
The promotional efforts of companies to sell their products and services to consumers over the internet.

Barack Obama is an avid BlackBerry user. This picture is indicative of the times we live in. Think of how often you see classmates and work colleagues walking down a hall with a smartphone in hand.

Enabling Better Service by Coordinating Remote Deliveries

With access to the internet, company activities may be geographically scattered but remain coordinated through a networked system that provides better service for customers. Many businesses, for example, coordinate activities from one centralized location, but their deliveries flow from several remote locations, often at lower cost. When you order furniture from an internet storefront—for example, a chair, a sofa, a table, and two lamps—the chair may come from a warehouse in Toronto, the lamps from a manufacturer in China, and the sofa and table from a supplier in North Carolina. Beginning with the customer's order, activities are coordinated through the company's network, as if the whole order were being processed at one place. This avoids the expensive in-between step of first shipping all the items to a central location.

Creating Leaner, More Efficient Organizations

Networks and technology are also leading to leaner companies with fewer employees and simpler structures. Because networks enable firms to maintain information linkages between employees and customers, more work and customer satisfaction can be accomplished with fewer people. Bank customers can access 24-hour information systems and monitor their accounts without employee assistance. Instructions that once were given to assembly workers by supervisors are now delivered to workstations electronically. Truck drivers delivering freight used to return to the trucking terminal to receive instructions from supervisors on reloading for the next delivery, but now instructions arrive on electronic screens in the trucks so drivers know in advance what will be happening next.

Enabling Increased Collaboration

Collaboration among internal units and with outside firms is greater when firms use collaboration software and other IT communications devices (we discuss these later in this appendix). Companies are learning that complex problems can be solved better through IT-supported collaboration, either with formal teams or spontaneous interaction among people and departments. The design of new products, for example, was once largely an engineering responsibility. Now it is a shared activity using information from people in marketing, finance, production, engineering, and purchasing who, collectively, determine the best design. For example, the design of Boeing's 787 Dreamliner aircraft is the result of collaboration, not just among engineers but also from passengers (who wanted electronic outlets to recharge personal electronic devices), cabin crews (who wanted more bathrooms and wider aisles), and air-traffic controllers (who wanted larger, safer airbrakes).

Enabling Global Exchange

The global reach of IT is enabling business collaboration on a scale that was unheard of just a few years ago. Consider Lockheed Martin's contract for designing the Joint Strike Fighter and supplying thousands of the planes in different versions for Canada, the United States, Britain, Italy, Denmark, and Norway. Lockheed can't do the job alone. Over the project's 20-year life, more than 1500 companies will supply everything from radar systems to engines to bolts. Web collaboration on a massive scale is essential for coordinating design, testing, and construction while avoiding delays, holding down costs, and maintaining quality.[7]

Improving Management Processes

IT has also changed the nature of the management process. At one time, upper-level managers didn't concern themselves with all of the detailed information filtering upward from the workplace because it was expensive to gather, slow in coming, and quickly became out of date. Rather, workplace management was delegated to middle and first-line managers.

With databases, specialized software, and networks, however, instantaneous information is accessible and useful to all levels of management. For example, consider *enterprise resource planning (ERP)*, a system for organizing and managing a firm's activities across product lines, departments, and geographic locations. The ERP stores real-time information on work status and upcoming transactions and notifies employees when action is required if certain schedules are to be met. It coordinates internal operations with activities of outside suppliers and notifies customers of upcoming deliveries and billings. Consequently, more managers use it routinely for planning and controlling operations. A manager at Hershey Foods, for example, uses ERP to check on the current status of any customer order for Hershey Kisses, to inspect productivity statistics for each workstation, and to analyze the delivery performance on any shipment. Managers can better coordinate company-wide performance because they can identify departments that are working well together and those that are lagging behind schedule and creating bottlenecks.

Providing Flexibility for Customization

IT has also created new manufacturing capabilities that enable businesses to offer customers greater variety and faster delivery cycles. Whether it's a personal computer from Dell, one of Nokia's phones, or a Rawlings baseball glove, today's design-it-yourself world has become possible through fast, flexible manufacturing using IT networks. At Timbuk2's website, for example, you can "build your own" custom messenger bag at different price levels with choices of size, fabric, colour combinations, accessories, liner material, strap, and even left- or right-hand access.[8] The principle is called **mass-customization**: Although companies produce in large volumes, each unit features the unique options the customer prefers. As shown in Figure B.1, flexible production and speedy delivery depend on an integrated network of information to coordinate all the activities among customers, manufacturers, suppliers, and shippers.

Providing New Business Opportunities

Not only is IT improving existing businesses, it is creating entirely new businesses. For big businesses, this means developing new products, offering new services, and reaching new clients. Only a few years ago, Google was a fledgling search engine. In 2010, the company had nearly $25 billion in cash and short-term investments and it was no longer simply a search engine company; Google had email (Gmail service) and other productivity software, the Android cellphone platform, and YouTube.[9]

The IT landscape has also presented small business owners with new e-business opportunities. More than 600 online marketplaces allow entrepreneurs to sell directly to consumers, bypassing conventional retail outlets, and enable B2B selling and trading with access to a worldwide customer base. To assist start-up businesses, eBay's services network is a ready-made online business model, not just an auction market. Services range from credit financing to protection from fraud and misrepresentation, information security, international currency exchanges, and post-sales management. These features enable users to complete sales transactions, deliver merchandise, and get new merchandise for future resale, all from the comfort of their own homes.

Technology continues to provide new and improved business models. For example, Instinet Inc. was a pioneer

MASS-CUSTOMIZATION
Although companies produce in large volumes, each unit features the unique options the customer prefers.

Figure B.1
Networking for mass-customization.

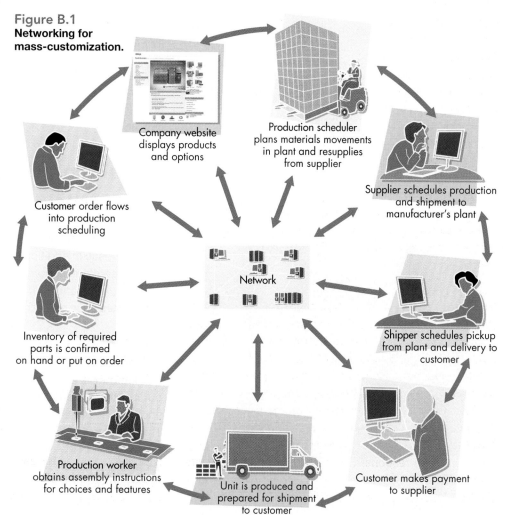

Company website displays products and options

Production scheduler plans materials movements in plant and resupplies from supplier

Supplier schedules production and shipment to manufacturer's plant

Customer order flows into production scheduling

Network

Shipper schedules pickup from plant and delivery to customer

Inventory of required parts is confirmed on hand or put on order

Customer makes payment to supplier

Production worker obtains assembly instructions for choices and features

Unit is produced and prepared for shipment to customer

in electronic trading. In 2010, it launched a service called Meet the Street, which matches companies with potential investors. This service competes directly with investment companies like the Royal Bank of Canada (RBC) and Goldman Sachs that are known for creating "road shows" (days packed with meetings with potential investors). The service enables business owners to book their own meetings, make travel arrangements, suggest dining spots, and use GPS technology to organize meetings efficiently to save time.[10]

Improving the World and Our Lives

Can advancements in IT really make the world a better place? Hospitals and medical equipment companies certainly think so. For example, when treating combat injuries, surgeons at Walter Reed National Military Medical Center in the U.S. rely on high-tech graphics displays that are converted into three-dimensional physical models

for pre-surgical planning. These 3-D mock-ups of shoulders, femurs, and facial bones give doctors the opportunity to see and feel the anatomy as it will be seen in the operating room, before they even use their scalpels.[11] Meanwhile, vitamin-sized cameras that patients swallow are providing doctors with computer images of the insides of the human body, helping them to make better diagnoses for such ailments as ulcers and cancer.[12]

Social Networking: Providing a Service

The many forms of social media—blogs, chats, and networks such as LinkedIn, Twitter, and Facebook—are no longer just playthings for gossips and hobbyists. As we examined in Chapter 8 (E-Business and Social Media Solutions box, "Job Recruitment in the Social Media Era") they're also tools for getting a job. The economic meltdown pushed millions of job seekers to online networking—tapping leads from friends, colleagues, and acquaintances—for contacts with companies that may be hiring. Peers and recruiters are networking using electronic discussion forums and bulletin boards at websites of professional associations and trade groups, technical schools, and alumni organizations.

Some social sites provide occupation-specific career coaching and job tips. For example, scientists are connecting with Epernicus, top managers use Meet the Boss, and graduate students are connecting with Graduate Junction.[13]

IT Building Blocks: Business Resources

Businesses today have a wide variety of IT resources at their disposal. In addition to the internet and email, these include communications technologies, networks, hardware devices, and software, as shown at technology media sites such as TechWeb.com.

The Internet's Other Communication Resources

The **internet** is a gigantic system of interconnected computers; these computers are connected by numerous applications utilizing different communications protocols. The most familiar internet protocols are **hypertext transfer protocol (HTTP)**—which is used for the **World Wide Web**, a branch of the internet consisting of interlinked hypertext documents, or webpages—and **simple message transfer protocol (SMTP)** and **post office protocol (POP)**, which are used to send and receive email. For

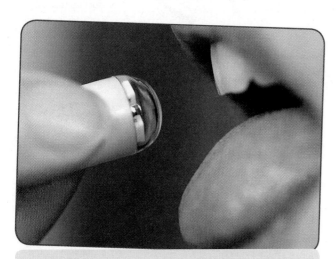

After this capsule is swallowed, the camera inside it can transmit 50 000 images during its eight-hour journey through the digestive tract.

thousands of businesses, the internet has replaced the telephone, fax machine, and standard mail as the primary communications tool.

The amount of traffic on the internet has increased dramatically over the years, and certain individuals, such as scientists, have found that it is often slow going when they try to transmit or manipulate large databases. So **Internet2** has been created, which is dramatically faster than the regular internet. Internet2 is generally available only to universities, corporations, and government agencies that have applications that put heavy demands on the internet (for example, videoconferencing).

The internet has spawned a number of other business communications technologies, including *intranets*, *extranets*, *electronic conferencing*, and *VSAT satellite communications*.

Intranets Many companies have extended internet technology by maintaining internal websites linked throughout the firm. These private networks, or **intranets**, are accessible only to employees and may contain confidential information on benefits programs, a learning library, production management tools, or product design resources. For firms such as Ford Motor Company, whose intranet is accessible to 200 000 people daily, sharing information on engineering, distribution, and marketing has reduced the lead time for getting new models into production and has shortened customer delivery times.[14]

Extranets **Extranets** allow outsiders limited access to a firm's internal information network. The most common application allows buyers to enter a system to see which products are available for sale and delivery, thus providing convenient product-availability information. Industrial suppliers are often linked into customers' information networks so that they can see planned production schedules and prepare supplies for customers' upcoming operations. **Enterprise portals** allow outsiders like customers to log on to a company's intranet. The extranet at Chaparral Steel, for example, lets customers shop electronically through its storage yards and gives them electronic access to Chaparral's planned inventory of industrial steel products.

Electronic Conferencing **Electronic conferencing** allows groups of people to communicate simultaneously from various locations via email, phone, or video, thereby eliminating travel time and saving money. One form, called *dataconferencing*, allows people in remote locations to work simultaneously on one document.

Videoconferencing allows participants to see one another on video screens while the conference is in progress. For example, Lockheed Martin's Joint Strike Fighter project, discussed earlier, uses internet collaboration systems with both voice and video capabilities. Although separated by oceans, partners can communicate as if they were in the same room while redesigning components and creating production schedules. Electronic conferencing is attractive to many businesses because it eliminates travel and saves money.

VSAT Satellite Communications Another internet technology businesses use to communicate is **VSAT satellite communications**. VSAT (short for *very small aperture terminal*) systems have a transmitter-receiver (*transceiver*) that sits outdoors with a direct line of sight to a satellite. The hub—a ground-station computer at the company's headquarters—sends signals to and receives signals from the satellite, exchanging voice, video, and data transmissions. An advantage of VSAT is privacy. A company that operates its own VSAT system has total control over communications among its facilities, no matter their location, without dependence on other companies. A firm might use VSAT to exchange sales and inventory information, advertising messages, and visual presentations between headquarters and store managers at remote sites.

Networks: System Architecture

A **computer network** is a group of two or more computers linked together, either hardwired or wirelessly, to share data or resources, such as a printer. The most common type

INTERNET2 Faster than regular internet, Internet2 is generally available only to universities, corporations, and government agencies that have applications with heavy demands.

INTRANETS An organization's private network of internally linked websites accessible only to employees.

EXTRANETS A system that allows outsiders limited access to a firm's internal information network.

ENTERPRISE PORTALS Enable customers to log on to a company's intranet.

ELECTRONIC CONFERENCING IT that allows groups of people to communicate simultaneously from various locations via email, phone, or video.

VSAT SATELLITE COMMUNICATIONS A network of geographically dispersed transmitter-receivers (transceivers) that send signals to and receive signals from a satellite, exchanging voice, video, and data transmissions.

COMPUTER NETWORK A group of two or more computers linked together by some form of cabling or by wireless technology to share data or resources, such as a printer.

of network used in businesses is a **client-server network**. In client-server networks, *clients* are usually the laptop or desktop computers through which users make requests for information or resources. *Servers* are the computers that provide the services shared by users. In big organizations, servers are usually assigned a specific task. For example, in a local university or college network, an *application server* stores the word-processing, spreadsheet, and other programs used by all computers connected to the network. A *print server* controls the printers, stores printing requests from client computers, and routes jobs as the printers become available. An *email server* handles all incoming and outgoing email. With a client-server system, users can share resources and internet connections—and avoid costly duplication.

Networks can be classified according to geographic scope and means of connection (either wired or wireless).

Wide Area Networks (WANs) Computers that are linked over long distances—province-wide or even nationwide—through telephone lines, microwave signals, or satellite communications make up what are called **wide area networks (WANs)**. Firms can lease lines from communications vendors or maintain private WANs. Walmart, for example, depends heavily on a private satellite network that links thousands of U.S. and international retail stores to its Bentonville, Arkansas, headquarters.

Local Area Networks (LANs) In **local area networks (LANs)**, computers are linked in a smaller area such as an office or a building. For example, a LAN unites hundreds of operators who enter call-in orders at TV's Home Shopping Network facility. The arrangement requires only one computer system with one database and one software system. **Virtual private networks (VPNs)** connect two or more LANs through a public network like the internet. This saves companies money because they don't have to pay for private lines, but it is important that strong security measures are in place so that unauthorized persons can't gain access.

Wireless Networks Wireless networks use airborne electronic signals to link network computers and devices. Like wired networks, wireless networks can reach across long distances or exist within a single building or small area. For example, the BlackBerry system shown in Figure B.2 consists of devices that send and receive transmissions on the **wireless wide area networks (WWANs)** of more than 100 service providers—such as Cellular One (United States), T-Mobile (United Kingdom and United States), and Vodafone (Italy)—in countries throughout the world. The wireless format that the system relies on to control wireless messaging is supplied by Research In Motion (RIM), the Canadian company that makes the BlackBerry, and is installed on the user-company's computer.[15] A *firewall* provides privacy protection. We'll discuss firewalls in more detail later in the appendix.

Wi-Fi *Hotspots* are locations, such as coffee shops, hotels, and airports, that provide wireless internet connections for people on the go. Each hotspot, or **Wi-Fi** (short for *wi*reless *fi*delity) access point, uses

Figure B.2
BlackBerry wireless internet architecture.

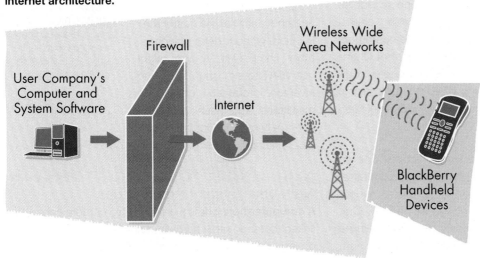

its own small network, called a **wireless local area network (wireless LAN or WLAN)**. Although wireless service is free at some hotspots, others charge a fee—a daily or hourly rate—for the convenience of Wi-Fi service.

Wi-Fi networks have many benefits, for example, employees can wait for a delayed plane in the airport and still be connected to the internet. However, Wi-Fi has limitations, including a short range of distance. In addition, thick walls, construction beams, and other obstacles can interfere with the signals sent out by the network. So, while a city may have hundreds of hotspots, your laptop must remain near one to stay connected. *WiMAX (worldwide interoperability for microwave access),* the next step in wireless advancements, will improve this distance limitation with its wireless range of about 50 kilometres.

Hardware and Software

Any computer network or system needs **hardware**—the physical components, such as keyboards, monitors, system units, and printers. In addition to the laptops, desktop computers, and BlackBerrys, *handheld computers* are also used in businesses. For example, Walmart employees roam store aisles using handhelds to identify, count, and order items, track deliveries, and update backup stock at distribution centres to keep store shelves replenished with merchandise.

The other essential in any computer system is **software**—programs that tell the computer how to function. Software includes *system software*, such as Microsoft Windows 7 for PCs, which tells the computer's hardware how to interact with the software. It also includes *application software*, which meets the needs of specific users (for example, Adobe Photoshop). Some application programs are used to address common, long-standing needs such as database management and inventory control, whereas others have been developed for a variety of specialized tasks ranging from mapping the underground structure of oil fields to analyzing the anatomical structure of the human body. For a subscription fee, companies can gain access to a large number of software application programs from application service providers (ASPs). They therefore don't have to spend a lot of money buying various software programs. Managed service providers (MSPs) go even further, and include management of a company's network servers.

One illustrative example of a software program is **computer graphics**, which converts numeric and character data into pictorial information like charts and graphs. They allow managers to see relationships more easily and generate clearer and more persuasive reports and presentations. As Figure B.3 shows, both types of graphics can convey different kinds of information—in this case, the types of materials that should be ordered by a picture framing shop like Artists' Frame Service.

Groupware—software that connects group members for email distribution, electronic meetings, message

WI-FI Short for wireless fidelity; a wireless local area network.

WIRELESS LOCAL AREA NETWORK (WIRELESS LAN OR WLAN) A local area network with wireless access points for PC users.

HARDWARE The physical components of a computer network, such as keyboards, monitors, system units, and printers.

SOFTWARE Programs that tell the computer's hardware what resources to use and how.

COMPUTER GRAPHICS Programs that convert numeric and character data into pictorial information like charts and graphs.

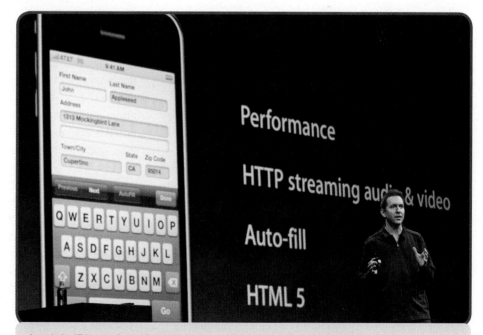

Apple's iPhone lags far behind in business usage compared to the BlackBerry but new versions are becoming more appealing. iPhones offer a larger keyboard, voice messaging and convenient text editing in addition to its key consumer features (iPod, movie viewing capacity etc.)

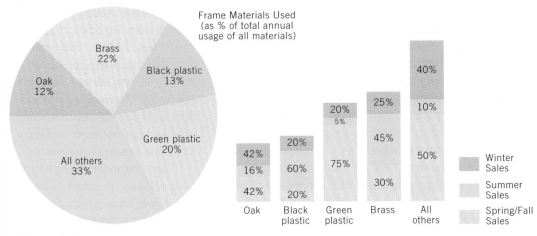

Figure B.3
Artists' Frame Service.

storing, appointments and schedules, and group writing—allows people to collaborate from their own desktop PCs, even if they're remotely located. It is especially useful when people work together regularly and rely heavily on information sharing. Groupware systems include IBM Lotus Domino, Microsoft Exchange Server, and Novell GroupWise.

Information Systems: Harnessing the Competitive Power of Information Technology

Business today relies on information management in ways that no one could foresee even a decade ago. Managers now treat IT as a basic organizational resource for conducting daily business. At major firms, every activity—designing services, ensuring product delivery and cash flow, evaluating personnel—is linked to *information systems*. An **information system (IS)** uses IT resources and enables managers to take **data**—raw facts and figures that by themselves may not have much meaning—and turn that data into **information**—the meaningful, useful interpretation of data. Information systems also enable managers to collect, process, and transmit that information for use in decision making.

One of the most widely publicized examples of the strategic use of information systems is Walmart. The IS drives down costs and increases efficiency because the same methods and systems are applied for all 5000-plus stores in Europe, Asia, and North America. Data on the billions of sales transactions—time, date, place—flows to company headquarters in Bentonville, Arkansas. Keeping track of nearly 700 million *stock keeping units* (SKUs) weekly, the information system enforces uniform reordering and delivery procedures—on packaging, timing, and quantities—for more than 30 000 suppliers. It also regulates the flow of the more than five billion cases through its distribution centres, and deliveries by nearly 8000 Walmart truck drivers, to its stores.

Beyond the firm's daily operations, information systems are also crucial in planning. Managers routinely use the IS to decide on products and markets for the next 5 to 10 years. The company's vast database enables marketing managers to analyze demographics, and it is also used for financial planning, materials handling, and electronic funds transfers with suppliers and customers.

Like most businesses, Walmart regards its information as an asset that's planned, developed, and protected. Therefore, it's not surprising that businesses have **information systems managers** who operate the systems used for gathering, organizing, and distributing information, just as they have production, marketing, and finance managers. These managers use many of the IT resources we discussed earlier to sift through this information and apply it to their jobs. The effective use of information is so critical that many companies have appointed **chief information officers** who are responsible for managing all aspects of information resources and information processes.

There are so many new challenges and opportunities for IT managers. For example, **cloud computing** is a major buzz word in IT circles and it has different meanings to different people. In essence, it refers to internet-based development and use of computer technology. Individuals have been using this approach for years with email and photo sharing (think Google and Flickr). Organizations are now taking a closer look at the prospects of shared data centres through internet technology. At the conceptual level, cloud computing means placing some infrastructure online and having someone else run it rather than doing it in-house. Some of the major advantages promised by this approach include lower costs, quicker set-up, easy scalability, easier software integration, reduced financial risk, decreased downtime, potential services for small business (that otherwise could not afford them), automatic updates that don't disrupt or endanger other systems, and empowered users. It should be interesting to see how this concept evolves into practice over the next few years.[16]

Leveraging Information Resources: Data Warehousing and Data Mining

Almost everything you do leaves a trail of information about you. Your preferences in movie rentals, television viewing, internet sites, and groceries; the destinations of your phone calls, your credit card charges, your financial status; personal information about age, gender, marital status, and even your health are just a few of the items about each of us that are stored in scattered databases. The behaviour patterns of millions of users can be traced by analyzing files of information gathered over time from their internet usage and in-store purchases.

Data Warehousing The collection, storage, and retrieval of such data in electronic files is called **data warehousing**. For managers, the data warehouse is a goldmine of information about their business. Indeed, Kroger Co., the Ohio-based grocery chain, collects data on customer shopping habits to find ways to gain greater customer loyalty. As part owner of a data-mining firm, Kroger accumulates information from its shopper cards, analyzes the data to uncover shopping patterns, and sends money-saving coupons to regular customers for the specific products they usually buy. Kroger's precision targeting pays off, especially in the recession economy. With a rate of coupon usage up to as much as 50 times the industry average, it's a money-saver for Kroger customers and boosts the company's sales, too.[17]

Data Mining After collecting information, managers use **data mining**—the application of electronic technologies for searching, sifting, and reorganizing pools of data to uncover useful information. Data mining helps managers plan for new products, set prices, and identify trends and shopping patterns. By analyzing what consumers actually do, businesses can determine what subsequent purchases they are likely to make and then send them tailor-made ads.

Information Linkages with Suppliers The top priority for Walmart's IS—improving in-stock reliability—requires integration of Walmart's and suppliers' activities with store sales. That's why Procter & Gamble, Johnson & Johnson, and other suppliers connect into Walmart's information system to observe up-to-the-minute sales data on individual items, by store. They can use the system's computer-based tools—spreadsheets, sales forecasting, and weather information—to forecast sales demand and plan delivery schedules. Coordinated planning avoids excessive inventories, speeds up deliveries, and holds down costs throughout the supply chain while keeping shelves stocked for retail customers.

Types of Information Systems

Since employees have a variety of responsibilities and decision-making needs, a firm's *information system* may actually be a set of several information systems that share data while serving different levels of the organization, different departments, or different operations. One popular information system is called the **transaction processing system (TPS)**, which processes information for many different, day-to-day business transactions like customer order-taking by online retailers, approval of claims at insurance companies, receiving

CHIEF INFORMATION OFFICERS Managers who are responsible for managing all aspects of information resources and information processes.

CLOUD COMPUTING Internet-based development and use of computer technology; at the conceptual level, it means placing some infrastructure online and having someone else run it rather than doing it in-house.

DATA WAREHOUSING The collection, storage, and retrieval of data in electronic files.

DATA MINING The application of electronic technologies for searching, sifting, and reorganizing pools of data to uncover useful information.

TRANSACTION PROCESSING SYSTEM (TPS) Applications of information processing for basic day-to-day business transactions.

and confirming reservations by airlines, and payroll processing.

Because they work on different kinds of problems, managers and their subordinates need access to the specialized information systems that satisfy their different information needs. In addition to different types of users, each business *function*—marketing, human resources, accounting, production, finance—has its own information needs, as do groups working on major projects. Each user group and department, therefore, may need a special IS. Two important groups are *know-ledge workers* and *managers*.

Information Systems for Knowledge Workers As we discussed in Chapter 8, *know-ledge workers* are employees for whom information and know-ledge are the raw materials of their work, such as engineers, scientists, and IT specialists who rely on IT to design new products or create new processes. These workers require **knowledge information systems**, which provide resources to create, store, use, and transmit new knowledge for useful applications—for instance, databases to organize and retrieve information, and computational power for data analysis.

Specialized support systems have also increased the productivity of knowledge workers. **Computer-aided design (CAD)** helps knowledge workers design products ranging from cellphones to jewellery to auto parts by simulating them and displaying them in 3-D graphics. The older method—making handcrafted prototypes from wood, plastic, or clay—is replaced with faster, cheaper prototyping: the CAD system electronically transfers instructions to a computer-controlled machine that builds the prototypes.

In archaeology, CAD is helping scientists uncover secrets hidden in fossils using 3-D computer models of skeletons, organs, and tissues constructed with digital data from CT (computed tomography) scans of dinosaur fossils. From these models, scientists have learned, for example, that the giant apatosaurus's neck curved downward, instead of high in the air as once thought. By seeing how the animals' bones fit together with cartilage, ligaments, and vertebrae, scientists are discovering more about how these prehistoric creatures interacted with their environment.[18]

Information Systems for Managers Each manager's information activities and IS needs vary according to his or her functional area (accounting, marketing, etc.) and management level. The following are some popular information systems used by managers for different purposes.

Management Information Systems Management **information systems (MISs)** support managers by providing reports, schedules, plans, and budgets that can then be used for making decisions, both short and long term. For example, at a publishing company, managers rely on detailed information—current customer orders, staffing schedules, employee attendance, production schedules, equipment status, and materials availability— for moment-to-moment decisions during the day. They require similar information to plan such mid-range activities as personnel training, materials movements, and cash flows. They also need to anticipate the status of the jobs and projects assigned to their departments. Many MIS—cash flow, sales, production scheduling, and shipping—are indispensable for helping managers complete these tasks.

For longer-range decisions involving business strategy, managers need information to analyze trends in the publishing industry and overall company performance. They need both external and internal information, current and future, to compare current performance data to data from previous years and to analyze consumer trends and economic forecasts.

Decision Support Systems Managers who face a particular kind of decision repeatedly can get assistance from **decision support systems (DSSs)**—interactive systems that create virtual business models and test them with different data to see how they respond. When faced with decisions on plant capacity, for example, managers can use a capacity DSS. The manager inputs data on anticipated sales, working capital, and customer-delivery requirements. The data flow into the DSS processor, which then simulates the plant's performance under the proposed data conditions. After experimenting with various data conditions, the DSS makes recommendations on the best levels of plant capacity for each future time period.

Artificial Intelligence **Artificial intelligence (AI)** refers to the development of computer systems to imitate human behaviour—in other words, systems that perform physical tasks, use thought processes, and learn. In developing AI systems, business specialists, modellers, and information-technology experts try to design computer-based systems capable of reasoning so that computers, instead of people, can perform certain activities. For example, a credit-evaluation system may decide which loan applicants are creditworthy and which are too risky, and it may then compose acceptance and rejection letters accordingly.

Some AI systems possess sensory capabilities, such as lasers that "see," "hear," and "feel." AND Corp. of Toronto has developed a software program—called Hnet—that can learn to recognize faces. This may seem like a simple thing, but millions of dollars had been spent on this problem, without success until AND Corp. developed the software. The system can be used to improve airport security and to track terrorists.[19]

The **expert system** is designed to imitate the thought processes of human experts in a particular field.[20] Expert systems incorporate the rules that an expert applies to specific types of problems, such as the judgments a physician makes when diagnosing illnesses. In effect, expert systems supply everyday users with "instant expertise." For example, Campbell's developed an expert system to mimic complex decision processes and save the expert knowledge that was going to be lost when a long-time expert soup maker announced his intention to retire.[21]

IT Risks and Threats

As with other technologies throughout history, IT has attracted abusers that are intent on doing mischief, with severity ranging from mere nuisance to outright destruction. Eager IT users everywhere are finding that even social networking and cell phones have a "dark side"—privacy invasion. Facebook postings of personal information about users can be intercepted and misused by intruders. Beacon caused a public uproar when it published peoples' online purchases publicly on their Facebook newsfeeds. This is a problem with cellphone advancements. Bluetooth connections allow savvy intruders to read a victim's text messages, listen in on live conversations, and even view unwary users' photos.[22] Smartphone sales are likely to surpass regular cellphone sales by 2015. This is presenting an increased challenge, since more personal information tends to be contained on these multipurpose devices.[23]

Businesses, too, are troubled with ITs dark side. Hackers break into computers, stealing personal information and company secrets, and launching attacks on other computers. Meanwhile, the ease of information sharing on the internet has proven costly for companies that are having an increasingly difficult time protecting their intellectual property, and viruses that crash computers have cost companies millions. In this section, we'll look at these and other IT risks.

Hackers

Breaking and entering no longer refers merely to physical intrusion. Today, it applies to IT intrusions as well. **Hackers** are cybercriminals who gain unauthorized access to a computer or network, either to steal information, money, trade secrets, or property, or to tamper with data. Another common hacker activity is to launch *denial of service (DoS) attacks*. DoS attacks flood networks or websites with bogus requests for information and resources, thereby shutting the networks or websites down and preventing legitimate users from accessing them.

Wireless mooching is a profitable industry for cybercriminals. In just five minutes, one newspaper reporter using a laptop found six unprotected wireless networks that were wide open to outside users.[24] Once inside an unsecured wireless network, hackers use it to commit identity theft and to steal credit card numbers, among other things. When police officers try to track down these criminals, they're long gone, leaving you, the network host, exposed to criminal prosecution.

Identity Theft

Once inside a computer network, hackers are able to commit **identity theft**, the unauthorized stealing of personal information (such as social insurance numbers and address) to get loans, credit cards, or other monetary benefits by impersonating the victim. Clever crooks get information on unsuspecting victims by digging in trash, stealing mail, or using *phishing* or *pharming* schemes to lure internet users to bogus websites. For instance,

ARTIFICIAL INTELLIGENCE (AI) The development of computer systems to imitate human thought and behaviour.

EXPERT SYSTEM A form of AI designed to imitate the thought processes of human experts in a particular field.

HACKERS Cybercriminal who gains unauthorized access to a computer or network, either to steal information, money, trade secrets, or property or to tamper with data.

IDENTITY THEFT Unauthorized stealing of personal information (such as social insurance number and address) to get loans, credit cards, or other monetary benefits by impersonating the victim.

a cybercriminal might send American Online subscribers an email notifying them of a billing problem with their accounts. When the customers click on the AOL Billing Center link, they are transferred to a spoofed (falsified) webpage, modelled after AOL's. The customers then submit the requested information—credit card number, social insurance number, and PIN—into the hands of the thief. Today, consumers are more aware of these scams, but they are still effective. Major organizations like the Canadian Bankers Association and the Competition Bureau are working with organizations to identify patterns and inform consumers.[25]

In Canada, the federal government created privacy legislation in the Personal Information Protection and Electronic Documents Act (PIPEDA) back in 2001. It was designed to promote e-commerce while protecting personal information. The Act outlines the rules for managing personal information in the private sector.[26]

Intellectual Property Theft

Nearly every company faces the dilemma of protecting product plans, new inventions, industrial processes, and other **intellectual property**—something produced by the intellect or mind that has commercial value. Its ownership and right to its use may be protected by patent, copyright, trademark, and other means. Intellectual property theft is evident when, for example, individuals illegally download unpaid-for movies, music, and other resources from file-swapping networks. But the activities are not limited to illegal entertainment downloads. For example, according to the U.S. Intelligence Agency, Chinese cyber spies steal about 40 to 50 billion dollars' worth of intellectual property each year.[27]

Computer Viruses, Worms, and Trojan Horses

Another IT risk facing businesses is rogue programmers who disrupt IT operations by contaminating and destroying software, hardware, or data files. Viruses, worms, and Trojan horses are three kinds of malicious programs that, once installed, can shut down any computer system. A *computer virus* exists in a file that attaches itself to a program and migrates from computer to computer as a shared program or as an email attachment. It does not infect the system unless the user opens the contaminated file, and users typically are unaware they are spreading the virus by file sharing. It can, for example, quickly copy itself over and over again, using up all available memory and effectively shutting down the computer.

Worms are a particular kind of virus that travel from computer to computer within networked computer systems, without your needing to open any software to spread the contaminated file. In a matter of days, the notorious Blaster worm infected some 400 000 computer networks, destroying files and even allowing outsiders to take over computers remotely. The worm replicates itself rapidly, sending out thousands of copies to other computers in the network. Travelling through internet connections and email address books in the network's computers, it absorbs system memory and shuts down network servers, web servers, and individual computers.

Unlike viruses, a *Trojan horse* does not replicate itself. Instead, it most often comes into the computer, at your request, masquerading as a harmless, legitimate software product or data file. Once installed, the damage begins. For instance, it may simply redesign desktop icons or, more maliciously, delete files and destroy information.

Spyware

As if forced intrusion isn't bad enough, internet users unwittingly invite spies—masquerading as a friendly file available as a giveaway or shared among individual users on their PCs. This so-called **spyware** is downloaded by users that are lured by "free" software. Once installed, it crawls around to monitor the host's computer activities, gathering email addresses, credit card numbers, passwords, and other inside information that it transmits back to someone outside the host system. Spyware authors assemble incoming stolen information to create their own "intellectual property" that they then sell to other parties to use for marketing and advertising purposes or for identity theft.[28]

Spam

Spam—junk email sent to a mailing list or a newsgroup (an online discussion group)—is a greater nuisance than postal junk mail because the internet is open to the public, email costs are negligible, and massive mailing lists are accessible through file sharing or by theft. Spam operators send unwanted messages ranging from explicit pornography to hate mail to advertisements to destructive computer viruses. In addition to wasting users' time, spam also consumes a network's bandwidth, thereby reducing the amount of data that can be transmitted in a fixed amount of time for useful purposes. U.S. industry experts estimate spam's damage in lost time and productivity at more than $140 billion worldwide in 2008 alone.[29]

IT Protection Measures

Security measures against intrusion and viruses are a constant challenge. Businesses guard themselves against intrusion, identity theft, and viruses by using *firewalls*, *special software*, and *encryption*.

Firewalls

Firewalls are security systems with special software or hardware devices designed to keep computers safe from hackers. A firewall is located where two networks—for example, the internet and a company's internal network—meet. It contains two components for filtering each incoming data:

1. The company's *security policy*—Access rules that identify every type of message that the company doesn't want to pass through the firewall.

2. A *router*—A table of available routes or paths, a "traffic switch" that determines which routes or paths on the network to send each message to after it is tested against the security policy.

Only those messages that meet the conditions of the user's security policy are routed through the firewall and permitted to flow between the two networks. Messages that fail the access test are blocked and cannot flow between the two networks.

Preventing Identity Theft

Internet privacy experts say that a completely new identity verification system is needed to stop the rising tide of internet identity theft. One possibility is an "infocard," which would act like a credit card and would allow websites to verify a customer's identity without keeping personal information on the customer. While foolproof prevention is impossible, steps can be taken to reduce the chance that you will be victimized. A visit to the Identity Theft Resource Center (www.idtheftcenter.org) is a valuable first step to get information on everything from scam alerts to victim issues—including assistance on lost and stolen wallets—to media resources, current laws, and prevention of identity theft in the workplace.

Preventing Viruses: Anti-Virus Software

Many viruses take advantage of weaknesses in operating systems in order to spread and propagate. Network administrators must make sure that the computers on their systems are using the most up-to-date operating system that includes the latest security protection. Combating viruses, worms, and Trojan horses has become a major industry for systems designers and software developers. Installation of **anti-virus software** products protects systems by searching incoming email and data files for "signatures" of known viruses and virus-like characteristics. Contaminated files are discarded or placed in quarantine for safekeeping.

Protecting Electronic Communications: Encryption Software

Unprotected email can be intercepted, diverted to unintended computers, and opened, revealing contents to intruders. Protective software is available to guard against those intrusions, adding a layer of security by encoding emails so that only intended recipients can open them. An **encryption system** works by scrambling an email message so that it looks like garbled nonsense to anyone who doesn't possess the key.

Avoiding Spam and Spyware

To help their employees avoid privacy invasion and to improve productivity, businesses often install anti-spyware and spam filtering software on their systems. Dozens of anti-spyware products provide protection—software such as Webroot's Spy Sweeper and Microsoft Windows Defender—but they must be continually updated to keep pace with new spyware techniques. While it cannot be prevented entirely, spam is abated by many internet service providers (ISPs) that ban the spamming of ISP subscribers.

While computer security devices—spam filters, data encryption, firewalls, and anti-virus software—catch

FIREWALL Security system with special software or hardware devices designed to keep computers safe from hackers.

ANTI-VIRUS SOFTWARE Product that protects systems by searching incoming emails and data files for "signatures" of known viruses and virus-like characteristics.

ENCRYPTION SYSTEM Software that assigns an email message to a unique code number (digital fingerprint) for each computer so only that computer, not others, can open and read the message.

a vast number of attempted intrusions, many threats remain, both for individuals and for businesses. In difficult economic times, both individuals and businesses are taken in by schemes that they would likely ignore if they weren't under financial pressure. For example, fake websites, cellphones, and internet-based phones promise high-paying jobs, low-cost loans, and can't-miss lotteries. Cellphone text messages lure bank customers into telephoning account information, saying victims' credit cards have been deactivated. Internet-based phone users receive fake caller-IDs of real hospitals, government agencies, banks, and other businesses in a new form of telephone phishing that talks victims into revealing personal information. Cyber-thieves are using "targeting" (also known as spear phishing) to identify wealthy individuals and professional money managers. Victims receive friendly sounding emails containing contaminated attachments that, once opened, infect their computers, exposing bank account and other identity information to scammers.

Part 3: Managing Operations and Information

Goal of the Exercise

This part of the business plan project asks you to think about your business in terms of both accounting concepts and information technology (IT) needs and costs. See Appendix B for material on IT.

Managing Operations and Information

An increasingly important part of a business plan is a consideration of how IT—computers, the internet, software, and so on—influences businesses. This part of the business plan asks you to assess how you will use technology to improve your business. Will you, for example, use a database to keep track of your customers? How will you protect your business from hackers and other IT security risks?

This part of the business plan also asks you to consider the costs of doing business, such as salaries, rent, and utilities. You'll also be asked to complete the following financial statements:

- *Balance Sheet.* The balance sheet is a foundation for financial reporting. This report identifies the valued items of the business (its *assets*) as well as the debts that it owes (its *liabilities*). This information gives the owner and potential investors a snapshot into the health of the business.

- *Income Statement (or Profit-and-Loss Statement).* This is the focus of the financial plan. This document will show you what it takes to be profitable and successful as a business owner for your first year.

Your Assignment

mybusinesslab

Step 1

Open the saved Business Plan file you have been working on.

Step 2

For the purposes of this assignment, you will answer the following questions in Managing Operations and Information:

1. What kinds of IT resources will your business require?

   Hint: Think about the employees in your business and what they will need in order to do their jobs. What computer hardware and software will they need? Will your business need a network and an internet connection? What type of network? Refer to Appendix B for a discussion on IT resources you may want to consider.

2. How will you use IT to keep track of your customers and potential customers?

   Hint: Many businesses—even small businesses—use databases to keep track of their customers. Will your business require a database? What about other information systems? Refer to Appendix B for more information on these topics.

3. What are the costs of doing business? Equipment, supplies, salaries, rent, utilities, and insurance are just some of these expenses. Estimate what it will cost to do business for one year.

   Hint: The Business Plan Student Template provides a table for you to insert the costs associated with doing business. Note that these are just estimates—just try your best to include accurate costs for the expenses you think will be a part of doing business.

4. How much will you charge for your product? How many products do you believe that you can sell in one year (or how many customers do you think your business can attract)? Multiply the price that you will charge by the number of products that you hope to sell or the amount you hope each customer will spend. This will give you an estimate of your *revenues* for one year.

   Hint: You will use the amounts you calculate in the costs and revenues questions in this part of the plan in the accounting statements in the next part, so be as realistic as you can.

5. Create a balance sheet and an income statement (profit-and-loss statement) for your business.

Hint: You will have two options for creating these reports. The first option is to use the Microsoft Word versions that are found within the Business Plan Student Template itself. The second option is to use the specific Microsoft Excel templates created for each statement, which are found on the book's MyBusinessLab. These Excel files are handy to use because they already have the worksheet calculations preset—all you have to do is plug in the numbers and the calculations will be performed automatically for you. If you make adjustments to the different values in the Excel worksheets, you'll automatically see how changes to expenses, for example, can improve the bottom line.

6. Create a floor plan of the business. What does it look like when you walk through the door?

Hint: When sketching your floor plan, consider where equipment, supplies, and furniture will be located.

7. Explain what types of raw materials and supplies you will need to run your business. How will you produce your good or service? What equipment do you need? What hours will you operate?

Hint: Refer to the discussion of operations in Chapter 10 for information to get you started.

8. What steps will you take to ensure that the quality of the product or service stays at a high level? Who will be responsible for maintaining quality standards?

Hint: Refer to the discussion of quality improvement and total quality management in Chapter 10 for information to get you started.

Note: Once you have answered the questions, save your Word document. You'll be answering additional questions in later chapters.

Tree Planters

At Touchwood Lake, Alberta, 36 rookie tree planters (as well as a group of veteran planters) meet Cal Dyck, who has contracts to plant 7 million white and black spruce seedlings in Alberta and Saskatchewan. The trees won't be ready for harvest for 90 years. The tree-planting industry was born in the 1970s when the idea of sustainable forestry caught on. Originally, convicts were used, but then the forestry companies found out that hippies were cheaper.

During a two-day orientation session, Cal gives the students a lot of information about tree planting. He knows most of them want to make a lot of money in a short period of time, and he tells them they can do that if they are highly motivated and committed to working hard (planters can burn up to 7000 calories per day). Students are paid between 10 and 25 cents per tree, depending on the terrain. For a $30-per-day charge, Cal will feed the workers and move them around to various planting sites. He also provides hot showers.

Among the rookies at the orientation are three friends: Misha (who is studying journalism at Concordia), Megan (a student at Emily Carr University in Vancouver), and Lianne (also a student at the Emily Carr University). They will soon learn about the frailty of the human body in the business of tree planting (blisters, tendonitis, twisted ankles, etc.). The orientation also includes all-important demonstrations about how to properly plant a seedling. Spacing the seedlings, planting them at the right depth, choosing the right type of soil, and having the seedlings at the right temperature are all important considerations. The rookies train as a group, but then they're on their own and can work at their own pace. Their work is constantly checked for quality. If planting is not done right, it must be redone.

The rookies plant for just four hours during their first day on the job. While rookies are learning how to plant, they may plant less than 100 trees a day, but an experienced veteran can plant 3000 trees in a day. These high-volume planters—called "pounders" because of their intense work ethic—can earn $15 000 during the summer season. They set high production goals for themselves and that motivates them to work hard.

For the rookies, the first week is already starting to blur. They eat, sleep, and plant. The work cycle is four days on and one day off. Within just a few weeks, some rookies are already starting to wonder why they are in the bush, especially on days when the rain is pouring down and they are soaked through. At Kananaskis, Alberta, work slows down because the terrain is rough and steep. It's only halfway through the season, but some planters already have bad cases of tendonitis from the repeated motion of jamming their shovel into the ground as they plant seedlings. Already 8 of the 36 rookies have quit.

Lianne has made $2500 so far, and she is one of the top rookie planters. By season's end, Lianne will have planted over 98 000 trees. Megan (Lianne's school buddy) is starting to waver. She is fighting a sinus infection and is not even making minimum wage. Misha has decided to quit. A friend of hers is getting married back east and she will not return after the wedding. A week later, Megan quits as well.

At Candle Lake, Saskatchewan, the planting crews are behind schedule as the season nears its end. They still have 1.2 million trees to plant, and the ranks of rookie planters are thinning fast. Only 14 of 36 rookies are still on the job. Smaller work crews mean more work for those who are left, and the opportunity to make more money. After more than three months in the bush, each rookie who is still on the job has planted thousands of trees. Lianne has learned to stop calculating her daily earnings. Brad, a veteran planter, says that he admires the rookies who have pulled through. He says that it's amazing that people can be brought into the bush from the city to do this kind of work.

Video Resource: "Tree Planters," *The National* (May 25, 2007).

Questions for Discussion

1. Explain what the terms "productivity" and "quality" mean. How are they related in the actual practice of tree planting?

2. Consider the following statement: *"The productivity and quality of rookie tree planters is very low, and the turnover rate is very high. Tree planting companies should therefore hire only experienced tree planters."* Do you agree or disagree with the statement? Defend your answer.

3. Why do you think tree planters are paid on a piece-rate basis? What are the advantages and disadvantages of paying tree planters this way? (Review the relevant material in Chapter 8 before answering this question.)

4. Explain the various forms of employee behaviour. How does each one of these forms of behaviour impact the productivity and quality of tree planters? (Review the relevant material in Chapter 9 before answering this question.)

African Accountants

In Canada's business jungle, all tracks lead to Bay Street, where lions of modern industry reign. Accountants keep Bay Street's books, but the heat is on to keep better books. Accountants don't like people who bring in shoeboxes full of receipts and then ask the accountant to organize them. Instead, accountants want the material organized before they try to do any calculations. But all this organizing costs money, and small- and mid-sized businesses don't usually have the money to pay for it.

For George Wall, of Wall & Associates, finding enough casual workers to do data organization and entry was a big challenge. He had to pay them up to $20 an hour, and that service was too pricey for many of his clients. But what if Wall could find workers who would do this work for one-tenth the hourly wage he had to pay people in Toronto? He found the solution by adopting global outsourcing. It works like this: When that shoebox arrives, each piece of paper is first fed into a high-speed scanner, then stored on a server, and then sent to the internet. While Bay Street sleeps, the material is sent to Kampala, Uganda, where the data are keyed in by African accountants who are paid only about $1 a day.

In a freshly painted office in Kampala, a dozen computers have just been taken out of their boxes, and a dozen workers have just been hired. Their boss is 20-something Abu Luaga, a Ugandan with a commerce degree who has the contract to do accounting work for Wall & Associates. He teaches the new hires what to do. His start-up funds came from his family, and he got involved with Wall & Associates through his connections with a Canadian business consultant.

There is much competition from other developing countries to get this kind of business. But his workers are keen, and they're already trained as bookkeepers. They're eager to see what the developed world has to offer, but many have never had a computer before and need training so that they can recognize various financial documents and learn Canadian accounting jargon. They're also being trained to think the way Canadian businesses do. As well, Luaga reminds them about deadlines and privacy. Because these workers are dealing with sensitive information, no cellphones are allowed in the office and the copying or saving of files or images is prohibited.

What are the implications of all this information flowing from the first world to the developing world and back again? It may be just the kind of miracle Uganda needs. The telecommunications industry has been a bright spot in the Ugandan economy, but Ugandans still make only about $1 a day. The country still relies on money earned by exporting coffee, and the government is dependent on foreign donors for part of its budget. Officials admit that the technical skills of workers aren't as good as those of people in some Asian countries, but this system allows educated Ugandans to work in their home country.

Luaga's workers say the work has already changed their career prospects. But not all Canadian clients have jumped at the chance to zip their documents to Africa. George Wall is convinced they will eventually be comfortable with the idea, and Luaga is banking on it. He's leasing bigger and better office space because he thinks that a new office and clients in Canada will impress other potential clients in Africa.

Video Resource: "African Accountants," *Venture* (February 16, 2003).

Questions for Discussion

1. What is the difference between financial and managerial accounting? Is the work that the African accountants are doing financial or managerial accounting? Explain.

2. Why might Canadian clients be reluctant to have Wall & Associates send their data to Africa for organizing? What can George Wall do to respond to their concerns?

3. Suppose that you read a newspaper editorial condemning the practice of sending documents to Africa on the grounds that this was yet another example of exporting Canadian jobs overseas to low-wage countries. How would you respond?

Managing Marketing

What is the first thing you think of when you hear the names Coffee Crisp, Crest, UFC, and EA Sports? You probably didn't hesitate before picturing a chocolate bar, toothpaste, mixed martial arts, and video games. Your rapid association of brand names and the goods or services they provide is a tribute to the effectiveness of the marketing managers of the firms that produce these goods. These and many other names have become household words because companies have developed the right products to meet customers' needs, have priced those products appropriately, have made prospective customers aware of the products' existence and qualities, and have made the products readily available.

Part Summary

Part 4, Managing Marketing, provides an overview of the many elements of marketing, including developing, pricing, promoting, and distributing various types of goods and services.

■ We begin in **Chapter 12, Understanding Marketing Processes and Consumer Behaviour**, by examining the ways in which companies distinguish their products, determine customer needs, and address consumer buying preferences.

■ Then, in **Chapter 13, Developing and Promoting Goods and Services**, we explore the development of different types of products, the effect of brand names and packaging, how promotion strategies help a firm meet its objectives, and the advantages and disadvantages of several promotional tools.

■ Finally, in **Chapter 14, Pricing and Distributing Goods and Services**, we examine pricings strategies. We also consider the various outlets business firms use to distribute their products, and we discuss the problems of storing and transporting goods to distributors.

Understanding Marketing Processes and Consumer Behaviour

After reading this chapter, you should be able to:

LO-1   Explain the concept of *marketing*.

LO-2   Explain the purpose of a *marketing plan* and identify the four components of the *marketing mix*.

LO-3   Explain *market segmentation* and show how it is used in target marketing.

LO-4   Explain the purpose and value of *marketing research*.

LO-5   Describe the key factors that influence the *consumer buying process*.

LO-6   Describe the *international* and *small-business marketing mixes*.

SCANLIFE

lululemon: A Clear Marketing Strategy, Even in Trying Times

Chip Wilson founded lululemon after taking a rejuvenating yoga class in 1998. After two decades in the ski, snowboard, and skate business, he made an abrupt change and built this yoga-inspired athletic gear retailer. The first outlet opened in Vancouver's Kitsilano area in 2000. By 2010, lululemon had well over 100 stores in Canada, the U.S., Australia, and China with revenues of $453 million. At the time, CEO Christina Day was proudly pointing to a same-store sales increase of 29 percent over the previous year. She also indicated that these results reflected the strength of the brand and its mission to focus on quality, design, innovation, and unique positioning. Who could argue with her? lululemon had carved a clearly identifiable niche and transformed people's buying behaviour while creating a lifestyle community.

lululemon strives to be more than just a retailer. According to the company, the intent is to elevate the world from mediocrity to greatness. Strong words for a clothing retailer. Its mission is to create components for people to live longer, healthier, and more fun lives. To further distinguish

How Will This Help Me?

Marketing is a business activity that focuses on providing value so customers will purchase goods and services offered for sale. If you understand the marketing methods and ideas that are presented in this chapter, you will benefit in two ways: (1) you'll be better prepared to enhance your career by using effective marketing ideas, both as an *employee* and as a *manager*, and (2) you'll be a more informed *consumer* with greater awareness of how businesses use marketing to influence your purchases.

itself, lululemon has developed a mantra, a manifesto, ambassadors, and a community hub to get the message out. Their values are a major stretch (no pun intended) from the tainted corporate image that defines so many firms these days.

In this chapter we will introduce you to the four Ps of marketing: product, price, place, and promotion. Let's take a look at how lululemon addresses these strategic pillars. From day one, Chip Wilson set out to provide superior products for his target consumer. It was clear to Chip that traditional sweatpants were totally unfit for the job, and an opportunity was identified. But he needed to educate consumers and offer better alternatives than the pure cotton clothing most people were wearing in yoga studios. His previous experience in developing technical athletic fabrics led to the creation of a design studio that moonlighted as a yoga studio in the evenings. Experts were consulted; yoga instructors were given clothing and enlisted as product testers. The efforts paid off. lululemon created a fabric called "luon," which is moisture wicking, pre-shrunk, has improved stretching ability, and maintains its shape. Today, lululemon makes products from Luxtreme, Coolmax, Silverscent, and Beechlu (to name a few); these fabrics are lighter weight and antibacterial.

lululemon offers important services to supplement its goods and build its community. Every outlet offers weekly complimentary yoga classes. In addition, they offer running clinics, boot camps, and Pilates courses. lululemon still consults yogis and elite athletes; a continuous improvement approach is the foundation of its product development cycle. Even the brand name was developed in this manner. Before the original launch, it surveyed 100 individuals to select the name and logo from a list of 20 options. Clearly, lululemon is a firm by the people, for the people.

In terms of place or distribution, over 100 retail outlets are being supplemented by 25 new showrooms, in 2010 alone, in key locations like Florida, California, Texas, and Vancouver. These showrooms are not permanent but rather leased spaces that aim to test new market locations and create buzz. In 2009, the successful launch of lululemon's e-commerce site was another major step in improving distribution. At the same time, the expansion of its wholesale business, to more yoga studios and gyms, helped create stronger ties and increased selling avenues. lululemon was also investing in its supply chain to ensure that popular products were kept in stock.

If you are thinking that lululemon has spent huge sums of money on advertising to achieve success, think again. lululemon uses virtually no traditional advertising, with the exception of strategically placed ads in highly targeted magazines like *Yoga Journal*. The company benefited from buzz generated by the 2010 Vancouver Winter Olympic Games held in its hometown. lululemon took advantage with two key stores located in high-traffic areas. Other promotional approaches are also being used. According to the CEO, a single email notification to clients about a new product can generate more than $6000 of sales.

lululemon focuses on consumer-generated buzz. It has an ambassador program designed for loyal devotees that embody the lifestyle. You can go to the website and read about or get in touch with hundreds of ambassadors. In addition, there are approximately 60 "elite" ambassadors like Olympians Clara Hughes, Jennifer Heil, and Thomas Grandi. There are plenty of other ways to communicate with a yogi or fellow devotees; the website creates synergy with all modern communication tools including basic blogging and the ever-popular social media sites Twitter, Facebook, and Flickr.

High-end quality is usually accompanied by high-end prices. lululemon's products are expensive and the company is unapologetic; the focus is on value, not price. Having a strategy is one thing, but sticking to it is something else. Many organizations overreact to current market circumstances and forget who they are. In the face of the most recent recession and price pressure from competitors, lululemon stood firm. Prices were kept high.

Sticking to a core strategy does not mean being stagnant. lululemon temporarily held back on expansion plans and focused on quality improvements, but by 2010 the expansion plans were gaining steam again. In the meantime, lululemon invested in its website and product development by enhancing its running business. In 2011 the firm expects to earn 25 percent of revenues from this source. lululemon continues to look at the big picture and focus on the long-term strategy. It embodies and displays the confidence that it tries to instil in its members through the lifestyle. It will be interesting to see how this company evolves over the next decade.

LO-1 What Is Marketing?

What images come to mind when you think of marketing? If you are like most people, you probably think of advertising for something like detergent or soft drinks. But marketing includes much more than advertising. **Marketing** is the process of planning and executing the conception, pricing, promotion, and distribution of ideas, goods, and services to create exchanges that satisfy individual and organizational objectives.

A company that employs the **marketing concept** is coordinated to achieve one goal—to serve its present and potential customers at a profit. This concept means that a firm must get to know what customers really want and closely follow evolving tastes. The various departments of the firm—marketing, production, finance, and human resources—must operate as a well-coordinated system that is unified in the pursuit of customer satisfaction.

Providing Value and Satisfaction

Consumers buy products that offer the best value when it comes to meeting their needs and wants. **Value** compares a product's benefits with its costs. *Benefits* include not only the features of the product or service but also the emotional satisfaction associated with owning, experiencing, or possessing it. *Costs* include the price, the expenditure of the buyer's time, and the emotional costs of making a purchase decision. The satisfied buyer perceives the benefits derived from the purchase to be greater than its costs. Thus, the simple but important ratio for value:

Value = Benefits/Costs

To understand how marketing creates value for customers, we need to know the kind of benefits that buyers get from a firm's goods or services. As we saw in Chapter 10, products provide consumers with time, place, ownership, and form utility. These utilities yield products that satisfy human wants or needs.

Goods, Services, and Ideas

Marketing of tangible goods is obvious in our everyday life. You walk into a department store and a woman with a clipboard and a bottle of perfume asks if you'd like to try a new brand of cologne. A pharmaceutical company proclaims the virtues of its new cold medicine. Your local auto dealer offers you a special deal. These **consumer goods** are products that you, the consumer, buy for personal use. Firms that sell their products to the end user are engaged in *consumer marketing*.

Marketing is also important for **industrial goods**—items that are used by companies for production purposes or further assembly. Conveyors, lift trucks, and earth movers are all industrial goods, as are components and raw materials such as integrated circuits, coal, steel,

and plastic. Firms that sell their products to other manufacturers are engaged in *industrial marketing*.

Marketing is also relevant for **services**—intangible products such as time, expertise, or some activity that you can purchase. *Service marketing* has become a major growth area in Canada. Insurance companies, airlines, investment counsellors, health clinics, and exterminators are a few examples of companies that engage in service marketing. In today's digital age, services come in many forms. The E-Business and Social Media Solutions box below highlights a very popular service delivery format.

Finally, marketing is also used to promote *ideas*. Television ads remind us that teaching is an honourable profession, that drinking and driving is irresponsible behaviour, and that smoking is detrimental to our health.

MARKETING Planning and executing the development, pricing, promotion, and distribution of ideas, goods, and services to create exchanges that satisfy both buyers' and sellers' objectives.

MARKETING CONCEPT The idea that the whole firm is directed toward serving present and potential customers at a profit.

VALUE Relative comparison of a product's benefits versus its costs.

CONSUMER GOODS Products purchased by individuals for their personal use.

INDUSTRIAL GOODS Products purchased by companies to use directly or indirectly to produce other products.

SERVICES Intangible products, such as time, expertise, or an activity, that can be purchased.

New technologies create new products, such as the Chinese cellphone "gas station" kiosk pictured above. Called *shouji jiayouzhan* in Chinese, these kiosks allow consumers to recharge their cellphones the way they would refuel their cars. The screens on the kiosks also provide marketers with a new way to display ads for waiting customers.

Apps, Apps, and More Apps: New Age Product Opportunities

Apple transformed the music industry with its successful marketing of the iPod and the creation of iTunes. Within a few years, music executives went from opponents to allies with a growing reliance on Apple to propel the industry into the future. Unfortunately for them, Apple had other plans. With iPod sales projected to flatten, Apple turned its attention to its newer iPhone device and the huge potential of applications (apps). The iPhone's success is clear. Back in 2008, the 3G iPhone sold over one million units in its first weekend. With each iPhone contract worth approximately $2000 to the service provider, Apple effectively created $2 billion worth of revenue streams for its partners in three days. In 2010, Apple sold 1.7 million iPhone G4s in the first three days of that launch, and new generation iPhones will keep revenues flowing for years. The launch of the iPad tablet in 2010 provided a new and exciting outlet, but Apple also had a great opportunity on the content side. In 2009, Apple had already amassed 10 000 apps, but this figure ballooned to well over 150 000 by mid-2010.

Most of you can list dozens if not hundreds of your favourite apps. The range is impressive. During the 2010 Vancouver Winter Olympic Games, the "cowbell" app was popular at the alpine skiing events. The "cigarette lighter" app is now a staple at music concerts. Dominos Pizza has an app that allows you to order pizza and have it delivered today or even a week from now. The "Shazam" app can help you download music or identify a song playing on the radio. There are sports scores, cooking tips, stock quotes, and much more. According to Gartner Inc., a technology industry research firm, smart phone owners are expected to download 4.5 billion apps in 2010, generating $7 billion in revenue. This figure is expected to grow to $30 billion by 2013.

How did Apple manage to develop so many apps so quickly? On the consumer side, people were excited by the touch screen and advanced graphics offered by the products. The gadget-loving tech generation had found a platform that fit their endless thirst for information and entertainment. It was a tool for increased social connectivity in an easily transportable format. How could this product be denied?

Apple has proven that it can identify, develop, and exploit opportunities: it quickly seized this one. Apple created a generous profit-sharing plan that provides

The increased size and capabilities of devices like the Apple iPad are opening up new opportunities for App developers. By 2011 the pace of development had accelerated and the number of Apple apps had already reached 300,000.

the developer with 70 percent of the revenue generated by its apps. This provides the profit incentive that has pushed individuals and firms to create new applications. So while Apple had 150 000 separate applications in its stable, BlackBerry could offer only approximately 5000 apps; the Google Android format had 25 000 apps.

Who is taking advantage of this business opportunity? Like the Yukon Gold Rush of the 1890s, everyone and anyone with a dream is entering this market space. Ethan Nicolas developed a game called iShoot and quit his job after earning $37 000 in a single day. Over three million people downloaded the free version of his game and over 320 000 eventually bought an extended version at a cost of $3 each. Major gaming companies like EA Sports are providing content like NBA Live. Old technology companies, like Marvel Comics, are finding new ways to deliver their products with the help of the iPad's large, user-friendly format. Whether we are talking about individuals with a dream or organizations with problems to solve, there is a potential solution in the world of apps. Once again, Apple is leading the way.

Critical Thinking Questions

1. What are your favourite apps? List and explain what makes them effective and/or useful.
2. Form a group of three or four and come up with a new application that you believe would meet the needs of a particular target group. Explain.

Relationship Marketing

Marketing often focuses on single transactions for products, services, or ideas, but **relationship marketing** emphasizes longer-term relationships with customers and suppliers. Stronger relationships, including stronger economic and social ties, can result in greater long-term satisfaction and retention of customers.[1] Harley-Davidson, for example, offers social incentives through the Harley Owners Group (HOG), the largest motorcycle club in the world, with over one million members and 1348 dealer-sponsored chapters globally and counting. HOG, explain Harley marketers, "is dedicated to building customers for life. HOG fosters long-term commitments to the sport of motorcycling by providing opportunities for our customers to bond with other riders and develop long-term friendships."[2]

LO-2 Strategy: The Marketing Mix

Although many individuals contribute to the marketing of a product, a company's **marketing managers** are typically responsible for planning and implementing the marketing activities that result in the transfer of goods or services to customers. These activities culminate in the **marketing plan**: a detailed and focused strategy for gearing marketing activities to meet consumer needs and wants. Marketing begins, therefore, when a company identifies a consumer need and develops a product to meet it.

In planning and implementing their strategies, marketing managers rely on four principal elements. These four elements—called the *four Ps of marketing*—are *product* (developing goods, services, and ideas), *pricing*, *promotion*, and *place* (distribution).[3] The sellers' four Ps are a mirror image of the buyers' four Cs: *customer solution* (product), *customer cost* (price), *customer convenience* (place), and *customer communication* (promotion).[4] Together, these elements are known as the **marketing mix** (see Figure 12.1).

The importance of these four elements varies, depending on the product being sold. Price might play a large role in selling fresh meat but a very small role in selling newspapers. Distribution might be crucial in marketing gasoline but not so important for lumber. Promotion is vital in toy marketing but of little consequence in marketing nails. The product is important in every case, but probably less so for toothpaste than for cars.

Product Marketing begins with a **product**—a good, a service, or an idea designed to fill a consumer need or want. Meeting consumer needs is a constant challenge, and often means changing existing products to keep pace with changing markets and competitors. Marketers try to promote particular features of products to distinguish them from their competitors in the marketplace.

Product differentiation is the creation of a feature or image that makes a product differ enough from competitive products to attract consumers. For example, Volvo automobiles provide enhanced safety features to set them apart from competitors. In recent advertisements featuring two older, nostalgic gentlemen, TD Canada Trust emphasized their non-traditional extended banking hours as a clear source of differentiation for its service-oriented business model.

One company has developed a system that allows its customers at retail home centres and lumber yards to custom-design decks and shelving. As a result, the company has differentiated a commodity—two-by-fours—by turning them into premium products. *Mass-customization* allows marketers to provide products that satisfy very specific consumer needs. We discuss products and product development in more detail in Chapter 13. Take a look at the boxed insert entitled "Guelph Thinks Green," which

Figure 12.1
Choosing the marketing mix for a business.

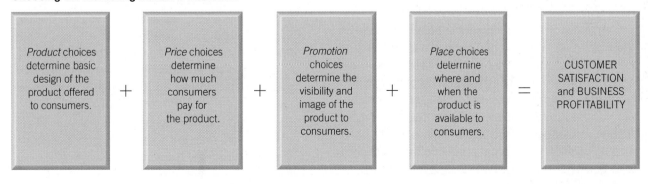

Product choices determine basic design of the product offered to consumers. + *Price* choices determine how much consumers pay for the product. + *Promotion* choices determine the visibility and image of the product to consumers. + *Place* choices determine where and when the product is available to consumers. = CUSTOMER SATISFACTION and BUSINESS PROFITABILITY

describes the efforts by Green World Solutions (GWS) to create environmentally friendly solutions.

Price Price refers not only to the actual amount of money that consumers pay for a product or service but also to the total value of the things that consumers are willing to give up in return for being able to have the benefits of the product or service. For example, if a person wants to buy a car, he or she might take money out of a savings account in order to pay for it. The value of the interest he or she would have earned on the savings account is part of the value that the customer gives up in order to own the car. Car manufacturers are always looking for ways to attract consumers. For example, when BMW Canada sets prices for its 3 Series line of cars, it needs to consider the competition. Recently, the Acura TL was offering $3000 rebates and the Audi A4 was available at 2.9 percent financing.[5] Determining the best price at which to sell a product is a difficult balancing act. From a manufacturer's point of view, prices must support the organization's operating, administrative, research, and marketing costs. On the other hand, prices cannot be so high that consumers turn to competing products.

Both low- and high-price strategies can be effective, depending on the situation. For example, Canadian Tire maintained healthy sales in patio furniture and barbecues during the most recent recession by stocking more lower-priced items and scaling back more expensive items.[6] At the same time, de Grisogono was launching The Meccanico watch in style, by winning the Prix du

---

THE GREENING OF BUSINESS

Guelph Thinks Green

The majority of plastics that have been manufactured in the last hundred years are still in existence. (As little as 4 percent of plastics have been recycled and only 2 percent have been incinerated.) The remaining masses are either buried, blowing around, sitting in a landfill, or floating in our oceans. Today's consumers are starting to look for ways to reduce waste.

A group of University of Guelph students decided to look more closely at a niche market to try to address waste issues. Green World Solutions (GWS) was created by Kwasi Danso, Jonathan Wolff, and Ashley van Herten, who recognized that in order to make a difference to the environment, consumers must become collectively accountable for their actions. GWS has aligned itself with the patent holder of a revolutionary additive that makes plastic biodegradable and has begun discussions and pricing strategies for manufacturing a variety of household items.

One product idea was a pet waste bag, but before the idea could be launched GWS needed to conduct significant market research to determine the product's competitiveness and feasibility. What it found was surprising: most of the biodegradable pet waste bags on the market were not biodegradable in a landfill. The ideal environment for the breakdown of the materials could be found only in commercial composts. This new revelation did not make sense to GWS, since consumers were led to believe the products currently on the market would biodegrade when left in garbage cans. This recognition that current product offerings needed to be improved gave GWS the basis for demonstrating to consumers that its product was superior to existing products.

GWS is testing this biodegradable additive with additional products in order to help various industries make better environmental choices. As this is a new market and environmental interest is at an all-time high, GWS is also spending considerable time and effort in creating a strong, recognizable brand image as an environmentally conscious company. Its name is descriptive and appealing to the target audience, and the logo shows imagery of a clean blue and green earth.

GWS has incorporated and is commencing production of biodegradable waste bags. The next steps for GWS are to actively promote environmental consumerism and to spread awareness of the importance of consumers taking responsibility for their own polluting activities. GWS foresees tremendous opportunity in the biodegradable retail plastic industry.

Critical Thinking Questions

1. What are the 4 Ps of marketing? Which one do you think was most important in this case?
2. What are some of the concerns that businesses would have when undertaking new initiatives like those at GWS? What concerns might consumers have?
3. Research the waste management industry. What can you learn from the companies' websites about the benefits of new biodegradable plastics?

Although BMW is consistent with its premium price policy, it must be conscious of the various offers that its competitors are providing, especially in difficult times.

Public at a prestigious competition in Geneva. The company proclaims that The Meccanico is the world's most complicated watch and it retails for about $200 000 or roughly as much as a Ferrari. The company had expected to sell approximately 177 watches but had only managed to sell 35, with another 60 orders in place, in the first six months.[7] Low prices will generally lead to a larger volume of sales. High prices will usually limit the size of the market but will increase a firm's profits per unit. In some cases, however, high prices may actually attract customers by implying that the product is especially good or rare. We will discuss pricing in more detail in Chapter 14.

Place (Distribution) In the marketing mix, *place* refers to **distribution**. Placing a product in the proper outlet (e.g., a retail store) requires decisions about warehousing, inventory control, and transportation that is needed to get the product from the producer to the consumer. Firms must also make decisions about the *channels* through which they distribute products. Many manufacturers sell goods to other companies, which in turn distribute them to retailers. Others sell directly to major retailers such as Rona, Walmart, or Safeway. Still others sell directly to final consumers. We explain distribution decisions further in Chapter 14.

Promotion The most visible component of the marketing mix is **promotion**, which refers to those activities that are designed to sell products and services to consumers. Promotional tools include advertising, personal selling, sales promotions, publicity, and public relations. Chapter 13 explores the promotion of products in more depth.

By providing both distribution and advertising for Grand & Toy, this truck plays a dual role in the company's marketing strategy.

LO-3 Target Marketing and Market Segmentation

Marketing managers realize that they cannot be "all things to all people" because people have different tastes, interests, goals, and lifestyles. The marketing concept's recognition of consumers' various needs and wants leads marketing managers to think in terms of **target markets**—groups of people with similar wants and needs. Target marketing clearly requires **market segmentation**—dividing a market into categories of customer types or "segments." For example, Mr. Big & Tall sells to men who are taller and heavier than average. Special-interest magazines are oriented toward people with certain interests like fishing, home decorating, or gardening.

GEOGRAPHIC
VARIABLES
Geographical units that
may be considered in a
segmentation strategy.

DEMOGRAPHIC
VARIABLES Charac-
teristics of populations
that may be considered
in developing a seg-
mentation strategy.

MULTICULTURAL
MARKETING Market-
ing activities directed at
various identifiable eth-
nic groups in Canada.

Table 12.1 Demographic Market Segmentation

Age	Under 5; 5–11; 12–19; 20–34; 35–49; 50–64; 65+
Education	Grade school or less; some high school; graduated high school; some college or university; college diploma or university degree; advanced degree
Family life cycle	Young single; young married without children; young married with children; older married with children under 18; older married without children under 18; older single; other
Family size	1, 2–3, 4–5, 6+
Income	Under $15 000; $15 000–$24 999; $25 000–$34 999; $35 000–$44 999; $45 000 and over
Nationality	Including but not limited to African, Asian, British, Eastern European, French, German, Irish, Italian, Latin American, Middle Eastern, and Scandinavian
Race	Including but not limited to Inuit, Asian, black, and white
Religion	Including but not limited to Buddhist, Catholic, Hindu, Jewish, Muslim, and Protestant
Sex	Male, female
Language	Including but not limited to English, French, Inuktitut, Italian, Ukrainian, and German

Once they have identified market segments, companies may adopt a variety of product strategies. Some firms decide to provide a range of products to the market in an attempt to market their products to more than one segment. For example, General Motors of Canada offers compact cars, vans, trucks, SUVs, luxury cars, and sports cars with various features and prices. Its strategy is to provide an automobile for nearly every segment of the market. In contrast, some businesses restrict production to one small market segment (or niche). Rolls-Royce understands that only a small number of people are willing to pay $310 000 for an exclusive touring limousine. Rolls-Royce makes no attempt to cover the entire range of possible products; instead, it markets only to a very small segment of the automobile market.

Identifying Market Segments

The members of a market segment must share some common traits or behaviours that will affect their purchasing decisions. In identifying market segments, researchers look at geographic, demographic, psychographic, and product-use variables.

Geographic Variables **Geographic variables** are the geographical units, from countries to neighbourhoods, that may be important in a segmentation strategy. For example, the heavy rainfall in British Columbia prompts its inhabitants to purchase more umbrellas than people living in Arizona's desert climate. Urban dwellers have less demand for pickup trucks than do their rural counterparts. Sailboats sell better along both coasts than they do in the Prairie provinces. These patterns affect marketing decisions about what products to offer, at what price to sell them, how to promote them, and how to distribute them. For example, consider the marketing of down parkas in rural Saskatchewan. Demand will be high, price competition may be limited, local newspaper advertising may be very effective, and the best location may be one easily reached from several small towns.

Demographic Variables **Demographic variables** describe populations by identifying characteristics such as age, income, gender, ethnic background, marital status, race, religion, and social class as detailed in Table 12.1. Note that these are objective criteria that cannot be altered. Marketers must work with or around them.

Depending on the marketer's purpose, a segment can be a single classification (e.g., age 20–34) or a combination of categories (e.g., age 20–34, married with children, earning $25 000–$34 999). Foreign competitors are gaining market share in auto sales by appealing to young buyers (under 30) with limited incomes (under $30 000). While companies such as Hyundai and Kia are winning entry-level customers with high quality and generous warranties, Volkswagen targets under-35 buyers with its entertainment-styled VW Jetta.[8] The Bank of Montreal is paying particular attention to the large baby boomer population (born between 1947 and 1966), which represents approximately 40 percent of the working population. Specialized services and products are being developed to serve the growing retirement needs of this group.[9]

Canada's great ethnic diversity requires companies to pay close attention to ethnicity as a segmentation variable. Visible minorities in Canada control $76 billion in annual buying power, and to be effective in **multicultural marketing**, companies must understand the underlying values that ethnic minority customers hold.[10] These consumers can be precisely targeted using one of the 370 media outlets geared toward 87 ethnic groups in Canada. Ethnic TV stations include the Fairchild Network (Cantonese and Mandarin) and ATN (South Asian). There are 44 language groups represented in 228 publications ranging from Punjabi to Italian. There are 66 languages represented on 57 radio stations across the country, including CHIN in Toronto, CFMB in Montreal, and CJVB in Vancouver.[11]

Coffee Shops

Yuppie Target
(Market Size)

Commuter Target
(Market Size)

(+customized) (slow) — leisure — relax — meeting-place — convenience — express — (+fast) (standardized)

Starbucks
(cappuccino)
(lounge chairs)
(classical music)
(chocolate treats)

Tim Hortons
1. Fast: "Always have time,"
basic coffee, drive thru
2. Fresh: "Always Fresh," 20 minutes
to prepare coffee/food
3. Friendly: customer service

Figure 12.2
Product positioning.

Psychographic Variables Members of a market can also be segmented according to **psychographic variables** such as lifestyles, opinions, interests, and attitudes. One company that used psychographic variables to revive its brand is Burberry, whose plaid-lined gabardine raincoats have been a symbol of British tradition since 1856. During the past decade, Burberry repositioned itself as a global luxury brand like Gucci and Louis Vuitton. The strategy calls for luring top-of-the-line, fashion-conscious customers. Burberry pictures today's luxury-product shopper as a world traveller who identifies with prestige fashion brands and monitors social and fashion trends in magazines like *Harper's Bazaar*.[12] Robert Polet, chief executive of the Gucci Group, agrees with this strategy: "We're not in the business of selling handbags. We are in the business of selling dreams."[13]

Psychographics are particularly important to marketers because, unlike demographics and geographics, they can sometimes be changed by marketing efforts. Many companies have succeeded in changing some consumers' opinions by running ads highlighting products that have been improved directly in response to consumer desires. For example, Las Vegas began courting the gay community a few years ago as part of a broader effort to target a range of minority audiences. Studies showed that the gay and lesbian travel market was among the most lucrative. According to research from Community Marketing Inc., a gay and lesbian market research company, gay and lesbian travel accounts for $55 billion of the overall U.S. travel market.[14]

Product-Use Variables This fourth way of segmenting looks at why people purchase the product in question, how they use the product, and their brand loyalty to

the product.[15] For example, a woman buying an *athletic* shoe will probably not care much about its appearance, but she will care a great deal about arch support, traction offered by the sole, and sturdiness. In contrast, a woman buying a *casual* shoe will want it to look good but be comfortable. A woman buying a *dress* shoe may require a specific colour or style and accept some discomfort and a relatively fragile shoe.

Whatever basis is used for segmenting a market, care must be taken to *position* the product correctly. **Product positioning** is based on the important attributes that consumers use to assess the product. For example, a low-priced car like a Ford Focus tends to be positioned on the basis of *economy*, while a Porsche is positioned in terms of *high performance*. The product positioning chart in Figure 12.2 shows that Tim Hortons emphasizes a standardized product and provides fast service to people in a hurry, while Starbucks provides more customized products in more leisurely surroundings.

Market Segmentation: A Caution
Segmentation must be done carefully. A group of people may share an age category, income level, or some other segmentation variable, but their spending habits may be quite different. Look at your friends in school. You may all be approximately the same age, but you have different needs and wants. Some of you may wear cashmere sweaters while others wear sweatshirts. The same holds true for income. University professors and truck drivers earn about the same level of income; however, their spending patterns, tastes, and wants are generally quite different.

In Canada, the two dominant cultures—English and French—have historically shown significant differences in consumer attitudes and behaviour. Researchers have found that compared with English Canadians, French Canadians are more involved with home and family, attend the ballet more often, travel less, eat more chocolate, and are less interested in convenience food. But this does not

MARKET RESEARCH
The systematic study of what buyers need and how best to meet those needs.

SECONDARY DATA
Information already available to market researchers as a result of previous research by the firm or other agencies.

PRIMARY DATA
Information developed through new research by the firm or its agents.

OBSERVATION
A market research technique involving viewing or otherwise monitoring consumer buying patterns.

necessarily mean that companies must have different product offerings in Quebec. The adoption process for new products varies from one individual to another according to socio-economic and demographic characteristics.

Marketers are very interested in a person's system of values because values can have a big influence on an individual's tendency to adopt a new product. One study using business school students from France, Quebec, and the rest of North America identified three types of consumers: the conservatives, the dynamics, and the hedonists. The conservatives are typically those consumers who are least likely to adopt new products, while the hedonists (pleasure seekers) are categorized as innovators and are the most likely to adopt new products. Individuals in the dynamics category are somewhat likely to adopt new products but are often seen as imitators.[16]

LO-4 Market Research

Market research, which is the study of what buyers need and how best to meet those needs, can address any element in the marketing mix. Business firms spend millions of dollars each year trying to figure out their customers' habits and preferences. Market research can greatly improve the accuracy and effectiveness of market segmentation.[17] For example, comic books have historically not been of much interest to girls, but DC Comics and Marvel Entertainment are convinced they can change that after observing the success of upstart companies like Tokyopop and Viz Media, which produce translated Japanese comics called *manga*. These companies have succeeded in attracting female readers by having "girl-friendly" content and by distributing their products in both comic book shops and mainstream bookstores.[18]

The Research Process
Market research can occur at almost any point in a product's existence, but it is most frequently used when a new or altered product is being considered. There are five steps in performing market research:[19]

1. *Study the current situation.* What is the need and what is currently being done to meet it?

2. *Select a research method.* In choosing a method, marketers must bear in mind the effectiveness and costs of different methods.

3. *Collect data.* **Secondary data** are information already available as a result of previous research by the firm or other organizations. For example, Statistics Canada publishes a great deal of data that are useful for business firms. Using secondary data can save time, effort, and money. But in some cases, secondary data are unavailable or inadequate, so **primary data**—new research by the firm or its agents—must be obtained. When the Metro grocery chain wanted to increase sales among a key target group—the yoga set (i.e., health-conscious women)—it added three metres of space for yogourt in its coolers while reducing space for products like margarine. The resulting data showed no loss in margarine sales but significant growth in yogourt sales.[20]

4. *Analyze the data.* As we learned in Chapter 11, data are not useful until they have been organized into information.

5. *Prepare a report.* This report normally includes a summary of the study's methodology and findings, various alternative solutions (where appropriate), and recommendations for an appropriate course of action.

Research Methods
The four basic types of methods used by market researchers are *observation*, *survey*, *focus groups*, and *experimentation*.

Observation Probably the oldest form of market research is simple **observation**. It is also a popular research method because it is relatively low in cost, often drawing on data that must be collected for some other reason, such as reordering. In earlier times, when a store owner noticed that customers were buying red children's wagons, not green ones, the owner reordered more red wagons, the manufacturer's records showed high sales of red wagons, and the marketing department concluded that customers wanted red wagons. But observation is now much more sophisticated. For example, Procter & Gamble sent video crews into about 80 households in the U.K., Germany, and China to capture people's daily routines and product interaction. P&G can use this information to develop new products to satisfy needs that consumers didn't even know they had.[21]

Retail guru Paco Underhill collects approximately 50 000 hours of video every year for customers like Walmart, Best Buy, and Gap.[22] Using video equipment to observe consumer behaviour is called *video mining*. It is being adopted by many retailers in North America, who use hidden cameras to determine the percentage of shoppers who buy and the percentage who only browse. They do this by comparing the number of people taped with the number of transactions the store records. Some consumer organizations are raising privacy concerns about this practice, since shoppers are unaware that they are being taped.[23]

Survey Sometimes observation of current events is not enough and marketers need to conduct a **survey** to find out what consumers want. When Sara Lee Corp. acquired Kiwi shoe polish, it surveyed 3500 people in eight countries about their shoe care needs. It learned that people do not care as much about the shine on their shoes as they do about how fresh and comfortable they are on the inside. The firm has since unveiled several new products under the Kiwi name and is doing quite well.[24]

The heart of any survey is a questionnaire that contains carefully constructed questions designed to give the company honest answers about specific research issues. Surveys can be expensive to carry out and may vary widely in their accuracy. Because no firm can afford to survey everyone, marketers must carefully select a representative group of respondents. In the past, surveys have been mailed to individuals for their completion, but online surveys are now gaining in popularity because the company gets immediate results and because the process is a less intrusive way of gathering data. At Hudson's Bay Company, customers can use online surveys to tell HBC how happy or unhappy they are about the service they received at any of The Bay's department stores. The company can then make any changes that are needed to keep customers happy. The Bay used to hire mystery shoppers to find out how well it was serving the public, but that program was ended when the online survey system was adopted.[25]

Focus Groups Many firms also use **focus groups**, where 6 to 15 people are brought together to talk about a product or service. A moderator leads the group's discussion, and employees from the sponsoring company may observe the proceedings from behind a one-way mirror. The comments of people in the focus group are taped, and researchers go through the data looking for common themes. The people in the focus group are not usually told which company is sponsoring the research. When Procter & Gamble was developing a new air freshener, it asked people in focus groups to describe their "desired scent experience." They discovered that people get used to a scent after about half an hour and no longer notice it. P&G used this information to develop Febreze Scentstories, which gives off one of five scents every 30 minutes.[26]

Consumers don't necessarily tell the truth when participating in focus groups or when filling out surveys. They may say one thing and think something else. This has led marketers to look at other ways of gathering information. For example, Sensory Logic Inc. studies facial expressions and eye movements to determine what consumers really think of a product.[27]

Experimentation **Experimentation** compares the responses of the same or similar individuals under different circumstances. For example, a firm that is trying to decide whether to include walnuts in a new candy bar probably would not learn much by asking people what they thought of the idea. But if it made some bars with nuts and some without and then asked people to try both, the responses could be very helpful.[28]

Understanding Consumer Behaviour

Market research in its many forms can be of great help to marketing managers in understanding how the common traits of a market segment affect consumers' purchasing decisions. Why do people buy a certain product? What desire are they fulfilling with the product? Is there a psychological or sociological explanation for why consumers purchase one product and not another? These questions and many others are addressed in the area of marketing known as **consumer behaviour**, which focuses on the decision process customers use when deciding what products to buy.

Influences on Consumer Behaviour

To understand consumer behaviour, marketers draw heavily on the fields of psychology and sociology. Four influences are most active, and marketers use them to explain consumer choices and predict future purchasing behaviour:

1. *Psychological influences* include an individual's motivations, perceptions, ability to learn, and attitudes.
2. *Personal influences* include lifestyle, personality, economic status, and life-cycle stage.
3. *Social influences* include family, opinion leaders (people whose opinions are sought by others), and reference groups such as friends, co-workers, and professional associates.
4. *Cultural influences* include culture (the "way of living" that distinguishes one large group from another),

SURVEY A market research technique based on questioning a representative sample of consumers about purchasing attitudes and practices.

FOCUS GROUP A market research technique involving a small group of people brought together and allowed to discuss selected issues in depth.

EXPERIMENTATION A market research technique in which the reactions of similar people are compared under different circumstances.

CONSUMER BEHAVIOUR The study of the process by which customers come to purchase and consume a product or service.

subculture (smaller groups, such as ethnic groups, with shared values), and social class (the cultural ranking of groups according to criteria such as background, occupation, and income).

Although these factors can have an impact on a consumer's choices, their effect on actual purchases varies. Some consumers regularly purchase certain products because they are satisfied with their performance. Such people are less subject to influence and stick with brand names they have experience with. On the other hand, as we saw in the opening case about lululemon, the clothes you wear often reflect social and psychological influences on your consuming behaviour.

LO-5 The Consumer Buying Process

Researchers who have studied consumer behaviour have constructed models that help marketing managers understand how consumers come to purchase products. Figure 12.3 presents one such model. At the foundation of this and similar models is an awareness of the psychosocial influences that lead to consumption. Ultimately, marketing managers use this information to develop marketing plans.

Problem/Need Recognition The buying process begins when a consumer becomes aware of a problem or need. For example, after strenuous exercise, you may recognize that you are thirsty and need refreshment. After the birth of twins, you may find your one-bedroom apartment too small for comfort. After standing in the rain to buy movie tickets, you may decide to buy an umbrella. Need recognition also

occurs when you have a chance to change your purchasing habits. For example, the income from your first job after graduation will let you purchase items that were too expensive when you were a student. You may also discover a need for professional clothing, apartment furnishings, and cars. Visa and the Bay recognize this shift and therefore market their credit cards to graduates.

Information Seeking Having recognized a need, consumers seek information. This search is not always extensive. If you are thirsty, you may ask where the vending machine is, but that may be the extent of your information search. Other times, you simply rely on your memory for information. If you are thirsty after a workout, Gatorade probably comes to mind because of all the ads you've seen reminding you that it is great way to replenish lost fluids. Before making major purchases, however, most people seek additional information. For example, if you move to a new city, you will want to find out who is the best local dentist, physician, hair stylist, or butcher. To get this information, you may check with acquaintances, co-workers, and relatives. Before buying an exercise bike, you may read the latest *Consumer Reports*—a public source of consumer ratings—on such equipment. You may also ask market sources such as the salesclerk or rely on direct experience. You might test-ride the bike to learn more before you buy.[29] The internet has become an important source of information; 80 percent of Canadians rely on the internet to gather information.[30]

Evaluation of Alternatives If you are in the market for a set of golf clubs, you probably have some idea

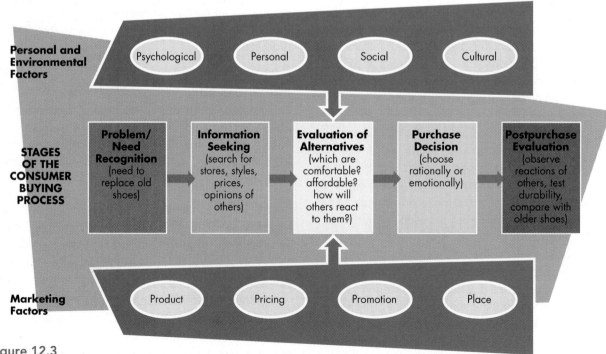

Figure 12.3
The consumer buying process.

of who produces clubs and how they differ. You may have accumulated some of this knowledge during the information-seeking stage and combined it with what you knew before. Based on product attributes such as colour, price, prestige, quality, and service record, you will decide which product best meets your needs.

Purchase Decision Ultimately, you make a purchase decision. "Buy" decisions are based on rational and emotional motives. **Rational motives** involve a logical evaluation of product attributes like cost, quality, and usefulness. **Emotional motives** like fear, sociability, imitation of others, and aesthetics can lead to less-than-ideal purchase decisions. Many spur-of-the-moment decisions are emotionally driven. You might buy mouthwash to avoid embarrassment. You might buy the same brand of jeans as your friends to "fit in." And you might buy a chocolate milkshake simply because you like the taste.

Post-Purchase Evaluation Marketing does not stop with the sale of a product or service but includes the process of consumption. What happens *after* the sale is very important. A marketer wants consumers to be happy after the consumption of the product so that they will buy the product again. In fact, since consumers do not want to go through a complex decision process for every purchase, they often choose a product they have used and liked.

Not all consumers are satisfied with their purchases. Dissatisfied consumers may complain, file a lawsuit, or publicly criticize the product and the company. They are unlikely to purchase the product again, and they are much more likely to speak about their negative experience with a product than are satisfied customers about their positive experience. People can complain about products or services at www.complaints.com or on social media sites. Dissatisfied customers can have a very negative impact on a company's marketing effort. **Word of mouth marketing** (also known as **buzz marketing**) is a very powerful marketing tool. It can, however, be the most devastating, since businesses cannot control it.[31] The Exercising Your Ethics feature at the end of the chapter describes a situation where the customer's buying process did not fit with the marketing methods being used by the company. The result was an unhappy customer.

Companies need to be proactive to satisfy their consumers. After a very tough year full of embarrassing recalls, Toyota Canada began offering customers free maintenance for two years or 48 000 kilometres on select 2010 vehicles. This approach is often used by high-end auto manufacturers. This response could be effective for three reasons: (1) it allows Toyota to identify unsatisfied customers and fix their problems before they spread negative word of mouth, (2) it is relatively inexpensive—in essence, four oil changes, and (3) it ensures that customers will get

into the habit of visiting the dealership; a behaviour that can be very lucrative after the two-year period expires.[32]

LO-6 The International Marketing Mix

Marketing products internationally means mounting a strategy to support global business operations. Obviously, this is no easy task. Foreign customers differ from domestic buyers in language, customs, business practices, and consumer behaviour. When they decide to go global, marketers must therefore reconsider each element of the marketing mix.

International Products

Some products (e.g., Heineken and Coca-Cola) can be sold in many countries with virtually no changes, but often only a redesigned (or completely different) product will meet the needs of foreign buyers. To sell its computers in Japan, Apple had to develop a Japanese-language operating system.

Mattel, the maker of Barbie dolls, is one company that has learned some interesting lessons about the international market. When it conducted focus groups with kids in dozens of countries, it found that worldwide demand existed for many of the same products. Mattel discovered, in essence, that children have similar tastes no matter where they live. Mattel's experience with its famous Barbie doll is illustrative. The dolls sold in Japan had always had black hair and Asian features, not the blonde, blue-eyed appearance of Barbie dolls sold in North America. This seemed to make intuitive sense, but now Mattel is finding that the original Barbie doll is selling just as well in Asia as in North America. But there are still important differences between countries, and they cannot be ignored. For example, German children aren't attracted to action toys the way Canadian and American children are. There are also differences within basic product lines. American kids want Nascar toy cars, while European children want Formula One models.

International Pricing

When pricing for international markets, marketers must handle all the considerations of domestic pricing while

Feathercraft is a small British Columbia manufacturer that has been successful selling kayaks in the Japanese market.

also considering the higher costs of transporting and selling products abroad. Some products cost more overseas than in Canada because of the added costs of delivery. In contrast, products like jet airplanes are priced the same worldwide because delivery costs are incidental; the huge development and production costs are the major considerations regardless of customer location.

International Promotion

Some standard Canadian promotional techniques like advertising do not always succeed in other countries. In fact, some Europeans believe that a product must be shoddy if a company does *any* advertising. International marketers must also be aware that cultural differences can cause negative reactions to products that are advertised improperly. For example, since many Europeans are offended by television commercials that show weapons or violence, Dutch commercials for toys do not feature the guns and combat scenes that are commonplace on Saturday morning television in North America. Meanwhile, cigarette commercials that are banned from Canadian and U.S. television are thriving in many Asian and European markets.

Symbolism can be a surprising consideration. In France, for instance, yellow flowers suggest infidelity. In Mexico, they are signs of death—an association made in Brazil by the colour purple. Clearly, product promotions must be carefully matched to the customs and cultural values of each country.

International Distribution

In some industries, delays in starting new distribution networks can be costly. Therefore, companies with existing distribution systems often enjoy an advantage over new businesses. Several companies have gained advantages in time-based competition by buying existing businesses. Procter & Gamble, for example, saved three years of start-up time by buying Revlon's Max Factor and Betrix cosmetics, both of which are well established in foreign markets. P&G can thus immediately use these companies' distribution and marketing networks for selling its own brands in the United Kingdom, Germany, and Japan. On the other hand, Coca-Cola has been a major player on the international distribution scene for decades and it's a good thing. While sales have been sluggish in North America, the firm is benefiting from major growth in China and India. North America sales now account for only 18 percent of Coca-Cola's profits.[33]

Other companies contract with foreign firms or individuals to distribute and sell their products abroad. Foreign agents may perform personal selling and advertising, provide information about local markets, or serve as exporters' representatives. But having to manage interactions with foreign personnel complicates a marketing manager's responsibilities. In addition, packaging practices in Canada must sometimes be adapted to withstand the rigours of transport to foreign ports and storage under conditions that differ radically from domestic conditions.

Small Business and the Marketing Mix

Many of today's largest firms were yesterday's small businesses. McDonald's began with one restaurant, a concept, and one individual (Ray Kroc) who had a lot of foresight. Behind the success of many small firms lies a skilful application of the marketing concept and careful consideration of each element in the marketing mix.

Small-Business Products

Some new products—and firms—are doomed from the start simply because few consumers want or need what they have to offer. Too often, enthusiastic entrepreneurs introduce products that they and their friends like, but they fail to estimate realistic market potential. Other small businesses offer new products before they have clear pictures of their target markets and how to reach them. They try to be everything to everyone, and they end up serving no one well. In contrast, sound product planning has paid off for many small firms. "Keep it simple" is a familiar key to success—that is, fulfill a specific need and do it efficiently.

Small-Business Pricing

Haphazard pricing that is often little more than guesswork can sink even a firm with a good product. Most often, small-business pricing errors result from a failure to predict operating expenses accurately. Owners of failing businesses have often been heard to utter statements like, "I didn't realize how much it costs to run a business!" and "If I price the product high enough to cover my expenses, no one will buy it!" But when small businesses set prices by carefully assessing costs, many earn very satisfactory profits—sometimes enough to expand or diversify.

Small-Business Promotion

Successful small businesses plan for promotional expenses as part of start-up costs. Some hold costs down by taking advantage of less expensive promotional methods. Local newspapers are sources of publicity when they publish articles about new or unique businesses. Other small businesses have succeeded by identifying themselves and their products with associated groups, organizations, and events. Thus a custom-crafts gallery might join with a local art league and local artists to organize public showings of their combined products. Social media sites are providing new inexpensive outlets for promotion of small businesses as well.

Small-Business Distribution

Problems in arranging distribution can also make or break small businesses. Perhaps the most critical aspect of distribution is facility location, especially for new service businesses. The ability of many small businesses—retailers, veterinary clinics, gourmet coffee shops—to attract and retain customers depends heavily on the choice of location.

In distribution, as in other aspects of the marketing mix, smaller companies may have advantages over larger competitors. They may be quicker in applying service technologies. Everex Systems Inc. sells personal computers to wholesalers and dealers through a system the company calls "Zero Response Time." Phone orders are reviewed every two hours so that the factory can adjust assembly to match demand.

Summary of Learning Objectives

1. **Explain the concept of *marketing*.** Marketing is the process of planning and executing the conception, pricing, promotion, and distribution of ideas, goods, and services to create exchanges that satisfy individual and organizational goals. Marketing can be used to promote consumer and industrial goods.

2. **Explain the purpose of a *marketing plan* and identify the four components of the *marketing mix*.**

Marketing managers plan and implement all the marketing activities that result in the transfer of products to customers. These activities culminate in the marketing plan. Marketing managers rely on the four Ps of marketing (marketing mix). (1) *Product:* a good, a service, or idea. Product differentiation is the creation of a feature or image that makes a product differ from competitors. (2) *Pricing:* strategically selecting the most appropriate price. (3) *Place (Distribution):* activities concerned with getting a product from the producer to the consumer. (4) *Promotion:* techniques used to communicate information about products to customers.

3. **Explain *market segmentation* and show how it is used in target marketing.** Marketers think in terms of target markets—groups of people who have similar wants and needs. Target marketing requires market segmentation—dividing a market into customer types or "segments." Four of the most important influences are (1) *geographic variables,* (2) *demographic variables,* (3) *psychographic variables,* and (4) *behavioural variables.*

4. **Explain the purpose and value of *marketing research.*** Market research is the study of what buyers need and the best ways to meet those needs. This process involves (1) studying the current situation, (2) selecting a research method, (3) collecting and analyzing data, and (4) preparing the report. The four most common research methods are observation, surveys, focus groups, and experimentation.

5. **Describe the key factors that influence the consumer buying process.** Consumer behaviour is the study of the process by which customers decide to purchase products. The result is a focus on four major influences on consumer behaviour: (1) *psychological*

influences, (2) *personal influences,* (3) *social influences,* and (4) *cultural influences.* By identifying which influences are most active in certain circumstances, marketers try to explain consumer choices and predict future purchasing behaviour.

6. **Describe the *international* and *small-business marketing mixes.*** When going global, marketers must reconsider each element of the marketing mix: (1) *product:* sell products abroad without changes or redesign the product, (2) *price:* consider the higher costs of transporting and selling abroad, (3) *distribution:* companies can gain advantages by buying businesses already established in foreign markets, and (4) *promotion:* can the ad campaign be transported abroad, or does it need to be totally redesigned?

Behind the success of many small firms lies an understanding of each element in the marketing mix: (1) *small-business products:* understanding what customers need and want, (2) *small-business pricing:* errors usually result from failure to project operating expenses perhaps the most critical aspect is facility location, (3) *small-business distribution:* the ability of many small businesses to attract and retain customers depends on it, and (4) *small-business promotion:* successful small businesses plan for promotional expenses as part of start-up costs.

Questions and Exercises

Questions for Analysis

1. Why and how is market segmentation used in target marketing?

2. Select an everyday product (such as books, iPods, skateboards, dog food, or shoes). Show how different versions of your product are aimed toward different market segments. Explain how the marketing mix differs for each segment.

3. Consider a service product, such as transportation, entertainment, or health care. What are some ways that more customer value might be added to this product? Why would your improvements add value for the buyer?

4. How does the branding and packaging of convenience, shopping, and specialty goods differ? Why? Give examples of actual products to defend your answer.

5. If you were starting a small business, what are the key marketing pitfalls you would try to avoid?

6. Select a product or service that you use regularly. Explain the relative importance of each of the four elements in the marketing mix (product, price, promotion, and place). Then select another product and determine the extent to which the relative emphasis changes. If it changed, why did it change?

Application Exercises

7. Interview the marketing manager of a local business. Identify the degree to which this person's job is focused on each element in the marketing mix.

8. Select a product made by a foreign company and visit its website. What is the product's target market? What is the basis on which the target market is segmented? Do you think that this basis is appropriate? How might another approach be beneficial? Why?

9. Interview someone who has recently purchased or is in the process of purchasing a car. Identify the actions that your subject took at each stage of the consumer buying process. Did the manufacturer help simplify the process? How? Is the consumer experiencing post-purchase regret?

10. Visit the websites of three major banks and identify how they help their clients gather information to ease the home-buying process (e.g., mortgage products and services).

Building Your Business Skills

Dealing in Segments and Variables

Goal

To encourage students to analyze the ways in which various market segmentation variables affect business success.

Situation

You and four partners are thinking of purchasing a heating and air conditioning (H/AC) dealership that specializes in residential applications priced between $2000 and $40 000. You are now in the process of deciding where that dealership should be. You are considering four locations: Miami, Florida; Toronto, Ontario; Vancouver, British Columbia; and Dallas, Texas.

Method

Step 1 Working with four classmates (your partnership group), conduct library research to learn how H/AC makers market their residential products. Check for articles in *The Globe and Mail*, *Canadian Business*, *Wall Street Journal*, and other business publications.

Step 2 Continue your research. This time, focus on the specific marketing variables that define each prospective location. Check Statistics Canada data at your library and on the internet and contact local chambers of commerce (by phone and via the internet) to learn about the following factors for each location:

- Geography
- Demography (especially age, income, gender, family status, and social class)
- Psychographic variables (lifestyles, interests, and attitudes)

Step 3 Meet with group members to analyze which location holds the greatest promise as a dealership site. Base your decision on your analysis of market segment variables and their effects on H/AC sales.

Follow-Up Questions

1. Which location did you choose? Describe the market segmentation factors that influenced your decision.

2. Identify the two variables you believe will have the greatest impact on the dealership's success. Why are these factors so important?

3. Which factors were least important in your decision? Why?

4. When equipment manufacturers advertise residential H/AC products, they often show them in different climate situations (in winter, summer, or high-humidity conditions). Which market segments are these ads targeting? Describe these segments in terms of demographic and psychographic characteristics.

Exercising Your Ethics

A Big Push for Publicity

The Situation

Marsden Corp. is known as a "good citizen" and prides itself on publicity it receives from sponsoring community projects. The company's executive vice-president, Jane Martin, has just been named chairperson of annual fundraising for the Coalition for Community Services (CCS), which is a group of community service organizations that depend on voluntary donations. In the highly visible chairperson's role, Martin has organized the support of officials at other firms to ensure that the fundraising target is met or surpassed.

The Dilemma

Martin began a meeting of 30 department managers to appeal for 100 percent employee participation in CCS giving in the fundraising drive. As follow-up the week before the drive officially started, she met with each manager, saying, "I expect you to give your fair share and to ensure that all your employees do likewise. I don't care what it takes, just do it. Make it clear that employees will at least donate cash. Even better, get them to sign up for weekly payroll deductions to the CCS fund because it nets more money than one-time cash donations."

Nathan Smith was both surprised and confused. As a newly appointed department manager, he was unsure how to go about soliciting donations from his 25 employees. Remembering Martin's comment, "I don't care what it takes, just do it," Nathan wondered what to do if someone did not give. Personally, too, he was feeling uneasy. How much should he give? With his family's pressing financial needs, he would rather not give money to CCS. He began to wonder if his donation to CCS would affect his career at Marsden.

Team Activity

Assemble a group of four to five students and assign each group member to one of the following roles:

- Nathan Smith (employee)
- Jane Martin (employer)
- Director of CCS (customer)
- Marsden stockholder (investor)
- Marsden CEO (if your group has five members)

Action Steps

1. Before discussing the situation with your group, and from the perspective of your assigned role, consider whether there are any *ethical issues* with Marsden's fundraising program. If yes, write them down.

2. Before discussing the situation with your group, and from the perspective of your assigned role, consider whether there are any *problems* likely to arise from Marsden's fundraising program. If yes, write them down.

3. Share the ethical issues and problems you identified with the group. Did the different roles result in different ethical issues and problems?

4. For the various ethical issues that were identified, decide as a group which one is the most important for Marsden to resolve. Likewise, for potential problems that were identified, which is the most important one for Marsden?

5. From an ethical standpoint, what does your group recommend to resolve the most important ethical issue? How should the most important problem be resolved? Identify the advantages and drawbacks of your recommendations.

Dell Facing Serious Challenges

For over a quarter of a century, Dell's successful model has been documented in countless articles and books. Quite simply, Dell has been a symbol of efficient distribution and customer service. However, this tremendous reputation has suffered in recent years as Dell has lost ground to competitors like HP and Acer. Before we examine what has gone wrong, let's take a look at the origins of Dell's success.

From the outset, Michael Dell's vision recognized a market with different kinds of potential users—the business sector, non-business organizations such as schools and other institutions, as well as the growing segment of PC users in homes—each with different needs and resources. Choosing to focus more on the business and institutional segments, Dell envisioned a then-unheard-of combination of service features for PC customers: high-quality products, lowest cost, ease in ordering and receiving products, live interaction with expert technical assistance for building a PC "the way you like it," super-fast deliveries, and after-the-sale communications to ensure product performance and to keep users informed about upgrades to enhance their PCs.

The market response was overwhelming, resulting in Dell's dominant position as industry leader. Dell's

unique vision for integrating all stages of marketing—development of the product and related services, pricing, selling to consumers directly via telephone or the internet, delivering directly to customers from efficient manufacturing plants, and promotional messages for product awareness and use—were unmatched by competitors that struggled to copy Dell's way of doing business.

A few years ago, Dell launched itself into the broader consumer electronics market for even greater revenue growth. Giant electronics retailers like Best Buy may have been concerned that Dell's customer-friendly business model would carry over into LCD TVs, DVD recorders, MP3 players, and digital cameras. The potential range of products is enormous: music, movies, photos, and other entertainment are increasingly digital and have become compatible extensions of PCs. Chairman and CEO Michael Dell had clearly identified a new strategic opportunity: "There is a whole new ballgame in the convergence of computing and consumer electronics, and it's a world we are comfortable in."

But would they succeed? Some experts thought the crossover into consumer products could be a problem because, unlike Gateway's and Hewlett-Packard's focus on the consumer segment, Dell's primary PC focus has been on business and institutional markets. A classic example of a failed crossover is IBM's ill-fated attempt in the 1980s to woo consumers with its downsized PC Jr. With hugely successful sales and technical support for business customers, IBM never understood the consumer market, and Big Blue's efforts proved a mismatch that ended with the withdrawal of the PC Jr. from the marketplace in the late 1990s. But in this case the risks were largely offset by Dell's brand familiarity in both business and consumer markets.

For masses of electronics lovers, Dell's entry came as welcome news. After all, competition drives down profit margins and prices. Retailers and e-tailers, in contrast, experienced what might be called "reverse sticker shock." Sellers enjoying net profit margins of 25 to 40 percent on consumer electronics may have to survive on the modest 10 percent margin to which PC sellers are accustomed. That would leave lots of room for Dell to push electronics prices down, gain large volume sales, and reap high total profits while competing firms in the industry try to imitate its low-price–high-value business model. At least, that was the plan.

The arguments were rational and the strategy seemed to fit the converging needs of the consumer. So what happened? It's still early to pass a final judgment, but the results are very disturbing. With Dell's attention focused on new greener pastures, the competition swooped in and stole market share. In 2010, Dell had dropped from a dominant position in PC sales to third place behind HP and Acer. Dell could briefly console itself in the thought that shipments were up by 5.2 percent that year. Unfortunately, reality set in when the comparative results were examined. The companies they were now chasing, HP and Acer, were up 28 percent and 23 percent respectively. In addition, the fourth- and fifth-ranked competitors, Lenovo and Toshiba, were up 42 and 30 percent respectively. With these statistics it was clear that Dell was in trouble and any minor gains it had made in electronics were being overshadowed by major losses in its primary market.

By mid-2010, the outlook was not getting any rosier, with increased price pressure coming, in particular, from Acer and higher component costs threatening margins further. Without its accustomed dominant position there was legitimate concern that Dell could no longer buy components at favourable prices versus the competition; a long-time source of competitive advantage. Meanwhile, over at Hewlett-Packard the results were positive. HP beat industry estimates and it was raising sales and profit estimates for the upcoming year.

The results were telling a negative story, which was in stark contrast to what had become the norm for Dell. But Dell was reformulating and looking for long-term solutions. After all, the initial move into electronics was taken to search for higher-margin products. In 2009, Dell bought Perot Systems Corp., an information technology and business solutions company, for US$3.9 billion. In 2010, Dell struck a deal with AT&T to bring its first-ever smart phone, which was already available in China and Brazil, to the U.S. Dell had also signed a deal with telecommunication provider Telefonica to develop and expand distribution of "smart mobile devices" (smart phones, tablets, and netbooks) in Europe and Latin America.

Dell is clearly moving forward. But would these moves pay off? Was the company spending enough energy on its core market? Was it willing to continue to sacrifice its former leadership position in PC sales for emerging growth opportunities? Would a move into the fiercely competitive and crowded smart phone market pay off? As Dell was answering these questions, and many more, competitors in all of these markets were formulating their own strategies to meet their goals. Only time will tell if Dell is on the right track or if its decline will continue.

Questions for Discussion

1. In this chapter we have discussed the important concepts of targeting, segmenting, and positioning. In groups of three or four, identify where Dell's brand is positioned in the minds of your classmates.

2. Over the years, Dell's success was based on a combination of strategic elements. Which of the four Ps was the key element in the success of the company? Explain how the company delivers value to consumers.

3. Identify the main factors favouring success for Dell's bold move into the North American smart phone market. What prominent factors suggest major problems or even failure in this attempt?

4. Debate: Divide into two groups and defend one of the following statements. (1) Dell should go back to its roots and focus primarily on sales of its computers, laptops, and notebooks. (2) In order for Dell to succeed it must continue to expand and pursue new opportunities such as the smart phone business.

SCANLIFE

chapter

13

Developing and Promoting Goods and Services

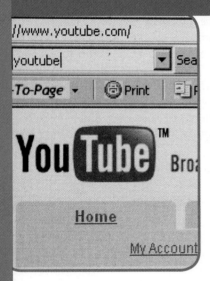

After reading this chapter, you should be able to:

LO-1 Identify a *product*, distinguish between *consumer* and *industrial products*, and explain the *product mix*.

LO-2 Describe the *new product development process* and trace the stages of the *product life cycle*.

LO-3 Explain the importance of *branding, packaging,* and *labelling*.

LO-4 Identify the important objectives of *promotion* and discuss the considerations in selecting a *promotional mix*.

LO-5 Describe the key *advertising media*.

LO-6 Outline the tasks involved in *personal selling*.

LO-7 Describe the various types of *sales promotions* and distinguish between *publicity* and *public relations*.

SCANLIFE

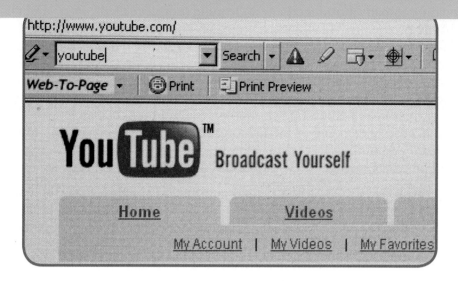

Psst! Did You Hear the Latest?

Word of mouth is probably the oldest form of advertising. Ever since the first brand names were developed hundreds of years ago, consumers have been exchanging information about positive and negative product features. In the eighteenth and nineteenth centuries, marketing was very fragmented and most products were promoted only in local areas at retailers like the general store. Word-of-mouth advertising was therefore mostly confined to local or regional markets because existing technology did not allow consumers to be well connected.

By the 1930s, the development of radio, and later television, allowed businesses to market their products nationwide. Word of mouth did not disappear, but it was overshadowed by mass marketing. More recently, word-of-mouth advertising has again gained prominence, mainly because of the internet. PQ Media predicts that in the United States, spending on word-of-mouth advertising will be $3.7 billion in 2011 as companies recognize the emerging importance of social networking sites like YouTube and Facebook and personal blogs.

Word-of-mouth advertising is relatively cheap, and the messages that it carries are trusted by those who hear them. A Nielsen study showed that 78 percent of consumers trust word-of-mouth messages. Newspapers were trusted by 63 percent of consumers, television by 56 percent, and text ads on cellphones by only 18 percent.

Word of mouth is a double-edged sword. If consumers are spreading positive messages about a product, sales will likely soar. For example, Nike spent very little money advertising its Presto line of stretchy sneakers, but kids and teens spread the word to each other about the shoes and the fashion statement they could make by having them. If, however, consumers are spreading negative messages, sales will suffer. The movie *Snakes*

How Will This Help Me?

By understanding the material in this chapter, you can benefit in three ways: (1) as an *employee* and as a *manager*, you'll be better able to use the concepts of developing and promoting products in your career; (2) as a *consumer*, you'll have a clearer picture of how the complex process of new product development and promotion leads to more consumer choice; and (3) as an *investor*, you'll be better prepared to evaluate a company's marketing program and its competitive potential before buying the company's stock.

on a Plane, which starred Samuel L. Jackson, bombed at the box office partly because word of mouth focused on how bad the film was.

Procter & Gamble—which is famous for its television commercials—is very active in word-of-mouth advertising. When the company introduced a new cleaning product called Dawn Direct Foam, it provided information about the product to Vocalpoint, a group of 450 000 brand "evangelists" who talk up P&G products. The new product launch was a success. P&G has another word-of-mouth unit called Tremors, which includes over 200 000 teenagers who are active on social networks. These individuals are often early adopters of new products. P&G is planning to use Canada as a testing ground for online advertising spending; especially in light of the fact that an Ipsos Reid survey showed that Canadian consumers spend 39 percent of their media consumption time on the internet, 26 percent on TV, and 11 percent on print media. This large percentage of media consumption time spent on the internet means great opportunities for word of mouth.

Many other companies also recognize the importance of word-of-mouth advertising:

- Algordonza is a Swiss-based company that makes artificial diamonds from the carbon found in the ashes of people who have been cremated. It sells about 700 diamonds each year to friends and relatives of the deceased. The company does not advertise but relies on word of mouth to make people aware of its product.

- Volkswagen Canada cancelled a scheduled advertising campaign for its Eos automobile because the cars were rapidly being sold due to positive word of mouth.

- Google did no marketing of Gmail; instead they gave Gmail accounts to certain "power users" and the resulting word of mouth increased demand for the service.

A group called The Influencers is Canada's first word-of-mouth community. It has created its own word-of-mouth campaign for promoting word-of-mouth advertising and cites various interesting statistics:

- The average person has 56 word-of-mouth conversations each week.

- Ninety-three percent of customers say word of mouth is the most trustworthy source of product information.

- Word of mouth is rated as the most reliable of 15 different marketing influences.

- Seventy-seven percent of word-of-mouth advertising is face to face.

- Forty-four percent of Canadians avoid buying products that overwhelm them with advertising.

LO-1 What Is a Product?

In developing the marketing mix for products—goods, services, or ideas—marketers must consider what consumers really buy when they purchase products. Only then can they plan their strategies effectively. We begin where product strategy begins—with an understanding of product *features* and *benefits*. Next, we will describe the major *classifications of products*, both consumer and industrial. Finally, we will discuss the most important component in the offerings of any business—its *product mix*.

VALUE PACKAGE
Product marketed as a bundle of value-adding attributes, including reasonable cost.

Features and Benefits

Products are much more than just *visible* features and benefits. In buying a product, consumers are also buying an image and a reputation. The marketers of Swatch Chrono watch are well aware that brand name, packaging, labelling, and after-the-purchase service are also indispensable parts of their product. Advertisements remind consumers that they don't just get "real" features like shock and water resistance, quartz precision, and Swiss craftsmanship; they also get Swatch's commitment that its products will be young and trendy, active and sporty, and stylistically cool and clean.

Today's consumer regards a product as a bundle of attributes which, taken together, marketers call the **value package**. Increasingly, buyers expect to receive products with greater *value*—with more benefits at reasonable costs. For example, the possible attributes in a personal computer value package are things like easy access, choice of colour, attractive software packages, fast ordering via the internet, and assurance of speedy delivery. Although the computer includes physical *features*—like processing devices and other hardware—most items in the value package are services or intangibles that collectively add value by providing *benefits* that increase the customer's satisfaction.

Look at the ad in Figure 13.1 for Public Mobile. In this ad, the technical features of mobile phones are not emphasized. Rather, the ad focuses on the benefits that buyers will get by using Public Mobile (for example, no contract). These benefits are being marketed as part of a complete value package.

Classifying Goods and Services
Product buyers fall into two groups: buyers of *consumer* products and buyers of *industrial* products. Consumer and industrial buying processes and marketing approaches are quite different.

Classifying Consumer Products Consumer products are commonly divided into three categories that reflect buyers' behaviour: *convenience*, *shopping*, and *specialty* goods.

- **Convenience goods** (such as milk and newspapers) and **convenience services** (such as those offered by fast-food restaurants) are consumed rapidly and regularly. They are relatively inexpensive and are purchased frequently and with little expenditure of time and effort.

- **Shopping goods** (such as HDTVs and tires) and **shopping services** (such as insurance) are more expensive and are purchased less frequently than convenience goods and services. Consumers often compare brands in different stores. They also evaluate alternatives in terms of style, performance, colour, price, and other criteria.

- **Specialty goods** (such as wedding gowns) and **specialty services** (such as catering for wedding receptions) are important and expensive purchases. Consumers usually decide on precisely what they want and will accept no substitutes. They will often go from store to store, sometimes spending a great

deal of time and money to get exactly the product they want.

Classifying Industrial Products Industrial products can be divided into two categories: *expense items* and *capital items*.

- **Expense items** are materials and services that are consumed within a year. The most obvious expense items are industrial goods used directly in the production process, for example, bulkloads of tea processed into tea bags. In addition, *support materials* help to keep a business running without directly entering the production process. Oil, for instance, keeps the tea-bagging machines running but is not used in the tea bags. Similarly, *supplies*—pencils, brooms, gloves, paint—are consumed quickly and regularly by every business. Finally, *services* such as window cleaning, equipment installation, and temporary office help are essential to daily operations. Because these items are used frequently, purchases are often automatic and require little decision making.

- **Capital items** are "permanent"—expensive and long-lasting—goods and services. All these items have expected lives of more than a year—typically up to several years. Expensive buildings (offices,

CONVENIENCE GOODS AND SERVICES Relatively inexpensive consumer goods or services that are bought and used rapidly and regularly, with minimal search effort.

SHOPPING GOODS AND SERVICES Moderately expensive consumer goods or services that are purchased infrequently, causing consumers to spend some time comparing their prices.

SPECIALTY GOODS AND SERVICES Very expensive consumer goods or services that are purchased rarely, and require an extensive search.

EXPENSE ITEMS Relatively inexpensive industrial goods that are consumed rapidly and regularly.

CAPITAL ITEMS Expensive, long-lasting industrial goods that are used in producing other goods or services and have a long life.

Figure 13.1
Public Mobile ad.

factories), fixed equipment (water towers, baking ovens), and accessory equipment (computers, airplanes) are capital goods. Capital services require long-term commitments. They include purchases for employee food services, building and equipment maintenance, or legal services.

The Product Mix

The group of products a company has available for sale, be it consumer or industrial, is known as the firm's **product mix**. Black & Decker makes toasters, vacuum cleaners, electric drills, and a variety of other appliances and tools. Nike has introduced a whole line of sports-related products like baseball gloves and bats, hockey sticks, basketballs, and in-line skates.

A **product line** is a group of products that are closely related because they function in a similar manner or are sold to the same customer group. ServiceMaster was among the first successful home services that offered mothproofing and carpet cleaning. Subsequently, the company expanded into other closely related services for homeowners—lawn care (TruGreen, ChemLawn), pest control (Terminix), and cleaning (Merry Maids).

Companies may extend their horizons and identify opportunities outside existing product lines. The result is *multiple* (or *diversified*) *product lines*. After years of serving residential customers, ServiceMaster has added business and industry services (landscaping and janitorial), education services (management of schools and institutions, including physical facilities and financial and personnel resources), and health-care services (management of support services—plant operations, asset management, laundry/linen supply—for long-term care facilities). Multiple product lines allow a company to grow rapidly and can help to offset the consequences of slow sales in any one product line.

LO-2 Developing New Products

All products and services—including once-popular TV shows like *Friends*, *The Sopranos*, and *Lost*—eventually reach the end of their life cycle and expire. Firms must therefore develop and introduce streams of new products. Levi's was once Canada's most popular brand of jeans, but the company failed to keep pace with changing tastes and lost market share. The company got back on track when it introduced their Signature brand of casual clothing. The brand has become very popular, and Levi's has opened Signature stores in several countries.

While new product development is critical, it is also very risky. Consider the battle between Toshiba (HD DVD) and Sony (Blu-ray) for global dominance of high-definition DVDs. Both companies invested millions of dollars in their respective products, and experts predicted that there would be a prolonged fight between the two companies. But in less than two years, Toshiba gave up the fight and stopped producing its product. Why? Because Sony was successful in convincing movie studios like Warner to release movies only in the Blu-ray format. Major retail outlets like Walmart and Netflix also announced they would sell only the Blu-ray format. Sony's success with Blu-ray is in marked contrast to its failure in the 1980s to get its Betamax format adopted for VCRs. In that earlier fight, Sony lost out when consumers preferred the VHS format.[1]

The Time Frame of New Product Development

Companies often face multi-year time horizons and high risks when developing new products. The Tesla roadster was officially approved for sale in Canada in 2010. What is it? It's an electric roadster that costs $125 000 and can go from zero to 60 mph in 3.7 seconds. Unfortunately, profits are not approaching that quickly. Tesla sold a little less than 1000 cars from 2008 to 2010, worldwide. At the beginning of 2010, the company was trying to raise $100 million in an initial public offering but it is clear that this is a long-term investment. In a recent statement, Tesla indicated that it does not expect to be able to claim tax deductions it has earned in recent years before they expire in 2024. In other words, the product is evolving but its financial success is not around the corner.[2]

The airplane manufacturing business can be quite profitable but it is a long and complicated process to launch a new model. In 2004, Montreal-based Bombardier announced that it would build a new CSeries line of regional passenger jets. In 2006, it shelved the project, but it restarted it in 2007. In 2008, Bombardier announced that it had received the first orders for the new plane but that it would not enter service until 2013.[3] Two other commercial airplane manufacturers have also had delays with their new planes. Boeing's 787 Dreamliner was originally set for release in 2008, but a strike by machinists and incomplete work by suppliers delayed the introduction of the new plane until 2010. Boeing's main competitor, Airbus, experienced its own problems. It had to redesign its A350, which pushed back the planned start of production by nearly three years.[4]

The Tesla Roadster combines sleek design with an environmentally friendly electric package. Quite a combination, but will enough consumers pay $125 000 for the car to make it a long-term success?

The Seven-Step Development Process

To increase their chances of developing a successful new product, many firms adopt some variation on a basic seven-step process (see Figure 13.2):

1. *Product ideas.* Product development begins with a search for ideas. Product ideas can come from consumers, the sales force, research and development people, or engineering personnel.

2. *Screening.* In this stage, the goal is to eliminate product ideas that don't match the firm's abilities, expertise, or objectives. Representatives from marketing, engineering, and production must have input at this stage.

3. *Concept testing.* Once the top concepts have been selected, companies use market research to solicit consumer input and identify key benefits as well as an appropriate price level.

4. *Business analysis.* This stage involves developing estimates of costs versus benefits. The aim is not to determine precisely how much money the product

Product Mortality Rates It takes about 50 new product ideas to generate one product that finally reaches the market. Even then, only a few of these survivors become *successful* products. Many seemingly great *ideas* have failed as *products*. Indeed, creating a successful new product has become increasingly difficult—even for the most experienced marketers. Why? The number of new products hitting the market each year has increased dramatically, and thousands of new household, grocery, and drugstore items are introduced annually. But at any given time, the average supermarket carries a total of only 20 000 to 25 000 different items. Because of lack of space and customer demand, about 9 out of 10 new products will fail. Those with the best chances are innovative and deliver unique benefits.

Speed to Market The more rapidly a product moves from the laboratory to the marketplace, the more likely it is to survive. By introducing new products ahead of competitors, companies quickly establish market leaders that become entrenched in the market before being challenged by late-arriving competitors. **Speed to market**—that is, a firm's success in responding to customer demand or market changes—is very important. One study estimated that a product that is only three months late to the market (three months behind the leader) loses 12 percent of its lifetime profit potential. A product that is six months late loses 33 percent.[5]

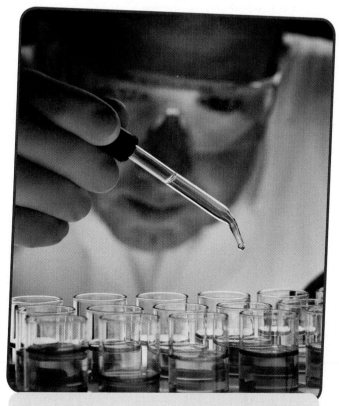

Pharmaceutical companies spend large amounts of money on research and development, yet bring relatively few products to market.

will make, but to see whether the product can meet minimum profitability goals.

5 *Prototype development.* At this stage, product ideas begin to take shape. Using input from the concept-testing phase, engineering and/or research and development produce a preliminary version of the product. Prototypes can be extremely expensive, often requiring extensive handcrafting, tooling, and development of components.

6 *Product testing and test marketing.* Using what it learned from the prototype, the company goes into limited production of the item. This stage is very costly, since promotional campaigns and distribution channels must be established for test markets. But test marketing gives a company its first information on how consumers will respond to a product under real market conditions.

7 *Commercialization.* If test-marketing results are positive, the company will begin full-scale production and marketing of the product. Gradual commercialization, with the firm providing the product to more and more areas over time, prevents undue strain on the firm's initial production capabilities.

The Product Life Cycle

The **product life cycle (PLC)** is the idea that successfully commercialized products have a limited profit-producing life for a company. This life may be a matter of months, years, or decades, depending on the ability of the product to attract customers over time. Products such as Kellogg's Corn Flakes, Coca-Cola, Ivory soap, and Caramilk chocolate bars have had extremely long productive lives.

Stages in the Product Life Cycle

The product life cycle is a natural process in which products are born, grow in stature, mature, and finally decline and die.[6]

The life cycle is typically divided into four states through which products pass as they "age" in the market. In Figure 13.3a, the four phases of the PLC are applied to several products with which you are familiar.

1 *Introduction.* The introduction stage begins when the product reaches the marketplace. During this stage, marketers focus on making potential consumers aware of the product and its benefits. Because of extensive promotional and development costs, profits are nonexistent. But the use of social media tools like Twitter and YouTube is providing cost-efficient alternatives for companies to generate attention and buzz.

2 *Growth.* If the new product attracts and satisfies enough consumers, sales begin to climb rapidly. During this stage, the product begins to show a profit. Other firms in the industry move rapidly to introduce their own versions. Heavy promotion is often required to build brand preference over the competition.

3 *Maturity.* Sales growth begins to slow. Although the product earns its highest profit level early in this stage, increased competition eventually leads to price cutting and lower profits. Marketing communications

Figure 13.2
The new product development process.

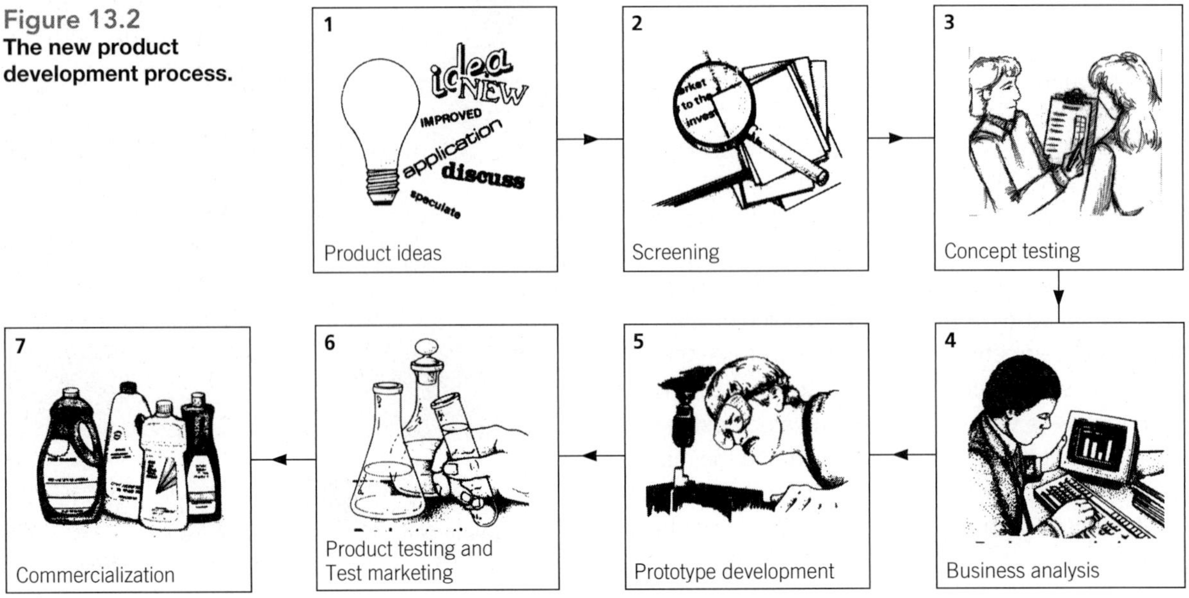

1 Product ideas
2 Screening
3 Concept testing
4 Business analysis
5 Prototype development
6 Product testing and Test marketing
7 Commercialization

tend to focus on reminder advertising. Toward the end of this stage, sales start to fall.

4. *Decline.* During this final stage, sales and profits continue to fall. New products in the introduction stage take sales away. Companies remove or reduce promotional support (ads and salespeople) but may let the product linger to milk the remaining profits.

Figure 13.3b plots the relationship of the PLC to a product's typical sales, costs, and profits. Although the early stages of the PLC often show no profit, successful products usually continue to generate profits until the decline stage. For most products, profitable life spans are short—thus, the importance placed by so many firms on the constant replenishment of product lines. At some point, the company must decide to cease production of a product in the decline stage. For example, in 2003, sales of digital cameras surpassed film cameras for the first time, and Kodak announced stoppage of film camera production after decades as the market leader.

Figure 13.3
The product life cycle: stage, sales, cost, and profit.

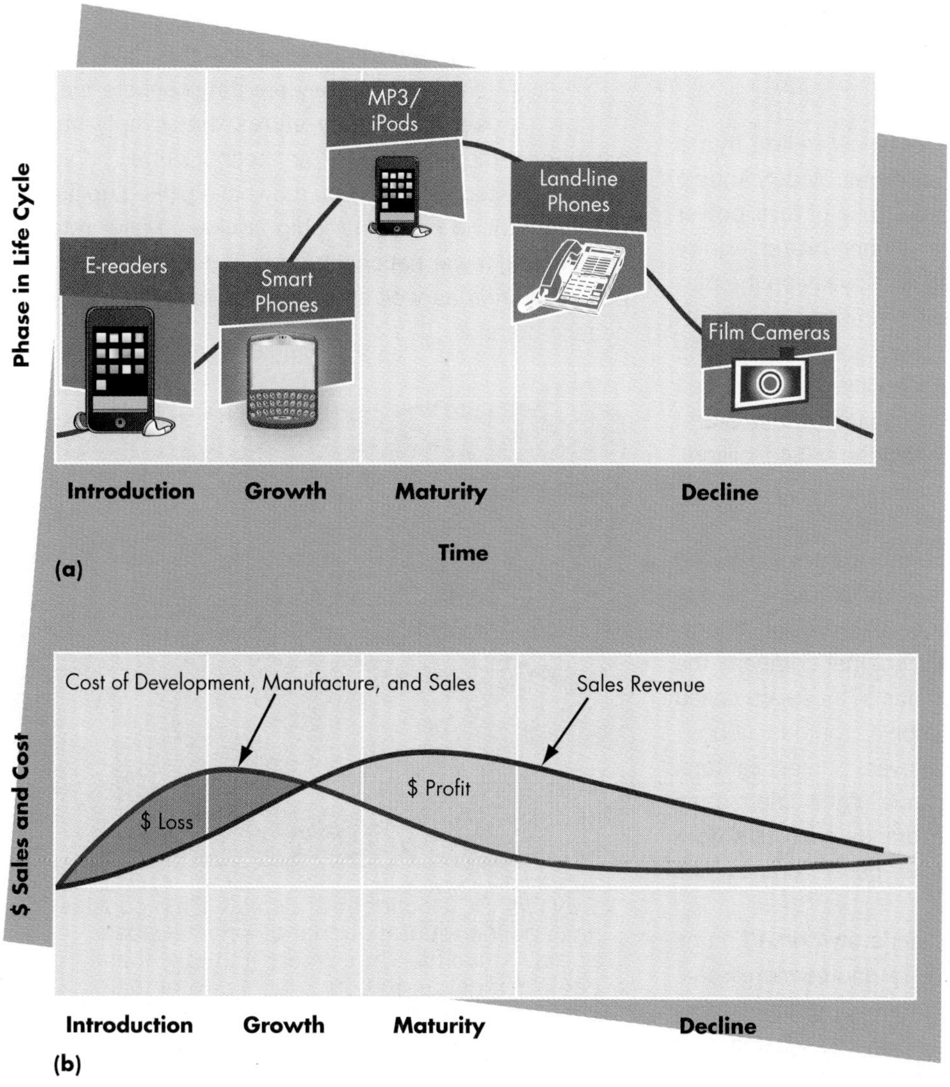

(a)

(b)

LO-3

Identifying Products

As noted earlier in the chapter, developing the features of a product is only part of a marketer's job. Identifying that product in consumers' minds through the use of brand names, packaging, and labelling is also important.

Branding Products

Branding is the use of symbols to communicate the qualities of a particular product made by a particular producer. In 2010, technology companies were at the top of the brand value list. According to Millward Brown Optimor, which creates the BrandZ Top 100 Global Brands Ranking, the three most successful brands in the world were Google, IBM, and Apple. (Take a look at the branding exercise in Figure 13.4.) Three Canadian brands made the Top 100: BlackBerry (#14), RBC (#36), and TD (#71).[7] Countries can also be branded. In the 2009 Country Brand Index, Canada ranked second (the U.S. was first).[8]

Companies sometimes change the name of a popular brand because it is "tired," or because of legal requirements. For example, when Circuit City acquired 874 Canadian RadioShack stores, a court ruling required that it drop the RadioShack name. Circuit City decided to rename the stores The Source by Circuit City. Scott Paper changed the name of Cottonelle, Canada's best-selling brand of toilet paper, to "Cashmere" when a licensing agreement with Kimberly-Clark expired.[9]

Adding Value through Brand Equity Many companies that once measured assets in terms of cash,

How many of these brand logos are you able to recognize?

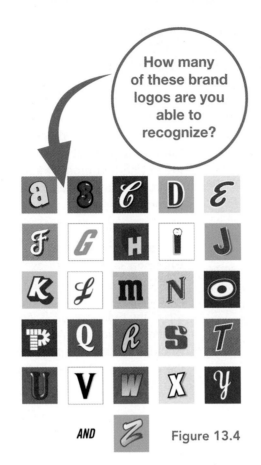

AND

Figure 13.4

supermarket chain in Britain, introduced its own private brand of cola that looks strikingly like the one used by Coke. The product is made by Cott Corporation of Toronto, which also makes the American Choice label for Walmart. Loblaw Companies Ltd. created a line of upscale products under the private brand President's Choice (PC). If you want Loblaws' famous PC Decadent chocolate chip cookies, you need to visit a Loblaws outlet or one of its subsidiaries. Shoppers Drug Mart has tried to copy the success of President's Choice with its private label brands: Life for a wide range of products and Quo for cosmetics.[11] In fact, Shoppers Drug Mart has set a goal to increase its private-label shelf space to 25 percent of overall product offerings. These brands are often 25 percent cheaper for consumers and yet the profit margins tend to be 15 percent higher for the company. This is a clear win-win scenario.[12] Private brands account for 19 percent of the overall market and $10.9 billion in the grocery market.[13]

Generic brands are also gaining more shelf space; they are the products that you see in grocery stores that simply state a category name like "bacon" or "peanut butter." If you've been to Costco recently, you may have picked up its very popular generic chocolate chip cookies. Major retailers are carrying fewer national brands and more of their own private brands as well as these less-expensive, no-frills generic brands.

buildings, equipment, and inventories now realize that a strong brand is an equally important asset. Widely known and admired brands are valuable because of their power to attract customers. Those with higher **brand equity** generate greater brand awareness and loyalty on the part of consumers, have larger market shares than competing brands, and are perceived to have greater quality. In a 2009 survey of Canadian brand equity, the top three companies were the Royal Bank of Canada (whose brand equity was valued at $5.3 billion), BlackBerry ($4.6 billion), and TD Canada Trust ($4.0 billion).[10]

Types of Brand Names **National brands** are those that are produced and distributed by the manufacturer across the entire country (e.g., Scotch tape, Crest). When a company with a well-known brand sells another company the right to place that brand on its products, these are called **licensed brands**. Harley-Davidson's famous logo—emblazoned on boots, eyewear, gloves, purses, lighters, and watches—brings the motorcycle maker more than $210 million annually. Along with brands such as Coors and Ferrari, licensing for character-based brands like Spider-Man is equally lucrative.

Private brands carry the retailer's own brand name even though they are manufactured by another firm. Sears has two well-known private brands—Craftsman tools and Kenmore appliances. J. Sainsbury PLC, the largest

Loblaws' PC Decadent Chocolate Chip cookies have built a reputation that all private-label brands strive for. Consumers that love these cookies must go to Loblaws, or one of their subsidiaries, to buy them.

Brand Loyalty **Brand loyalty** means that when customers need a particular item, they will go back and buy the same brand. Brand loyalty exists at three levels: *brand awareness* (customers recognize the brand), *brand preference* (consumers have a favourable attitude toward the brand), and *brand insistence* (consumers demand the brand and will go out of their way to get it). Brand insistence implies consumer trust in a brand. Canadians have less trust than they did 20 years ago, but some well-known brands like Kellogg's, BlackBerry, and Apple are still viewed positively.[14]

Brand loyalty is strong in several sports, including baseball, basketball, and soccer, and fans respond to marketing efforts by companies like Nike and Adidas. But in some other sports (e.g., skateboarding) brand loyalty is difficult to develop. Because skateboarders go through a lot of boards each year, they are reluctant to buy brand-name boards, which cost three to five times what "blank" boards cost. The International Association of Skateboard Companies estimates that 50 to 70 percent of all boards sold are blank, not branded.[15]

Brand loyalty can have a major impact on a company's profits. In the beer industry, each market share point is worth about $25 million in profit. This is why beer brands have such fierce competitive battles.[16]

E-Business and International Branding The expensive and fierce struggle for brand recognition is very evident in the branding battles among major internet players. Collectively, the top internet brands—Google, Yahoo!, and Amazon—spend billions each year. For example, Cisco Systems Inc. developed a successful promotional campaign that increased its brand awareness by 80 percent. The campaign also lifted Cisco's reputation as an internet expert above that of Microsoft and IBM.[17]

Firms that sell products internationally face a growing branding strategy issue. They must consider how product names will translate in various languages. Chevrolet learned this lesson decades ago when it entered the Spanish market with the Nova. This name was not well received simply because "no va" translates into "it does not go."[18] Recently, the 2010 Buick Lacrosse was launched and the name is catching attention in Quebec for the wrong reasons. In French slang, lacrosse is a term for pleasuring yourself. What's even more surprising is that GM was aware of this unfortunate naming issue and originally released the car in 2005 as the Buick Allure. But in an effort to cut down marketing costs it ignored the potential embarrassment and decided to launch the Lacrosse in 2010.[19]

Differences in approaches to brand names are evident even within countries. When Headspace Marketing Inc. asked 1000 Quebecers to rate how well 12 brands had adapted to the needs and expectations of Quebecers,

they found that the top three brands were Tim Hortons, Canadian Tire, and Bureau en Gros/Staples (in that order). Tim Hortons ranked much higher than Starbucks (which ranked last), even though Tim Hortons did very little to adapt its product line to the Quebec market and Starbucks did a lot. However, Tim Hortons got involved with community charities and activities and used Quebec actors in its ad campaigns. This apparently made the Tim Hortons brand "resonate" better with Quebecers.[20]

The experience of Tim Hortons is not unusual. Consider the "brand wars" between Coke and Pepsi in Quebec. Coke sells better than Pepsi in most places in the world, but not in Quebec. Why is that? Perhaps it's because Pepsi customizes its advertisements to meet distinct Québécois tastes. One now-famous ad shows what happens when a European tourist orders a Coke in Quebec: a hush comes over the restaurant, wildlife stops in the forest, and traffic comes to a halt. The waiter finally opens a Pepsi for the tourist, who then says, "Ah! Ici, c'est Pepsi."[21]

Trademarks, Patents, and Copyrights

Because brand development is very expensive, a company does not want another company using its name and confusing consumers into buying a substitute product.

Many companies apply to the Canadian government and receive a **trademark**, the exclusive legal right to use a brand name. Trademarks are granted for 15 years and may be renewed for further periods of 15 years, but only if the company continues to protect its brand name. In 2008, a European court ruled that the construction toys made by LEGO can no longer be protected by trademark law. Montreal-based Mega Brands Inc., which makes a competitive product called Mega-Bloks, had challenged LEGO's trademark.[22]

Just what can be trademarked is not always clear. If the company allows the name to lapse into common usage, the courts may take away protection. Common usage occurs when the company fails to use the ® (registered) symbol for its brand. It also occurs if the company fails to correct those who do not acknowledge the brand as a trademark. Windsurfer, a popular brand of sailboards, lost its trademark, and the name can now be used by any sailboard company. The same thing has happened to other names that were formerly brand names—trampoline, yo-yo, thermos, snowmobile, kleenex, and aspirin. But companies like Xerox, Coca-Cola, Jell-O, and Scotch tape have successfully defended their brand names.

BRAND LOYALTY Customers' recognition of, preference for, and insistence on buying a product with a certain brand name.

TRADEMARK The exclusive legal right to use a brand name.

PATENT Protects an invention or idea for a period of 20 years.

COPYRIGHT Exclusive ownership rights granted to creators for the tangible expression of an idea.

PACKAGING The physical container in which a product is sold, including the label.

LABELS That part of a product's packaging that identifies the product's name and contents and sometimes its benefits.

CONSUMER PACKAGING AND LABELLING ACT A federal law that provides comprehensive rules for packaging and labelling of consumer products.

A **patent** protects an invention or idea for a period of 20 years. The cost is $1600 to $2500 and it takes 18 months to three years to secure a patent from the Canadian Intellectual Property Office.[23] Patents can be very valuable. In 2006, Research In Motion agreed to pay $612.5 million to NTP Inc., a U.S. firm that claimed RIM was infringing on some patents that NTP held.[24] In 2010, RIM was found not guilty by a judge in the U.K. for a claim by Motorola.[25] In yet another patent dispute, Pfizer Inc. reached an agreement in 2008 with an Indian generic drug maker that will keep a cheaper version of the cholesterol-lowering drug Lipitor out of the U.S. market until 2011. Sales revenues of Lipitor are about US$13 billion annually, so this is a very important deal for Pfizer.[26]

Copyrights give exclusive ownership rights to the creators of books, articles, designs, illustrations, photos, films, and music. Computer programs and even semiconductor chips are also protected. Copyrights extend to creators for their entire lives and to their estates for 50 years thereafter. Copyrights apply to the tangible expressions of an idea, not to the idea itself. For example, the idea of cloning dinosaurs from fossil DNA cannot be copyrighted, but Michael Crichton, the author of *Jurassic Park*, could copyright his novel because it is the tangible result of the basic idea.

There is much debate about how copyrights apply to material that appears on the internet. In 2005, the U.S.-based Authors Guild and several publishers sued Google, claiming that its book-scanning project was infringing on their copyrights. In 2008, Google agreed to pay US$125 million to settle the lawsuits. Google can now make available millions of books online.[27] The issue of file sharing is making copyright a big issue these days. New laws and new interpretations of old ones will redefine the role of copyright over the next few years.

Packaging Products

With a few exceptions, including fresh fruits and vegetables, structural steel, and some other industrial products, almost all products need some form of **packaging** to be transported to the market. Packaging serves as an in-store advertisement that makes the product attractive, clearly displays the brand, identifies product features and benefits, and reduces the risk of damage, breakage, or spoilage. It is the marketer's last chance to say "buy it" to the consumer. Packaging costs can be as high as 15 percent of the total cost to make a product, and features like resealable tops can add 20 percent to the price. In 2009, Tropicana learned that consumers were fond of the company's classic logo with the orange and straw as the centrepiece. When they tried to replace it with a new design, consumers responded with emails, letters, and complaints. PepsiCo, which owns Tropicana, immediately reversed the decision.[28]

Companies are paying close attention to consumer concerns about packaging. Beyond concerns about product tampering, packaging must be tight enough to withstand shipping, but not so tight that it frustrates consumers when they try to open the package. Nestlé—which spends more than $6 billion annually on packaging—spent nine months coming up with a new easier-opening lid and an easier-to-grip container for its new Country Creamery ice cream.[29]

Labelling Products

Labels *identify*, *promote*, and *describe* the product. The federal government regulates the information on package labels. The **Consumer Packaging and Labelling Act** has two main purposes: (1) to provide a comprehensive set of rules for packaging and labelling of consumer products, and (2) to ensure that the manufacturer provides full and factual information on labels. All pre-packaged products must state in French and English the quantity enclosed in metric units, as well as the name and description of the product.

Sellers are very sensitive about what is on the label of the products they sell. For example, the maple leaf is on all beer that Labatt Brewing Co. Ltd. sells in Canada—except in Quebec. There, the label has a stylized sheaf of wheat instead. Interestingly, the maple leaf is much more prominent on Labatt's beer sold in the United States.[30] Many companies use different labels for their products in Quebec than they do for products sold elsewhere in Canada.

LO-4 Promoting Products and Services

The ultimate objective of promotion is to increase sales. However, marketers also use promotion to increase consumer awareness of their products, to make consumers more knowledgeable about product features, and to persuade consumers to like and actually purchase their products. Today's value-conscious customers gain benefits when the specific elements in the promotional mix are varied so as to communicate value-added benefits in its products. Burger King shifted its promotional mix by cutting back on advertising and using those funds for customer discounts. Receiving the same food at a lower price is "value added" for Burger King's customers. Many companies, like Hallmark Cards, experience seasonal sales patterns. By increasing their promotional activities in slow periods, they can achieve a more stable sales volume throughout the year. As a result, they can keep their production and distribution systems running evenly.

The boxed insert entitled "Promoting a Green Business Image" describes how companies communicate information about their green initiatives to consumers.

Promotional Strategies

Once a firm's promotional objectives are clear, it must develop a promotional strategy to achieve these objectives. Promotional strategies may be of the push or pull variety. A company with a **push strategy** will "push" its product to wholesalers and retailers, who

PUSH STRATEGY A promotional strategy in which a company aggressively pushes its product through wholesalers and retailers, which persuade customers to buy it.

THE GREENING OF BUSINESS

Promoting a Green Business Image

Canadian businesses are increasingly promoting themselves as "green" enterprises. For example, the Fur Council of Canada—which emphasizes its ties with Native Canadians and its made-in-Canada attributes—is promoting itself as a green industry with billboard and print advertisements that stress the sustainability of the fur industry.

Convincing customers that a business is green is becoming increasingly difficult because consumers have become quite cynical, and because watchdog groups carefully scrutinize green claims. The 2010 Canadian Green Gap Index survey found that an overwhelming majority of Canadians either couldn't name a green retailer or didn't think any retailer was deserving of the label. A Gandalf Group survey of 1500 Canadians found that the majority of consumers think that (a) environmental claims by businesses are just a marketing ploy, and (b) labelling regulations are needed so buyers can understand what terms like "eco-friendly" actually mean.

One oil company that has had great difficulties with its green image is BP. Its slogan "Beyond Petroleum" promotes its green image, but BP is involved in extracting oil from the Alberta oil sands, which Greenpeace has called "the greatest climate crime in history." BP was also cited for environmental offences several times during the last decade. All of these problems were evident even before a fire in 2006 at a BP refinery in Texas that killed 15 workers, and the much more highly publicized explosion on its deepwater drilling rig in the Gulf of Mexico in 2010 that killed 11 workers and

created an environmental catastrophe when millions of litres of oil were released into the ocean.

The term *greenwashing* has been coined to describe the practice of exaggerating or making false claims about the environmental impact of a product or service. EnviroMedia publishes a Greenwashing Index that ranks the eco-friendly advertising claims of various companies. In response to concerns about greenwashing, the Canadian Competition Bureau, in cooperation with the Canadian Standards Association, has drafted industry guidelines that will require companies to back up their environmental claims with scientific evidence. The new guidelines will create national definitions for terms like "recyclable" and will also prohibit vague claims about products (for example, "our product is non-toxic").

Critical Thinking Questions

1. What is your reaction to the Fur Council of Canada's green advertising campaign? What would you say to an animal rights activist who is outraged at the claims the Fur Council is making?
2. Consider the following statement: *"The Competition Bureau's plan to create national guidelines to define terms like 'recyclable' is well intentioned, but it will not work in practice because companies will figure out ways to get around the rules and still make unwarranted claims about how green they are."* Do you agree or disagree with the statement? Explain your reasoning.

PULL STRATEGY A promotional strategy in which a company appeals directly to customers, who demand the product from retailers, which demand the product from wholesalers.

PROMOTIONAL MIX That portion of marketing concerned with choosing the best combination of advertising, personal selling, sales promotions, and publicity to sell a product.

ADVERTISING Paid, non-personal communication by which an identified sponsor informs an audience about a product.

ADVERTISING MEDIUM The specific communication device—television, radio, internet, newspapers, direct mail, magazines, billboards—used to carry a firm's advertising message to potential customers.

then persuade customers to buy it. In contrast, a company with a **pull strategy** appeals directly to customers, who demand the product from retailers, who in turn demand the product from wholesalers, who in turn demand the product from the manufacturer. Advertising "pulls" while personal selling "pushes."

Makers of industrial products often use a push strategy, while makers of consumer products often use a pull strategy. Many large firms use a combination of the two strategies. For example, Coca-Cola uses advertising to create consumer demand (pull) for its various beverages—Coke, Fruitopia, Dasani, and PowerAde. It also pushes wholesalers and retailers to stock these products.

The Promotional Mix

As we noted in Chapter 12, there are four basic types of promotional tools: *advertising*, *personal selling*, *sales promotions*, and *publicity and public relations*. The best combination of these tools—the best **promotional mix**—depends on many factors. The company's product, the costs of different tools versus the promotions budget, and characteristics in the target audience all play a role. Figure 13.5 summarizes the

effective promotional tools for each stage of the consumer buying process (discussed in Chapter 12).

LO-5 Advertising Promotions

Advertising is paid, non-personal communication by which an identified sponsor informs an audience about a product. You can probably remember many jingles and slogans from your early childhood. If a friend tells you that he or she has dandruff, you may instinctively tell them to use Head and Shoulders shampoo. Companies have been planting messages in your head for years. Like it or not, we are all a little bit brainwashed. Consumers remember brand names more easily if the company has a catchy advertising slogan. Buckley's Cough Mixture is well known in Canada. You remember the slogan, don't you? "It tastes awful, and it works." Advertising can convince customers to try a company's product or service, but it has limits. It is the customers' experience with the product or service that determines whether they will make repeat purchases. Let's take a look at the different types of advertising media, noting some of the advantages and limitations of each one.

Advertising Media

In developing advertising strategies, marketers must consider what is the best **advertising medium** for their message. IBM, for example, uses television and internet ads to keep its name fresh in consumers' minds. But it also uses newspaper and magazine ads to educate consumers on products' abilities and trade publications to introduce new software. An advertiser selects media with a number of factors in mind. The marketer must first ask:

Figure 13.5
The consumer buying process and the promotional mix.

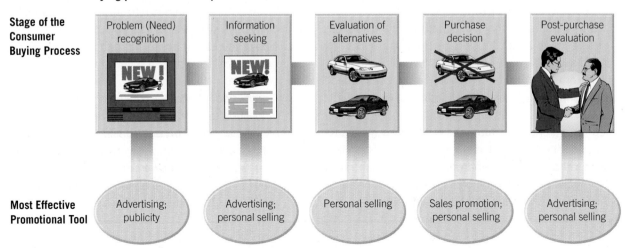

Stage of the Consumer Buying Process	Problem (Need) recognition	Information seeking	Evaluation of alternatives	Purchase decision	Post-purchase evaluation
Most Effective Promotional Tool	Advertising; publicity	Advertising; personal selling	Personal selling	Sales promotion; personal selling	Advertising; personal selling

Which medium will reach the people I want to reach? If a firm is selling hog-breeding equipment, it might choose a business magazine read mostly by hog farmers. If it is selling silverware, it might choose a magazine for brides like *Let's Get Married* (or *Marions-Nous*). If it is selling toothpaste, the choice might be a general audience television program or a general audience magazine such as *Reader's Digest* (or *Sélection du Reader's Digest*). Each advertising medium has its own advantages and disadvantages. In the following paragraphs, we will examine the various media formats. In addition, Table 13.1 provides a summary of their advantages and disadvantages.

Newspapers Newspapers are a widely used advertising medium; in 2008, Canadian advertisers spent $2.5 billion on this medium. Unfortunately this figure was nearly 3 percent lower than in the previous year and continued a downward trend.[31] Newspapers offer excellent coverage, since each local market has at least one daily newspaper, and many people read the paper every day. This medium offers flexible, rapid coverage, since ads can change from day to day. Newspapers also offer believable coverage, since ads are presented next to news. In addition, a larger percentage of individuals with higher education and income level tend to read newspapers on a daily basis. For example, newspapers attract a 47 percent readership from individual households with an income of $75 000 or above, as opposed to only a 5 percent readership of individual households under $20 000.[32] However, newspapers do not generally allow advertisers to target their audience very precisely. In recent years, the volume of classified ads placed in newspapers has declined as

advertisers have shifted their emphasis to the internet. The *Toronto Star* has tried to counter this trend by giving a free internet posting to anyone who buys a classified ad in the newspaper.[33]

Television Television allows advertisers to combine sight, sound, and motion, thus appealing to multiple senses. (Ads can use many techniques to emphasize motion. There was a great Cadillac ad that focused on motion by turning off the sound for seven seconds and capturing viewer attention in a unique manner.) Information on viewer demographics for a particular program allows advertisers to promote to their target audiences. National advertising is done on television because it reaches more people than any other medium. One disadvantage of television is that too many commercials cause viewers to confuse products. In addition, viewers who record programs on DVRs (digital video recorders) often fast-forward through the ads appearing on the TV shows they have recorded. This is a growing concern, since 35 percent of Canadians are expected to have this device by 2012.[34] The brevity of TV ads also makes television a poor medium to educate viewers about complex products.

Spending on television advertising in Canada totalled $3.3 billion in 2008.[35] Television is the most expensive advertising medium. In 2010, a 30-second commercial during the NFL Super Bowl cost about $3 million, up from $1.3 million in 1998. Perhaps it was coincidental, but Pepsi decided to pass on the opportunity after 23 consecutive years of participation.[36] To buy a national 30-second spot in Canada for the Super Bowl costs approximately $110 000; a comparable Grey Cup spot cost about $65 000.[37]

Table 13.1 Media Strengths and Weaknesses

Advertising	Strengths	Weaknesses
Television	Program demographics allow for customized ads Large audience	Most expensive
Magazines	Often reread and shared Variety of ready market segmentation	Require advanced planning Little control over ad placement
Newspapers	Broad coverage Ads can be changed daily	Quickly discarded Broad readership limits ability to target specific audience
Direct mail	Targeted audience Personal messages Predictable results	Easily discarded Environmentally irresponsible
Internet	Targeted audience Measurable success	Nuisance to consumers Easy to ignore
Radio	Inexpensive Large audience Variety of ready market segmentation	Easy to ignore Message quickly disappears
Outdoor	Inexpensive Difficult to ignore Repeat exposure	Presents limited information Little control over audience

A combination of additional unmeasured media—catalogues, sidewalk handouts, skywriting, telephone calls, ads on PDAs, special events, movies, and door-to-door communication—are not included.

In examining the TV medium, we should also consider product placement, which involves using brand-name products as part of the actual storyline of TV shows. This approach has been growing. Shows like *Survivor* and *American Idol* are noticeably full of placements. *American Idol* contestants are interviewed in the Coca-Cola room and the judges drink from prominently placed Coca-Cola glasses. The contestants film a music video featuring a Ford car or truck each week, which is presented as part of the show. Finally, the audience is invited to vote using AT&T. In all, there were over 4100 plugs in one recent season of *American Idol*.[38] In the early days of TV, live commercials featured actors selling the merits of products. Decades later, in an attempt to break through the clutter, it appears as if this old technique has been revived and updated.

Direct Mail **Direct mail** involves flyers or other types of printed advertisements mailed directly to consumers' homes or places of business. Direct mail allows the company to select its audience and personalize its message. The goal is to generate an immediate response and to have the customer contact a firm directly. Although many people discard "junk mail," targeted recipients with stronger-than-average interest are more likely to buy. Although direct mail involves the largest advance costs of any advertising technique, it does appear to have the highest cost-effectiveness. With "fax attacks," advertisers can send their "mail" messages electronically via fax machines and get higher response rates than they would if they used Canada Post. Targeted emails are also serving this purpose. Advertisers spent $1.7 billion on direct mail promotion in 2008.[39]

Radio According to BBM research, radio reaches 81 percent of Canadians on a daily basis; the average Canadian spends 159 minutes listening to the radio during a typical workday.[40] Radio ads are fairly inexpensive, and since most radio is programmed locally, this medium gives advertisers a high degree of customer selectivity. For example, radio stations are already segmented into listening categories such as classic rock, country and western, jazz, talk, news, and religious programming. Radio only permits an audio presentation and ads are over quickly. As well, people tend to use the radio as "background" while they are doing other things, so they may pay little attention to advertisements. Spending on radio advertisements totalled $1.5 billion in Canada in 2008.[41]

Subscriber-based satellite radio poses a significant long-term threat to the traditional radio model.

Magazines The many different magazines on the market provide a high level of consumer selectivity. The person who reads *Popular Photography* is more likely to be interested in the latest specialized lenses from Canon than is a *Gourmet* magazine subscriber. Magazine advertising allows for excellent reproduction of photographs and artwork that not only grab buyers' attention but may also convince them of the product's value. Magazines also provide advertisers space for detailed product information. Magazines have a long life and tend to be passed from person to person, thus doubling and tripling the number of exposures. *Reader's Digest* has the largest readership in Canada, followed by *Canadian Living* (*Chatelaine* and *Canadian Geographic* are tied for third).[42] Spending on magazine advertisements totalled $692 million in Canada in 2008. This figure represents a 4 percent decline from the previous year; it was the sharpest decline of any medium in that timeframe.[43]

Outdoor Advertising Outdoor advertising—billboards; signs; and advertisements on buses, taxis, and subways—is relatively inexpensive, faces little competition for customers' attention, and is subject to high repeat exposure. Outdoor advertising has also gone high-tech. Winnipeg-based Sidetrack Technologies Inc. has developed a system of 360 digital strips that are placed at intervals along subway walls. When a train passes by, the strips blend together, creating the impression of watching a video. The strips can be changed remotely, thus allowing a company like McDonald's to advertise Egg McMuffins in the morning and Big Macs during the afternoon commute.[44]

Titan Worldwide has developed an LED display that shows commercials on New York City buses. The display contains GPS technology, so it can target audiences based on the time of day and postal code where the bus is located. The technology will also be introduced to Canada and Ireland.[45] Many billboards now feature animation and changing images, and today's billboard messages are cheaper because they can be digitally printed in colour in large quantities. On the downside, outdoor ads can present only limited information, and sellers have little control over who sees their advertisements. Outdoor advertising in Canada totalled $463 million in 2008.[46]

Word of Mouth **Word-of-mouth (WOM) advertising** occurs when consumers talk to each other about products they are using. According to the Word of Mouth Marketing Association, there are several varieties of WOM advertising, including buzz marketing (using high-profile news to get consumers talking about a product), viral marketing

Speed and creativity have given billboards like these a new prominence in the world of advertising media. Instead of relying on highly skilled human artists, outdoor ad sellers can now commission digital creations that not only turn heads but cost less than most other media. Whereas it used to take a month to launch a billboard-based campaign, it now takes just days.

(consumers passing product information around on the internet), product seeding (providing free product samples to influential consumers), and cause marketing (involving consumers who feel strongly about a cause such as reducing poverty).[47]

Consumers form very strong opinions about products as a result of conversations with friends and acquaintances, so when consumers start talking about a new product or idea, the information can build momentum and spread like wildfire. This "spreading the word" can happen without any expenditure of money by the company selling the product in question. However, companies spend money developing formal word-of-mouth advertising campaigns because they recognize how powerful they are. The now-famous Evolution ad for Dove soap (which showed an "ordinary" girl being transformed into a goddess) was posted on YouTube instead of traditional media. It was eventually viewed by 300 million people and generated huge publicity for the brand. The only cost to the company was that incurred in making the video.[48] Toronto-based Hook Communications launched its Voice over Internet Protocol (VOIP) service in 2010 with an incentive to spread the word. Customers are being asked to provide the emails of friends and then Hook sends friendly messages on their behalf. If two people join the service, the referrer receives a year of free service and $100 in loyalty rewards.[49]

The Internet Online ad sales were valued at $1.6 billion in Canada in 2008.[50] The growth in this area has been substantial and the power of this approach is unquestionable. To understand the transformational power of this medium, consider the strategic fortress of TV advertising: the Super

Bowl. By 2010, even this sacred advertising event had changed. Instead of tightly guarding their secret campaigns for the big day, many companies are now creating teaser campaigns on YouTube and Facebook, to build interest, weeks before the event. In addition, the immense audience is being directed from TV to the internet during the game. For example, Budweiser Canada used the Super Bowl to drive people to its Facebook page in order to enter a live contest that concluded at the end of the game.[51] The long-promised power of the online ad world is not a myth. (Yes, Virginia, there is an Internet Clause). For a detailed example, take a look at the E-Business and Social Media Solutions Box entitled "Batman Embraces the Internet Age."

MySpace is using "hypertargeting" to categorize users into different categories like "rodeo watcher" or "scrapbook enthusiast." Live Nation, a concert promoter, saw increased traffic on its Coldplay page after it placed ads on MySpace that were directed at fans of Coldplay and similar bands. This sounds very positive for marketers, but privacy concerns have arisen about technologies that track consumers as they surf the web. For example, a company called NebuAd has developed ad-tracking software that has gotten the attention of critics who claim that it violates wiretap laws.[52]

Internet advertising offers advantages for both buyers and sellers. For buyers, advantages include *convenience*, *privacy*, *selection*, *easily accessible information*, and *control*. For sellers, advantages include *reach*, *direct distribution*, *reduced expenses*, *relationship building* (with customers on interactive websites), *flexibility*, and *feedback* (sellers can measure the success of messages by counting how many people see each ad and track the number of click-throughs to their own websites).[53]

Online marketing can be profitable for companies, but what happens when consumers turn against them? With so many individuals participating in social networking sites like Facebook and MySpace and keeping personal blogs, it's increasingly common for a single unhappy customer to wage war against a company for selling faulty products or providing poor service. Individuals may post negative reviews of products on blogs, upload angry videos outlining complaints on YouTube, or join public discussion forums where they can voice their opinion. While companies benefit from the viral spread of good news, they must also be on guard against an online backlash that can damage their reputation.[54]

Virtual Advertising Another method of advertising, called *virtual advertising*, uses digital implants of brands or products onto live or taped programming, giving the illusion that the product is part of the show. With this technique, an advertiser's product can appear as part of the

MEDIA MIX The combination of media through which a company chooses to advertise its products.

television show—when viewers are paying more attention—instead of during commercial breaks. In a televised basketball game, the digital image of a brand—for example, the round face of a Rolex watch or an Acura hubcap—can be electronically enlarged and superimposed on centre court without physically changing the playing floor. For recorded movies, digital images can be inserted easily. A Reitmans shopping bag can be digitally added to the table in a kitchen scene, or a Sony HDTV can be superimposed on the wall for display during a dramatic scene in the den.[55]

Other Advertising Media and Approaches Mobile phone ads are growing in importance for obvious reasons.

There are 21.5 million Canadian wireless phone subscribers, which translates into a 67.5 percent penetration rate. In addition, with more of these users moving to smart phones, the range of ad possibilities are improving.[56]

A combination of many additional media—including catalogues, sidewalk handouts, Yellow Pages, skywriting, special events, and door-to-door communications—make up the remaining advertisements to which Canadians are exposed. The combination of media that a company chooses for advertising is called its **media mix**. Although different industries use different mixes, most depend on multiple media to advertise their products and services. As you can read in the Entrepreneurship and New Ventures boxed insert, advergaming is also a major venue for advertising. There were approximately 130 million console and computer gamers in North America in 2010, with a projected 170 million expected by 2013.[57]

E-BUSINESS AND SOCIAL MEDIA SOLUTIONS

Batman Embraces the Internet Age

The five Batman movies released between 1989 and 2008 grossed more than $1.6 billion worldwide. It would be understandable, then, if the producers decided to reduce the marketing budget for film number six. If ever a movie could be expected to market itself, it would be *The Dark Knight*. Instead, the producers teamed with 42 Entertainment, a California-based creator of alternate reality games, to immerse fans in one of the most elaborate viral marketing campaigns ever conceived. The fun began over a year before the movie opened, with the appearance of posters and a website "supporting" one of the film's characters, Harvey Dent, in his campaign for district attorney of Gotham City. Visitors to the website quickly discovered a link to a similar site—www.whysoserious.com—that appeared to have been vandalized by the movie's main villain, the Joker.

The emergence of the Joker set in motion a series of games in which fans vied with one another to solve puzzles. The fastest fans received cellphones that let them access information that led them deeper into the puzzle. Meanwhile, the websites multiplied: fake newspapers with articles like "Batman Stops Mob Melee," safety tips from the Gotham Police Department, even a link to Betty's House of Pies—a restaurant that plays a small but crucial role in the movie's plot.

The appeal of viral marketing, according to Jonathan Waite, owner of the Alternate Reality Gaming Network, is that "you're not a passive onlooker; you're taking an active role. And any time you take an active role, you're emotionally connecting." Or, as one blogger put it, "I've never been a fan of the Batman series, but this sort of thing makes me want to go see it."

The Dark Knight's innovative marketing campaign helped catapult the movie to a record-breaking box office debut, earning over $158 million in its opening weekend. Domestically and internationally, the film was a great success, earning more than $873 million worldwide. That was more than half the money earned by the previous five Batman movies combined.

This is not an isolated case; companies are clearly paying attention to the enhanced power of an old tool. Word of mouth in the e-business social media age is just beginning to gain strength and explore possibilities.

Critical Thinking Question

1. Have you participated in the spread of a viral campaign recently? Describe the ad and the reasons why you sent the content to a friend.

Personal Selling Promotions

Virtually everyone has done some selling. Perhaps you had a lemonade stand or sold candy for the drama club. Or you may have gone on a job interview, selling your abilities and services as an employee to the interviewer's company. In personal selling, a salesperson communicates one to one with a potential customer to identify the customer's need and match that need with the seller's product.

Personal selling—the oldest form of selling—provides the personal link between seller and buyer. It adds to a firm's credibility because it gives buyers a contact person who will answer their questions. Because it involves personal interaction, personal selling

PERSONAL SELLING
Promotional tool in which a salesperson communicates one to one with potential customers.

ENTREPRENEURSHIP AND NEW VENTURES

Fuelling the World of Branded Entertainment

The casual gaming industry develops non-violent, easy-to-play video games that appeal to a wide variety of users. Industry sales are $2.3 billion, expected annual growth is 20 percent, and the worldwide market is about 200 million people. Fuel Industries of Ottawa, Ontario, founded in 1999, has positioned itself as an up-and-comer in this industry by winning contracts that typically would be awarded to big-name companies like DreamWorks Animation and Pixar Animation Studios. The company's success has not gone unnoticed. In 2008, *Canadian Business* magazine recognized Fuel as one of the country's fastest growing businesses.

Fuel doesn't just develop online video games. Rather, it is pioneering a model of branded online entertainment (referred to as "advergames"). Essentially, an advergame is an online video game and advertising rolled into one. The theory behind the concept is simple: if consumers are having fun while interacting with the entertainment, they are more likely to remember and feel positive toward the brand. Instead of trying to make an impression during a traditional 60-second commercial, advergames keep consumers engaged for up to 600 seconds! Many companies are beginning to see the benefits of this marketing strategy.

Fuel was launched into the branded digital promotion business when it created an advergame called Fairies and Dragons that helped McDonald's promote its Happy Meal in 40 European countries. With every Happy Meal, kids received a fairy or dragon toy along with a CD-ROM that contained three games and 10 hours of game play. That approach differed noticeably from the usual tactic of licensing characters from established entertainment companies like Disney. Plans are underway to launch the same concept for McDonald's in other regions, including Australia, Japan, and North America.

Since their success with McDonald's, Fuel has done similar work for U.S. toy company Jakks Pacific's branded game Girl Gourmet Cupcake Maker. The company is also behind the development of Spark City, an online game targeted to tween girl gamers. This virtual world is part of the All Girl Arcade website. The branded element appears through the integration with television and retail. As an example, Fuel is adding a movie theatre to Spark City and the agency is in talks with broadcasters and film companies looking to run trailers in the theatre.

So, what's the cost to get your brand into Spark City? It could be anywhere between $25 000 and $200 000. But is there a risk of virtual world burnout among customers as branded sites flourish? According to Virtual Worlds Management, a Texas-based company, the future looks good, but "the cream will definitely rise to the top." Therefore, if a company chooses this strategy, as with any product, branded sites need to be developed to address the needs and wants of the selected target market.

Critical Thinking Questions

1. How can marketers build relationships with customers through newer methods of virtual advertising like advergames?
2. What are the advantages and disadvantages of internet advertising?

SALES PROMO-TIONS Short-term promotional activities designed to stimulate consumer buying or cooperation from distributors and other members of the trade.

requires a level of trust between the buyer and the seller. When a buyer feels cheated by the seller, that trust has been broken and a negative attitude toward salespeople in general can develop.

Personal selling is the most expensive form of promotion per contact because presentations are generally made to one or two individuals at a time. Personal selling expenses include salespeople's compensation and their overhead (travel, food, and lodging). The average cost of an industrial sales call has been estimated at nearly $300.[58] The Exercising Your Ethics exercise at the end of the chapter describes an interesting personal selling dilemma.

Costs have prompted many companies to turn to *telemarketing*: using telephone solicitations to conduct the personal selling process. Telemarketing is useful in handling any stage of this process and in arranging appointments for salespeople. It cuts the cost of personal sales visits to industrial customers, who require about four visits to complete a sale. Such savings are stimulating the growth of telemarketing, which provides 150 000 jobs in Canada and generates $25 billion in annual sales. Telemarketing returns $6.25 for every dollar spent.[59]

Because many consumers are annoyed by telemarketing pitches, a do-not-call registry was set up in Canada in 2008, and six million people quickly registered. Heavy fines can be levied on companies that ignore the new rules. A survey by VoxPop showed that 80 percent of Canadians who registered now receive fewer telemarketing calls than they used to.[60] However, in 2009, it was discovered that some unscrupulous marketers were actually using the registry to call people. Michael Geist, a Canada research chair in internet and e-commerce law at the University of Ottawa, says the government's registry is flawed.[61]

LO-7 Sales Promotions

Sales promotions are short-term promotional activities designed to stimulate consumer buying or cooperation from distributors, sales agents, or other members of the trade. They are important because they increase the likelihood that buyers will try products. They also enhance product recognition and can increase purchase size and amount. For example, soap is often bound into packages of four with the promotion, "Buy three and get one free."

To be successful, sales promotions must be convenient and accessible when the decision to purchase occurs. If Harley-Davidson has a one-week motorcycle promotion and you have no local dealer, the promotion is neither convenient nor accessible to you, and you will not buy. But if Herbal Essences offers a 20 percent–off coupon that you can save for use later, the promotion is convenient and accessible. Like anything else, too much of a good thing can be destructive. The Bay has been criticized for holding too many scratch-and-save "Bay Days." The goal of such programs is to generate immediate sales, as people are given an incentive to buy now or buy before the end of the weekend. But in the case of the Bay, many customers have been conditioned to expect these sales. The end result is that

Once the master of mass-marketing (especially the 30-second TV spot), Coca-Cola has bowed to audience fragmentation and the invention of DVR's, which allow people to skip TV ads altogether. Coke has begun experimenting with alternative approaches to promotion, focusing on events and activities that can be integrated into the daily routines of targeted consumers. In Europe, the company posts interactive websites built around music, and in the United States it has installed Coke Red Lounges in a few select malls, offering teenagers exclusive piped-in music, movies, and videos.

some customers delay purchase, waiting for the next sale. This is clearly not the goal of a sales promotion program.

Types of Sales Promotions The best-known sales promotions are *coupons*, *point-of-purchase displays*, *purchasing incentives* (such as free samples, trading stamps, and premiums), *trade shows*, and *contests and sweepstakes*.

- **Coupons** are certificates entitling the bearer to stated savings off a product's regular price. Coupons may be used to encourage customers to try new products, to attract customers away from competitors, or to induce current customers to buy more of a product. They appear in newspapers and magazines and are often sent through direct mail.

- To grab customers' attention as they walk through a store, some companies use **point-of-purchase (POP) displays.** Displays located at the end of the aisles or near the checkout in supermarkets are POP displays. POP displays often coincide with a sale on the item(s) being displayed. They make it easier for customers to find a product and easier for manufacturers to eliminate competitors from consideration. The cost of shelf and display space, however, is becoming more and more expensive.

- Free samples and premiums are *purchasing incentives*. Free samples allow customers to try a product without any risk. They may be given out at local retail outlets or sent by manufacturers to consumers via direct mail. **Premiums** are free or reduced-price items, such as pens, pencils, calendars, and coffee mugs, given to consumers in return for buying a specified product. For example, during one promotion, Molson Canadian included a free T-shirt with certain packages of its beer.[62] Premiums may not work as well as originally hoped, since customers may only temporarily switch to a brand simply to get the premiums that company is offering.

- Industries sponsor **trade shows** for their members and customers. Trade shows allow companies to rent booths to display and demonstrate their products to customers who have a special interest in the products or who are ready to buy. Trade shows are relatively inexpensive and are very effective, since the buyer comes to the seller already interested in a given type of product. International trade shows are becoming more important.

- Customers, distributors, and sales representatives may all be persuaded to increase sales of a product through the use of *contests*. For example, distributors and sales agents may win a trip to Hawaii for selling the most pillows in a month.

Publicity and Public Relations

Much to the delight of marketing managers with tight budgets, **publicity** is free. Moreover, because it is presented in a news format, consumers see publicity as objective and believable. However, marketers may have little control over bad publicity, and that can have a very negative impact. For example, a YouTube video showing what appeared to be a Guinness beer commercial portrayed several people in a suggestive sexual arrangement with the title "Share One with a Friend." Guinness was quick to distance itself from the fake advertisement, saying that was not how it wanted its product portrayed. In another case, the restaurant chain Olive Garden was placed in a difficult position when it received favourable publicity from Playboy Playmate Kendra Wilkinson, who at that time was one of Hugh Hefner's three live-in girlfriends and who was featured in the E! series *The Girls Next Door*. She gave several on-air plugs, but the restaurant was concerned because Wilkinson's reputation at the time was not consistent with the company's wholesome, family-friendly image.[63]

In contrast to publicity, **public relations** is company-influenced publicity. It attempts to create goodwill between the company and its customers through public-service announcements that enhance the company's image. For example, a bank may announce that senior citizens' groups can have free use of a meeting room for their social activities. As well, company executives may make appearances as guest speakers representing their companies at professional meetings and civic events. They also may serve as leaders in civic activities like the United Way campaign and university fundraising.

Corporate sponsorships of athletic events also help promote a company's image. Roots has been successful

COUPON A method of sales promotion featuring a certificate that entitles the bearer to stated savings off a product's regular price.

POINT-OF-PURCHASE (POP) DISPLAY A method of sales promotion in which a product display is located in a retail store in order to encourage consumers to buy the product.

PREMIUM A method of sales promotion in which some item is offered free or at a bargain price to customers in return for buying a specified product.

TRADE SHOW A method of sales promotion in which members of a particular industry gather for displays and product demonstrations designed to sell products to customers.

PUBLICITY Information about a company, a product, or an event transmitted by the general mass media (with no direct cost to the company).

PUBLIC RELATIONS Company-influenced information directed at building goodwill with the public or dealing with unfavourable events.

AMBUSH MARKETING Occurs when a company launches an advertising campaign to coincide with a major event, like the Olympics; it capitalizes on viewer interest without paying an official sponsorship fee.

GLOBAL PERSPECTIVE Company's approach to directing its marketing toward worldwide rather than local or regional markets.

in getting high-profile individuals to wear its products. These sponsorships rely on a positive brand association to the event; however, sometimes sponsors can be frustrated by a competitor that benefits from the same exposure without paying official sponsor fees, a practice known as **ambush marketing**. The Royal Bank was an official sponsor of the 2010 Winter Olympic Games, so when Scotiabank launched a national photo contest to display Canadian pride, cleverly timed to benefit from the exposure of the games, the Olympic organizing committee took notice.[64] Most large firms have a department to manage their relations with the public and to present a desired company image.

International Promotional Strategies

As we saw in Chapter 5, in recent decades we have witnessed a profound shift from "home-country" marketing to "multi-country" and now to "global" marketing. Nowhere is this rapidly growing global orientation more evident than in marketing promotions, especially advertising.

Emergence of the Global Perspective

Every company that markets products in several countries faces a basic choice: use a *decentralized approach*, maintaining separate marketing management for each country or region, or adopt a *global perspective*, directing a coordinated marketing program at one worldwide audience. Thus, the **global perspective** is a philosophy that directs marketing toward worldwide rather than local or regional markets.

The Movement toward Global Advertising A truly global perspective means designing products for multinational appeal—that is, genuinely global products.[65] A few brands, such as Coca-Cola, McDonald's, Mercedes-Benz, and Rolex, enjoy recognition as truly global brands. One universal advertising program is more efficient and cost-effective than developing different programs for many countries, but global advertising is not feasible for many companies. Four factors make global advertising a challenging proposition:

- *Product variations.* Even if a product has universal appeal, some variations, or slightly different products, are usually preferred in different cultures. *Cosmopolitan* magazine has 58 editions, in 34 languages, and is distributed to 100 countries.[66] Many companies have found that without a local or national identity, universal ads don't cause consumers to buy. Coca-Cola's "think global, act local" strategy and Nestlé's approach to small-scale local advertising call for ads tailored to different areas. Such ads are designed to produce variations on a universal theme while appealing to local emotions, ideas, and values. Advertising agencies have set up worldwide agency networks that can coordinate a campaign's central theme while allowing regional variations.

- *Language differences.* Compared with those in other languages, ads in English require less print space and airtime because English is an efficient and precise language. Also, translations are often inexact or confusing. When Coke first went to China, the direct translation of *Coca-Cola* came out "bite the wax tadpole."

Before creating an international advertisement like this Chinese ad for Coca-Cola, it is crucial to research what differences—such as meaning of words, traditions, and taboos—exist between different societies. For example, German manufacturers of backpacks label them as "body bags," which is not terribly enticing to the Canadian consumer. Gerber baby food is not sold in France because the French translation of gerber is "to vomit."

- *Cultural receptiveness.* There are differences across nations regarding the mass advertising of sensitive products (birth control or personal hygiene products), not to mention those for which advertising may be legally restricted (alcohol, cigarettes). A Canadian in Paris may be surprised to see nudity in billboard ads and even more surprised to find that France is the only country in the European Union that bans advertising and selling wine on the internet. In the EU and through much of Asia, comparative advertising is considered distasteful or even illegal.

- *Image differences.* Any company's image can vary from nation to nation, regardless of any advertising appeals for universal recognition. American Express, IBM, and Nestlé have better images in the United States than in the United Kingdom, where Heinz, Coca-Cola, and Ford have better images.

PEARSON mybusinesslab

To improve your grade, visit the MyBusinessLab website at www.pearsoned.ca/mybusinesslab. This online homework and tutorial system allows you to test your understanding and generates a personalized study plan just for you. It provides you with study and practice tools directly related to this chapter's content. MyBusinessLab puts you in control of your own learning! Test yourself on the material for this chapter at www.pearsoned.ca/mybusinesslab.

Summary of Learning Objectives

1. **Identify a *product*, distinguish between *consumer* and *industrial products*, and explain the *product mix.*** A *product* is a good, service, or idea that is marketed to fill consumer needs and wants. Customers buy products because of the *value* that they offer. *Consumer products* are divided into three categories that reflect buyer behaviour: *convenience goods*, *shopping goods,* and *specialty goods*. Industrial products include *expense items* and *capital items*. The group of products that a company makes available for sale is its *product mix*.

2. **Describe the *new product development process* and trace the stages of the *product life cycle.*** Many firms adopt some version of a basic seven-step process: (1) *product ideas*, (2) *screening*, (3) *concept testing*, (4) *business analysis*, (5) *prototype development*, (6) *product testing and test marketing*, and (7) *commercialization*.

   The *product life cycle (PLC)* is a series of four stages characterizing a product's profit-producing life: (1) *introduction*, (2) *growth*, (3) *maturity*, and (4) *decline*.

3. **Explain the importance of *branding, packaging*, and *labelling.*** *Branding* is a process of using symbols to communicate the qualities of a particular product. With a few exceptions, a product needs some form of *packaging*, a physical container in which it is sold, advertised, or protected. Every product has a *label* on its package that identifies its name, manufacturer, and contents; like packaging, labelling can help market a product.

4. **Identify the important objectives of *promotion* and discuss the considerations in selecting a *promotional mix.*** Besides the ultimate objective of increasing sales, marketers may use promotion to accomplish any of the following four goals: (1) *communicating information*, (2) *positioning products*, (3) *adding value*, and (4) controlling sales volume.

5. **Describe the key *advertising media.*** The most common media—television, newspapers, direct mail, radio, magazines, outdoor advertising, internet, mobile—differ in their cost and their ability to segment target markets. The combination of media through which a company advertises is its *media mix*.

6. **Outline the tasks involved in *personal selling.*** In *personal selling*, a salesperson communicates one to one with potential customers to identify their needs and align them with a seller's products. It adds to a firm's credibility because it allows buyers to interact and ask questions. Unfortunately, expenses are high so many companies have turned to *telemarketing*.

7. **Describe the various types of *sales promotions* and distinguish between *publicity* and *public relations.*** *Sales promotions* are short-term promotional activities designed to stimulate consumer buying or

cooperation from members of the trade. They increase the likelihood that buyers will try pro-ducts; they also enhance product recognition and can increase purchase size and amount. The following are the best-known forms of promotions: (1) *coupons*, (2) *point-of-purchase (POP) displays*, (3) *free samples*, (4) *premiums*, (5) *trade shows*, and (6) *contests*.

Publicity is a promotional tool in which information about a company or product is created and transmitted by general mass media. It is free, and because it is presented in a news format, consumers often see it as objective and credible. However, marketers often have little control over it, and it can be as easily detrimental as beneficial. *Public relations* is company-influenced publicity that seeks to build good relations with the public and deal with unfavourable events.

Questions and Exercises

Questions for Analysis

1. What impact do the different levels of brand loyalty (recognition, preference, insistence) have on the consumer buying process described in Chapter 12?

2. Why would a business use a "push" strategy rather than a "pull" strategy?

3. Is publicity more or less available to small firms than to larger firms? Why?

4. How would you expect the branding, packaging, and labelling of convenience, shopping, and specialty goods to differ? Why? Give examples to illustrate your answers.

5. Select a good or service that you have purchased recently. Try to retrace the relevant steps in the buyer decision process as you experienced it. Which steps were most important to you? Which steps were least important?

6. Sales promotions and advertising are both part of the promotional mix. How do the short-term objectives of sales promotions differ from advertising efforts?

Application Exercises

7. Interview the manager of a manufacturing firm that produces at least three or four different products. Identify each of the company's products in terms of their stage in the product life cycle. Are all the products in the same stage, or does the company have products in each stage?

8. Select a product that is sold nationally. Identify as many media sources used in its promotion as you can. Which medium is used most often? On the whole, do you think the campaign is effective? What criteria did you use to make your judgment about effectiveness?

9. Interview the owner of a local small business. Identify the company's promotional objectives and strategies, and the elements in its promotional mix. What changes, if any, would you suggest? Why?

10. Identify two advertising campaigns that have recently been conducted by similar businesses in your area. Go online to gather more information and watch ads on YouTube, and/or clip ads in newspapers and magazines. Survey students as to which company had a more effective ad campaign. Summarize the findings and explain why you think one was better than the other.

TEAM EXERCISES

Building Your Business Skills

Greeting Start-Up Decisions

Goal

To encourage students to analyze the potential usefulness of two promotional methods—personal selling and direct mail—for a start-up greeting card company.

Situation

You are the marketing adviser for a local start-up company that makes and sells specialty greeting cards in a city of 400 000. Last year's sales totalled 14 000 cards, including personalized holiday cards, birthday cards, and special-events cards for individuals. Although revenues increased last year, you see a way of further boosting sales by expanding into card shops, grocery stores, and gift shops. You see two alternatives for entering these outlets:

1. Use direct mail to reach more individual customers for specialty cards.

2. Use personal selling to gain display space in retail stores.

Your challenge is to persuade the owner of the start-up company to use the alternative you believe is the more financially sound decision.

Method

Step 1 Get together with four or five classmates to research the two kinds of product segments: *personalized cards* and *retail store cards*. Find out which of the two kinds of marketing promotions will be more effective for each segment. What will be the reaction to each method by customers, retailers, and card company owners?

Step 2 Draft a proposal to the company owner. Leaving budget and production details to other staffers, list as many reasons as possible for adopting a direct mail strategy. Then list as many reasons as possible for adopting a personal selling strategy. Defend each reason. Consider the following reasons in your argument:

■ *Competitive environment:* Analyze the impact of other card suppliers that offer personalized cards and cards for sale in retail stores.

■ *Expectations of target markets:* Who buys personalized cards, and who buys ready-made cards from retail stores?

■ *Overall cost of the promotional effort:* Which method—direct mail or personal selling—will be more costly?

■ *Marketing effectiveness:* Which promotional method will result in greater consumer response?

Follow-Up Questions

1. Why do you think some buyers want personalized cards? Why do some consumers want ready-made cards from retail stores?

2. Today's computer operating systems provide easy access to software for designing and making cards on home computers. How does the availability of this product affect your recommendation?

3. What was your most convincing argument for using direct mail? For using personal selling?

4. Can a start-up company compete in retail stores against industry giants such as Hallmark?

Exercising Your Ethics

Cleaning Up in Sales

The Situation

Selling a product—whether a good or a service—requires the salesperson to believe in it, to be confident of his or her sales skills, and to keep commitments made to clients. Because so many people and resources are involved in delivering a product, numerous uncertainties and problems can give rise to ethical issues. This exercise encourages you to examine some of the ethical issues that can surface in the selling process for industrial products.

The Dilemma

Cleaning Technologies Corporation (CTC) is a U.S.-based company that manufactures equipment for industrial cleaners. The Canadian division of CTC has hired Denise Skilsel and six other recent graduates that have just completed the sales training program for a new line of high-tech machinery that CTC has developed. As a new salesperson, Skilsel is eager to meet potential clients, all of whom are professional buyers for companies—such as

laundries and dry cleaners, carpet cleaners, and military cleaners—that use CTC products or those of competitors. Skilsel is especially enthusiastic about several facts that she learned during training: CTC's equipment is the most technically advanced in the industry, carries a 10-year performance guarantee, and is safe—both functionally and environmentally.

The first month was difficult but successful. In visiting seven firms, Skilsel successfully closed three sales, earning large commissions and praise from the sales manager. Moreover, after listening to her presentations, two more potential buyers gave verbal commitments and were about to sign for much bigger orders than any Skilsel had closed to date. As she was catching her flight to close those sales, Skilsel received two calls—one from a client and one from a competitor. The client, just getting started with CTC equipment, was having some trouble: employees stationed nearby were getting sick when the equipment was running. The competitor told Skilsel that the U.S. Environmental Protection Agency (EPA) had received complaints from some of CTC's customers that the new technology was environmentally unsafe because of noxious emissions.

Team Activity

Assemble a group of four students and assign each group member to one of the following roles:

- Denise Skilsel: CTC salesperson (employee)
- CTC sales manager (employer)
- CTC customer
- CTC investor

Action Steps

1. Before discussing the situation with your group, and from the perspective of your assigned role, consider what you would recommend Skilsel say to the two client firms she is scheduled to visit. Write down your recommendation.

2. Gather your group together and reveal each member's recommendation.

3. Appoint someone to record the main points of agreement and disagreement. How do you explain the results? What accounts for any disagreement?

4. Identify any ethical issues involved in group members' recommendations. Which issues, if any, are more critical than others?

5. From an ethical standpoint, what does your group finally recommend Skilsel say to the two client firms she is scheduled to visit? Explain your result.

6. Identify the advantages and drawbacks resulting from your recommendations.

BUSINESS CASE 13

Measuring the Effectiveness of Advertising

Businesses spend a lot of money each year on advertising, so it is not surprising that they want to know what effect it is having. For example, marketers are asking advertising agencies more probing questions about advertising campaigns and media buys: how are the media plans developed, who buys the current media mix, and how have they performed? Faced with growing accountability to perform, ad agencies are imposing more accountability on media outlets. Local and national TV may no longer rely solely on Nielsen ratings as evidence for ad effectiveness; more convincing proof of performance would show how much they contribute to advertiser's sales. Newspapers, magazines, radio, and other media will also be asked for more convincing evidence. New ways to test the effects of media on consumer attention, persuasion and consumer thinking, and responsiveness in buying behaviour are in the development stage. Reliable measurements will allow media planners in advertising agencies to compare bottom-line results from alternative media expenditures—newspapers, internet, radio, magazines, TV—and to pinpoint the best combination of media buys.

In general, advertisers want to know what television programs consumers are watching, or what websites they are visiting. If it can be demonstrated that some TV shows or websites are more popular than others, advertisers will pay more to have their ads appear in those places.

Nielsen Media Research is the most well-known company providing information on television viewing habits. It gets its revenues by selling its viewer data to advertising agencies, television networks, and cable companies. In the past, the system involved having selected viewers write down the channel number they were watching and who was watching TV each quarter-hour of the day. But this system was cumbersome, and consumers often

Measuring audiences has evolved over the years and media competition is complex.

made errors when filling out forms. The system gradually began to break down as technology changed. For example, when remote controls became popular, so did channel surfing, but channel surfing is virtually impossible to reflect in a diary. The introduction of digital video recorders (DVRs) and the delivery of shows via cellphone, computer, and iPad has made Nielsen's old system obsolete.

Nielsen initially responded to criticisms by attaching electronic meters to household TVs. The meter determined what channel was being watched and who was watching, but viewers still had to punch in a pre-assigned number on their remote control whenever they started to watch. These meters likely improved the accuracy of in-home viewing data, but they did not address the growing problem of measuring viewing habits of people who were not at home but who were still watching TV. For example, measuring the viewing habits of students who live away from home at university is not easy. Nielsen also doesn't monitor viewing in offices, bars, hotels, prisons, and many other out-of-home venues.

Cable companies argue that Nielsen's system doesn't accurately capture the large number of people who watch cable TV. Differences can be substantial with different measuring systems. For example, in a side-by-side analysis in New York City, an episode of *The Simpsons* on the Fox network showed a 27 percent decline when the new electronic meters were used, but shows on Comedy Central cable saw gains of 225 percent using the same electronic measurement.

In Montreal and Quebec City, consumers are being paid to carry a pager-sized device that records each advertisement they see or hear and every store or restaurant they go into. BBM Canada is using something called the Personal Portable Meter (PPM) to determine television ratings. These devices listen for cues that broadcasters have embedded in their broadcasts and enable BBM to assess television viewing outside peoples' homes (it has also been introduced for radio listeners). The new system allows advertisers to eventually correlate the advertisements people hear with the products they buy. They can therefore determine how effective their advertisements are.

Nielsen announced that it would introduce new technology that would allow it to capture DVR viewing on a daily basis. It will also begin measuring video-on-demand and testing ways of measuring viewing on the internet and on hand-held devices such as iPods and cellphones. If these new measuring systems show significantly different viewing patterns than historical data, it will result in even more advertising dollars shifting to new media. Nielsen also has invested in a company called NeuroFocus, which is developing a system for scanning the human brain to determine if people are paying attention to (and remembering) ads they see.

But even if these improvements are made, some critics will not be happy. The vice-president at one advertising space–buying company says that the only thing that is important to measure is "live" viewing. The use of DVRs has led to a sharp drop in "live" television viewing, and people who are watching a DVR program may not even be watching the ads. Not surprisingly, TV companies disagree with that assessment. They argue that ad rates should be determined by the total viewership an ad gets.

Two web measurement services—comScore and Nielsen Online—gather data on internet use by getting people to agree to let their online surfing and purchasing patterns be monitored. The behaviour of these individuals is then extrapolated to the larger population. Since this method is similar to the traditional assessment method that Nielsen used to measure television-viewing habits, there are also concerns about its accuracy. To overcome these concerns, Google introduced Google Analytics to more accurately measure internet use. It shows which websites various target audiences visit and helps advertisers figure out the best places to place online ads. Google's system uses data

from web servers and allows for a better understanding of how the internet is used by consumers. Both comScore and Nielsen Online charge advertisers for the data they provide, but Google provides information free of charge. Google also introduced a new system to help advertisers determine how web surfers respond to the ads they see on the various sites they visit. The system works by comparing people who have seen the ads with people who haven't.

No system is perfect, and it is clear that using web servers to gather data has some problems of its own. For example, measurement is based on "cookies" (tracking data), but some users delete cookies and then another cookie is attached when they later revisit a website. This can lead to overstatement of the number of website visits. As well, the system has trouble telling whether a website visit is from an actual consumer or from a technology that visits different websites.

One of the potentially serious problems with gathering data about consumer behaviour is "click fraud." It can occur in several ways, such as when a web developer repeatedly clicks on a website in order to make it seem like there is a great deal of interest in it. Or computers can be programmed to repeatedly click on ads to simulate a real consumer clicking on ads on a web page. When this happens, advertisers get a bigger bill but no extra sales revenue. When click fraud occurs, the money spent on advertising is obviously wasted. Click Forensics Inc., a click fraud reporting service, reports that the click fraud rate is about 16 percent. But Google claims that only 2 out of 10 000 clicks are fraudulent.

Questions for Discussion

1. The viewership data that Nielsen develops is important in determining how much advertisers pay to place their ads on TV. What are the advantages and disadvantages of the system? Are there alternative systems that might work better? Explain.

2. The argument has been made that counting DVR viewing isn't useful because people don't watch program advertisements when using a DVR and because advertisements simply don't have the same urgency as they do when the program actually airs. Do you agree or disagree with this argument? Give reasons. Whatever your position, how do you think uncertainty over issues like this influence the value of the data that are produced? What could be done to improve the data?

3. Suppose that you are buying advertising space on TV. Would you be more likely to accept Nielsen data for, say, sports programs than you would for dramas? Explain. What kind of biases might you have and why?

4. What are the strong and weak points of measuring viewership for internet advertisements?

SCANLIFE

chapter

14

Pricing and Distributing Goods and Services

After reading this chapter, you should be able to:

LO-1 Identify the various *pricing objectives* that govern pricing decisions and describe the price-setting tools used in making these decisions.

LO-2 Discuss *pricing strategies* and *tactics* for existing and new products.

LO-3 Explain the *distribution mix*, the different *channels of distribution*, and the different *distribution strategies* that businesses use.

LO-4 Explain the differences among *wholesalers*, *agents/brokers*, and *retailers*.

LO-5 Identify the different types of *retail stores* and the activities of *e-intermediaries*.

LO-6 Define *physical distribution* and describe the major activities in *warehousing* operations.

LO-7 Compare the five basic forms of *transportation* and explain how distribution can be used as a marketing strategy.

SCANLIFE

Buyers and Sellers Jockey for Position

Retail shoppers want to get the lowest price possible, and retailer sellers want to get the highest price possible to protect their profit margins. As a result, there is always a certain level of tension between sellers of goods and the customers who buy them. During the recession that started in 2008, this tension reached a new level.

Stores continue to trumpet low prices as they always have, but they don't want to attract just the "cherry-picking" customers (those that go from store to store buying only on-sale items). Rather, retailers want customers who buy a variety of products because this allows the retailer to keep profit margins higher. When you go into a Zellers store, for example, you might see boxes of canned Coke near the entrance with a bargain price of three for $9.99. But you'll have to look harder to find the discount price of $58.97 on Sesame Street's Elmo. As you are looking for Elmo, the store hopes you will find some other item that you need that is not on sale.

Walmart tries to cope with cherry-picking consumers by placing products that customers might overlook close to high-demand items (e.g., placing reduced-price slippers next to higher-priced boots). Canadian Tire and Loblaw have also noted the cherry-picking trend. In addition to strategically placing on-sale items, retailers can cope with cherry pickers by limiting quantities (e.g., "one per customer"), advertising higher-margin items, and developing promotional programs that encourage shoppers to buy a broad range of products.

Retailers aren't the only ones struggling with low margins. Manufacturers are also faced with pricing dilemmas. For example, when Unilever Canada Ltd. was faced with big cost increases in the price of soybean oil used in Hellmann's mayonnaise, it debated about whether it should increase the price or simply absorb the cost increase. It finally decided

How Will This Help Me?

By understanding the material presented in this chapter, you will benefit in three ways: (1) as a *consumer*, you will have a better understanding of how a product's development, promotion, and distribution affect its selling price, (2) as an *investor*, you'll be better prepared to evaluate a company's marketing program and its competitive potential before buying the company's stock, and (3) as an *employee and/or manager*, you'll be able to use your knowledge about product pricing and distribution to further your career.

to do neither. Instead, it kept the price the same but decreased the size of the mayonnaise jar from 950 ml to 890 ml and changed the container from glass to plastic (which cut manufacturing costs).

This practice has become very common because marketers believe that people don't notice the change in *quantity* like they do the change in *price*. Other examples of this strategy are as follows:

- Kimberly-Clark Corp. cut the price of its diapers, but cut the quantity in the package even more (this was, in effect, a 5 percent price increase).
- General Motors started charging extra for antilock brakes instead of including them at no charge as it used to (this also constituted a price increase).
- Wrigley reduced the number of pieces in a pack of Juicy Fruit gum from 17 to 15 while keeping the price the same.
- Tropicana reduced the size of its orange juice container from 2.84 litres to 2.63 litres but kept the price the same.
- General Mills introduced smaller boxes for Cheerios and Wheaties, and Kellogg did the same with many of its cereals; both retained their former pricing.

In November 2008, only 2 of the 30 companies that make up the Dow-Jones Industrial Average had higher stock prices than they did in November 2007, before the recession hit. Those two companies—McDonald's and Walmart—are legendary for their low prices, and both of them benefited as consumers "traded down" to cheaper meals and consumer products as a result of the recession. There are many other examples as well. Consider the recent success of so-called dollar stores—retailers that offer ultra-cheap prices on a limited selection of goods. These include stores like The Silver Dollar, Dollarama, and Buck or Two. Sales revenues for this type of retail outlet have doubled in the last five years, and the number of stores has tripled. While dollar stores originally targeted low-income shoppers, they now are appealing to buyers at all income levels, and they are gaining the attention of companies that once ignored them. Procter & Gamble, for example, created a special version of Dawn dish soap that sells for $1, and Kraft Foods sells boxes of macaroni and cheese in dollar stores.

Pricing issues are very significant in the cigarette industry. For many years, the North American cigarette market has been an oligopoly that is dominated by a few very large tobacco companies like Imperial Tobacco, R.J. Reynolds, Philip Morris, Brown & Williamson, and Lorillard Tobacco. The pricing strategy that has historically been used by these companies is to increase prices to maintain (or increase) profits. This strategy worked for decades because customers were very loyal to their favourite brand. But now some new cigarette manufacturing companies have entered the market and are pricing their cigarettes as much as 50 percent lower than the "majors." The majors are likely to have less control over the market than they used to, and they are going to have much more difficulty simply raising prices in the future.

LO-1 Pricing Objectives and Tools

In **pricing**, managers decide what the company will receive in exchange for its products. There are several objectives that might influence a firm's pricing decisions, and several major tools that companies can use to meet whatever pricing objectives are set.

Pricing to Meet Business Objectives

Different companies have different **pricing objectives**. Two of the most common objectives are *profit-maximizing* pricing and *market share pricing*. Pricing decisions may also be influenced by the need to survive in the marketplace, by social and ethical concerns, and even by corporate image.

Profit-Maximizing Objectives Pricing to maximize profits is tricky. If prices are set too low, the company will sell all of its output, but it may miss the opportunity to make additional profit on each unit. If prices are set too high, the company will make a large profit on each item but it may not sell all its output. To avoid these problems, companies try to set prices to sell the number of units that will generate the highest possible total profits, given prevailing market conditions. For example, Coca-Cola tested a vending machine that automatically raised the price of a Coke as the temperature climbed. It also tried setting prices at different vending machines at different levels, depending on how many customers used the machine.[1] The Ottawa Senators increased prices 20 percent for games against the Toronto Maple Leafs and the Detroit Red Wings.[2]

In the United Kingdom, one auto insurer has introduced a system where car insurance premiums vary depending on how much, where, and when a person drives. For example, a 40-year-old driver who is driving on a divided highway at 2 p.m. might pay only one pence per mile to drive, but a teenager driving at 1 a.m. would pay dramatically more (about one *pound* per mile).[3] In Canada, Skymeter Corp. is developing a technology that tracks how far a car travels and where it parks. A GPS unit on the car's dashboard makes the measurements. The system does away with the need for highway toll booths and parking attendants.[4]

In calculating profits, managers weigh receipts against costs for materials and labour used to create the product. But they also consider the capital resources (plant and equipment) that the company must tie up to generate that level of profit. The costs of marketing (such as maintaining a large sales staff) can also be substantial. Concern over the efficient use of these resources has led many firms to set prices so as to achieve a targeted level of return on sales or capital investment.[5]

Market-Share Objectives Some companies initially set low prices for new products. They are willing to accept minimal profits—even losses—to get buyers to try their products. These companies are using price to establish **market share**—a company's percentage of the total market sales for a specific product. Even with established products, market share objectives may outweigh profits in setting price. For a product like Philadelphia cream cheese, dominating a market means that consumers are more likely to buy it because they are familiar with a well-known, highly visible brand name.

Retailers like Walmart are also concerned about market share. In 2010, Walmart cut prices in order to attract customers who were shopping for food at supermarkets instead of at Walmart.[6] And Toyota cut prices in 2010 in an attempt to regain market share (which had declined from 18.9 percent in December 2009 to 12.8 percent in February 2010) after millions of its cars were recalled due to reports of uncontrollable acceleration.[7]

Price-Setting Tools

Whatever a company's objectives, managers must measure the potential impact of various prices before deciding on a final price. Two basic tools are often used for this purpose: *cost-oriented pricing* and *break-even analysis*. As a rule, these tools are combined to identify prices that will allow the company to reach its objectives.

Cost-Oriented Pricing Cost-oriented pricing considers the firm's desire to make a profit and takes into account the need to cover production costs. A video store manager, for instance, would begin to price DVDs by calculating the cost of making them available to shoppers. Included in this figure would be store rent, employee wages, utilities, product displays, insurance, and, of course, the cost of buying DVDs from the manufacturer.

Let's assume that the cost from the manufacturer is $8 per DVD. If the store sells DVDs for this price, it will not make any profit. Nor will it make a profit if it sells DVDs for $8.50 each, nor even for $10 or $11. The manager must account for product and other costs and set a figure for profit. Together, these figures constitute markup. In this case, a reasonable markup of $7 over costs would result in a $15 selling price. Markup is usually stated as a percentage of selling price. Markup percentage is thus calculated as follows:

Markup percentage = Markup/Sales price

In the case of our DVD retailer, the markup percentage is 46.7:

Markup percentage = $7/$15 = 46.7%

In other words, out of every dollar taken in, 46.7 cents will be gross profit for the store. From this profit, the store must still pay rent, utilities, insurance, and all other costs. Markup can also be expressed as a percentage of cost: The $7 markup is 87.5 percent of the $8 cost of a DVD ($7 divided by $8).

Using low-cost, direct-to-consumer selling and market share pricing, Dell profitably dominated the personal computer market while its competitors sold through traditional retailers (which added costs that prevented them from matching Dell's low prices).

In some industries, cost-oriented pricing doesn't seem to be relevant. When you go to a movie, for example, you pay the same price for each film you see. But it may cost as little as $2 million or as much as $200 million to make a film. Shouldn't the admission price be based on how much the film cost to make? After all, you pay a lot more for a BMW 5 Series automobile than you do for a Honda Civic because the BMW costs more to make. But for movies, the market seems to be the overriding consideration (i.e., consumers are simply not willing to pay more than a certain amount to see a movie, no matter how much it cost to make). In other situations, however, price is not a major consideration for the consumer (see the boxed insert entitled "Men and Cars").

Break-Even Analysis: Cost–Volume–Profit Relationships If a firm uses cost-oriented pricing, it will cover its **variable costs**—costs that change with the number of goods or services produced or sold. It will also make some money toward paying its **fixed costs**—costs that are unaffected by the number of goods or services produced or sold. But how many units must the company sell before all of its fixed costs are covered and it begins to make a profit? To determine this figure, it needs a **break-even analysis**.

ENTREPRENEURSHIP AND NEW VENTURES

Men and Cars: Unrequited Love

Men have always had a bit of a love affair with their cars, but the customers of Auto Vault are downright obsessive. You would be too if you had $500 000 invested in a Lamborghini or some other exotic coupé. Auto Vault, a Toronto-based secure car storage facility for luxury automobiles and motorcycles, is owned and operated by Gary Shapiro. He got the idea for Auto Vault when working in sales at a high-end auto dealership. Potential customers complained that money wasn't the issue when it came to making a purchase; rather, the problem was where they would store the vehicle. Shapiro's company was launched in 2004, and it has been experiencing steady growth since inception, expanding from 80 customers at the end of its first year of operations to 400 in 2008.

For a $229 monthly fee, customers can purchase Auto Vault's Gold Package, which includes an exterior dust cover, interior mats and steering wheel cover, access to dedicated staff, secure parking, security monitoring, valet delivery, and detailing. For $299/month, you can get all the features of the Gold Package, plus tire pressure monitoring, battery and fluid checks, scheduled vehicle start-ups, and visual inspections.

Auto Vault's customers are really purchasing peace of mind. They trust Shapiro and they like him. "I was once called 'likable' in a newspaper article. . . . I hope I am, it would make it easier to convince someone to hand over the keys to a $500 000 car and their American Express card," says Shapiro. He is also known for his discretion; people are not told who owns which car, and some of his customers even have cars that are unknown to their families. Finally, the location is secret and disclosed to customers only after Shapiro meets with them.

As part of his service offering, Shapiro also likes to maintain personal contact with his clients and this is done through his handling of all incoming calls. "Word spread that I take good care of people," he said. This has helped him to get referrals, and according to Shapiro, he doesn't have to push his product; customers come to him. His next venture is a $15 million storage facility to be converted into parking condos. For $40 000, plus monthly maintenance fees, prestige car owners can purchase their own customized unit (average size is 400 square feet). Shapiro's imagination for what his car condo can offer has no boundaries. He's talking about such features as decor to match your car colour, 24-hour concierge service, a detailing service, and common areas with large screen TVs, among others. This romance between men and cars . . . it must be true love! And price is no object.

Critical Thinking Questions

1. Describe the various pricing strategies and distribution options that are available to companies. Which pricing and distribution strategies were adopted by Auto Vault?

2. Do you think Shapiro's pricing reflects the market he is targeting? Why or why not?

To continue with our video store example, suppose again that the variable cost for each DVD (in this case, the cost of buying the DVD from the producer) is $8. This means that the store's annual variable costs depend on how many DVDs are sold—the number of DVDs sold multiplied by the $8 cost per DVD. Assume that fixed costs for keeping the store open for one year are $100 000. These costs are unaffected by the number of DVDs sold; costs for lighting, rent, insurance, and salaries are steady no matter how many DVDs the store sells. How many DVDs must be sold to cover both fixed and variable costs and to start to generate some profit? The answer is the **break-even point**, which is 14 286 DVDs. We arrive at this number through the following equation:

$$\text{Breakeven point (in units)} = \frac{\text{Total Fixed Cost}}{\text{Price} - \text{Variable Cost}}$$

$$= \frac{\$100\ 000}{\$15 - \$8} = 14\ 286\ \text{DVDs}$$

Figure 14.1 shows the break-even point graphically. If the store sells fewer than 14 286 DVDs, it loses money for the year. If sales exceed 14 286 DVDs, profits grow by $7 for each DVD sold. If the store sells exactly 14 286 DVDs, it will cover all of its costs but will earn zero profit. Zero profitability at the break-even point can also be seen by using the following profit equation:

$$\text{Profit} = \frac{\text{Total}}{\text{Revenue}} - \left(\begin{matrix} \text{Total} & & \text{Total} \\ \text{Fixed} & + & \text{Variable} \\ \text{Cost} & & \text{Cost} \end{matrix} \right)$$

$$= (14\ 286\ \text{DVDs} \times \$15) - (\$100\ 000\ \text{Fixed Cost} + [14\ 286\ \text{DVDs} \times \$8\ \text{Variable Cost}])$$

$$\$0 = (\$214\ 290) - (\$100\ 000 + \$114\ 288)$$

(rounded to the nearest whole DVD)

The video store owner would certainly like to hit the break-even quantity as early as possible so that profits will start rolling in. Why not charge $30 per DVD and reach the break-even point earlier? The answer lies in the downward-sloping demand curve we discussed in Chapter 1. At a price of $30 per DVD, sales at the store would drop. Before setting a price, the manager must consider how much DVD buyers are willing to pay and what the store's competitors charge.

LO-2 Pricing Strategies and Tactics

In this section, we discuss *pricing strategy* (pricing as a planning activity that affects the marketing mix) as well as some basic *pricing tactics* (ways in which managers implement a firm's pricing strategies).

Pricing Strategies

How important is pricing as an element in the marketing mix? Because pricing has a direct impact on revenues, it is extremely important. Moreover, it is a very flexible tool. It is easier to change prices than to change products or distribution channels. Different pricing strategies can result in widely differing prices for products that are very similar.

Pricing Existing Products A firm has three basic options available in pricing its existing products. It can set prices above the prevailing market price charged for similar products, below the market price, or at the market price. Companies pricing above the market play on customers' beliefs that higher price means higher quality. Companies such as Godiva (chocolates) and Rolls-Royce have succeeded with this pricing philosophy. In contrast, both Budget and Discount promote themselves as low-priced alternatives to Hertz and Avis.

Pricing New Products Companies introducing new products into the market have to consider two contrasting pricing policy

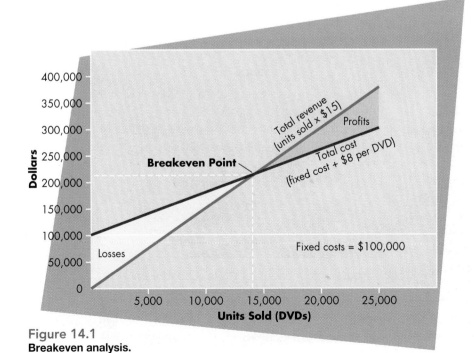

Figure 14.1
Breakeven analysis.

options: coming in with either a very high price or a very low one. **Price skimming**—setting an initially high price to cover costs and generate a profit—may generate a large profit on each item sold. The revenue is often needed to cover development and introduction costs. High-definition television (HDTV) is an example. In contrast, **penetration pricing**—setting an initially low price to establish a new product in the market—seeks to create consumer interest and stimulate trial purchases.

When Carbonite Inc. started its online backup service, it charged "one flat low price" no matter how many computer files you needed to back up.[8] To attract customers, Apple iTunes' initial policy was to price all songs at $0.99, but now it prices older tunes at $0.69 and currently popular tunes for $1.29.

Fixed versus Dynamic Pricing
The fixed pricing system is still used by most companies, but in the electronic marketplace dynamic pricing has been introduced as an alternative. Dynamic pricing is feasible because the flow of information on the internet notifies millions of buyers around the world of instantaneous changes in product availability.[9] To attract sales that might be lost under the fixed-price structure, sellers can alter prices privately on a one-to-one, customer-to-customer basis.[10] For example, at Priceline.com, consumers can state a price (below the published fixed price) that they are willing to pay for airfare. An airline can complete the sale by accepting the bid price. Progressive Casualty Insurance Company has introduced what is perhaps the ultimate dynamic pricing system. It sets insurance rates for drivers based on their real-time driving behaviour—information that is generated by the automobile's GPS system.[11]

Pricing Tactics
Regardless of its pricing strategy, a company may adopt one or more *pricing tactics*. Companies selling multiple items in a product category often use **price lining**—offering all items in certain categories at a limited number of prices. With price lining, a department store, for example, predetermines three or four *price points* at which a particular product will be sold. For example, all men's suits might be priced at $175, $250, or $400.

Psychological pricing is based on the idea that customers are not completely rational when making buying decisions. For example, the long-standing tactic of **odd-even pricing** assumes that customers think that a price of $99.95 is significantly lower than a price of $100. But Walmart is going against this trend. In an attempt to make it easier for money-conscious customers to calculate their bill before they get to the cash register, Walmart is rounding prices to the nearest dollar on many products.[12]

Another tactic is to offer a **discount** in an attempt to stimulate sales. In recent years, *cash discounts* have

Roy Cooper scours the markets of Quito, Ecuador for tapestries, baskets, and religious relics. He then sells them on the internet, usually at substantial markups, by privately negotiating prices with buyers.

If the manufacturer says a product should retail for $349, why doe every retailer sell it for, say, $229? Such discrepancies between a manufacturer's suggested retail price and the actual retail price are the norm in the electronics industry and consumers have come to expect discounted prices. But if no one charges suggested retail prices, are customers really getting a discount?

become popular. Stores also offer *seasonal* discounts to stimulate the sales of products during times of the year when most customers do not normally buy the product. *Trade discounts* are available to companies or individuals in a product's distribution channel. For example, wholesalers, retailers, and interior designers pay less for fabric than the typical consumer does. *Quantity discounts* involve lower prices for purchases in large quantities. Discounts for cases of motor oil or soft drinks at retail stores are examples of quantity discounts.

LO-3 The Distribution Mix

The success of any product is affected not only by its price but also by its **distribution mix**—the combination of distribution channels by which a firm gets products to end users.

Intermediaries and Distribution Channels

Intermediaries are the individuals and firms that help to distribute a producer's goods. **Wholesalers** sell products to other businesses, which resell them to final consumers. **Retailers** sell products directly to consumers. While some firms rely on independent intermediaries, others employ their own distribution networks and sales forces. Intermediaries are appearing in places where most people might think they aren't needed. A Canadian company called Imagine This Sold Ltd. provides expertise to people who are trying to sell items on eBay. This company exists because trading has become so competitive on eBay that more expertise is needed to succeed than a lot of people thought.[13]

Distribution of Goods and Services

A **distribution channel** is the path that a product follows from producer to end user. Figure 14.2 shows how four popular distribution channels can be identified according to the kinds of channel members involved in getting products to buyers. All channels begin with a producer and end either with a consumer or an industrial (business) user.

Channel 1: Direct Distribution In a **direct channel**, the product travels from the producer to the consumer or industrial buyer without intermediaries. Using their own sales forces, companies such as Avon, Dell, Geico, and Tupperware use this channel. Direct distribution is prominent on the internet for thousands of products ranging from books and automobiles to insurance and vacation packages sold directly by producers to users. Most business goods, especially those bought in large quantities, are sold directly by the manufacturer to the industrial buyer.

Channel 2: Retail Distribution Producers often distribute consumer products through retailers. Goodyear and Levi's have their own retail outlets. Large outlets such as Walmart buy merchandise directly from producers and sell to consumers. Many industrial buyers also rely on Channel 2 as they shop at office supply retailers such as Staples, Office Depot, and Office Max.

Channel 3: Wholesale Distribution Channel 2 was once the most widely used method of nondirect distribution.

Figure 14.2
Channels of distribution.

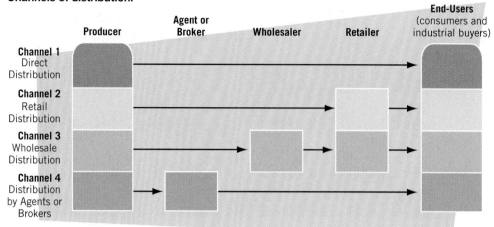

But it requires a large amount of floor space, both for storing merchandise and for displaying it in stores. Faced with the rising cost of store space, many retailers found that they could not afford both retail and storage space. Thus, wholesalers entered the distribution network to take over more of the storage function. The combination convenience store/gas station is an example of Channel 3. With approximately 90 percent of the space used to display merchandise, only 10 percent is left for storage and office facilities. Wholesalers relieve the space problem by storing merchandise for retailers and restocking store displays frequently.

Channel 4: Distribution by Agents or Brokers

Channel 4 uses *sales agents* or *brokers* who represent producers and sell to consumers, industrial users, or wholesalers. They receive commissions based on the prices of the goods they sell. **Sales agents** generally deal in the related product lines of a few producers, and form long-term relationships to represent those producers and meet the needs of steady customers. Vancouver-based Uniglobe Travel International, a travel agency representing airlines, car-rental companies, hotels, and tour companies, books flight reservations and arranges complete recreational travel services for consumers. The firm also services companies whose employees need lodging and transportation for business travel. In contrast to agents, **brokers** match numerous sellers and buyers as needed, often without knowing in advance who they will be. Both the real estate industry and stock exchanges rely on brokers to match buyers and sellers.

The Pros and Cons of Nondirect Distribution Each intermediary in the distribution chain makes a profit by charging a markup or commission. Thus, nondirect distribution means higher prices. Intermediaries, however, can provide *added value* by saving consumers both time and money. Moreover, the value accumulates with each link in the supply chain. Intermediaries provide time-saving information and make the right quantities of products available where and when consumers need them. Consider Figure 14.3, which illustrates the problem of making chili without the benefit of a common intermediary—the supermarket. As a consumer, you would obviously spend a lot more time, money, and energy if

At Delphi Automotive Systems, Jessica Prince assembles fuel pumps according to a process that she helped engineers and consultants design. The auto parts are shipped directly from the plant to an auto manufacturer, illustrating a direct channel of distribution.

you tried to gather all the ingredients from one producer at a time.

Eliminating intermediaries does not magically eliminate the tasks they perform and the costs they incur in performing those tasks. In this do-it-yourself era, more and more people are trying to save money by opting to sell their homes without using the services of a real estate agent. Since the agent's fee is normally between 5 and 6 percent of the purchase price of the house, the savings can be substantial. But the seller then has to do all the work that brokers would normally do to earn their fee.

Intermediaries like real estate agents provide an essential service, but not necessarily a *low-cost* service. E-brokers, who charge a flat rate that is far below what traditional real estate brokers charge, have emerged. It is not surprising that this development has been viewed with alarm by traditional real estate agents. What's worse, in 2010, the Canadian Competition Bureau filed a complaint with the Competition Tribunal, alleging that the Canadian Real Estate Association (CREA) was engaging in anti-competitive restrictions that were designed to maintain high fees for traditional real estate brokers by cutting e-brokers out of the CREAs Multiple Listing Service.[14] Real estate agents may soon have to face the fact that the internet has a lot of power to make data free and open.[15]

Distribution Strategies

The choice of a distribution strategy determines the amount of market exposure the product gets and the cost of that exposure. **Intensive distribution** occurs when a product is distributed through as many channels and channel members as possible. As Figure 14.4 shows, Caramilk chocolate bars flood the market through many different outlets. Intensive distribution is normally used for low-cost consumer goods such as candy and magazines. In contrast, **exclusive distribution** occurs when a manufacturer grants the exclusive right to distribute or sell

a product to one wholesaler or retailer in a given geographic area. For example, Jaguar automobiles are sold by only a single dealer servicing a large metropolitan area. **Selective distribution** falls between intensive and exclusive distribution. A company that uses this strategy selects only wholesalers and retailers who will give special attention to the product in terms of sales efforts, display position, etc. This method is usually embraced by companies like Black & Decker, whose product lines do not require intense market exposure to increase sales.

Channel Conflict and Channel Leadership

Channel conflict occurs when members of the distribution channel disagree over the roles they should play or the rewards they should receive. John Deere, for example, would no doubt object if its dealers began distributing Russian and Japanese tractors. Channel conflict may also arise if one member has more power than the others or is viewed as receiving preferential treatment. Such conflicts defeat the purpose of the system by disrupting the flow of goods to their destinations. Usually, one channel member—the **channel captain**—is the most powerful

Figure 14.3
Advantages of intermediaries.

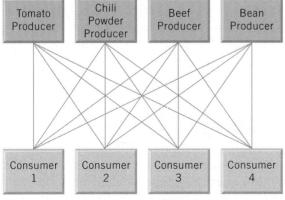

PURCHASE OF GOODS WITHOUT INTERMEDIARIES

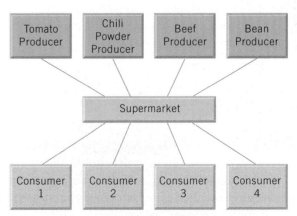

PURCHASE OF GOODS WITH INTERMEDIARIES

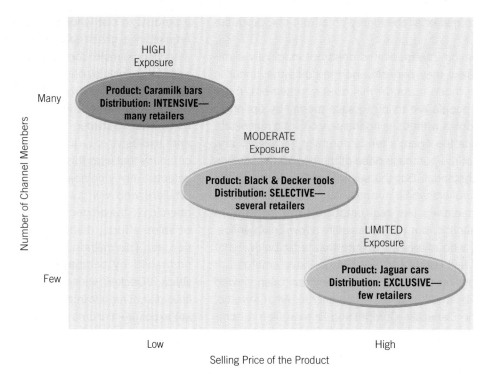

Figure 14.4
Amounts of market exposure from the three kinds of distribution.

in determining the roles and rewards of other members. The channel captain might be a manufacturer, or
it might be a large retailer like Walmart that generates
large sales volumes.

Vertical marketing systems (VMSs) are designed
to overcome the problems of channel conflict. In a VMS,
separate businesses join to form a unified distribution
channel, with one member coordinating the activities
of the whole channel. In a *corporate VMS*, all stages in
the channel are under single ownership. The Limited,
for example, owns both the production facilities that
manufacture its apparel and the retail stores that sell it.
In a *contractual VMS*, channel members sign contracts
agreeing to specific duties and rewards. The Independent
Grocers Alliance (IGA), for example, consists of
independent retail grocers joined with a wholesaler who
contractually leads—but does not own—the VMS. Most
franchises are contractual VMSs.

of services to their customers, who are buying products
for resale to consumers or other businesses. In addition to storing and providing an assortment of products,
wholesalers may offer delivery, credit, product information, and merchandising services such as marking prices
and setting up displays. **Merchant wholesalers** take title
to merchandise, that is, they buy and own the goods they
resell to other businesses.

In contrast, **agents and brokers** (including internet
e-brokers) do not own the merchandise they sell. Rather,
they serve as sales and merchandising arms for producers who do not have their own sales forces. The value
of agents and brokers lies in their knowledge of markets
and their merchandising expertise. They show sale items
to potential buyers and, for retail stores, they provide
such services as shelf and display merchandising and
advertising layout. They remove open, torn, or dirty packages, arrange products neatly, and generally keep goods
attractively displayed. Many supermarket products are
handled through brokers.

LO-4 Wholesaling

Now that you know something about distribution
channels, we can look more closely at the role of intermediaries. As noted earlier, wholesalers are independent
companies that buy products from manufacturers and sell
them to other businesses. Wholesalers provide a variety

LO-5 Retailing

You may not have had much contact with wholesalers,
but like most Canadians, you buy nearly all the goods
and services you consume from retailers. Most retailers

are small operations, often consisting of just the owners and part-time help. But there are some very large retailers, and these account for billions of dollars of sales each year. Walmart is the largest retailer in Canada.

Types of Retail Outlets

Canadian retail operations vary widely by type as well as size. We can classify them in various ways: by their pricing strategies, location, range of services, or range of product lines. Choosing the right types of retail outlets is a crucial aspect of every seller's distribution strategy. There are three main classifications of retail outlets: *product line retailers*, *bargain retailers*, and *convenience stores*.

Product Line Retailers Retailers featuring broad product lines include **department stores** like the Bay, which are organized into specialized departments like shoes, furniture, women's clothing, and so on. Stores are usually large, handle a wide range of goods, and offer a variety of services, such as credit plans and delivery. Similarly, **supermarkets** like Loblaws, Sobeys, and Safeway are divided into departments of related products: food products, household products, and so forth. They stress low prices, self-service, and wide selection. In contrast, **specialty stores** are small stores that carry one line of related products. They serve specific market segments with full product lines in narrow product fields and often feature knowledgeable sales personnel. Sunglass Hut International stores, for example, have a deep selection of competitively priced sunglasses.

Bargain Retailers **Bargain retailers** carry wide ranges of products and come in many forms. The first **discount houses** sold large numbers of items (such as TVs and other appliances) at substantial price reductions to cash-only customers. As name-brand items became more common, they offered better product assortments while still transacting cash-only sales in low-rent facilities. As they became more firmly entrenched, they began moving to better locations, improving their decor, and selling better-quality merchandise at higher prices. They also began offering a few department store services, such as credit plans and noncash sales.

Catalogue showrooms mail catalogues to attract customers into showrooms to view display samples, place orders, and wait briefly while clerks retrieve orders from attached warehouses. **Factory outlets** are manufacturer-owned stores that avoid wholesalers and retailers by selling merchandise directly from factory to consumer.

Wholesale clubs like Costco offer large discounts on a wide range of brand-name merchandise to customers who pay annual membership fees.

Convenience Stores Neighbourhood food retailers, such as Mac's and 7-Eleven, are **convenience store** chains, which offer ease of purchase. They stress easily accessible locations, extended store hours, and speedy service. They differ from most bargain retailers in that they do not feature low prices. Like bargain retailers, they control prices by keeping in-store service to a minimum. In 2009, more than 2300 convenience stores closed across Canada, partly because contraband cigarettes siphoned off about $2.5 billion in sales. The Canadian Convenience Stores Association estimates that half of Ontario's cigarette sales and 40 percent of Quebec's are cheap black-market cigarettes on which no tax has been paid.[16]

The boxed insert entitled "The Bag Controversy" contains some surprising facts about the different types of bags that retailers provide for customers.

Nonstore Retailing

Not all goods and services are sold in stores. In fact, some of the nation's largest retailers sell all or most of their products without bricks-and-mortar stores. For example, certain types of consumer goods—soft drinks, candy, and cigarettes—lend themselves to distribution in vending machines. However, vending machine sales still represent only a small proportion of all retail sales.

Direct-Response Retailing In **direct-response retailing**, companies contact customers directly

DEPARTMENT STORES Large retail stores that offer a wide variety of high-quality items divided into specialized departments.

SUPERMARKETS Large retail stores that offer a variety of food and food-related items divided into specialized departments.

SPECIALTY STORES Small retail stores that carry one line of related products.

BARGAIN RETAILERS Retail outlets that emphasize low prices as a means of attracting consumers.

DISCOUNT HOUSES Bargain retail stores that offer major items such as televisions and large appliances at discount prices.

CATALOGUE SHOWROOM A bargain retail store in which customers place orders for items described in a catalogue and pick up those items from an on-premises warehouse.

FACTORY OUTLETS Bargain retail stores that are owned by the manufacturers whose products they sell.

WHOLESALE CLUBS Huge, membership-only, combined retail wholesale operations that sell brand-name merchandise.

CONVENIENCE STORES Retail stores that offer high accessibility, extended hours, and fast service on selected items.

DIRECT-RESPONSE RETAILING A type of retailing in which firms make direct contact with customers both to inform them about products and to receive sales orders.

to inform them about products and to receive sales orders. The oldest form of retailing, **direct selling**, is still used by companies like Avon and Tupperware that sell door-to-door or through home-selling parties. Avon has more than 4 million sales reps in 100 countries,[17] and Tupperware has more than 60 000 salespeople just in Russia.[18] The Fuller Brush Company was started in 1906 by Arthur Fuller, a self-described "country bumpkin" from Nova Scotia. The company used to be well known in door-to-door selling, but sweeping changes in North American society—women leaving the home to work, mass retailing, and the globalization of business—caused the company to fall on hard times. Two of its most famous salesmen were the Reverend Billy Graham and disc jockey Dick Clark.

Mail order (or **catalogue marketing**) is another popular form of direct-response retailing. So is **telemarketing**—the use of the telephone to sell directly. It is growing rapidly

THE GREENING OF BUSINESS

The Bag Controversy

Canadians use 55 million plastic bags each *week*. Concerns about plastic bags have motivated retailers to take action. Consider the following examples:

■ Cities as different as San Francisco, California, and Leaf Rapids, Manitoba, have banned the use of plastic bags; several grocers in Nova Scotia are also considering the move.

■ Walmart and many other retailers are training their cashiers to ask customers if they even need a bag of any kind.

■ Loblaws has sold more than 14 million reusable bags, and the number of plastic bags given to customers has been reduced by 20 percent.

■ Many stores, including IKEA and No Frills charge customers for plastic bags and try to encourage consumers to use reusable bags.

■ Mountain Equipment Co-op wants to convince customers to stop using disposable bags altogether, so it makes a five-cent donation to environmental groups each time a customer declines to take a plastic bag.

In spite of these trends, there is actually no consensus about which type of bag is the most environmentally friendly: paper bags, plastic bags, or reusable cloth. At first glance, it might seem obvious that plastic bags are the worst because they have generated the most negative publicity. It might also seem obvious that reusable cloth or canvas bags are the best because they can be reused. But each type of bag has advantages and disadvantages. To determine which type of bag is best requires a consideration of many factors, including input and output costs, distribution costs, and reclamation costs.

To give you an idea of the complexity of the issue, consider a few facts. Since plastic bags are made from fossil fuels, they can take up to 1000 years to degrade. Even when they do degrade, the toxins they contain get into the soil. They are also an eyesore when they blow around landfills and elsewhere. Paper bags are better than plastic bags because they are made from natural materials, while plastic bags are synthetic. But the production of paper bags generates 70 percent more emissions and 50 percent more water pollution than plastic bags. Eco-friendly reusable cotton bags also have problems because cotton requires a lot of water (and pesticides) to grow. As well, they may also contain bacterial contaminants (one study showed that 30 percent of reusable bags had unsafe levels of bacterial contaminants, and 40 percent contained yeast or mould). Plastic bags do not have either of these problems. Given all these advantages and disadvantages, it is difficult for consumers to know which alternative is best.

Use of plastic bags is not the only issue facing retailers. Consumers are also starting to demand that retailers provide more eco-friendly packaging that is biodegradable, recycled, or reusable. One alternative to traditional plastic bottles is polyethylene terephthalate plastic bottles, which can be produced from recycled material. And remember that old-fashioned glass is 100 percent recyclable. Consumers also want less packaging overall, whatever type it is.

Critical Thinking Question

1. All things considered, which shopping bag do you think is best: plastic, paper, or reusable cloth bags? Defend your answer.

in Canada and Great Britain, but suffered a downturn in the United States with recent state and national do-not-call registries. **E-intermediaries** are internet-based channel members who perform one or both of the following functions: (1) they collect information about sellers and present it to consumers, or (2) they help deliver internet products to buyers. Three important types of e-intermediaries are *syndicated sellers*, *shopping agents*, and *e-retailers*.

Syndicated Sellers **Syndicated selling** occurs when one website offers another a commission for referring customers. Expedia.com, the world's leading online travel service, shows a list of car rental companies such as Dollar Rent A Car on its website. When Expedia customers click on the Dollar banner for a car rental, they are transferred from the Expedia site to the Dollar site. Dollar pays Expedia a fee for each booking that comes through this channel. Although the new intermediary increases the cost of Dollar's supply chain, it adds value for customers. Travellers avoid unnecessary cyber-space searches and are efficiently guided to a car-rental agency.[19]

Shopping Agents **Shopping agents (e-agents)** help internet consumers by gathering and sorting information. Although they don't take possession of products, they know which websites and stores to visit, give accurate comparison prices, identify product features, and help consumers complete transactions by presenting information in a usable format—all in a matter of seconds. PriceScan.com is among the better-known cyber-shopping agents, but there are many others as well. Since e-agents have become so plentiful, unsure shoppers are turning to rating sites such as eSmarts.com that evaluate and compare e-agents.

E-commerce intermediaries called *business-to-business (B2B) brokers* have also emerged for business customers. The pricing process between B2B buyers and sellers of commodities can be outsourced, for example, to an internet company like Ariba. As a pricing broker, Ariba links any large-volume buyer with potential suppliers that bid to become the supplier for the buyer. Client companies (the commodity buyers), such as Quaker Oats or Emerson Electric, pay Ariba a fixed annual subscription fee and receive networking into Ariba's auction headquarters, where real-time bids come in from suppliers at remote locations. The website provides up-to-date information until the bidding ends with the low-price supplier. In conducting the pricing transactions electronically, Ariba doesn't take possession of any products. Rather, it brings together timely information and links businesses to one another.[20]

Electronic Retailing **Electronic retailing** (also called *e-tailing*) allows consumers to shop from home using the internet. Sears Canada, one of the most popular e-tailers in Canada, offers more than 10 000 items for sale on its website.[21] E-tailing is made possible by communications networks that let sellers post product information on consumers' personal computers. E-tailing sales are increasing as more people shop online with their personal computers.

Electronic Catalogues **E-catalogues** use the internet to display products for both retail and business customers. Using electronic displays (instead of traditional mail catalogues), gives millions of users instant access to pages of product information. The seller avoids mail-distribution and printing costs, and once an online catalogue is in place, there is little cost in maintaining and accessing it. Recognizing these advantages, about 85 percent of all cataloguers are now on the internet, with sales via websites accounting for 10 percent of all catalogue sales. Popular consumer e-catalogues include JCPenney, L.L. Bean, and Victoria's Secret. Top B2B e-catalogues include Dell and Office Depot.[22]

Internet-Based Stores It is estimated that in 2010, Canadians bought nearly $12 billion worth of goods and services over the internet. As large as this number seems, it still represents less than 5 percent of the total dollars that consumers spent on goods and services in 2010.[23] But growth is rapid. At Sears Canada, for example, online sales in 2010 were about 10 percent of Sears' total sales, up from about 2 percent as recently as 2005.[24] Forrester Research predicts that e-commerce sales will keep growing at a 10 percent compounded annual rate through 2014, and that e-commerce sales will represent 8 percent of retail sales by 2014.[25] More information on the growth of e-business is presented in the boxed insert entitled "Exploiting E-Distribution Opportunities."

TELEMARKETING Use of the telephone to sell directly to consumers.

E-INTERMEDIARIES Internet-based distribution-channel members that collect information about sellers and present it in convenient form to consumers and/or help deliver internet products to consumers.

SYNDICATED SELLING Occurs when a website offers other websites a commission for referring customers.

SHOPPING AGENT (E-AGENT) A type of intermediary that helps internet consumers by gathering and sorting information they need to make purchases.

ELECTRONIC RETAILING Non-store retailing in which information about the seller's products and services is connected to consumers' computers, allowing consumers to receive the information and purchase the products in the home.

E-CATALOGUES Non-store retailing that uses the internet to display products and services for both retail shoppers and business customers.

Exploiting E-Distribution Opportunities

When retailers initially got into online selling, they often kept their sites separate from traditional outlets. But this led to confusion when customers were unable to exchange items in stores. Similarly, today organizations are struggling with the implementation of social media strategies. Here are some recent developments in e-distribution:

- Amazon is the poster child for e-distribution success. It is the key destination for book and DVD sales and has a growing presence in everything from glassware to patio furniture. Amazon's development of the Kindle e-reader further demonstrates its willingness to embrace new distribution trends. Amazon created the Kindle even though it had no previous experience in hardware development.

- Walmart transformed the traditional retail landscape, and it is now serious about online sales as well. It announced its intentions by slashing prices to $9 on 10 hot upcoming books. Walmart is using these books as loss leaders to gain attention and drive traffic to its e-store. It clearly plans to attack Amazon's position.

- Sears Canada has leveraged its traditional strength in catalogue sales with internet distribution. Today the company is focused on creating "an endless aisle." Sears Canada recently hired 80 e-commerce specialists, many from rivals like Indigo and Home Depot. It plans to double online sales in the next five years. Sears is taking advantage of the poor online presence of competitors like the Bay.

- In 2010, Procter & Gamble surprised retailers by announcing that it would sell hundreds of its brands, including Tide and Pampers, in its new e-store. This places P & G in direct competition with its retailers. P & G executives argue that the site will actually provide consumer research, which could benefit loyal retailers.

- HMV was slow to embrace digital music distribution. In Canada, HMV Digital was launched in 2009 (iTunes.ca launched in 2004). When the music industry switched from records to CDs, HMV made a seamless transition. But it did not react quickly to this new distribution challenge and suffered. HMV is now trying to regain strength; it has an uphill battle, but it's a step in the right direction.

New technology continues to revolutionize distribution relationships. For example, the fastest-growing cellphone activity is shopping directly from mobile devices. Success today is measured by a company's ability to identify challenges and opportunities, and to develop solutions that satisfy consumers and the bottom line. It's not an easy task.

Critical Thinking Questions

1. What are the strengths and weaknesses of e-distribution?
2. Have you ever purchased items from any of these sites? Were your experiences positive or negative? Explain.

Ice.com, a Montreal-based company, is a typical internet-based store that sells mid- and low-priced jewellery over the internet, mostly to U.S. customers. The company is profitable because it deals in products that are high-value, high-margin, small-size, and easy to ship to customers.[26]

Using the internet to do *comparison shopping* is increasing rapidly. Internet sites like Ask Jeeves, Google, and Yahoo allow consumers to compare prices and products before making a purchase. E-commerce is still in its infancy, and there is a lot of room for growth.

More than 30 000 Canadians are "small retailers" who make a significant portion of their annual income by selling goods and services on sites like eBay, Kijiji, and craigslist. But they often do not pay income or sales tax on their sales, so both the Canada Revenue Agency and the federal government are losing millions of dollars in tax revenues each year. The Federal Court of Appeal has ordered eBay to provide information on people who sell more than $1000 per month on its site.[27] eBay is also planning to retreat from its recently adopted strategy of selling new goods over the internet, and will return to its original strategy of being the web's flea market.[28]

Electronic Storefronts and Cybermalls Today, a seller's website is an **electronic storefront** (or *virtual storefront*) from which consumers collect information about products and buying opportunities, place orders, and pay for purchases. Producers of large product lines, such as Dell, dedicate storefronts to their own product lines. Other sites, such as Newegg.com—which offers computer and other electronics equipment—are category sellers whose storefronts feature products from many manufacturers.

Search engines like Yahoo! serve as **cybermalls**: collections of virtual storefronts representing diverse products. After entering a cybermall, shoppers can navigate by choosing from a list of stores (e.g., L.L. Bean or Lands' End), product listings (e.g., computers or MP3 players), or departments (e.g., apparel or bath and beauty). When your virtual shopping cart is full, you check out and pay your bill. The value-added properties of cybermalls are obvious: speed, convenience, 24-hour access, and efficient searching.

Interactive and Video Marketing Today, both retail and B2B customers interact with multimedia sites using voice, graphics, animation, film clips, and access to live human advice. One good example of **interactive marketing** is LivePerson.com, a leading provider of real-time sales and customer service for over 3000 websites. When customers log on to the sites of Bell Canada, Toyota, Earthlink, Hewlett Packard, and Microsoft—all of which are LivePerson clients—they can enter a live chat room where a service operator initiates a secure one-to-one text chat. Questions and answers go back and forth to help customers get answers to specific questions before deciding on a product. Another form of interaction is the so-called banner ad that changes as the user's mouse moves about the page, revealing new drop-down, check, and search boxes.

Video marketing, a long-established form of interactive marketing, lets viewers shop at home through home-shopping channels that display and demonstrate products and allow viewers to phone in or email orders. One U.S. network, QVC, also operates in the United Kingdom, Germany, Mexico, and South America.

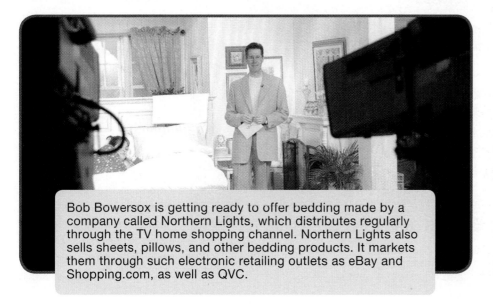

Bob Bowersox is getting ready to offer bedding made by a company called Northern Lights, which distributes regularly through the TV home shopping channel. Northern Lights also sells sheets, pillows, and other bedding products. It markets them through such electronic retailing outlets as eBay and Shopping.com, as well as QVC.

Physical Distribution

Physical distribution refers to the activities needed to move products efficiently from manufacturer to consumer. The goals of physical distribution are to keep customers satisfied, to make goods available when and where consumers want them, and to keep costs low. Companies are continually experimenting with physical distribution to improve efficiency and open new markets. For example, Maersk Line and Aqualife AS have partnered to create a transport system to ship seafood from Canada's east coast aquaculture companies to customers in Europe. Specialized tanks on board the ships oxygenate water without having to use pumps. The new system will help to open new markets for aquaculture products grown in Canada.[29] Another example: Coca-Cola Co. decided to take over Coca-Cola Enterprises (CCE)—which focused on bottling and distribution—because Coca-Cola Co. thought it could better manage its various brands and cut distribution costs. Pepsi had done the same thing with its bottlers in 2009.[30]

ELECTRONIC STOREFRONT A seller's website in which consumers collect information about products and buying opportunities, place sales orders, and pay for their purchases.

CYBERMALLS Collections of virtual storefronts representing diverse products.

INTERACTIVE MARKETING Selling products and services by allowing customers to interact with multimedia websites using voice, graphics, animation, film clips, and access to live human advice.

VIDEO MARKETING Selling to consumers by showing products on television that consumers can buy by telephone or mail.

PHYSICAL DISTRIBUTION Those activities needed to move a product from the manufacturer to the end consumer.

Physical distribution includes *warehousing* and *transporting operations,* as well as *distribution for e-customers.*

Warehousing Operations

Storing or **warehousing** products is a major function of distribution management. There are two basic types of warehouses: *private* and *public*. **Private warehouses** are owned by and provide storage for just one company, be it a manufacturer, a wholesaler, or a retailer. Most are used by large firms that deal in mass quantities and need storage regularly. **Public warehouses** are independently owned and operated. Companies that use these warehouses pay for the actual space used. Public warehouses are popular with firms that need such storage only during peak business periods. They are also used by manufacturers that want to maintain stock in numerous locations to get their products to many markets quickly. Within these two categories, we can further divide warehouses according to their use as *storage warehouses* (which provide storage for extended periods) or as *distribution centres* (which store products whose market demand is constant and high).

LO-7 Transportation Operations

The highest cost faced by many companies is that of physically moving a product, so cost is a major consideration in managing transportation operations. In 2010,

Walmart decided to take over the delivery of products to its stores from any manufacturer where Walmart could do the job cheaper. These savings will be used to further cut prices at its retail stores.[31] When managing transportation operations, firms must also consider other factors such as the nature of the product, the distance it must travel, the speed with which it must be received, and customer wants and needs. These vary across different transportation modes.

Transportation Modes The major transportation modes are *trucks*, *railroads*, *planes*, *water carriers*, and *pipelines*. Differences in cost are most directly related to the speed of delivery.

Trucks The advantages of trucks include flexibility, fast service, and dependability. Nearly all areas of Canada, except the far north, can be reached by truck. Trucks are a particularly good choice for short-distance distribution and more expensive products. Large furniture and appliance retailers in major cities, for example, use trucks to shuttle merchandise between their stores and to make deliveries to customers. Trucks can, however, be delayed by bad weather. They also are limited in the volume they can carry in a single load.

Planes Air is the fastest available transportation mode, and in Canada's far north, it may be the only available transportation. Other advantages include greatly reduced costs in packing, handling, unpacking, and final preparations necessary for sale to the consumer. Also, inventory carrying costs can be reduced by eliminating the need to store certain commodities. In recent years, a whole new industry has evolved to meet the customers' need to receive important business papers and supplies "overnight." Fresh fish, for example, can be flown to restaurants each day, avoiding the risk of spoilage that comes with packaging and storing a supply of fish. Air freight, however, is the most expensive form of transportation. Spanish apparel chain Zara is willing to pay the extra cost because it can get new merchandise to stores in Europe within 24 hours by using air freight. Because Zara minimizes the inventory it carries, it doesn't have to cut prices to move

Modern long-haul trucks have satellite capabilities, anti-collision radar, vehicle-detection sensors, computers for shifting through 10 speeds, and roomy cabs with sleepers, refrigerators, and microwave ovens.

out-of-date apparel items, so it earns higher margins on the products it sells.[32]

Railroads Railroads have been the backbone of our transportation system since the late 1800s. They are now used primarily to transport heavy, bulky items such as cars, steel, and coal. They are limited by fixed, immovable rail tracks.

Water Carriers Water transportation is the least expensive, but slowest, way to ship. Boats and barges are mainly used for extremely heavy, bulky materials and products (like sand, gravel, oil, and steel) for which transit times are unimportant. The St. Lawrence Seaway is a vital link in Canada's water transportation system, and water transportation is particularly important in Canada's far north. For example, barges deliver commodities like fuel oil to various isolated hamlets along the western edge of Hudson's Bay during the summer months, and Northern Transportation Company Ltd. moves freight on the Athabasca River because of demand created by the oil sands projects in northern Alberta.[33]

Pipelines Like water transportation, pipelines are slow in terms of overall delivery time. They are also completely inflexible, but they do provide a constant flow of the product and are unaffected by weather conditions. Traditionally, this delivery system has transported liquids and gases. Lack of adaptability to other products and limited routes make pipelines a relatively unimportant transportation method for most industries.

Intermodal Transportation Intermodal transportation—the combined use of different modes of transportation—has come into widespread use. For example, shipping by a combination of truck and rail ("piggy-back"), water and rail ("fishy-back"), or air and rail ("birdy-back") has improved flexibility and reduced costs.

INTERMODAL TRANSPORTATION The combined use of different modes of transportation.

ORDER FULFILLMENT All activities involved in completing a sales transaction, beginning with making the sale and ending with on-time delivery to the customer.

Distribution for E-Customers

New e-commerce companies often focus on sales, only to discover that delays in after-the-sale distribution cause customer dissatisfaction. **Order fulfillment** begins when the sale is made. It involves getting the product to each customer in good condition and on time. But the volume of a firm's transactions can be huge, and fulfillment performance—in terms of timing, content, and terms of payment—has been a source of irritation to many e-business customers.

To improve on-time deliveries, many businesses maintain distribution centres and ship from their own warehouses. Other e-tailers, however, outsource order filling to distribution specialists, such as the giant UPS e-logistics and the much smaller CaseStack, to gain reliable performance. Both CaseStack and UPS process orders, ship goods, provide information about product availability and order status, and handle returns. To perform these tasks, the client's computer system must be networked with that of the distribution specialist.

Physical Distribution as a Marketing Strategy

Distribution is an increasingly important way of competing for sales. Instead of just offering advantages in product features and quality, price, and promotion, many firms have turned to distribution as a cornerstone of business strategy. This approach means assessing and improving the entire stream of activities—wholesaling, warehousing, and transportation—that are required to get products to customers.

A container train crosses the Salmon River Bridge in New Brunswick.

Consider, for example, the distribution system of National Semiconductor, one of the world's largest computer-chip makers. Finished microchips are produced in plants around the world and shipped to customers, such as IBM, Toshiba, and Compaq, which also run factories around the globe. Chips originally sat waiting at one location after another—on factory floors, at customs, in distributors' facilities, and in customers' warehouses. Typically, they travelled 20 000 different routes on as many as 12 airlines and spent time in 10 warehouses before reaching customers. National has streamlined the system by shutting down six warehouses and now air freights chips worldwide from a single centre in Singapore. Every activity—storage, sorting, and shipping—is run by FedEx. By outsourcing the activities, National's distribution costs have fallen, delivery times have been reduced by half, and sales have increased.

Summary of Learning Objectives

1. **Identify the various *pricing objectives* that govern pricing decisions and describe the price-setting tools used in making these decisions.** The two main pricing objectives are *pricing to maximize profits* and *pricing to achieve market share objectives*. Price-setting tools include *cost-oriented pricing* (considering both the firm's desire to make a profit and the need to cover production costs), and *break-even analysis* (assessing total costs versus revenues for various sales volumes).

2. **Discuss *pricing strategies* and *tactics* for existing and new products.** The three options for pricing existing products are *pricing above the market, pricing below the market,* and *pricing at the market*. Companies *pricing new products* must often choose between *price skimming* (setting an initially high price to cover costs and generate a profit) or *penetration pricing* (setting an initially low price to establish a new product in the market). *Pricing tactics* include *price lining* (offering all items in certain categories at a limited number of prices), *psychological pricing* (appealing to buyers' perceptions of relative prices), and *discounting* (reducing prices to stimulate sales).

3. **Explain the *distribution mix*, the different *channels of distribution*, and the different *distribution strategies* that businesses use.** In selecting a *distribution mix*, a firm may use all or any of four *channels of distribution*. Channel 1 involves direct sales to consumers; Channel 2 includes a *retailer*; Channel 3 involves both a retailer and a *wholesaler*; and Channel 4 includes an *agent* or *broker* who enters the system before the wholesaler and retailer. *Distribution strategies* include *intensive, exclusive,* and *selective distribution*, which differ in the number of products and channel members involved and in the amount of service performed in the channel.

4. **Explain the differences among *wholesalers, agents/brokers,* and *retailers*.** *Wholesalers* are independent companies that buy products from manufacturers and sell them to other businesses. Wholesalers take title to the goods they sell, and they may also extend credit as well as store, repackage, and deliver products to other members of the channel. *Agents and brokers* do not own the merchandise they sell. Rather, they serve as sales and merchandising arms for producers that do not have their own sales forces. *Retailers* sell products directly to consumers.

5. **Identify the different types of *retail stores* and the activities of *e-intermediaries*.** Retail operations are classified as *product line retailers* (including department stores, supermarkets, and specialty stores),

bargain retailers (including discount houses, catalogue showrooms, factory outlets, warehouse clubs), and convenience stores. Non-store retailing includes direct-response retailing, mail order, telemarketing, direct selling, electronic retailing, e-catalogues, electronic storefronts, and cybermalls. E-intermediaries are internet-based channel members that perform functions like collecting information about sellers and presenting it to consumers, or helping to deliver internet products. They include syndicated selling (a website offers other websites a commission for referring customers), shopping agents (who help internet consumers by gathering and sorting information), and business-to-business brokers (who are intermediaries for business customers).

6. **Define physical distribution and describe the major activities in warehousing operations.** Physical distribution—the activities needed to move products from manufacturer to consumer—include warehousing (the storage of goods) and transportation of goods (including the movement of goods to e-customers). Private warehouses are owned and used by a single manufacturer, wholesaler, or retailer. Public warehouses are independently owned and operated and permit companies to rent only the space they need. Storage warehouses provide storage for extended periods. Distribution centres store products whose market demand is constant and high.

7. **Compare the five basic forms of transportation and explain how distribution can be used as a marketing strategy.** There are five modes of transportation, and differences in cost are most directly related to delivery speed. The advantages of trucks include flexibility, fast service, and dependability. Railroads are now used primarily to transport heavy, bulky items such as cars and steel. Planes provide the fastest mode of transportation, but air freight is the most expensive form of transportation. Water carriers are the least expensive but the slowest. Pipelines are slow and inflexible but provide a constant flow of products and are unaffected by weather. Many firms regard distribution as a cornerstone of their business strategy. This approach means assessing and streamlining the entire range of activities involved in getting products to customers.

Questions and Exercises

Questions for Analysis

1. How do cost-oriented pricing and break-even analysis help managers measure the potential impact of prices?

2. What general factors motivate marketing managers to price their products at, above, or below prevailing market prices?

3. From the manufacturer's point of view, what are the advantages and disadvantages of using intermediaries to distribute products? What are the advantages and disadvantages from the end-user's point of view?

4. Identify several products in each of the three distribution strategy categories (intensive, selective, and exclusive). What are the characteristics of the products in each category? Is there a pattern? Explain.

5. How do the activities of e-agents (internet shopping agents) or brokers differ from those of traditional agents/brokers?

6. A retailer buys a product from a manufacturer for $25 and sells it for $45. What is the markup percentage? Explain what the term "markup percentage" means.

Application Exercises

7. Consider the various kinds of non-store retailing. Give examples of two products that typify the kinds of products sold to consumers through each form of non-store retailing. Are different products best suited to each form of non-store retailing? Explain.

8. Novelties Ltd. produces miniature Canadian flag decals. The fixed costs for their latest project are $5000. The variable costs are $0.70/flag, and the company should be able to sell them for $2 apiece. How many flags must Novelties Ltd. sell to break even? How many flags must the company sell to make a profit of $2000? If the maximum number of flags the company can sell is 5000, should it get involved in this project?

9. Select a product with which you are familiar and analyze various possible pricing objectives for it. What information would you want to have if you were to adopt a profit-maximizing objective? A market-share objective?

10. Interview the manager of a local manufacturing firm. Identify the firm's distribution strategy and the channels of distribution that it uses. Where applicable, describe the types of wholesalers or retail stores used to distribute the firm's products.

Building Your Business Skills

Are You Sold on the Net?

Goal

To encourage students to consider the value of online retailing as an element in a company's distribution system.

Situation

As the distribution manager of a privately owned clothing manufacturer specializing in camping gear and outdoor clothing, you are convinced that your product line is perfect for online distribution. However, the owner of the company is reluctant to expand distribution from a successful network of retail stores and a catalogue operation. Your challenge is to convince the boss that retailing via the internet can boost sales.

Method

Step 1 Join together with four or five classmates to research the advantages and disadvantages of an online distribution system for your company. Among the factors to consider are the following:

- The likelihood that target consumers are internet shoppers. Camping gear is generally purchased by young, affluent consumers who are comfortable with the web.

- The industry trend to online distribution. Are similar companies doing it? Have they been successful?

- The opportunity to expand inventory without increasing the cost of retail space or catalogue production and mailing charges.

- The opportunity to have a store that never closes.

- The lack of trust many people have about doing business on the web. Many consumers are reluctant to provide credit card data over the web.

- The difficulty that electronic shoppers have in finding a website when they do not know the store's name.

- The certainty that the site will not reach consumers who do not use computers or who are uncomfortable with the web.

Step 2 Based on your findings, write a persuasive memo to the company's owner stating your position about expanding to an online distribution system. Include information that will counter expected objections.

Follow-Up Questions

1. What place does online distribution have in the distribution network of this company?

2. In your view, is online distribution the wave of the future? Is it likely to increase in importance as a distribution system for apparel companies? Why or why not?

Exercising Your Ethics

The Chain of Responsibility

The Situation

Because several stages are involved when distribution chains move products from supply sources to end consumers, the process offers ample opportunity for ethical issues to arise. This exercise encourages you to examine some of the ethical issues that can emerge during transactions among suppliers and customers.

The Dilemma

A customer bought an expensive wedding gift at a local store and asked that it be shipped to the bride in another province. Several weeks after the wedding, the customer contacted the bride, who had not confirmed the arrival of the gift. It hadn't arrived. Charging that the merchandise had not been delivered, the customer requested a refund from the retailer. The store manager uncovered the following facts:

- All shipments from the store are handled by a well-known national delivery firm.

- The delivery firm verified that the package had been delivered to the designated address two days after the sale.

- Normally, the delivery firm does not obtain recipient signatures; deliveries are made to the address of record, regardless of the name on the package.

The gift giver argued that even though the package had been delivered to the right address, it had not been delivered to the named recipient. It turns out that, unbeknownst to the gift giver, the bride had moved. It stood to reason, then, that the gift was in the hands of the new occupant at the bride's former address. The manager informed the gift giver that the store had fulfilled its obligation. The cause of the problem, she explained, was the incorrect address given by the customer. She refused to refund the customer's money and suggested that the customer might want to recover the gift by contacting the stranger who received it at the bride's old address.

Team Activity

Assemble a group of four students and assign each group member to one of the following roles:

- Customer (the person who had originally purchased the gift)

- Employee (of the store where the gift was purchased)

- Bride (the person who was supposed to receive the gift)

- Customer service manager (of the delivery company)

Action Steps

1. Before hearing any of your group's comments, and from the perspective of your assigned role, decide whether there are any ethical issues in this situation. If so, write them down.

2. Before hearing any of your group's comments, and from the perspective of your assigned role, decide how this dispute should be resolved.

3. Together with your group, share the ethical issues that were identified. What responsibilities does each party—the customer, the store, and the delivery company—have in this situation?

4. What does your group recommend be done to resolve this dispute? What are the advantages and disadvantages of your recommendations?

BUSINESS CASE 14

Changing Distribution Channels in the Music Business

Physical distribution of music in the form of CDs is rapidly declining, and digital distribution of music is rapidly increasing. A report by PriceWaterhouseCoopers LLP (PWC) predicts that by 2011 physical music sales in Canada will decline to just $275 million. That's down from $572 million as recently as 2007. The *increase* in digital music delivery has been dramatic. In 2007, digital music sales were just $122 million in Canada (that was only one-fourth of the volume of physical music sales). The PWC study predicts that by 2011 digital sales from sites such as iTunes will increase to $366 million (that will be more than physical music sales).

Music piracy is getting worse as consumers share music on the internet, and this is hastening the decline of traditional music sales. During the period 1999–2009, for example, CD sales declined 50 percent in Canada. In contrast, worldwide digital music sales have increased more than tenfold since 2004. In response to the decline in traditional music formats, record stores have shifted

their emphasis away from CDs and toward DVDs and video games.

The evolution of retail music sales shows how dramatically changes in technology can influence channels of distribution. For decades, consumers visited music stores, looked over the merchandise, and then decided what to buy (originally breakable records, then vinyl records, then eight-track tapes, then cassettes, and finally CDs). Then came internet stores offering thousands of titles in CDs and cassettes. Customers searched the lists, placed orders electronically or over the phone, and then received their music by mail.

Then came an online music service called Napster, where customers downloaded free software onto their computers that allowed them to put their music on Napster's website and trade with anyone else who was live on the internet at the same time. Not surprisingly, recording industry executives were not impressed with this new channel of distribution. They argued that file-sharing denied music artists the royalties they were due. The threat from Napster was seen as so great that the Recording Industry Association of America (RIAA) decided to prosecute. The courts soon shut Napster down for copyright infringement. But the victory was short-lived, and other file-sharing services like Morpheus, KaZaA, and Grokster popped up.

To combat illegal downloading, the recording industry launched two online music services—MusicNet and Pressplay. If customers used MusicNet, they paid $9.95 a month and got 100 downloads (but couldn't copy them and the deal expired at the end of the month). If they used Pressplay, they got 100 downloads for $24.95 per month (and the right to burn 20 tracks to a CD). Other similar services are offered by iTunes (the industry leader), Microsoft, Yahoo!, and a rejuvenated Napster.

The recording industry also filed lawsuits against Grokster and StreamCast Networks (the makers of Morpheus), and in 2005 the U.S. Supreme Court ruled that the entertainment industry could sue companies like Grokster and Morpheus. A few months later, Grokster agreed to shut down and pay $50 million to settle piracy complaints by the music industry. Grokster then announced plans to launch a legal service called 3G, which would require customers to pay a fee to get access to songs that could be downloaded.

In 2009, a Swedish court delivered another blow to illegal file sharing when it found four men guilty of illegally posting online a pirated copy of the film *X-Men Origins: Wolverine*. Their website—called Pirate Bay—indexed songs, movies, and TV shows. It is visited by more than 22 million people each day. The men were sentenced to one year in jail and ordered to pay $3.6 million in damages to various entertainment companies.

But will the Swedish court ruling stop the illegal downloading of music? Grokster and Morpheus software is in the hands of millions of consumers who can still engage in illegal downloading, and more file-sharing software becomes available all the time. For example, a relatively new Canadian file-sharing service called isoHunt has become one of the world's most visited websites. Overseas programmers also offer new software to consumers and they are beyond the reach of the law in North America. A survey by Forrester Research found that 80 percent of the respondents said they were not going to stop free downloading.

Music companies should never underestimate how clever consumers can be when they are highly motivated to get something for free. Consider what happened with Apple's iTunes software. There is an option on the software called "share my music," which allows users to make their library of songs available to any other computer running iTunes. The software allows people to *listen* to other peoples' collection of music, but not to *copy* it. Or so Apple thought when it developed the software. Then, some clever programmers figured out a way to get around the restriction and they started using iTunes software to facilitate illegal downloading.

It is hard to predict how this story will end.

Questions for Discussion

1. Consider the traditional channels of distribution for music albums. Which channel elements are most affected by the presence of services like KaZaA and Morpheus? Explain how those elements are affected.

2. Why is the music industry so concerned about internet distribution? Are there any opportunities for the recording industry in internet distribution?

3. Develop arguments opposing the legality of services offered by Morpheus. Then take the reverse position and develop arguments in favour of these services.

4. What types of ethical or social-responsibility issues does file sharing raise?

5. What other products, besides music albums, are the most likely candidates for distribution on the internet, now and in the future?

SCANLIFE

Part 4: Managing Marketing

Goal of the Exercise

So far, your business has an identity, you've described the factors that will affect your business, and you've examined your employees, the jobs they'll be performing, and the ways in which you can motivate them. Part 4 of the business plan project asks you to think about marketing's 4 Ps—product, price, place (distribution), and promotion—and how they apply to your business. You'll also examine how you might target your marketing toward a certain group of consumers.

Exercise Background:
Part 4 of the Business Plan

In Part 1, you briefly described what your business will do. The first step in Part 4 of the plan is to more fully describe the product (good or service) you are planning to sell. Once you have a clear picture of the product, you'll need to describe how this product will stand out in the marketplace—that is, how will it differentiate itself from other products?

In Part 1, you also briefly described who your customers would be. The first step in Part 4 of the plan is to describe your ideal buyer, or target market, in more detail, listing their income level, education level, lifestyle, age, and so forth. This part of the business plan project also asks you to discuss the price of your products, as well as where the buyer can find your product.

Finally, you'll examine how your business will get the attention and interest of the buyer through its promotional mix—advertising, personal selling, sales promotions, and publicity and public relations.

This part of the business plan encourages you to be creative. Have fun! Provide as many details as you possibly can, as this reflects an understanding of your product and your buyer. Marketing is all about finding a need and filling it. Does your product fill a need in the marketplace?

Your Assignment

PEARSON
mybusinesslab

Step 1

Open the saved Business Plan file you have been working on.

Step 2

For the purposes of this assignment, you will answer the following questions in Part 4: Managing Marketing:

1. Describe your target market in terms of age, education level, income, and other demographic variables.

   Hint: Refer to Chapter 12 for more information on the aspects of target marketing and market segmentation that you may want to consider. Be as detailed as possible about who you think your customers will be.

2. Describe the features and benefits of your product or service.

   Hint: As you learned in Chapter 13, a product is a bundle of attributes—features and benefits. What features does your product have—what does it look like and what does it do? How will the product benefit the buyer?

3. How will you make your product stand out in the crowd?

   Hint: There are many ways to stand out in the crowd, such as having a unique product, outstanding service, or a great location. What makes your great idea special? Does it fill an unmet need in the marketplace? How will you differentiate your product to make sure that it succeeds?

4. What pricing strategy will you choose for your product, and what are the reasons for this strategy?

   Hint: Refer to Chapter 14 for more information on pricing strategies and tactics. Since your business is new, so is the product. Therefore, you probably want to choose between price skimming and penetration pricing. Which will you choose, and why?

5. Where will customers find your product or service? (That is, what issues of the distribution mix should you consider?)

   Hint: If your business does not sell its product directly to consumers, what types of retail stores will sell your product? If your product will be sold to another business, which channel of distribution will you use? Refer to Chapter 14 for more information on aspects of distribution you may want to consider.

6. How will you advertise to your target market? Why have you chosen these forms of advertisement?

Hint: Marketers use several different advertising media—specific communication devices for carrying a seller's message to potential customers— each having advantages and drawbacks. Refer to Chapter 13 for a discussion of the types of advertising media you may wish to consider here.

7. What other methods of promotion will you use, and why?

Hint: There's more to promotion than simple advertising. Other methods include personal selling, sales promotions, and publicity and public relations. Refer to the discussion of promotion in Chapter 13 for ideas on how to promote your product that go beyond just advertising.

Note: Once you have answered the questions, save your Word document. You'll be answering additional questions in later chapters.

The "Feel-Better" Bracelet

Q-Ray advertisements say that its "Serious Performance Bracelet" is designed to help people play, work, and live better." The advertisements say that the $200 bracelet—which makes people feel better by balancing natural positive and negative forces—is ionized using a special secret process. Golfers claim that the bracelet reduces their pain, so *Marketplace* went looking for answers at the golf course. Sandra Post, a champion golfer, is a paid spokesperson for the bracelet. When Wendy Mesley of *Marketplace* interviews her, Post emphasizes the jewellery aspect of the Q-Ray, not its pain-relief qualities. Mesley also interviews golfers Frank and Sam. Frank tells her that the bracelet has reduced his arthritis pain, but Sam (who also wears one of the bracelets) thinks the pain relief is mostly in peoples' heads.

Advertising that a product provides pain relief is a tricky business. Even though a lot of people wear the Q-Ray for pain relief, the company cannot advertise that its product relieves pain unless there are medical studies that clearly show this. And there are no such studies. Until 2006, people in Q-Ray ads said that the bracelet had cured their pain. But now they can't say that because the U.S. Federal Trade Commission ruled that such advertising is deceptive.

Andrew Park is the man who brought the Q-Ray to North America, and now his son Charles is marketing the product in Canada. Park says that 150 000 Q-Rays have been sold in Canada at a price of $200 each. In an interview with Mesley, Park says that the company does not make pain relief claims for the product in its advertisements. But then Mesley shows a hidden camera film clip to Park where he is making a pain relief claim during the shooting of an infomercial. Park says that he believes that the product reduces pain, and that if you believe the bracelet will relieve your pain, it will. Mesley also plays a hidden camera clip showing retail salespeople telling customers that the Q-Ray reduces the pain of arthritis. Park says he can't control what retailers tell their customers.

Marketplace also asked Christopher Yip, an engineer at the University of Toronto, to test a Q-ray bracelet to determine if it was ionized. Yip found that it did not hold an electrical charge and was therefore not

ionized. When Park is confronted with this evidence, he says that he never claimed that the bracelet would hold an electrical charge. Rather, he simply says that the bracelet is ionized using an "exclusive ionization process." Hidden camera film of retail salespeople shows them explaining ionization by saying things like "it picks up the iron in your blood and speeds up circulation" and "negative ions are collected in the ends of the bracelet." Retail salespeople say they aren't sure what ionization is.

Mesley also shows Park a hidden camera interview with the Q-Ray sales coordinator. The coordinator mentions several types of pain that Q-Ray bracelet relieves—migraine, carpal tunnel, and arthritis. Park says that he will have to meet with the sales coordinator and inform her that she cannot make these pain-relief claims.

Video Resource: "Buyer Belief," *Marketplace* (November 14, 2007).

Questions for Discussion

1. Is the Q-Ray bracelet a convenience, shopping, or specialty good? Explain your reasoning. Also analyze the "value package" provided by the Q-Ray bracelet.

2. Briefly describe the variables that are typically used to segment markets and what each involves. Which variable is Q-Ray using?

3. Consider the following statement: *"People suffering from chronic pain need hope, and a product like Q-Ray provides hope. Even though it might be difficult to prove that the bracelet relieves pain, if people believe the product will reduce their pain that might become a self-fulfilling prophecy and the person's pain will be relieved. So, companies like Q-Ray should not be prohibited from advertising that their product has pain-relieving qualities."* Do you agree or disagree with this statement? Defend your answer.

4. Which of the 4 Ps is most important in the marketing of the Q-Ray bracelet? Explain your reasoning.

Shall We Dance?

Baby boomers (people born between 1947 and 1966) now make up one-third of Canada's population, and they control 55 percent of the disposable income in Canada. The needs and wants of this demographic group have created many new business opportunities in the health, leisure, and security industries. Many entrepreneurs are now chasing "boomer bucks."

Consider Beverly and Robert Tang, who are former North American dance champions. They want to capitalize on boomers' love of dancing. Their timing is good, since television has boosted interest in ballroom dancing with immensely popular shows like *Dancing with the Stars*. The Tangs want to cash in on the dance craze by targeting baby boomers (mostly women), because boomers have the money to spend on dancing lessons. And they want their company—Dancescape—to be a world-class dance lifestyle company that is the basis for a global dance brand.

It's Thursday night at a Ukrainian church hall, and baby boomers are dancing under the instruction of the Tangs. The Tangs spend a lot of time giving instruction, but they have also invested $20 000 to make a learn-to-dance video. It's already selling in the U.S. and they're working on Canadian and U.K. distribution. A key element of their plan is three websites where dancers can shop, socialize, and download dance videos. The Tangs hope their website will be the new "Facebook for dancers." But to build their brand and build their business, they need $1.4 million. They manage to get an audience with Tim Draper, a venture capitalist who has made millions on the internet. He likes karaoke, and he invested in Hotmail, so they know he's open to new ideas. To prepare for their meeting with him, they hire a brand coach to help them prepare their sales pitch. Unfortunately, after working with them, the coach thinks the Tangs aren't ready to meet with Draper. The coach thinks they are spending so much time running the business that they don't have time to refine and polish their sales pitch.

On pitch day, Tim Draper gets an impromptu lesson from Beverly and also listens to Robert's sales pitch. The sales pitch gets off to a rocky start when Robert calls Tim "Steve" on two occasions. That is very embarrassing. Draper listens carefully to Robert's sales pitch, but makes no commitment. But he doesn't give them a flat "no" either. The Tangs are still hopeful Draper may come through.

Marketplace talks with two experts about the prospects of success for Dancescape. Lina Ko works for National Public Relations, a company that does surveys with boomers. She also has a blog that provides insights into Canadian consumers' needs and wants. The other expert is Robert Herjavec, who owns a computer company. He says it's good that the Tangs are doing something they love, because "you should love what you do and you'll never work a day in your life." But, he observes, that doesn't automatically mean that you'll have a viable business doing what you love. He notes that the Tangs are promoting dancing to the boomer generation, but they are trying to do it using the technology of the younger generations. He is not convinced that boomers are technologically savvy enough for this to work. He also has concerns because he wants to see young people dancing, not boomer-age people. He thinks the Tangs need a viral marketing idea that will have broad appeal. Selling their videos through niche stores limits their market and is inconsistent with their goal of being a global brand.

Ko disagrees with Herjavec, and says that the perception that boomers are not technically savvy is incorrect. She also notes that the dancing concept is good because boomers are interested in exercising and dancing is good exercise. Dancing also makes people feel younger than they really are. The targeting of women is also a good idea because women have a big influence on family purchase decisions. But Ko thinks that the Tangs should revamp their language. Boomers don't want to hear the word "retirement." Rather they want to reinvent themselves. Ko says too that the Tangs need to further segment the boomer market because boomers in their forties are quite different from boomers in their sixties.

Video resource: "Boomer Bonanza," *Fortune Hunters* (March 8, 2008).

Questions for Discussion

1. What is the difference between goods, services, and ideas? Are the Tangs marketing a good, a service, or an idea? Explain your reasoning.

2. Which of the 4 Ps of marketing do you think is most important in the case of dancing lessons? Explain your reasoning.

3. Which variables do marketers generally use to identify market segments? Which variables are being used by the Tangs? Be specific.

Managing Financial Issues

Management of the financial transactions of a business firm is absolutely critical to the firm's survival. Whether it involves raising money to start a new firm, accurately assessing the riskiness of the firm's investments, or monitoring the firm's activities in securities markets, financial management is a key business activity.

Part Summary

Part 5, Managing Financial Issues, provides an overview of the importance of money and banking in the modern business environment, how firms raise and manage money, how they define and manage risk, and how they use Canadian securities markets to meet their financial needs.

- In **Chapter 15, Money, Banking, and Securities Markets,** we explore the nature of money, its creation through the banking system, and the role of the Bank of Canada in the nation's financial system. We also look at the securities markets in which Canadian firms raise long-term funds, how these markets operate, and how they are regulated.

- In **Chapter 16, Financial Decisions and Risk Management,** we look at the reasons businesses need funds and how financial managers raise both long- and short-term funds. We also examine the kinds of risks businesses encounter and the ways in which they deal with these risks.

chapter

15

Money, Banking, and Securities Markets

After reading this chapter, you should be able to:

LO-1 Define *money* and identify the different forms it takes in Canada's money supply.

LO-2 Understand the different kinds of *financial institutions* that make up the Canadian financial system and explain the services they offer.

LO-3 Explain the functions of the *Bank of Canada* and describe the tools it uses to control the money supply.

LO-4 Discuss the value of *common stock* and *preferred stock* to stockholders and describe the secondary market for each type of security.

LO-5 Describe the investment opportunities offered by *bonds*, *mutual funds*, and *commodities*.

LO-6 Explain the process by which securities are bought and sold.

SCANLIFE

Money, Money, Money

Money has been important in business (and family) transactions for thousands of years. Various objects have served as money, including pig tusks (New Guinea), whale teeth (Fiji Islands), large stones (Islands of Yap in the western Pacific Ocean), cows (Ireland), and cowrie shells (China). Objects that have been used as money typically have one (or more) of the following characteristics: they are rare (e.g., gold or silver), hard to get (e.g., whale teeth), or have some intrinsic beauty that makes them desirable (e.g., feathers from a beautiful bird).

Some items that we would consider odd are still used for money. For example, the teeth of spinner dolphins are used as money in the Solomon Islands of the South Pacific. One dolphin tooth is equal to about two Solomon Islands dollars (a dollar was worth about US$0.13 in 2010). The governor of the Central Bank of the Solomon Islands says people keep dolphin teeth as a "store of wealth" in much the same way that people in most countries put money in the bank. A pig costs about 50 dolphin teeth, while just a handful of dolphin teeth are needed to buy some yams and cassava. Counterfeiting is an issue in the Solomon Islands just as it is in industrialized societies (counterfeiters try to pass off the teeth of fruit bats as the real thing).

The demand for dolphin teeth as currency is driven by a couple of unique aspects of Solomon Island society. First, tribal disputes that result in the loss of property or human life are often settled by paying compensation, in teeth, rather than in dollars. Second, teeth are the currency of choice when young men choose a bride (a bride costs at least 1000 teeth). Each dolphin yields only about 20 teeth, so many dolphins need to be killed each year to balance supply and demand. Henry Suku-fatu is a dolphin hunter who sells about 1000 teeth a month. He says he can't keep up with demand, which is why the exchange value of teeth is rising.

In most societies today, metal coins and paper money predominate. But have you ever wondered how a country decides what denominations of

How Will This Help Me?

By understanding the material in this chapter, you will benefit in two ways: (1) as a *consumer*, you'll learn what money is, where it comes from, how the supply of money grows, and the kinds of services that are available to you from the financial services industry; (2) as an *investor*, you'll be better prepared to evaluate investment opportunities that will improve your personal financial situation.

coins and paper money it should have? One model—called D-metric—uses the average day's net pay to make suggestions about the denomination structure of a country's currency. For example, if the average day's pay in a country is $100, the D-metric model recommends that the lowest denomination should be the nickel, and that a $500 bill should be introduced. The model also recommends introducing a $5 coin when the average day's net pay reaches $150. Another model looks at other factors, including cultural preferences, the impact of other methods of paying for things (credit and debit cards), and the average size of exchange transactions. It provides similar recommendations.

A Bank of Canada study back in 2005 suggested that Canada should drop the penny because it is more trouble than it is worth, and it is costing Canadian society about $130 million each year. New Zealand stopped making the penny in 1987 and Australia in 1990. France, Norway, and Britain have also eliminated low-denomination coins. But in Canada, there is still a lot of demand for pennies. The production of pennies has actually increased in recent years because people are not recirculating them. In 2009 alone, the Royal Canadian Mint produced 948 million pennies. In 2008, a report from the Desjardin Group proposed eliminating the nickel, replacing the $5 bill with a coin, adding a 20-cent piece, making the 50-cent piece smaller, and introducing a $200 bill.

The United States is also dealing with the question of denominations for their currency. Many people wonder why the United States is still using a $1 bill and note that it is out of step with many other industrialized countries. For example, the smallest bill used in the 15 countries in the euro zone is the five-euro note (worth US$6.18 in 2010). In Britain, the smallest bill is the five-pound note (worth US$7.27 in 2010), and in Japan, it's the 1000-yen note (worth about US$11.28 in 2010). It is estimated that if the United States switched to a $1 coin like Canada has done, it would save taxpayers there about $522 million a year in production expenses. Each dollar bill costs about 4 cents to produce, and it has a life span of only about 21 months. In contrast, a coin costs more to produce (about 20 cents), but lasts 30 years or more.

The use of coins and paper money dominate in modern society. But the barter system—exchanging goods and services instead of paying money for them—is still evident. For example, a painter might agree to paint a plumber's house if the plumber will fix the painter's leaky pipes. Barter was common in ancient societies, and it is making something of a comeback. In the 1990s, when Russia was trying to move away from a command economy and toward a market-based economy, barter accounted for more than half of the business transactions. When the recession began in 2008, barter exchanges reported a big jump in the number of transactions that were taking place. Barter became more important even in North America because during an economic downturn participants want to conserve cash.

High-tech barter organizations like International Monetary Systems and U-Exchange.com make it possible for people from around the world to get involved in the barter economy. For example, Rich Rowley of Tacoma, Washington, offered to provide new home construction, remodelling, home repairs, home maintenance, and commercial improvements in return for things like tickets to sporting events, vacations, land, medical and dental care, a boat, and a motor home. Participants can build up credits that they can use for future transactions. The trade publication Barternew.com estimates that in the United States, bartering is worth more than $3 billion annually.

LO-1 What Is Money?

When someone asks you how much money you have, what do you say? Do you count the bills and coins in your pockets? Do you mention the funds in your chequing and savings accounts? What about stocks, or bonds, or your car? Taken together, the value of everything you own is your personal *wealth*. Not all of it, however, is *money*.

The Characteristics of Money

As we saw in the opening case, many different objects have been used as money in different societies. Modern money usually takes the form of stamped metal or printed paper—Canadian dollars, British pounds—that is issued by governments. The Chinese were using metal money to represent the objects they were exchanging as early as 1100 BCE. Coins probably came into use in China sometime around 600 BCE and paper money around 1200 CE. Just about any object can serve as **money** if it is portable, divisible, durable, and stable. To understand why these qualities are important, imagine using something that lacks these features (e.g., a 35-kilogram salmon).

■ *Portability.* If you wanted to use the salmon to buy goods and services, you would have to carry a

35-kilogram fish from shop to shop. Modern currency, in contrast, is lightweight and easy to handle.

- *Divisibility.* Suppose you wanted to buy a hat, a book, and some milk from three different stores using salmon as money. How would you divide the fish? First, out comes a cleaver at each store. Then, you would have to determine whether a kilogram of its head is worth as much as a kilogram from its middle. Modern currency is easily divisible into smaller parts with fixed values for each unit. In Canada, a dollar can be exchanged for 4 quarters, 10 dimes, 20 nickels, 100 pennies, or any combination of these coins.

- *Durability.* Fish seriously fail the durability test. Each day, whether or not you "spend" it, the salmon will be losing value (and gaining scents). Modern currency does not spoil, it does not die, and, if it wears out, it can be replaced with new coins and paper money.

- *Stability.* If salmon were in short supply, you might be able to make quite a deal for yourself. But in the middle of a salmon run, the market would be flooded with fish. Since sellers would have many opportunities to exchange their wares for salmon, they would soon have enough fish and refuse to trade for salmon. While the value of the paper money we use today has fluctuated over the years, it is considerably more stable.

The Functions of Money

What if a successful fisherman needs a new sail for his boat? In a *barter economy*—where goods are exchanged directly for one another—he would have to find someone who not only needs fish but who is willing to exchange a sail for it. If no sail maker wants fish, the fisherman must find someone else—say, a shoemaker—who wants fish and will trade for it. Then the fisherman must hope that the sail maker will trade for his new shoes. Contrast this with a money economy, where the fisherman would sell his catch, receive money, and exchange it for goods like a new sail. Thus, the barter economy is relatively inefficient. This example demonstrates the three functions of money:

- *Medium of exchange.* Like the fisherman "trading" money for a new sail, we use money as a way of buying and selling things. Without money, we would be stuck in a barter system.

- *Store of value.* Pity the fisherman who catches a fish on Monday and wants to buy a few bars of candy on, say, the following Saturday. By then, the fish would have spoiled and be of no value. In the form of currency, however, money can be used for future purchases and so "stores" value.

- *Unit of account.* Finally, money lets us measure the relative values of goods and services. It acts as a unit of account because all products can be valued and accounted for in terms of money. For example, the concepts of "$1000 worth of clothes" or "$500 in labour costs" have universal meaning because everyone deals with money every day.

The Spendable Money Supply: M-1

For money to serve as a medium of exchange, a store of value, or a unit of account, buyers and sellers must agree on its value. The value of money, in turn, depends in part on its supply (how much money is in circulation). When the money supply is high, the value of money drops. When the money supply is low, the value of money increases.

It is not easy to measure the supply of money, nor is there complete agreement on exactly how it should be measured. The "narrow" definition of the money supply is called **M-1**, which includes only the most liquid forms of money: currency and demand deposits (chequing accounts) in banks. As of April 2010, M-1 totalled $539.4 billion in Canada.[1]

Currency is paper money and coins issued by the Canadian government. It is widely used to pay small bills. Canadian currency—which clearly states "This note is legal tender"—is money the law requires a creditor to accept in payment of a debt. Counterfeiting of paper currency is now a worldwide problem, partly because new technologies like scanners and colour copiers allow counterfeiters to make real-looking bills rather easily. In 2009, there were over 1.48 billion Bank of Canada notes in circulation; over 67 000 counterfeit bills were detected.[2] A survey conducted by SES Canada Research Inc. found

MONEY Any object generally accepted by people as payment for goods and services.

M-1 Only the most liquid forms of money (currency and demand deposits).

CURRENCY Paper money and coins issued by the government.

This 100-kilogram gold coin—produced by the Royal Canadian Mint—is the largest gold coin ever produced. It is 99.99 percent pure gold and sells for $3 million.

CHEQUE An order instructing the bank to pay a given sum to a specified person or firm.

DEMAND DEPOSITS Money in chequing accounts; counted as M-1 because such funds may be withdrawn at any time without notice.

M-2 Everything in M-1 plus savings deposits, time deposits, and money market mutual funds.

TIME DEPOSIT A deposit that requires prior notice to make a withdrawal; cannot be transferred to others by cheque.

MONEY MARKET MUTUAL FUNDS Funds operated by investment companies that bring together pools of assets from many investors to buy short-term, low-risk financial securities.

that 18 percent of Canadians have received a counterfeit bill, and 39 percent felt that it was likely that they would receive a counterfeit bill at some point.[3] In an attempt to reduce counterfeiting, the Bank of Canada has issued new $20 and $5 bills with more sophisticated security features.[4]

A **cheque** is an order instructing the bank to pay a given sum to a specified person or firm. Cheques enable buyers to make large purchases without having to carry large amounts of cash. Money in chequing accounts, known as **demand deposits**, is counted in M-1 because such funds may be withdrawn at any time without notice.

M-1 Plus the Convertible Money Supply: M-2

M-2 includes everything in M-1 plus items that cannot be spent directly but that are easily converted to spendable forms: *time deposits*, *money market mutual funds*, and *savings deposits*. M-2 accounts for nearly all the nation's money supply. As this overall supply of money increases, more is available for consumer purchases and business investment. When this supply decreases, less is available for consumer purchases and business investment. As of April 2010, M-2 totalled $967.5 billion in Canada.[5]

Unlike demand deposits, **time deposits** require prior notice of withdrawal and cannot be transferred by cheque. The supply of money in time deposits (e.g., *certificates of deposit [CDs]*) grew rapidly in the 1970s and 1980s as interest rates rose to 15 percent. But when interest rates dropped in the late 1990s, consumers began putting more of their money into mutual funds.

Money market mutual funds are operated by investment companies that bring together pools of assets from many investors. The fund buys a collection of short-term, low-risk financial securities. Ownership of and profits (or losses) from the sale of these securities are shared among the fund's investors. These funds attracted many investors in the 1980s and 1990s because of high payoffs. But the sharp decline in the stock market in 2001–2002 and again in 2008, and more importantly the environment of low interest rates, meant reduced consumer interest in money market mutual funds.

Credit Cards: Plastic Money?

Although not included in M-1 or M-2, credit—especially credit cards—has become a major factor in the purchase of consumer goods in Canada. The use of MasterCard, Visa, American Express, and credit cards issued by individual businesses has become so widespread that many people refer to credit cards as "plastic money." In 2008, Canadians spent $267 billion using credit cards.[6] Credit cards are actually a *money substitute*; they serve as a temporary medium of exchange but are not a store of value. With the recent financial crisis as an incentive, the Canadian government is planning to adopt a new code of conduct to further regulate credit and debit cards.[7]

In 2009, Canadians held 72 million credit cards.[8] Visa is the world's biggest credit card company with 56.7 billion transactions registered in 2009, more than MasterCard and American Express combined.[9] Worldwide, the total value of goods purchased with Visa cards is above $3 trillion annually.[10]

Credit cards are big business for two reasons. First, they are quite convenient for consumers. Second, credit cards are extremely profitable for issuing companies because of fees they collect. Some cards charge annual fees to holders, and all of them charge interest on unpaid balances. Depending on the issuer, cardholders pay interest rates ranging from 11 to 20 percent. Merchants who accept credit cards also pay fees to card issuers.

Banks like the Bank of Montreal, the Canadian Imperial Bank of Commerce, the Bank of Nova Scotia, and TD Canada Trust are the biggest issuers of Visa cards in Canada. Each time a card is used, the banks receive an "interchange" fee, which is a percentage of the purchase value of the transaction. The banks use these fees to offset costs they incur with loyalty and points programs. There is an ongoing battle for market share among Canada's major banks as they issue credit cards, so banks are continually offering more perks. However, as the perks improve for consumers, banks pass on their costs to retailers in the form of higher interchange fees. For example, the fees paid by the owner of the Bloor Street Diner in Toronto on Visa transactions increased from 1.51 percent to 1.86 percent, including interchange fees (the annual payout of credit card fees is about $120 000). The owner feels that he simply has to take Visa credit cards or he will lose business.[11] Credit card companies collected $4.5 billion in fees in 2008.[12]

Credit card fraud is an increasing concern for both consumers and retailers. The Interac Association estimated that credit and debit card fraud cost financial institutions over $100 million in 2007.[13] Sometimes criminals pay retail workers to steal information from customers' credit cards. Then that information is used to purchase thousands of dollars' worth of goods over the internet or through mail-order

The hub of operations at Amazon.com is this 840 000 square-foot warehouse, where workers can ship as many as 11 000 boxes an hour. The key to the efficiency of the facility is technology—all orders are processed electronically. The most important technology of all may be the credit card. If you had nothing but cash, you'd find it hard to shop on the internet, and internet retailers who depend on credit card transactions (like Amazon, Dell, and eBay) couldn't exist in a cash-only world.

houses. By the time the credit card holder gets his or her next bill, the thieves are long gone. Another approach is to use a card reader. When a credit card is swiped through the reader, key information about the cardholder is produced. Then a counterfeit card is made and used.[14]

To deal with these problems, credit card companies have developed a new encryption technology. In 2008, holders of CIBC Visa, Royal Bank Visa, and BMO MasterCard began receiving new high-tech, crime-deterring credit cards with a computer chip embedded in them. Two million of the new cards were sent to customers, and millions more will be sent out in the next couple of years. Royal Bank said its customers will receive the new chip cards when their old ones expire. With the new system, consumers won't swipe their cards as they used to. Rather, they will insert the credit card in a reader, then punch in a personal identification number (PIN) just as they do with their debit card. Once it is approved, they will remove the card from the reader. There is no signature required. A pilot project in Kitchener–Waterloo, Ontario, involved the use of more than 170 000 chip cards and 3500 reading devices at various retailers. There was an 80 percent decrease in fraudulent activity in areas where the new cards were being used.[15] More detail about credit cards is provided in Appendix C.

LO-2 The Canadian Financial System

Many forms of money, especially demand deposits and time deposits, depend on the existence of financial institutions to provide a broad spectrum of services to both individuals and businesses. In this section, we describe the major types of financial institutions, explain how they work, and describe some of the special services they offer. We also explain their role as creators of money and discuss the regulation of the Canadian banking system.

CHARTERED BANK
A privately owned, profit-seeking firm that serves individuals, non-business organizations, and businesses as a financial intermediary.

Financial Institutions

There are several types of financial institutions in Canada, but the main function of all of them is to facilitate the flow of money from sectors with surpluses to those with deficits by attracting funds into chequing and savings accounts. Incoming funds are loaned to individuals and businesses and perhaps invested in government securities.

For many years, the financial community in Canada was divided rather clearly into four distinct legal areas. These "four financial pillars" are (1) chartered banks, (2) alternate banks (i.e., trust companies and credit unions/*caisses populaires*), (3) life insurance companies and other specialized lending and saving intermediaries (i.e., factors, finance companies, venture capital firms, mutual funds, and pension funds), and (4) investment dealers. We will discuss each of these financial institutions in detail later in this chapter, but it is important to understand that many changes have taken place in the financial services industry in the last couple of decades; the differences across the four divisions has been blurred.

Changes Affecting Financial Institutions

The crumbling of the four financial pillars began in 1980 when changes were made to the Bank Act. In the years since then, many other changes have been made. For example, banks are now permitted to own securities dealers, to establish subsidiaries to sell mutual funds, and to sell commercial paper (see Chapter 16). Trust companies have declined in importance, and many trust companies have been bought by banks or insurance companies. The largest trust company—Canada Trust—merged with the Toronto-Dominion Bank and is now called TD Canada Trust.

Financial Pillar #1— Chartered Banks

A **chartered bank** is a privately owned, profit-seeking financial intermediary that serves individuals, businesses, and non-business organizations. Chartered banks are

TRUST SERVICES
The management of funds left in the bank's trust.

LETTER OF CREDIT
A promise by a bank to pay money to a business firm if certain conditions are met.

BANKER'S ACCEPTANCE
A promise that a bank will pay a specified amount of money at a future date.

ELECTRONIC FUNDS TRANSFER (EFT)
A combination of computer and communications technology that transfers funds or information into, from, within, and among financial institutions.

AUTOMATED BANKING MACHINES (ABMS)
Electronic machine that allows bank customers to conduct account-related activities 24 hours a day, 7 days a week.

the largest and most important financial institution in Canada. In March 2010, Canadian chartered banks had assets totalling $1.98 trillion.[16] Chartered banks offer chequing and savings accounts, make loans, and provide many services to their customers. They are the main source of short-term loans for business firms.

Unlike the United States, where there are hundreds of banks, each with a few branches, in Canada there are only a few banks, each with hundreds of branches. The five largest Canadian banks account for about 90 percent of total bank assets. *Schedule I* banks are those that are Canadian-owned and have no more than 10 percent of voting shares controlled by a single interest. *Schedule II* banks are those that may be domestically owned but do not meet the 10 percent limit, or may be foreign-controlled. Several foreign banks have set up Schedule II subsidiaries in Canada. The Act limits foreign-controlled banks to deposits that do not exceed 8 percent of the total domestic assets of all banks in Canada.

Services Offered by Banks

The banking business is highly competitive; therefore, banks no longer just accept deposits and make loans. Most banks now offer pension services, trust services, international services, financial advice, and electronic money transfer.

Pension Services Most banks help customers establish savings plans for retirement. Banks serve as financial intermediaries by receiving funds and investing them as directed by customers. They also provide customers with information on investment possibilities.

Trust Services Many banks offer **trust services**—the management of funds left "in the bank's trust." In return for a fee, the trust department will perform such tasks as making your monthly bill payments and managing your investment portfolio. Trust departments also manage the estates of deceased persons.

International Services The three main international services offered by banks are *currency exchange*, *letters of credit*, and *banker's acceptances*. Suppose that a Canadian company wants to buy a product from a French supplier. For a fee, it can use one or more of three services offered by its bank:

1 It can exchange Canadian dollars for euros at a Canadian bank and then pay the French supplier in euros.

2 It can pay its bank to issue a **letter of credit**—a promise by the bank to pay the French firm a certain amount if specified conditions are met.

3 It can pay its bank to draw up a **banker's acceptance**, which promises that the bank will pay some specified amount at a future date.

Financial Advice Many banks, both large and small, help their customers manage their money. Depending on the customer's situation, the bank may recommend different investment opportunities. The recommended mix might include guaranteed investment certificates, mutual funds, stocks, and bonds. Today, bank advertisements often stress the role of banks as financial advisers.

Electronic Funds Transfer **Electronic funds transfer (EFT)** combines computer and communication technology to transfer funds or information into, from, within, and among financial institutions. In addition to internet banking, examples include *automated banking machines*, *pay-by-phone*, *direct deposits and withdrawals*, *point-of-sale transfers*, and *smart cards*.

Automated Banking Machines (ABMs) ABMs (also called automated teller machines—ATMs) let you bank at almost any time of day or night. There are over 17 000 ABM machines in Canada and many of them are located inside the more than 6000 Canadian bank branches. However, there are plenty of independent "white label" machines that usually charge higher fees. In 2010, First-Ontario Credit Union launched a new version it called the Personal Assistant Teller (PAT). This system provides a video link with a teller who can talk to the consumer about loans or listen to complaints in addition to offering the traditional ABM transactions.[17]

Pay-by-Phone These systems let you telephone your financial institution and pay certain bills or transfer funds between accounts.

Direct Deposits and Withdrawals This system allows you to authorize in advance specific, regular deposits and withdrawals. You can arrange to have paycheques and social assistance cheques automatically deposited and recurring expenses, such as insurance premiums and utility bills, automatically paid.

Point-of-Sale Transfers These let you pay for retail purchases with your **debit card**, a type of plastic money that immediately reduces the balance in the user's bank account when used. There are more than four billion debit card transactions each year. There were more than 21 million active debit cards in Canada in 2009 and approximately 1 percent of these cards were affected by fraud.[18] Debit cards are convenient but should be used with basic caution.

Smart Cards **Smart cards** (e.g., phone cards)—also known as "electronic purses" or "stored-value cards"—can be programmed with "electronic money" at ATM machines or with special telephone hookups. After using your card to purchase an item, you can then check an electronic display to see how much money is left. European and Asian consumers are the most avid users. In North America, smart cards are most popular in gas pump payments, followed by prepaid phone service, ATMs, self-operated checkouts, and automated banking services.[19] Analysts predict that in the near future smart cards will function as much more than electronic purses.

E-Cash Electronic money, known as **e-cash**, is the money that moves along multiple channels of consumers and businesses via digital electronic transmissions. The money flows from the buyer to the seller's e-cash funds, which are instantaneously updated and stored on a microchip. Although e-cash transactions are cheaper than handling cheques, there are potential problems in the form of hackers and system crashes.

Figure 15.1 summarizes the services that chartered banks offer. Banks are chartered by the federal government and are closely regulated when they provide these services.

Bank Loans

Banks are the major source of short-term loans for business. Although banks make long-term loans to some firms, they prefer to specialize in providing short-term funds to finance inventories and accounts receivable. A *secured* loan is backed by collateral (e.g., accounts receivable). If the borrower cannot repay the loan, the bank sells the collateral. An *unsecured* loan is backed only by the borrower's promise to repay it. Only the most credit-worthy borrowers can get unsecured loans.

Borrowers pay interest on their loans. Large firms with excellent credit records pay the **prime rate of interest**, which is the lowest rate charged to borrowers. This rate changes often because of changes in the demand and supply of loanable funds, as well as Bank of Canada policies. The so-called "Big Six" Canadian banks (Royal Bank, CIBC, Bank of Montreal, Bank of Nova Scotia, TD Canada Trust, and National Bank of Canada) typically act in concert with respect to the prime rate.

Banks as Creators of Money

Financial institutions provide a special service to the economy—they create money. They don't mint bills and coins, but by taking in deposits and making loans, they *expand the money supply*. We will first look at how this expansion process works, assuming that banks have a **reserve requirement**, that they must keep a portion of their chequable deposits in vault cash or as deposits with the Bank of Canada. (The reserve requirement was dropped in 1991 and the implications of this change are described later.)

DEBIT CARD A type of plastic money that immediately on use reduces the balance in the user's bank account and transfers it to the store's account.

SMART CARDS A credit card-sized computer that can be programmed with "electronic money."

E-CASH Money that moves among consumers and businesses via digital electronic transmissions.

PRIME RATE OF INTEREST The lowest rate charged to borrowers.

RESERVE REQUIREMENT The requirement (until 1991) that banks keep a portion of their chequable deposits in vault cash or as deposits with the Bank of Canada.

Figure 15.1

Examples of services offered by many chartered banks and trust companies.

- Long- and short-term loans
- Automated teller machines
- Safeguard property entrusted to it
- Debit and credit cards
- Savings accounts
- Guaranteed investment certificates

- Chequing accounts
- Buy and sell securities for customer accounts
- Exchange Canadian dollars for foreign currencies
- Exchange foreign currencies for Canadian dollars
- Advise customers on financial matters

Devout Muslims can't pay or receive interest, a fact that complicates banking operations. Because money has to work to earn a return, institutions like the Shamil Bank in Bahrain invest deposits directly in such ventures as real estate and then pay back profit shares rather than interest. Buying a car is possible through a complex arrangement in which the bank takes temporary ownership and then sells the car to the individual at a profit. Mortgage arrangements are similar but even more complicated.

But what happens if there is no reserve requirement? At the extreme, it means that banks could (theoretically) create infinite amounts of money because they wouldn't have to keep any in reserve. But banks will not do this because it is risky. So, in practice, the dropping of the reserve requirement simply means that banks will be able to create more money than they did when there was a reserve requirement.

Other Changes in Banking

Substantial changes in addition to those already described are taking place in banking, including *deregulation*, *changes in customer demands*, and *changes in international banking*.

Deregulation Deregulation has allowed banks to alter their historical role as intermediaries between depositors and borrowers. Canada's banks are diversifying to provide more financial products to their clients. Training bankers to be effective in this environment is necessary. For example, over 100 executives at TD Canada Trust attended a Harvard University course that taught them to think like investment bankers. The Bank of Montreal conducted a similar course for over 400 executives. Deregulation has been a change for Canadian banks and in an interesting twist, the "Big Six" banks actually asked the government to get tougher with mortgage rules to cool off the housing market in early 2010 by raising the minimum down payment from 5 percent to 10 percent and reducing amortization maximum periods from 35 to 30 years.[20]

Changes in Consumer Demands Consumers are no longer content to keep money in a bank when they can get more elsewhere. They are turning to electronic banks like ING Direct and President's Choice Financial (a Loblaw subsidiary) that pay higher interest on savings accounts. Such companies can pay higher rates because they don't incur the costs associated with having branches like traditional banks do.

Traditional banks are responding to this new competition by selling a growing array of services in their branches. For example,

Suppose you saved $100, took it to a bank, and opened a chequing account. Let's assume for the moment that there is a reserve requirement, and that it is 10 percent. Your bank must therefore keep $10 of your $100 deposit in reserve, so it has only $90 to lend to other borrowers. Now suppose a person named Jennifer Leclerc borrows $90 from your bank. She now has $90 added to her chequing account. Assume that she writes a cheque for $90 payable to Canadian Tire. Canadian Tire's bank ends up with a $90 deposit, and that bank is also required to keep $9 in reserve. It therefore has $81 to lend out to someone else. This process of deposit expansion can continue as shown in Figure 15.2, and your original deposit of $100 could result in an increase of $1000 in new deposits for all banks in the system.

Figure 15.2
How the chartered banking system creates money.

Deposit	Money Held in Reserve by Bank	Money to Lend	Total Supply
$100.00	$10.00	$90.00	$190.00
90.00	9.00	81.00	271.00
81.00	8.10	72.90	343.90
72.90	7.29	65.61	409.51
65.61	6.56	59.05	468.56

the Bank of Montreal started providing bereavement services. If a customer's mother dies, BMO offers a service that takes care of everything from the funeral planning to redirecting the deceased person's mail.[21] Banks are finding new ways to attract and serve their clientele in order to remain competitive and attract a new generation that does not have the same loyalties as previous generations. Read the E-Business and Social Media Solutions boxed insert entitled "Online and Mobile Banking Solutions Straight to the Consumer."

Online and Mobile Banking Solutions Straight to the Consumer

In the past decade, the banking industry has embraced technology. Why? Each time Apple launches a device, or a new generation of an old device (e.g., iPhone or iPad), people line up. Overnight campouts were once reserved for major music concerts. But such images demonstrate a simple fact: consumers have a growing connection with technology. Here are some key statistics to back this up. In 2010:

- 70 percent of Canadians were using mobile devices
- 17 percent of Canadians were already using smart phones (with a 22 percent increase projected by year-end)
- 78 percent of Canadians were using online banking services

Only 10 percent of Canadian consumers were using mobile banking services in 2010, but that number is expected to grow quickly. Many experts predict that mobile banking will eventually surpass online banking. So how can banks take advantage of such trends?

In the U.S., some banks are enabling clients to email a photo of a cheque from their mobile devices, to be deposited, without an actual visit. Banks in Canada were not standing still. CIBC was the first Canadian bank to launch a mobile banking application for the iPhone platform. A few years back, RBC designed a peer-to-peer website for students, with a slogan to match: "Not your parents' banking site." RBC was also one of the first Canadian banks to create a Facebook group, called RBC Campus Connections. TD Canada Trust created an equivalent group called the Money Lounge, where students can win trips or discuss the merits of making their first RRSP investment. These relationships help students learn in a non-threatening manner. This sort of contact is important. According to an Ipsos Reid poll, 44 percent of Canadians have an account at the bank where they opened their first account. Opportunities to mine data are also a significant part of building such relationships.

The discount brokerage divisions are also trying to exploit opportunities. For example, BMO InvestorLine offers video demonstrations for clients. RBC Dominion Securities has created practice accounts where prospective investors can manage an imaginary $100 000 portfolio. Banks are also offering online seminars and webinars, as well as online tutorials. A simulation video game called Financial Football was released in New York to help students learn how to balance their chequebooks; the game uses the graphics and rules of professional football. It was sponsored by Visa but it is yet another possible tool for banks to engage consumers, drive traffic to their sites, and build brand loyalty. One thing is clear: banks are now fighting a whole new battle for your financial loyalty.

Critical Thinking Question

1. Have you used a banking smart phone application or visited a bank-sponsored social media group? How effective do you think these tools are for the consumer? For the banks?

Banks also want to get much more involved in selling insurance, but as of 2010, the Bank Act prohibited banks from selling insurance *in their branch offices* (they are allowed to sell insurance at other locations). Canadian banks are being "creative" in keeping insurance and banking activities separate (but not too separate). In Oakville, Ontario, Royal Bank of Canada consumers who enter the branch will notice the RBC bank on the right and RBC Insurance on the left. The two operations are separated by only a glass wall. Dan Danyluk, the CEO of the Insurance Brokers Association of Canada, says that RBC's strategy is ignoring the intent of the law. He argues that credit-granting institutions like banks should not be allowed to sell insurance in their branches because they may try to tie the buying of, say, car insurance to the approval of the loan to buy the car.[22] The government agrees and in 2010 it sent a message by banning banks from selling unauthorized insurance on their websites.[23]

All of this activity is transforming the profit base of banks. In the past, they made most of their money from the spread between interest rates paid to depositors and the rates charged on loans. Investment banking, on the other hand, is fee-based. Banks are making a larger proportion of their profits from fees, and this is blurring the traditional boundary between banks and securities firms.

Changes in International Banking Canada's banks are going to experience increased competition because foreign banks are now allowed to do business in Canada. Canadian banks are responding to this threat with a variety of tactics, including attempts to merge with one

another. But bank mergers have been blocked by the federal government because it feared the mergers would reduce competition and harm consumers. Despite the setback, banks are cooperating to spread their fixed costs. For example, Syncor Services is a joint venture between three of the "Big Six" banks that provides cheque-clearing services across Canada.[24]

LO-3 The Bank of Canada

The **Bank of Canada**, formed in 1935, is Canada's central bank. It has a crucial role in managing the Canadian economy and in regulating certain aspects of chartered bank operations. The Bank of Canada is managed by a board of governors composed of a governor, a deputy governor, and 12 directors appointed from different regions.

The rate at which chartered banks can borrow from the Bank of Canada is called the **bank rate**, or **rediscount rate**. It serves as the basis for establishing the chartered banks' prime interest rates. In practice, chartered banks seldom have to borrow from the Bank of Canada. However, the bank rate is an important instrument of monetary policy as a determinant of interest rates.

The Money Supply and the Bank of Canada The Bank of Canada plays an important role in managing the money supply in Canada (see Figure 15.3). If the Bank of Canada wants to *increase* the money supply, it can buy government securities. The people who sell these bonds then deposit the proceeds in their banks. These deposits increase banks' reserves and their willingness to make loans. The Bank of Canada can also lower the bank rate; this action will cause increased demand for loans from businesses and households because these customers borrow more money when interest rates drop.

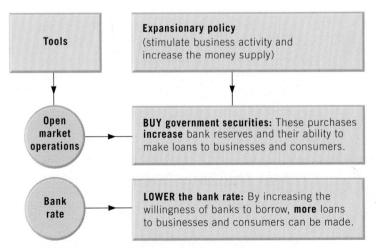
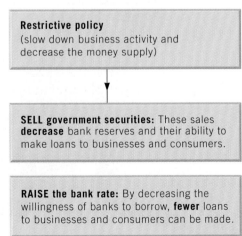

Figure 15.3
Bank of Canada monetary policy actions.

If the Bank of Canada wants to *decrease* the money supply, it can sell government securities. People spend money to buy bonds, and these withdrawals bring down banks' reserves and reduce their willingness to make loans. The Bank of Canada can also raise the bank rate; this action will cause decreased demand for loans from businesses and households because these customers borrow less money when interest rates rise.

Financial Pillar #2— Alternate Banks

Trust Companies

A **trust company** safeguards property—funds and estates—entrusted to it. It may also serve as trustee, transfer agent, and registrar for corporations and provide other services. For example, a corporation selling bonds to investors appoints a trustee, usually a trust company, to protect the bondholders' interests. A trust company can also serve as a transfer agent and registrar for corporations. A *transfer agent* records changes in ownership of a corporation's shares of stock, and a *registrar* certifies to the investing public that stock issues are correctly stated and comply with the corporate charter. Other services include preparing and issuing dividend cheques to stockholders and serving as trustee for employee profit-sharing funds. Trust companies also accept deposits and pay interest on them. As noted previously, trust companies have declined in importance during the last couple of decades.

Credit Unions/Caisses Populaires

Credit unions and *caisses populaires* are cooperative savings and lending associations formed by a group with common interests. They are important because they lend money to businesses and to consumers (who use the money to buy durable goods such as cars and furniture from businesses). Members (owners) can add to their savings accounts by authorizing deductions from their paycheques or by making direct deposits. They can borrow short-term, long-term, or mortgage funds from the credit union. Credit unions invest substantial amounts of money in corporate and government securities and sell certificates of deposits to the general public. According to a Moody's Investor Services report, credit unions are gaining popularity because they offer many services available at banks and they tend to pay dividends to their members when they make profits. In 2010, credit unions accounted for 16 percent of domestic deposits and 19 percent of mortgages.[25]

Financial Pillar #3—Specialized Lending and Savings Intermediaries

Life Insurance Companies

A **life insurance company** shares risk with its policyholders in return for payment of a premium by policyholders. It lends some of the money it collects from premiums to borrowers. Life insurance companies are substantial investors in real estate mortgages and in corporate and government bonds. Next to chartered banks, they are the largest financial intermediaries in Canada. We discuss insurance in Chapter 16.

Factoring Companies

An important source of short-term funds for many firms is factoring companies. A **factoring company** (or **factor**) buys accounts receivable (amounts due from credit customers) from a firm. It *pays* less than the face value of the accounts but *collects* the entire face value of the accounts. The difference, minus the cost of doing business, is the factor's profit. A firm that sells its accounts receivable to a factor shifts the risk of credit loss to the factor. If an account turns out to be uncollectible, the factor suffers the loss.

Financial Corporations

A **sales finance company** specializes in financing instalment purchases made by individuals and firms. When you buy durable goods from a retailer on an instalment plan with a sales finance company, the loan is made directly to you. The item itself serves as security for the loan. Sales finance companies enable firms to sell on credit, even though the firms could not afford to finance credit sales on their own. General Motors Acceptance Corporation (GMAC) is a sales finance company that finances instalment contracts resulting from sales made by General Motors. Industrial Acceptance Corporation is a large Canadian sales finance company.

A **consumer finance company** makes personal loans to consumers. Often, the borrower pledges no security (collateral) for the loan. For larger loans, collateral may be required. These companies do not make loans to businesses, but they do provide the financing that allows consumers to buy goods and services from businesses. Household Finance Corporation is an example of a consumer finance company.

Venture Capital Firms

A **venture capital firm** provides funds for new or expanding firms that seem to have significant potential. For example, Google announced in 2009 that it had started a venture capital fund to support "young companies with awesome potential."[26] Venture capital firms may demand an ownership stake of 50 percent or more before they will buy into a company. Because financing new, untested businesses is risky, venture capital firms also want to earn a higher-than-normal return on their investment. They may insist that they be given at least one seat on the board of directors to observe how their investment is faring. Venture capital firms look for companies with growth potential that could lead to substantial increases in stock value.

Venture capital firms obtain their funds from initial capital subscriptions, from loans from other financial intermediaries, and from retained earnings. The amount of venture capital that is raised varies according to economic conditions. In 2009, venture capital firms raised a total of $1.01 billion in Canada, but this continued a negative trend and represented the lowest levels in 14 years.[27] Canada's venture capital industry has been experiencing serious problems over the past few years. Many Canadian entrepreneurs have turned to U.S.-based venture capital companies for funding.[28] In the first quarter of 2010, the energy and environmental technology sector was one bright spot that was experiencing major growth in venture capital funding.[29]

Pension Funds

A **pension fund** accumulates money that will be paid out to plan subscribers at some time in the future. The money collected is invested in corporate stocks and bonds, government bonds, or mortgages until it is to be paid out.

Financial Pillar #4— Investment Dealers

Investment dealers (called stockbrokers or underwriters) are the primary distributors of new stock and bond issues (the underwriting function). They also facilitate secondary trading of stocks and bonds, both on stock exchanges and on over-the-counter stock and bond markets (the brokerage function). These functions are described in more detail later in this chapter.

Other Sources of Funds

Government Financial Institutions and Granting Agencies

In Canada, a number of government suppliers of funds are important to business. In general, they supply funds to new and/or growing companies. However, established firms can also use some of them.

The *Business Development Bank of Canada (BDC)* makes term loans, primarily to smaller firms judged to have growth potential but unable to secure funds at reasonable terms from traditional sources. It provides proportionally more equity financing and more management counselling services. A variety of provincial industrial development corporations also provide funds to developing business firms in the hope that they will provide jobs in the province. A number of federal and provincial programs are specifically designed to provide loans to agricultural operators. Most of these, with the exception of farm improvement loans that guarantee bank loans to farmers, are long-term loans for land purchase.

The federal government's *Export Development Corporation* finances and insures export sales for Canadian companies. The *Canada Mortgage and Housing Corporation (CMHC)* is involved in providing and guaranteeing mortgages. The CMHC is particularly important to the construction industry. Governments are also involved in providing grants to business operations.

International Sources of Funds

The Canadian capital market is just one part of the international capital market. Canadian provinces borrow extensively in foreign markets such as those in London and New York. Canadian corporations likewise find it attractive to borrow in foreign markets. Foreign sources of funds have been important in the economic development of Canada. Although many groups and individuals have expressed concern about foreign ownership of Canadian businesses, projections of Canada's future capital requirements indicate that we will continue to need these funds. Canadian financial institutions will continue to play a large role in making these funds available.

International Banking and Finance

Banks and other financial institutions play an important role in the international movement of money and in the value that is placed on the currency of various countries. Each nation tries to influence its currency exchange rates for economic advantage in international trade. The subsequent country-to-country transactions result in an *international payments* process that moves money between buyers and sellers on different continents.

Exchange Rates and International Trade

The value of a given currency such as the Canadian dollar reflects the overall supply and demand for Canadian dollars both at home and abroad. This value changes with economic conditions worldwide; therefore, firms watch for trends. In early 2010, the Canadian dollar fluctuated between US$0.92 and US$0.99, but at one point in 2007 it was valued at US$1.10. This was up sharply from its 2002 value of US$0.63.

The Law of One Price When a country's currency is overvalued, its exchange rate is higher than warranted by its economic conditions, and its high costs make it less competitive. In contrast, an undervalued currency means low costs and low prices. When a currency becomes overvalued, a nation's economic authorities may *devalue* the nation's currency. This causes a decrease in the country's exchange value, making it less expensive for other countries to buy the country's products. If a nation's currency is undervalued, the government can *revalue* the currency, which will make it more expensive for other countries to buy its products.

But how do we know whether a currency is overvalued or undervalued? One method involves a simple concept called the **law of one price**: the principle that identical products should sell for the same price in all countries. In other words, if the different prices of a Rolex watch in different countries were converted into a common currency, the common-denominator price should be the same everywhere.

A simple example that illustrates over- and undervalued currencies is the Big Mac Index, published annually in *The Economist*. The index lists a variety of countries and their Big Mac prices in terms of U.S. dollars. In March 2010, a Big Mac cost $3.58 in the United States. If a Big Mac in another country costs more than $3.58, the currency is overvalued; if it costs less than $3.58, the currency is undervalued. In 2010, the most overvalued currencies were Norway ($6.87), Switzerland ($6.16),

and the Eurozone ($4.62). Canada ranked fourth at ($4.06). The most undervalued currencies were China, Malaysia, and Thailand. These different values mean that, in theory, you could buy Big Macs in China and sell them in Norway at a profit. If you did that, the demand for burgers would increase in China, driving up the price to match the other countries. In other words, the law of one price would set it (see Table 15.1).[30]

> **LAW OF ONE PRICE**
> The principle that identical products should sell for the same price in all countries.

The International Payments Process

Transactions among buyers and sellers in different countries are simplified through the services provided by their banks. For example, payments from buyers flow through a local bank that converts them from the local currency into the foreign currency of the seller. Likewise, the local bank receives and converts incoming money from the banks of foreign buyers. This *international payments process* is shown in Figure 15.4.[31]

Step 1 A Canadian olive importer withdraws $1000 from its chequing account to buy olives from a Greek exporter. The local Canadian bank *converts* those dollars into euros at the current exchange rate (0.76704 euros per dollar).

Step 2 The Canadian bank sends the cheque for 767.04 euros (EUR 767.04 = 0.76704 multiplied by 1000) to the exporter in Greece.

Steps 3 and 4 The exporter sends olives to its Canadian customer and deposits the cheque in its local Greek bank. While the exporter now has euros that can be spent in Greece, the importer has olives to sell in Canada. At the same time, a separate transaction is being made between a Canadian machine exporter and a Greek olive oil producer. This time, the importer/exporter roles are reversed between the two countries: the Greek firm needs to *import* a $1000 olive oil press from Canada.

Steps 5 and 6 EUR 767.04 withdrawn from a local Greek bank account is converted into $1000 Canadian and sent via cheque to the Canadian exporter.

Steps 7 and 8 The olive oil press is sent to the Greek importer, and the importer's cheque is deposited in the Canadian exporter's local bank account.

The International Bank Structure

There is no worldwide banking system that is comparable, in terms of policymaking and regulatory power, to the system of any single industrialized nation. Rather, worldwide banking stability relies on a loose structure of agreements among individual countries or groups of countries. In addition, local standards and laws vary

Table 15.1 Big Mac Currency Index

Country	Big Mac Prices		Implied PPP* of the Dollar	Actual Dollar Exchange Rate Jan 31st	Under (–) / Over (+) Valuation Against the Dollar, %
	In Local Currency	In Dollars			
United States[†]	$3.22	3.22			
Argentina	Peso 8.25	2.65	2.56	3.11	–18
Australia	A$3.45	2.67	1.07	1.29	–17
Brazil	Real 6.4	3.01	1.99	2.13	–6
Britain	£1.99	3.90	1.62[‡]	1.96[‡]	+21
Canada	C$3.63	3.08	1.13	1.18	–4
Chile	Peso 1,670	3.07	519	544	–5
China	Yuan 11.0	1.41	3.42	7.77	–56
Colombia	Peso 6,900	3.06	2,143	2,254	–5
Costa Rica	Colones 1,130	2.18	351	519	–32
Czech Republic	Koruna 52.1	2.41	16.2	21.6	–25
Denmark	DKr27.75	4.84	8.62	5.74	+50
Egypt	Pound 9.09	1.60	2.82	5.70	–50
Estonia	Kroon 30	2.49	9.32	12.0	–23
Euro area[§]	€ 2.94	3.82	1.10**	1.30**	+19
Hong Kong	HK$12.0	1.54	3.73	7.81	–52
Hungary	Forint 590	3.00	183	197	–7
Iceland	Kronur509	7.44	158	68.4	+131
Indonesia	Rupiah 15,900	1.75	4,938	9,100	–46
Japan	¥280	2.31	87.0	121	–28
Latvia	Lats 1.35	2.52	0.42	0.54	–22
Lithuania	Litas 6.50	2.45	2.02	2.66	–24
Malaysia	Ringgit 5.50	1.57	1.71	3.50	–51
Mexico	Peso 29.0	2.66	9.01	10.9	–17
New Zealand	NZ$4.60	3.16	1.43	1.45	–2
Norway	Kroner 41.5	6.63	12.9	6.26	+106
Pakistan	Rupee 140	2.31	43.5	60.7	–28
Paraguay	Guarani 10,000	1.90	3,106	5,250	–41
Peru	New Sol 9.50	2.97	2.95	3.20	–8
Philippines	Peso 85.0	1.74	26.4	48.9	–46
Poland	Zloty 6.90	2.29	2.14	3.01	–29
Russia	Rouble 49.0	1.85	15.2	26.5	–43
Saudi Arabia	Riyal 9.00	2.40	2.80	3.75	–25
Singapore	S$3.60	2.34	1.12	1.54	–27
Slovakia	Crown 57.98	2.13	18.0	27.2	–34
South Africa	Rand 15.5	2.14	4.81	7.25	–34
South Korea	Won 2,900	3.08	901	942	–4
Sri Lanka	Rupee 190	1.75	59.0	109	–46
Sweden	SKr32.0	4.59	9.94	6.97	+43
Switzerland	SFr6.30	5.05	1.96	1.25	+57
Taiwan	NT$75.0	2.28	23.3	32.9	–29
Thailand	Baht 62.0	1.78	19.3	34.7	–45
Turkey	Lire 4.55	3.22	1.41	1.41	nil
UAE	Dirhams 10.0	2.72	3.11	3.67	–15
Ukraine	Hryvnia 9.00	1.71	2.80	5.27	–47
Uruguay	Peso 55.0	2.17	17.1	25.3	–33
Venezuela	Bolivar 6,800	1.58	2,112	4,307	–51

Sources: McDonald's; *The Economist*

*Purchasing-power parity: local price divided by price in United States. [†]Average of New York, Atlanta, Chicago, and San Francisco; [‡]Dollars per pound; [§]Weighted average of prices in euro area; **Dollars per euro.

Figure 15.4
The international payments process.

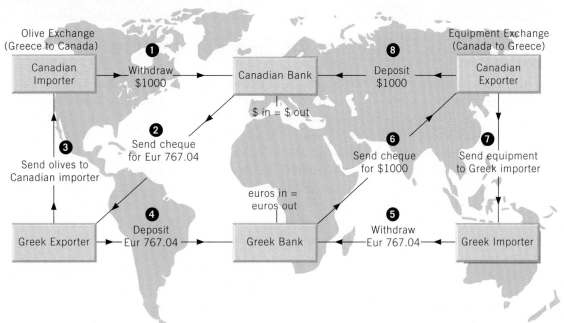

greatly. Read the Managing in Turbulent Times boxed insert entitled "Canadian vs. U.S. Banks."

The World Bank and the IMF Two United Nations agencies, the World Bank and the International Monetary Fund, help to finance international trade. Unlike true banks, the **World Bank** actually provides only a very limited scope of services. For instance, it funds national improvements by making loans to build roads, schools, power plants, and hospitals. The resulting improvements eventually enable borrowing countries to increase productive capacity and international trade.

The **International Monetary Fund (IMF)** is a group of some 186 nations that have combined their resources for the following purposes:

- to promote the stability of exchange rates
- to provide temporary, short-term loans to member countries
- to encourage members to cooperate on international monetary issues
- to encourage development of a system for international payments

Securities Markets

So far in this chapter we have talked about the importance of money, the various organizations in the Canadian financial system, and international finance. We now turn our attention to securities markets, where the role of money is very obvious. Stocks and bonds are both known as **securities** because they represent a secured (asset-based) claim on the part of investors. Collectively, the market in which stocks and bonds are sold is called the *securities market*.

Primary and Secondary Markets for Securities

Primary securities markets handle the buying and selling of new stocks and bonds by firms or governments. When new securities are sold to one buyer or a small group of buyers, these *private placements* allow the businesses that use them to keep their plans confidential.

Investment Banking Most new stocks and some bonds are sold to the public market. To bring a new security to market, the issuing corporation must obtain approval from a provincial securities commission. It also needs the services of an investment banker. **Investment bankers** serve as financial specialists in issuing new securities. Well-known institutions like RBC Dominion Securities and TD Securities provide the following services:

WORLD BANK
A United Nations agency that provides a limited scope of financial services, such as funding national improvements in undeveloped countries.

INTERNATIONAL MONETARY FUND (IMF) United Nations agency consisting of about 186 nations that have combined resources to promote stable exchange rates, provide temporary short-term loans, and serve other purposes.

SECURITIES Stocks, bonds, and mutual funds representing secured, or asset-based, claims by investors against issuers.

PRIMARY SECURITIES MARKET Market in which new stocks and bonds are bought and sold

INVESTMENT BANKERS Financial specialists in issuing new securities.

Canadian vs. U.S. Banks: Quite a Difference

As the worldwide recession deepened in 2009, increasing concern was expressed that many U.S. banks were in financial trouble. That news was in sharp contrast to the situation in Canada, where the top five Canadian banks earned $18.9 billion in profits. Meanwhile, the top five U.S. banks lost $37 billion. A 2009 World Economic forum report ranked the Canadian banking system as the soundest in the world. (The U.S. ranked fortieth.)

There are three major reasons for the differences in performance between U.S. and Canadian banks. First, Canadian banks are more strictly regulated than U.S. banks. For example, Canadian banks must maintain a bigger cushion to absorb potential losses, and their shares must be widely held. The Office of the Superintendent of Financial Institutions, Canada's banking regulator, gets credit for being very conservative and keeping a close watch on the activities of Canadian banks. There is a bit of irony here, because the characteristics of the Canadian banking system, which have worked well in the recent financial crisis, are the same characteristics that Canadian consumers have complained about for years.

Second, the U.S. and Canadian banking industries are structured differently. In the U.S., there are thousands of banks, and most of them have just one (or a few) branches. In contrast, in Canada there are very few banks, but each one has hundreds of branches. The large number of banks in the U.S. made it difficult to determine how big the problems were when the recession hit in 2008. By the time it became clear that

there were major problems, drastic action was needed to fix them. Multibillion-dollar bailouts were provided for financial institutions as the U.S. tried to cope with bank problems, and President Obama admitted that the Canadian banking system was managed much better than the U.S. banking system. Canadian banks in the U.S.—Royal Bank's RBC Bank, Bank of Montreal's Harris Bank, and Toronto Dominion's TD Bank—all noted a surge in deposits as their U.S. rivals struggled with financial problems.

Third, Canadian laws limited the amount of foreign competition that Canadian banks have to face, so Canadian banks did not feel compelled to take on the kinds of risky mortgages that got U.S. banks into trouble. As well, the risk-averse nature of Canadian banks served them well when the recession hit. When they did get involved, they showed the risky mortgages on their balance sheets so the public knew exactly what their financial condition was.

Critical Thinking Questions

1. Is there a trade-off between bank responsiveness to customers and customer satisfaction with banks?

2. Consider the following statement: "*Governments around the world should continuously apply very strict standards for banks, even in good economic times, so that the kinds of financial problems that developed in the U.S. will not happen again.*" Do you agree with the statement? Explain your reasoning.

SECONDARY SECURITIES MARKET The sale and purchase of previously issued stocks and bonds.

1 They advise companies on the timing and financial terms for a new issue.

2 By underwriting (buying) the new securities, investment bankers bear some of the risk of issuing a new security.

3 They create the distribution network that moves the new securities through groups of other banks and brokers into the hands of individual investors.

New securities represent only a small portion of securities traded. The market for existing stocks and bonds—the **secondary securities market**—is handled by organizations like the Toronto Stock Exchange. We will consider the activities of these markets later in this chapter.

LO-4 Stocks

Each year, millions of investors buy and sell the stocks of thousands of Canadian and international companies. This widespread ownership has become possible because of the availability of different types of stocks and because markets have been established for conveniently buying and selling them. In this section, we will focus on *common* and *preferred stock* as securities and the *stock exchanges* where they are bought and sold.

Common Stock

Individuals and companies buy a firm's common stock, hoping that the stock will increase in value (a capital gain) and/or will provide dividend income. Stock values are expressed in three ways: *par value, market value,* and *book value.*

Par Value The face value of a share of stock, its **par value**, is set by the issuing company's board of directors. Each company must preserve money in the amount of its stock's par value in its retained earnings, and cannot distribute it as dividends.

Market Value A stock's real value is its **market value**—the current price of a share in the stock market. The price of a stock can be influenced by both objective factors (company profits) and by subjective factors, including *rumours* (e.g., claims that a company has made a big gold strike), *investor relations* (publicizing the positive aspects of a company's financial condition to financial analysts and financial institutions), and *stockbroker recommendations* (a recommendation to buy a stock may increase demand and cause its price to increase, while a recommendation to sell can decrease demand and cause the price to fall). None of these actions is illegal.

Overall, the market value of stocks can show different movements during different decades. For example, in the 1930s, the S&P Financial Index experienced a 41.2 percent decline. The only other negative decade occurred in the 2000s, which showed a 24.1 percent decline; it is referred to by some as the "lost decade." Conversely, the 1990s were a time of great prosperity, with a 308.5 percent increase.[32]

The **market capitalization** of a company's stock is computed by multiplying the number of a company's outstanding shares times the market value of each share. Because stock prices change every day, so does market capitalization. The Royal Bank topped the Canadian list in 2009 with a market capitalization of approximately $54 billion.[33]

Book Value *Stockholders' equity* is the sum of a company's common stock par value, retained earnings, and additional paid-in capital. The **book value** of common stock represents stockholders' equity divided by the number of shares. Book value is used as a comparison indicator because, for successful companies, the market value is usually greater than its book value. Thus, when market price falls to near book value, some investors buy the stock on the principle that it is underpriced and will increase in value in the future.

Preferred Stock

Preferred stock is usually issued with a stated par value, such as $100. Dividends paid on preferred stock are usually expressed as a percentage of the par value. For example, if a preferred stock with a $100 par value pays a 6 percent dividend, stockholders would receive an annual dividend of $6 on each share.

Some preferred stock is *callable*, meaning the issuing firm can require the preferred stockholders to surrender their shares in exchange for a cash payment. The amount of this cash payment, known as the *call price*, is specified in the agreement between the preferred stockholders and the firm.

Stock Exchanges

A **stock exchange** is an organization of individuals formed to provide an institutional setting in which stock can be bought and sold. The exchange enforces certain rules to govern its members' trading activities. Most exchanges are non-profit corporations established to serve their members. To become a member, an individual must purchase one of a limited number of "seats" on the exchange. Only members (or their representatives) are allowed to trade on the exchange. In this sense, because all orders to buy or sell must flow through members, they have a legal monopoly. Memberships can be bought and sold like other assets.

A **stockbroker** receives buy and sell orders from those who are not members of the exchange and executes the orders. In return, the broker earns a commission from the order placer. Like many products, brokerage assistance can be purchased at either discount or at full-service prices. Buying 200 shares of a $20 stock costs an investor between $6.99 to $19.99 in fees at Scotia iTRADE, and up to $100 at a full-service brokerage firm. Price differences are obvious even among the discount brokers, but the highest discount price is well below the price of the full-service broker.[34]

Discount brokerage services cost less because sales personnel receive fees or salaries, not commissions. Unlike many full-service brokers, discount brokers do not offer investment advice or person-to-person sales

---

PAR VALUE The arbitrary value of a stock set by the issuing company's board of directors and stated on stock certificates; used by accountants but of little significance to investors.

MARKET VALUE The current price of one share of a stock in the secondary securities market; the real value of a stock.

MARKET CAPITALIZATION The dollar value (market value) of stocks listed on a stock exchange.

BOOK VALUE Value of a common stock expressed as total stockholders' equity divided by the number of shares of stock.

STOCK EXCHANGE A voluntary organization of individuals formed to provide an institutional setting where members can buy and sell stock for themselves and their clients in accordance with the exchange's rules.

STOCKBROKER An individual licensed to buy and sell securities for customers in the secondary market; may also provide other financial services.

consultations. However, they offer automated online services: stock research, industry analysis, and screening for specific types of stocks. *Online trading* is popular because of convenient access, fast no-nonsense transactions, and the opportunity for self-directed investors to manage their own investments while paying low fees.

Canadian Stock Exchanges

The *Toronto Stock Exchange (TSX)* is the largest stock exchange in Canada. It is made up of about 110 individual members who hold seats. The securities of most major corporations are listed here. A company must pay a fee before it can list its security on the exchange. The TSX has recently gained strength from an unexpected source: During the last economic recession many U.S. companies looked north and listed on the TSX to take advantage of Canada's relatively strong economic climate.[35]

Foreign Stock Exchanges

Many foreign countries also have active stock exchanges, and several foreign stock exchanges—most notably those in the United States and United Kingdom—trade far more shares each day than the TSX does.

The New York and American Stock Exchanges

For many people, "the stock market" means the *New York Stock Exchange (NYSE)*. It was founded in 1792 and is located at the corner of Wall Street and Broad Street. In May 2010, the market value of shares traded on the NYSE was US$11.6 billion. Only firms meeting certain minimum requirements—earning power, total value of outstanding stock, and number of shareholders—are eligible for listing on the NYSE.[36]

Other Foreign Stock Exchanges

In 1980, the U.S. stock market accounted for more than half the value of the *world* market in traded stocks. Market activities, however, have shifted as the value of shares listed on foreign exchanges continues to grow rapidly. The annual dollar value of trades on exchanges in London, Tokyo, and other cities is now in the trillions. In fact, the London exchange exceeds even the NYSE in number of stocks listed. Exchanges are also flourishing in cities from Shanghai to Warsaw, but risk levels in some markets are very high. The Chinese stock market has been compared to a casino, and it is plagued with corruption, lax government regulation, and financially troubled companies. In 2010, the Chinese stock market lost 19 percent of its value in just one month.[37]

The Over-the-Counter Market

The **over-the-counter (OTC)** market is so called because its original traders were somewhat like retailers—they kept supplies of shares on hand and, as opportunities arose, sold them over the counter to interested buyers. Even today, the OTC market has no trading floor. It consists of many people in different locations who hold an inventory of securities that are not listed on any of the major exchanges. The OTC market consists of independent dealers who own the securities that they buy and sell at their own risk.

NASDAQ

The **National Association of Securities Dealers Automated Quotation (NASDAQ)** is the world's first electronic stock market.[38] The NASDAQ telecommunications system operates the NASDAQ Stock Market by broadcasting trading information on an intranet to over 350 000 terminals worldwide. NASDAQ orders are paired and executed on a computer network. The stocks of nearly 3700 companies are traded by NASDAQ. Many newer firms are listed here when their stocks first become available in the secondary market. Highly traded listings include Apple, Microsoft, Intel, RIM, Baidu, and Netflix.[39]

Founded in 1792 and located at the corner of Wall and Broad Streets in New York City, the NYSE sees billions of shares change hands each day.

BONDS

A **bond** is an IOU—a written promise that the borrower will pay the lender, at some stated future date, a sum of money (the principal) and a stated rate of interest. Bondholders have a claim on a corporation's assets and earnings that comes before the claims of common and preferred stockholders. All corporations issue common stock, but not all issue bonds. Stockholders provide equity (ownership) capital, while bondholders are lenders (although they are also considered "investors" as far as the securities market is concerned). Stock certificates represent ownership, while bond certificates represent indebtedness.

Bonds differ from one another in terms of maturity date and risk level. To help bond investors make assessments, several services rate the quality of bonds from different issuers. Table 15.2 shows ratings by Moody's and Standard & Poor's. The rating measures the bond's *default risk*—the chance that one or more promised payments will be deferred or missed altogether. The financial crisis of 2008 revealed some significant problems with bond rating agencies. The credibility of companies like Moody's and Standard & Poor's declined because they gave overly favourable ratings to mortgage-backed securities that were actually very risky. People who made investments based on the ratings lost billions of dollars when bonds they thought were safe turned out not to be.[40] Standard & Poor's is revamping its procedures to help investors understand the difference between traditional corporate bonds and the so-called *structured securities* that turned out to be much riskier than anyone thought.[41]

Government Bonds

Government bonds—for example, Canada Savings Bonds—are among the safest investments available. However, securities with longer maturities are somewhat riskier than short-term issues because their longer lives expose them to more political, social, and economic changes. All federal bonds are backed by the Canadian government. Government securities are sold in large blocks to institutional investors, who buy them to ensure desired levels of safety in portfolios. In January 2010, it was reported that net foreign inflows into Canadian bonds was $86.3 billion. This was the highest level since 1988. In recent years, Canadian bonds have become increasingly attractive for foreign investors, especially Americans (75 percent of the inflows), because of Canada's relatively healthy finances and economy.[42]

Provincial and local governments also issue bonds (called *municipal bonds*) to finance school and transportation systems and a variety of other projects. Banks invest in bonds nearing maturity because they are relatively safe, liquid investments. Pension funds, insurance companies, and private citizens also make longer-term investments in municipal bonds.

Corporate Bonds

Corporate bonds are a major source of long-term financing for Canadian corporations. They usually have maturity dates of 10, 20, or 30 years. Longer-term corporate bonds are somewhat riskier than shorter-term bonds. Unlike stocks, nearly all secondary trading in bonds occurs in the over-the-counter market rather than on organized exchanges. Like stocks, market values and prices of bonds change daily. The direction of bond prices moves opposite to interest rate changes—as interest rates move up, bond prices tend to go down. The prices of riskier bonds fluctuate more than those of higher-grade bonds and often exceed the interest rate of the economy. Corporate bonds may be categorized in two ways: (1) according to methods of interest payment, and (2) according to whether they are *secured* or *unsecured*.

Interest Payment: Registered and Bearer Bonds **Registered bonds** register the names of holders with the company, which simply mails out cheques. Certificates are of value only to registered holders. **Bearer (or coupon) bonds** require bondholders to clip coupons from certificates

> **BOND** A written promise that the borrower will pay the lender, at a stated future date, the principal plus a stated rate of interest.
>
> **REGISTERED BONDS** The names of holders are registered with the company.
>
> **BEARER (OR COUPON) BONDS** Require bondholders to clip coupons from certificates and send them to the issuer to receive interest payments.

Table 15.2 **Bond Ratings**				
	High Grade	**Medium Grade (Investment Grade)**	**Speculative**	**Poor Grade**
Moody's	Aaa Aa	A Baa	Ba B	Caa to C
Standard & Poor's	AAA AA	A BBB	BB B	CCC to D

and send them to the issuer in order to receive payment. Coupons can be redeemed by anyone, regardless of ownership.

Bond Security Borrowers can reduce the risk of their bonds by pledging assets to bondholders in the event of default. **Secured bonds** can be backed by mortgages or other specific assets. If the corporation does not pay interest when it is due its assets can be sold and the proceeds used to pay the bondholders. Unsecured bonds are called **debentures**. No specific property is pledged as security for these bonds. Holders of unsecured bonds generally have claims against property not otherwise pledged in the company's other bonds. Accordingly, debentures have inferior claims on the corporation's assets. Financially strong corporations often use debentures.

The Retirement of Bonds

Maturity dates on bonds of all kinds may be very long. But at some point, all bonds must be paid off. In terms of maturity dates, there are three types of bonds: *callable*, *serial*, and *convertible*.

Callable Bonds The issuer of a **callable bond** has the right at almost any time to call the bonds in and pay them off at a price stipulated in the bond indenture (contract). Issuers are most likely to call in existing bonds when the prevailing interest rate is lower than the rate being paid on the bond. But the price the issuer must pay to call in the bond, the *call price*, usually gives a premium to the bondholder. For example, a bond might have a $100 face value and be callable by the firm for $108.67 any time during the first year after being issued. The call price and the premium decrease annually as the bond nears maturity.

Bonds are often retired by the use of a **sinking-fund provision** in the bond indenture. This method requires the issuing company to put a certain amount of money into a special bank account each year. At the end of a number of years, the money in this account (including interest) is sufficient to redeem the bonds. Failure to meet the sinking-fund provision places the bond issue in default.

More choices
and more options
than ever before

Perfect for the secure part of your RRSP

NEW CANADA SAVINGS BONDS
YOU'RE ON SOLID GROUND.

Canada

Private corporations are not the only organizations that issue bonds. The Government of Canada issues Canada Savings Bonds to finance its debt.

Bonds with sinking funds are generally regarded as safer investments than bonds without them.

Serial and Convertible Bonds As an alternative to sinking funds, some corporations issue serial or convertible bonds. In a **serial bond** issue, the firm retires portions of the bond issue at different predetermined dates. For example, in a $100 million serial bond issue maturing in 20 years, the company may retire $5 million of the issue each year.

Convertible bonds can be converted to common stock, at the option of the bondholder. Since this option gives bondholders a chance for capital gains, the company can offer lower interest rates when issuing these bonds. Suppose that in 2004, Canadian Arctic Explorations sold a $100 million issue of 4.5 percent convertible bonds. The bonds were issued in $1000 denominations; they mature in 2014. At any time before maturity, each debenture of $1000 is convertible into 19.125 shares of the company's common stock. Assume that between October 2004 and March 2011, the stock price ranged from a low of $28 to a high of $67. In that time, then, 19.125 common shares had a market value ranging from $535 to $1281. In other words, the bondholder could have exchanged the $1000 bond in return for stock to be kept or sold at a possible profit (or loss).

LO-5 Other Investments

Although stocks and bonds are very important, they are not the only marketable securities for businesses. Financial managers are also concerned with investment opportunities in *mutual funds*, *hedge funds, commodities*, and *stock options*.

Mutual Funds

Mutual funds pool investments from individuals and other firms to purchase a portfolio of stocks, bonds, and short-term securities. For example, if you invest $1000 in a mutual fund that has a portfolio worth $100 000, you own 1 percent of the portfolio. Mutual funds usually have portfolios worth many millions of dollars. Investors in **no-load funds** are not charged a sales commission when they buy into or sell out of the mutual fund. **Load funds** carry a charge of between 2 and 8 percent of the invested funds. Mutual funds give small investors access to professional financial management. Their managers have up-to-date information about market conditions and the best large-scale investment opportunities.

Mutual funds vary by the investment goals they stress. Some stress safety and invest in treasury bills and other safe issues that offer income (liquidity). Other funds seek higher current income and are willing to sacrifice some safety. Still other mutual funds stress growth. Aggressive-growth mutual funds seek maximum capital appreciation; they sacrifice current income and safety and invest in new companies, and other high-risk securities.

Ethical Funds Mutual funds that stress socially responsible investing are called **ethical funds**. They will not invest in cigarette manufacturers or companies that make weapons, for example, and instead focus on investing in companies that produce safe and useful products and show concern for their employees, for the environment, and for human rights. While many companies offer such investments, The Ethical Funds Company is dedicated to this mission.

Hedge Funds

Hedge funds are private pools of money that try to give investors a positive return regardless of stock market performance. Hedge funds often engage in risky practices like *short-selling* (essentially betting that a company's stock price will go down) and *leveraging* (borrowing money against principal). Historically, interest in hedge funds has been limited to wealthy people (called "accredited investors") who are assumed to be very knowledgeable about financial matters and are able to weigh the risks of investing. But recently, hedge funds have begun marketing their products to the average investor with something called "principal-protected notes." They guarantee that investors will get their original investment back at a certain time, but they do not guarantee that any additional returns will be forthcoming. Some hedge funds have been in the news for all the wrong reasons. For example, an Ontario Securities Commission panel ruled that two executives from the now-defunct Norshield Asset Management Ltd. knowingly misled their clients and investigators and failed to keep proper books. Losses are estimated at $159 million from 1900 retail investors.[43]

Commodities

Futures contracts—agreements to purchase a specified amount of a commodity at a given price on a set date in the future—are available for commodities ranging from coffee beans and live hogs to propane and platinum, as well as for stocks. Since selling prices reflect traders' beliefs about the future, prices of such contracts are very volatile, and futures trading is very risky.

For example, on January 3, 2010, the price of gold was $1100 per ounce, and futures contracts for July 2010 gold were selling for $1075 per ounce. This price would reflect investors' judgment that gold prices would be slightly lower in July. Now suppose that you purchased a 100-ounce gold futures contract in January for $107 500 ($1075 × 100). If in March 2011, the July gold futures sold for $1150, you could sell your contract for $115 000. Your profit after the two months would be $7500. Of course, if the futures contract had been selling for less than $1075, you would have lost money.

Margins Usually, buyers of futures contracts need not put up the full purchase amount. Rather, the buyer posts

MUTUAL FUND Any company that pools the resources of many investors and uses those funds to purchase various types of financial securities, depending on the fund's financial goals.

NO-LOAD FUND A mutual fund in which investors are not charged a sales commission when they buy into or sell out of the fund.

LOAD FUND A mutual fund in which investors are charged a sales commission when they buy into or sell out of the fund.

ETHICAL FUNDS Mutual funds that stress socially responsible investing.

HEDGE FUNDS Private pools of money that try to give investors a positive return regardless of stock market performance.

FUTURES CONTRACTS Agreement to purchase specified amounts of a commodity (or stock) at a given price on a set future date.

MARGIN The percentage of the total sales price that a buyer must put up to place an order for stock or a futures contract.

STOCK OPTION The purchased right to buy or sell a stock.

CALL OPTION The purchased right to buy a particular stock at a certain price until a specified date.

PUT OPTION The purchased right to sell a particular stock at a certain price until a specified date.

a smaller amount—the **margin**—that may be as little as $3000 for contracts of $100 000. Let us look again at our gold futures example. If you had posted a $3300 margin for your July gold contract, you would have earned a $7500 profit on that investment of $3300 in only two months. However, you also took a big risk involving two big *ifs*: If you had held on to your contract until July *and* if gold had dropped, say to $1025, you would have lost $5000 ($107 500 – $102 500). If you had posted a $3300 margin to buy the contract, you would have lost that entire margin and would owe an additional $1700.

Between 75 and 90 percent of all small-time investors lose money in the futures market.

The boxed insert entitled "Green Trading" describes a different kind of trading that is being increasingly debated.

Stock Options

A **stock option** is the right to buy or sell a stock. A **call option** gives its owner the right to buy a particular stock at a certain price, with that right lasting until a particular date. A **put option** gives its owner the right to sell a particular stock at a specified price, with that right lasting until a particular date. These options are traded on several stock exchanges.

Suppose that you thought the price of Research In Motion (RIM) (which sold for $63.79 per share on May 28, 2010) was going to go up. You might buy a call option giving you the right to buy 100 shares of RIM any time in the next two months at a so-called *strike price* of $75.

THE GREENING OF BUSINESS

Green Trading

Traders are accustomed to using financial markets for investing in just about everything—ranging from pork bellies to movie production—in the hope of gaining a profit. However, new financial markets for commodities known as *carbon credits* are not driven by just the profit motive but also by a sense of social responsibility. The economic incentives of emissions trading (ET) bring together both environmental polluters and green companies in an effort to save the planet and turn a profit.

Here's how it works. Regulators in various countries are setting limits on the amounts of several industrial pollutants that can be released into the atmosphere, including carbon dioxide (CO_2), sulphur dioxide, and mercury. A leading example is the European Union's Emissions Trading Scheme (ETS), which was started by the European Commission in 2005 to meet the EU's obligations for carbon reductions in accordance with the Kyoto Protocol on Climate Change. The ETS annually sets a cap for the total amount of CO_2 emission allowed for each EU country and for each business in that country. The country totals and the EU total cannot exceed the caps.

Individual companies are issued a permit containing a number of credits that represent the right to emit a certain amount of CO_2. Any company producing below its CO_2 cap can sell its surplus credits to other, more pollution-prone companies that need more credits to keep operating without going over their cap. This is where the trading opportunities arise. It's like a stock exchange that quickly matches up buyers and sellers, in this case buyers and sellers of emissions credits.

With emissions trading, environmentally oriented companies sell unneeded emissions allowances and gain a financial return on their past investment for reducing pollution. Such companies view environmental cleanup not as an expense but as a responsible investment. Other companies that have previously avoided making such investments face higher costs as they bid for others' unused carbon credits. The trading scheme has created a new financial incentive for the development of cleaner industries that reduce carbon emissions and other greenhouse gases.

Critical Thinking Questions

1. What are the advantages of emissions trading? What are the disadvantages?
2. What has been the experience of the European Union to date with emissions trading?
3. What is the Canadian government doing about introducing emissions trading?

If the stock rose to $85 before July, you would exercise your call option. Your profit would be $10 per share ($85 – $75) less the price you paid to buy the option. However, if the stock price fell instead of rising, you would not exercise your call option because RIM would be available on the open market for less than $75 per share. Your stock option would be "under water"; that is, it would be worthless. You would lose whatever you paid for the option. In recent years, there has been much negative publicity about stock options that are *given* to executives to motivate them to work hard for the company.

LO-6 Buying and Selling Securities

The process of buying and selling stocks, bonds, and other financial instruments is complex. You need to gather information about possible investments and match them to your investment objectives. Then you must decide whether you want to use a broker to buy and sell stocks, or whether you want to do it yourself.

Using Financial Information Services

Have you ever looked at the financial section of your daily newspaper and found yourself wondering what all those tables and numbers mean? If you cannot read stock and bond quotations, you probably should not invest in them. Fortunately, this skill is easily mastered.

Stock Quotations Figure 15.5 shows the type of information newspapers provide about daily market transactions of individual stocks. The corporation's name is shown along with the number of shares sold, the high and low prices of the stock for that trading day, the closing price of the stock, and the change from the closing price on the previous day.

Bond Quotations Bond prices also change daily. These changes form the *coupon rate*, which provides information for firms about the cost of borrowing funds. Prices of domestic corporation bonds, Canadian government bonds, and foreign bonds are reported separately. Bond prices are expressed in terms of 100, even though most have a face value of $1000. Thus a quote of 85 means that the bond's price is 85 percent of its face value, or $850.

A corporate bond selling at 155¼ would cost a buyer $1552.50 ($1000 face value multiplied by 1.5525), plus commission. The interest rate on bonds is also quoted as a percentage of par, or face, value. Thus "6½s" pay 6.5 percent of par value per year. Typically, interest is paid semi-annually at half of the stated interest or coupon rate.

The market value (selling price) of a bond at any given time depends on three things: its stated interest rate, the "going rate" of interest in the market, and its redemption or maturity date. A bond with a higher stated interest rate than the going rate on similar quality bonds will probably sell at a premium above its face value—its selling price will be above its redemption price. A bond with a lower stated interest rate than the going rate on similar quality bonds will probably sell at a discount—its selling price will be below its redemption price. How much the premium or discount is depends largely on how far in the future the maturity date is. The maturity date is shown after the interest rate. Figure 15.6 shows the type of information daily newspapers provide.

Figure 15.5
How to read a daily stock quotation.

Company	Volume	High	Low	Close	Change
Four Seasons	633	67.49	65.27	66.15	–1.13
Goldcorp	35 233	31.99	30.65	31.15	+0.83
GW Life	54	25.80	25.57	25.80	–0.22
Hudson Bay	32 376	15.06	15.00	15.04	–0.02
Vale Inco	**18 640**	**58.82**	**57.01**	**58.05**	**+0.84**
Ipsco	4341	106.40	104.09	105.75	–0.25
Jean Cou	6918	14.56	14.31	14.31	–0.06
Kinross	72 321	13.68	12.92	13.10	+0.27

■ *Stock*
Vale Inco (Name of Company).

■ *Volume*
18 640 (total number of shares traded on this date [in 100's].

■ *High and Low*
During the trading day, the highest price was $58.82 and the lowest price was $57.01.

■ *Close*
At the close of trading on this date, the last price paid per share was $58.05.

■ *Net Change*
Difference between today's closing price and the previous day's closing price. Price increased by 84 cents per share.

MARKET INDEX
A measure of the market value of stocks; provides a summary of price trends in a specific industry or of the stock market as a whole.

BULL MARKET
A period of rising stock prices; a period in which investors act on a belief that stock prices will rise.

BEAR MARKET
A period of falling stock prices; a period in which investors act on a belief that stock prices will fall.

DOW JONES INDUSTRIAL AVERAGE (DJIA) Market index based on the prices of 30 of the largest firms listed on NYSE.

S&P/TSX INDEX
An average computed from 225 large Canadian stocks from various industry groups.

STANDARD & POOR'S COMPOSITE INDEX (S&P 500)
Market index based on the performance of 400 industrial firms, 40 utilities, 40 financial institutions, and 20 transportation companies.

NASDAQ COMPOSITE INDEX
Value-weighted market index that includes all NASDAQ-listed companies, both domestic and foreign.

Figure 15.6
How to read a bond quotation.

Issuer	Coupon	Maturity	Price	Yield
		GOVERNMENT OF CANADA		
Canada	5.00	June 1, 14	103.71	4.45
Canada	8.00	June 1, 27	145.92	4.58
		PROVINCIALS		
Hy Que	6.50	Feb. 15, 11	108.55	4.50
Man	7.75	Dec. 22, 25	135.19	4.93
		CORPORATE		
BC Tel	**9.65**	**Apr 8, 22**	**138.49**	**6.48**
Loblaw	6.65	Nov. 8, 27	107.91	5.99

- *Issuer*
  Company name is British Columbia Telephone.
- *Coupon*
  The annual rate of interest at face value is 9.65 percent.
- *Maturity*
  The maturity date is April 8, 2022.
- *Price*
  On this date, $138.9 was the price of the last transaction.
- *Yield*
  The yield is computed by dividing the annual interest paid by the current market price.

Bond Yield Suppose you bought a $1000 par-value bond in 1995 for $650. Its stated interest rate is 6 percent, and its maturity or redemption date is 2015. You therefore receive $60 per year in interest. Based on your actual investment of $650, your yield is 9.2 percent. If you hold it to maturity, you get $1000 for a bond that originally cost you only $650. This extra $350 increases your true, or effective, yield.

Market Indexes Although they do not indicate how specific securities are doing, **market indexes** provide a useful summary of trends in specific industries and the stock market as a whole. Such information can be crucial in choosing investments. For example, market indexes reveal bull and bear market trends. **Bull markets** are periods of upward-moving stock prices. The years 1981–89, 1993–99, and 2004–06 were bull markets. Periods of falling stock prices are called **bear markets**. The years 1972–74, 1991–92, 2000–02, and 2007-09 were bear markets.

The Dow Jones Industrial Average The most widely cited market index is the **Dow Jones Industrial Average (DJIA)**. The Dow is the sum of market prices for 30 of the largest industrial firms listed on the NYSE. By tradition, the Dow is an indicator of blue-chip (top quality) stock price movements. Because of the small number of firms it considers, however, it is a limited gauge of the overall stock market. The Dow increased sharply in the 1990s. It reached 11 000 early in 2000 but dropped to less than 8000 in 2002. By mid-2010, it stood at 11 100.

The S&P/TSX Average The **S&P/TSX index** is an average computed from 225 large Canadian stocks from various industry groups.[44] The index has also been very volatile during the last few years. It moved sharply upward during the bull market of the 1990s and topped 11 000 in the summer of 2000. It then dropped to 6500 by the end of 2000. By mid-2010, it had risen to 12 700.

The S&P 500 Standard & Poor's Composite Index (S&P 500) consists of 500 stocks, including 400 industrial firms, 40 utilities, 40 financial institutions, and 20 transportation companies. The index average is weighted according to market capitalization of each stock, so the more highly valued companies exercise a greater influence on the index.

The NASDAQ Composite Because it considers more stocks, some stock market observers regard the **NASDAQ Composite Index** as the most important of all market indexes. Unlike the Dow and the S&P 500, all NASDAQ-listed companies are included in the index. The NASDAQ market has been very volatile. In early 2000, it reached 5000, but by 2001 had dropped to just 1300. In mid-2010 it stood at only 2050.

Buying and Selling Stocks

Based on your own investigations and/or recommendations from your broker, you can place many types of orders. A **market order** requests the broker to buy or sell a certain security at the prevailing market price at the time. A **limit order** authorizes the purchase of a stock only if its price is less than or equal to a given limit. For example, a limit order to buy a stock at $80 per share means that the broker is to buy it if and only if the stock becomes available for a price of $80 or less. Similarly, a stop order instructs the broker to sell a stock if its price falls to a certain level. For example, a **stop order** of $85 on a particular stock means that the broker is to sell it if and only if its price falls to $85 or below.

You can also place orders of different sizes. A **round lot** order requests 100 shares or some multiple thereof. Fractions of a round lot are called odd lots. Trading **odd lots** is usually more expensive than trading round lots, because an intermediary called an odd-lot broker is often involved, which increases brokerage fees.

The business of buying and selling stocks is changing rapidly. Formerly, a person had to have a broker to buy and sell stocks. More and more individuals are now buying and selling stocks on the internet, and traditional brokers are worried that before long, customers will avoid using their services.

Financing Securities Purchases

When you place a buy order of any kind, you must tell your broker how you will pay for the purchase. You might maintain a cash account with your broker. Then, as stocks are bought and sold, proceeds are added into the account and commissions and costs of purchases are withdrawn by the broker. You can also buy shares on credit.

Margin Trading As with futures contracts, you can buy stocks on *margin*—putting down only a portion of the stock's price. You borrow the rest from your broker, who, in turn, borrows from the banks at a special rate and secures the loans with stock. Suppose you purchased $100 000 worth of stock in WestJet. Let's also say that you paid $50 000 of your own money and borrowed the other $50 000 from your broker at 10 percent interest. Valued at its market price, your stock serves as your collateral. If shares have risen in value to $115 000 after one year, you can sell them and pay your broker $55 000 ($50 000 principal plus $5000 interest). You will have $60 000 left over. Your original investment of $50 000 will have earned a 20 percent profit of $10 000. If you had paid the entire price out of your own pocket, you would have earned only a 15 percent return.

Although investors often recognize possible profits to be made in margin trading, they sometimes fail to consider that losses can be amplified. If the value of your initial WestJet investment of $100 000 had instead fallen to $85 000 after one year, you would have lost 15 percent if you had paid out of pocket. However, if you had used

margin trading, you would have lost $20 000 ($5000 interest payment + $15 000 share decrease) on a $50 000 investment, which amounts to a 40 percent loss.

The rising use of margin credit by investors was a growing concern during the bull market of 2004–06. Investors focused on the upside benefits but were not sensitive enough to the downside risks. Especially at online brokerages, inexperienced traders were borrowing at an alarming rate, and some were using the borrowed funds for risky and speculative day trading. So-called *day traders* visited websites online to buy and sell a stock in the same day (so-called *intraday trades*), seeking quick in-and-out fractional gains on large volumes (many shares) of each stock. While some day traders were successful, most ended up as financial losers.

Short Sales In addition to money, brokerages also lend buyers securities. A **short sale** begins when you borrow a security from your broker and sell it (one of the few times it is legal to sell what you do not own). At a given time in the future, you must restore an equal number of shares of that issue to the brokerage, along with a fee.

For example, suppose that in June you believe the price of Bombardier stock will soon fall. You order your broker to sell short 1000 shares at the market price of $5 per share. Your broker will make the sale and credit $5000 to your account. If Bombardier's price falls to $3.50 per share in July, you can buy 1000 shares for $3500 and give them to your broker, leaving you with a $1500 profit (before commissions). The risk is that Bombardier's price will not fall but will hold steady or rise, leaving you with a loss.

Securities Regulation

In 1912, the Manitoba government was a Canadian pioneer in making laws applying mainly to the sale of new securities. Under these "**blue-sky laws**," corporations issuing securities must back them up with something

---

MARKET ORDER An order to a broker to buy or sell a certain security at the current market price.

LIMIT ORDER An order to a broker to buy a certain security only if its price is less than or equal to a given limit.

STOP ORDER An order to a broker to sell a certain security if its price falls to a certain level or below.

ROUND LOT The purchase or sale of stock in units of 100 shares.

ODD LOT The purchase or sale of stock in units of other than 100 shares.

SHORT SALE Selling borrowed shares of stock in the expectation that their price will fall before they must be replaced, so that replacement shares can be bought for less than the original shares were sold for.

BLUE-SKY LAWS Laws regulating how corporations must back up securities.

PROSPECTUS
A detailed registration statement about a new stock filed with a provincial securities exchange; must include any data helpful to a potential buyer.

INSIDER TRADING
The use of special knowledge about a firm to make a profit on the stock market.

more than the blue sky. Similar laws were passed in other provinces. Provincial laws also generally require that stockbrokers be licensed and securities be registered before they can be sold. In each province, issuers of proposed new securities must file a prospectus with the provincial securities exchange. A **prospectus** is a detailed registration statement that includes information about the firm, its operation, its management, the purpose of the proposed issue, and any other data helpful to a potential buyer of these securities. The prospectus must be made available to prospective investors.

The Ontario Securities Act contains disclosure provisions for new and existing issues, prevention of fraud, regulation of the Toronto Stock Exchange, and takeover bids. It also prohibits **insider trading**, which is the use of special knowledge about a firm to make a profit in the stock market. The Toronto Stock Exchange provides an example of self-regulation by the industry. The TSX has regulations concerning listing and delisting of securities, disclosure requirements, and issuing of prospectuses for new securities.

Unlike the United States with its Securities and Exchange Commission (SEC), Canada does not yet have a comprehensive federal regulatory body. In fact, Canada is the only country in the industrialized world that does not have a single regulator.[45] But in 2010, the federal government continued to move toward a new national securities act complete with a governing body called the Canadian Securities Regulatory Authority (CSRA). Reactions have been mixed, with the RCMP claiming that the Act does not go far enough to address criminal activity in securities trading. Time will tell, but it is clearly a step in the right direction.[46]

PEARSON
mybusinesslab

To improve your grade, visit the MyBusinessLab website at **www.pearsoned.ca/mybusinesslab**. This online homework and tutorial system allows you to test your understanding and generates a personalized study plan just for you. It provides you with study and practice tools directly related to this chapter's content. MyBusinessLab puts you in control of your own learning! Test yourself on the material for this chapter at **www.pearsoned.ca/mybusinesslab**.

Summary of Learning Objectives

1. **Define *money* and identify the different forms it takes in Canada's money supply.** Any item that is portable, divisible, durable, and stable satisfies the four basic characteristics of *money*. Money also serves three functions: a medium of exchange, a store of value, and a unit of account. The nation's money supply is often determined by two measures. *M-1* includes liquid (or spendable) forms of money: currency (bills and coins), demand deposits, and other "chequable" deposits. *M-2* includes M-1 plus items that cannot be directly spent but that can be easily converted to spendable forms: time deposits, money market funds, and savings deposits. *Credit* must also be considered as a factor in the money supply.

2. **Understand the different kinds of *financial institutions* that make up the Canadian financial system and explain the services they offer.** There are four financial pillars in Canada: chartered banks, alternate banks, life insurance companies, and investment dealers. Chartered banks are the most important source of short-term funds for business firms. They create money in the form of expanding demand deposits. The four types of financial institutions offer services like financial advice, brokerage services, electronic funds transfer, pension and trust services, and lending of money.

3. **Explain the functions of the *Bank of Canada* and describe the tools it uses to control the money**

supply. The Bank of Canada manages the Canadian economy, controls the money supply, and regulates certain aspects of chartered banking operations. If the Bank of Canada wants to increase the money supply, it can buy government securities or lower the bank rate. If it wants to decrease the money supply, it can sell government securities or increase the bank rate.

4. **Discuss the value of *common stock* and *preferred stock* to stockholders and describe the secondary market for each type of security.** *Common stock* gives investors the prospect of capital gains and dividend income. Common stock values are expressed in three ways: *par value, market value,* and *book value. Preferred* stock is less risky than common stock. Both common and preferred stock are traded on *stock exchanges* (and in *over-the-counter [OTC] markets*). "Members" who hold seats on exchanges act as *brokers*—agents who execute buy-and-sell orders—for non-members.

5. **Describe the investment opportunities offered by *bonds*, *mutual funds*, and *commodities*.** Like stocks and bonds, *mutual funds* offer investors different levels of risk and growth potential. *Load funds* require investors to pay commissions of 2 to 8 percent; *no-load funds* do not charge commissions when investors buy in or out. *Futures contracts*—agreements to buy specified amounts of commodities at given prices on preset dates—are traded in the *commodities market.* Commodities traders often buy on *margins,* percentages of total sales prices that must be put up to order futures contracts.

6. **Explain the process by which securities are bought and sold.** Investors generally use such financial information services as newspapers and online stock, bond, and OTC quotations. *Market indexes* such as the Toronto Stock Exchange index, the Dow Jones Industrial Average, the Standard & Poor's Composite Index and the NASDAQ Composite provide useful summaries of trends. Investors can then place different types of orders. *Market orders* are orders to buy or sell at current prevailing prices. Investors can issue *limit* or *stop orders* that are executed only if prices rise or fall below specified levels. *Round lots* are purchased in multiples of 100 shares. *Odd lots* are purchased in fractions of round lots. Securities can be bought on margin or as part of *short sales.*

Questions and Exercises

Questions for Analysis

1. What specific changes in banking are shifting banks away from their historical role?

2. Do we really need all the different types of financial institutions we have in Canada? Could we make do with just chartered banks? Why or why not?

3. Should credit cards be counted in the money supply? Why or why not? Support your answer by using the definition of money.

4. Should banks be regulated, or should market forces be allowed to determine the money supply? Defend your answer.

5. Suppose you decided to invest in common stocks as a personal investment. Which kind of broker—full-service or online discount—would you use for buying and selling stock? Why?

6. Choose a stock from the TSX and find a newspaper listing of a recent day's transactions for the stock. Explain what each element in the listing means.

Application Exercises

7. Start with a $1000 deposit and assume a reserve requirement of 15 percent. Now trace the amount of money created by the banking system after five lending cycles.

8. Interview several consumers to determine which banking services and products they use (debit cards, ATMs, smart cards, etc.). If interviewees are using these services, determine the reasons. If they are not, find out why not.

9. Interview the manager of a local chartered bank branch. Identify the ways in which the Bank of Canada helps the bank and the ways in which it limits the bank.

10. Contact a broker for information about setting up a personal account for trading securities. Prepare a report on the broker's requirements for placing buy/sell orders, credit terms, cash account requirements, services available to investors, and commissions/fees schedules.

Building Your Business Skills

Market Ups and Downs

Goal

To encourage students to understand the forces that affect fluctuations in stock prices.

Situation

Investing in stocks requires an understanding of the various factors that affect stock prices. These factors may be intrinsic to the company itself or part of the external environment.

- Internal factors relate to the company itself, such as an announcement of poor or favourable earnings, earnings that are more or less than expected, major layoffs, labour problems, management issues, and mergers.

- External factors relate to world or national events, such as the threat of war, the BP oil spill in the Gulf of Mexico, weather conditions that affect sales, the Bank of Canada's adjustment of interest rates, and employment figures that were higher or lower than expected. By analyzing these factors, you will often learn a lot about why a stock did well or why it did poorly. Being aware of these influences will help you anticipate future stock movements.

Method

Step 1 Working alone, choose a common stock that has experienced considerable price fluctuations in the past few years. Here are several examples: BP, Amazon.com, RIM, and Apple. Find the symbol for the stock and the exchange on which it is traded.

Step 2 Visit the Globe Investor website (or a similar site) and gather information on the particular stock and study its trading pattern. You can also visit your library and find the *Daily Stock Price Record*, a publication that provides a historical picture of daily stock closings. There are separate copies for the various stock exchanges.

Step 3 Find four or five days over a period of several months or even a year when there have been major price fluctuations in the stock. (A two- or three-point price change from one day to the next is considered major.) Then research what happened on that day that might have contributed to the fluctuation. A good place to start is *The Globe and Mail* or *The Wall Street Journal*.

Step 4 Write a short analysis that links changes in stock price to internal and external factors. As you analyze the data, be aware that it is sometimes difficult to know why a stock price fluctuates.

Step 5 Get together with three other students who studied different stocks. As a group, discuss your findings, looking for fluctuation patterns.

Follow-Up Questions

1. Do you see any similarities in the movement of the various stocks during the same period? For example, did the stocks move up or down at about the same time? If so, do you think the stocks were affected by the same factors? Explain your thinking.

2. Based on your analysis, did internal or external factors have the greater impact on stock price? Which factors had the longer-lasting effect? Which factors had the shorter effect?

3. Why do you think it is so hard to predict changes in stock price on a day-to-day basis?

Exercising Your Ethics

Serving Two Masters: Torn between Company and Client

The Situation

Employees in financial services firms are sometimes confronted by conflicting allegiances between the company and its clients. In managing customers' stock portfolios, the best timing for buy and sell decisions for clients' financial positions may not be the most profitable for the financial manager's firm. Investment managers, as a result, must choose a "right" course of action to reconcile conflicting interests.

The Dilemma

George Michaels is a customer portfolio manager employed by Premier Power Investments Company. His 35 clients—individual investors—have portfolios with market values ranging from $200 000 to $2 million in stocks, bonds, and mutual funds. Clients generally rely on George's recommendations to buy, sell, or hold each security based on his knowledge of their investment goals and risk tolerance, along with his experience in keeping up with market trends and holding down transactions costs. Premier Power Investments Company earns sales commissions ranging from 2 to 4 percent of market value for each buy and sell transaction.

On Monday morning, George's boss, Vicky Greene, informs him that due to Premier Power Investments Company's sagging revenues, it is to everyone's benefit to increase the number of transactions in customers' portfolios. She suggests that he find some different and attractive securities to replace existing securities for his customers. As George thinks about possible ways for accelerating his buy and sell recommendations, he has concerns about the motivation behind Vicky's comments. He is unsure what to do.

Team Activity

Assemble a group of four students and assign each group member to one of the following roles:

- George Michaels (employee)
- Vicky Greene (employer)
- Portfolio owner (customer)
- Owner (one of many outside shareholders of Premier Power Investments Company)

Action Steps

1. Before discussing the situation with your group, and from the perspective of your assigned role, consider whether there are any ethical issues in this situation. If yes, write them down.

2. Return to your group and reveal ethical issues that were identified by each member. Be especially aware of how different roles resulted in different kinds of ethical issues. Why might role differences result in dissimilar priorities on ethical issues?

3. For the various ethical issues that were identified, decide as a group which one is the most important for Premier Power Investments to resolve. Which issue is second in importance?

4. From an ethical standpoint, what does your group finally recommend be done to resolve the most important ethical issue? To resolve the second most important ethical issue?

Stock Market Games and the Dark Side of Financial Advising

The stock market is supposed to be a place where you can increase your assets over time if you invest wisely and have patience. But some people don't want to trust their financial situation to unpredictable markets, so they come up with creative (often illegal) ways to manipulate the market to ensure that they will get a positive outcome. Unfortunately, it only takes the bad behaviour of a few people to make it seem like the stock market is a haven for con artists. In the following paragraphs, several classic frauds are briefly described.

Diverting Investors' Funds

Vincent Lacroix, the founder of Norbourg Asset Management Inc., was found guilty in 2008 of diverting $115 million from Norbourg into accounts that he and his wife controlled. Some investors lost their entire life savings. Lacroix was sentenced to 12 years in prison and fined $255 000, but he is appealing the sentence. The case was brought against Lacroix by the Autorité des marchés financiers (AMF), which is the securities watchdog in Quebec. The AMF itself is the target of a class action suit that claims that it didn't do enough to protect small investors.

Ponzi Schemes

In 2009, Bernie Madoff confessed to running a Ponzi scheme that bilked investors out of $50 billion. A Ponzi scheme attracts investors by promising them that they will make very large returns, much larger than can normally be made. Investors who join the scheme early may indeed make large returns because they are being paid with money that is being contributed by later investors. But eventually the scheme collapses, and almost everyone loses their investment. For most of the period from 1990 to 2008, Madoff reported to investors that they were making 12 percent annually on their investment. That was about double what investors could normally be expected to make. But it is alleged that Madoff never invested anyone's money in anything. Rather, he simply falsified financial reports and told people that their "investments" were doing fine. Many charitable organizations and rich individuals lost millions of dollars each as a result of their investment with Madoff.

Closer to home, in 2010, Earl Jones was sentenced to 11 years after his scheme cost 158 Montreal investors

a total of $50 million. He promised investors 12 percent returns but never invested a penny for them. Upon hearing the sentence, his own brother, Bevon Jones, said that he thought the sentence was too lenient and that his brother should never see the light of day. Bevon Jones lost $1 million in this scheme.

Insider Trading

Andrew Rankin was an investment banking star with RBC Dominion Securities when he was charged with insider trading and "tipping" his friend Daniel Duic about several big corporate deals that were about to take place. Using the information provided by Rankin, Duic made over $4 million in profit by buying and selling the stocks of these companies at opportune times. When this was discovered, Duic made a deal with the Ontario Securities Commission to testify against his friend. Rankin was convicted of "tipping" and was sentenced to six months in jail. However, he appealed, and the Ontario Securities Commission agreed to withdraw the criminal charges and he was spared jail time. Rankin was also fined $250 000 and barred for life from working in the securities industry.

In another insider trading case, Barry Landen of Agnico-Eagle Mines was found guilty after he sold shares he owned before it became publicly known that the company was going to report poor results. He was sentenced to 45 days in jail and fined $200 000.

In a third case, Glen Harper, the president of Golden Rule Resources Ltd., was found guilty of insider trading. He had sold $4 million worth of shares in his company after he found out that its supposedly huge gold find in Ghana was in doubt. When Harper sold his shares, the price of Golden Rule's stock was about $13 per share. After the bad news became public, the stock fell to $0.10 a share. Harper was sentenced to one year in prison and fined nearly $4 million.

High-Closing

In this scheme, just before the stock exchange closes a trader buys enough shares of a given stock so that the price of that stock rises above the price of the previous trade. This makes it look as if the stock has upward momentum. The motivation to "high-close" a stock can be strong for money managers, because they are under intense pressure to increase the value of their portfolios so they can demonstrate high performance and attract more clients. The temptation is particularly strong at year-end because money managers' annual bonuses are tied to their performance.

"Salting" Gold Mines

In a classic case, David Walsh started a small gold-mining company in Calgary that he called Bre-X. After claiming that core samples showed that the company had found a major gold deposit in Indonesia, the price of the stock rose from $0.27 a share to nearly $300 a share. But it eventually became clear that the core samples had been tampered with and that there was no gold at the site. The shares of Bre-X quickly became worthless and investors lost millions.

Questions for Discussion

1. What factors determine the market price of a share of stock? Which of those factors were at work in the cases described above that dealt with the issue of stock prices?

2. What is the difference between debt and equity financing? Are the situations described above examples of debt or equity issues? Explain.

3. Consider the following statement: *"Insider trading should not be illegal. In a free-market economy, individuals who have the motivation and intelligence to gather information that allows them to make a lot of money should not be prevented from capitalizing on the information they have collected."* Do you agree or disagree with the statement? Explain your reasoning.

SCANLIFE

chapter

16

Financial Decisions and Risk Management

After reading this chapter, you should be able to:

LO-1 Describe the responsibilities of a *financial manager*.

LO-2 Distinguish between *short-term (operating)* and *long-term (capital)* expenditures.

LO-3 Identify four sources of *short-term financing* for businesses.

LO-4 Distinguish among the various sources of *long-term financing* and explain the risks involved in each.

LO-5 Discuss some key issues in financial management for small businesses.

LO-6 Explain how *risk* affects business operations and identify the five steps in the *risk-management process*.

SCANLIFE

The Source of a Meltdown, the Joy of a Bounce Back, and the Prospects Ahead

A financial crisis began in the United States in September of 2008 and quickly spread to the world economy. Stock markets dropped disastrously, investment banks failed, and consumer and business credit became very difficult to obtain. For most people, the crisis was sudden and unexpected, and they did not understand what had gone wrong. Overall, the cause was a combination of regulatory failure, low interest rates, and greed on the part of financial institutions and individuals. But in the next 18 months, a confusing combination of events occurred: (1) an apparent low was reached, (2) stocks then rose very sharply, and (3) volatility returned once again. Some were preaching that the market was working out the kinks, but many experts feared the worst and reminded anyone who would listen of lessons from 1929, 1930, and the historical mess that followed.

The seeds of the 2008 financial meltdown were actually sown back in 2000, when the tech bubble burst and a recession ensued. The Bank of Canada, the U.S. Federal Reserve, and central banks around the world cut interest rates to encourage investment and get their economies moving again. It worked, but the low interest rates caused a boom in real estate values in the United States. Many people who had previously not been able to get a mortgage suddenly found that banks were eager to lend them money. Not surprisingly, the increased demand for houses caused home prices to increase. Low interest rates also caused investors to look for ways to make a greater return on their money, and that often led them to higher-risk investments that gave a greater return.

How Will This Help Me?

The opening case shows the importance of understanding and managing risk with respect to the financial activities of business firms. The material in this chapter will benefit you in two ways: (1) you will be better able to use your knowledge about finance in your career as both an *employee* and as a *manager*, and (2) you will be a more informed *consumer*, with greater awareness of how businesses use financial instruments to support their activities.

The increase in housing prices was very pronounced in the United States because of the activity of companies like the Federal National Mortgage Association (nicknamed Fannie Mae) and the Federal Home Mortgage Corporation (nicknamed Freddie Mac). Fannie Mae was formed during the Great Depression of the 1930s to encourage banks to extend credit to homeowners. It was privatized in 1968. Freddie Mac was formed in 1970 to prevent monopolization in the home mortgage market. As time went on, these two companies (which together guarantee nearly half the mortgages in the United States) made increasingly risky loans to homeowners, and this added to the problem.

During the period from 2003 to 2006, almost anyone in the United States could qualify for a mortgage (even though they couldn't actually make their monthly payments). These mortgages came to be called NINJA loans (because the borrower had no income, no job, and no assets). Brokers who arranged such loans had a big incentive to do so—they received from $1000 to as much as $10 000 for each loan they arranged. Investment banks and other financial institutions started borrowing money so they could lend it to all the people who wanted to buy houses. These financial institutions then issued assets (called collateralized debt obligations, or CDOs) to cover their costs. These CDOs were marketed to investors as being very safe because the collateral backing them up was the homes that had been purchased with the money. This would not have been a problem if housing prices had continued to rise, but they didn't, and here's why: the mortgages came with very low "teaser" rates for the first year or two, after which the rate of interest charged increased sharply. Once people got into the third or fourth year of their mortgage, their monthly costs went way up and they couldn't make their payments. So they defaulted on their loans and the banks wound up foreclosing on the homes. This caused a drop in demand for homes, which caused housing prices to drop. As time passed, more and more people got into trouble because many of them owed more on their mortgage than the new lower value of their home. Many simply walked away from their homes and stopped making payments.

When housing prices dropped, financial institutions had to borrow more money to make up for the reduced value of their CDO assets. But by then investors had become aware of the problems and were reluctant to loan money to anybody. Because banks held so much bad debt, they were also unwilling to loan money (to consumers and to each other), and this caused a liquidity crisis. The London Interbank Offered Rate (LIBOR) is the rate large banks charge each other when making loans; in September 2008, the rate went as high as 6 percent, which indicated considerable mistrust between banks.

The crisis was worsened by credit default swaps. These are essentially insurance against defaults on mortgage loans, and they work like this: Let's say that an investor buys bonds from Corporation X. The investor can buy a credit default swap from a company like American International Group (AIG) that guarantees that the investor will get his or her money back if Corporation X defaults on its bond payments. The investor pays AIG a fee (the equivalent of an insurance premium). Because the aforementioned CDOs were assumed to be very safe investments, very low premiums were charged for credit default swaps. When the housing market went bust, the companies that sold credit default swaps were in big financial trouble because they had to come up with collateral for all those defaulted mortgages (which they had earlier assumed would never be in default). For example, AIG had $300 billion of credit default swaps on its books, and it charged far too little for them.

Stock markets plunged as the credit crisis worsened, and this meant huge losses for Canadians who had bought stocks. This development was particularly problematic for people who were about to retire because the value of their stocks declined by as much as 50 percent in just a few months. By the end of 2008, most economists were predicting a deep and lengthy recession for the world economy.

The financial difficulties also caused the bankruptcy of large investment banks like Bear Stearns and Lehman Brothers. Merrill Lynch & Co. was also in trouble and was taken over by Bank of America. Fannie Mae, Freddie Mac, and AIG were essentially taken over by the U.S. government (total cost: $285 billion). But the bailout of individual companies was not enough. It was becoming apparent that the entire world's financial system was getting very close to a complete meltdown. To deal with the crisis, U.S. legislators agreed to form a $700 billion bailout fund that gave the U.S. Treasury the authority to buy up so-called "toxic" mortgages and other bad debts that were held by banks. The central governments of Britain, Germany, France, and Italy also developed multibillion-dollar bailout plans. The idea was that if banks around the world were relieved of their bad debts, they would start loaning money again to people who wanted to buy houses, and that would stabilize the housing markets. Loans would also encourage consumers to start buying again, and that demand would create jobs in both goods- and service-producing companies.

A funny thing happened in 2009; stocks rose sharply. For example, the TSX composite was up 35 percent for the year and up approximately 54 percent since reaching lows in March. By mid 2010, the market was trading at around 11 700, up significantly from 7724 a year earlier, but pretty much where it ended the previous year. But everything was not calm. There was a lot of volatility in the market. Part of it was being sparked by the sovereign debt crisis in Europe. Greece stood at the epicentre of this latest shock, which remained in the headlines for months. However, this new crisis was not about one small nation. It forced investors and governments to look at their own debt shortcomings and the shortcomings of their key trading partners. In an environment of fear everyone tries to minimize risk. The panic that often follows leads to devastating results in markets.

Legitimate questions loomed. Was the bounce back real or artificial? To support citizens and corporations, governments spent money and took on great debt levels to flood the markets with cash. Bailouts became a part of daily conversation. Spending was out of control. In 2010, total public and private debt per person amounted to $23 324 in Canada, $44 759 in the United States, and a whopping $147 898 in Britain.

What did this all mean? At the time, some people were pointing to eerie parallels between 2010 and 1930, when the stock market increased by over 50 percent, from 1929 lows, before subsequently plunging even further than those original lows. Government mismanagement and inadequate regulation was a major issue at that time as well. Others were more optimistic. But it was clearly a risky period for investors and corporations in the markets.

LO-1 The Role of the Financial Manager

Financial managers plan and control the acquisition and dispersal of the company's financial assets. The business activity known as **finance** (or corporate finance) typically involves four responsibilities:

1. determining a firm's long-term investments
2. obtaining funds to pay for those investments
3. conducting the firm's everyday financial activities
4. managing the risks that the firm takes

Objectives of the Financial Manager

A financial manager's overall objective is to increase a firm's value and stockholders' wealth. Financial managers do many specific things to increase a firm's value: collect funds, pay debts, establish trade credit, obtain loans, control cash balances, and plan for future financial needs. Whereas accountants create data to reflect a firm's financial status, financial managers make decisions for improving that status. Financial managers must ensure that a company's revenues exceed its costs—in other words, that it earns a profit. In sole proprietorships and partnerships, profits translate directly into increases in owners' wealth. In corporations, profits translate into an increase in the value of common stock.

Responsibilities of the Financial Manager

The various responsibilities of the financial manager in increasing a firm's wealth fall into three general categories: *cash flow management*, *financial control*, and *financial planning*.

Cash Flow Management To increase a firm's value, financial managers must ensure that it always has enough funds on hand to purchase the materials and human resources that it needs to produce goods and services. Funds that are not needed immediately must be invested to earn more money. This activity—**cash flow management**—requires careful planning. If excess cash balances are allowed to sit idle instead of being invested, a firm loses the interest that it could have earned. One study revealed that companies averaging $2 million in annual sales typically hold $40 000 in non-interest-bearing accounts. Larger companies hold even larger sums. By putting idle cash to work, firms not only gain additional income, they also avoid having to borrow from outside sources. The savings on interest payments can be huge.

Financial Control Because things never go exactly as planned, financial managers must be prepared to make adjustments for actual financial changes that occur each day. **Financial control** is the process of checking actual performance against plans to ensure that the desired

FINANCIAL MANAGERS Those managers responsible for planning and overseeing the financial resources of a firm.

FINANCE The business function involving decisions about a firm's long-term investments and obtaining the funds to pay for those investments.

CASH FLOW MANAGEMENT Managing the pattern in which cash flows into the firm in the form of revenues and out of the firm in the form of debt payments.

FINANCIAL CONTROL The process of checking actual performance against plans to ensure that the desired financial status is achieved.

financial outcome occurs. For example, planned revenues based on forecasts usually turn out to be higher or lower than actual revenues. Why? Simply because sales are unpredictable. Control involves monitoring revenue inflows and making appropriate financial adjustments. Higher-than-expected revenues, for instance, may be deposited in short-term interest-bearing accounts, or they may be used to pay off short-term debt. Otherwise earmarked resources can be saved or put to better use. In contrast, lower-than-expected revenues may necessitate short-term borrowing to meet current debt obligations.

Budgets are often the backbone of financial control (see Chapter 11). The budget provides the "measuring stick" against which performance is evaluated. The cash flows, debts, and assets not only of the whole company but of each department are compared at regular intervals against budgeted amounts. Discrepancies indicate the need for financial adjustments so that resources are used to the best advantage.

Financial Planning The cornerstone of effective financial management is the development of a **financial plan**, which describes a firm's strategies for reaching some future financial position. In constructing the plan, a financial manager must ask several questions:

- What funds are needed to meet immediate plans?
- When will the firm need more funds?
- Where can the firm get the funds to meet both its short- and long-term needs?

To answer these questions, a financial manager must develop a clear picture of why a firm needs funds. Managers must also assess the relative costs and benefits of potential funding sources. In the following sections, we examine the main reasons for which companies generate funds and describe the main sources of business funding, both for the short and long term.

LO-2 Why Businesses Need Funds

Every company needs money to survive. Failure to make a contractually obligated payment can lead to bankruptcy and the dissolution of the firm. But the successful financial manager must distinguish between two kinds of financial outlays: *short-term (operating)* expenditures and *long-term (capital)* expenditures.

Short-Term (Operating) Expenditures
A firm incurs short-term expenditures regularly in its everyday business activities. To handle these expenditures, financial managers must pay attention to *accounts payable*, *accounts receivable*, and *inventories*.

Accounts Payable In Chapter 11, we defined *accounts payable* as unpaid bills owed to suppliers plus wages and taxes due within a year. For most companies, this is the largest single category of short-term debt. To plan for funding flows, financial managers want to know in advance the amounts of new accounts payable, as well as when they must be repaid. For information about such obligations and needs—say, the quantity of supplies required by a certain department in an upcoming period—financial managers must rely on other managers. The Team Ethics exercise at the end of the chapter presents an interesting dilemma regarding accounts payable.

Accounts Receivable As we also saw in Chapter 11, *accounts receivable* refers to funds due from customers who have bought on credit. A sound financial plan requires financial managers to project accurately both how much credit is advanced to buyers and when they will make payments. For example, managers at Kraft Foods must know how many dollars worth of cheddar cheese Safeway supermarkets will order each month; they must also know Safeway's payment schedule. Because accounts receivable represents an investment in products for which a firm has not yet received payment, they temporarily tie up its funds. Clearly, the seller wants to receive payment as quickly as possible.

Credit Policies Predicting payment schedules is a function of **credit policy**—the rules governing a firm's extension of credit to customers. This policy sets standards as to which buyers are eligible for what type of credit. Typically, credit is extended to customers who have the ability to pay and who honour their obligations. Credit is denied to firms with poor payment histories.

Credit policy also sets payment terms. For example, credit terms of "2/10, net 30" mean that the selling company offers a 2 percent discount if the customer pays within 10 days. The customer has 30 days to pay the regular price. Under these terms, the buyer would have to pay only $980 on a $1000 invoice on days 1 to 10, but all $1000 on days 11 to 30. The higher the discount, the more incentive buyers have to pay early. Sellers can thus adjust credit terms to influence when customers pay their bills.

Inventories Between the time a firm buys raw materials and the time it sells finished products, it ties up funds in **inventory**—materials and goods that it will sell within the year. Failure to manage inventory can have grave financial consequences. Too little inventory of any kind can cost a firm sales, while too much inventory means tied-up funds that cannot be used elsewhere. In extreme cases, a company may have to sell excess inventory at low prices simply to raise cash.

The basic supplies a firm buys to use in its production process are its **raw materials inventory**. Levi Strauss's raw materials inventory includes huge rolls of denim. **Work-in-process inventory** consists of goods partway through the production process. Cut-out but not-yet-sewn jeans are part of the work-in-process inventory at Levi's. Finally, **finished goods inventory** are the items that are ready for sale (completed blue jeans ready for shipment to Levi dealers).

Long-Term (Capital) Expenditures

Companies need funds to cover long-term expenditures for fixed assets. As noted in Chapter 11, fixed assets are items that have a lasting use or value, such as land, buildings, and machinery. Long-term expenditures are usually more carefully planned than short-term outlays because they pose special problems. They differ from short-term outlays in the following ways, all of which influence the ways that long-term outlays are funded:

- unlike inventories and other short-term assets, they are not normally sold or converted to cash
- their acquisition requires a very large investment
- they represent a binding commitment of company funds that continues long into the future

In 2010, General Motors decided to invest $200 million in its St. Catharines, Ontario, engine plant in order to install a new flexible assembly line for a new generation of V8 engines. This is part of a strategy that involved $850 million being invested in five North American plants. It also came just a week after GM had announced that it repaid the loan portion ($8 billion) of its $60 billion government bailout.[1]

LO-3 Sources of Short-Term Funds

Firms can call on many sources for the funds they need to finance day-to-day operations and to implement short-term plans. These sources include *trade credit*, *secured and unsecured loans*, and *factoring of accounts receivable*.

Trade Credit

Accounts payable are not merely an expenditure. They are also a source of funds to the company, which has the use of both the product purchased and the price of the product until the time it pays its bill. **Trade credit**, the granting of credit by one firm to another, is effectively a short-term loan. Trade credit can take several forms.

- The most common form, **open-book credit**, is essentially a "gentlemen's agreement." Buyers receive merchandise along with invoices stating credit terms. Sellers ship products on faith that payment will be forthcoming.

- When sellers want more reassurance, they may insist that buyers sign legally binding **promissory notes** before merchandise is shipped. The agreement states when and how much money will be paid to the seller.

- The **trade draft** is attached to the merchandise shipment by the seller and states the promised date and amount of payment due. To take possession of the merchandise, the buyer must sign the draft. Once signed by the buyer, the document becomes a **trade acceptance**. Trade drafts and trade acceptances are useful forms of credit in international transactions.

Secured Short-Term Loans

For most firms, bank loans are a vital source of short-term funding. Such loans almost always involve a promissory note in which the borrower promises to repay the loan plus interest. In **secured loans**, banks also require the borrower to put up collateral—to give the bank the right to seize

COLLATERAL
Any asset that a lender has the right to seize if a borrower does not repay a loan.

PLEDGING ACCOUNTS RECEIVABLE
Using accounts receivable as collateral for a loan.

UNSECURED LOAN
A short-term loan in which the borrower is not required to put up collateral.

LINE OF CREDIT
A standing agreement between a bank and a firm in which the bank specifies the maximum amount it will make available to the borrower for a short-term unsecured loan; the borrower can then draw on those funds, when available.

REVOLVING CREDIT AGREEMENT
A guaranteed line of credit for which the firm pays the bank interest on funds borrowed, as well as a fee for extending the line of credit.

COMMERCIAL PAPER
A method of short-run fundraising in which a firm sells unsecured notes for less than the face value and then repurchases them at the face value within 270 days; buyers' profits are the difference between the original price paid and the face value.

certain assets if payments are not made. Inventories, accounts receivable, and other assets (e.g., stocks and bonds) may serve as **collateral** for a secured loan.

Secured loans allow borrowers to get funds when they might not qualify for unsecured credit. Moreover, they generally carry lower interest rates than unsecured loans.

Inventory as Collateral When a loan is made with inventory as a collateral asset, the lender lends the borrower some portion of the stated value of the inventory. Inventory is more attractive as collateral when it can be readily converted into cash. Boxes full of expensive, partially completed lenses for eyeglasses are of little value on the open market. Meanwhile, a thousand crates of canned tomatoes might well be convertible into cash.

Accounts Receivable as Collateral When accounts receivable are used as collateral, the process is called **pledging accounts receivable**. In the event of non-payment, the lender may seize the receivables (funds owed the borrower by its customers). If these assets are not enough to cover the loan, the borrower must make up the difference. This option is especially important to service companies such as accounting firms and law offices. Because they do not maintain inventories, accounts receivable are their main source of collateral. Typically, lenders that will accept accounts receivable as collateral are financial institutions with credit departments capable of evaluating the quality of the receivables.

Factoring Accounts Receivable A firm can raise funds rapidly by *factoring* (that is, selling) its accounts receivable. The purchaser of the receivables (called a *factor*) might, for example, buy $40 000 worth of receivables for 60 percent of that sum ($24 000). The factor profits to the extent that the money it eventually collects exceeds the

amount it paid. This profit depends on the quality of the receivables, the cost of collecting them, and interest rates.

Unsecured Short-Term Loans

With an **unsecured loan**, the borrower does not have to put up collateral. In many cases, however, the bank requires the borrower to maintain a *compensating balance*—the borrower must keep a portion of the loan amount on deposit with the bank in a non-interest-bearing account.

The terms of the loan—amount, duration, interest rate, and payment schedule—are negotiated. To receive an unsecured loan, a firm must ordinarily have a good banking relationship with the lender. Once an agreement is made, a promissory note will be executed and the funds transferred to the borrower. Although some unsecured loans are one-time-only arrangements, many take the form of *lines of credit*, *revolving credit agreements*, or *commercial paper*.

Lines of Credit A standing agreement with a bank to lend a firm a maximum amount of funds on request is called a **line of credit**. With a line of credit, the firm knows the maximum amount it will be allowed to borrow if the bank has sufficient funds. The bank does not guarantee that the funds will be available when requested. For example, suppose that RBC gives Sunshine Tanning Inc. a $100 000 line of credit for the coming year. By signing promissory notes, Sunshine's borrowings can total up to $100 000 at any time. The bank may not always have sufficient funds when Sunshine needs them. But Sunshine benefits from the arrangement by knowing in advance that the bank regards the firm as creditworthy and will lend funds to it on short notice.

Revolving Credit Agreements Revolving credit agreements are similar to bank credit cards for consumers. Under a **revolving credit agreement**, a lender agrees to make some amount of funds available on demand to a firm for continuing short-term loans. The lending institution guarantees that funds will be available when sought by the borrower. In return, the bank charges a *commitment fee*—a charge for holding open a line of credit for a customer even if the customer does not borrow any funds. The commitment fee is often expressed as a percentage of the loan amount, usually 0.5 to 1 percent of the committed amount. For example, suppose that RBC agrees to lend Sunshine Tanning up to $100 000 under a revolving credit agreement. If Sunshine borrows $80 000, it still has access to $20 000. If it pays off $50 000 of the debt, reducing its debt to $30 000, then $70 000 is available. Sunshine pays interest on the borrowed funds and also pays a fee on the unused funds in the line of credit.

Commercial Paper Some firms can raise short-term funds by issuing commercial paper. Since **commercial paper** is backed solely by the issuing firm's promise to pay, it is an option for only the largest and most creditworthy firms. Here's how it works: Corporations issue commercial paper with a face value. Companies that buy commercial paper pay less than that value. At the end of a specified period (usually 30 to 90 days but legally up to 270 days), the issuing company buys back the paper—*at the face value*. The difference between the price the buying company paid and the face value is the buyer's profit. For example, if Air Canada needs to borrow $10 million for 90 days, it might issue commercial paper with a face value of $10.2 million. Insurance companies with $10 million excess cash will buy the paper. After 90 days, Air Canada would pay $10.2 million to the insurance companies.

LO-4 Sources of Long-Term Funds

Firms need long-term funding to finance expenditures on fixed assets—the buildings and equipment necessary for conducting business. They may seek long-term funds through *debt financing* (outside the firm) or through *equity financing* (from internal sources), or *hybrid financing* (a middle ground). In making decisions about sources of long-term funds, companies must consider the *risk–return relationship*.

Debt Financing

Long-term borrowing from outside the company—**debt financing**—is a major component of most firms' long-term financial planning. The two primary sources of such funding are long-term loans and the sale of bonds.

Long-Term Loans Most corporations get their long-term loans from a chartered bank, usually one with which the firm has developed a long-standing relationship. But credit companies, insurance companies, and pension funds also grant long-term business loans.

Long-term loans are attractive to borrowers for several reasons:

- the number of parties involved is limited, so loans can often be arranged quickly
- the duration of the loan is easily matched to the borrower's needs
- if the firm's needs change, loans usually contain clauses making it possible to change terms

Long-term loans also have some disadvantages. Large borrowers may have trouble finding lenders to supply enough funds. Long-term borrowers may also have restrictions placed on them as conditions of the loan. They may have to pledge

long-term assets as collateral. And they may have to agree not to take on any more debt until the borrowed funds are repaid.

Interest Rates Interest rates are negotiated between the borrower and lender. Although some bank loans have fixed rates, others have floating rates tied to the prime rate that they charge their most creditworthy customers (see Chapter 15). For example, a company may negotiate a loan at prime +1 percent. If prime is 3 percent at that particular time, the company will pay 4 percent (3 percent + 1 percent). The prime rate itself goes up and down as market conditions change.

DEBT FINANCING
Raising money to meet long-term expenditures by borrowing from outside the company; usually takes the form of long-term loans or the sale of corporate bonds.

CORPORATE BOND
A promise by the issuing company to pay the holder a certain amount of money on a specified date, with stated interest payments in the interim; a form of long-term debt financing.

Corporate Bonds A **corporate bond** is a contract—a promise by the issuing company or organization to pay the holder a certain amount of money on a specified date. Most bonds pay interest semi-annually or annually. If it fails to make a bond payment, the company is in default. In many cases, bonds may not be redeemed for 30 years.

Corporate bonds are the major source of long-term debt financing for most corporations. Bonds are attractive when companies need large amounts of funds for long periods of time. The issuing company gets access to large numbers of lenders through nationwide bond markets. But bonds involve expensive administrative and selling costs. They also may require very high interest payments if the issuing company has a poor credit rating.

The proceeds from this corporate bond can be used to purchase fixed assets that are necessary for the production of goods and services.

Table 16.1 Stockholders' Equity for Sunshine Tanning

Common Stockholders' Equity, 2003	
Initial common stock (500 shares issued @ $20 per share, 2003)	$10 000
Total stockholders' equity	$10 000
Common Stockholders' Equity, 2009	
Initial common stock (500 shares issued @ $20 per share, 2003)	$10 000
Additional paid-in capital (500 shares issued @ $100 per share, 2009)	50 000
Total stockholders' equity	$60 000

Bond Indenture The **bond indenture** spells out the terms of a bond, including the amount to be paid, the interest rate, and the maturity (payoff) date. The indenture also identifies which of the firm's assets, if any, are pledged as collateral. Because of the risk of default, debt financing appeals most strongly to companies that have predictable profits and cash flow patterns. For example, demand for electric power is quite steady from year to year and predictable from month to month. Thus, provincial hydro-electric utility companies enjoy steady streams of income and can carry substantial amounts of debt.

With the equity markets in turmoil, many companies were turning to the bond market in 2010. According to Colleen Campbell of BMO Nesbitt Burns, the bond market was in the midst of the highest demand she had seen in her 30-year career. In 2009, bond sales stood at $148 billion, up from $118 billion a year earlier.[2]

Equity Financing

Sometimes, looking inside the company for long-term funding is preferable to looking outside. In most cases, **equity financing** takes the form of issuing common stock or of retaining the firm's earnings. Both options involve putting the owners' capital to work.

Issuing Common Stock By selling shares, the company gets the funds it needs to buy land, buildings, and equipment. When shareholders purchase common stock, they seek profits in the form of both dividends and increases in the price of the stock. In 2010, Kanata, Ontario–based Mitel Networks Corporation, which specializes in communications for small- and medium-sized businesses, was looking to sell about 18.5 million shares to raise $180 million to pay down some of its existing heavy debt load.[3]

Let's look at a particular example in detail. Suppose that Sunshine Tanning's founders invested $10 000 in buying the original 500 shares of common stock (at $20 per share) in 2003. If the company used these funds to buy equipment and succeeded financially, by 2009 it may have needed further funds for expansion. A pattern of profitable operations and regularly paid dividends enabled Sunshine to raise $50 000 by selling 500 new shares of stock for $100 per share. This additional paid-in capital would increase the total shareholders' equity to $60 000, as shown in Table 16.1.

The use of equity financing via common stock can be expensive because paying dividends is more expensive than paying bond interest. Why? Interest paid to bondholders is a business expense and, hence, a tax deduction for the firm. Stock dividends are not tax-deductible. So, as you can see, financial managers and executives can spend considerable time in deciding on the question of debt or equity financing.

Retained Earnings Another approach to equity financing is to use *retained earnings*. These earnings represent profits not paid out in dividends. Using retained earnings means that the firm will not have to borrow money and pay interest on loans or bonds. A firm that has a history of reaping much higher profits by successfully reinvesting retained earnings may be attractive to some investors. But the smaller dividends that can be paid to shareholders as a result of retained earnings may decrease demand for—and thus the price of—the company's stock. In 2010, Hertz bought out the Dollar Thrifty Automotive Group for US$1.17 billion. About 80 percent of that deal was financed with cash from Hertz, with the remaining 20 percent coming in the form of Hertz stock.[4]

In mid 2010, China's CNOOC Ltd. share price was $136, and there were 44.67 billion common shares out-standing. Its market cap was over $7 trillion.

Let's revisit our Sunshine Tanning example. If the company had net earnings of $50 000 in 2010, it could pay a $50-per-share dividend on its 1000 shares of common stock. But if it plans to remodel at a cost of $30 000 and retains $30 000 of earnings to finance the project, only $20 000 is left to distribute for stock dividends ($20 per share).

Since equity funding can be expensive, why don't firms rely totally on debt capital? Because long-term loans and bonds carry fixed interest rates and represent a fixed promise to pay regardless of the profitability of the firm. If the firm defaults on its obligations, it may lose its assets and go into bankruptcy. In 2009, CanWest Global announced that it was halting interest payments of $30.4 million to bondholders as it tried to recapitalize the company and avoid bankruptcy. The firm said it might replace the old debt with new debt, guaranteeing that bondholders would get their money from cash that CanWest was planning to generate by selling some of its assets.[5]

Hybrid Financing: Preferred Stock

Preferred stock is a hybrid investment because it has some of the features of corporate bonds and some features of common stock. As with bonds, payments on preferred stock are for fixed amounts, such as $6 per share per year. Unlike bonds, however, preferred stock never matures. It can be held indefinitely, like common stock. And dividends need not be paid if the company makes no profit. If dividends are paid, preferred stockholders receive them first in preference to dividends on common stock. A major advantage of preferred stock to the issuing corporation is its flexibility. It secures funds for the firm without relinquishing control, since preferred stockholders have no voting rights. It does not require repayment of principal, or the payment of dividends in lean times.

Choosing Between Debt and Equity Financing

Financial planning involves striking a balance between debt and equity financing to meet the firm's long-term need for funds. Because the mix of debt and equity provides the firm's financial base, it is called the **capital structure** of the firm. Financial plans contain targets for the capital structure, such as 40 percent debt and 60 percent equity. But choosing a target is not easy. A wide range of debt-versus-equity mixes is possible.

The most conservative strategy is to use all equity financing and no debt because a company has no formal obligations for financial payouts. But as we have noted, equity is a very expensive source of capital. The riskiest strategy would be to use all debt financing. While less expensive than equity funding, indebtedness increases the risk that a firm will be unable to meet its obligations and will go bankrupt. Somewhere between the two extremes, financial planners try to find a mix that will maximize stockholders' wealth. Figure 16.1 summarizes

CAPITAL STRUCTURE
Relative mix of a firm's debt and equity financing.

Figure 16.1
Comparing debt and equity financing.

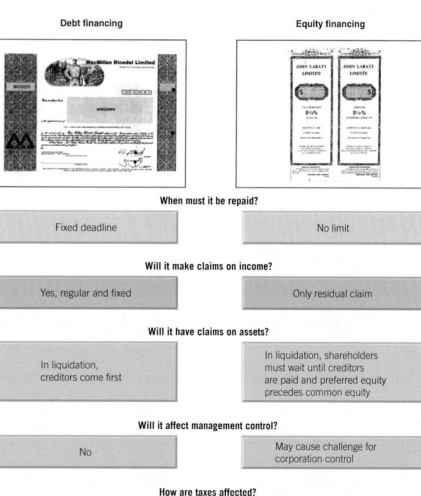

Debt financing	Equity financing
When must it be repaid?	
Fixed deadline	No limit
Will it make claims on income?	
Yes, regular and fixed	Only residual claim
Will it have claims on assets?	
In liquidation, creditors come first	In liquidation, shareholders must wait until creditors are paid and preferred equity precedes common equity
Will it affect management control?	
No	May cause challenge for corporation control
How are taxes affected?	
Bond interest is deductible	Dividends are not deductible
Will it affect management flexibility?	
Yes, many constraints	No, few constraints

RISK–RETURN
RELATIONSHIP
Shows the amount of
risk and the likely rate
of return on various
financial instruments.

the factors management takes into account when deciding between debt and equity financing. The boxed insert entitled "An Online Community for People 50 and Older" describes one small company's fundraising dilemma.

The Risk–Return Relationship

While developing plans for raising capital, financial managers must be aware of the different motivations of individual investors. Why do some individuals and firms invest in stocks while others invest only in bonds? Investor motivations determine who is willing to buy a given company's stocks or bonds.

Everyone who invests money is expressing a personal preference for safety versus risk. Investors give money to firms and, in return, anticipate receiving future cash flows.

Some cash flows are more certain than others. Investors generally expect to receive higher payments for higher uncertainty. They do not generally expect large returns for secure investments such as government-insured bonds. Each type of investment, then, has a **risk–return relationship**. Figure 16.2 shows the general risk–return relationship for various financial instruments.

Figure 16.2
The risk–return relationship.

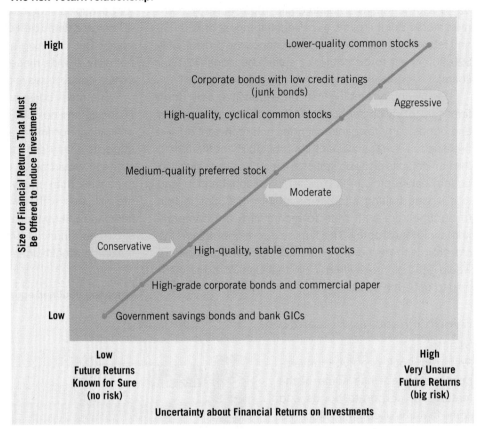

ENTREPRENEURSHIP AND NEW VENTURES

An Online Community for People 50 and Older

The social networking site Facebook began specifically for college students, and over 80 percent of its users are under the age of 35. That's one reason Kelly and Jeff Lantz founded 55-Alive!, a social networking site for users over 50 years old. Launched in 2005, the company had a meagre $5000 in revenues in its first year. The following year, revenues jumped to $30 000 as the site's activities expanded into instant messaging, blogging, and chat rooms for member-created groups. Two groups that are widely subscribed to are "Man's Best Friend" and "Widow/Widower" forums.

So what's next? To date, 55-Alive! is financed with the Lantzes' own money and has just one part-time employee. Kelly and Jeff project a need for at least $250 000 of outside funding to expand the site's content and to hire someone to help with sales ads. Despite its early success, 55-Alive! still receives only 100 000 visits per month, just a small fraction of Facebook's 100 million daily users. While Facebook seems to continue to appeal largely to a younger demographic, it has been experiencing significant growth in the 35–54 age category.

Critical Thinking Questions

1. What possible sources of financing are available to 55-Alive!?

2. How important is it that Kelly and Jeff develop a business plan to help secure this money?

High-grade corporate bonds rate low in terms of risk on future returns but also low on size of expected returns. The reverse is true of junk bonds, those with a higher risk of default.

Risk–return differences are recognized by financial planners, who try to gain access to the greatest funding at the lowest possible cost. By gauging investors' perceptions of their riskiness, a firm's managers can estimate how much it must pay to attract funds to their offerings. Over time, a company can reposition itself on the risk continuum by improving its record on dividends, interest payments, and debt repayment.

LO-5 Financial Management for Small Businesses

Most new businesses have inadequate funding. Why are so many start-ups underfunded? Entrepreneurs often underestimate the value of establishing *bank credit* as a source of funds and use *trade credit* ineffectively. In addition, they often fail to consider *venture capital* as a source of funding, and they are notorious for not *planning cash flow needs* properly. Many of them are also not aware of government programs that are available for support. For example, programs like the Canada Small Business Funding Program enable entrepreneurs to receive up to $350 000 worth of loans and up to $500 000 for the purchase of real property. Each year the program provides approximately 10 000 loans for over $1 billion of financing.[6] Of course, companies that do not apply, or are unaware of the program, get $0 even if they are good potential candidates.

Establishing Bank Credit and Trade Credit

Some banks have liberal credit policies and offer financial analysis, cash-flow planning, and knowledgeable advice. Some provide loans to small businesses in bad times and work to keep them going. Obtaining credit, therefore, begins with finding a bank that can—and will—support a small firm's financial needs. Once a *line of credit* is obtained, the small business can seek more liberal credit policies from other businesses. Sometimes suppliers give customers longer credit periods—say, 45 or 60 days rather than 30 days. Liberal trade credit terms with their suppliers lets firms increase short-term funds and avoid additional borrowing from banks.

Start-up firms without proven financial success usually must present a business plan to demonstrate creditworthiness.[7] As we saw in

Chapter 4, a business plan is a document that tells potential lenders why the money is needed, the amount needed, how the money will be used to improve the company, and when it will be paid back.

Venture Capital

Many newer businesses—especially those undergoing rapid growth—cannot get the funds they need through borrowing alone. They may, therefore, turn to *venture capital*—outside equity funding provided in return for part ownership of the borrowing firm (see Chapter 4).

Planning for Cash-Flow Requirements

All businesses should plan for their cash flows, but it is especially important for small businesses to do so. Success or failure may hinge on anticipating times when cash will be short and when excess cash is expected. Figure 16.3 shows possible cash inflows, cash outflows, and net cash position (inflows minus outflows), month by month, for Slippery Fish Bait Supply. In this highly seasonal business, bait stores buy heavily from Slippery during the spring and summer months. Revenues outpace expenses, leaving surplus funds that can be invested. During the fall and winter, expenses exceed revenues. Slippery must borrow funds to keep going until sales revenues pick up again in the spring. Comparing predicted cash inflows from sales with outflows for expenses shows the firm's monthly cash-flow position.

Figure 16.3
Cash flow for Slippery Fish Bait Supply Company.

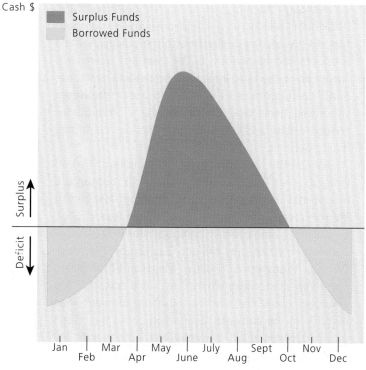

Cash $

- Surplus Funds
- Borrowed Funds

Surplus | Deficit

Jan Feb Mar Apr May June July Aug Sept Oct Nov Dec

A Quicken Course in Accountability

After deciding to hold himself accountable for designing new products, Scott Cook created some unique methods to ensure he'd meet those design obligations when he founded a company back in 1983. Cook is the former CEO of Intuit, the $3.1 billion company whose well-known software tools—Quicken and Quickbooks—have changed the way we manage our financial lives.

Cook initially envisioned three core principles for product design that eventually led to superb commercial success:

- First: It's the customer that's most important. Listen to the customer and design the product for customer value.

- Second: Be open-minded in identifying all competing ways the customer could perform the task, not just the obvious ways.

- Third: Simplify and improve the product so it provides the easiest way for the customer to complete the task to be performed.

From the beginning, Cook believed these principles would lead to superior, user-friendly preferred products that customers would buy and use. Accordingly, customer acceptance of the products would be the ultimate measure of success or failure of product designs for which Cook was accountable.

Although the firm was selling computer software, Cook didn't restrict his vision to just software competitors. As the second design principle stipulates, Intuit's products had to perform better than any alternative way of doing the task, including competitors' software, hand calculators, and pencil-and-paper methods. Otherwise, users wouldn't prefer Intuit's products for cheque writing and the many other financial tasks they had to perform.

While the initial version of Quicken worked well, Cook's insistence on pleasing customers meant that he wasn't satisfied. Seeking user-based improvements, the first design principle was applied by assigning employees in computer stores to observe consumers when they bought Quicken off the shelf. Cook's imaginative "Follow Me Home" program surprised customers when they were asked if the employee could come home with them to watch their reaction to the software. Everything about the user's experience was noted, beginning with ease or difficulty in opening the package, reading instructions, installing

Scott Cook, Intuit founder and chairman of the executive committee.

the software on a computer, using it, and even turning away to write with pencil and paper. Cook insisted that anything preventing ease of use, no matter how small, was Intuit's fault, not the customer's. So watching for even the tiniest display of displeasure or frustration, the employee silently observed the user's facial expressions, body language, vocal reactions, pauses, and re-reading of instructions in each stage from opening the shrink-wrapped package to using the product.

Guided by what was learned from "Follow Me Home," the third principle was invoked for simplifying and improving Quicken. As word spread about the software's success with personal finance on home computers, entrepreneurs started using it—making changes to suit their needs—for financial management tasks in their companies. Once again, by listening to these new customers, Intuit modified the software into a new product—Quickbooks—especially designed for business financial management. Because these companion tools—Quicken and Quickbooks—are the most popular in the industry, the firm's $3.1 billion sales revenues and market leadership are evidence that Cook fulfilled the product-design obligations for which he was accountable.

Critical Thinking Questions

1. Choose two consumer products that you use and come up with specific suggestions for pursuing accountability in the way that Cook did for his company's products. Be specific.

2. Does Cook's view of "accountability" seem extreme? Is there a downside to such aggressive accountability?

By anticipating shortfalls, a financial manager can seek advance funds and minimize their cost. By anticipating excess cash, a manager can plan to put the funds to work in short-term, interest-earning investments. The Managing in Turbulent Times box describes how one entrepreneur was successful by helping other individuals organize their financial matters.

LO-6 Risk Management

Risk—uncertainty about future events—is a factor in every manager's job because nearly every managerial action raises the possibility for either positive or negative outcomes. Risk management is therefore essential.[8] Firms devote considerable resources not only to recognizing potential risks but also to positioning themselves to make the most advantageous decisions regarding risk.

The financial crisis that erupted in 2008 caused many firms to take a second look at their risk-management practices. For example, the Caisse de dépôt et placement du Québec incurred heavy losses in 2008 as a result of its involvement in currency- and stock-related derivatives and the commercial paper crisis.[9] The Bank of Montreal (BMO) also had problems and reported write-downs of $490 million. That was on top of the $850 million charge it incurred as the result of fraud committed by one of its traders. As a result of the losses, BMO did a complete review of its risk-management systems and procedures. Bill Downe, the CEO, admitted that BMO got involved in some business activities that were beyond the company's risk tolerance and strategic plan.[10]

According to a survey of 600 executives conducted by Toronto-based recruitment firm Watson Gardner Brown, the most difficult jobs to staff are in the risk management and compliance areas. Why? Firms are increasing the size of these divisions because of the scandals and the meltdown in some securities in recent years. Institutional investors are demanding more attention to risk oversight before they will trust their funds to such organizations. Finding enough highly qualified people to fill these spots, even with generous salaries, has been a challenge.[11]

Coping with Risk

Businesses constantly face two basic types of risk: **Speculative risks**, such as financial investments, involve the possibility of gain or loss. **Pure risks** involve only the possibility of loss or no loss. For example, designing and distributing a new product is a speculative risk. The product may fail or succeed. The chance of a warehouse fire is a pure risk.

For a company to survive and prosper, it must manage both types of risk in a cost-effective manner. We can thus define the process of **risk management** as "conserving the firm's earning power and assets by reducing the threat of losses due to uncontrollable events."[12]

The risk-management process usually involves five steps.

Step 1: Identify Risks and Potential Losses Managers analyze a firm's risks to identify potential losses. For example, a firm with a fleet of delivery trucks can expect that one of them will eventually be involved in an accident. The accident may cause bodily injury to the driver or others, and may cause physical damage to the truck or other vehicles.

Step 2: Measure the Frequency and Severity of Losses and Their Impact To measure the frequency and severity of losses, managers must consider both past history and current activities. How often can the firm expect the loss to occur? What is the likely size of the loss in dollars? For example, our firm with the fleet of delivery trucks may have had two accidents per year in the past. If it adds more trucks to its fleet, it may reasonably expect the number of accidents to increase.

Step 3: Evaluate Alternatives and Choose Techniques That Will Best Handle Losses Having identified and measured potential losses, managers are in a better position to decide how to handle them. They generally have four choices: *risk avoidance*, *control*, *retention*, or *transfer*.

Risk Avoidance A firm opts for **risk avoidance** by declining to enter or by ceasing to participate in a risky activity. For example, the firm with the delivery trucks could avoid any risk of physical damage or bodily injury by closing down its delivery service. Similarly, a pharmaceutical maker may withdraw a new drug for fear of liability lawsuits.

Risk Control When avoidance is not practical or desirable, firms can practise **risk control**—say, the use of loss-prevention techniques to minimize the frequency of

RISK Uncertainty about future events.

SPECULATIVE RISK An event that offers the chance for either a gain or a loss.

PURE RISK An event that offers no possibility of gain; it offers only the chance of a loss.

RISK MANAGEMENT Conserving a firm's (or an individual's) financial power or assets by minimizing the financial effect of accidental losses.

RISK AVOIDANCE Stopping participation in or refusing to participate in ventures that carry any risk.

RISK CONTROL Techniques to prevent, minimize, or reduce losses or the consequences of losses.

losses. A delivery service, for instance, can prevent losses by training its drivers in defensive-driving techniques, mapping out safe routes, and conscientiously maintaining its trucks.

Risk Retention When losses cannot be avoided or controlled, firms must cope with the consequences. When such losses are manageable and predictable, they may decide to cover them out of company funds. The firm is thus said to "assume" or "retain" the financial consequences of the loss: hence the practice known as **risk retention**. For example, the firm with the fleet of trucks may find that each vehicle suffers vandalism totalling $300 per year. Depending on its coverage, the company may find it cheaper to pay for repairs out of pocket rather than to submit claims to its insurance company.

Risk Transfer When the potential for large risks cannot be avoided or controlled, managers often opt for **risk transfer**. They transfer the risk to another firm—namely, an insurance company. In transferring risk to an insurance company, a firm pays a *premium*. In return, the insurance company issues an insurance policy—a formal agreement to pay the policyholder a specified amount in the event of certain losses. In some cases, the insured party must also pay a *deductible*—an agreed-upon amount of the loss that the insured must absorb prior to reimbursement. Thus, the truck company may buy insurance to protect itself against theft, physical damage to trucks, and bodily injury to drivers and others involved in an accident.

Every year in Canada, well over $1 billion is lost to insurance fraud. The insurance industry estimates that between $10 and $15 of every $100 you pay in premiums goes to cover fraud losses. The Canadian Coalition Against Insurance Fraud (CCAIF) exists to curb this fraud. CCAIF members include mutual and private insurance companies, public automobile insurers, and representatives from health care, law enforcement, and consumer advocacy groups. Part of the CCAIF's mandate is to ensure that consumers are aware of the connection between insurance fraud and higher insurance rates. Working with Crime Stoppers, the CCAIF offers a reward to tipsters who provide information leading to the discovery of fraud.

Step 4: Implement the Risk-Management Program The means of implementing risk-management decisions depend on both the technique chosen and the activity being managed. For example, risk avoidance for certain activities can be implemented by purchasing those activities from outside providers, such as hiring delivery services instead of operating delivery vehicles. Risk control might be implemented by training employees and designing new work methods and equipment for on-the-job safety. For situations in which risk retention is preferred, reserve funds can be set aside out of revenues. When risk transfer is needed, implementation means selecting an insurance company and buying the right policies.

Step 5: Monitor Results Because risk management is an ongoing activity, follow-up is always essential. New types of risks emerge with changes in customers, facilities, employees, and products. Insurance regulations change, and new types of insurance become available. Consequently, managers must continually monitor a company's risks, re-evaluate the methods used for handling them, and revise them as necessary.

Summary of Learning Objectives

1. **Describe the responsibilities of a *financial manager*.** A financial manager's overall objective is to increase a firm's value and stockholders' wealth. They must ensure that earnings exceed its costs so that the firm generates a profit. The responsibilities of the financial manager fall into two general *categories:* (1) *cash-flow management,* and (2) *financial control.*

2. **Distinguish between *short-term (operating)* and *long-term (capital)* expenditures.** *Short-term (operating)* expenditures are incurred in a firm's everyday business activities. To handle these expenditures, managers must pay attention to accounts payable, accounts receivable, and inventories. *Long-term (capital)* expenditures are required to purchase fixed assets.

3. **Identify four sources of *short-term financing* for businesses.** The four sources of short-term financing are *trade credit, secured short-term loans, factoring accounts receivable,* and *unsecured short-term loans.*

4. **Distinguish among the various sources of *long-term financing* and explain the risks involved in each.** Firms may seek long-term funds to pay for fixed assets through two channels: (1) *debt financing,* and (2) *equity financing.* All-debt financing is the most speculative, while all-equity is the most conservative. The use of *preferred stock* is a "hybrid" approach; it has features of both corporate bonds and common stocks.

5. **Discuss some key issues in financial management for small businesses.** Obtaining credit begins with finding a bank to support a small firm's financial needs. Once a *line of credit* is obtained, the small business can seek more liberal credit policies from other businesses. Obtaining long-term loans is more difficult for new businesses than for established companies, and start-ups pay higher interest rates than older firms. To demonstrate that it's a good credit risk, a start-up must usually present a *business plan.*

6. **Explain how *risk* affects business operations and identify the five steps in the *risk-management process*.** Businesses face two basic types of *risk:* (1) *speculative risks,* and (2) *pure risks. Risk management* entails conserving earning power and assets by reducing the threat of losses due to uncontrollable events. The process has five steps: Step 1: *Identify risks and potential losses.* Step 2: *Measure the frequency and severity of losses and their impact.* Step 3: *Evaluate alternatives.* Step 4: *Implement the risk-management program.* Step 5: *Monitor results.*

Questions and Exercises

Questions for Analysis

1. In what ways do the two sources of debt financing differ from each other? How do they differ from the two sources of equity financing?

2. Describe the relationship between investment risk and return. In what ways might the risk–return relationship affect a company's financial planning?

3. What is the basic relationship between the amount of risk associated with a project and the likelihood of gains (or losses) on the project? Explain how several financial instruments (GICs, common stocks, preferred stocks, corporate bonds) illustrate this basic relationship.

4. How would you decide on the best mix of debt and equity for a company?

5. Why would a business "factor" its accounts receivable?

6. What are the risks and benefits associated with the sources of short-term funds (trade credit, secured and unsecured loans, and factoring accounts receivable)? How do these risks and benefits compare with those associated with sources of long-term funds (debt and equity)?

Application Exercises

7. Interview the owner of a small local business. Identify the types of short-term and long-term funding that this firm typically uses. Why has the company made these particular financial management decisions?

8. Interview the owner of a small local business. Ask this person to describe the risk-management process that he or she follows. What role, for example, is played by risk transfer? Why has the company made the risk-management decisions that it has?

9. Go to Sedar.com and find the balance sheets of two corporations operating in the same industry. Determine the relative emphasis each company has placed on raising money through debt versus equity. Why might these differences exist?

10. Interview a risk manager of a large firm and ask him or her the following questions: What risks do you think your firm faces? How does your firm manage these risks? How have your policies changed over the years to adjust for new risk levels?

TEAM EXERCISES

Building Your Business Skills

Understanding Risk-Management Issues

Goal
To encourage students to gain a better understanding of the major financial and risk-management issues that face large companies.

Method
During the last few years, all of the following companies reported financial problems relating to risk management:

- Air Canada
- Bombardier
- EarthLink
- BP

Step 1 Working alone, research one of the companies listed above to learn more about the financial risks that were reported in the news.

Step 2 Write a short explanation of the risks and financial-management issues faced by the firm you researched.

Step 3 Join in teams with students who researched other companies and compare your findings.

Follow-Up Questions

1. Were there common themes in the "big stories" in financial management?

2. What have the various companies done to minimize future risks and losses?

Exercising Your Ethics

Doing Your Duty When Payables Come Due

The Situation
Sarah Keats is the vice-president of finance at Multiverse, a large firm that manufactures consumer products. On December 15, 2010 (two weeks before the end of the fiscal year), she attends an executive committee meeting at which Jack Malvo, the CEO, expresses concern that the firm's year-end cash position will be less favourable than projected. The firm has exceeded analysts' performance expectations in each of his eight years at the helm, and Malvo is determined that stockholders will never be disappointed as long as he is CEO. The purpose of the meeting is to find solutions to the cash problem and decide on a course of action.

The Dilemma

To open the meeting, Malvo announces, "We have just two weeks to reduce expenses or increase revenues. We need a $100 million swing to get us where market analysts predicted we'd be on cash flows for the year. Any suggestions?"

In the discussion that ensues, it is noted that Multiverse owes $150 million to about 80 companies that supply component parts and other operating supplies to Multiverse. The money is due before year-end. Sarah Keats says, "Our cash outflows for the year will be lower if we delay paying suppliers, which will help the bottom line. And, it's like getting a free loan." The procurement director, Julie Levin, expresses the following concern: "Our agreements with suppliers call for faithful payments at designated times, and many of the smaller firms depend on receiving that cash to meet their obligations. Also, we've worked hard for two years at improving relationships with all suppliers, and that effort could go down the drain if we don't meet our financial commitments as promised."

As the meeting draws to a close, Malvo announces, "Keep me posted on any unexpected developments, but if nothing helpful comes up in the next few days, let's go ahead and withhold supplier payments for three weeks."

Team Activity

Assemble a group of four students and assign each group member one of the following roles:

- Jack Malvo (CEO of Multiverse)
- Sarah Keats (vice-president of finance)
- Julie Levin (procurement director)
- A stockholder of Multiverse

Action Steps

1. Before discussing the situation with your group, and from the perspective of your assigned role, decide whether there are any ethical issues here.

2. Before discussing the situation with your group, and from the perspective of your assigned role, decide what action you think should be taken. Write down your recommended action.

3. Gather your group together and reveal, in turn, each member's comments and recommendations.

4. Appoint someone to record the main points of agreement and disagreement within the group. How do you explain the results? What accounts for any disagreements?

5. From an ethical standpoint, what does your group recommend?

BUSINESS CASE 16

The Commercial Paper Crisis

Commercial paper is sold to investors on the promise that the issuing organization will pay back the principal (plus interest) in the near future (usually 30 or 60 days). In effect, the issuer might say something like this: If you loan my company $99, in one month my company will give you $100. So, the investor earns $1 of interest in one month on a $99 loan. Both individuals and organizations buy commercial paper because they want to put their extra cash into a liquid (and safe) short-term investment that will earn interest until they need the money.

In recent years, a variation of this basic system was developed. Asset-backed commercial paper (ABCP) is issued by companies (called conduits) that sold subprime mortgages to people with poor credit ratings. They then packaged these mortgages together with other, more traditional loans (on credit cards, automobiles, and regular home mortgages) and sold them as collateralized debt obligations (CDOs) to investors. These products were

Baffinland Iron Mines Corporation was one of many companies to suffer during the ABCP crisis through no fault of its own. It bought $43.8 million of ABCP to earn interest on extra cash but got a big surprise when the issuer was unable to pay on time.

much riskier than traditional commercial paper, but investors typically didn't know that.

In 2007, problems developed in the Canadian commercial paper market as a result of problems in the U.S. subprime mortgage market (where people who wouldn't usually qualify for mortgage money got money to buy a house). People who wanted to buy a home but had a poor credit rating got subprime mortgages with low interest "teaser" rates for the first two years. But those rates then rose to market rates for the remaining years of the mortgage. When people with subprime mortgages started defaulting, because they couldn't afford the higher interest rates, the subprime market collapsed. Foreclosures increased and the returns that normally would have been earned on these mortgages dropped sharply. And since these subprime mortgages were included in commercial paper that was sold to investors, the conduits couldn't pay their investors as they had promised. When word got out about this problem, investors refused to "roll over" their commercial paper (i.e., they wouldn't agree to keep their money in commercial paper for another 30 or 60 days) because they felt that it was too risky. The conduits thus experienced a sharp decline in the money they had available. They then went to their liquidity providers (Canadian banks) to get more money, but the banks argued that since the whole commercial paper market hadn't seized up (just the non-bank part of the market), they weren't obliged to provide the conduits with any money. The result was that many holders of commercial paper did not receive their principal and interest when they thought they would.

Many individuals who bought ABCP were assured by their financial advisers or by the Canadian bond rating firm DBRS that it was AAA-rated and was as safe as guaranteed investment certificates (GICs). DBRS was later criticized for giving such high ratings to such risky investments. Many other investors didn't even know they owned any ABCP until they tried to get some of their money and were told it was "frozen." For example, Angela Speller, a retiree in Victoria, B.C., invested almost $1 million in ABCP and expected to be able to withdraw money as she needed it. But now she fears she will have to wait years to see her money.

Baffinland Iron Mines Corp. is typical of companies that discovered they were not going to get their money when they wanted it. The company mines iron ore deposits on Baffin Island and needs money to buy equipment of all kinds to carry on its regular operations. The company bought $43.8 million of ABCP to earn interest on extra cash that it had. One month later, some of the proceeds of the ABCP (principal plus interest) that were supposed to be paid to Baffinland were not paid because the company Baffinland had bought the ABCP from was unable to pay. This created a major cash shortage at Baffinland that hindered its exploration activities.

Another example is Petrolifera Petroleum Ltd. of Calgary. The company invested about $37 million in ABCP, but when $31 million of the notes came due, they were not paid.

Caisse de dépôt et placement du Québec had the greatest exposure to the ABCP securities market (perhaps as much as $13 billion). Other organizations with some exposure included Nav Canada ($368 million), Ontario Power Generation Inc. ($102 million), and Canada Post ($27 million). Major Canadian banks had exposure too. The Canadian Imperial Bank of Commerce revealed that it lost $1 billion.

One way to solve the problem was to simply convert short-term commercial paper into longer-term debt and then gradually pay off investors. But that solution ignores the very reason that investors buy commercial paper in the first place (i.e., short-term liquidity). A group called the Pan-Canadian Investors Committee was formed for the purpose of resolving the commercial paper mess. In April 2008, the committee announced that noteholders had voted in favour of a plan designed to solve the problem, but in September, the financial crisis hit and that further delayed settlement. Finally, in December, the committee announced a formal agreement to restructure $33 billion of ABCP by exchanging short-term notes for longer-term ones. Purdy Crawford, the chair of the group, said that most individuals and companies would likely get all their money back if they held the restructured notes to maturity. The agreement requires the federal government and the provinces of Quebec, Ontario, and Alberta to provide over $4 billion to ensure that the $32 billion in ABCP is actually restructured.

In 2010, long after the ABCP financial mess, investors were still a bit skeptical about commercial paper. The DBRS did not expect a solid rebound in the market until 2011 at the earliest. Canaccord Financial Inc., which sold ABCP paper to retail clients before this market essentially froze, disposed of its ABCP assets and effectively closed the book. It was trying to forget or at least distance itself from a time when clients were legitimately yelling for their funds.

Questions for Discussion

1. Why do investors buy commercial paper? Why did some investors buy non-bank commercial paper?

2. How does the commercial paper crisis demonstrate the risk–return principle?

3. Explain how problems in the U.S. subprime mortgage market caused difficulties in the Canadian commercial paper market.

4. Should Canada's federal government become more involved in regulation of the commercial paper market so problems like the one described above won't happen again? Defend your answer.

SCANLIFE

Appendix C
Managing Your Personal Finances

For many people, the goal of financial success isn't *being* wealthy; it's the things that they can *do* with wealth. That's why chapter one in so many financial success stories deals with a hard reality: Like it or not, dealing with personal finances is a life-long job. As a rule, it involves a life-altering choice between two options:

- committing to the rational management of your personal finances—controlling them as a way of life and helping them grow
- letting the financial chips fall where they may and hoping for the best (which seldom happens)

Not surprisingly, option one results in greater personal satisfaction and financial stability. Ignoring your finances, on the other hand, invites frustration, disappointment, and, quite often, acute financial distress.

Taking Your Finances Personally

In Chapter 16, we explored some basic financial-management activities, including the role of financial managers in cash flow management, financial planning and control, and debt and equity financing. We discussed the activities of financial managers—clarifying financial goals, determining short-term and long-term funding needs, and managing risk. Many of the principles of *organizational* finance pertain to *personal* finance as well. Recall, for example, the principle of reducing organizational financial risk by diversifying investments.

In managing your own finances and pursuing your own personal financial goals, you must consider the activities that we'll revisit in the following sections: cash management, financial planning and control, investment alternatives, and risk management. We start by describing a key factor in success: the personal financial plan. Then we'll detail the steps in the planning process and relate them to some core concepts and crucial decisions in personal financial management.

Building Your Financial Plan

Financial planning is the process of looking at your current financial condition, identifying your goals, and anticipating your requirements for meeting those goals. Once you've determined the assets you need to meet your goals, you'll then identify the best sources and uses of those assets for eventually reaching your goals. Because your goals and financial position will change as you enter different life stages, your plan should always make room for revision. Figure C.1 summarizes a step-by-step approach to personal financial planning.

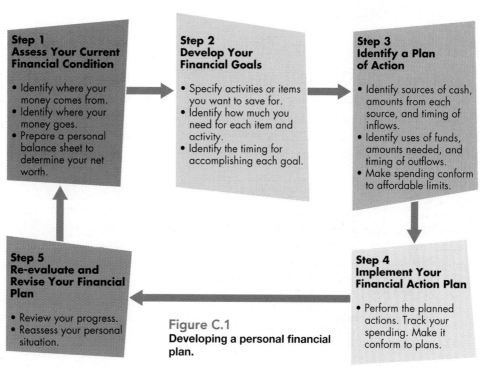

Step 1
Assess Your Current Financial Condition

- Identify where your money comes from.
- Identify where your money goes.
- Prepare a personal balance sheet to determine your net worth.

Step 2
Develop Your Financial Goals

- Specify activities or items you want to save for.
- Identify how much you need for each item and activity.
- Identify the timing for accomplishing each goal.

Step 3
Identify a Plan of Action

- Identify sources of cash, amounts from each source, and timing of inflows.
- Identify uses of funds, amounts needed, and timing of outflows.
- Make spending conform to affordable limits.

Step 4
Implement Your Financial Action Plan

- Perform the planned actions. Track your spending. Make it conform to plans.

Step 5
Re-evaluate and Revise Your Financial Plan

- Review your progress.
- Reassess your personal situation.

Figure C.1
Developing a personal financial plan.

Knowing Your Net Worth

Begin by assessing your current financial position (Step 1). Your personal net worth is the value of all your assets minus all your liabilities or debts. Bear in mind that personal net worth doesn't refer to the resources that you plan to manage in the future (as in a budget); it's a measure of *your wealth* at the present time. The worksheet in Figure C.2 provides some sample calculations for developing your own personal "balance sheet." Because assets and liabilities change over time, updating your balance sheet not only allows you to monitor changes but also provides more accurate information for realistic budgeting and planning.

Using Your Net Worth to Set and Evaluate Goals

Your personal balance sheet lets you review your *current* overall financial condition. Once you know where you presently stand, you can move on to Step 2 in financial planning: setting specific goals for the future by calculating *changes in net worth*. The worksheet in Figure C.3 allows for goal setting in three time frames: *immediate* (within one year), *intermediate* (within five years), and *long term* (over more than five years). This kind of planning should encourage you to set measurable goals and completion times when calculating your future financial needs. It also lets you set priorities for rationing your resources if, at some point, you don't have the wherewithal to pursue all of your goals.

Because subsequent planning steps—beginning with Step 3 (identifying a plan of action) and including implementation—will affect assets and liabilities, your balance sheet will change over time. That's why it needs periodic updating to reflect your current net worth, to monitor your progress, and to help you start a new planning cycle.

The Time Value of Money

The time value of money is perhaps the single most important concept in personal finance. It's especially relevant for setting financial goals and evaluating investments. The concept of *time value* recognizes the basic fact that, while it's invested, money grows by earning interest or yielding some other form of return. Thus, whenever you make everyday purchases, you're

Figure C.2
Worksheet for calculating net worth.

Assets: What You Own		Example Numbers	Your Numbers
LIQUID ASSETS:			
1. Cash	$	300	_____
2. Savings	+	3,700	_____
3. Chequing	+	1,200	_____
INVESTMENTS:			
4. RRSP	+	12,400	_____
5. Securities	+	500	_____
6. Retirement Plan	+	—	_____
7. Real Estate (other than primary residence)	+	—	_____
HOUSEHOLD:			
8. Cars (market value)	+	18,000	_____
9. House (market value)	+	—	_____
10. Furniture	+	3,400	_____
11. Personal Property	+	6,600	_____
12. Other assets		—	_____
13. Total Assets (add lines 1-12)		**= $46,100**	_____
Liabilities (Debt): What You Owe			
CURRENT LIABILITIES:			
14. Credit-card balance	$	1,300	_____
15. Unpaid bills due	+	1,800	_____
16. Alimony and child support	+	—	_____
LONG-TERM LIABILITIES:			
17. Home mortgage	+	—	_____
18. Home equity loan	+	—	_____
19. Car loan	+	4,100	_____
20. Student loan	+	3,600	_____
21. Other liabilities	+	2,400	_____
22. Total Liabilities (add lines 14-21)		**= $13,200**	_____
Net Worth			
23. Total Assets (line 13)		$46,100	_____
24. Less: Total Debt (line 22)	–	13,200	_____
25. Results: Net Worth		**= $32,900**	_____

Name the Goal	Financial Requirement (amount) for This Goal	Time Frame for Accomplishing Goal	Importance (1= highest, 5 = lowest)
Immediate Goals:			
Live in a better apartment	_____	_____	_____
Establish an emergency cash fund	_____	_____	_____
Pay off credit-card debt	_____	_____	_____
Other	_____	_____	_____
Intermediate Goals:			
Obtain adequate life, disability, liability, property insurance	_____	_____	_____
Save for wedding	_____	_____	_____
Save to buy new car	_____	_____	_____
Establish regular savings program (5% of gross income)	_____	_____	_____
Save for university/college for self	_____	_____	_____
Pay off major outstanding debt	_____	_____	_____
Make major purchase	_____	_____	_____
Save for home remodeling	_____	_____	_____
Save for down payment on a home	_____	_____	_____
Other	_____	_____	_____
Long-Term Goals:			
Pay off home mortgage			
Save for university/college for children	_____	_____	_____
Save for vacation home	_____	_____	_____
Increase personal net worth to $___ in ___ years.	_____	_____	_____
Achieve retirement nest egg of $___ in ___ years.	_____	_____	_____
Accumulate fund for travel in retirement	_____	_____	_____
Save for long-term care needs	_____	_____	_____
Other	_____	_____	_____

Figure C.3
Worksheet for setting financial goals.

giving up interest that you could have earned with the same money if you'd invested it instead. From a financial standpoint, "idle" or uninvested money—money that could be put to work earning more money—is a wasted resource.

Why Money Grows The value of time stems from the principle of compound growth—the compounding of interest paid over given time periods. With each additional time period, interest payments accumulate and earn even more interest, thus multiplying the earning capacity of

the investment. Let's say, for example, that you invest $1 today at 10 percent annual interest. As you can see from Table C.1, you'll have $1.10 at the end of one year (your $1 original investment plus $0.10 in interest).

If you reinvest your whole $1.10, you'll earn interest on both your first year's interest and your original investment. During year 2, therefore, your savings will grow to $1.21 (your $1.10 reinvestment plus $0.11 in interest). Obviously, each year's interest will be greater than the previous year's. The interest accumulated over a single time period may seem rather modest, but when you add it up over many periods, the growth can be impressive.

Table C.1 Timetable for Growing $1.00

n	1%	2%	4%	6%	8%	10%
1	1.010	1.020	1.040	1.060	1.080	1.100
2	1.020	1.040	1.082	1.124	1.166	1.210
3	1.030	1.061	1.125	1.191	1.260	1.331
4	1.041	1.082	1.170	1.262	1.360	1.464
5	1.051	1.104	1.217	1.338	1.469	1.611
6	1.062	1.126	1.265	1.419	1.587	1.772
7	1.072	1.149	1.316	1.504	1.714	1.949
8	1.083	1.172	1.369	1.594	1.851	2.144
9	1.094	1.195	1.423	1.689	1.999	2.358
10	1.105	1.219	1.480	1.791	2.159	2.594
15	1.161	1.346	1.801	2.397	3.172	4.177
20	1.220	1.486	2.191	3.207	4.661	6.727
25	1.282	1.641	2.666	4.292	6.848	10.834
30	1.348	1.811	3.243	5.743	10.062	17.449

Note:
n = Number of time periods
% = Various interest rates

After about 7½ years at 10 percent, your original $1 will have doubled. In other words, if you had invested $10 000, you'd have $20 000.

You should understand that this one-time investment of $10 000 would be worth $174 490 ($10 000 × 17.449) at 10 percent annual compound interest after 30 years (e.g., tax free in an RRSP account). If, however, you left it lying in a bank account earning 1 percent, that same $10 000 would be worth only $13 480 ($10 000 × 1.348) after 30 years. How is that possible? Take a close look at the following section, which describes a very important concept: the rule of 72.

The Rule of 72 How long does it take to double an investment? A handy rule of thumb is called the "Rule of 72." You can find the number of years needed to double your money by dividing the annual interest rate (in percent) into 72. If, for example, you reinvest annually at 8 percent, you'll double your money in about nine years:

72/8 = 9 years

The Rule of 72 can also calculate how much interest you must get if you want to double your money in a given number of years. Simply divide 72 by the desired number of years. Thus, if you want to double your money in 10 years, you need to get 7.2 percent in interest:

72/10 = 7.2 percent interest

Finally, the Rule of 72 highlights the downside as well as the upside of the compound- growth principle. The process means greater wealth for savers but increased indebtedness for borrowers. As we have seen, for example, an 8 percent rate doubles the principal every nine years:

72/8 = 9 years

Over a period of 36 years, the amount doubles four times:

36/9 = 4 times

At 4 percent, in contrast, it doubles only twice over 36 years. Table C.2 charts the accumulation of the difference—$16 000 versus $4000—between investments (or loans) made at 8 percent versus 4 percent. The lesson for the personal-finance manager is clear: When investing (or saving), seek higher interest rates because money doubles more frequently; when borrowing, seek lower interest rates because indebtedness grows more slowly. If you are risk averse and do not want to invest in higher risk investments (stocks, mutual funds), at a minimum move your funds from basic savings accounts that pay 1 to 2 percent to government bonds that will average 4 to 6 percent over a 30-year span. Even in this conservative scenario a 6 percent average return for the $10 000 investment would be $57 430 rather than $13 480; that is still a significant improvement. If you understand the power of compound interest and make the correct debt reduction and investment appreciation decisions it will make a huge difference in your financial future. Always remember the Rule of 72!

Making Better Use of Your Time Value Most people want to save for the future, either for things they need

Table C.2 The Power of Doubling

Initial Investment (or Initial Unpaid Debt) = $1000	
Number of Times Doubled	Value after Doubling
1	$2000
2	$4000
3	$8000
4	$16 000

(down payment on a house, university or college tuition, retirement nest egg) or for nonessentials (luxury items and recreation). Needless to say, the sooner you get started, the greater your financial power will be. You will have taken advantage of the time value of money for a longer period of time.

Consider the following illustration. Co-workers Ellen and Barbara are both planning to retire in 25 years. Let's assume that they are planning for a 10 percent annual return on investment (stock markets in North America have averaged about 10 percent over the past 75 years, with higher returns in some years and losses in others). Their savings strategies, however, are different. Whereas Barbara begins saving immediately, Ellen plans to start later but invest larger sums. Barbara will invest $2000 annually for each of the next five years (years 1–5), for a total investment of $10 000. She'll let interest accumulate through year 25. Ellen, meanwhile, wants to live a little larger by spending rather than saving for the next 10 years. Then, for years 11–20, she'll start saving $2000 annually, for a total investment of $20 000. She, too, will allow annual returns to accumulate until year 25, when both she and Barbara retire. Will Ellen have a larger retirement fund in year 25 because she's ultimately contributing twice as much as Barbara?

Not by a long shot. Barbara's retirement wealth will be much larger—$90 358 versus Ellen's $56 468—even though she invested only half as much ($10 000 versus $20 000). We explain the disparity by crunching all the numbers in Figure C.4. As you can see, Barbara's advantage lies in timing—namely, the length of her savings program. Her money is invested longer—over a period of 21 to 25 years—with interest compounding over that range of time. Ellen's earnings are compounded over a shorter period—6 to 15 years. Granted, Ellen may have had more fun in years 1 to 5, but Barbara's retirement prospects look brighter.

Time Value as a Financial-Planning Tool

How much must you set aside today to accumulate enough money for something you want tomorrow? By its very nature, financial planning takes into account not only future needs (retirement, vacations, a wedding, major purchases) but also sources of funds for meeting those needs. Timing, however, is important. The timing of financial transactions will determine whether your

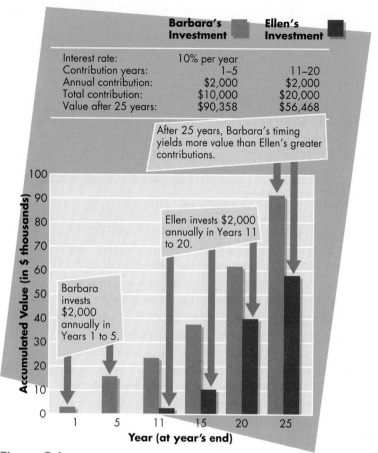

Figure C.4
Compounding money over time.

plan works or doesn't work the way you intend. Start by considering the time value of money at the outset of your planning cycle. In this respect, various time-based tables for financial calculations are quite useful.[1] As we saw with Table A.1 and the previous example, investment growth is based on interest rates. Let's look at another example to see how we can use this tool for financial planning.

Having recently inherited $50 000, Jason wants to invest for his old age. Specifically, he wants to accumulate a $200 000 nest egg by the time he reaches 55 (30 years from now). He also wants to spend some of the money while he's young enough to enjoy it, but he doesn't know how much he'll have left to spend after he's determined the amount needed to meet his retirement goal.

To help Jason with his planning, we first need to focus on our 30-year investment; thus $n = 30$ in Table C.1. As you can see, the accumulated value of that investment depends on the annual interest rate. At 4 percent, for instance, the growth factor is 3.243. Over 30 years, therefore, $1 invested now will grow to $3.243. Our question, then, is this: If $1 invested now yields $3.243, how many dollars must we invest now to accumulate $200 000 in 30 years? The answer is fairly simple. If $1 provides $3.243

Table C.3 Nest Egg Worksheet

	Investment Returns (annual rate)			Your numbers %
	Conservative 4%	Moderate 6%	Optimistic 8%	
Ending amount after 30 years:	$200 000	$200 000	$200 000	—
Growth factor (from table):	3.243	5.743	10.062	—
Amount* to invest now (end amount/growth factor):	$61 671**	$34 825	$19 877	—
	($200 000/3.243)	($200 000/5.743)	($200 000/10.062)	

*Rounded to nearest whole dollar.
**This amount is greater than the available $50 000.

in 30 years, and if we want to accumulate $200 000, we divide $200 000 by $3.243 to determine that Jason needs to invest $61 671 to reach his retirement goal.

Jason's worksheet, which is shown in Table C.3, reveals trial calculations made with three different interest rates—conservative, moderate, optimistic—available from alternative investments. As you can see, a 4 percent return on investment won't provide the desired $200 000. If he gets only 4 percent, Jason would have to invest $61 671; but, as we know, he has only $50 000. As a matter of fact, if he invested the entire $50 000 at 4 percent, he'd end up with just $162 150 ($50 000 × $3.243 = $162 150), which is well below his $200 000 goal.

Thus, Jason has two choices: find a higher-paying investment or, if he's willing to settle for 4 percent, reduce the amount of his desired nest egg. To make his decision, Jason can use the trial data contained in Table C.3. Projecting an investment at 8 percent, he needs to allocate only about $20 000 to start his nest egg and still have more than $30 000 for other uses. If he considers the 8 percent investment too risky, he may opt for the safer 6 percent return; in that case, he'd still have $15 175 left ($50 000 − $34 825).

Conserving Money by Controlling It

Several steps in the financial planning process call for conserving money by paying attention to where it goes—by keeping spending within affordable limits and understanding what you're spending your money on.[2] As too many people have found out the hard way, a major pitfall in any financial plan is the temptation to spend too much, especially when credit is so easy to get. Consumers often lose track of how much they spend, and, to make matters worse, some don't consider the costly finance charges associated with easy credit. Because many credit-card

issuers target university and college students and recent graduates with tempting offers appealing to the desire for financial independence, we'll use the following section to explain the financial costs entailed by credit cards. Keep in mind, however, that the same lessons apply equally to home-equity loans, consumer finance agreements, and other sources of credit.

Credit Cards: Keys to Consumer Satisfaction or Fiscal Handcuffs?

Although some credit cards don't charge annual fees, all of them charge interest on unpaid (outstanding) balances. Because credit-card debt is one of the most expensive sources of funds, you need to understand the costs before you start charging instead of being surprised when you open the bill. For one thing, many card users don't realize how much interest they're paying or how long it will take them to pay off their bills.

Table C.4 reprints a page from Bankrate.com's credit card calculator. Using the table as a guide, let's consider the following situation. Suppose you owe $5000 for credit-card purchases and your card company requires a minimum monthly payment of 5 percent of the unpaid balance. The interest rate is 18 percent APR (annual percentage rate) on the outstanding balance. (By the way, these aren't too high. Some rates are well above 20 percent.)

Thus, Table C.4 reflects an account with $5000 outstanding balance at the end of last month. This is the amount on which your interest of 18 percent APR is charged. Remember, too, that your card company requires a minimum monthly payment (minimum payment due—or MPD) of 5 percent (of the current balance). Let's assume that you pay only the monthly minimum and ask ourselves two questions:

1. How many months will it take to pay off the $5000?
2. How much interest will you have paid when you do pay it off?

Table C.4 Paying Off Credit Card Debt

| Balance = $5,000 | MPD 3% | | MPD 5% | | MPD 10% | |
APR	Months	Costs	Months	Costs	Months	Costs
6%	144	$5,965.56	92	$5,544.58	50	$5,260.74
9%	158	$6,607.24	96	$5,864.56	51	$5,401.63
12%	175	$7,407.50	102	$6,224.26	53	$5,550.32
18%	226	$9,798.89	115	$7,096.70	55	$5,873.86
21%	266	$11,704.63	123	$7,632.92	57	$6,050.28

Note:
MPD = Minimum Payment Due
APR = Annual Percentage Rate

In Table C.4, the column labelled "MPD 5%" reveals that at 18 percent APR it will take you 115 months to pay off $5000. That's approximately 9½ years! And remember, this number assumes that your balance gradually diminishes to zero because you add no other purchases to the card. Your total payment of $7096.70 covers your $5000 debt plus interest charges. An immediate cash payoff, therefore, would avoid $2096.70 in interest payments.

Why does repayment take so long? In Table C.5, we run through some sample calculations for the first two months in your 115-month repayment process. As you can see, your minimum monthly payment decreases because your ending balance gets smaller with each monthly payment. Your $250 payment in February includes $75 in interest owed on the $5000 balance in the previous month. At 18 percent APR, interest on $5000 would be $900 for a year ($0.18 \times \$5000$), but for one month (January), it's only $1/12$ of that amount—$75. You're paying the rest of your February instalment of $175 ($250 − 75) on the principal amount, thereby reducing the month-end balance to $4825. If we carry out these calculations over 115 months, we find that, when your account is paid in full, you've made "payments on principal" of $5000 and interest payments of $2096.70.

Practise Paying Off Your Debt Using the method illustrated in Table C.5, you should be able to answer the following questions about credit-card repayment (answers appear at the end of the appendix):

1. According to the data in Table C.5, your minimum monthly payment for April would be which of the following? [select one] (a) $232.81; (b) $253.47; (c) $230.56; (d) $226.18.

2. According to the data in Table C.5, for April, the interest owed on your previous balance would be which of the following? [select one] (a) $70.43; (b) $71.94; (c) $69.84; (d) $68.32.

3. According to the data in Table C.5, for April, your ending balance owed on principal would be which of the following? [select one] (a) $4182.16; (b) $4493.16; (c) $4517.22; (d) $4334.97.

Table C.5 Calculating Minimum Monthly Payments

Month	Minimum Monthly Payment (5% of Previous Ending Balance)	=	Interest Owed on Previous Balance* ($1/12 \times 18\%$) × Previous Balance)	+	Payment on Principal	Ending Balance Owed on Principal
January	—		—		—	$5000
February	$250 [0.05 × $5000]	=	$75 [$1/12$ × 0.18 × $5000]	+	$175	$4825 [5000 – 175]
March	$241.25 [0.05 × 4825]	=	$72.38 [$1/12$ × 0.18 × 4825]	+	$168.87	$4656.13 [4825 – 168.87]

*Monthly interest is calculated using $1/12$ of annual interest rate.

Save Your Money: Lower Interest Rates and Faster Payments

A closer look at Table C.4 confirms two principles for saving money that you can apply when borrowing from any source, not just credit cards: Look for lower interest rates and make faster repayments.

Seeking Lower Interest Rates Because higher interest rates obviously mean more expensive money, you save money with lower interest rates (money that you can use for other things). With a little research, you'll find that potential creditors charge different rates (ranging from below 10 percent to over 20 percent APR). How much can you save? Look again at Table C.4 and compare the cost of borrowing $5000 at 18 percent with the cost of borrowing it at 9 percent. If you assume the same 5 percent minimum monthly payment, how much interest does 9 percent save you over the life of the repayment? The answer is $1232.14 ($864.56 instead of $2096.70). That's a nearly 59 percent savings.

Making Faster Payments Because money has a time value, lenders charge borrowers according to the length of time for which they borrow. In general, longer lending periods increase the cost, while shorter periods are cheaper. Accordingly, borrowers often speed up payments to cut interest costs. Using Table C.4, for example, compare the costs of the "5% MPD" (required monthly payment of 5 percent on the remaining balance) with the faster "10% MPD." The faster schedule cuts the repayment period from 115 to 55 months and, at 18 percent APR, reduces interest costs by $1222.84 (7096.70 − 5873.86).

What if you combined both faster repayment and the lower interest rate (9 percent versus 18 percent)? You'd cut your total interest cost to just $450.30—a savings of $1695.07 over the amount you'd pay if you made slower repayments at the higher rate.

Financial Commitments of Home Ownership

Should you rent or buy the roof you need over your head? The answer to that question involves a variety of considerations, including life stage, family needs, career, financial situation, and preferred lifestyle. If you decide to buy, for example, you have to ask yourself how much house you can afford. To answer that question, you need to ask yourself a number of questions about your personal financial condition and your capacity for borrowing.

To Buy or Not to Buy: That Is the Question

Renting is attractive because you can move in without making an initial investment (or at least making a hefty down payment). That's why it's a popular choice among young adults, especially singles with limited budgets and people whose lifestyles aren't congenial to settling down in a fixed location. Flexibility, mobility, and freedom from obligations of maintenance and upkeep are important advantages. Financially speaking, however, rent payments are cash outflows that provide future financial benefits to owners instead of renters.

By the same token, first-time homebuyers cite the prospect of future financial gain as an attractive reason for buying. The financial inducements are in fact powerful, including home equity, increasing property values, and tax advantages. You can see whether buying is a good idea for you by consulting a "rent-versus-buy calculator" on the web, such as the one at www.ginniemae.gov. By letting you try various interest rates, down payments, loan lengths, and rental costs, calculators specify the financial advantages of renting or buying under a wide range of financial circumstances.

Many younger adults with children report that they choose to buy because they want privacy, space, and the freedom to choose a neighbourhood. Finally, most home buyers say that they get satisfaction from a sense of ownership—from having their own property. Table C.6 summarizes the key considerations in deciding whether to rent or buy a place to live.

In addition to loan payments, the typical demands of ownership—time and other resources for maintaining and improving a home—tend to cut into the money left over for recreation, eating out, taking vacations, and so on. You can reduce the financial pressure by calculating in advance a realistic price range—one that not only lets you buy a house but also lets you live a reasonably pleasant life once you're in it.

How Much House Can You Afford?

Buying a home is the biggest investment most people ever make. Unfortunately, many make the mistake of buying a house that they can't afford, resulting in unnecessary stress and even devastating financial loss. This happened on a massive scale in the U.S. housing downfall of 2007–2009: millions of home buyers had borrowed beyond their means by getting larger loans than they could afford. Borrowers were aided by lenders using loose credit standards, unlike the time-proven standards presented below, leading to unrealistic repayment requirements. Borrowers' incomes were too small to

Table C.6 To Buy or Not to Buy

Renting	Buying
• No down payment to get started	• Must make payments for mortgage, property taxes, and insurance
• Flexibility to leave	• Equity builds up over time
• No obligation for upkeep or improvements	• More privacy
• No groundskeeping	• Value of property may increase
• Easy cash-flow planning (a single monthly payment)	• Financial gains from selling house can be exempt from taxes
• May provide access to recreation and social facilities	• Greater control over use of property and improvements
• Rental conditions may be changed by owner	• The home can become a source of cash by refinancing with another mortgage loan or a home-equity loan
• Timing for repairs controlled by owner	

meet monthly payments, especially when interest rates (and thus payments) increased, and when unemployment increased in the recession. They lost their homes.

Most people need a loan to buy a house or a condominium. A **mortgage loan** is a loan that's secured by the property—the home—being purchased. Because the size of a loan depends on the cost of the property, both borrowers and lenders want to know whether the buyer can afford the house they want. How can you determine how much you can afford? One time-tested (though conservative) rule of thumb cautions the buyer to keep the price below 2½ times his or her annual income. Thus, if your income is $48 000, look for a house priced below $120 000.

Any such calculation, however, will give you just a rough estimate of what you can afford. There are other considerations. What you can afford also depends on how much money you have for a down payment and how much you can borrow. Lending institutions use two guidelines for estimating a buyer's borrowing capacity: (1) the borrower's ability to meet the recurring costs of buying and owning, and (2) other long-term debt that the buyer has already incurred.

PITI What are those recurring costs? Every month, the homeowner must pay principal, interest, taxes, and insurance—PITI, for short. Because all four costs are greater for more expensive homes, the buyer's monthly obligation depends on how much house he or she has bought. The size of principal and interest payments depends on the mortgage amount, the length of the mortgage loan, and the interest rate. Obviously, if you borrow a fixed amount, the larger your monthly payment, the faster you'll pay off your loan. As Table C.7 shows, monthly payments on conventional loans are lower for longer-term loans and higher for higher interest rates.

MORTGAGE LOAN A loan that is secured by the home that is being purchased.

Table C.7 Monthly Payment on a $10 000 Loan

| Interest Rate (%) | Length of Loan | | | | |
	3 Years	5 Years	10 Years	20 Years	30 Years
5.0	$299.71	$188.71	$106.07	$66.00	$53.68
6.0	304.22	193.33	111.02	71.64	59.96
6.5	306.49	195.66	113.55	74.56	63.21
7.0	308.77	198.01	116.11	77.53	66.53
8.0	313.36	202.76	121.33	83.65	73.38
9.0	318.00	207.58	126.68	89.98	80.47
10.0	322.67	212.47	132.16	96.51	87.76
11.0	327.39	217.42	137.76	103.22	95.24
12.0	332.14	222.44	143.48	110.11	102.86

In evaluating loan applications, lenders use PITI calculations to estimate the buyer's financial capacity—his or her ability to meet monthly payments. To determine how much someone is likely to lend you, calculate 28 percent of your gross monthly income (that is, before taxes and other deductions). If your PITI costs don't exceed that figure, you'll probably get the loan. With a monthly gross income of $4000, for example, your PITI costs shouldn't exceed $1120 (28 percent of $4000). Additional calculations show a house price of $162 382 is the most this borrower can afford. Figure C.5 gives a sample calculation, and you should be able to make step-by-step computations by plugging your own numbers into the worksheet.

Other Debt In evaluating financial capacity, lenders also look at any additional outstanding debt, such as loans and credit-card bills. They will generally accept indebtedness (including PITI) up to 36 percent of gross income. Because PITI itself can be up to 28 percent, you might be allowed as little as 8 percent in other long-term debt. With your $4000 monthly gross income, your total debt should be less than $1440 ($1120 for PITI and $320 for other debt). If your total debt exceeds $1440, you may have to settle for a smaller loan than the one you calculated with the PITI method. Websites such as http://mortgages.interest.com provide mortgage calculators for testing interest rates, lengths of loans, and other personal financial information.

Cashing Out from Tax Avoidance (Legally)

Personal expenditures always require cash outflows; some also reduce your tax bill and save you some cash. Registered Retirement Savings Plans (RRSPs), Tax-Free Savings Accounts (TFSAs), and Registered Education Savings Plans (RESPs) have this effect. (Before you

Figure C.5
Worksheet for PITI calculations.

ASSUMPTIONS:

30-year mortgage
Closing costs (fees for property, survey, credit report, title search,
          title insurance, attorney, interest advance, loan origination) = $5,000
Funds available for closing costs and down payment = $25,000
Interest rate on mortgage = $6\frac{1}{2}$% per year
Estimated real estate taxes = $200 per month
Estimated homeowner's insurance = $20 month

Example Numbers		Your Numbers
1. Monthly income, gross (before taxes or deductions)........$4,000		_____
2. Apply PITI ratio (0.28 x amount on line 1) to determine borrower's payment capacity: 0.28 x $4,000 = ...$1,120		_____
3. Determine mortgage payment (principal and interest) by subtracting taxes and insurance from PITI (line 2)...–$ 220		_____
4. Result: Maximum mortgage payment (principal and interest).................................. $900		_____
5. Using Table C.5 find the monthly mortgage payment on a $10,000 loan at $6\frac{1}{2}$% interest for 30 years.. $63.21		_____
6. Since each $10,000 loan requires a $63.21 monthly payment, how many $10,000 loans can the borrower afford with the $900 payment capacity? The answer is determined as follows: $900.00/$63.21 = 14.2382 loans of $10,000 each		_____
7. Result: Maximum allowable mortgage loan [calculated as follows: 14.2382 loans (from line 6 above) x $10,000 per loan] = ...$142,382		_____
8. Result: Maximum house price borrower can afford using PITI (amount of house that can be bought with available funds):		
From loan...........................$142,382 From down payment............$ 25,000 Less closing cost.................–$ 5,000		_____ _____ _____
...............$162,382		_____

commit any money to these instruments or activities, check with an expert on tax regulations; they change from time to time.)

Registered Retirement Savings Plans (RRSPs)

The Registered Retirement Savings Plan (RRSP) program was created by the federal government to provide incentive for Canadians to save money. How does it work? Contributors are able to deduct up to 18 percent of their previous year's salary up to a maximum of $22 000 each year. For example, Sally is 30 years old and earns a salary of $85 000. If she contributes $15 000 into an RRSP investment she will be taxed as if she only earned $70 000. In other words, the other $15 000 is shielded from taxes. This brings down her tax payment and enables her to have more money working for her in her name. In addition, this $15 000 (and any subsequent investments) will grow tax-free for the next 30 to 35 years until she retires.[3]

Tax-Free Savings Accounts (TFSAs)

In 2009, the Canadian government created the TFSA program, which enables individuals to contribute up to $5000 per year. This investment vehicle does not provide a tax deduction, like an RRSP, but it allows investment income and capital gains to grow tax-free. Unlike RRSPs, taxes are not applied even when the funds are withdrawn. However, as some people have discovered, the $5000 per year cap must be respected or else taxes will be applied.[4]

Registered Education Savings Plans (RESPs)

The RESP program enables parents to put money aside for a child's post-secondary education many years before the funds will be needed. The contributions can grow tax-free. However, it gets a bit complicated if the child does not pursue post-secondary studies. There is the possibility of transferring to a sibling under a family plan and the account can be open for up to 36 years. The initial contributions are not tax-deductible.

Protecting Your Net Worth

With careful attention, thoughtful saving and spending, and skilful financial planning (and a little luck), you can build up your net worth over time. In addition to steps for accumulating net worth, therefore, every financial plan should consider steps for preserving it. One approach involves the risk–return relationship that we discussed in Chapter 16. Do you prefer to protect your current assets, or are you willing to risk them in return for greater growth? At various life stages, and whenever you reach a designated level of wealth, you should adjust your asset portfolio to conform to your risk and return preferences—conservative, moderate, or aggressive. Another approach is life insurance.

Life Insurance

You can also think of life insurance as a tool for financial preservation. A life insurance policy is a promise to pay beneficiaries after the death of an insured party. In return, of course, insurance companies collect *premiums*—payments from the insurance purchaser—during his or her lifetime.

What Does Life Insurance Do? From a personal-finance perspective, the purpose of life insurance is to replace income upon the death of the policyholder. Accordingly, the amount of insurance you need depends on how many other people rely on your income. Insurance, for example, is crucial for the married parent who is a family's sole source of income. On the other hand, a single person with no financial dependents needs little or no insurance and will probably prefer to put money into higher-paying investments.

How Much Should I Buy? To estimate the amount you need, begin by adding up all of the annual expenses—rent, food, clothing, transportation, schooling, debts to be paid—that you pay for the dependents who would survive you. Then multiply the total by the number of years that you want the insurance to cover your dependents. Typically, this sum will amount to several times your current annual income. Thus, many policyholders, especially during the life stages of highest need—are insured for 10 to 20 times their annual salaries.

Two Basic Types of Insurance *Term insurance* pays a predetermined benefit when death occurs during the stipulated term—say, 10, 20, or 30 years—covered by the policy. If the insured outlives the term, the policy loses its value and simply ceases. When it is in force, however, the insured knows that it will provide funds to beneficiaries if he or she dies. Premiums for term life insurance are significantly lower than premiums for whole life insurance.

Unlike term life, *whole-life insurance*—also known as *cash-value insurance*—remains in force as long as premiums are paid. In addition to paying a death benefit, whole life accumulates cash value over time—a form of savings. Once the insured reaches a point at which he or she no longer needs the coverage, paid-in money can be withdrawn. Whole-life savings, however, earn less interest than most alternative forms of investment.

Another important distinction should be made here. If you buy term insurance you can invest your savings (extra funds from lower premiums versus whole life) into your own account, in your own name, and build equity. If something were to happen to the policyholder the beneficiaries would get the insurance payment and would also get the personal investment funds. A whole-life–policy holder would be given the face value of the policy but any savings in the policy would cease to exist and would be kept by the insurance company. In essence, those savings funds belong to the insurance company. That is why many policies charge interest if you borrow from your insurance policy account (because it's not really yours).

How Much Does It Cost? The cost of insurance, of course, depends on how much you buy. But it also depends on your life expectancy and other risk factors that insurers determine statistically. Premiums are higher for people whose life expectancies are shorter, whether because of gender, age, weight, occupation, or pre-existing health conditions.

The lower cost of term insurance is an important consideration, not just for people on limited incomes, but also for those seeking higher returns from other types of investment. To get the best match between your policy and your personal situation, therefore, you should evaluate the terms and conditions of a variety of policies. You can get convenient comparisons on websites such as IntelliQuote.com (www.intelliquote.com).

Answers to "Practise Paying Off Your Debt"

1. Item (a) is the correct answer, obtained as follows:

    Minimum monthly payment
    (5% of previous ending balance):
    April $232.81 = (0.05 \times \$4656.13)$

2. Item (c) is the correct answer, obtained as follows:

    Interest owed on previous balance
    ($\frac{1}{12} \times 0.18$ previous balance):
    April $69.84 = (\frac{1}{12} \times 0.18 \times \$4656.13)$

3. Item (b) is the correct answer, obtained as follows:

    Payment on principal   *Ending balance owed on*

    (monthly payment −   *principal* (previous balance −

    monthly interest)   (payment on principal)

    April $162.97 = ($232.81 − $69.84)$ $4493.16

                   = ($4656.13 − $162.97)

Part 5: Managing Financial Issues

Goal of the Exercise

In this final part of the business plan project, you'll consider how you'll finance your business as well as create an executive summary for your plan.

Exercise Background: Part 5 of the Business Plan

In a previous part of the business plan, you discussed the costs of doing business, as well as how much revenue you expect to earn in one year. It's now time to think about how to finance the business. To get a great idea off the ground requires money. But how will you get these funds?

You'll then conclude this project by creating an *executive summary*. The purpose of the executive summary is to give the reader a quick snapshot into your proposed business. Although this exercise comes at the end of the project, once you're done writing it, you'll end up placing the executive summary at the *beginning* of your completed business plan.

Your Assignment

mybusinesslab

Step 1

Open the saved Business Plan file you have been working on.

Step 2

For the purposes of this assignment, you will answer the following questions, shown in Part 5: Managing Financial Issues.

1. How much money will you need to get your business started?

   Hint: Refer to Part 3 of the plan, where you analyzed the costs involved in running your business. Approximately how much will you need to get your business started?

2. How will you finance your business? For example, will you seek out a bank loan? Borrow from friends? Sell stocks or bonds initially or as your business grows?

   Hint: Refer to Chapter 15 for information on securities such as stocks and bonds. Refer also to Chapters 4 and 16 for more information on sources of short-term and long-term funds.

3. Now, create an executive summary for your business plan. The executive summary should be brief—no more than two pages—and cover the following points:

   - The name of your business
   - Where your business will be located
   - The mission of your business
   - The product or service you are selling
   - Who your ideal customers are
   - How your product or business will stand out in the crowd
   - Who the owners of the business are and what experience they have
   - An overview of the future prospects for your business and industry

   Hint: At this point, you've already answered all of these questions, so what you need to do here is put the ideas together into a "snapshot" format. The executive summary is really a sales pitch—it's the investor's first impression of your idea. Therefore, as with all parts of the plan, write in a clear and professional way.

   Congratulations on completing the business plan project!

Debt Nation

We are a nation in debt, so *Marketplace* examined the finances of three Canadian families. Here are their stories.

Wayne and Theresa

Wayne and Theresa earn about $85 000 a year between them, but they are struggling with a total debt of $343 000 (mortgages, taxes, and loans). Wayne finishes furniture and Theresa works 25 hours a week from home. When Wayne has lots of work, they get by, but when he doesn't, there are problems because they simply buy too many things. Theresa feels very insecure about their financial situation. When unexpected expenses come up, stress levels increase. For example, when Wayne's van broke down, he borrowed money from Household Finance at a high interest rate.

A financial adviser (John) talks to Wayne and Theresa about their debt problems. He observes that their mortgage is not getting smaller as time passes. He says they simply must make higher payments on their mortgage to reduce the amount they owe. He also notes that some of their credit cards carry a 30 percent interest rate. He says they should cut up their credit cards because they have become addicted to credit card debt. John says that Wayne is too easygoing about their debt level, and fears that he won't follow through on plans to reduce the family's debts.

Wayne and Theresa also talk to a psychologist (Sherrell). She says they behave like ostriches, and they need to get their heads out of the sand and analyze their situation. She recommends that the two of them take 30 minutes each week so that Theresa can bring Wayne up to speed about her concerns about their financial situation. They both admit that they haven't cut up their credit cards. They say they just can't give them up.

Joanne and Travis

Joanne and Travis live in a farmhouse in the country. Travis is a musician and Joanne is often unemployed. They are trying to pay off debts of about $186 000 (credit cards, car loans, and mortgages). Joanne is a shopaholic (she likes vintage dresses), and she shops whether she's on a high or feeling low. She says she buys things she doesn't need (like a drill from Canadian Tire that was on sale). Like Wayne and Theresa, unexpected expenses have caused Joanne and Travis additional stress. For example, their septic tank had to be drained, and that cost several hundred dollars that they didn't have.

John, the financial adviser, talks to Joanne and Travis about their problems. He discovers that Travis earns between $15 000 and $25 000 each year. John tells them to pay off their high-interest debt by selling part of their property, but Joanne and Travis like their country acreage.

Sherrell, the psychologist, says that Joanne's obsession with shopping must stop if they hope to get out of their financial hole. Sherrell says that the great lie of the consumer mentality is that "If I shop, I'll feel better, and the feeling will last." She tells Joanne she must take control of her debt. Sherrell tells Joanne to create a "mad money" jar that can be used when Joanne feels the urge to shop. When the jar has no money in it, Joanne is not allowed to shop.

Hannalaura

Hannalaura is a teacher who wants to retire soon but knows she can't afford to. Her total debt is about $187 000. She also wants to take her daughter on a trip to England. She initially got into trouble when a nasty marriage breakup cost her $50 000 (she added that debt to her existing mortgage). She doesn't want her children to have to look after her during her retirement.

John, the financial adviser, visits Hannalaura and tells her she won't likely be able to get out of debt before she retires. He tells her that the trip to England is out of the question, and that she should finish three more university credits she needs for a degree because that will help her earn more money. But Hannalaura is reluctant.

Sherrell, the psychologist, notes that very few people can follow financial advice. She thinks that Hannalaura has a lot of unresolved anger about her past experiences and feels rather helpless about not being able to change things in her life. Sherrell tells her that she must spend less and save more for her retirement. Sherell is afraid that Hannalaura will not change.

Video Resource: "Debt Nation," *Marketplace* (January 15, 2006).

1. Identify several reasons why people get into financial difficulty. Which reason applies to which family? Is there a common underlying reason for these three families?

2. Consider the following statement: *"Credit card companies should cancel the credit card of any consumer whose credit card balance exceeds $10 000. This will prevent the consumer from falling more deeply into debt."* Do you agree or disagree with this statement? Explain your reasoning.

3. Sherrell, the psychologist, says that very few people follow financial advice. Why do you think that people don't follow financial advice?

4. How successful do you think each family will be as they attempt to resolve their financial problems? (After you have turned in your answers, your instructor will give you an update on the three families.)

VIDEO CASE V-2

Card Tricks

Do you think that you're credit card savvy? Do you know what's in the fine print in cardholders' agreements? Meet four people who got so fed up with hidden fees and rising interest rates on their credit cards that they decided to do something about it.

David Caldarelli was mistakenly charged double for a highway toll. When he sent in his monthly credit card payment, he did not pay for the highway toll overcharge. When he got his next statement, he was shocked to discover that he had been charged $23 dollars in interest (even on the part of the total bill he had already paid). When he inquired about the charge, he was informed that since he had not paid the entire bill, he was charged interest on his total month's charges. He discovered that if you don't pay every penny you owe on your monthly statement, the next month you will be charged interest as if you hadn't paid anything. He was therefore being charged interest on money that he had already paid back. He discovered that this provision was in his cardholder agreement, but these agreements are complex (almost as if they are written by lawyers for lawyers). David complained about this, and was successful in getting the $23 charge cancelled (a one-time goodwill gesture, he was told). David learned to beware of the partial payment.

Paul Cassano got hit with a fee of a different kind. He stayed at a hotel in New York and left an imprint of his card. But when he checked out, he paid in cash and the hotel cancelled the charge on his credit card. When he got his Visa bill a month later, there was a charge for $42.36 that he couldn't figure out. He inquired and discovered that he had been charged an extra fee for using his credit card in the U.S. It is called a currency conversion fee (this fee is on top of the usual currency exchange rate). He sued Visa on the basis that he had been charged an undisclosed 1.65 percent fee when he first charged his hotel room, and then again when he had cancelled that and paid cash. That fee is now disclosed. A similar lawsuit against CIBC cost that bank $19.5 million. After it lost, CIBC upped its conversion fee.

Victor Moge is concerned that interest rates on unpaid credit card balances keep going up, even as interest rates on many other things are going down. His MBNA card rate used to be 15.99 percent, but now it's 19.99 percent. He discovered that credit card companies can raise your rate whenever they want. Some companies have raised the rate by five percentage points in one jump (for example, if the person misses a payment). The prime rate would never go up that fast, but the rate charged on credit cards has nothing to do with the prime rate. The debt that consumers rack up on credit cards is unsecured, so the card providers want to reduce the risk that you will not pay your bill. If you are carrying a high balance, they get worried that you might not pay your bill. They cover that risk by charging higher interest rates (there is a legal ceiling—60 percent).

Sheri Aberback-Ptack pays her American Express monthly credit card bill on time, but when she was charged $11.00 interest for a supposedly late payment, she looked into the situation. She discovered that even if you pay your bill on time, the credit card company may not record the payment until a few days later. If that few days later is after the due date, you are charged interest. She was upset and brought in her lawyer. He says American Express should have to assume the cost of any processing delay on their part. On another occasion, Sheri paid her bill two days earlier so she wouldn't get charged interest. But she was still charged interest because the payment wasn't actually processed before the due date. She says the customer should not have to guess how many days ahead they have to pay their bill in order to avoid interest charges. So, the payment due date is an illusion. If you don't send the money before the due date (or even if you do), you might get charged a late payment fee. Sheri and her lawyer are preparing a class action suit against the company.

Since none of the credit card companies or banks would talk to *Marketplace*, it went to the director of public affairs for the Canadian Bankers Association. She observed that credit card debt is unsecured, so the rates customers are charged vary quite a bit, depending on how much risk credit card companies think they are exposed to. She also noted that credit card interest rates have nothing to do with the prime rate, and it's up to the card user to determine whether he or she wants to carry a balance or pay the entire bill each month.

How do you avoid losing in the credit card game? One strategy is to talk to your bank about options like a line of credit or a low-interest credit card. If you can't get either of those, you should look around for cheaper alternatives at other banks or other credit card companies.

Video Resource: "Card Tricks," *Marketplace* (February 27, 2005).

Questions for Discussion

1. Credit cards are often referred to as "plastic money." Explain why credit cards do not actually qualify as "money."

2. Think about the situation that was encountered by each of the four individuals profiled above. Do you think the individual or the credit card company had the most defensible position? Explain your reasoning for each case.

3. Consider the following statement: *"If consumers don't pay off their credit card balance each month, that's their decision, and they shouldn't complain about the interest they are charged. They should just stop spending so much money and pay off their bill each month (or just stop using their credit card). Demanding more restrictive legislation on credit card companies is not the answer. Consumers get into debt because they spend more than they can afford."* Do you agree or disagree with the statement. Explain your reasoning.

Notes, Sources, and Credits

Endnotes

Chapter 1

1. "Canada's 500 Largest Corporations," *The Financial Post*, June 2009, 42–43.

2. Richard Blackwell, "Canada Ranks High in Low Business Costs," *The Globe and Mail*, March 31, 2010, B5.

3. Robert A. Collinge and Ronald M. Ayers, *Economics by Design: Principles and Issues*, 2nd ed. (Upper Saddle River, NJ: Prentice Hall, 2000), 41–42; Michael J. Mandel, "The New Economy," *BusinessWeek,* January 31, 2000, 73–77.

4. Richard I. Kirkland Jr., "The Death of Socialism," *Fortune*, January 4, 1988, 64–72.

5. Andres Oppenheimer, "Latin America Is Skeptical," *The Orlando Sentinel*, February 20, 2006, A19.

6. James Kynge, "Private Firms' Growth in China Striking: Report," *National Post*, May 11, 2000, C14.

7. See Karl E. Case and Ray C. Fair, *Principles of Economics*, 5th ed. (Upper Saddle River, NJ: Prentice Hall, 1999), 69–74; Robert A. Collinge and Ronald M. Ayers, *Economics by Design: Principles and Issues*, 2nd ed. (Upper Saddle River, NJ: Prentice Hall, 2000), 51–52.

8. Andres Oppenheimer, "While Latin America Nationalizes, India Opens Up," *Orlando Sentinel*, January 22, 2007, A11.

9. Barry Critchley, "Canada Post Should Be Privatized: OECD; Productivity Issue," *National Post*, March 11, 2010, FP2.

10. John Greenwood, "Study Cites Privatization in Productivity Gains," *National Post*, June 26, 2009, FP1.

11. *Bank of Canada Banking and Financial Statistics*, Series G1, Government of Canada Fiscal Position, April 2010, S84.

12. *The Financial Post*, June 2009, 82.

13. "UFC May Have Long Wait to Crack Ontario Market," thestar.com, May 23, 2010, www.thestar.com/printarticle/783892.

14. Andy Hoffman, "Labatt Convicted in Quebec Discount Beer Case," *The Globe and Mail*, November 24, 2005, B10.

15. Jim Middlemiss, "Don't Get Caught Offside in Rules Changes; Wrong Advice on Competition Act Could Be Costly," *National Post*, March 23, 2009, FP6. For an analysis of the current situation in the U.S. regarding resale price maintenance, see Joseph Pereira, "Price-Fixing Makes Comeback after Supreme Court Hearing," *The Wall Street Journal*, August 18, 2008, A1, A12.

16. Hollie Shaw, "Bogus Ads: If You Mislead the Consumer, Be Ready to Suffer the Financial Fallout," *National Post*, May 22, 2009, FP12.

17. Shirley Won and Jacquie McNish, "Antitrust Watchdog Loses Beer Battle," *The Globe and Mail*, March 29, 2007, B1, B6.

18. Steven Chase and Jacquie McNish, "Prentice Probes Watchdog's Court Conduct," *The Globe and Mail*, January 30, 2008, B1–B2.

19. John Gray, "Texas Fold 'Em," *Canadian Business*, October 9–22, 2006, 44–46.

20. "Video Gaming: The Next Level," *Venture*, March 20, 2005.

21. "Alberta Film, TV Production Faces Decline," May 19, 2010, CBC News, www.cbc.ca/arts/film/story/2010/05/18/alberta-film-production-decline.html.

22. Jennifer Allen, "New Lobby Rules Mean More Work for Lawyers," *The Globe and Mail*, August 13, 2008, B5.

23. "Canada's Maple Syrup Output Rises in '09," *National Post*, March 11, 2010, FP6.

24. For a detailed analysis of the rise in food prices, see Sinclair Stewart and Paul Waldie, "The Byzantine World of Food Pricing: How Big Money Is Wreaking Havoc," *The Globe and Mail*, May 31, 2008, B4–B7.

25. See Paul Heyne, Peter J. Boettke, and David L. Prychitko, *The Economic Way of Thinking*, 10th ed. (Upper Saddle River, NJ: Prentice Hall, 2003), 190, 358–359.

26. Karl E. Case and Ray C. Fair, *Principles of Economics*, 6th ed., updated (Upper Saddle River, NJ: Prentice Hall, 2003), 300–309.

27. *Hoover's Handbook of World Business 2002* (Austin: Hoover's Business Press, 2002), 74–75.

28. Timothy Aeppel, "Show Stopper: How Plastic Popped the Cork Monopoly," *The Wall Street Journal*, May 1, 2010, A1.

29. "Royal Mail's Reign Comes to an End," *The Globe and Mail*, January 2, 2006, B7.

30. Eric Bellman, "As Economy Zooms, India's Postmen Struggle to Adapt," *The Wall Street Journal*, October 3, 2006, A1, A12.

31. For an in-depth analysis of the history of Canadian business, see Michael Bliss, *Northern Enterprise* (Toronto: McClelland and Stewart, 1987).

32. Matt Hartley, "The Cloud Is the Great Equalizer; 'It's Everywhere,'" *National Post*, May 25, 2010, FP14.

Chapter 2

1. Eric Reguly, "As Ash Spreads, So Does Damage," *The Globe and Mail*, April 19, 2010, B1.

2. See Jay B. Barney and William G. Ouchi, eds., *Organizational Economics* (San Francisco: Jossey-Bass, 1986), for a detailed analysis of linkages between economics and organizations.

3. Karl E. Case and Ray C. Fair, *Principles of Economics*, 6th ed., updated (Upper Saddle River, NJ: Prentice Hall, 2003), 432–433.

4. Karl E. Case and Ray C. Fair, *Principles of* Economics, 6th ed., updated (Upper Saddle River, NJ: Prentice Hall, 2003), 15.

5. Karl E. Case and Ray C. Fair, *Principles of Economics*, 6th ed., updated (Upper Saddle River, NJ: Prentice Hall, 2003), 15.

6. Richard Blackwell, "The 'R' Word," *The Globe and Mail*, October 16, 2008, B5.

7. Bank of Canada Banking and Financial Statistics, Table H1 (May 2010): S96.

8. Matthew McLearn, "Our Dangerous Addiction to GDP," *Canadian Business*, October 12, 2009, 23.

9. Green Economics website, www.greeneconomics.ca/gpi, accessed June 9, 2010; Barry Marquardson, "GDP Fails as a Measurement," *The Globe and Mail*, July 16, 1998, B2.

10. Conference Board of Canada website, www.conferenceboard.ca/hcp/details/economy/income-per-capita.aspx, accessed June 7, 2010.

11. Olivier Blanchard, *Macroeconomics*, 3rd ed. (Upper Saddle River, NJ: Prentice Hall, 2003), 24–26.

12. OECD website, http://stats.oecd.org/Index.aspx?DatasetCode=LEVEL, accessed June 9, 2010; Kevin Lynch, "Canada's Productivity Trap," *The Globe and Mail*, January 29, 2010, B1.

13. Jay Heizer and Barry Render, *Operations Management*, 6th ed. (Upper Saddle River, NJ: Prentice Hall, 2001), 15–16.

14. Statistics Canada website, www40.statcan.gc.ca/l01/cst01/gblec02a-eng.htm, accessed June 9, 2010.

15. Greg Hitt and Murray Hiebert, "U.S. Trade Deficit Ballooned to a Record in 2005," *The Wall Street Journal*, February 11–12, 2006, A1, A10.

16. Neil Reynolds, "Stimulating Our Way into a Crisis," *The Globe and Mail*, February 18, 2009, B2.

17. Paul Viera, "Federal Deficit for 2009 Smaller than Expected, Finance Department Says," *The Financial Post*, May 29, 2010.

18. Canadian Federal Budget website, www.budget.gc.ca/2010/pdf/budget-planbudgetaire-eng.pdf, accessed June 9, 2010.

19. Neil Reynolds, "U.S. Debt: Don't Worry, Be Happy (till 2017)," *The Globe and Mail*, April 3, 2009, B2.

20. Celia Dugger, "Life in Zimbabwe: Wait for Useless Money, Then Scour for Food," *The New York Times*, October 2, 2008, A1, A14.

21. Geoffrey York, "How Zimbabwe Slew the Dragon of Hyperinflation," *The Globe and Mail*, March 23, 2009, B1.

22. Tavia Grant, "A Snapshot of How We Spend," *The Globe and Mail*, April 20, 2010, B2; Tavia Grant, "Lard in 1913, Plasma TV Now: CPI Tracks Changes," *The Globe and Mail*, April 21, 2005, B1, B15.

23. Bruce Little, "There's Been a Huge Shift in How Consumers Spend," *The Globe and Mail*, July 5, 2004, B4. Figure 2.3 shows how inflation has varied over the last 20 years in Canada.

24. Statistics Canada website, www.statcan.gc.ca/subjects-sujets/labour-travail/lfs-epa/t100604a1-eng.htm, accessed June 10, 2010.

25. Jeremy Torobin and Tavia Grant, "Slow Jobs Growth, Growing Debt Fears: U.S., European Recoveries Show Signs of Strain," *The Globe and Mail*, June 5, 2010, B1, B5.

26. Julie Jargon, "Seeking Sweet Savings," *The Wall Street Journal*, October 2, 2007, B1–B2.

27. Statistics Canada, *Industrial Research and Development: Intentions*, Catalogue no. 88-202-X, Table 4, Concentration of Total Intramural Research and Development Expenditures by Companies Size (Ottawa: Minister of Industry, 2010), www.statcan.gc.ca/pub/88-202-x/2009000/tablesectlist-listetableauxsect-eng.htm.

28. Statistics Canada, *Industrial Research and Development: Intentions* (Ottawa: Minister of Industry, 2009). www.statcan.gc.ca/pub/88-202-x/2009000/t003-eng.htm.

29. Statistics Canada, 2008, *Industrial Research and Development: Intentions*, Catalogue no. 88-202-X, Table 4, Concentration of Total Intramural Research and Development Expenditures by Companies Size, www.statcan.gc.ca/pub/88-202-x/2009000/t050-eng.htm.

30. Invest in Ontario, "Canadian Industrial Intramural R&D Expenditures, Selected Industries," www.investinontario.com/siteselector/bcrd_508.asp.

31. Intel website, Moore's Law, www.intel.com/technology/mooreslaw/, accessed June 11, 2010.

32. Tavia Grant, "Wishful Thinking, a Tax Credit That Doesn't End," *The Globe and Mail*, January 20, 2010, B5.

33. Michael Babad, "How Ontario's Drug Reforms Could Hit Shoppers Drug Mart," *The Globe and Mail*, April 8, 2010, B1; Marina Strauss, "Cost-Lowering Drug Reform Expected to Hit Shoppers," *The Globe and Mail*, July 23, 2009, B5.

34. Geoffrey York, "Nationalization Talks Put Miners on Edge," *The Globe and Mail*, February 2, 2010, B3.

35. David Ebner, "BP Spill Causes Trans-atlantic Tensions," *The Globe and Mail*, June 11, 2010, B5; Eric Reguly, "Now Come the Lawyers," *The Globe and Mail*, June 5, 2010, B1, B4; Peter Coy and Stanley Reed, "Lessons of the Spill," *Bloomberg BusinessWeek*, May 10–16, 2010.

36. Richard Blackwell, "The Greening of the Corner Office," *The Globe and Mail*, March 26, 2007, B1, B4.

37. Michael Porter, *Competitive Strategy: Techniques for Analyzing Industries and Competitors* (New York: The Free Press, 1980).

38. Judy Strauss and Raymond Frost, *E-Marketing* (Upper Saddle River, NJ: Prentice Hall, 2001), 245–246.

39. Lee J. Krajewski and Larry P. Ritzman, *Operations Management: Strategy and Analysis*, 6th ed. (Upper Saddle River, NJ: Prentice Hall, 2002), 3–4.

40. Lee J. Krajewski and Larry P. Ritzman, *Operations Management: Strategy and Analysis*, 6th ed. (Upper Saddle River, NJ: Prentice Hall, 2002), Chapter 3.

41. Gordon Pitts, "Kraft CEO Still Digesting Cadbury Takeover," *The Globe and Mail*, June 7, 2010, B8.

42. Tim Kiladze, "Takeover Activity Eases Off," *The Globe and Mail*, June 11, 2010, B6.

43. Andrew Willis, "Couche-Tard Shows No Stomach for Casey's Fight," *The Globe and Mail*, June 9, 2010, B16.

44. Lawrence Surtees, "Takeover Concern Prompts BCE Poison Pill Plan," *The Globe and Mail*, February 25, 2000, B5.

45. "Culture of Fun Benefits Clients, Staff," *National Post*, October 27, 2008, FP12.

Chapter 3

1. Sinclair Stewart, "CIBC Sues 6 Former Employees, Alleges They Took Confidential Data, Recruited Colleagues to Upstart Genuity," *The Globe and Mail*, January 6, 2005, B1, B4.

2. Howard Levitt, "Managers Have Duty to Remain Loyal to Employer; Court Penalizes Merrill Lynch for Taking RBC Staff," *National Post*, November 12, 2008, FP15.

3. Ronald Ebert and Ricky Griffin, *Business Essentials* (Upper Saddle River, NJ: Prentice Hall, 2009).

4. Thomas Donaldson and Thomas W. Dunfee, "Toward a Unified Conception of Business Ethics: An Integrative Social Contracts Theory," *Academy of Management Review*, Vol. 19, Issue 2 (1994): 252-284.

5. "Drug Companies Face Assault on Prices," *The Wall Street Journal*, May 11, 2000, B1, B4.

6. John Saunders, "Bitter Air Carrier Dogfight Heads to Court," *The Globe and Mail*, July 8, 2004, B3.

7. Andrew Crane, "Spying Doesn't Pay; Intelligence Gathering Is Still an Ethical and Legal Minefield," *National Post*, November 11, 2008, FP12.

8. Mike Esterl and David Crawford, "'Rocky Future' Ahead as Siemens Probe Widens," *The Globe and Mail*, April 27, 2007, B7; David Crawford and Mike Esterl, "At Siemens, Witnesses Cite Pattern of Bribery," *The Wall Street Journal*, January 31, 2007, A1, A10.

9. Ann Zimmerman and Anita Raghavan, "Diamond Group Widens Probe of Bribe Charges," *The Wall Street Journal*, March 8, 2006, B1–B2.

10. Steve Ladurantaye, "Maple Leaf Battered by Meat Recall Costs," *The Globe and Mail*, October 30, 2008, B3; Kristine Owram, "Maple Leaf Claims 'Progress' after Recall," *The Globe and Mail*, February 25, 2009, B5.

11. Mark Schwartz, "Heat's on to Get an Effective Code," *The Globe and Mail*, November 27, 1997, B2.

12. Julie Schmidt, "Nike's Image Problem," *USA Today*, October 4, 1999, 1B, 2B.

13. Alix M. Freedman, "As Unicef Battles Baby-Formula Makers, African Infants Sicken," *The Wall Street Journal*, December 5, 2000, A1, A18.

14. Jeffrey S. Harrison and R. Edward Freeman, "Stakeholders, Social Responsibility, and Performance: Empirical Evidence and Theoretical Perspectives," *Academy of Management Journal*, Vol. 42, Issue 5, 1999, 479–485; also David P. Baron, *Business and Its Environment*, 3rd ed. (Upper Saddle River, NJ: Prentice Hall, 2000).

15. Richard Blackwell, "The Double-Edged Sword of Corporate Altruism," *The Globe and Mail*, November 10, 2008, B5.

16. Milton Friedman, *Capitalism and Freedom* (Chicago: University of Chicago Press, 1962).

17. Jeremy Main, "Here Comes the Big New Cleanup," *Fortune*, November 21, 1988, 102-118.

18. Neil Reynolds, "The Dirty Truth of China's Energy," *The Globe and Mail*, March 28, 2007, B2.

19. Bill Curry, "Ottawa Wants Kyoto Softened," *The Globe and Mail*, May 12, 2006, A1, A7.

20. Jeffrey Ball, "U.N. Effort to Curtail Emissions in Turmoil," *The Wall Street Journal*, April 12-13, 2008, A1, A5.

21. Patricia Adams, "The Next Big Scam," *National Post*, January 13, 2010, FP15.

22. Lauren Etter, "For Icy Greenland, Global Warming Has a Bright Side," *The Wall Street Journal*, July 18, 2006, A1, A12.

23. "Going Green Losing Its Shine Among World's Citizens: Poll," *Winnipeg Free Press*, November 28, 2008, A20.

24. Richard Blackwell, "Canada Becoming a Wind Powerhouse," *The Globe and Mail*, March 9, 2007, B3.

25. Catherine Collins, "The Race for Zero," *Canadian Business*, March 1991, 52-56.

26. "Syncrude Guilty in Duck Deaths," *Winnipeg Free Press*, June 26, 2010, A10; also Tim Shufelt, "Trial Goes Far Beyond Ducks; Syncrude Case Affects All Tailings Pond Users," *National Post*, March 19, 2010, FP1.

27. Egle Procuta, "One Man's Garbage Is Another's Gold," *The Globe and Mail*, April 11, 2006, B7.

28. Geoffrey Scotton, "Cleanups Can Hurt, Companies Warned," *The Financial Post*, June 25, 1991, 4.

29. Marc Huber, "A Double-Edged Endorsement," *Canadian Business,* January 1990, 69-71.

30. Daniel Machalaba, "As Old Pallets Pile Up, Critics Hammer Them as New Eco-Menace," *The Wall Street Journal*, April 1, 1998, A1.

31. Claudia Cattaneo, "Talisman Braces for Jungle Standoff: Threats of Violence," *National Post*, November 14, 2008, FP1.

32. Barrry Critchley, "Gold Industry Eager to Send CSR Message," *National Post*, May 25, 2010, FP2.

33. Emily Steel, "Nestlé Takes a Beating on Social Media Sites," *The Wall Street Journal*, March 29, 2010, B5.

34. Steve Ladurantaye, "Maple Leaf Battered by Meat Recall Costs," *The Globe and Mail*, October 30, 2008, B3.

35. Nicholas Casey, Nicholas Zamiska, and Andy Pasztor, "Mattel Seeks to Placate China with Apology on Toys," *The Wall Street Journal*, September 22-23, 2007, A1, A7.

36. John Wilke, "U.S. Probes Ice Makers Collusion Case," *The Wall Street Journal*, August 7, 2008, B1, B10.

37. Paul Waldie, "Chocolate Bar Makers Probe over Prices," *The Globe and Mail*, November 28, 2007, B1, B10.

38. "Chocolate Makers Face Legal Challenges," *The Globe and Mail*, February 20, 2008, B9.

39. Jason Magder, Jack Branswell, and Ken Meaney, "Gas Firms Guilty of Price-Fixing," *Winnipeg Free Press*, June 13, 2008, A15.

40. Jacquie McNish and Jeff Gray, "'Quaint' Canada Called No Match for Price-Fixers," *The Globe and Mail*, January 27, 2010, B11.

41. Jonathan Cheng, "False Ads: Chinese Consumers Awaken to a Western Problem," *The Wall Street Journal*, July 8, 2005, B9.

42. Peter Darke, "Rise of the Skeptical Consumer," *National Post*, June 23, 2009, FP6.

43. Shawn McCarthy, "Crackdown on New York's Canal Street," *The Globe and Mail*, August 30, 2004, B1, B11.

44. Holly Shaw, "Buzzing Influencers," *National Post*, March 13, 2008, FP12.

45. Tim Barker, "Word-of-Mouth Advertising Grows in Influence, Concern," *Orlando Sentinel*, March 17, 2006, A1, A19.

46. Michael McCarthy and Lorrie Grant, "Sears Drops Benetton after Controversial Death Row Ads," *USA Today*, February 18, 2000, 2B.

47. Shona McKay, "Willing and Able," *Report on Business,* October 1991, 58–63.

48. J. Southerst, "In Pursuit of Drugs," *Canadian Transportation*, November 1989, 58–65.

49. Joshua Gallu and Dawn Kopecki, "Whistleblower Awarded Record US$5.1 Million; Firm Fined US$2.3 Billion; Former Salesman Was Appalled by Pfizer's Tactics," *National Post*, September 4, 2009, FP3.

50. Brent Jang and Patrick Brethour, "This WestJet Staffer Blew the Whistle on His Employer's Corporate Spying: He's Still Waiting for Someone to Say Thanks," *The Globe and Mail*, October 18, 2006, A1, A12.

51. Boyd Erman, "Whistleblower Hotline Opens," *The Globe and Mail*, May 26, 2009, B5.

52. Janet McFarland, "Former Agnico Executive Sentenced to Jail Time," *The Globe and Mail*, January 30, 2009, B3.

53. Jacquie McNish, "Grmovsek Faces Record Sentence," *The Globe and Mail*, November 7, 2009, B7.

54. Greg Farrell, "Enron Law Firm Called Accounting Practices 'Creative,'" *USA Today*, January 16, 2002.

55. Daniel Stoffman, "Good Behaviour and the Bottom Line," *Canadian Business,* May 1991, 28–32.

56. "Great-West Life, London Life and Canada Life Donate $100,000 to the Salvation Army to Help Provide a Brighter Christmas for Many Across Canada," Canada Newswire, December 18, 2008.

57. "McHappy Day Raises $3 Million for Charities," *National Post*, May 8, 2010, FP18.

58. Diana McLaren, "Spirit of Philanthropy Is Thriving," *The Globe and Mail*, December 10, 2008, B7.

59. "Survey Shows Canadian Businesses Engaged in Meeting Community Need," Canada Newswire, February 7, 2008, 1.

60. Tom Kierans, "Charity Begins at Work," *Report on Business,* June 1990, 23.

61. Theresa Ebden and Dawn Walton, "Walkerton Recipient of New-Style Corporate Giving," *The Globe and Mail*, June 3, 2000, B1, B6.

62. Alan Muller and Gail Whiteman, "Exploring the Geography of Philanthropic Disaster Response: A Study of Fortune Global 500 Firms," *Journal of Business Ethics*, 2009, 84: 589–603.

63. Diane McLaren, "Doing Their Part—with Goals in Mind," *The Globe and Mail*, December 10, 2008, B7.

64. Bruce Owen, "Camp Tim on Its Way," *Winnipeg Free Press*, May 28, 2010, A6.

65. Kira Vermond, "A Great Way to Engage Your Employees," *The Globe and Mail*, July 26, 2008, B16.

66. Sandra Waddock and Neil Smith, "Corporate Responsibility Audits: Doing Well by Doing Good," *Sloan Management Review,* Winter 2000: 75–85.

67. Richard Blackwell, "The Double-Edged Sword of Corporate Altruism," *The Globe and Mail*, November 10, 2008, B5.

68. Alison Arnot, "The Triple Bottom Line," *CGA*, January–February 2004, 27–32.

69. Richard Blackwell, "GE Tops of 'Sustainable' Companies," *The Globe and Mail*, January 28, 2010, B2.

70. "Hydro One Tops Best 50 Corporate Citizens in Canada List for 2009," www.corporateknights.ca.

Chapter 4

1. Tavia Grant, "Call It the Entrepreneurial Era," *The Globe and Mail*, March 30, 2010, B.

2. Statistics Canada, *Business Dynamics in Canada*, Catalogue no. 61-534-XIE (Ottawa: Minister of Industry, 2006).

3. P.D. Reynolds, S.M. Camp, W.D. Bygrave, E. Autio, and M. Hay, *Global Entrepreneurship Monitor: 2001 Executive Report* (Kansas City, MO: Kauffman Center for Entrepreneurial Leadership, 2001); P.D. Reynolds, M. Hay, W.D. Bygrave, S.M. Camp, and E. Autio, *Global Entrepreneurship Monitor: 2000 Executive Report* (Kansas City, MO: Kauffman Center for Entrepreneurial Leadership, 2000).

4. Industry Canada, *Key Small Business Statistics* (Ottawa: Public Works and Government Services Canada, 2006), 24.

5. Industry Canada, *Key Small Business Statistics*, 2010, http://dsp-psd. pwgsc.gc.ca/collection_2010/ic/ Iu186-1-2010-1-eng.pdf (2009), 5, accessed June 23, 2010.

6. Monica Diochon, Teresa Menzies, and Yvon Gasse, "Exploring the Relationship between Start-Up Activities and New Venture Emergence: A Longitudinal Study of Canadian Nascent Entrepreneurs," *International Journal of Management and Enterprise Development,* Vol. 2, Issue 3/4 (2005): 408–426.

7. Industry Canada, *Key Small Business Statistics* (Ottawa: Small Business and Tourism Branch Canada, 2009), 23.

8. Queen's University business website, www.business.queensu.ca/news/2009/ 01-14-09-BSME.php.

9. Nancy M. Carter, William B. Gartner, and Paul D. Reynolds, "Firm Founding," in W.B. Gartner, K.G. Shaver, N.M. Carter, and P.D. Reynolds, eds., *Handbook of Entrepreneurial Dynamics: The Process of Business Creation* (Thousand Oaks, CA: Sage, 2004), 311–323.

10. William D. Bygrave and C.W. Hofer, "Theorizing about Entrepreneurship," *Entrepreneurship Theory and Practice,* Vol. 16, Issue 2 (Winter 1991): 14; Donald Sexton and Nancy Bowman-Upton, *Entrepreneurship: Creativity and Growth* (New York: Macmillan, 1991), 7.

11. Fred Vogelstein, "How Mark Zuckerberg Turned Facebook into the Web's Hottest Platform," *Wired*, September 6, 2007, www.wired. com/techbiz/startups/news/2007/ 09/ff_facebook?currentPage=3; Ellen McGirt, "Hacker, Dropout, CEO," *Fast Company*, May 2007, www.fastcompany.com/magazine/115/open_features-hacker-dropout-ceo.html.

12. Heritage Foundation Index of Economic Freedom website, www.heritage. org/index/ranking.aspx, accessed June 23, 2010.

13. Angela Dale, "Self-Employment and Entrepreneurship: Notes on Two Problematic Concepts," in Roger Burrows, ed., *Deciphering the Enterprise Culture* (London: Routledge, 1991), 45, 48; Holt 1992, 11.

14. Donald Sexton and Nancy Bowman-Upton, *Entrepreneurship: Creativity and Growth* (New York: Macmillan, 1991), 11; Kao, 1991, 21.

15. Allan A. Gibb, "The Enterprise Culture and Education: Understanding Enterprise Education and Its Links with Small Business, Entrepreneurship and Wider Educational Goals," *International Small Business Journal,* Vol. 11, Issue 3 (1993): 13–34; Donald Sexton and Nancy Bowman-Upton, *Entrepreneurship: Creativity and Growth* (New York: Macmillan, 1991).

16. Terrence Belford, "Intrapreneurs Combine Big-Biz Clout with Entrepreneurial Style," *CanWest News* (March 23, 2005). Retrieved June 25, 2006, from CBCA Current Events database. (Document ID: 1009719591.)

17. Industry Canada, Small Business Research and Policy, Key Small Business Statistics, Table 3 (Ottawa: Public Works and Government Services Canada, 2008), www.ic.gc.ca/eic/site/sbrp-rppe.nsf/eng/rd02300.html.

18. Industry Canada, Small Business Research and Policy, Key Small Business Statistics (Ottawa: Public Works and Government Services Canada, 2010), http://dsp-psd.pwgsc.gc.ca/collection_2010/ic/Iu186-1-2010-1-eng.pdf.

19. Statistics Canada website, Employment by Class of Worker and Industry, www.statcan.gc.ca/daily-quotidien/100507/t100507a2-eng.htm, accessed June 23, 2010.

20. Industry Canada, Small Business Research and Policy, Key Small Business Statistics (Ottawa: Public Works and Government Services Canada, 2006), 10.

21. William B. Gartner, Kelly G. Shaver, Nancy M. Carter, and Paul D. Reynolds, *Handbook of Entrepreneurial Dynamics* (Thousand Oaks, CA: Sage, 2004), ix.

22. Industry Canada, Small Business Research and Policy, Key Small Business Statistics (Ottawa: Public Works and Government Services Canada, 2006), 10.

23. Industry Canada, Key Small Business Statistics (Ottawa: Public Works and Government Services Canada, 2009), 3.

24. Richard Bloom, "Building a Future on Sweet Dreams," *The Globe and Mail,* October 21, 2004, B9.

25. Lauren McKeon, "Tied to Home," *Canadian Business*, April 14, 2008, 33.

26. RBC website, Female Entrepreneur Awards, www.theawards.ca/cwea/past-winners.cfm, accessed June 24, 2010.

27. Roma Luciw, "Stay-at-Home Moms Stay the Business Course," *The Globe and Mail*, March 3, 2007, B10.

28. BDC website, Young Entrepreneurs Award, www.bdc.ca, accessed June 24, 2010.

29. Ben Barry website, www.benbarry.com, accessed June 24, 2010; Sarah Kennedy, "Self-Styled Pioneer Aims to Alter Face of Fashion," *The Globe and Mail*, July 1, 2002, B12.

30. Tell Us About Us website, www.tellusaboutus.com, accessed June 24, 2010; Geoff Kirbyson, "Market-Research Firm Lands Major Contract," *The Winnipeg Free Press*, July 19, 2004, D7.

31. Donald F. Kuratko and Richard M. Hodgetts, *Entrepreneurship: Theory, Process, Practice,* 7th ed. (Mason, OH: Thomson South-Western, 2007), 118–125; John A. Hornday, "Research about Living Entrepreneurs," in *Encyclopedia of Entrepreneurship*, Calvin Kent, Donald Sexton, and Karl Vesper, eds. (Englewood Cliffs, NJ: Prentice Hall, 1982), 26–27; Jeffry A. Timmons and Stephen Spinelli, *New Venture Creation: Entrepreneurship for the 21st Century* (Boston: McGraw-Hill Irwin, 2007), 9.

32. J.D. Kyle, R. Blais, R. Blatt, and A.J. Szonyi, "The Culture of the Entrepreneur: Fact or Fiction," *Journal of Small Business and Entrepreneurship,* 1991: 3–14.

33. R.H. Brockhaus and Pam S. Horwitz, "The Psychology of the Entrepreneur," in *The Art and Science of Entrepreneurship*, D.L. Sexton and Raymond W. Smilor, eds. (Cambridge, MA: Ballinger, 1986); William B. Gartner, "What Are We Talking about When We Talk about Entrepreneurship?" *Journal of Business Venturing,* Vol. 5, Issue 1 (1990): 15–29; Allan A. Gibb, "The Enterprise Culture and Education: Understanding Enterprise Education and Its Links with Small Business, Entrepreneurship and Wider Educational Goals," *International Small Business Journal,* Vol. 11, Issue 3 (1993): 13–34; J.C. Mitchell, "Case and Situation Analysis," *Sociological Review,* Vol. 31, Issue 2 (1983): 187–211.

34. Donald Sexton and Nancy Bowman-Upton, *Entrepreneurship: Creativity and Growth* (New York: Macmillan, 1991); Karl H. Vesper, *New Venture Strategies* (Englewood Cliffs, NJ: Prentice Hall, 1990); W.D. Bygrave and C.W. Hofer, "Theorizing about Entrepreneurship," *Entrepreneurship Theory and Practice,* Vol. 16, Issue 2 (Winter 1991): 14.

35. Walter Good, *Building a Dream* (Toronto: McGraw-Hill Ryerson, 1998), 40.

36. Wayne A. Long and W. Ed McMullan, *Developing New Ventures* (San Diego: Harcourt Brace Jovanovich, 1990), 374–375.

37. "Sally Fox: Innovation in the Field," www.vreseis.com/sally_fox_story.htm, accessed June 27, 2006.

38. Rasha Mourtada, "Tested to the Limit," *The Globe and Mail*, April 14, 2009, B4.

39. Michael E. Porter, "Know Your Place," *Inc.,* Vol. 13, Issue 9 (September 1992): 90–93.

40. Howard H. Stevenson, H. Irving Grousbeck, Michael J. Roberts, and Amarnath Bhide, *New Business Ventures and the Entrepreneur* (Boston: Irwin McGraw-Hill, 1999), 19.

41. Howard H. Stevenson, H. Irving Grousbeck, Michael J. Roberts, and Amarnath Bhide, *New Business Ventures and the Entrepreneur* (Boston: Irwin McGraw-Hill, 1999), 21.

42. Marc J. Dollinger, *Entrepreneurship: Strategies and Resources* (Upper Saddle River, NJ: Prentice Hall, 1999), 94–101.

43. Thomas W. Zimmerer and Norman M. Scarborough, *Essentials of Entrepreneurship and Small Business Management*, 4th ed. (Upper Saddle River, NJ: Pearson Prentice Hall), 359.

44. Michael E. Porter, "Know Your Place," *Inc.*, Vol. 13, Issue 9 (September 1992): 90-93.

45. Saxx Apparel website, www.saxxapparel.com, accessed June 18, 2010; Rasha Mourtada, "Help Me Get an Angel in My Underwear," *The Globe and Mail*, January 28, 2008, B13.

46. Canada's Venture Capital and Private Equity website, www.cvca.ca/files/Downloads/Final_English_Q4_2009_VC_Data_Deck.pdf, accessed June 24, 2010.

47. Steve Ladurantaye, "New Rules Set Stage for Wave of Foreign Capital," *The Globe and Mail*, March 6, 2010, B1.

48. Business Development Bank of Canada website, www.bdc.ca, accessed June 24, 2010.

49. Karl H. Vesper, *New Venture Mechanics* (Englewood Cliffs, NJ: Prentice Hall, 1993), 105.

50. Jeffry A. Timmons, *New Venture Creation* (Boston: Irwin McGraw-Hill, 1999), 277.

51. Lisa Stephens, "With Some Shape Shifting, This Company Has Legs," *The Globe and Mail*, October 5, 2005, B10.

52. George Anders, Carol Hymowitz, Joann Lublin, and Don Clark, "All in the Family," *The Wall Street Journal*, August 1, 2005, B1, B4.

53. Harvey Schacter, "Honey, You're Fired," *The Globe and Mail*, October 18, 2010, E5.

54. Tony Wilson, "Legal Advice on Starting a Franchise," *The Globe and Mail*, March 16, 2010.

55. Harvey's website, http://harveysfranchising.ca/eng/franchising_2.php, accessed June 24, 2010.

56. "Top 10 Corporations in Canada, 2010," *The Financial Post*, Special Edition, June 2010, 40.

57. "Rankings for Corporate Governance Practices," *The Globe and Mail*, June 18, 2010, B7.

58. Brent Jang, "Porter's IPO: Figuring the Flight Plan," *The Globe and Mail*, April 19, 2010, B9; Scott Deveau, "Porter's Aviation Grounds IPO," *The Financial Post*, June 2, 2010.

59. Andrew Willis, "Market Survey Indicates Eager Demand for IPO's," *The Globe and Mail*, January 6, 2010, B9.

60. "Clearwater Foods Going Private," *National Post*, August 15, 2008, www.nationalpost.com/story-printer.html?id=725985.

61. Terry Pedwell, "Income Trusts Face Tough Rules," *Winnipeg Free Press*, November 1, 2006, B7.

62. Shirley Won, "Looking for Gems in 'Under-loved' Trust Sector," *The Globe and Mail*, June 18, 2010, B13.

63. "An Overview of Available Business Structures," www.umanitoba.ca/afs/agric_economics/MRAC/structures.html#Cooperatives.

64. Industry Canada, *Key Small Business Statistics* (Ottawa: Public Works and Government Services Canada, 2009), 12.

65. Kevin Marron, "Want to Succeed? Read This," *The Globe and Mail*, October 19, 2005, E1, E5. Several excellent articles on starting and operating a small business are found in Section E, "Report on Small Business" in *The Globe and Mail*, October 19, 2005.

66. See Norman M. Scarborough and Thomas W. Zimmerer, *Effective Small Business Management: An Entrepreneurial Approach*, 7th ed. (Upper Saddle River, NJ: Prentice Hall, 2003).

67. Virginia Galt, "Business Bankruptcies Fall in Canada," *The Globe and Mail*, May 13, 2009, B4.

Chapter 5

1. John W. Miller and Marcus Walker, "China Passes Germany as Top Exporter," *The Globe and Mail*, January 6, 2010, B8.

2. Jiri Maly, "Five Trends That Will Shape the Global Economy," *The Globe and Mail*, June 7, 2010, B5.

3. World Bank website, http://web.worldbank.org/WBSITE/EXTERNAL/DATASTATISTICS/0,contentMDK:20420458~menuPK:64133156~pagePK:64133150~piPK:64133175~theSitePK:239419,00.html, accessed March 21, 2010; Ricky Griffin and Michael W. Pustay, *International Business: A Managerial Perspective*, 5th ed. (Upper Saddle River, NJ: Prentice Hall, 2007).

4. Thomas Friedman, *The World Is Flat* (New York: Farrar, Straus, and Giroux, 2005).

5. Barrie McKenna, "China, India Crowd G7 in Driver's Seat," *The Globe and Mail*, July 19, 2006, B11; Andrew Batson, "China's Rise as Auto-Parts Power Reflects New Manufacturing Edge," *The Wall Street Journal*, August 1, 2006, A1, A6.

6. Paul Brent, "A Few BRICS Short of a Load," *Canadian Business*, November 23, 2009, 21; Courtland L. Bovee, John V. Thill, and George Dracopoulos, *Business in Action*, 2nd ed. (Don Mills, ON: Pearson Education, 2008), Chapter 2; Shirley Won, "BRIC May Cure Any Resource Sector Ills," *The Globe and Mail*, November 22, 2007, B17; Andrew Mills, "The Face of Brazil's Ascent," *The Globe and Mail*, March 12, 2010, B11.

7. Tom Krishner, "Indian Car Maker May Land Jaguar, Land Rover," *The Globe and Mail*, January 4, 2008, B3.

8. Jason Bush, "Ikea in Russia: Enough Is Enough," *BusinessWeek*, July 13, 2009, 33.

9. Tavia Grant and Brian Milner, "Why Brazil Stands Out," *The Globe and Mail*, June 10, 2010, B1, B6.

10. Ricky W. Griffin and Michael W. Pustay, *International Business: A Managerial Perspective*, 2nd ed. (Reading, MA: Addison-Wesley, 1999), Chapter 3; Dominick Salvatore, *International Economics*, 6th ed. (Upper Saddle River, NJ: Prentice Hall, 1998), 27-33; Karl E. Case and Ray C. Fair, *Principles of Economics*, 5th ed. (Upper Saddle River, NJ: Prentice Hall, 1999), 813-817.

11. This section is based on Michael Porter, *The Competitive Advantage of Nations* (Boston: Harvard Business School Press, 1990), Chapters 3 and 4; Warren J. Keegan, *Global Marketing Management*, 6th ed. (Upper Saddle River, NJ: Prentice Hall, 1999), 312-321; John J. Wild, Kenneth L. Wild, and Jerry C.Y. Han, *International Business: An Integrated Approach* (Upper Saddle River, NJ: Prentice Hall, 2000), 175-178.

12. World Economic Forum website, www.weforum.org/en/initiatives/gcp/Global%20Competitiveness%20Report/index.htm, accessed March 21, 2010.

13. Bank of Canada website, http://test.bankofcanada.ca/pdf/bfs.pdf, Table J2, *Bank of Canada Banking and Financial Statistics* (March 2010): S-112, accessed March 28, 2010.

14. Karl E. Case and Ray C. Fair, *Principles of Economics*, 5th ed. (Upper Saddle River, NJ: Prentice Hall, 1999), 818–821.

15. Jeremy Torobin, "Dollar at Par: The New Normal," *The Globe and Mail*, March 18, 2010, B1, B6; Bank of Canada website, www.bankofcanada.ca/cgi-bin/famecgi_fdps, accessed March 27, 2010.

16. LuAnn LaSalle, "Clearwater Eyes Productivity to Offset High Loonie," *The Globe and Mail*, March 24, 2010, B1.

17. Gordon Pitts, "How Captain High Liner Beat the Dollar Odds," *The Globe and Mail*, March 16, 2010, B1–B4.

18. Geoffrey York, "McCain Laying Down Its Chips on African Strategy," *The Globe and Mail*, December 22, 2009, B3.

19. Mark MacKinnon, "RIM's Indonesian Bonanza," *The Globe and Mail*, March 25, 2010, B1.

20. Diane Francis, "China Learns the Lingo," *The National Post*, January 16, 2010, FP2; Shirley Won, "Small Firms Beating a Path to the Middle Kingdom," *The Globe and Mail*, August 31, 2004, B7.

21. Ray August, *International Business Law: Text, Cases, and Readings*, 3rd ed. (Upper Saddle River, NJ: Prentice Hall, 2000), 192–197.

22. Fortune 500 website, Global 500 Rankings, http://money.cnn.com/magazines/fortune/global500/2009/index.html, accessed March 28, 2010.

23. Warren J. Keegan, *Global Marketing Management*, 6th ed. (Upper Saddle River, NJ: Prentice Hall, 1999), 290–292; Ricky W. Griffin and Michael W. Pustay, *International Business: A Managerial Perspective*, 2nd ed. (Reading, MA: Addison-Wesley, 1999), 427–431; John J. Wild, Kenneth L. Wild, and Jerry C.Y. Han, *International Business: An Integrated Approach* (Upper Saddle River, NJ: Prentice Hall, 2000), 454–456.

24. Ricky W. Griffin and Michael W. Pustay, *International Business: A Managerial Perspective*, 2nd ed. (Reading, MA: Addison-Wesley, 1999), 431–433;

25. Shirley Won, "Small Firms Beating a Path to the Middle Kingdom," *The Globe and Mail*, August 31, 2004, B7.

26. Shirley Won, "Small Firms Beating a Path to the Middle Kingdom," *The Globe and Mail*, August 31, 2004, B7.

27. Gaurav Raghuvanshi and Eric Bellman, "Wal-Mart Tiptoes into India's Marketplace," *The Globe and Mail*, February 21, 2010, B13.

28. John J. Wild, Kenneth L. Wild, and Jerry C.Y. Han, *International Business: An Integrated Approach* (Upper Saddle River, NJ: Prentice Hall, 2000), Chapter 7; Ricky W. Griffin and Michael W. Pustay, *International Business: A Managerial Perspective*, 2nd ed. (Reading, MA: Addison-Wesley, 1999), 436–439.

29. Carolynne Wheeler, "Bombardier Laid Track Long Ago for Deal in China," *The Globe and Mail*, October 1, 2009, B1; Bertrand Marotte, "Bombardier Speeds Ahead in China," *The Globe and Mail*, September 29, 2009, B1.

30. Eric Beauchesne, "Foreign Control of Economy Hits 30-Year High," *Winnipeg Free Press*, November 19, 2005, B7.

31. Janet McFarland, "Corporate Canada Easy Prey for Foreign Buyers, *The Globe and Mail*, February 27, 2008, B1–B2.

32. Roma Luciw, "Hollowed Out Fears? Relax, Foreigners Lead on Hiring," *The Globe and Mail*, July 14, 2006, B1–B2.

33. Gordon Pitts, "Mixed Messages on Danger of Foreign Takeovers," *The Globe and Mail*, September 18, 2006, B1, B3. For an extensive analysis of the effect of foreign takeovers of Canadian business firms, see Roger Martin and Gordon Nixon, "Who, Canada," *The Globe and Mail*, July 2, 2007, B1–B3.

34. John Partridge, "Foreign Takeover Fears Played Down," *The Globe and Mail*, August 22, 2007, B3.

35. Marcus Gee, "Green Hats and Other Ways to Blow a Deal in China," *The Globe and Mail*, August 27, 2007, B1.

36. Steven Chase, "Canada Slaps Duties on Chinese-Made Barbecues," *The Globe and Mail*, August 28, 2004, B2.

37. Peter Kennedy, "Softwood Decision Gets Mixed Reviews," *The Globe and Mail*, December 8, 2005, B6.

38. Jennifer Ditchburn, "Canada, U.S. Pen Deal to End Lumber Dispute," *The Winnipeg Free Press*, July 2, 2006, A6.

39. Paul Veira, "Emerson Warns Lumber Leaders of 'Consequences,'" *The Financial Post*, August 1, 2006, FP1, FP5; also Steve Merti, "Lumber Exporters Taste Sting of Softwood Deal," *The Winnipeg Free Press*, September 22, 2006, B5.

40. "WTO Strikes Down U.S. Cotton Subsidy Appeal," *The Globe and Mail*, March 4, 2005, B10.

41. Scott Kilman and Roger Thurow, "To Soothe Anger over Subsidies, U.S. Cotton Tries Wooing Africa," *The Wall Street Journal*, August 5, 2005, A1, A6.

42. Simon Tuck, "Farmers to WTO: If It Ain't Broke . . . ," *The Globe and Mail*, August 9, 2004, B1–B2.

43. Anthony DePalma, "Chiquita Sues Europeans, Citing Banana Quota Losses," *The New York Times*, January 26, 2001, C5; Brian Lavery, "Trade Feud on Bananas Not as Clear as It Looks," *The New York Times*, February 7, 2001, W1; David E. Sanger, "Miffed at Europe, U.S. Raises Tariffs for Luxury Goods," *The New York Times*, March 4, 1999, A1, A5.

44. Wendy Stueck, "Mining Firms Hit Again by Chavez Threat," *The Globe and Mail*, September 23, 2005, B4; also Barrie McKenna, "A Nation of Big Riches, Bigger Risks," *The Globe and Mail*, September 24, 2005, B4.

45. Konrad Yakabuski, "Quebec Courts Margarine War," *The Globe and Mail*, October 14, 1997, B1, B4.

46. Kevin Doherty, "Yellow Margarine Ban to Be Lifted in Quebec," *Montreal Gazette*, July 8, 2008, B1; Bertrand Marotte, "Ontario Calls for Dispute Panel in Quebec Margarine Battle," *The Globe and Mail*, March 26, 2002, B10.

47. Neville Nankivell, "Spilled Milk over Provincial Trade," *National Post*, April 24, 2000, C9.

48. Gerry Stobo, "Cross-Border Mobility," *CGA*, May–June 2005: 13–16.

49. Gary McWilliams, "Wal-Mart Era Wanes Amid Big Shifts in Retail," *The Wall Street Journal*, October 3, 2007, A1, A17.

50. Thestar.com website, "UFC May Have Long Wait to Crack Ontario Market," www.thestar.com/sports/wrestling/ufc/article/783892—ufc-may-have-long-wait-to-crack-ontario-market, accessed July 9, 2010.

51. Dawn Walton, "Builders Most Likely to Bribe, Report Finds," *The Globe and Mail*, January 21, 2000, B5.

52. Nicholas Bray, "OECD Ministers Agree to Ban Bribery as Means for Companies to Win Business," *The Wall Street Journal*, May 27, 1997, A2.

53. Elaine Kurtenbach, "Rio Workers Get Harsh Sentences," *The Globe and Mail*, March 29, 2010, B1: Elaine Kurtenbach, "Rio Tinto Exec Admits to Some Bribery Charges," *The Globe and Mail*, March 23, 2010, B12.

54. "Canada Ties for First in List of Countries Resistant to Corrupt Business," *National Post*, December 10, 2008, FP2; "Russian Firms Most Prone to Bribery, Survey Finds," *The Globe and Mail*, December 10, 2008, B14.

55. Transparency International website, www.transparency.org/policy_research/surveys_indices/cpi/2009, accessed May 25, 2010.

56. "EU Fines Banana Importers for Cartel Actions," *The Globe and Mail*, October 16, 2008, B11; "EU Imposes Highest Fine over Auto Glass Cartel," *The Globe and Mail*, November 13, 2008, B9; "Oil Companies Fined by EU over 'Paraffin Mafia' Cartel," *The Globe and Mail*, October 2, 2008, B7.

57. Toby Heaps, "Potash Politics," *Corporate Knights*, Winter 2009, 19–23.

58. Canadian Press, "China Decries U.S. Duties on Steel Pipes," *The Globe and Mail*, January 1, 2010, B4.

59. Peter Wonacott, "Downturn Heightens China–India Tension on Trade," *The Wall Street Journal*, March 20, 2009, A8.

60. Peter Wonacott, "Downturn Heightens China–India Tension on Trade," *The Wall Street Journal*, March 20, 2009, A8.

61. "New Global Trade Regulator Starts Operations Tomorrow," *Winnipeg Free Press*, December 31, 1994, A5.

62. Barrie McKenna, "Boeing's WTO Win May Prove a Hollow Victory," *The Globe and Mail*, September 5, 2009, B5.

63. "US Hails WTO Victory over China," *The Globe and Mail*, December 22, 2009, B5.

64. John Miller, "Global Trade Talks Fail as New Giants Flex Muscle," *The Wall Street Journal*, July 30, 2008, A1, A12.

65. Michelle MacAfee, "Trade Protest Turns Violent," *Winnipeg Free Press*, July 29, 2003, A9.

66. Europa website, http://europa.eu/index_en.htm, accessed March 23, 2010.

67. Bruce Little, "Free-Trade Pact Gets Mixed Reviews," *The Globe and Mail*, June 7, 2004, B3.

68. Barrie McKenna, "Dead End for Free Trade," *The Globe and Mail*, May 17, 2008, B4–B5.

69. Rachel Pulfer, "NAFTA's Third Amigo," *Canadian Business*, June 15, 2009, 27.

Chapter 6

1. Chris Knight, "McDonald's New Recipe for Success; The Golden Arches Has Fought Its Way Back, Not with the Burger, but with Coffee, Snack Wraps, and a Restaurant Facelift," *National Post*, September 5, 2009, FP1.

2. Grant Buckler, "Workplace Wheel of Fortune," *The Globe and Mail*, December 18, 2007, B8.

3. *Hoover's Handbook of American Business 2006* (Austin: Hoover's Business Press, 2006).

4. Alex Taylor III, "How a Top Boss Manages His Day," *Fortune*, June 19, 1989, 95–100.

5. Harvey Schachter, "Turning a Company Inside Out," *The Globe and Mail*, May 18, 2009, B4.

6. "2009 All-Star Execs," *Canadian Business*, November 23, 2009, 59.

7. Roma Luciw, "No. 1 Employee Not Always Your No. 1 Manager," *The Globe and Mail*, February 17, 2007, B10.

8. The experiences of these and other bosses are described in a CBS television series entitled "Undercover Boss" that premiered in 2010. It depicts the experiences business executives have when working with entry-level employees (who don't know they are working with the president). The program summarizes the lessons the CEOs learned. Another series, the "Big Switcheroo" on CBC, portrays situations where bosses trade jobs with lower-level workers.

9. www.cbc.ca/money/story/2010/01/04/executive-compensation- average-salary-ceo.html#ixzz0lroe33Ns.

10. Rick Spence, "As a Leader, Are You a Cop or a Coach? Top Secret Meet Reveals Great Coaches Are Rare," *National Post*, July 21, 2009, FP11.

11. Jerry Useem, "Boeing vs. Boeing," *Fortune,* October 2, 2000, 148-160; "Airbus Prepares to 'Bet the Company' as It Builds a Huge New Jet," *The Wall Street Journal*, November 3, 1999, A1, A10.

12. Charles P. Wallace, "Adidas—Back in the Game," *Fortune*, August 18, 1997, 176-182.

13. Barry M. Staw and Jerry Ross, "Good Money after Bad," *Psychology Today,* February 1988: 30-33.

14. Gerry McNamara and Philip Bromiley, "Risk and Return in Organizational Decision Making," *Academy of Management Journal*, Vol. 42 (1999): 330-339.

15. Brian O'Reilly, "What It Takes to Start a Startup," *Fortune*, June 7, 1999, 135-140.

16. Sinclair Stewart and Derek DeCloet, "It's Mr. Focus v. Mr. Diversification," *The Globe and Mail*, June 3, 2006, B4.

17. Michael Porter, *Competitive Strategy: Techniques for Analyzing Industries and Competitors* (New York: The Free Press, 1980).

18. Bertrand Marotte, "Gildan Takes T-Shirt Making to the Cutting-Edge of Casual Apparel," *The Globe and Mail*, July 3, 2004, B3.

19. "Cruise-Ship Delays Leave Guests High and Dry," *The Wall Street Journal*, October 24, 1997, B1, B10; *Hoover's Handbook of American Business 2000* (Austin: Hoover's Business Press, 2000), 1512-1513.

20. Any Hoffman, "Potash Strike Leaves Slippery Side Effects," *The Globe and Mail*, November 17, 2008, B1.

21. Steve Ladurantaye, "Maple Leaf Battered by Meat Recall Costs," *The Globe and Mail*, October 30, 2008, B3.

22. Kristine Owram, "Maple Leaf Claims 'Progress' after Recall," *The Globe and Mail*, February 25, 2009, B5.

23. Ric Dolphin, "His Race, His Rules," *Canadian Business*, May 1988, 32.

24. Isadore Sharp, "Quality for All Seasons," *Canadian Business Review*, Spring 1990: 21–23.

25. Bruce McDougall, "The Thinking Man's Assembly Line," *Canadian Business*, November 1991, 40–44.

26. Peter Verburg, "Prepare for Take-off," *Canadian Business*, December 25, 2000, 95–99.

27. Sanam Islam, "Execs See Link to Bottom Line: Gap Is Closing; More Firms Keen to Be Seen as Best Corporate Culture," *National Post*, November 12, 2008, FP16.

28. Wallace Immen, "Half of Workers Don't Fit In," *The Globe and Mail*, October 22, 2008, C2.

29. Derek Sankey, "Cult-Like Culture Is Key," *The Financial Post*, July 28, 2008, www.nationalpost.com/story-printer.html?id=684225.

30. "Golden Rule Is Measure of Success: 10 Most Admired Corporate Cultures," *National Post*, December 3, 2008, FP16; Calvin Leung, "Culture Club," *Canadian Business*, October 9–22, 2006, 115, 116, 118, 120.

31. Sinclair Stewart and Andrew Willis, "Hunkin Is De-Risking the Place," *The Globe and Mail*, December 11, 2004, B4.

32. Carrie Tait, "CIBC Shuffles the Deck," *National Post*, January 8, 2008, www.nationalpost.com/story.

33. Bernard Simon and Jonathan Wehatley, "Heading in Opposite Directions," *Financial Times*, March 11, 2010, 10.

Chapter 7

1. Robert L. Simison, "Ford Rolls Out New Model of Corporate Culture," *The Wall Street Journal*, January 13, 1999, B1, B4.

2. Joann Muller, "Ford: Why It's Worse than You Think," *BusinessWeek*, June 25, 2001, 80–84.

3. John A. Wagner and John R. Hollenbeck, *Management of Organizational Behavior* (Englewood Cliffs, NJ: Prentice Hall, 1992), 563–565.

4. Jay Diamond and Gerald Pintel, *Retailing*, 6th ed. (Upper Saddle River, NJ: Prentice Hall, 1996), 83–84.

5. "Nike Redefines Its Regions Amid Spending Pullback," *The Globe and Mail*, March 21, 2009, B7.

6. Michael E. Raynor and Joseph L. Bower, "Lead from the Center," *Harvard Business Review*, May 2001: 93–102.

7. Bruce Horovitz, "Restoring the Golden-Arch Shine," *USA Today*, June 16, 1999, 3B.

8. *Hoover's Handbook of American Business 2006* (Austin: Hoover's Business Press, 2006); Brian Dumaine, "How I Delivered the Goods," *Fortune Small Business*, October 2002.

9. Lee Hawkins, "Reversing 80 Years of History, GM Is Reining in Global Fiefs," *The Wall Street Journal*, October 6, 2004, A1, A14.

10. Donna Fenn, "The Buyers," *Inc.*, June 1996: 46–48.

11. "Teck to Drop Cominco, Split into Five Units," *The Globe and Mail*, October 2, 2008, B7.

12. Nelson Wyatt, "Bell Canada Plan Creates 3 Divisions," *The Winnipeg Free Press*, May 8, 2003, B7.

13. J. Galbraith, "Matrix Organization Designs: How to Combine Functional and Project Forms," *Business Horizons*, 1971: 29–40; H.F. Kolodny, "Evolution to a Matrix Organization," *Academy of Management Review* 4 (1979): 543–553.

14. Interview with Tom Ward, operations manager for Genstar Shipyards.

15. Diane Brady, "Martha Inc.," *BusinessWeek*, January 17, 2000, 62–66.

16. Miguel Helft, "Yahoo Chief Rearranges Managers Once Again," *The New York Times*, February 27, 2009, B5.

17. Gail Edmondson, "Danone Hits Its Stride," *BusinessWeek*, February 1, 1999, 52–53.

18. Thomas A. Stewart, "See Jack. See Jack Run," *Fortune*, September 27, 1999, 124–127.

19. James P. Sterba, "At the Met Opera, It's Not Over Till the Fat Man Folds," *The Wall Street Journal*, January 1998, 1, 6.

20. Jerald Greenberg and Robert A. Baron, *Behavior in Organizations: Understanding and Managing the Human Side of Work*, 7th ed. (Upper Saddle River, NJ: Prentice Hall, 2000), 308–309.

21. Tyler Hamilton, "Welcome to the World Wide Grapevine," *The Globe and Mail*, May 6, 2000, B1, B6.

Chapter 8

1. See Angelo S. DeNisi and Ricky W. Griffin, *Human Resource Management* (Boston: Houghton Mifflin, 2001), for a complete overview.

2. Susanna Kelley, "In RIM's Ravaged Heartland, Good Jobs Go Begging," *The Globe and Mail*, November 12, 2009, B4.

3. Grant Robertson, "Changing of the Guard," *The Globe and Mail*, March 17, 2010, B1.

4. Patrick Brethour and Heather Scoffield, "Plenty of Work, Not Enough Bodies," *The Globe and Mail*, August 21, 2006, B4.

5. Tavia Grant, "Companies Sound Upbeat Note on Hiring," *The Globe and Mail*, June 8, 2010, B5.

6. Elizabeth Church, "Store Owners Struggle with Staffing," *The Globe and Mail*, November 25, 1996, B6.

7. Kira Vermond, "Get This: Lame Summer Internships Now Sizzle," *The Globe and Mail*, July 19, 2008, B17.

8. Wallace Immen, "Prospective Hires Put to the Test," *The Globe and Mail*, January 26, 2005, C1, C2.

9. Wallace Immen, "Prospective Hires Put to the Test," *The Globe and Mail*, January 26, 2005, C1, C2.

10. Katie Rook, "Curveball Job Questions: How Not to Strike Out," *The Globe and Mail*, September 3, 2005, B9.

11. Ogilvy Renault website, www.ogilvyrenault.com/en/; Emily Sternberg, Anouk Violette, William Hlibchuk, "Drug and Alcohol Testing by Employers in Canada—A Legal Issues Pulse-Check," May 28, 2008, accessed July 2, 2010; Canadian Human Rights Commission

Policy on Alcohol and Drug Testing, June 2002, P1-16.

12. David Hutton, "Job Reference Chill Grows Icier," *The Globe and Mail*, June 18, 2008, B1.

13. Bertrand Marotte, "From the Cockpit to the OR: CAE's Diversification," *The Globe and Mail*, May 25, 2010, B3.

14. Tavia Grant, "Weekend Workout: Reverse Mentoring," *The Globe and Mail*, July 11, 2009, B14.

15. Abby Ellin, "Training Programs Often Miss the Point on the Job," *The New York Times*, March 29, 2000, C12.

16. Kira Vermond, "Taking a Full-Circle Look at Work Reviews," *The Globe and Mail*, November 24, 2007, B18.

17. Harvey Schacter, "Why Performance Reviews Get an F," *The Globe and Mail*, June 30, 2010, B22; Walllace Immen, "A Failing Grade for Performance Reviews," *The Globe and Mail*, May 14, 2010, B14.

18. "2009 Executive Compensation," *The Globe and Mail*, May 25, 2010, B7.

19. Boyd Erman, "Shareholders Win Voice on CEO Pay at 3 Big Banks," *The Globe and Mail*, February 27, 2009, B1.

20. Joann Lublin, "Say on the Boss's Pay," *The Wall Street Journal*, March 7, 2008, B1–B2.

21. Heather Scoffield, "New National Refrain: Can I Help You?" *The Globe and Mail*, May 27, 2008, B1, B6.

22. Andrew Willis, "Record Bonus Pool Building at Canada's Banks," *The Globe and Mail*, June 2, 2010, B11.

23. Cathryn Atkinson, "The Total Package: Anatomy of a Great Place to Work," *The Globe and Mail*, July 2, 2008, B6.

24. Jennifer Myers, "The Right Way to Reward," *The Globe and Mail*, April 3, 2010, B13.

25. Canada's Economic Action Site website, www.actionplan.gc.ca/initiatives/eng/index.asp?mode=2&initiativeID=77, accessed June 30, 2010.

26. Craig McInnes, "Pumped Up and Ready to Pay Out," *Vancouver Sun*, January 12, 2009.

27. Virginia Galt, "Companies, Unions, Expect Little Relief," *The Globe and Mail*, September 15, 2004, B4.

28. Virginia Galt, "Gift of Time Pays off for Savvy Employers," *The Globe and Mail*, December 28, 2004, B3.

29. Virginia Galt, "Gift of Time Pays off for Savvy Employers," *The Globe and Mail*, December 28, 2004, B3.

30. Erin White, "Sabbaticals: The Pause That Refreshes," *The Wall Street Journal*, August 2, 2005, B1, B4.

31. Kamal Dib, "Diversity Works," *Canadian Business*, March 29, 2004, 53-54.

32. Catalyst website, www.catalyst.org/publication/, accessed July 1, 2010.

33. Richard Blackwell and Brent Jang, "Top Court Sides with Airline Attendants," *The Globe and Mail*, January 27, 2006, B1, B6.

34. Jennifer Peltz, "Fired NY Banker's Suit, and Suits, Raise Eyebrows," *The Globe and Mail*, June 29, 2010, B5.

35. CBC website, "Mandatory Retirement Fades in Canada," www.cbc.ca/canada/story/2009/08/20/mandatory-retirement-explainer523.html, August 20, 2009, accessed July 1, 2010.

36. Omar El Akkad, "A Woman's Work May Never Be Done," *The Globe and Mail*, March 28, 2006, B1, B4.

37. Michael Moss, "For Older Employees, On-the-Job Injuries Are More Often Deadly," *The Wall Street Journal*, June 17, 1997, A1, A10.

38. Jill Mahoney, "Visible Majority by 2017," *The Globe and Mail*, March 23, 2005, A1, A7.

39. Max Boisot, *Knowledge Assets* (Oxford: Oxford University Press, 1998).

40. Statistics Canada website, www40.statcan.ca/l01/cst01/labor12-eng.htm, accessed July 1, 2010.

41. Tavia Grant, "Financial Crisis Sparks More Demand for Temps at the Top," *The Globe and Mail*, November 14, 2008, B16.

42. Citizenship and Immigration Canada website, www.cic.gc.ca/english/work/index.asp, accessed July 1, 2010.

43. Aaron Bernstein, "When Is a Temp Not a Temp?" *BusinessWeek*, December 7, 1998, 90–92.

44. David Lipsky and Clifford Donn, *Collective Bargaining in American Industry* (Lexington, MA: Lexington Books, 1981).

45. Human Resources and Skills Development Canada website, www.hrsdc.gc.ca/eng/labour/labour_relations/info_analysis/union_membership/index2009.shtml, accessed July 1, 2010; Patrick Brethour and Heather Scoffield, "Plenty of Work, Not Enough Bodies," *The Globe and Mail*, August 21, 2006, B4.

46. Elizabeth Church, "Store Owners Struggle with Staffing," *The Globe and Mail*, November 25, 1996, B6.

47. Kira Vermond, "Get This: Lame Summer Internships Now Sizzle," *The Globe and Mail*, July 19, 2008, B17.

48. Greg Keenan, "CAW Rewriting Playbook to Keep Factories Running," *The Globe and Mail*, September 5, 2006, B3.

49. Virginia Galt, "Worn-Out Middle Managers May Get Protection," *The Globe and Mail*, January 3, 2005, B1, B8.

50. Paul Waldie, "How Health Costs Hurt the Big Three," *The Globe and Mail*, March 22, 2005, B1–B2; Virginia Galt, "Companies, Unions Expect Little Relief," *The Globe and Mail*, September 15, 2004, B4.

51. David Ebner, "Potash Workers Ratify Deal That Changes Little," *The Globe and Mail*, November 15, 2008, B7.

52. Paul Waldie, "China's Workers Pressing Their Case—and Winning," *The Globe and Mail*, June 30, 2010, B1, B6.

53. Jack Mintz, "The Perils of the Picket Line," *Canadian Business*, February 27–March 12, 2006, 15.

54. Alison Auld, "N.S. Nurses Defy Strike Law," *The Globe and Mail*, June 28, 2001, B1, B2.

55. "Petro-Canada Workers Locked Out Last Year Advised to Accept Contract," *National Post*, December 20, 2008, FP2.

56. Murray McNeill, "Hotel Workers Sever Relationship with Union," *The Winnipeg Free Press*, July 22, 2005, B14.

57. "Staff Shuns Offer, Magna Plant to Close," *The Globe and Mail*, March 19, 2009, B4.

58. "Potash Corp., Union Seek Mediator to Get Contract Talks Back on the Rails," *National Post*, July 31, 2008, www.nationalpost.com/story-printer.html?id=690890.

59. "Ottawa Names Arbitrator to Decide Exit Package Terms for Air Canada Workers," *National Post*, August 20, 2008, www.nationalpost.com/story-printer.html?id=735135.

Chapter 9

1. "Bosses: Killing Them with Kindness Pays Off," *The Globe and Mail*, October 8, 2008, C3.

2. Daniel Goleman, *Emotional Intelligence: Why It Can Matter More than IQ* (New York: Bantam Books, 1995); also Kenneth Law, Chi-Sum Wong, and Lynda Song, "The Construct and Criterion Validity of Emotional Intelligence and Its Potential Utility for Management Studies," *Journal of Applied Psychology*, 2004: 483–496.

3. Daniel Goleman, "Leadership That Gets Results," *Harvard Business Review*, March–April 2000: 78–90.

4. "Half of Canadians Love Their Jobs," *The Globe and Mail*, February 17, 2010, B20.

5. "Canadians Ranked No. 3 in Satisfaction with Their Current Employer," *National Post*, April 14, 2010, FP5.

6. Doris Burke, Corey Hajim, John Elliott, Jenny Mero, and Christopher Tkaczyk, "The Top Ten Companies for Leaders," *Fortune*, October 1, 2007, money.cnn.com/galleries/2007/fortune/0709/gallery.leaders_global_topten.fortune/index.html.

7. Barbara Moses, "A Cruise with the Boss? A Box of Timbits? Time to Get Serious about Rewarding Employees," *The Globe and Mail*, April 28, 2010, B16.

8. Frederick W. Taylor, *Principles of Scientific Management* (New York: Harper and Brothers, 1911).

9. See Daniel Wren, *The History of Management Thought*, 5th ed. (New York: John Wiley & Sons, 2004).

10. Douglas McGregor, *The Human Side of Enterprise* (New York: McGraw-Hill, 1960).

11. Abraham Maslow, "A Theory of Human Motivation," *Psychological Review* (July 1943): 370–396.

12. Frederick Herzberg, Bernard Mausner, and Barbara Bloch Snydeman, *The Motivation to Work* (New York: Wiley, 1959).

13. Victor Vroom, *Work and Motivation* (New York: Wiley, 1964); Craig Pinder, *Work Motivation* (Glenview, IL: Scott, Foresman, 1984).

14. J. Stacy Adams, "Toward an Understanding of Inequity," *Journal of Abnormal and Social Psychology*, Vol. 75, Issue 5 (1963): 422–436.

15. Andy Holloway, "How the Game Is Played," *Canadian Business*, April 2, 2001, 26–35.

16. Brent Jang, "'WestJetters' Reap Rewards for Wild-Weather Work," *The Globe and Mail*, January 8, 2009, B7.

17. Deena Waisberg, "Tip of the Hat to Excellence: Employers Get Creative with Rewards to Keep Top Performers," *National Post*, November 19, 2008, FP15.

18. For more information on some of the potential problems with goal setting, see Drake Bennett, "Do Goals Undermine Good Management?" *National Post*, March 24, 2009, FP10; also Wallace Immen, "The Goal: To Set Goals That Really Can Be Met," *The Globe and Mail*, March 20, 2009, B12.

19. Interviews with Sterling McLeod and Wayne Walker, senior vice-presidents of sales for Investors Group Financial Services.

20. Tavia Grant, "Workplace Democracy," *The Globe and Mail*, May 30, 2009, B14.

21. Brent Jang, "High-Flying WestJet Morale Gets Put to the Test," *The Globe and Mail*, November 25, 2005, B3.

22. Virginia Galt, "Change Is a Good Thing When Everyone Is Involved," *The Globe and Mail*, June 25, 2005, B11.

23. Tavia Grant, "Workplace Democracy," *The Globe and Mail*, May 30, 2009, B14.

24. Robert Grant, "AES Corporation: Rewriting the Rules of Management," *Contemporary Strategy Analysis* (Hoboken, NJ: John Wiley & Sons, 2007), www.blackwellpublishing.com/grant/docs/17AES.pdf.

25. Patricia Kitchen, "Tap Your Employees," *Orlando Sentinel*, March 14, 2007, F1.

26. Mary Teresa Bitti, "The Power of Teamwork," *National Post*, December 18, 2009, FP12.

27. Tom Peters, *Liberation Management* (New York: Alfred Knopf, 1992), 238–239.

28. Charles Snow, Scott Snell, Sue Canney Davison, and Donald Hambrick, "Use Transnational Teams to Globalize Your Company," *Organizational Dynamics*, Spring 1996, 61.

29. Gregory Moorhead and Ricky W. Griffin, *Organizational Behavior*, 6th ed. (Boston: Houghton Mifflin, 2001), Chapter 7.

30. For a discussion of team effectiveness, see Nancy Langton and Stephen Robbins, *Organizational Behaviour*, 4th Canadian ed. (Toronto: Pearson Canada, 2006), 217–230.

31. Gregory Moorhead and Ricky W. Griffin, *Organizational Behavior*, 6th ed. (Boston: Houghton Mifflin, 2001), Chapter 7.

32. A.B. Drexler and R. Forrester, "Teamwork—Not Necessarily the Answer," *HR Magazine*, January 1998, 55–58.

33. Gregory Moorhead and Ricky W. Griffin, *Organizational Behavior*, 6th ed. (Boston: Houghton Mifflin, 2001), Chapter 7.

34. Ricky Griffin, *Task Design* (Glenview, IL: Scott, Foresman, 1982).

35. Richard J. Hackman and Greg Oldham, *Work Redesig n* (Reading, MA: Addison-Wesley, 1980).

36. Kira Vermond, "Punching in on the Variable Clock," *The Globe and Mail*, March 22, 2008, B14.

37. Tavia Grant, "Lower Costs, Higher Morale Benefits of Four-Day Work Week," *The Globe and Mail*, August 18, 2008, B4.

38. Paul Lima, "With New Advances in Technology, Why Are We Still Jumping in the Car?" *The Globe and Mail*, October 20, 2008, E9.

39. Joyce Rosenberg, "Out of Sight, on Your Mind: Learning to Trust Telecommuters," *The Globe and Mail*, September 20, 2008, B19.

40. Paul Lima, "With New Advances in Technology, Why Are We Still Jumping in the Car?" *The Globe and Mail*, October 20, 2008, E9.

41. "Productivity Rises for Teleworkers: Survey," *The Globe and Mail*, October 15, 2008, C7.

42. Randi Chapnik Myers, "The Back and Forth of Working from Home," *The Globe and Mail*, March 8, 2008, B16.

43. Margot Gibb-Clark, "Satellite Office a Hit with Staff," *The Globe and Mail*, November 18, 1991, B4.

44. Dawn Walton, "Survey Focuses on Job Sharing," *The Globe and Mail*, June 10, 1997, B4.

45. John Kotter, "What Leaders Really Do," *Harvard Business Review*, December 2001: 85-94.

46. Ronald Heifetz and Marty Linsky, "A Survival Guide for Leaders," *Harvard Business Review*, June 2002: 65-74.

47. Frederick Reichheld, "Lead for Loyalty," *Harvard Business Review*, July–August, 2001: 76-83.

48. S.A. Kirkpatrick and E.A. Locke, "Leadership: Do Traits Matter?" *Academy of Management Executive*, May 1991: 48-60.

49. Daniel Goleman, "What Makes a Leader?" *Harvard Business Review*, November–December 1998: 93-99.

50. David Dorsey, "Andy Pearson Finds Love," *Fast Company*, August 2001, 78-86.

51. David A. Waldman and Francis J. Yammarino, "CEO Charismatic Leadership: Levels-of-Management and Levels-of-Analysis Effects," *Academy of Management Review*, Vol. 24 (1999): 266-285.

52. Ronald Ebert and Ricky Griffin, *Business Essentials,* 7th ed. (Upper Saddle River, NJ: Prentice Hall, 2009), 129.

53. Jane Howell and Boas Shamir, "The Role of Followers in the Charismatic Leadership Process: Relationships and Their Consequences," *Academy of Management Review*, January 2005: 96-112.

54. J. Richard Hackman and Ruth Wageman, "A Theory of Team Coaching," *Academy of Management Review*, April 2005: 269-287.

55. "How Women Lead," *Newsweek*, October 24, 2005, 46-70.

56. Madelaine Drohan, "What Makes a Canadian Manager?" *The Globe and Mail*, Feburary 25, 1997, B18.

57. Rebecca Walberg, "Canada's Management Dividend," *National Post*, November 17, 2009, FP14.

58. Sinclair Stewart, "Passed By at TD, CEO Hits Stride in New York," *The Globe and Mail*, December 5, 2006, B1, B21; also Zena Olijnyk, Mark Brown, Any Holloway, Calvin Leung, Alex Mlynek, Erin Pooley, Jeff Sanford, Andrew Wahl, and Thomas Watson, "Canada's Global Leaders," *Canadian Business*, March 8–April 10, 2005, 37-43.

Chapter 10

1. *Our Time: GE Annual Report*: 2004 (Fairfield, CT: General Electric Co., 2005), 4-5.

2. Judy Strauss and Raymond Frost, *Marketing on the Internet* (Upper Saddle River, NJ: Prentice Hall, 1999), 266-271.

3. Susan Carey, "The Case of the Vanishing Airport Lines," *Wall Street Journal*, August 9, 2007, B1).

4. Mark Lander, "Slovakia No Longer a Laggard in Automaking," nytimes.com, April 13, 2004, www.nytimes.com/2004/04/13/business/worldbusiness.

5. Hollie Shaw, "The Way Toyota Builds Cars," *National Post*, October 13, 2009, FP1.

6. Christina Passariello, "Louis Vuitton Tries Modern Methods on Factory Lines," *The Wall Street Journal*, October 9, 2006, A1, A15.

7. Neal Boudette, "Chrysler Gains Edge by Giving New Flexibility to Its Factories," *The Wall Street Journal*, April 11, 2006, A1, A15.

8. Greg Keenan, "Ford's New Maxim: Flex Manufacturing," *The Globe and Mail*, May 10, 2006, B3.

9. Lou Michel, "WNY's Trash, China's Treasure," *The Buffalo News*, July 20, 2008.

10. Don Marshall, "Time for Just in Time," *PIM Review*, June 1991: 20-22; Gregg Stocker, "Quality Function Deployment: Listening to the Voice of the Customer," *APICS: The Performance Advantage*, September 1991: 44-48.

11. "The Disney Institute," April 25, 2000, www.disney.go.com/DisneyWorld/DisneyInstitute/ProfessionalPrograms/DisneyDifference/index.html.

12. Bruce Little, "Stock Answers," *The Globe and Mail*, June 6, 1995, B12.

13. Marina Strauss, "Low Fills/High Stakes," *The Globe and Mail*, May 12, 2010, B1.

14. www.stats.oecd.org/Index.aspx?DatasetCode=LEVEL.

15. Don Drummond, "What Comes after the Great Recession?" *National Post*, June 30, 2009, FP13.

16. Harvey Enchin, "Canada Urged to Stop Living off Fat of the Land," *The Globe and Mail*, October 25, 1991, B1, B6.

17. Jon Hilsenrath, "Behind Surging Productivity: The Service Sector Delivers," *The Wall Street Journal*, November 7, 2003, A1, A8.

18. Peter Kennedy, "Canfor Goes High Tech to Cut Costs," *The Globe and Mail*, July 29, 2000, 3.

19. Lee J. Krajewski and Larry P. Ritzman, *Operations Management: Strategy and Analysis*, 5th ed. (Reading, MA: Addison-Wesley, 1999), 229-230.

20. Bruce McDougall, "The Thinking Man's Assembly Line," *Canadian Business*, November 1991, 40.

21. Ted Wakefield, "No Pain, No Gain," *Canadian Business*, January 1993, 50-54.

22. Ben Casselman and Russell Gold, "Unusual Decisions Set Stage for BP Disaster," *The Wall Street Journal*, May 27, 2010, A1.

23. Thomas Foster Jr., *Managing Quality: An Integrative Approach* (Upper Saddle River, NJ: Prentice Hall, 2001), 325-339.

24. Thomas Foster Jr., *Managing Quality: An Integrative Approach* (Upper Saddle River, NJ: Prentice Hall, 2001), 325–329.

25. James Evans and James Dean Jr., *Total Quality: Management, Organization, and Strategy*, 2nd ed. (Cincinnati, OH: South-Western, 2000), 230.

26. Margot Gibb-Clark, "Hospital Managers Gain Tool to Compare Notes," *The Globe and Mail*, September 9, 1996, B9.

27. Del Jones, "Baldrige Award Honors Record 7 Quality Winners," *USA Today*, November 26, 2003, 6B.

28. "Customer Service You Can Taste," *Canadian Business*, July 1991, 19–20.

29. www.iso.org/iso/iso_members.

30. Roberta S. Russell and Bernard W. Taylor III, *Operations Management*, 4th ed. (Upper Saddle River, NJ: Prentice Hall, 2003), 137–140.

31. Sunil Chopra and Peter Meindl, *Supply Chain Management: Strategy, Planning, and Operation*, 6th ed. (Upper Saddle River, NJ: Prentice Hall, 2001), 3–6; Lee J. Krajewski and Larry P. Ritzman, *Operations Management: Strategy and Analysis*, 5th ed. (Reading, MA: Addison-Wesley, 1999), Chapter 11; Roberta S. Russell and Bernard W. Taylor III, *Operations Management*, 4th ed. (Upper Saddle River, NJ: Prentice Hall, 2003), Chapter 7; and Thomas Foster Jr., *Managing Quality: An Integrative Approach* (Upper Saddle River, NJ: Prentice Hall, 2001), Chapter 9.

32. Sunil Chopra and Peter Meindl, *Supply Chain Management: Strategy, Planning, and Operation*, 6th ed. (Upper Saddle River, NJ: Prentice Hall, 2001), Chapter 20.

33. Christina Passariello, "Louis Vuitton Tries Modern Methods on Factory Lines," *The Wall Street Journal*, October 9, 2006, A1, A15.

Chapter 11

1. Ronald Hilton, *Managerial Accounting*, 2nd ed. (New York: McGraw-Hill, 1994), 7.

2. "Canada's Chartered Accountants Congratulate 2,701 Candidates Who Passed the 2008 Uniform Evaluation," www.cica.ca/index.cfm?ci_id=48153&la_id=1&print=true.

3. "CGA-Canada Announces 2008 Fellowship Recipients," www.newswire.ca/en/releases/archive/February2009/05/c5463.html.

4. Certified Management Accountants of Canada website, www.cma-canada.org.

5. Hollie Shaw, "Accounting's Big Bang Moment: Switch from GAAP," *National Post*, September 24, 2009, FP1.

6. Virginia Galt, "It's Crunch Time as Accounting Changes Loom," *The Globe and Mail*, June 17, 2010, B10.

7. Al Rosen, "Cooking with IFRS," *Canadian Business*, July 20, 2009, 12.

8. Rachel Sanderson, "IASB Softens Stance on Accounting Convergence," *Financial Times*, February 16, 2010, 16.

9. David Milstead, "A Close Inspection of Shoppers' Revenue Accounting," *The Globe and Mail*, May 17, 2010, B8.

10. Charles T. Horngren, Walter T. Harrison Jr., and Linda Smith Bamber, *Accounting*, 5th ed. (Upper Saddle River, NJ: Prentice Hall, 2002), 11–12, 39–41.

11. Charles T. Horngren, Walter T. Harrison Jr., and Linda Smith Bamber, *Accounting*, 5th ed. (Upper Saddle River, NJ: Prentice Hall, 2002), 17–20.

12. Billie Cunningham, Loren Nikolai, and John Bazley. *Accounting: Information for Business Decisions* (Fort Worth, TX: Dryden, 2000), 133–134.

13. Charles T. Horngren, Walter T. Harrison Jr., and Linda Smith Bamber, *Accounting*, 4th ed. (Upper Saddle River, NJ: Prentice Hall, 1999), 201–202.

Appendix B

1. Omar El Akkad, "Canadian Internet Usage Grows," *The Globe and Mail*, May 11, 2010, B9.

2. Ian Marlow and Jacquie McNish, "Canada's Digital Divide," *The Globe and Mail*, April 3, 2010, B1, B4.

3. Philip Kotler, Gary Armstrong, and Peggy H. Cunningham, *Principles of Marketing*, 6th Canadian ed. (Toronto: Pearson, 2005), 88.

4. Simon Tuck, "Security Rated Top On-Line Fear," *The Globe and Mail*, July 5, 1999, B5.

5. James Hagerty and Dennis Berman, "New Battleground in Web Privacy War: Ads That Snoop," *The Wall Street Journal*, August 27, 2003, A1, A8.

6. Mike Lazaridis, "Because Someone Had to Stand Up for All Those Frustrated Engineers," *Inc.*, April 2005, 98; "BlackBerry Subscribers Surge to over Three Million," May 9, 2005, www.blackberry.com/news/press/2005/pr-09_05_2005-01.shtml.

7. "Northrop Grumman Awards International Contracts for F-35 Joint Strike Fighter," *Northrop Grumman News Release*, September 29, 2005, www.irconnect.com/noc/pages/news_printer.html?=86963&print=1; Faith Keenan and Spencer E. Ante, "The New Teamwork," *BusinessWeekOnline*, February 18, 2002.

8. Laura Northrup, "Timbuk2 Really, Really Wants You to Be Happy with Their Bags," *The Consumerist*, June 5, 2009, at www.consumerist.com/5280357/timbuk2_really-really-wants-you-to-be. Emily Walzer, "Have It Your Way," *SGB*, Vol. 38, Issue 1 (January 2005): 42.

9. David Milstead, "A Rocket, a Meteor—Or a One Trick Pony?" *The Globe and Mail*, January, 29, 2010, B9.

10. Boyd Erman, "Online Brokerage Muscles in on the Road Show," *The Globe and Mail*, March 29, 2010, B5.

11. 3D Systems, "3D Systems Helps Walter Reed Army Medical Center Rebuild Lives," July 6, 2005, www.3dsystems.com.

12. 3D Systems, "3D Systems Helps Walter Reed Army Medical Center Rebuild Lives," www.3dsystems.com/appsolutions/casestudies/walter_reed.asp; also Hannah Hickey, "Camera in a Pill Offers Cheaper, Easier Window on Your Insides," UWNews.org, January 24, 2008, http://uwnews.org/article.asp?articleid=39292.

13. David LaGesse, "How to Turn Social Networking into a Job Offer," *U.S. News & World Report*, May 11, 2009, www.usnews.com/articles/business/careers/2009/05/11/how-to.

14. "ABN AMRO Mortgage Group Offers One Fee to Ford Motor Company Employees," *Mortgage Mag*, February 14, 2005, www.mortgagemag.com/n/

502_003.htm; also "An Intranet's Life Cycle," morebusiness.com, June 16, 1999, www.morebusiness.com/getting_started/website/d928247851.brc.

15. Figure B.2 is a modified version of diagrams on the BlackBerry website, Research In Motion Ltd., technical images, www.blackberry.com/images/technical/bes_exchange_arthitecture.gif.

16. Gayle Balfour, "The Wisdom of the Cloud," *Backbone*, May 2009, 16–20; SalesForce.com website, www.salesforce.com/cloudcomputing/, accessed July 7, 2010.

17. "Kroger Tailors Ads to Its Customers," *Columbia Daily Tribune*, January 12, 2009, 7B.

18. Jo Merchant, "Virtual Fossils Reveal How Ancient Creatures Lived," *NewScientist*, May 27, 2009, www.newscientist.com/article/mg20227103.500-virtual-fossils-reveal- how-ancient-creatures-lived.html.

19. Geoffrey Rowan, "Unique Software Thinks Like a Human," *The Globe and Mail*, December 31, 1996, B1, B4.

20. Kenneth C. Laudon and Jane P. Laudon, *Essentials of Management Information Systems*, 3rd ed. (Upper Saddle River, NJ: Prentice Hall, 1999), 383–388; E. Wainwright Martin, et al. *Managing Information Technology: What Managers Need to Know*, 3rd ed. (Upper Saddle River, NJ: Prentice-Hall, 1999), 225–227.

21. Emily Smith, "Turning an Expert's Skills into Computer Software," *BusinessWeek*, October 7, 1985, 104–107.

22. Phuong Tram, "Facebook and Privacy Invasions," Imprint Online, June 15, 2008, http://imprint.uwaterloo.ca/index.php?option=com_content&task=view&id=2570&Itemid=57; also Jacqui Cheng, "Canadian Group: Facebook a Minefield of Privacy Invasion," May 30, 2008, http://arstechnica.com/tech-policy/news/2008/05/canadian-group-files-complaint-over-facebook-privacy.ars; also "Cell Phones a Much Bigger Privacy Risk than Facebook," Fox News, February 20, 2009, www.foxnews.com/printer_friendly_story/0,3566,497544,00.html.

23. Danny Bradbury, "Predicting 2010," *Backbone* magazine, March 2010, 23.

24. Alex Leary, "Wi-Fi Cloaks a New Breed of Intruder," *St. Petersburg Times*, July 4, 2005, www.sptimes.com/2005/07/04/State/Wi_Fi_cloaks_a_new_br.shtml.

25. "Fraud Prevention," *The Globe and Mail*, March 29, 2010, FP1.

26. Treasury Board of Canada Secretariat website, www.tbs-sct.gc.ca/pgol-pged/piatp-pfefvp/course1/mod2/mod2-3-eng.asp, accessed July 6, 2010.

27. Siobhan Gorman, "The Cold War Goes Digital—and Corporate," *The Globe and Mail*, January 14, 2010, B7.

28. www.webopedia.com/TERM/S/spyware.html.

29. "Ferris Research and Abaca Technology Corporation Hold Anti-Spam Webinar," *NewswireToday*, April 9, 2008, www.newswiretoday.com/news/32531/.

Chapter 12

1. Philip Kotler, *Marketing Management*, 11th ed. (Upper Saddle River, NJ: Prentice Hall, 2003), 76–78.

2. *Harley-Davidson Inc.: 2009 Annual Report* (Milwaukee: Harley-Davidson, 2009), 7; Philip Kotler, *Marketing Management: Analysis, Planning, Implementation, and Control*, 9th ed. (Upper Saddle River, NJ: Prentice Hall, 1997), 12–13, 48–51.

3. Philip Kotler, *Marketing Management: Analysis, Planning, Implementation, and Control*, 7th ed. (Upper Saddle River, NJ: Prentice Hall, 1991).

4. Philip Kotler and Peggy Cunningham, *Marketing Management* (Toronto: Prentice Hall, 2004), 18.

5. Greg Keenan, "BMW Canada Seeks Top Luxury Spot," *The Globe and Mail*, June 15, 2009, B5.

6. Marina Strauss, "Canadian Tire Targets the Price Sensitive," *The Globe and Mail*, May 15, 2009, B4.

7. Eric Reguly, "Hard Time: Makers of Luxury Watches Clock a Slow Return to Sales Health," *The Globe and Mail*, February 2, 2010, B1.

8. Chris Isadore, "Sweet Spot: Luxury SUV's Are Hot," *CNN/Money*, www.cnnmoney.com, January 7, 2004.

9. Rasha Moutarda, "Gerontologists Go Beyond the Numbers," *The Globe and Mail*, February 19, 2010, B9.

10. Aparita Bhandari, "Ethnic Marketing—It's More than Skin Deep," *The Globe and Mail*, September 7, 2005, B3.

11. Canadian Media Directors Council, *Media Digest, 2009–2010*, Ethnic Media, P16 (Toronto: Marketing, 2009), 40, www.cmdc.ca/pdf/Media_Digest_2009.pdf.

12. Lauren Goldstein, "Dressing up an Old Brand," *Fortune*, November 9, 1998, 154–156.

13. Peter Gumbel, "Mass vs. Class," *Fortune*, September 17, 2007, 82.

14. Tamara Audi, "Las Vegas Goes All Out to Attract Gay Travelers," *The Wall Street Journal*, November 2, 2007, B1.

15. Philip Kotler, *Marketing Management*, 11th ed. (Upper Saddle River, NJ: Prentice Hall, 2003), 292–294.

16. Naoufel Daghfous, John V. Petrof, and Frank Pons, "Values and Innovations: A Cross-cultural Study," *The Journal of Consumer Marketing*, Vol. 16, Issue 4 (2009): 314–331.

17. Lauren Goldstein, "Dressing up an Old Brand," *Fortune*, November 9, 1998, 154–156.

18. Matt Phillips, "Pow! Romance! Comics Court Girls," *The Wall Street Journal*, June 8, 2007, B1.

19. John Morton, "How to Spot the Really Important Prospects," *Business Marketing*, January 1990: 62–67.

20. Marina Strauss, "You, in the Yoga Pants, Metro Is Watching You," *The Globe and Mail*, November 19, 2009, B1.

21. Emily Nelson, "P&G Checks Out Real Life," *The Wall Street Journal*, May 17, 2001, B1, B4.

22. Susan Berfield, "Getting the Most Out of Every Shopper," *BusinessWeek*, February 9, 2009, P45.

23. Joseph Pereira, "Spying on the Sales Floor," *The Wall Street Journal*, December 21, 2004, B1, B4.

24. Julie Jargon, "Kiwi Goes beyond Shine in Effort to Step up Sales," *The Wall Street Journal*, December 20, 2007, B1.

25. Marina Strauss, "Mining Customer Feedback, Firms Go Undercover and Online," *The Globe and Mail*, May 13, 2004, B1, B25.

26. Deborah Ball, Sarah Ellison, and Janet Adamy, "Probing Shoppers' Psyche," *The Wall Street Journal*, October 28, 2004, B1, B8.

27. Peter Morton, "Marketing at Face Value," *National Post*, July 11, 2007, FP3.

28. Emily Nelson, "P&G Checks Out Real Life," *The Wall Street Journal*, May 17, 2001, B1, B4.

29. Robyn Greenspan, "The Web as a Way of Life," May 21, 2002, www.cyberatlas.com.

30. Omar El Akkad, "Canadian Internet Usage Grows," *The Globe and Mail*, May 11, 2010, B9.

31. Thomas Russell, Glenn Verrill, and W. Ronald Lane, *Kleppner's Advertising Procedure*, 11th ed. (Englewood Cliffs, NJ: Prentice Hall, 1990); James Engel, Martin Warshaw, and Thomas Kinnear, *Promotional Strategy*, 6th ed. (Homewood, IL: Richard D. Irwin, 1987).

32. AutoNorth website, "Toyota Canada Offers Free Scheduled Maintenance on All Models," January 6, 2010, www.autonorth.ca, accessed April 19, 2010.

33. John Heinzl, "Analysts See Signs of Fizz Returning to Coke," *The Globe and Mail*, July 10, 2009, B1.

Chapter 13

1. Barrie McKenna and Matt Hartley, "Stringer Makes His Mark," *The Globe and Mail*, February 20, 2008, B1, B6; Richard Siklos, "How Did Sony Win the HD War?" *The Globe and Mail*, February 29, 2008, B7; Matt Hartley, "The Spoils of Format Wars Sweet but Fleeting," *The Globe and Mail*, March 13, 2010, B1, B6.

2. Greg Keenan, "Electruc Roadster Approved in Canada," *The Globe and Mail*, January 26, 2010, B9; David Milstead, "Tesla Admits It Has a Rough Road Ahead," *The Globe and Mail*, February 5, 2010, B9; David Welch, "A Long Bet on Electric Cars," *BusinessWeek*, October 12, 2009, P32.

3. Eric Reguly, "Beaudoin's Big, Bold Bet," *The Globe and Mail*, July 14, 2008, B1, B10.

4. Susanna Ray, "Dreamliner a Scheduling Nightmare; Delayed yet Again; Boeing This Time Cites Strike and Fastener Problem," *National Post*, December 12, 2008, FP12.

5. James C. Anderson and James A. Narus, *Business Market Management: Understanding, Creating, and Delivering Value* (Upper Saddle River, NJ: Prentice Hall, 1999), 203–206.

6. Philip Kotler, *Marketing Management*, 11th ed. (Upper Saddle River, NJ: Prentice Hall, 2003), 328–339.

7. "Technology Firms Dominate Top 10 Brand Value List," *The Globe and Mail*, April 29, 2010, B1: Millward Brown website, www.millwardbrown.com/Libraries/Optimor_BrandZ_Files/2010_BrandZ_Top100_Report.sflb.ashx, accessed May 11, 2010.

8. *Country Brand Index: 2009*, www.countrybrandindex.com/press-release.

9. Keith McArthur, "How to Survive an Identity Crisis," *The Globe and Mail*, November 14, 2005, B1, B11.

10. "Canada's Most Valuable Brands 2009," Brand Finance Canada, Spring 2009, www.finance.com/Uploads/pdfs/BrandFinanceCanadaMostValuableBrands2009.pdf.

11. Marina Strauss, "Shoppers Sees Gold in Private Labels," *The Globe and Mail*, January 3, 2005, B1–B2.

12. Courtland Bovee, John V. Thill, and George Dracopoulos, *Business in Action*, 2nd ed. (Don Mills, ON: Pearson Education, 2008), 332.

13. Marina Strauss, "(Re)Making a Name in No Name," *The Globe and Mail*, March 21, 2009, B3.

14. Readers Digest website, Most Trusted Brands 2010, www.readersdigest.ca/trustedbrand/html/winners.html, accessed April 25, 2010.

15. Paul Glader, "Avid Boarders Bypass Branded Gear," *The Wall Street Journal*, July 27, 2007, B1–B2.

16. Keith McArthur, "Why Molson Is Crying in Its Beer," *The Globe and Mail*, July 10, 2004, B4.

17. John Frook, "Cisco Scores with Its Latest Generation of Empowering Tools," *B to B*, August 20, 2001, 20.

18. Cyndee Miller, "Little Relief Seen for New Product Failure Rate," *Marketing News*, June 21, 1993, 1; Nancy J. Kim, "Back to the Drawing Board," *The Bergen [New Jersey] Record*, December 4, 1994, B1, B4.

19. MSN website, Steve Mertl, "Buick LaCrosse's French Slang Meaning Latest Example of Pitfalls of Car Names," http://autos.ca.msn.com/news/canadian-press-automotive-news/article.aspx?cp-documentid=22011666, accessed April 25, 2010.

20. Marina Strauss, "The Secret to Gaining Success in Quebec," *The Globe and Mail*, September 27, 2005, B4.

21. Konrad Yakabuski, "How Pepsi Won Quebec," *The Globe and Mail*, August 28, 2008, B1–B2.

22. "Mega Brands Wins Case over Lego," *The Globe and Mail*, November 13, 2008, B3.

23. Canadian Intellectual Patent Office (CIPO) website, www.cipo.ic.gc.ca/eic/site/cipointernet-internetopic.nsf/eng/Home, accessed April 25, 2010; Canadian Western Diversification Canada website, www.wd.gc.ca/eng/7133.asp, accessed April 25, 2010.

24. Paul Waldie, "How RIM's Big Deal Was Done," *The Globe and Mail*, March 6, 2006, B1, B14.

25. Globe and Mail website, "Judge Rules for RIM in Patent Dispute," February 3, 2010, www.theglobeandmail.com, accessed April 25, 2010.

26. Avery Johnson, "Pfizer Buys More Time for Lipitor," *The Wall Street Journal*, June 19, 2008, B1.

27. "Google to Pay US$125 Million to Settle Copyright Lawsuits Over Book Project," *National Post*, October 29, 2008, FP6.

28. Stuart Elliott, "Tropicana Discovers Some Buyers Are Passionate about Packaging," *The Wall Street Journal*, November 17, 2005, B1, B5.

29. Deborah Ball, "The Perils of Packaging: Nestlé Aims for Easier Openings," *The Wall Street Journal*, February 23, 2009.

30. Keith McArthur, "Oh? Canada? Ads Beg to Differ," *The Globe and Mail*, July 1, 2004, B1, B18.

31. Canadian Media Directors Council, *Media Digest, 2009–2010*, Net Advertising Volume by Medium, P13 (Toronto:

Marketing, 2009), 14, www.cmdc.ca/pdf/Media_Digest_2009.pdf.

32. Canadian Media Directors Council, *Media Digest, 2009–2010*, Daily Newspapers, P13 (Toronto: Marketing, 2009), 40, www.cmdc.ca/pdf/Media_Digest_2009.pdf.

33. Andrew Wahl, "Red All Over," *Canadian Business*, February 13–26, 2006, 53–54.

34. Susan Krashinsky, "Reports of TV's Death Greatly Exaggerated," *The Globe and Mail*, April 13, 2010, B1.

35. Canadian Media Directors Council, *Media Digest, 2009–2010*, Canadian Market Data, P12 (Toronto: Marketing, 2009), 40, www.cmdc.ca/pdf/Media_Digest_2009.pdf.

36. Suzanne Vranica, "Pepsi Taking a Time-Out from Super Bowl Ads," *The Globe and Mail*, December 17, 2009, B9.

37. Marina Strauss, "Super Bowl Clobbers the Grey Cup," *The Globe and Mail*, January 26, 2008, B3.

38. Ronald Grover, "American Idol's Ads Infinitum," *BusinessWeek*, May 28, 2008, 38–39.

39. Canadian Media Directors Council, *Media Digest, 2009–2010*, Net Advertising Volume by Medium, P13 (Toronto: Marketing, 2009), 28, http://www.cmdc.ca/pdf/Media_Digest_2009.pdf.

40. Canadian Media Directors Council, *Media Digest, 2009–2010*, Net Advertising Volume by Medium, P13 (Toronto: Marketing, 2009), 28, http://www.cmdc.ca/pdf/Media_Digest_2009.pdf.

41. Canadian Media Directors Council, *Media Digest, 2009–2010*, Net Advertising Volume by Medium, P13 (Toronto: Marketing, 2009), 28, www.cmdc.ca/pdf/Media_Digest_2009.pdf.

42. James Adams, *"Reader's Digest* Still Rules Magazine Roost," *The Globe and Mail*, March 27, 2009, B2.

43. Canadian Media Directors Council, *Media Digest, 2009–2010*, Net Advertising Volume by Medium, P13 (Toronto: Marketing, 2009), 28, www.cmdc.ca/pdf/Media_Digest_2009.pdf.

44. Matt Hartley, "Tunnel Visionaries," *The Globe and Mail*, January 31, 2008, B18.

45. "30 Second Spot: Dispatches from the World of Media and Advertising," *The Globe and Mail*, October 31, 2008, B8.

46. Aaron O. Patrick, "Technology Boosts Outdoor Ads as Competition Becomes Fiercer," *The Wall Street Journal*, August 23, 2006, A1, A10; Grant Robertson, "Growth in Internet Ads Outpaces All Others," *The Globe and Mail*, June 23, 2006, B4; Canadian Media Directors Council, *Media Digest, 2009–2010*, Net Advertising Volume by Medium, P13 (Toronto: Marketing, 2009), 28, www.cmdc.ca/pdf/Media_Digest_2009.pdf.

47. Mike Blaney blog, "Word of Mouth Advertising," www.themarketingguy.wordpress.com/2007/10/09/word-of-mouth-advertising.

48. Sarah Scott, "Ready for Their Close-Up," *Financial Post Business*, September 2007, 40–45.

49. Simon Houpt, "Tell a Friend: Companies Flock to Word-of-Mouth Marketing," *The Globe and Mail*, April 16, 2010, B6.

50. Canadian Media Directors Council, *Media Digest, 2009–2010*, Net Advertising Volume by Medium, P13 (Toronto: Marketing, 2009), 28, www.cmdc.ca/pdf/Media_Digest_2009.pdf.

51. Simon Houpt, "Super Bowl Marketers Are Changing Their Game," *The Globe and Mail*, February 5, 2010, B5.

52. Amol Sharma and Emily Steel, "Ads Critical to MySpace," *The Wall Street Journal*, August 4, 2008, B5.

53. P. Kotler, G. Armstrong, and P. Cunningham, *Principles of Marketing*, 6th Canadian ed. (Toronto: Pearson, 2005), 89–91.

54. Ronald Ebert and Ricky Griffin, *Business Essentials* (Upper Saddle River, NJ: Prentice Hall, 2009), 161.

55. Stuart Elliott, "Real or Virtual? You Call It," *The New York Times*, October 1, 1999, C1, C6.

56. Canadian Media Directors Council, *Media Digest, 2009–2010*, Internet and Mobile Media, P74 (Toronto: Marketing, 2009), 40, www.cmdc.ca/pdf/Media_Digest_2009.pdf.

57. Canadian Media Directors Council, *Media Digest, 2009–2010*, In-Game Advertising, P76 (Toronto: Marketing, 2009), 40, www.cmdc.ca/pdf/Media_Digest_2009.pdf.

58. "Regulators Wary of Ads Rapping Rivals," *The Globe and Mail*, May 23, 1991, B4.

59. Simon Avery, "Do Not Call List Could Give Boost to Direct Mail," *The Globe and Mail*, September 29, 2008, B3.

60. Hollie Shaw, "Do Not Call List a Ringing Success," *National Post*, March 13, 2009, FP12.

61. Oliver Moore, "Clement Blasts Do-Not-Call Scammers," *The Globe and Mail*, January 26, 2009, A4.

62. John Heinzl, "Beer Firms Rethink Giveaways," *The Globe and Mail*, March 3, 2003, B1, B5.

63. Grant Robertson, "Thanks, but No Thanks," *The Globe and Mail*, August 29, 2008, B5; Rebecca Dana, "When You're Here, You're Family—but What about a Playboy Model?" *The Wall Street Journal*, August 13, 2008, A1, A14.

64. Tasmyn Burgmann, "Olympic Organizers on Lookout for Ambush Marketing," thestar.com, http://olympics.thestar.com/2010/article/753866-olympic-organizers-on-lookout-for-ambush-marketing, accessed May 11, 2010.

65. Warren J. Keegan, *Global Marketing Management*, 7th ed. (Upper Saddle River, NJ: Prentice Hall, 2002), Chapter 14.

66. *Cosmopolitan* website, www.cosmomediakit.com/r5/home.asp, accessed April 25, 2010.

Chapter 14

1. Constance Hays, "Coke Tests Weather-Linked Pricing," *The Globe and Mail*, October 29, 1999, B11.

2. Stefan Fatsis, "The Barry Bonds Tax: Teams Raise Prices for Good Games," *The Wall Street Journal*, December 3, 2002, D1, D8.

3. Lawrence Solomon, "Revolution on the Road: Pay-per-Mile Insurance," *National Post*, October 14, 2006, FP15.

4. David George-Cosh, "Cisco Joins Skymeter to Help Unsnarl City Traffic," *National Post*, October 6, 2008, www.nationalpost.com/story-printer.html?id=862402.

5. Stephen Kindel, "Tortoise Gains on Hare," *Financial World,* February 23, 1988, 18–20.

6. Eric Lam, "Wal-Mart Stores Set to Reduce Prices to Win Back Customers From Rivals," *National Post*, March 16, 2010, FP8.

7. Greg Keenan, "Toyota's Discounts Ignite New Car War," *The Globe and Mail*, March 4, 2010, B3.

8. "About Carbonite," http://www.carbonite.com/about/.

9. Judy Strauss and Raymond Frost, *E-Marketing*, 2nd ed. (Upper Saddle River, NJ: Prentice Hall, 2001), 166–167; Eloise Coupey, *Marketing and the Internet* (Upper Saddle River, NJ: Prentice Hall, 2001), 281–283.

10. Judy Strauss, Adel El-Ansary, and Raymond Frost, *E-Marketing*, 3rd ed. (Upper Saddle River, NJ: Prentice Hall, 2003), 320–323.

11. George Stalk, "How 'Dynamic' Pricing Can Give Your Company an Edge," *The Globe and Mail*, September 7, 2009, B6.

12. "Wal-Mart Rounds Prices to Lure Shoppers," *The Globe and Mail*, April 15, 2009, B12.

13. Marina Strauss, "Taking 'e' Out of E-commerce: Meet the eBay Middleman," *The Globe and Mail*, October 6, 2004, B1, B19.

14. "Plans Shake Pillars of Real Estate; Proposals from Both Sides Would Overhaul Industry," *National Post*, February 12, 2010, FP1. For more information on this issue, see "How an Epic Battle Began," *National Post*, May 1, 2010, FP1, and Steve Ladurantaye, "Do-It-Yourselfers Are Shaking Up an Industry; Real Eastate Agents Are Fighting Back," *The Globe and Mail*, May 20, 2010, B1.

15. Steve Ladurantaye, "The Battle to Unlock the Housing Market," *The Globe and Mail*, January 30, 2010, B1.

16. Bertrand Marotte, "Contraband Killing Convenience Stores," *The Globe and Mail*, April 7, 2010, B9.

17. Direct Selling Association website, www.dsa.org.

18. Gordon Pitts, "Tupperware Shows the World How to Party," *The Globe and Mail*, February 9, 2008, B3.

19. Expedia.com website, June 23, 2005, www.expedia.com.

20. Ann Bednarz, "Acquisitions Tighten Supply-Chain Market," *Network World,* February 9, 2004, 21–22.

21. Marina Strauss, "E-tailing in Age of Refinement," *The Globe and Mail*, August 3, 2005, B6.

22. "Did You Know?" *Catalog News.com*, www.catalog-news.com, April 8, 2002; Judy Strauss and Raymond Frost, *E-Marketing,* 2nd ed. (Upper Saddle River, NJ: Prentice Hall, 2001), 140.

23. "Marina Strauss, "Turning to the Web for 'An Endless Aisle,'" *The Globe and Mail*, February 13, 2010, B3.

24. "Marina Strauss, "Turning to the Web for 'An Endless Aisle,'" *The Globe and Mail*, February 13, 2010, B3.

25. Erick Schonfeld, "Forrester Forecast: Online Retail Sales Will Grow to $250 Billion by 2014," March 8, 2010, www.techcrunch.com/2010/03/08.

26. Zena Olijnyk, "Dot-Com Wonder Boys, *Canadian Business,* April 14, 2003, 30–36.

27. Vito Pilieci, "Taxman Eyes Internet Sellers," *Winnipeg Free Press*, November 18, 2008, B5.

28. Geoffrey Fowler, "EBay Retreats in Web Retailing," *The Wall Street Journal*, March 12, 2009, A1, A11.

29. Bertrand Marotte, "Reeling in Fresh Customers," *The Globe and Mail*, April 20, 2010, B3.

30. David Milstead, "Coke Gets Back into the Bottling Business," *The Globe and Mail*, February 26, 2010, B10.

31. "Walmart to Assume Product Shipping," *National Post*, May 22, 2010, FP4.

32. Kerry Capell, "Zara Thrives by Breaking All the Rules," *Bloomberg Businessweek*, April 26, 2010.

33. Gordon Jaremko, "River Highway in Canada's North Open for Business," *The Winnipeg Free Press*, July 25, 2006, B10.

Chapter 15

1. Bank of Canada Banking and Financial Statistics, Series E1, Selected Monetary Aggregates, May 2010, S54.

2. Bank of Canada Banking and Financial Statistics, Series B4, Statistics Pertaining to Counterfeit Bank of Canada Notes, May 2010, S14.

3. Dean Beeby, "Canadians Worry about Counterfeit Cash: Survey," *Winnipeg Free Press*, June 26, 2006, B8.

4. Omar El Akkad, "Canada's $5 Bill Offers New Security Features," *The Globe and Mail*, April 5, 2006, B5.

5. Bank of Canada Banking and Financial Statistics, Series E1, Selected Monetary Aggregates, May 2010, S52.

6. Rita Trichur, "Canadians Struggling to Dig Out of Debt," *Winnipeg Free Press,* December 12, 2009.

7. Tara Perkins, "Card Payment Players Clash over Code," *The Globe and Mail*, January 18, 2010, B5.

8. Euromonitor website, www.euromonitor.com/, accessed July 10, 2010.

9. www.wikinvest.com/stock/Visa_(V), accessed September 7, 2010.

10. Boyd Erman, "Visa's IPO Taps into the World's Love of Plastic," *The Globe and Mail*, February 26, 2008, B1, B6.

11. Tara Perkins, "Credit Card Perks Putting the Squeeze on Retailers," *The Globe and Mail*, June 24, 2008, B1, B5.

12. "Retailers Want Ottawa to Regulate Debit and Credit Card Fees," *CBC.ca*, www.cbc.ca/consumer/story/2009/04/21/fees.html.

13. Danny Bradbury, "Better Safeguards in the Cards; Credit Card Safety," *National Post*, March 12, 2009, FP12.

14. Tom Lowry, "Thieves Swipe Credit with Card Readers," *USA Today*, June 28, 1999, 1B.

15. Geoff Kirbyson, "High-Tech Credit Cards Latest Crime-Fighting Tool," *Winnipeg Free Press*, December 23, 2008, A5.

16. Bank of Canada Banking and Financial Statistics, Series C1, Chartered Bank Assets, May 2010, S17.

17. Tara Perkins and Grant Robertson, "The Bank Machine with a Personal Touch," *The Globe and Mail*, June 3, 2010, B5.

18. The Canadian Bankers website, www.cba.ca/en/consumer-information/42-safeguarding-your-money/

59-debit-card-fraud, accessed May 28, 2010.

19. "Statistics for Smart Cards," ePaynews.com, June 14, 2004, www. epaynews.com/statistics/scardstats.html.

20. Marina Strauss, "Need a Mortgage with Those Tools?" *The Globe and Mail*, February 6, 2010, A1, A9.

21. Tara Perkins, "They'll Even Plan Your Funeral," *The Globe and Mail*, September 29, 2007, B4–B6.

22. Tara Perkins, "A Piece of Drywall Away from Being Part of the Branch," *The Globe and Mail*, April 26, 2008, B6.

23. Business News Network website, "Ottawa Bans Insurance Sales on Bank Websites," May 27, 2010, www.bnn.ca/ news/17916.html, accessed July 10, 2010.

24. Karen Horcher, "Reconstruction Zone," *CGA*, June 1997, 19.

25 Jamie Sturgeon, "Credit Unions Could Rival Canada's Big Banks, Moody's Says," *National Post*, April 28, 2010, FP5.

26. "Google VC Fund Looking for 'Young Companies with Awesome Potential,'" *National Post*, April 1, 2009, FP2.

27. Canada's Venture Capital and Private Equity Association website, www. cvca.ca/resources/statistics/, accessed May 29, 2010.

28. David George-Cosh, "Lean Times for Tech Startups: VC's Offer Ideas on How to Kickstart the Industry," *National Post*, January 16, 2009, FP4; Stephen Hurwitz, "Misadventure Capitalism: A Byzantine Cross-Border Investment Regime Is Killing the Canadian Venture-Capital and Technology Industries," *National Post*, May 1, 2009, FP11.

29. "Venture Capital Investment IN Q1 2010: Slower Decline," Canada's Venture Capital and Private Equity Association website, May 18, 2010, www. cvca.ca/files/News/CVCA_Q1_2010_ VC_Press_Release_FINAL.pdf, accessed May 29, 2010.

30. *The Economist* website, Big Mac Index, March 18, 2010, www. economist.com/daily/chartgallery/ displaystory.cfm?story_id=15715184, accessed May 29, 2010.

31. Robert J. Carbaugh, *International Economics*, 5th ed. (Cincinnati: South-Western, 1995), Chapter 11.

32. David Parkinson, "The Lost Decade," *The Globe and Mail*, December 31, 2009, B1.

33. *Canadian Business* website, Investor 500 Rankings, http:// list.canadianbusiness.com/ rankings/investor500/2009/q1/ top-500/market-value/Default. aspx?sp2=1&d1=d&sc1=4, accessed May 29, 2010.

34. Louise Lee and Lauren Young, "Is Schwab's Latest Come-on Enough?" *BusinessWeek*, June 7, 2004, 44.

35. Ben Levinsohn, "Beating a Path to Toronto's Exchanges," *BusinessWeek*, May 19, 2008, 52.

36. NYSE website, www.nyse.com/ about/listed/lcddata.html?ticker=EL, accessed May 29, 2010.

37. David Berman, "After China Breaks," May 17, 2010, The Globe and Mail Blog, www.theglobeandmail.com/ globe-investor/markets/markets-blog/ after-china-brakes/article1571458/.

38. NASDAQ website, June 25, 2000, www.nasdaq.com/about/timeline.stm.

39. NASDAQ website, www.nasdaq. com, accessed May 29, 2010.

40. Aaron Lucchetti, "As Housing Boomed, Moody's Opened Up," *The Wall Street Journal*, April 11, 2008, A1, A15.

41. Boyd Erman, "DBRS to Roll Out a New Road Map on Risk," *The Globe and Mail*, February 8, 2008, B1, B6.

42. Matt Walcoff and Suzanne Woolley, "O Canada," *Bloomberg Business Week*, April 25, 2010, 59.

43. Janet McFarland, "OSC Rules Norshield Hedge Fund Misled Investors," *The Globe and Mail*, March 9, 2010, B6.

44. Richard Blackwell, "TSE 300 Shift Will Shrink Index," *The Globe and Mail*, January 31, 2002, B17.

45. Richard Mackie, "Ontario Pursues Single Regulator," *The Globe and Mail*, December 22, 2003, B1, B4.

46. Janet McFarland, "Act's Police Powers Applauded," *The Globe and Mail*, May 28, 2010, B3.

Chapter 16

1. Greg Keenan, "GM Invests in St. Catharines Engine Plant," *The Globe and Mail*, April 27, 2010, B12.

2. Boyd Erman, "Safety First: The Mantra for Markets in 2010," *The Globe and Mail*, March 4, 2010, E1, E5.

3. Ommar El Akkad, "Mitel Makes Second Try at IPO," *The Globe and Mail*, April 22, 2010, B12.

4. Ashley Heher, "Hertz Agrees to Buy Rival Dollar Thrifty," *The Globe and Mail*, April 27, 2010, B8.

5. Andrew Willis, "CanWest Halts Bondholder Payments," *The Globe and Mail*, March 13, 2009, B3.

6. Industry Canada website, www.ic. gc.ca, accessed May 31, 2010.

7. Norman M. Scarborough and Thomas W. Zimmerer, *Effective Small Business Management: An Entrepreneurial Approach*, 6th ed. (Upper Saddle River, NJ: Prentice Hall, 2000), esp. 298–300.

8. Richard S. Boulton, Barry D. Libert, and Steve M. Samek, "Managing Risk in an Uncertain World," *Upside*, June 2000, 268–278.

9. Gordon Pitts and Bertrand Marotte, "Has Sabia Jumped from the Frying Pan into the Fire?" *The Globe and Mail*, March 14, 2009, www.globeinvestor. com/servlet/story/GAM.20090314. RSABIA14/GIStory/.

10. Tara Perkins, "BMO Retreats to Its Low-Risk Roots," *The Globe and Mail*, March 5, 2008, B5.

11. Joe Castaldo, "Bay Street Hurt by Talent Deficit," *Canadian Business*, December 9, 2009, 15.

12. Thomas P. Fitch, *Dictionary of Banking Terms*, 2nd ed. (Hauppauge, NY: Barron's, 1993), 531.

Appendix C

1. Chris Arthur J. Keown, Personal Finance, 3rd ed. (Upper Saddle River, NJ: Pearson Prentice Hall, 2004), 600–609.

2. Christopher Farrell, "No Need to Hit the Panic Button," *BusinessWeek*, July 26, 2004, 76–84.

3. Canada Revenue Agency website, www.cra-arc.gc.ca, accessed July 4, 2010.

4. Canada Revenue Agency website, www.cra-arc.gc.ca/tx/rgstrd/tfsa-celi/bt-eng.html, accessed July 4, 2010.

Source Notes

Chapter 1

Opportunities and Challenges in the Mobile Phone Market
LuAnn LaSalle, "BlackBerry's Out of Touch with Consumers: Analysts," *Winnipeg Free Press*, June 26, 2010, B8; "RIM Thumbs Its Way into the Top Five Mobile Handset Makers in First Quarter," *National Post*, May 1, 2010, FP5; Carrie Tait, "RIM Aims to Corner Market, Lazaridis Says: Trade Show Opens; Analysts Still Wary of Growing Competition," *National Post*, April 28, 2010, FP8; Don Vialoux and John Vialoux, "New Products May Help RIM Regain Its Cool: Big Valuation Gap; iPhone Sales Put Rocket under Apple Shares," *National Post*, April 24, 2010, FP8; "Research In Motion History," http://en.wikipedia.org/wiki/Research_In_Motion, accessed January 23, 2010; "Timeline: The History of Research in Motion," http://forums.crackberry.com/f2/timeline-history-research-motion-7162/, accessed January 23, 2010; Grant Robertson, "Smart-Phone Application Scores Big," *The Globe and Mail*, January 15, 2010, B4; Omar El Akkad, "Note to Teens: Blame Canada," *The Globe and Mail*, January 9, 2010, B3; Omar El Akkad, "RIM Suffers BlackBerry Backlash Sparked by Service Disruptions," *The Globe and Mail*, December 24, 2009, B1; Omar El Akkad, "RIM's Move on Main St. Gains Pace," *The Globe and Mail*, December 18, 2009, B1; "Google Enters Smartphone Market War; 'Fight for Scale'"; Android Mobile Phone a Challenge to Apple, RIM," *National Post*, December 15, 2009, FP5; "RIM Aims to Tap Chinese Millions: Despite Fakes," *National Post*, December 9, 2009, FP1; Omar El Akkad, "RIM Signs Deal to Peddle BlackBerry in China," *The Globe and Mail*, December 8, 2009, B3; Bob Willis, "Patent Lawsuit Against RIM Could See BlackBerry Ban in U.S. Market," *National Post*, December 4, 2009, FP4; "Klausner Technologies Sues Motorola, RIM Over Visual Voicemail Patents," *National Post*, November 24, 2009, FP5; Simon Avery, "RIM Plans Buyback to Tackle Sinking Share Price," *The Globe and Mail*, November 6, 2009, B16; Omar El Akkad, "Bad Day for RIM and Its BlackBerry," *The Globe and Mail*, November 3, 2009, B10; Paul Vieira, "Fallen Heroes Litter Tech Battlefield; RIM Latest to Feel Heat, but It's Too Early to Panic," *National Post*, November 3, 2009, FP1; Bruce Dowbiggin, "BlackBerry Plugs Its Neighbours at Score," *The Globe and Mail*, November 2, 2009, S7; Simon Avery, "'Optimistic' RIM Unveils Storm 2 Smart Phone," *The Globe and Mail*, October 16, 2009, B3; Fabrice Taylor, "RIM's Best Days Are Behind It," *The Globe and Mail*, October 9, 2009, B9; John Greenwood, "High Hopes Rock RIM; Shares Slump on Failure to Hit Expectations on Sales, Earnings," *National Post*, September 25, 2009, FP1; Simon Avery, "RIM Leader of Smart Phone Pack," *The Globe and Mail*, September 24, 2009, B15; Simon Avery, "Nokia Plays Defence with Launch of New Gadget," *The Globe and Mail*, August 25, 2009, B3; Joe Castaldo, "RIM Rocks Out," *Canadian Business*, Winter 2007/2008, 15; John Gray, "RIM," *Canadian Business*, September 10, 2007, 10; Joe Castaldo, "RIM's Test of Faith," *Canadian Business*, April 9, 2007, 29.

Entrepreneurship and New Ventures: A Shrine to Wine
"Alexander Dumas," The Modern Library website, www.randomhouse.com/modernlibrary/library/author.pperl?authorid=7552, accessed May 20, 2009; "Doing Business Abroad," Foreign Affairs and International Trade website, www.tradecommissioner.gc.ca/eng/services.jsp, accessed May 20, 2009; "Genuwine Cellars Captivates Discriminating Tastes—Robb Denomme wins BDC's Young Entrepreneur Award for Manitoba," *Canada NewsWire*, Proquest Database, October 21, 2008, accessed May 20, 2009; Jean-Rene Halde, "BDC's Young Entrepreneur Awards," *Canadian Business*, November 24, 2008, Vol. 81, Issue 20, 19; "Savouring the Taste of Success: Meet Manitoba Winner Robbie Denomme," BDC Etc., December 2008–January 2009, www.genuwinecellars.com/genuwineintheNEWS.html, accessed May 20, 2009; "Uncorking Success in Foreign Markets," Foreign Affairs and International Trade website, www.dfait-maeci.gc.ca/commerce/success/genuwine-en.asp, accessed May 20, 2009; "Wine Proverbs and Quotes," Life in Italy website, www.lifeinitaly.com/wines/wine-quotes.asp, accessed May 20, 2009.

E-Business and Social Media Solutions: Virtual Goods: An Emerging E-Market Ari Levy and Joseph Galante, "Who Wants to Buy a Digital Elephant," *Bloomberg BusinessWeek*, March 8, 2010, 64–65; Ari Levy, Brian Womack, and Joseph Galante, "A Cash Crop for Facebook," *Bloomberg BusinessWeek*, March 8, 2010, 65; Douglas McMillan "Zynga and Facebook: It's Complicated," *Bloomberg BusinessWeek*, April 26–May 2, 2010, 50–51; BBC News website, "Sales of Virtual Goods Boom in the US," accessed October 22, 2009; CBC News website, "Bottled Water: Quenching a Planet's Thirst," accessed August 20, 2008.

Figure 1.3 Adapted from Karl E. Case and Ray C. Fair, *Principles of Economics*, 8th ed., updated (Upper Saddle River, NJ: Prentice Hall, 2007), 103–105.

Managing in Turbulent Times: The High Price of High Prices Sarah McBride, "Copper Caper: Thieves Nab Art to Sell for Scrap," *The Wall Street Journal*, May 1, 2008, A1, A14; Bob Davis and Douglas Belkin, "Food Inflation, Riots Spark Worries for World Leaders," *The Wall Street Journal*, April 14, 2008 A1, A11; Lauren Etter, "Rice Prices Are Steaming, with Many Implications," *The Wall Street Journal*, December 15–16, 2007, B1, B5; Patrick Barta and Jane Spencer, "As Alternative Fuels Heat up, Environmental Concerns Grow," *The Wall Street Journal*, December 5, 2006, A1, A13; Joel Millman, "Metal Is So Precious That Scrap Thieves Now Tap Beer Kegs," *The Wall Street Journal*, March 14, 2006, A1, A15.

Business Case 1: Are We Running Out of Oil? Claudia Cattaneo, "Peak Oil Demand Theory in Vogue," *National Post*, January 26, 2009, FP1; John Lyons and David Luhnow, "Brazil May Be the Globe's Next Big Spigot," *The Globe and Mail*, May 23, 2008, B8; Neil King and Peter Fritsch, "IEA Set to Lower Global Oil Supply Forecast," *The Wall*

Street Journal, May 22, 2008, B11; "New Method to Extract Gas Hydrates," *Winnipeg Free Press*, April 17, 2008, A6; Neil King, "A Rosy View of Oil Supply," *The Globe and Mail*, January 17, 2008, B7; Russell Gold and Ann Davis, "Oil Officials See Limit Looming on Production," *The Wall Street Journal*, November 19, 2007, A1, A17; Judy Monchuk, "Slew of Deals Shows Oil Sands Fever Not Breaking," *The Globe and Mail*, August 6, 2007, B3; Shawn McCarthy, "Canada's Oil Boom Has Legs, IEA Says," *The Globe and Mail*, July 10, 2007, B1, B16; Neil Reynolds, "Peak Oil Doomsayers Fall Silent as Reserves Grow Ever Larger," *The Globe and Mail*, April 11, 2007, B2; Robert Hirsch, "Peaking of World Oil Production: Recent Forecasts," *WorldOil*, Vol. 228 (April 2007); Patrick Brethour, "Peak Oil Theorists Don't Know Jack," *The Globe and Mail*, September 6, 2006, B1, B6; Michael Lynch, "Oil Discovery Forecasts Doomed," *The Globe and Mail*, May 28, 2005, B6; Peter Tertzakian, "Canada: Energy Superpower?" *The Globe and Mail*, May 28, 2005, B6; Barrie McKenna, "Welcome to the Age of Scarcity," *The Globe and Mail*, May 21, 2005, B15; Haris Anwar, "Supply: Are Saudi Reserves Drying Up?" *The Globe and Mail*, May 21, 2005, B19.

Chapter 2

Air Canada's Challenging Environment: Competition, Economic Crisis, Fuel Prices, Volcanoes, and More Brent Jang, "Air Canada Pushes for Greater Transatlantic Traffic," *The Globe and Mail*, December 18, 2009, B1; Slobodan Lekic, "Volcanic Ash Forces More Delays, Rerouting of Transatlantic Flights," *The Globe and Mail*, May 9, 2010, B1; Robin Millard, "Volcanic Ash Cancels, Delays More Flights," *National Post*, May 9, 2010; Brent Jang, "Air Canada's Problems Pile Up," *The Globe and Mail*, February 19, 2009, B1; CBC News website, "Volcanic Ash Costs Air Canada $20M over 5 Days," www.cbc.ca/world/story/2010/04/19/ash-cloud-airlines-cost.html, April 19, 2010; Air Canada Annual Report 2009, www.aircanada.com/en/about/investor/documents/2009_ar.pdf, accessed June 12, 2010; Air Canada website, "Air Canada Best Airline in North America in International Survey,"

www.aircanada.com/en/about/media/facts/awards/index.html.

Figure 2.3 Bank of Canada website, CPI Statistics, www.bankofcanada.ca/en/cpi.html, accessed June 10, 2010.

The Greening of Business: The Hydrogen Fuel Cell Tomoko Hosaka, "Honda's New Fuel Cell Car Goes Hollywood," *The Globe and Mail*, June 17, 2008, B11; Yuri Kageyama, "Toyota's Hybrid Sales Top 1 Million Vehicles," *Winnipeg Free Press*, June 8, 2007, B16; Peter Kennedy, "Ballard's Celebrated Drive Hits a Bumpy Road," *The Globe and Mail*, July 17, 2004, B6; Peter Kennedy, "GM Aims to Finish First in Fuel Cell Race," *The Globe and Mail*, June 10, 2003, B5; Chris Nuttall-Smith, "Waiting for the Revolution," *Report on Business*, February 2003, 44–54; Jeffrey Ball, "Hydrogen Fuel May Be Clean, but Getting It Here Looks Messy," *The Wall Street Journal*, March 7, 2003; Rebecca Blumenstein, "Auto Industry Reaches Surprising Consensus: It Needs New Engines," *The Wall Street Journal*, January 5, 1998, A1, A10.

Entrepreneurship and New Ventures: Nova Scotia's Golden Nectar: Glen Breton Rare Susan Krashinsky, "Scotch Whisky Snobs Shudder as Glen Breton Toasts Win," *The Globe and Mail*, June 12, 2009, B1; "Nothing Shady about This Glen, Court Rules," *The Globe and Mail*, January 24, 2009, B7; "Cape Breton Distillery Toasts Scotch Shortage," cbc.ca, November 6, 2008, www.cbc.ca/canada/nova-scotia/story/2008/11/06/glenora-scotch.html; "Cape Breton Distiller Fighting to Defend Product's Name," CanWest News, April 7, 2008; "Scotch Whisky Association Filing Appeal in Dispute with N.S. Distiller," Canada NewsWire, March 9, 2007; Keith McArthur, "Could Name Dispute Put N.S. Whisky on the Rocks?" *The Globe and Mail*, December 16, 2006, B7; Brian Flinn, "Battle of the Glen Shapes up over Nova Scotia Distiller," CanWest News, July 9, 2004, 1; Rod Currie, "Distillery Produces Single Malt Whisky in Cape Breton Highlands," Canada NewsWire, April 29, 2002; Corinne McLean, "Turning Liquid Silver into Gold: Glenora Captures the Spirit of Scotland," *Plant*, Vol. 59, Issue 15 (2000): 12; Allan Lynch, "Scotch on the Rocks," *Profit*, Vol. 10, Issue 8 (1991): 38.

E-Business and Social Media Solutions: Corus Entertainment

Looking for Listeners and Revenues in New Places Grant Robertson, "Corus Looks to iTunes to Boost Web Traffic," *The Globe and Mail*, May 12, 2009, B12; Susan Krashinsky, "New Bidders Make Play for Radio Stations," *The Globe and Mail*, June 9, 2010, B4; Corus Entertainment website, www.corusent.com/home/Radio/tabid/1663/Default.aspx, accessed June 11, 2010; Corus Entertainment Annual Report 2009, www.corusent.com/home/Corusent Files%5Cfiles%5CCorporate%20-%20 Annual%20Reports/Corus_AR09.pdf, accessed June 11, 2010.

Business Case 2: Inflation, Deflation, and the Validity of the CPI Allan Robinson, "Deflation Risk Helps Curb Interest Rates," *The Globe and Mail*, April 13, 2010, B1; Phil Green, "Hiding Inflation," *National Post*, April 29, 2010, FP11; Louise Egan, "Consumer Prices Decline," *Montreal Gazette*, September 18, 2009, B1; "Deflation Threat Persists Despite Signs of Revival," *National Post*, April 16, 2009, FP4; Allan Robinson, "Negative Inflation Rate Expected," *The Globe and Mail*, January 16, 2009, B10; Alia McMullen, "Japan Drawn Back into Vortex of Deflation," *National Post*, December 20, 2008, FP2; Eric Beauchesne, "Rising Food Prices Pack Punch," *Winnipeg Free Press*, July 24, 2008, B5; David Parkinson, "China Positioned to Unleash Global Deflation," *The Globe and Mail*, November 13, 2008, B12; George Athanassakos, "Confusion Reigns with Deflation-Inflation Conundrum," *The Globe and Mail*, November 6, 2008, B11; Heather Scoffield, "Now Canada Faces the Demons," *The Globe and Mail*, July 16, 2008, B5; Heather Scoffield, "Shock Move Sounds Inflation Alarm," *The Globe and Mail*, June 11, 2008, B1, B4; Andrew Batson, "Inflation, Spanning Globe, Is Set to Reach Decade High," *The Wall Street Journal*, April 10, 2008, A1, A12.

Chapter 3

What Really Happened at Livent? Jacquie McNish, "Convictions Seen as Much-Needed Regulatory Win," *The Globe and Mail*, March 26, 2009, B4; Janet McFarland, "ICAO Appeal Panel Upholds Deloitte Decision," *The Globe and Mail*, February 19, 2009, B9; Grant McCool and John Poirier, "Madoff Mess Manoeuvres,"

National Post, December 18, 2008, FP3; Shannon Kari, "Livent Defence Calls No Witnesses; Final Arguments," *National Post*, November 4, 2008, FP5; Janet McFarland, "File Listed Livent 'Problems': Investigator," *The Globe and Mail*, October 22, 2008, B9; Janet McFarland, "Livent Brass Pulled 'Numbers out of a Hat,'" *The Globe and Mail*, September 9, 2008, B2; Janet McFarland, "Ex-Livent Official Tells of 'Absurd' Plan," *The Globe and Mail*, September 3, 2008, B5; Janet McFarland, "Livent Staff Dodged Drabinsky's Controls, Lawyer Says," *The Globe and Mail*, July 18, 2008, B2; Janet McFarland, "Liven Software Was Altered, Court Hears," *The Globe and Mail*, July 17, 2008, B9; Janet McFarland, "Ad Firms Helped Livent, Ex-Official Says," *The Globe and Mail*, July 16, 2008, B7; Janet McFarland, "All His Time Spent on Fraud: Ex-Livent Official," *The Globe and Mail*, July 15, 2008, B4; Janet McFarland, "Ex-CFO Testified She Hid Fraud at Livent," *The Globe and Mail*, June 12, 2008, B3.

E-Business and Social Media Solutions: Ethics in the YouTube Age Erin Anderssen, "Daddy What Are We Downloading Today?" *The Globe and Mail*, May 17, 2010, B1, B3; Robert Thompson, "A Crushing Blow for Web Pirates," *Canadian Business*, March 1, 2010, 17; YouTube website, www.youtube.com/t/howto_copyright, accessed June 1, 2010.

Figure 3.2 David P. Baron, *Business and Its Environment*, 4th ed. (Upper Saddle River, NJ: Prentice Hall, 2003), 768.

Figure 3.3 Based on Andrew C. Revkin, "Who Cares about a Few Degrees?" *The New York Times*, December 12, 1997, F1.

The Greening of Business: This Is One Green (and Socially Responsible) Company! Hollie Shaw, "Keeping It Green; Outdoor-Recreation Retailer Finds Ways to Draw Customers," *National Post*, November 28, 2008, FP14; Laura Pratt, "Sustainability Reporting," *CGA*, September–October 2007, 18–21; Sharda Prashad, "Good Green Goals," *The Toronto Star*, April 22, 2007, www.thestar.com/printArticle/205855; Ralph Shaw, "Peak Performance (Mountain Equipment Co-op)," *Alternatives Journal*, Vol. 31, Issue 1 (January/February 2005): 19–20.

Managing in Turbulent Times: Counterfeit Products: Who's Accountable? "eBay Claims Court Victory in Belgium over L'Oreal in Counterfeit Goods Case," *National Post*, August 13, 2008, www.nationalpost.com/story-printer.html?id=718982; "EBay Quashes Tiffany Trademark Suit," *The Globe and Mail*, July 15, 2008, B6; "The End of Louis Vuitton on eBay?" etonline.com/news/2008/06/63035, accessed July 29, 2008; Maureen Fan, "China's Olympic Turnabout on Knockoffs," June 13, 2008, A1; Aileen McCabe, "China's Knock-Off Shops Help the Rich Scrape By," *Winnipeg Free Press*, April 19, 2008, C19; Daryl-Lynn Carlson, "The Costly Reality of Fakes," *The National Post*, December 5, 2007; Daryl-Lynn Carlson, "Canada's IP Protection Laws Soft," *The National Post*, December 5, 2007; Paul Waldie, "Court Clobbers Store for Selling Vuitton Fakes," *The Globe and Mail*, November 26, 2007, B3; Jonathan Cheng, "A Small Firm Takes on Chinese Pirates," *The Wall Street Journal*, July 5, 2007, B1–B2; Stacy Meichtry, "Swell or Swill?" *The Wall Street Journal*, August 10, 2006, B1–B2; Alessandra Galloni, "As Luxury Industry Goes Global, Knock-Off Merchants Follow," *The Wall Street Journal*, January 31, 2006, A1, A13; Alessandra Galloni, "Bagging Fakes and Sellers," *The Wall Street Journal*, January 31, 2006, B1–B2; Gordon Fairclough, "Tobacco Firms Trace Fakes to North Korea," *The Wall Street Journal*, January 27, 2006, B1–B2; Jeff Sanford, "Knock-Off Nation," *Canadian Business*, November 8–21, 2004, 67–71; Shawn McCarthy, "Crackdown on New York's Canal Street," *The Globe and Mail*, August 30, 2004, B1, B11.

Entrepreneurship and New Ventures: How Green Is That Orange? "Frequently Asked Questions," Arthur's Juice website, http://arthursjuice.ca/en_faq.asp, accessed May 12, 2009; The Packaging Association of Canada website, www.pac.ca/ePromos/NA09_Walmart_Sus_Conf_3info.htm#Travis_Bell, accessed May 12, 2009; Karen Davidson, "New Products Sport Green Nutrition," *The Grower*, May 1, 2009; Randy Ray, "Fresh Ideas for Green Manufacturing," *The Globe and Mail*, April 22, 2009, E10; Cleve Dheensaw, "100 Marathons Earn Place on Walk of Fame," *Times Colonist*,

October 11, 2008; Rick Spence, "Top 100 List Reveals Healthy Economy," *The Financial Post*, June 2, 2008, FP5; Ken Ramstead, "The Juices Are Flowing," *Canadian Grocer*, Vol. 121, Issue 3 (April 2007): 53.

Business Case 3: Pollution on the High Seas Bruce Stanley, "Ships Draw Fire for Rising Role in Air Pollution," *The Wall Street Journal*, November 27, 2007, A1, A16; Bill McAllister, "Alaska Still Out Front on Environmental Monitoring," *The Juneau Empire*, May 29, 2004; Marilyn Adams, "Former Carnival Exec Says He Was Fired for Helping Federal Inquiry," *USA Today*, November 8–10, 2003; Marilyn Adams, "Cruise-Ship Dumping Poisons Seas, Frustrates U.S. Enforcers," *USA Today*, November 8–10, 2003; Michael Connor, "Norwegian Cruise Line Pleads Guilty in Pollution Case," *Reuters*, December 7, 2002; "What Is a Dead Zone?" *Oceana Interactive,* June 10, 2004, www.oceana.org/index.cfm? sectionID 511&fuseaction59#25.

Chapter 4

Parasuco Jeans: The Story of a Born Entrepreneur Patricia Gajo, "Jean-Ius," *Nuvo,* Spring 2010, 72–73; Parasuco website, www.parasuco.com, accessed June 23, 2010; Kristin Laird, "Parasuco's New Ad Campaign Is in Ice," *Marketing,* March 19, 2009; Eva Freide, "Flattery or Fakery," *Montreal Gazette,* July 22, 2008; Daniel Geiger, *Real Estate Weekly,* "Duane Reade Takes Deal for Parasuco Space," www.rew-online.com/news/story.aspx?id=907, accessed March 26, 2010.

Table 4.1 "Queen's Releases List of Top Employers," *The Globe and Mail*, February 11, 2010, page 87. Courtesy of Queen's School of Business, http://business.queensu.ca/news/2010/02-10-2010-BSME-results.php.

Figure 4.1 Statistics Canada, Business Register, December 2008, 7; www.ic.gc.ca/eic/site/sbrp-rppe.nsf/vwapj/KSBS-PSRPE_July-Juillet2009_eng.pdf/$FILE/KSBS-PSRPE_July-Juillet2009_eng.pdf.

The Greening of Business: Small Businesses Go Green Green Enterprise Ontario website, http://greenenterprise.net/index.php, accessed June 18, 2010; Laura Ramsay, "Small Firms Can Go Green Too: There's Lots of Help

Out There," *The Globe and Mail*, October 14, 2008, E1; Burke Campbell, "Entrepreneur's Green Inspiration from the East," *National Post*, September 22, 2008, www.nationalpost.com/story-printer.html?id=812446.

Entrepreneurship and New Ventures: Spotlight on Mompreneurs Rasha Moutarda, "Mom's the Word for Marketing Frozen Baby Food," *The Globe and Mail*, April 21, 2010, B7; Alexandra Lopez-Pacheco, "Home-Preneurs Want It All: She Said," *National Post*, December 22, 2008, FP4; Melissa Martin, "Mompreneurial Spirit," *Winnipeg Free Press*, September 2, 2008, D1, D5; Green Please Inc. website, http://greenpleaseforyou.com/, accessed June 25, 2010; SavvyMom website, www.savvymom.ca/index.php/newsletter/a_winning_story, accessed June 20, 2010.

Table 4.3 Industry Canada website, Canadian Business Incubators, www.ic.gc.ca/eic/site/sbrp-rppe.nsf/eng/rd02276.html, accessed June 24, 2010.

E-Business and Social Media Solutions: New Age Entrepreneurs: The Rise of Twitter Susan Krashinski, "Making Money, 140 Characters at a Time" *The Globe and Mail*, April 14, 2010, B1, B6; Amber MacArthur, "What Twitter Ads Mean to You" *The Globe and Mail*, April 13, 2010, B1; Lyndsie Bourgon, "Tweeting Them Where It Hurts," *Canadian Business*, November 23, 2009, 22; Lisan Jutras, "How Will the Twitterati Deal with the Ad Men?" *The Globe and Mail*, April 18, 2010, B1, B3; Twitter website, www.twitter.com, accessed June 14, 2010; Hollie Shaw, "The Tweet Spot: Marketers Embrace Social Media," *The Financial Post*, October 30, 2009, B1, B3; Spencer E. Ante, "The Real Value of Tweets," *Bloomberg BusinessWeek*, January 18, 2010, P31; Jon Fine, "Twitter Makes a Racket: But Revenues?" *Bloomberg BusinessWeek*, April 20, 2009, P89.

Table 4.5 *Financial Post*, Special Edition, June 2010, 40. Material reprinted with the express permission of "The National Post Company", a division of Postmedia Network Inc.

Business Case 4: Family Business Burke Campbell, "Sisters Toast

Family Roots as Business Bears Fruit," *National Post*, September 29, 2008, www.nationalpost.com/story-printer.html?id=846427; Gabriel Kahn, "A Vintage Strategy Faces Modernity," *The Wall Street Journal*, April 5–6, 2008, A6; Chris Morris, "Rumours of Irving Family Corporate Breakup Swirl," *Winnipeg Free Press*, November 23, 2007, B14; Gordon Pitts and Jacquie McNish, "Shaking the Family Tree," *The Globe and Mail*, November 22, 2007, B1, B9; Gordon Pitts and Jacquie McNish, "Irving Brothers Look to Break up Empire," *The Globe and Mail*, November 21, 2007, B1, B6; Martin Peers, Matthew Karnitschnig, and Merissa Marr, "Shaken from the Family Tree," *The Globe and Mail*, July 20, 2007, B6; also Paul Waldie, "Mitchell's Feud Goes Public," *The Globe and Mail*, November 30, 2002, B3.

Chapter 5

Tim Hortons USA: Exporting a Strategic Model Is No Easy Task Scott Anderson, "Tim Hortons to Go 'Upscale' in Expansion," *The Globe and Mail*, March 6, 2010, B2: Jasmine Budak, "The Donut Offensive," *Canadian Business*, March 1, 2010, 36–38; Sunny Freeman, "Tim Hortons Rides Out Price Increases," *The Globe and Mail*, February 26, 2010, B7; Simon Houpt, "Tim Hortons: At the Intersection of Commerce and Culture," *The Globe and Mail*, March 6, 2010, B1: Susan Ma, "Tims Takes Manhattan," *The Globe and Mail*, July 27, 2009, B3; Jason Kirby, "Tim's Takes on America," *Maclean's*, March 12, 2008, B3; Tim Hortons website, www.timhortons.com/us/en/about/investors.html, accessed March 27, 2010.

Table 5.1 Statistics Canada website, www40.statcan.gc.ca/l01/cst01/gblec02a-eng.htm, accessed March 28, 2010.

Managing in Turbulent Times: The Crisis in Europe: Let the Name Calling Begin Patrick Donahue and Tony Czuuczka, "German Lawmakers Approve 1 Trillion Bailout," *The Globe and Mail*, May 22, 2010, B6; Mark Scott, "Europe's Delicate Dilemma," *BusinessWeek*, January 25, 2010, 56; "EU Puts the Screws to Greece over Deficit," *The Globe and Mail*, February 4, 2010, B13; Eric Reguly, "Bailing out PIIGS

Just Encourages Bad Behaviour," *The Globe and Mail*, December 24, 2009; Eric Reguly, "Europe's Debt Crisis Threat to Recovery," *The Globe and Mail*, February 5, 2010, B1; Eric Reguly, "Greece's Financial Woes Threaten EU Stability," *The Globe and Mail*, February 5, 2010, B1; Eric Reguly, "Europe to Launch a Bailout Fund," *The Globe and Mail*, March 9, 2010, B1; Elisa Martinuzzi, "Goldman Stars in This Greek Tragedy," *BusinessWeek*, March 1, 2010, 30.

Entrepreneurship and New Ventures: Epic Entrepreneurs: Have Camera, Will Travel Epic Global Media website, http://epicglobalmedia.com, accessed May 25, 2010; "Epic Newsgroup Inc. Charts New Territory—Sabrina Heinekey and Tiffany Steeves Win BDC's Young Entrepreneur Award for British Columbia," Canada NewsWire, October 16, 2007, 1; Brian Morton, "Media Export: Businesswomen Built Their Empire on Faraway Places," *The Telegram*, October 22, 2007, www.thetelegram.com/index.cfm?sid=73310&sc=82; Business Development Bank of Canada, "Young Entrepreneur," *Profits*, Vol. 27, Issue 2 (2007): 10; "Vancouver Pair Wins B.C. Prize for Entrepreneurs," *Business Edge*, Vol. 4, Issue 22 (2007), www.businessedge.ca/article.cfm/newsID/16611.cfm.

Table 5.2 *Financial Post Business*, Special Edition 2010, 67. Material reprinted with the express permission of "The National Post Company", a division of Postmedia Network Inc.

Business Case 5: Bombardier's Global Strategy Bombardier's Global Strategy: Eric Reguly, "Beaudoin's Big, Bold Bet," *The Globe and Mail*, July 14, 2008, B1, B10; Tu Thanh Ha, "A Power Plant That Is Quieter, Fuel Efficient but Still Years Away," *The Globe and Mail*, July 14, 2008, B1, B10; Shawn McCarthy and Eric Reguly, "Canadian Hopes, Global Risks," *The Globe and Mail*, July 14, 2008, A1, A6.

Chapter 6

Corporate Culture Christopher Swann, "You Can Trust Us Most: Survey," *National Post*, February 23, 2010, FP2; "Corporate Culture Gives an Edge: Despite Recession, Record Number of Nominations in Survey," *National Post*, November 12, 2009, FP12; Meagan Fitzpatrick, "RCMP 'Horribly Broken,' Need Fix Quickly: Report," *Winnipeg Free Press*, June 16, 2007, A9; Roma Luciw, "No. 1 Employee Not Always Your No. 1 Manager," *The Globe and Mail*, February 17, 2007, B10; Calvin Leung, "Culture Club," *Canadian Business*, October 9-22, 2006, 115-120; Andrew Wahl, "Culture Shock," *Canadian Business*, October 10-23, 2005, 115-116; Gordon Pitts, "It Boiled Down to a Culture Clash," *The Globe and Mail*, June 11, 2005, B5; Doug Nairne, "Mounties Riding the Vision Thing," *Winnipeg Free Press*, September 16, 1996, A5.

Managing in Turbulent Times: What Do Managers Actually Do? Henry Mintzberg, *The Nature of Managerial Work* (New York: Harper and Row, 1973); Harvey Schachter, "Monday Morning Manager," *The Globe and Mail*, November 8, 2005, B2.

Figure 6.4 Ricky W. Griffin, *Management*, 8th ed. (Boston: Houghton Mifflin, 2005), 282.

Figure 6.5 Based on Stephen P. Robbins and Mary Coulter, *Management*, 9th ed. (Upper Saddle River, NJ: Prentice Hall, 2007), 199.

Figure 6.6 Based on Thomas L. Wheelan and J. David Hunger, *Strategic Management and Business Policy*, 7th ed. (Upper Saddle River, NJ: Prentice Hall, 2000), 13.

The Greening of Business: Setting Green Goals Alexandra Lopez-Pacheco, "Planet-Friendly Offices," *National Post*, October 2, 2009, FP12; "Rona Wins Kudos on Green Initiative," *The Globe and Mail*, November 22, 2008, B7; Marjo Johne, "Shoppers Get a Brand New Bag," *The Globe and Mail*, October 20, 2008, E5; John Murphy, "Honda CEO Vies for Green Mantle," *The Wall Street Journal*, June 16, 2008, B1-B2; "Deadline Set for Big Polluters," *National Post*, December 13, 2007, www.nationalpost.com/news/canada/story.html?id-164992; "Going Green: The Future of the Retail Food Industry," *Agriculture and Agri-Food Canada*, www.ats.agr.gc.ca/us/4351_e.htm, July 2007; "Google Sets Goal of Making Renewables Cheaper than Coal," *Clean Edge News*, November 28, 2007, www.cleanedge.com/story.php?nID=5036;

Sharda Prashad, "Good Green Goals," *The Toronto Star*, April 22, 2007, www.thestar.com/printArticle/205855.

E-Business and Social Media Solutions: Print Media: Are E-Readers the Solution or a New Problem? Jordan Timm, "Indigo 2.0," *Report on Business*, March 1, 2010, 29; Susan Krashinski, "Upstart Kobo Aims at Kindle," *The Globe and Mail*, February 9, 2010, B7; Yukuri Iwatini Kane and Geoffrey A. Fowler, "Apple Foes Have Head Start on E-Content," *The Globe and Mail*, April 3, 2010, B5; John Barber, "Arrival of iPad Gives Publisher Clout in e-Book Pricing," *The Globe and Mail*, February 2, 2010, B5; John Barber, "Why Old Media Loves Apple's New Thing," *The Globe and Mail*, January 27, 2010, B7; "Taiwan's AsusTek Unveils iPad Competitor," *The Globe and Mail*, June 1, 2010, B10; Geoffrey A. Fowler, "iPad Enjoys Strong Start, but How Long?" *The Globe and Mail*, April 5, 2010, B7; Rachel Metz, "iPad Could Be Kindle's First Big Threat," *The Globe and Mail*, March 30, 2010, B10; Susan Krashinski, "Magazine Sales Hit Hard at Newsstands," *The Globe and Mail*, February 9, 2010, B7; Simon Avery, "Amazon Slides after iPad Launch," *The Globe and Mail*, February 3, 2010, 16; Omar El Akkad, "E-Reader Rivals Jostle for Position," *The Globe and Mail*, January 7, 2010, B7; Jason Kirby and Katie Engelhart, "Rupert Murdoch vs. the Internet," *Maclean's*, January 18, 2010, 40-42; Jim Harris, "Newspapers Are Suffering," *Backbone*, November 2009, 10; Marina Strauss, "Turning a Page into the Digital Age," *The Globe and Mail*, June 27, 2009, B3.

Entrepreneurship and New Ventures: From a Missouri Garage to Hollywood Photo-Kicks.com, http://photo-kicks.com/, accessed June 5, 2008; Inc.com 5000, www.lne.com/inc5000/2007/company-profile.html?id+200705920, accessed June 8, 2008; Joanne Schneider, "Action: Filmmakers Open Studios In Columbia," *Columbia Business Times*, February 20, 2009, www.columbiabusinesstimes.com/3527/2009/02/20/action-filmmakers-open-studios-in-columbia/.

Business Case 6: The Business of Bagging Customers Vanessa O'Connell, "Coach Targets China— and Queens," *The Wall Street Journal*,

May 29, 2008, B1; "Coach's Drive Picks up the Pace," *BusinessWeek*, March 29, 2004, 98-100; Julia Boorstin, "How Coach Got Hot," *Fortune*, October 28, 2003, 131-134; Marilyn Much, "Consumer Research Is His Bag," *Investor's Business Daily*, December 16, 2003; "S&P Stock Picks and Pans: Accumulate Coach," *Business Week*, October 22, 2003.

Chapter 7

Reorganizing the Irving Empire Chris Morris, "Rumours of Irving Family Corporate Breakup Swirl," *Winnipeg Free Press*, November 23, 2007, B14; Gordon Pitts and Jacquie McNish, "Shaking the Family Tree," *The Globe and Mail*, November 22, 2007, B1, B9; Gordon Pitts and Jacquie McNish, "Irving Brothers Look to Break up Empire," *The Globe and Mail*, November 21, 2007, B1, B6; Gordon Pitts, "Death, Departure Set Irving on New Path," *The Globe and Mail*, July 22, 2010, B1.

Managing in Turbulent Times: Product versus Geographical Departmentalization: What's the Right Choice? Joann Lublin, "Place vs. Product: It's Tough to Choose a Management Model," *The Wall Street Journal*, June 27, 2001, A1, A4; Richard Blackwell, "New CIBC Boss Promises Shakeup," *The Globe and Mail*, April 2, 1999, B1, B4; Rekha Bach, "Heinz's Johnson to Divest Operations, Scrap Management of Firm by Region," *The Wall Street Journal*, December 1997, B10-B12; Jana Parker-Pope and Joann Lublin, "P&G Will Make Jager CEO Ahead of Schedule," *The Wall Street Journal*, September 1998, B1, B8.

The Greening of Business: Green Structures "Manitoba Hydro Place Wins Best Tall Building Award for the Americas," *Insights*, August 2009, 1; Gerald Flood, "At One with the World," *Winnipeg Free Press*, April 19, 2009, B1-B2; Jay Somerset, "A Building with an Energy All Its Own," *The Globe and Mail*, November 11, 2008, B9; Marta Gold, "More Realtors Turning Green," *Winnipeg Free Press*, August 24, 2008, F2; Murray McNeill, "Green Is the New Green at Credit Union Branches," *Winnipeg Free Press*, August 20, 2008, B6, B8; "Delta Hotels Expands Green Initiatives with Hybrid Heating,"

August 15, 2008, www.sempapower. com/media/newsarticles; Peter Mitham, "Going for the Gold in Green," *The Globe and Mail*, August 5, 2008, B5; John D. Stoll, "Car Dealers Set 'Green' Blueprints," *The Wall Street Journal*, May 15, 2008, B1; "Going Green: The Future of the Retail Food Industry," Agriculture and Agri-Food Canada, July 2007, www.ats.agr.gc.ca/us/ 4351_e.htm.

Business Case 7: Structure Evolves at Frantic Films Randall King, "Frantic Films Sells Division," *Winnipeg Free Press*, November 28, 2007, B7; Interviews with Jamie Brown, CEO of Frantic Films; documents provided by Frantic Films.

Chapter 8

Are More Cracks Appearing in the Glass Ceiling? Simon Houpt, "Four Seasons Hotels Gets New CEO: 21-Year Veteran of the Company," *The Globe and Mail*, June 26, 2010, B2; Tavia Grant, "Mining for Women," *The Globe and Mail*, April 15, 2009, B19; Sandra Rubin, "What Will It Take to Crack the Glass Ceiling?" *The Globe and Mail*, December 17, 2008, B8; Wallace Immen, "One More Gap in Pay between Men and Women," *The Globe and Mail*, August 15, 2008, C1; Meagan Fitzpatrick, "Women Still Earning Less than Men: Statistics Canada," *Winnipeg Free Press*, May 2, 2008, A5; Konrad Yakabuski, "Meet the New Leading Lady of Finance," *The Globe and Mail*, March 27, 2008, B1–B2; "Women Less Likely to Aspire to Top Corporate Positions," Hudson Canada, March 6, 2008, http:// ca.hudson.com/node.asp?kwd=03-06-08- women-survey; Rudy Mezzetta, "Banks, Credit Unions Put Women in Top Spots," *Investment Executive*, February 2008; Matthew McClearn, "Mind the Gap," *Canadian Business*, November 5, 2007, 21–22; Margaret Wente, "It's Manly at the Top," *The Globe and Mail*, May 7, 2005, A21; Janet McFarland, "Women Still Find Slow Rise to Power Positions," *The Globe and Mail*, March 13, 2003, B1, B7; Virginia Galt, "Top Women Still Finding Barriers," *The Globe and Mail*, September 25, 2002, B7; Marie Drolet, "The Male–Female Wage Gap," *Perspectives on Labour and Income, Online Edition*, December 2001, www.statcan.gc.ca/pub/75-001-x/

01201/4095957-eng.html; Elizabeth Church, "Women Still Shut Out of Many Top Posts," *The Globe and Mail*, February 10, 2000, B15; Belle Rose Ragins, "Gender Gap in the Executive Suite: CEOs and Female Executives Report on Breaking the Glass Ceiling," *Academy of Management Executive*, February 1998, 28–42; Greg Keenan, "Ford Canada Gets New CEO," *The Globe and Mail*, April 9, 1997, B1; Greg Keenan and Janet McFarland, "The Boys' Club," *The Globe and Mail*, September 27, 1997, B1, B5; Greg Keenan, "Woman at the Wheel," *The Globe and Mail*, July 8, 1995, B1, B6.

The Greening of Business: Green Recruiting Greg McMillan, "The Greening of the Jobscape," *The Globe and Mail*, November 14, 2008, B7; Marjo Johne, "Show Us the Green, Workers Say," *The Globe and Mail*, October 10, 2007, C1; "Creating Jobs by Going Green," www.premier.gov.on.ca/ news/Product.asp?ProductID=1400.

E-Business and Social Media Solutions: Job Recruitment in the Social Media Era Wallace Immen, "Tweet Your Way to a Job" *The Globe and Mail*, May 19, 2010, B16; Tavia Grant, "LinkedIn Set to Open Shop in Canada," *The Globe and Mail*, March 29, 2010, B3; Tavia Grant, "Tweet-Tweet: Want Ads Singing a New Tune," *The Globe and Mail*, November 12, 2009, B1, B4; "LinkedIn: Balancing Friendships and Prospects," *The Globe and Mail*, February 4, 2009, C6; Matthew Boyle, "Enough to Make Monster Tremble," *BusinessWeek*, July 6, 2009, 43–45; Ijeoma Ross, "Online Recruiter Looks to Cast Wider Web," *The Globe and Mail*, May 12, 2008, B6; Susan Pinker, "Connecting Online: Small Investment, Big Return," *The Globe and Mail*, September 30, 2009, B20; Scott Morisson, "Taking a Page from Facebook," *The Globe and Mail*, December 30, 2009, B8.

Managing in Turbulent Times: The Importance of Perks Roma Luciw and John Partridge, "How to Keep Staff? More Perks, Of Course," *The Globe and Mail*, February 23, 2008, B17; Virginia Galt, "Statscan Studies Workplace Stress," *The Globe and Mail*, June 26, 2003, B3; David Leonhardt, "Did Pay Incentives Cut Both Ways?" *The New York Times*, April 7, 2002,

BU1–3; Dean Foust and Michelle Conlin, "A Smarter Squeeze?" *BusinessWeek*, December 31, 2001, 42–44; Tischelle George, "Bye-Bye Employee Perks," *Information Week*, October 15, 2001; Rick Perera, "Siemens Offers Workers 'Time-Outs' to Save Cash," *The Industry Standard*, August 31, 2001; Anne Howland, "There's No Place Like Work," *CGA*, July–August 2000, 21–25.

Business Case 8: Reports from the Walmart–Union Battlefield David Friend and Sunny Freeman, "Wal-Mart Canada to Create 6,500 Jobs," *The Globe and Mail*, February 24, 2010, B14; Terence Corcoran, "Wal-Mart Wins Big Union Battle," *National Post*, April 9, 2009, FP13; Marina Strauss, "UFCW Digs in Heels in Looming Retail Food Fight," *The Globe and Mail*, January 12, 2009, B1; Bert Hill, "Another Wal-Mart Unionized; Second for Quebec," *National Post*, December 20, 2008, FP6; Brent Jang, "CAW Eyes Union Drive at WestJet Airlines," *The Globe and Mail*, September 10, 2008, B3; Brent Jang, "WestJet Brushes Off Potential CAW Drive," *The Globe and Mail*, September 11, 2008, B5; Allison Lampert, "Unions Want More Wal-Mart Wins," *Winnipeg Free Press*, August 22, 2008, B8; Jean-Francois Bertrand, "Union Contract Imposed on Quebec Wal-Mart Store a First," *Winnipeg Free Press*, August 16, 2008, B10; "Arbitrator Sides with Wal-Mart Workers," *The Globe and Mail*, August 16, 2008, B7; Peter Rakobowchuk, "Early Closing of Unionized Wal-Mart Called Cowardly," *Winnipeg Free Press*, April 30, 2005, C15; Marina Strauss, "Wal-Mart Faces Another Unionized Store in Quebec," *The Globe and Mail*, January 20, 2005, B4; Barrie McKenna, "Unions Starting to Make Inroads at Wal-Mart," *The Globe and Mail*, August 23, 2004, B1, B12; Aldo Santin, "Wal-Mart vs. Union Battle Now Shifts to Manitoba," *Winnipeg Free Press*, August 5, 2004, B3; Patrick Brethour, "Wal-Mart Hails Saskatchewan Court Ruling in Union Drives," *The Globe and Mail*, July 28, 2004, B1, B20; Virginia Galt, "Wal-Mart Must Give Union Access," *The Globe and Mail*, May 13, 2003, B5; "Union Is Trying to Organize Staff at Wal-Mart," *Winnipeg Free Press*, May 13, 2003, A7; Zena Olijnyk, "CAW Walks Away from Wal-Mart," *National Post*, April 20, 2000, C5; Susan Bourettte, "Wal-Mart

Staff Want Out of Union," *The Globe and Mail*, April 23, 1999, B9; John Heinzl and Marina Strauss, "Wal-Mart's Cheer Fades," *The Globe and Mail*, February 15, 1997, B1, B4; Margot Gibb-Clark, "Why Wal-Mart Lost the Case," *The Globe and Mail*, February 14, 1997, B10.

Chapter 9

What Do Employees Want? Wallace Immen, "Meaning Means More than Money at Work: Poll," *The Globe and Mail*, February 27, 2009, B14; Wallace Immen, "Hey, Boss, Shine Your Shoes? Keep Me Around," *The Globe and Mail*, October 22, 2008, C3; Tavia Grant, "Favourite Perk? Not a BlackBerry," *The Globe and Mail*, September 10, 2008, C1; Wallace Immen, "Boomers, Gen-Yers Agree: It's All about Respect," *The Globe and Mail*, January 24, 2007, C1; Wallace Immen, "The Continuing Divide Over Stress Leave," *The Globe and Mail*, June 10, 2005, C1; also Jeff Buckstein, "In Praise of Praise in the Workplace," *The Globe and Mail*, June 15, 2005, C1, C5; also Virginia Galt, "This Just in: Half Your Employees Ready to Jump Ship," *The Globe and Mail*, January 26, 2005, B1, B9; also David Sirota, Louis Mischkind, and Michael Meltzer, "Nothing Beats an Enthusiastic Employee," *The Globe and Mail*, July 29, 2005, C1; also Virginia Galt, "Business's Next Challenge: Tackling Mental Health in the Workplace," *The Globe and Mail*, April 12, 2005, B1, B20; also Virginia Galt, "Canadian Take Dour View on Jobs, Bosses, Angels," *The Globe and Mail*, October 18, 2004, B1, B7; also Virginia Galt, "Worker Stress Costing Economy Billions, Panel Warns," *The Globe and Mail*, July 21, 2000, B9; "A Better Workplace," *Time*, April 17, 2000, 87.

Figure 9.3 A.H. Maslow, *Motivation and Personality*, 2nd ed. (Upper Saddle River, NJ: Prentice Hall, 1970). Reprinted by permission of Prentice Hall, Inc.

Entrepreneurship and New Ventures: Employee Engagement: The Ultimate Win–Win Leena Rao, "I Love Rewards Raises $5.9 Million for Employee Rewards Program," TechCrunch website, www.techcrunch.com/2009 /05/07/i-love-rewards-raises-59-million-for-employee-rewards-program/, accessed May 7, 2009; Chris Atchison, "Masters of One," *Profit*, Vol. 28, Issue 2 (May 2009), 18; "I Love Rewards Reports Record Results as Demand for Rewards and Recognition Programs Grows," *Canada NewsWire*, April 24, 2009; "I Love Rewards Named One of the World's Most Democratic Workplaces," *Marketwire*, April 14, 2009; Ari Weinzwig, "Ask Inc: Tough Questions, Smart Answers," *Inc.*, Vol. 29, Issue 12 (December 2007), 84; Ryan McCarthy, "'Help Wanted' Meets 'Buy It Now': Why More Companies Are Integrating Marketing and Recruiting," *Inc.*, Vol. 29, Issue 11 (November 2007), 50.

Managing in Turbulent Times: Encouraging Employees to Share Ideas Virginia Galt, "Ideas: Employees' Best-Kept Secrets," *The Globe and Mail*, June 18, 2005, B11; Frederick A. Starke, Bruno Dyck, and Michael Mauws, "Coping with the Sudden Loss of an Indispensable Worker," *Journal of Applied Behavioural Science*, Vol. 39, Issue 2 (2003): 208–229; Timothy Aeppel, "On Factory Floors, Top Workers Hide Secrets to Success," *The Wall Street Journal*, July 1, 2002, A1, A10; Christopher Robert, Tahira Probst, Joseph Martocchio, Fritz Drasgow, and John Lawler, "Empowerment and Continuous Improvement in the United States, Mexico, Poland, and India: Predicting Fit on the Basis of the Dimensions of Power Distance and Individualism, *Journal of Applied Psychology*, October 2000, 643–658; Timothy Aeppel, "Not All Workers Find Idea of Empowerment as Neat as It Sounds," *The Wall Street Journal*, September 8, 1997, A1, 13.

Table 9.1 Reprinted with permission of the Free Press, a division of Simon & Schuster Adult Publishing Group, from *A Force of Change: How Leadership Differs from Management*, by John P. Kotter. Copyright 1990 by John P. Kotter, Inc. All rights reserved.

Figure 9.7 Reprinted by permission of *Harvard Business Review*. Exhibit from "How to Choose Leadership Patterns," by Robet Tannenbaum & Warren Schmidt, May–June 1973. Copyright 1973 by the Harvard Business School Publishing Corporation. All rights reserved.

Figure 9.8 Copyright 1990 by the The Regents of the University of California, Reprinted from the *California Management Review*, Vol. 32, Issue 2. By the permission of the Regents.

Business Case 9: What about Telecommuting? Joyce Rosenberg, "Out of Sight, on Your Mind; Learning to Trust Telecommuters," *The Globe and Mail*, September 20, 2008, B19; "Productivity Rises for Teleworkers: Survey," *The Globe and Mail*, October 15, 2008, C7; Randi Chapnik Myers, "The Back and Forth of Working from Home," *The Globe and Mail*, March 8, 2008, B16; Paul Lima, "With New Advances in Technology, Why Are We Still Jumping in the Car?" *The Globe and Mail*, October 20, 2008, E9; Kira Vermond, "In Support of Ditching the Commute," *The Globe and Mail*, November 17, 2007, B23.

Chapter 10

Too Many Recalls Alexis Leondis, "Honda, Ford Leap over Toyota in U.S. Customer Loyalty Rankings," *National Post*, May 14, 2010, FP4; Greg Keenan and John Gray, "Toyota Faces Class-Action Suits," *Business News Network*, www.bnn.ca/news/15452.html, accessed February 1, 2010; Greg Keenan, "Toyota Executives Plan Media Blitz," *The Globe and Mail*, February 1, 2010, B1; Greg Keenan, "Toyota Scrambles for Remedy as Recall Grows," *The Globe and Mail*, January 30, 2010, B3; Paul Vieira, "Toyota Finds a Fix: Pedal Maker speeds Up Output as Recall Grows," *National Post*, January 29, 2010, FP1; Greg Keenan, "As Toyota Stumbles, Rivals Eye Gains," *The Globe and Mail*, January 29, 2010, B1; Greg Keenan, "Toyota Suspending Sales of Models Involved in Recall," *The Globe and Mail*, January 27, 2010, B12; "Toyota Retains Quality Crown over Ford, GM," *National Post*, June 23, 2009, FP12; John Lippert, Alan Ohnsman, and Kae Inoue, "Is Toyota the New GM? Founder's Grandson Thinks So," *The Globe and Mail*, June 23, 2009, B15; www.mattel.com; John Quelch, "Mattel: Getting a Toy Recall Right," August 27, 2007, Harvard Business School; Nicholas Casey, Nicholas Zamiska, and Andy Pasztor "Mattel Seeks to Placate China," *The Wall Street Journal*, September 22,

2007; Hari Bapuji and Paul W. Beamish, "Toy Recalls—Is China Really the Problem?" *Canada-Asia Commentary*, Issue 45 (September 2007); Paul W. Beamish and Hari Bapuji, "Toy Recalls and China: Emotion vs. Evidence," *Management and Organization Review*, Vol. 4, Issue 2 (July, 2008), 197–209.

E-Business and Social Media Solutions: Open Source Automobile Manufacturing "Be Open (Source)," *Report on Business*, November 2009, 62; Ian Harvey, "Outside Box, a Better Box," *Backbone*, January 2010, 11; Local Motors website, www.local-motors.com/, accessed June 4, 2010.

Entrepreneurship and New Ventures: The Unicycle Motorbike "Hold on Tight! The World's First Unicycle Motorbike," MailOnline website, April 29, 2008,www.dailymail.co.uk/news/article-562726/Hold-tight-The-worlds-unicycle-MOTORBIKE.html, accessed May 15, 2009; James F. Quinn, "Uno and Only: Start with a Motorcycle, Add 'Star Wars' and Give the Segway a Run for Its Futuristic Money," *Chicago Tribune* web edition, June 29, 2008, www.motorcycleenhancements.com/uno_chicago_ tribune /uno_chicago_tribune.htm#, accessed May 16, 2009; Mary Teresa Bitti, "The Brett Wilson Show," *National Post* website, January 9, 2009, www.nationalpost.com/related/topics/story.html ?id=1159190, accessed May 17, 2009; Trish Crawford, "Star Power for the Uno: Milton Teen's 'Cool' Electric Bike Creates Buzz," *The Hamilton Spectator*, June 3, 2008, A01; Trish Crawford, "Teenager's Electric Unicycle Creates One Singular Sensation: Science Fair Project Getting World Attention," *The Toronto Star,* June 3, 2008, A04; "Uno Inventory Lands $1.25 Million for Research Center," Milton Canadian Champion, November 21, 2008.

The Greening of Business: For the Greener Good www.walmart.ca/wms/microsite/GreenerGood/en/initiatives.html; Allison Linn, "Wal-Mart Pushes Suppliers to 'Go Green'; Company Uses Business-as-Usual Tactics to Drive Environmental Agenda," MSNBC.com, accessed April 18, 2007; "Is Wal-Mart Going Green? CEO Vows to Be 'Good Steward for the Environment' in Announcing Goals," MSNBC.com news services, accessed October 25; 2005.

Figure 10.6 www.stats.oecd.org/Index.aspx?DatasetCode=LEVEL.

Business Case 10: Quality Problems in Service Businesses Karen Howlett, "Ontario Launches Review of Travel Industry Watchdog Due to Conquest's Demise," *The Globe and Mail*, April 22, 2009; Ross Marowits, "Transat Cuts 53 Administrative Jobs," *The Canadian Press*, April 21, 2009; Keith Leslie, "Other Tour Operators 'Likely' Face Financial Problems: McGuinty," *The Globe and Mail*, April 21, 2009; Bob Cox, "FAA Knew of MD-80 Wiring Problem in 2003," *Airport Business,* April 14, 2008, www.airportbusiness.com/web/online/Top-News-Headlines/FAA-knew-of-MD-80-wiring-problem-in-2003/1$18873; MSNBC News Services, "American's MD-80s Cleared to Fly Again," April 14, 2008, www.msnbc.msn.com/id/24029455/; Brent D. Bowen and Dean E. Headley, "2008 Airline Quality Rating," April 2008, http://aqr.aero/aqrreports/2008aqr.pdf; "Survey: Airline Complaints Sky High" CBS News, April 7, 2008, www.cbsnews.com/stories/2008/04/07/business/main3996989.shtml; MSNBC News Services, "American Airlines Grounds Fleet of MD-80s," March 26, 2008, www.msnbc.msn.com/id/23808772/.

Chapter 11

What's the Latest on Pension Accounting? "OMERS Gains Don't Cover Deficit Hole; Obligations Grow Faster than Contributions," *National Post*, March 2, 2010, FP3; Janet McFarland, "Pension Plans Tagging Along with Surge in Stock Markets," *The Globe and Mail*, January 7, 2010, B3; Boyd Erman, "Teachers Books Worst-Ever Year after 18 percent Plunge," *The Globe and Mail*, April 3, 2009, B4; Janet McFarland, "Who's Responsible?" *The Globe and Mail*, March 6, 2009, B1; Lori McLeod, "Pension Plans Suffer Historic Losses," *The Globe and Mail*, January 9, 2009, A1; Janet McFarland, "Returns Forecast This Year Will Do Little to Offset 2008 Shortfalls," *The Globe and Mail*, January 14, 2009, B3; Janet McFarland, "Relief Falls Short, Pension Plans Warn," *The Globe and Mail*, November 28, 2008, B1;

Elizabeth Church, "Pension Funding Shortfall Increases Dramatically," *The Globe and Mail*, November 8, 2005, B5; Elizabeth Church, "Pension Fund Shortfall Soars in First Half," *The Globe and Mail*, November 23, 2005, B1, B7; Elizabeth Church, "Cost of Retiree Benefit Liabilities 'Sleeping Giant,'" *The Globe and Mail*, August 23, 2004, B4; Paul Waldie and Karen Howlett, "Reports Reveal Tight Grip of Ebbers on WorldCom," *The Globe and Mail*, June 11, 2003, B1, B7; Barrie McKenna, Karen Howlett, and Paul Waldie, "Probes Cite Ebbers in 'Fraud,'" *The Globe and Mail*, June 10, 2003, B1, B16; Elizabeth Church, "Accounting Overhaul Coming," *The Globe and Mail*, December 23, 2002, B1, B6; Richard Blackwell, "OSC Targets Tech Accounting," *The Globe and Mail*, September 26, 2000, B1, B6.

The Greening of Business: The Green Revolution Hits Accounting Ken Garen, "Are You Ready to Prosper?" *The Practical Accountant*, June 2008, SR29; Jeff Sanford, "The Next Pension Crisis," *Canadian Business*, August 13, 2007, Vol. 80, Issue 14/15, 62–63; Dom Serafini, "Regulations Are the Consumers' Best Friends," *Intermedia*, July 2004, 32, 2, ABI/INFORM Global, 23.

Managing in Turbulent Times: Opportunities in Forensic Accounting *Daily Gleaner*, A1, accessed March 6, 2009, from Canadian Newsstand Core database (Document ID: 1652944261); Randy Ray, "It Is a Sexy Environment and We Are the CSIs," *The Globe and Mail*, October 10, 2007, B8; Chartered Accountants of Canada website, www.cica.ca; Elisabeth Bumiller, "Bush Signs Bill Aimed at Fraud in Corporations," *The New York Times*, July 31, 2007; Kroll Investigative Services website, www.kroll.com; "Some Lottery Retailers Don't Obey the Rules; Winnings 20% Failed Anti-Cheating Test," February 28, 2009.

Business Case 11: Who Will Take the Blame? Amir Efrati, "Legal Experts See Roadmap," *The Wall Street Journal*, March 13–14, 2010, B3; Michael Corkery, "Executive Warned on Accounting," *The Wall Street Journal*, March 13–14, 2010, B1; "Resolution of Discipline Hearings (Since January 1, 2008)," www.ica.bc.ca/kb.php3?catid=1034, accessed January 27, 2010; Ken Mark, "Deloitte Will Appeal ICAO Ruling," *The Bottom Line*, February 2010, www.thebottomlinenews.ca/index.php?section=article&articleid=297, accessed January 29, 2010; Jeff Buckstein, "SOX Provision Holds Management's Feet to the Fire," *The Globe and Mail*, April 19, 2006, B13; Claire Gagne, "The Sarbanes-Oxley Act Restores Shine to Auditors' Reputation—and Fills Their Coffers," *Canadian Business*, September 27–October 10, 2004, 47–49; Karen Howlett, "Livent's Auditors Charged with Misconduct," *The Globe and Mail*, April 6, 2004, B1, B4; Karen Howlett, "Accounting Hearing Is Told Misconduct Charges Against Auditors Are 'Rubbish,'" *The Globe and Mail*, April 14, 2004, B3; Shawn McCarthy, "Investors Expect Too Much: Deloitte CEO," *The Globe and Mail*, October 17, 2005, B10; Elizabeth Church, "Accounting Overhaul Coming," *The Globe and Mail*, December 23, 2002, B1, B6; Richard Blackwell, "Auditing Firms Get Tighter Rules," *The Globe and Mail*, July 18, 2002, B1, B4; John Partridge and Karen Howlett, "CIBC Restricts Its Auditors," *The Globe and Mail*, March 1, 2002, B1, B4; Lily Nguyen, "Accountants Primed for Change," *The Globe and Mail*, February 4, 2002, B9; Richard Blackwell, "Accountants to Issue New Rules," *The Globe and Mail*, March 28, 2002, B1, B7; John Gray, "Hide and Seek," *Canadian Business*, April 1, 2002, 28–32; Steve Liesman, Jonathan Weil, and Michael Schroeder, "Accounting Debacles Spark Calls for Change: Here's the Rundown," *The Wall Street Journal*, February 6, 2002, A1, A8; Edward Clifford, "Big Accounting Firms Face Insurance Crunch," *The Globe and Mail*, November 13, 1993, B3; Patricia Lush, "Gap Widens Between Views on Auditor's Role in Canada," *The Globe and Mail*, February 14, 1986, B3; Chris Robinson, "Auditor's Role Raises Tough Questions," *The Financial Post*, June 22, 1985.

Chapter 12

lululemon: A Clear Marketing Strategy, Even in Trying Times
"Lululemon to Open 25 New Stores by June as Profits Nearly Triple," *Canadian Business*, March 25, 2010; Marina Strauss, "Lululemon Rides out Recession in Quality Fashion," *The Globe and Mail*, March 29, 2010, B1; Marina Strauss, "Lululemon Ramps up Plans to Hit the Net," *The Globe and Mail*, March 27, 2009, B8; lululemon website, www.lululemon.com, accessed April 22, 2010; Sunny Freeman, "Lululemon Targeting 45 Markets for Showroom Openings to Create Brand Buzz," *Canadian Business*, March 25, 2010; Sunny Freeman, "Ask the Legends: Chip Wilson," *Profit*, March 2010; Canadian Business website, accessed April 22, 2010; Marina Strauss, "New Mantra Pays Off for Lululemon," *The Globe and Mail*, December 10, 2009, B2; Aili McConnon, "Lululemon's Next Workout," *BusinessWeek*, June 9, 2008, 42–43; Marina Strauss, "Lululemon's Plan for Lean Times," *The Globe and Mail*, March 28, 2009, B3; Jennifer Wells, "Now Is Her Chance to Stretch," *The Globe and Mail*, April 3, 2008, B1, B4; John Partridge, "Lululemon Shops for New Retailing Head at Starbucks," *The Globe and Mail*, January 5, 2008, B8; Paul Waldie and Marina Strauss, "Lululemon Supplier Navigates Rocky Shoals," *The Globe and Mail*, November 16, 2007, B3.

E-Business and Social Media Solutions: Apps, Apps, and More Apps: New Age Product Opportunities
Hans Wagner, "iPhone 4: Numbers to Grow," *The Globe and Mail*, July 9, 2010; John Lorinc, "The Age of the App," *Report on Business*, April 2010, 47–50; Peter Burrows, "Apps Trump Tunes at Apple," *BusinessWeek*, September 28, 2009, 34; Jim Harris, "Talking about a Revolution," *Backbone*, December 2008, 10; Brian X. Chen, *Wired* website, "Coder's Half-Million-Dollar Baby Proves iPhone Gold Rush Is Still On," www.wired.com/gadgetlab/2009/02/shoot-is-iphone/, accessed April 22, 2010; Matt Asay, CNET News website, "Apple Channels Google, Microsoft to Attract Developers," http://news.cnet.com/8301-13505_3-20003211-16.html, accessed April 22, 2010; CNET News Website, Rick Broida, "I Ordered an iPad. What Apps Should I Install First?" http://reviews.cnet.com/8301-31747_7-20003145-243.html, accessed April 22, 2010; Omar El Akkad, "Apple Rides iPhone, Mac to Record Profit," *The Globe and Mail*, January 26, 2010, B1, B6.

The Greening of Business: Guelph Thinks Green American Pet Products Manufacturing Association-website, www.appma.org/press_industrytrends.asp; Blair Coursey, "North America: Plastic Waste—More Dangerous than Global Warming," *Ethical Corporation*, May 8, 2007.

Business Case 12: Dell Facing Serious Challenges Connie Guglielmo, "Dell Profit Margin Misses Estimates as Earnings Slip," *BusinessWeek*, February 18, 2010; Scott Moritz, "Hewlett-Packard Rings Dell's Bells," *The Globe and Mail*, November 24, 2009, B1; Jessica Mintz, "Dell Profit Plummets 63 Per Cent," *The Globe and Mail*, May 28, 2009, B8; Agam Shagh, "Dell Taking Smartphone Business to New Areas," *BusinessWeek*, April 14, 2010; Joel Hruska, "Apple, Dell Big Market Share Winners for the First Quarter," *Ars Technica*, April 17, 2008; Kevin Maney, "Dell to Dive into Consumer Electronics Market," *USA Today*, September 25, 2003, 1B–2B; David Teather, "Michael Dell Quits as Chief of His Own Company," *The Guardian*, March 5, 2004.

Chapter 13

Psst! Did You Hear the Latest?
Hollie Shaw, "Reaching Out via Web; Marketers Look for Creative Ways to Draw in Consumers," *National Post*, November 7, 2008, FP14; Nick Turner, "Cupcake Business Reaps Sweet Rewards: Location and Word of Mouth Key to Success," *National Post*, October 27, 2008, FP9; Sam Cage, "Word of Mouth Sells 'Remembrance' Gems," *National Post*, September 15, 2008; Sinclair Stewart, "Hey, Did You Hear about That Great New Toothpaste?" *The Globe and Mail*, November 20, 2007, B3; Erin White, "Word of Mouth Makes Nike Slip-On Sneakers Take Off," *The Globe and Mail*, June 7, 2001, B1, B4; Mike Blaney, "Word of Mouth Advertising," blog, www.themarketingguy.wordpress.com/2007/10/09/word-of-mouth-advertising; www.theinfluencers.ca/why_wom.php.

The Greening of Business: Promoting a Green Business Image Simon Haupt, "The Green Gap Is Wide Open: Survey Results Show That Canadian Companies Leave Public Perception Wanting," *The Globe and Mail*, June 1,

2010, B2; Hollie Shaw, "Making the Case that Wearing Fur Can Be Eco-Friendly," *Winnipeg Free Press*, December 5, 2008, B6; Daryl-Lynn Carlson, "Advertising Guidelines Target 'Greenwashing,'" *Winnipeg Free Press*, November 21, 2008, B6; Marina Strauss, "Standing Out in a Sea of Green," *The Globe and Mail*, August 16, 2008, B3; Randy Boswell, "Oilsands Ad 'Greenwash' Environment Group Crows," *The Globe and Mail*, August 14, 2008, C8; Richard Blackwell, "Eco-Friendly? Canadians Want to See the Proof," *The Globe and Mail*, July 28, 2008, B1, B3; Shawn McCarthy, "Oil Sands Tries Image Makeover," *The Globe and Mail*, June 24, 2008, B1, B7; Sharon Epperson, "BP's Fundamental but Obscured Energy Contradiction," cnbc.com, May 21, 2008, www.cnbc.com/id/24758394; Carly Weeks, "New Scrutiny for Green Claims," *The Globe and Mail*, March 11, 2008, B1, B6; "Oil Company BP Pleads Guilty to Environmental Crime," *International Herald Tribune*, November 29, 2007, www.iht.com/articles/ap/2007/11/30/business/NA-FIN-US-BP-Settlement-Alaska.php?page=1; Terry Macalister, "Greenpeace Calls BP's Oil Sands Plan An Environmental Crime," Guardian.co.uk, December 7, 2007, www.guardian.co.uk/business/2007/dec/07/bp.

E-Business and Social Media Solutions: Batman Embraces the Internet Age "Batman Film Series," May 23, 2008, http://en.wikipedia.org/wiki/Batman_%28film_series%29; Claude Brodesser-Akner, "Hyping Joker—Without Exploiting Heath's Death," *Advertising Age*, May 12, 2008, http://adage.com/article.php?article_id=126981; Chungaiz, blog, "New Batman Dark Knight Marketing Continues, Fantastic!" December 13, 2007, www.altogetherdigital.com/20071213/new-batman-dark-knight-marketing-continues-fantastic; Chris Lee, "The Dark Knight Marketing Blitz," *Los Angeles Times*, March 24, 2008, articles.latimes.com/2008/mar/24/entertainment/et-batmanviral24. See also http://batman.wikibruce.com/Timeline; www.42entertainment.com; http://whysoserious.com.

Entrepreneurship and New Ventures: Fuelling the World of Branded Entertainment Jonathan Paul, "RPGs Look for Brands to Play With," *Strat-*

egy, April 2009, 33; Frank Armstrong, "Fairytale Ending for Tiny Ottawa Firm," *The Globe and Mail*, November 11, 2008; Lana Castleman, "Virtual Worlds on the Menu at Kids Marketing Agencies," *KidScreen*, October 2008, 79; Lana Castleman, "McDonald's Is Lovin' Customer Content," *KidScreen*, May 2008, 26; Rob Gerlsbeck, "Fuel Industries," *Marketing* 112, 21 (2007): 22.

Business Case 13: Measuring the Effectiveness of Advertising Grant Surridge, "People, Lend Them Your Ears: More Accurate Radio Monitoring," *National Post*, November 26, 2008, FP1; Google analytics website, www.google.com/analytics/index.html, accessed April 27, 2010; Emily Steel, "Google Set to Roll Out Web-Measurement Tool," *The Wall Street Journal*, June 24, 2008, B14; Jennifer Wells, "The Brain Guy Wants to Get Inside Your Head," *The Globe and Mail*, March 15, 2008, B4–B5; "TV Networks Pay Back Advertisers," *National Post*, December 13, 2007; David George-Cosh, "Fighting Click Fraud: Is It Really Down for the Count?" *The Globe and Mail*, August 23, 2007, B7; Brooks Barnes, "New TV Ratings Will Produce Ad-Price Fight," *The Wall Street Journal*, December 22, 2005, B1, B3; Brooks Barnes, "Where're the Ratings, Dude?" *The Wall Street Journal*, March 7, 2005, B1, B6; Keith McArthur, "New TV Ratings Devices Know What You're Watching," *The Globe and Mail*, November 29, 2004, B1, B12; Keith McArthur, "Advertisers Wary of Plan to Fuse TV Ratings Systems," *The Globe and Mail*, July 13, 2004, B1, B20; Brooks Barnes, "For Nielsen, Fixing Old Ratings System Causes New Static," *The Wall Street Journal*, September 16, 2004, A1, A8; Elizabeth Jensen, "Networks Blast Nielsen, Blame Faulty Ratings for Drop in Viewership," *The Wall Street Journal*, November 22, 1996, A1, A8.

Chapter 14

Buyers and Sellers Jockey for Position "Consumers Trade Down, McDonald's Sales Go Up," *The Globe and Mail*, December 9, 2008, B12; Marina Strauss, "Stores Aim to Convert 'Cherry Pickers,'" *The Globe and Mail*, November 19, 2008, B11; Janet Adamy, "McDonald's Strategy to Take Sales from Pricier Restaurants Working,"

National Post, October 23, 2008, FP2; David Hutton, "Consumers Get Less Bang for Their Buck," *The Globe and Mail*, July 8, 2008, B2; Ann Zimmerman, "Behind the Dollar-Store Boom: A Nation of Bargain Hunters," *The Wall Street Journal*, December 13, 2004, A1, A10; Gordon Fairclough, "Four Biggest Cigarette Makers Can't Raise Prices as They Did," *The Wall Street Journal*, October 25, 2002, A1, A8; Timothy Aeppel, "After Cost Cutting, Companies Turn toward Price Increases," *The Wall Street Journal*, September 18, 2002, A1, A12.

Entrepreneurship and New Ventures: Men and Cars: Unrequited Love Auto Vault website, www.autovaultcanada.com/, accessed May 24, 2009; Deirdre Kelly, "Nowhere to Park the Lamborghini?" *The Globe and Mail*, September 20, 2008, M3; Jerry Langton, "Driven by Love of Hot Wheels: Entrepreneur Cashes in on Need for Secure Storage for Owners' Exotic Cars with Auto Vault, Car Condo," *The Toronto Star*, May 12, 2008, B1; Joshua Knelman, "Auto Focus: This 40,000 Square-Foot Car Park Protects Your Precious Ride from All the Elements—Criminal and Climactic," *Toronto Life*, May 2005, 27; "Storing Your 'Baby' for Winter," The Expositor website, www.brantfordexpositor.ca/PrintArticle.aspx?e=1283051, accessed May 24, 2009.

The Greening of Business: The Bag Controversy Diane Katz, "The Grocery-Bag Dilemma: Is Paper or Plastic Greener?" *Winnipeg Free Press*, July 26, 2009, A11; Marjo Johne, "Shoppers Get a Brand New Bag," *The Globe and Mail*, October 20, 2008, E5; "Going Green: The Future of the Retail Food Industry," *Agriculture and Agri-Food Canada*, www.ats.agr.gc.ca/us/4351_e.htm, July 2007.

E-Business and Social Media Solutions: Exploiting E-Distribution Opportunities Marina Strauss, "Turning to the Web or an Endless Aisle," *The Globe and Mail*, February 13, 2010, B3; Heather Green, "Amazon Aims to Keep You Clicking," *BusinessWeek*, March 2, 2009, 34; Geoffrey A. Fowler, "Amazon Aims to Become More than Books," *The Globe and Mail*, September 18, 2009, B9; Marina Strauss, "Wal-Mart's New e-Frontier," *The Globe and Mail*, October 17, 2009, B3; "P&G Jumping into Online Retail with New Test Site,"

The Globe and Mail, January 15, 2010, B6; Reena Jana, "Retailers Are Learning to Love Smartphones," *BusinessWeek*, October 26, 2009, 49.

Business Case 14: Changing Distribution Channels in the Music Business Jeff Gray, "Canada Rebuked as Haven for Digital Music Pirates," *The Globe and Mail*, April 29, 2010, B2; Barrie McKenna, "The (Legal) Music Fades Out for Canadians," *The Globe and Mail*, October 20, 2009, B14; Matt Hartley, "From Pirate Bay, a Torpedo to Illegal File Sharing," *The Globe and Mail*, April 18, 2009, B3; Grant Robertson, "Death Knell Sounds for CDs," *The Globe and Mail*, June 19, 2008, B3; Shawn McCarthy, "U.S. Court Shuts Door on Internet File-Sharing," *The Globe and Mail*, June 28, 2005, B3; also "File Sharing Firm Will Shut Down," *Winnipeg Free Press*, November 8, 2005, A11; also Nick Wingfield, "Online Music's Latest Tune," *The Wall Street Journal*, August 27, 2004, B1, B2; also Nick Wingfield, "New File-Swapping Software Limits Sharers to a Select Few," *The Wall Street Journal*, October 4, 2004, B1, B4; also Sarah McBride, "Stop the Music!" *The Wall Street Journal*, August 23, 2004, B1; also Vauhini Vara, "On Campus, iTunes Finds an Illicit Groove, *The Wall Street Journal*, August 23, 2004, B1–B2; also Nick Wingfield and Sarah McBride, "Green Light for Grokster," *The Wall Street Journal*, August 20, 2004, B1, B3; also Nick Wingfield, "The Day the Music Died," *The Wall Street Journal*, May 2, 2003, B8; "The End of File-Shares as We Know Them," *The Winnipeg Free Press*, July 4, 2003, A8; Ted Birdis, "Music Industry Escalates Net Fight," *The Winnipeg Free Press*, June 26, 2003, A12; Matthew Ingram, "Digital Music Industry Gets New Spin on Napster Judge's Decision," *The Globe and Mail*, February 26, 2002; Nick Wingfield, "Napster Boy, Interrupted," *The Wall Street Journal*, October 1, 2002, B1, B3; Anna Matthews and Charles Goldsmith, "Music Industry Faces New Threats on Web," *The Wall Street Journal*, February 21, 2003, B1, B4.

Chapter 15

Money, Money, Money "SMEs Turn to Bartering, Saving Cash," *National Post*, January 5, 2009, FP8; Tom Hundley,

"So Why Does the $1 Bill Still Exist?" *The Buffalo News*, July 20, 2008, D3; Yaroslav Trofimov, "Shrinking Dollar Meets Its Match in Dolphin Teeth," *The Wall Street Journal*, April 30, 2008, A1, A13; Roma Luciw, "Goodbye Penny, Hello $5 Coin?" *The Globe and Mail*, April 10, 2008, B5; Tara Perkins, "Lose the Loose Change? Bank Study Proposed Dropping Penny," *The Globe and Mail*, July 3, 2007, B3; "What Is Money?" Royal Canadian Mint website, http://www.mint.ca/store/dyn/PDFs/RCM_09AR_ENG_FA.pdf, accessed May 26, 2010; Annual Report, P44, The British Museum, www.britishmuseum.org/explore/themes/money/what_is_money.aspx.

E-Business and Social Media Solutions: Online and Mobile Banking Solutions Straight to the Consumer Tara Perkins and Ian Marlow, "Mobile Banking Makes Inroads," *The Globe and Mail*, February 8, 2010, B3; Rob Carrick, "Before You Hit 'Buy,'" *The Globe and Mail*, March 4, 2010, B7; Rob Carrick, "Ditching Your Adviser Has Never Been Easier," *The Globe and Mail*, August 27, 2009, B10; Valerie Bauman, "Video Game Helps Students Score in Fiscal Skills," *The Globe and Mail*, December 14, 2009, B6; Lauren Young, "Big Banks Take a Hint from Mint.com," *BusinessWeek*, October 12, 2009, P62; Tara Perkins, "School's in and Banks Wake Up," *The Globe and Mail*, September 3, 2007, B3.

Table 15.1 Economist.com, http://bigmacindex.org/year/2010-big-mac-index.htm. © The Economist Newspaper Limited, London, July 22, 2010, page 414.

Managing in Turbulent Times: Canadian vs. U.S. Banks: Quite a Difference Konrad Yakabuski, "You May Love Canada's Banks Now, but . . . ," *The Globe and Mail*, April 30, 2009, B2; Janet Whitman, "Maybe Canadian Banks Are the New Swiss Watches: Stability Played up and Paying Off," *National Post*, April 4, 2009, FP4; Tara Perkins, "Why Canadian Banks Work," *The Globe and Mail*, March 7, 2009, B1; Theresa Tedesco, "The Great Solvent North," *The New York Times*, February 28, 2009, A19.

The Greening of Business: Green Trading Ronald Ebert and Ricky Grif-

fin, *Business Essentials,* 7th ed. (Upper Saddle River, NJ: Prentice Hall, 2009), 227.

Business Case 15: Stock Market Games and the Dark Side of Financial Advising Ingrid Peritz, "Earl Jones Sentenced to 11 Years," *The Globe and Mail*, February 15, 2010, B1; Janet McFarland, "Former Agnico Executive Sentenced to Jail Time," *The Globe and Mail*, January 30, 2009, B3; Tara Perkins, "Former Trader Pleads Guilty in Fraud That Cost BMO $850 Million," *The Globe and Mail*, November 19, 2008, B1; Janet McFarland and Brent Jang, "Andrew Rankin: Barred from Trading Stocks, but Cleared of Criminal Charges," *The Globe and Mail*, February 22, 2008, B1, B4; Bertrand Marotte, "Mutual Fund Fraudster Gets 12 Years," *The Globe and Mail*, January 29, 2008, B1, B4; Richard Blackwell, "Firm, Ex-CEO Pay Millions in Penalties," *The Globe and Mail*, December 20, 2001, B1, B6; Richard Blackwell, "OSC Scores Trading Conviction," *The Globe and Mail*, July 22, 2000, B1–B2; Karen Howlett, Sinclair Stewart, and Paul Waldie, "Brokers Caught up in Police Probe," *The Globe and Mail*, June 20, 2003, B1, B20.

Chapter 16

The Source of a Meltdown, the Joy of a Bounce Back, and the Prospects Ahead Kevin Carmichael, "A World Awash in Debt," *The Globe and Mail*, November 28, 2009, B1; "The Big Global Screw-Up," *National Post*, February 24, 2009, FP11; Frank Partnoy, "Financial Reform: Lessons from 1929," *BusinessWeek*, October 12, 2009, 84; Malcolm Morisson, TSX Ends 2009 Trading Higher," Canadian Press, December 31, 2009; Tavia Grant, "Bailouts Tied to Curbing Executive Pay," *The Globe and Mail*, October 15, 2008, B4; Jonathan Ratner, "TSX Falls 35% in 2008," *The Financial Post*, December 31, 2008; Marcus Walker, Sara Schaefer-Munoz, and David Gauthier-Villars, "Bailout Price Tags Raise the Question: How?" *The Globe and Mail*, October 14, 2008, B11; Richard Blackwell, "From Subprime to Stock Swoon," *The Globe and Mail*, October 13, 2008, B3; Joel Schlesinger, "A Brief History of a Financial Meltdown," *Winnipeg Free Press*, October 12, 2008, B9; "Wall

Street's Rescue," *The Globe and Mail*, October 6, 2008, B4; "Contagion," *Winnipeg Free Press*, October 3, 2008, A15; "Investors Lost Billions, Large Banks and Brokerages Failed, Wall Street's Troubles Went Global," *The Globe and Mail*, October 1, 2008, B1; Rachel Puffer, "Easy Money," *Canadian Business*, September 29, 2008, 38; Janet Whitman, "Scramble to Start Financial Rescue," *National Post*, September 22, 2008, www.nationalpost.com; Eoin Callan, "Paulson Bailout Extended," *National Post*, September 22, 2008, www.nationalpost.com; Jeanne Aversa and Julie Davis, "U.S. Puts Taxpayer on Huge Hook," *Winnipeg Free Press*, September 20, 2008, B11; Kristine Owram, "Happy Days Here Again?" *Winnipeg Free Press*, September 20, 2008, B11; Barrie McKenna, "A Desperate Disease, a Desperate Remedy," *The Globe and Mail*, September 20, 2008, B5; Derek DeCloet, "Five Days That Shook the Financial World," *The Globe and Mail*, September 20, 2008, B2; Barrie McKenna, "Fannie, Freddie Stay in Free Fall on Bailout Talk," *The Globe and Mail*, August 21, 2008, B9.

Entrepreneurship and New Ventures: An Online Community for People 50 and Older 55-Alive website, accessed May 25, 2010; "Towne Square," 55-Alive!, www.55-alive.com/index.php; Peter Corbett, "2009 Facebook Demographics and Statistics Report: 276% Growth in 35–54 Year Old Users," iStrategyLabs, January 5, 2009, www.istrategylabs.com/2009-facebook-demographics-and-statistics-report-276-growth-in-35-54-year-old-users/; Dahlia Fahmy, "55-Alive! Wants to Be MySpace for the Baby Boomer Set," *Inc.*, October 1, 2007.

Managing in Turbulent Times: A Quicken Course in Accountability Intuit website, http://about.intuit.com/about_intuit/press_room/press_release/articles/2009/IntuitReports-Solid2009-FiscalYear-Results.html, accessed July 10, 2010; Michael S. Hopkins, "Because He Learns and Teaches" *Inc.*, April 2004, 119–120.

Business Case 16: The Commercial Paper Crisis Boyd Erman, "Canaccord Turns the Page on ABCP," *The Globe and Mail*, May 19, 2010; Boyd Erman, "Commercial Paper Market Shows Few Signs of Recovery," *The Globe and Mail*, April 10, 2010; Philip Ling, "$4.45 Billion Fund to Ensure ABCP Solution: Backstop in Place; Major Hurdle in Process Crossed, Purdy Says," *National Post*, December 27, 2008, FP4; Boyd Erman, "A Long, Tough Struggle Ends Finally, with a Deal," *The Globe and Mail*, December 26, 2008, B4; "Strategem Issues ABCP Warning," *National Post*, www.nationalpost.com/story-printer.html?id=209530; John Greenwood, "Frustrated as Hell," *National Post*, October 21, 2008, www.nationalpost.com/story-printer.html?id=895020; Janet McFarland, Boyd Erman, Karen Howlett, and Tara Perkins, "Ordinary People, an Extraordinary Mess," *The Globe and Mail*, August 9, 2008, B4–B6; David Friend, "Investors in ABCP Approve Restructuring," *Winnipeg Free Press*, April 26, 2008, B13; Boyd Erman, "DBRS to Roll Out a New Road Map on Risk," *The Globe and Mail*, February 8, 2008, B1, B6; Gary Norris, "Financial Rescue Has Holes," *Winnipeg Free Press*, December 26, 2007, B17; Duncan Mavin, "Subprime Torpedoes CIBC," *Winnipeg Free Press*, December 7, 2007, B1; Matthew McClearn, "The Asset-Backed Commercial Paper Crunch Has Burned Investors: Now Lawyer Purdy Crawford Is Trying to Sort Out the Mess," *Canadian Business*, November 5, 2007, 130–139; Thomas Watson, "Issues of Trust," *Canadian Business*, November 5, 2007, 141–147; Aaron Lucchetti and Kara Scannell, "Ratings Firms: A Dollar Short and Day Late?" *The Wall Street Journal*, September 26, 2007, C1–C2; Karen Mazurkewich and John Greenwood, "Caisse Top ABCP Holder," *National Post*, September 18, 2007, FP1, FP5; Peter Eavis, "Oh, the People You'll Blame," *Fortune*, September 17, 2007, 118–124; John Greenwood, "Banks Left on Hook in Credit Market Freeze," *National Post*, September 15, 2007, FP7; John Greenwood and Duncan Mavin, "Credit Rout Far from Over," *National Post*, September 12, 2007, FP1, FP13; Jeff Sanford, "How This Happened," *Canadian Business*, September 10, 2007, 87–88; Doug Alexander, "Banks Feel Heat of ABCP Meltdown," *National Post*, September 8, 2007, FP7; Tara Perkins, "Misguided, or Misunderstood?" *The Globe and Mail*, September 8, 2007, B4–B5; John Greenwood, "ABCP Losses Could Hit 50%," *National Post*, September 5, 2007, FP1, FP5; Kara Scannell and Deborah Solomon, "Unraveling the Subprime Mess," *The Wall Street Journal*, September 4, 2007, A6; "Mortgage Mayhem," *Fortune*, September 3, 2007, 82–83; Jon Birger, "Markdown," *Fortune*, September 3, 2007, 77–78; Shawn Tully, "Risk Returns with a Vengeance," *Fortune*, September 3, 2007, 51–56; Boyd Erman, "Commercial Paper Had Never Suffered for a Lack of Buyers and Sellers—Until Recent Liquidity Concerns Sent Investors Running for the Exits," *The Globe and Mail*, August 25, 2007, B2; John Greenwood, "Legal Actions Looming," *National Post*, August 24, 2007, FP1, FP3; Barbara Shecter, "Greenspan's Rate Cuts Helped Create a Culture of Debt That Ignored Borders and Was Ultimately Shunned as Too Risky," *National Post*, August 18, 2007, FP1, FP4; Sean Silcoff, "Warnings Were Issued Well Ahead of Crisis," *National Post*, August 18, 2007, FP1, FP3; Andrew Willis and Boyd Erman, "Credit Crunch Claims Victim in Canada," *The Globe and Mail*, August 14, 2007, B1, B4; David Wolf, "The Butterfly Market," *Canadian Business*, August 13–27, 2007, 15.

Photo Credits

Part One Hemera/Thinkstock, page 1

Chapter 1 BlackBerry®, RIM®, Research In Motion®, SureType®, SurePress™ and related trademarks, names and logos are the property of Research In Motion Limited and are registered and/or used in the U.S. and countries around the world, pages 2 & 3; Sculpies/Dreamstime.com, page 6, top left; Tinabelle/Dreamstime.com, page 6, top right; EschCollection Prime/Alamy/GetStock.com, page 6, bottom left; Prebranac/Dreamstime.com/GetStock.com, page 6, bottom right; Frederic J. Brown/AFP/Getty Images, page 10; Tim Pohl/iStockphoto, page 12; iStockphoto/Thinkstock, page 16; Masterfile, page 18; Ritz Sino/*The New York Times,* page 21; Hemera/Thinkstock, page 26

Chapter 2 Courtesy of Air Canada, pages 34 & 35; Bettmann/Corbis, page 42; Fredrik Renander/Alamy, page 49; Courtesy of Corus® Entertainment Inc., page 50; Chris Wattie/Reuters/Corbis, page 56

Name and Organization Index

Subject Index

buyers, 48
buying an existing business, 99
buzz marketing, 339

C

cafeteria-style benefit plans, 205
caisses populaires, 411
call option, 422
call price, 417, 420
callable bond, 420
callable stock, 417
campus interviews, 196
Canada
  balance of trade, 40, 119
  budget deficits, 40
  Canadian dollar, 120, 121
  Canadian *vs.* U.S. banks, 415
  capital requirements, 412
  competition policy, 11
  Corruption Perceptions Index, 129
  creditor nation, 40
  exports, 119*f*
  foreign buyouts, 125
  GDP per capita, 39
  global competitiveness
    ranking, 119
  government bailouts, 9
  as high-income country, 116
  history of business in Canada,
    18–22, 19*t*
  imports, 119*f*
  management of Canadian economy,
    42–43
  management styles, 241
  market economy in, 13–16
  mergers and acquisitions, 51
  mixed market economy, 10
  productivity levels, 274
  rate of price increases, 41*f*
  R&D spending, 43
  role in global economy, 116
  top foreign-controlled
    companies, 126*t*
  top small- and medium-sized
    employers, 87*t*
  top ten corporations, 102*t*
  venture capital industry, 412
  World Trade Organization, founding
    member of, 130
Canada Business Corporations Act,
  103–104
Canada Business program, 13
Canada Labour Code, 211–212
Canada Pension Plan, 204
Canada Savings Bonds, 420
Canada Small Business Funding
  Program, 443
Canada Water Act, 12
*Canadian Charter of Rights and
  Freedoms*, 212
Canadian dollar, 120, 121, 413

*Canadian Environmental Protection
  Act*, 70
Canadian financial system
  alternate banks, 411
  chartered banks, 405–411
  financial institutions, 405–412
  "four financial pillars," 405
  government financial institutions and
    granting agencies, 412
  investment dealers, 412
  other sources of funds, 412
  specialized lending and savings
    intermediaries, 411–412
Canadian Human Rights Act, 205,
  207, 212
Canadian Radio-television and
  Telecommunications Commission
  (CRTC), 10
Canadian stock exchanges, 418
Canadian Wheat Board, 10
cap and trade system, 68
capacity planning, 266
capital, 6
capital expenditures, 437
capital items, 350
capital market, 412
capital requirements, 94
capitalism, 8
carbon credits, 422
carbon dioxide emissions, 68, 68*f*
cartels, 129
cases. *See* business cases; opening
  cases; video cases
cash, 295
cash budget, 93
cash discounts, 379
cash flow management, 298, 435
cash-flow requirements, 443, 443*f*
cash flows from financing, 298
cash flows from investing, 298
cash flows from operations, 298
casual gaming industry, 363
catalogue marketing, 385
catalogue showrooms, 383
cause and effect diagrams, 275, 275*f*
cellular layout, 267
centralized organization, 177
certificates of deposit (CDs), 404
certified general accountant (CGA),
  290–291
certified management accountant
  (CMA), 291
chain of command, 172–173
change management, 164
channel captain, 382
channel conflict, 381–382
channels of distribution, 379–380, 379*f*
charismatic leadership, 239–240, 239*f*
charitable donations, 76
chartered accountant (CA), 290
chartered bank

automated banking machines
  (ABMs), 406
bank loans, 407
bank rate, 410
branch offices, 410
in Canada, 406
changes in banking, 408–409
consumer demand, changes in, 408–409
as creators of money, 407–408, 408*f*
defined, 406
deregulation, 408
direct deposits and withdrawals, 406
e-cash, 407
electronic funds transfer (EFT),
  406–407
financial advice, 406
international banking, 410
international services, 406
online and mobile banking
  solutions, 409
pay-by-phone, 406
pension services, 406
point-of-sale transactions, 407
services offered by, 406–407, 407*f*
smart cards, 407
trust services, 406
vs. U.S. banks, 415
chemical processes, 263
cheque kiting, 74, 404
chief executive officer (CEO), 103, 151
chief financial officer (CFO), 151
chief information officers, 314
chief operating officer (COO), 151
China, 117, 118
cigarette industry, 374
classical theory of motivation, 226
clerical processes, 263
client relationships, 234
client-server network, 311
cloud computing, 315
co-operative, 104–105
coaches, 240
code of ethics, 62, 64–65, 64*f*
COLA clauses, 213
collateral, 95, 438
collective bargaining
  bargaining cycle, 212–213
  bargaining zone, 213*f*
  benefits, 213
  compensation, 213
  contract issues, 213
  defined, 210
  failure of, 213–214
  history of, 211
  job security, 213
  management rights, 213
  management tactics, 214
  mediation and arbitration, 214–215
  other union issues, 213
  reaching agreement, 212–213
  union tactics, 214

ISO 9000, 279
ISO 9000:2000, 279
ISO 14000, 279
Italy, 121

J

Japan, 117
jeitinho, 62
job analysis, 195
job commitment, 225
job description, 195
job enrichment, 234
job evaluation, 203
job fair, 197
job redesign, 234
job rotation, 201
job satisfaction, 225
job security, 213
job sharing, 237
job shops, 267
job specialization, 173–174
job specification, 195
just-in-time (JIT) production
    systems, 272–273

K

Key Small Business Statistics, 87
knowledge information systems, 316
knowledge workers, 209
Kyoto Summit, 68

L

labels, 356
labour, 5
Labour Force Survey, 87
labour markets, and knowledge
    workers, 209
labour productivity, 273
labour shortage, 42
labour unions
    Canada Labour Code, 211–212
    collective bargaining, 210, 211,
      212–215
    dealing with organized labour,
      210–211
    decertification, 214
    defined, 210
    federal labour legislation, 211–212
    future of unions, 211
    historical steps for labour
      legislation, 211*t*
    legal environment, 211–212
    management tactics, 214
    provincial labour legislation, 212
    union hiring halls, 196
    union-management relations, 210
    union tactics, 214
    unionism today, 210
    as users of accounting information, 289
laissez-faire, 20
land pollution, 69–70

language barriers, 126
language differences, 366
law
    administrative law, 29
    business law. *See* business law
    common law, 29
    court system, 29
    defined, 29
    international law, 33
    sources of law, 29
    statutory law, 29
law of demand, 14
law of one price, 413
law of supply, 14
layout planning, 267–269, 267*f*
leadership
    approaches to, 237–238
    behavioural approach, 238
    Canadian *vs.* American management
      styles, 241
    channel leadership, 381–382
    charismatic leadership, 239–240, 239*f*
    coaches, leaders as, 240
    continuum, 239*f*
    cross-cultural leadership, 241
    defined, 237
    and effective organizations, 237
    employee-oriented, 238
    ethical leadership, 241
    and gender, 240
    leadership styles, 238
    managers and, 148
    and motivation, 237–242
    quality, leading for, 276
    recent trends, 239–242
    situational (contingency) approach, 238
    strategic leadership, 241
    task-oriented, 238
    trait approach, 238
    transactional leadership, 239
    transformational leadership, 239
    virtual leadership, 241–242
leading, 149
lean manufacturing, 267
learning organization, 184
lease, 31
legal context of HRM
    comparable worth, 207
    employee health and safety,
      207–208
    equal employment opportunity,
      205–206
    retirement, 208
    sexual harassment, 207
legal differences, 127–129
legislation
    anti-combines legislation, 20
    anti-discrimination laws, 205–206
    blue-sky laws, 426
    consumer protection legislation, 11–12
    corporations, influence of, 13

employee health and safety, 207–208
environmental protection
    legislation, 12
equal employment regulations,
    205–206
labour unions, 211–212, 211*t*
securities regulation, 425–426
sexual harassment, 207
letter of credit, 406
leverage, 299
leveraged buyouts, 299
leveraging, 421
liabilities, 293, 296
liaison, 148
licensed brands, 354
licensing arrangements, 124–125
life insurance company, 411
limit order, 425
limited liability, 104
limited partners, 101
limited partnership, 101
line authority, 178–179, 178*f*
line departments, 178
line of credit, 438, 443
liquidation plan, 32
liquidity, 294
load funds, 421
Lobbying Act, 13
lobbyist, 13
local area networks (LANs), 312
local communities, 66
local-content laws, 128–129
location planning, 266–267
lockout, 214
London stock exchange, 418
long-term (capital) expenditures, 437
long-term funds, 439–443
long-term goals, 157
long-term liabilities, 296
long-term loans, 439
long-term solvency ratios, 298–299
love money, 95
low-contact processes, 264
low-contact system, 264
low-income countries, 116
low middle-income countries, 116
luck, 106

M

M-1, 403–404
M-2, 404
magazines, 360
mail order, 385
make-to-order, 262
make-to-stock, 262
Malaysia, 117
Malcolm Baldrige National Quality
    Award, 278
management
    see also managers
    areas of management, 151–152